Computer Law

Fourth Edition

Edited by

Chris Reed

Professor of Electronic Commerce Law
Centre for Commercial Law Studies,
Queen Mary & Westfield College, University of London

Of Counsel to Tite & Lewis, London

and

John Angel

Senior Visiting Fellow
Centre for Commercial Law Studies
Queen Mary & Westfield College, University of London

Consultant to Clifford Chance

 Blackstone Press

Published by
Blackstone Press Limited
Aldine Place
London
W12 8AA
United Kingdom

Sales enquiries and orders
Telephone +44-(0)-20-8740-2277
Facsimile +44-(0)-20-8743-2292
e-mail: sales@blackstone.demon.co.uk
website: www.blackstonepress.com

ISBN 1 84174 016 0
© Chris Reed and John Angel 2000
The contributors hold the copyright for their respective chapters
First edition 1990
Second edition 1993
Third edition 1996
Fourth edition 2000
Reprinted 2001

The rights of the contributors to be identified as authors of this work have been asserted in accordance with ss. 77 and 78 of the Copyright, Designs and Patents Act 1988.

British Library Cataloguing in Publication Data
A CIP catalogue record for this book is available from the British Library

Typeset in 10/11 Plantin by Style Photosetting Ltd, Mayfield, East Sussex
Printed and bound in Great Britain by Antony Rowe Limited,
Chippenham and Reading

Contents

Preface

It is a striking illustration of the speed at which computer law develops that this fourth edition appears only ten years after the first — indeed, if the authors and editors could have found the strength, this might even have been the fifth or sixth edition. During the three and a half years since the third edition of this book, the pace of change has increased rapidly, and for that reason all the chapters bar one are either completely new or have been revised extensively. The exception is the chapter on semiconductor chip protection where, because of the relatively small number of players, there have been no developments of note.

We have taken the opportunity of this new edition to make a number of important changes to the structure and contents of the book. The original division of the technology acquisition topics into hardware and software contracts made sense in 1990, but over the last few years the trend towards integrated purchasing of systems has made this increasingly artificial. Contracts now often concentrate on the supply of information *services*, rather than on acquiring the technology needed to provide them. The book thus begins with chapters on the procurement of systems and of services, to match this market trend. In the field of intellectual property and related rights, databases have acquired a special regime of protection and thus warrant their own chapter. The impact of the Internet has been particularly dramatic in the last three years, and so the chapter on Electronic Data Interchange has been replaced by one on electronic commerce, and a new chapter included on the special legal position of Internet intermediaries. Finally, computing technology is now fulfilling its potential to transform the nature of work, and a chapter covering the effects on employment rights has been added.

A number of thanks are due, and I am particularly grateful to John Angel for accepting the role of co-editor and sharing the burden of producing this book. I would also like to thank the new authors who appear in this edition, adding new material or taking the place of those who were no longer able to contribute. This is also an appropriate place to record my gratitude to those

who have contributed to previous editions, and to those who have found the
time to update and extend their chapters — it is their collective efforts which
have made this book work over the years.

Chris Reed
Information Technology Law Unit,
Centre for Commercial Law Studies,
May 2000

Preface to the First Edition

The idea for this book came from teaching a course on the University of London LLM, and from conversations with practitioners working in the field of computer law. The problem seemed clear; the few books that existed on the subject were out of date, over simplistic, or covered the subject unevenly, and in some cases all three. What was needed was a book that provided a reasonably detailed coverage of all the important aspects of the subject, and it was needed soon. The solution also seemed simple; to gather together a team of authors, each of whom could offer specialist knowledge in some aspect of the field, and collectively produce a book which offered a broad coverage, but also went into the different areas in depth. My intention was that the book should interest and be useful to legal practitioners and those involved in the computer industry, as well as to students. How far this book succeeds in this aim is, of course, a matter that only the reader can judge.

I should like at the outset to point out that, although I relied on the individual authors to decide what topics should be dealt with in their own chapter, my task as editor was to coordinate the writing and to pull the book together into a harmonious whole. Bearing in mind particularly that they were generally writing in substantial ignorance of the precise contents of the other chapters, the responsibility for errors, particularly errors of omission, rests solely on my own shoulders. I should like to thank them all for the effort they put into this book, and in particular to thank Christopher Millard who made a number of valuable suggestions and helped at the planning stage as well as contributing his own chapter.

I should also like to thank my wife Jilly for her help in editing and proofreading, and for her patience during the months when I appeared more closely wedded to my word processor than to her. Thanks are also due to all at Blackstone Press, who listened sympathetically to many feeble excuses for the lateness of the manuscript and never nagged.

Chris Reed, November 1989

Contributors

THE EDITORS

Chris Reed is Professor of Electronic Commerce Law and Head of the Information Technology Law Unit at the Centre for Commercial Law Studies, Queen Mary and Westfield College, University of London. He joined the Centre in 1987 and is responsible for the University of London LLM courses in Information Technology Law, Internet Law, Electronic Banking Law and Telecommunications Law. Chris is also Of Counsel to the City of London law firm Tite & Lewis, a correspondent law firm of Ernst & Young.

Chris has published widely on many aspects of computer law. He is the author of *Electronic Finance Law* (Woodhead Faulkner, 1991) and *Digital Information Law: Electronic Documents and Requirements of Form* (Centre for Commercial Law Studies, 1996); and the co-editor of *Cross-Border Electronic Banking* (Lloyd's of London Press).

Chris was Joint Chairman of the Society for Computers and Law from 1997 to 2000, and in 1997–98 he acted as Specialist Adviser to the House of Lords Select Committee on Science and Technology. Chris participated as an Expert at the European Commission/Danish Government Copenhagen Hearing on Digital Signatures, represented the UK Government at the Hague Conference on Private International Law, has been an invited speaker at OECD and G8 international conferences, and has been consulted by various UK government departments on electronic commerce law reform. He was involved in research which led to the EU directives on electronic signatures and on electronic commerce.

John Angel is a Senior Visiting Fellow at the Information Technology Unit, Centre of Commercial Law Studies, Queen Mary & Westfield College, University of London, where he lectures on the LLM Internet Law, IT Law and Telecommunications Law courses. John is also a consultant to the Clifford Chance Online Services group and specialises in e-commerce law.

He managed a computer software company, and in addition to two law degrees, has an MSc in industrial and business studies from Warwick University.

John is General Editor of the *Outsourcing Practice Manual* (Sweet & Maxwell, 1998–2000), Joint Editor of the *Telecommunication Law Handbook* and *Telecommunications Law* (both published by Blackstone Press, 1998 and 2000 respectively) and Consultant Editor to *Electronic Business Law* (published monthly and online by Butterworths).

Previously John specialised in employment law and was a part-time Chairman of Industrial Tribunals for many years. He is a Fellow of the Institute of Personnel and Development.

THE AUTHORS

Justine Campbell, LLB is a solicitor in BT's legal department, and a senior member of the Competition Law and Public Policy Team. Prior to joining BT, she spent five years at Freshfields, qualifying into Freshfields' Competition Law Team, and working in both the London and Brussels offices. She specialises in competition law in the telecommunications and technology sectors, including national and EC merger control, commercial arrangements and monopolies investigations.

Simon Chalton is a solicitor and a consultant to Bird & Bird, a City of London law firm with special interests in computer law. His experience with computers and the law relating to information technology goes back to the late 1960s when he contributed to the specification and design of computer applications programs and their implementation, and served as a non-executive director and chairman of a software house. His experience includes advising on computer and software contracts, software licensing and software protection, computer-related disputes and data protection.

Simon has held office as Chairman of the Intellectual Property Committee of the British Computer Society, as Chairman of the National Computing Centre's Legal Group and as Chairman of the International Bar Association's Computer and Database Committee. In a European context he is a World Intellectual Property Organisation listed mediator, a Fellow of the Chartered Institute of Arbitrators and a Fellow of the Society for Advanced Legal Studies. In an American context he has served as a member of the Society for Information Management's Procurement Working Group and as a Vice-Chair within the Computer Division of the Economics of Law Practice Section of the American Bar Association. He is a Fellow of the American Bar Foundation and a Fellow of the College of Law Practice Management.

Simon is the senior founder co-author and co-editor of Sweet & Maxwell's Encyclopedia of Data Protection, and a co-author and co-editor of *Database Law* (Jordan Publishing: 1998). He contributes to other publications and professional journals relating to computer law, is an experienced practitioner and speaker at an international level, and writes extensively on the legal aspects of computing.

Andrew Charlesworth is Senior Lecturer in Information Technology Law, and Director of the Information Law and Technology Unit at the University of Hull Law School, where he teaches IT law and Law of Electronic Commerce modules on both the LL.B. and LL.M. degrees. He is a member of the Editorial Board of the *Journal of Information Law and Technology*, the International Advisory Panel of the *International Yearbook of Law, Computers & Technology* and the Correspondents Panel of the *Computer Law and Security Report*. In the past, he has been Associate Editor of the *International Yearbook of Law, Computers & Technology*, and a member of both the Executive Committee of the British & Irish Legal Education Technology Association (BILETA) and the General Council of the Society for Computers and Law (SCL). He has lectured on computer misuse, data protection, intellectual property, social exclusion and the information superhighway, and legal issues of the Internet and WWW, at conferences and seminars in Europe, North America, the Middle East and Australia.

Allison Coleman is a Senior Lecturer in Law at the University of Wales, Aberystwyth, where she is the University's advisor in Intellectual Property and Industrial Contracts. She is author of *The Legal Protection of Trade Secrets* (Sweet & Maxwell, 1992), *Intellectual Property Law* (Longman Law, Tax and Finance, 1994) and a co-author of *Professional Issues in Software Engineering* (3rd edn, Taylor and Francis, 2000). Allison acts as Intellectual Property consultant to a firm of solicitors and to a number of University companies concerned with the exploitation of intellectual property and is a member of the editorial board of *Information and Communications Technology Law*.

Tim Cowen is General Counsel of IGNITE. Former Chief Counsel, Competition Law & Public Policy, Tim has also held the post of Head of European Law for British Telecom, where he was responsible for all aspects of EU law and telecommunications regulations affecting the BT Group. He is a member of the International Chamber of Commerce Working Group on Computing and Telecommunications Law and of the CBI Competition Panel. Tim speaks and writes regularly on EU law and competition law as applied to the telecommunications & IT industry.

Lars Davies, MA, LLM, Research Fellow, joined the Information Technology Law Unit at the Centre for Commercial Law Studies, Queen Mary and Westfield College, University of London, in May 1995. He works in the area of electronic commerce, with particular reference to the Internet. Prior to becoming a lawyer, Lars worked in the computer industry as a technical support engineer. Aside from his work in the IT Law Unit, Lars also teaches on the LL.M. Internet Law, Information Technology Law and Telecommunications Law options. He also regularly speaks or lectures on these topics nationally and internationally. Lars is a consultant to the law firm Ashurst Morris Crisp.

David Engel is an Associate in the Media & Internet Litigation Group at Theodore Goddard, where he has worked since 1993. In addition to his media litigation practice, David advises on contentious and non-contentious Internet issues including the legal risks of employee access to e-mail and the Internet, website content, ISP liability and domain name disputes. He is a recent contributor to *E-mail@work* (Pearson, 2000). His articles on Internet-related legal issues have appeared in various publications, including *The Times*, *International Media Law*, *Computer Bulletin*, *Copyright World*, *Entertainment Law Review* and *Communications Law*.

Robert Hart, a Chartered Patent Agent and European Patent Attorney, is an independent consultant in intellectual property matters and Director of Intellectual Property International Limited. He was formerly Intellectual Property Development Executive for the Plessy Company Plc. He was inaugural chairman of the BCS Intellectual Property Committee, a member of the Chartered Institute of Patent Agents Software Protection Committee, and represents the BCS on the British Copyright Council. He represented IFIP and the WIPO Committee on the Legal Protection of Computer Software in Geneva, 1983, and the UK and the WIPO Working Group on Technical Questions Relating to the Legal Protection of Software in Canberra 1984. He has acted as a consultant to WIPO on the legal protection of semi-conductor products, representing UNICE at the WIPO experts meetings in 1986, 1987 and 1988. More recently he has acted as technical consultant to DG III of the Commission of the European Communities on the Directive on the legal protection of computer programs and the Directive on the legal protection of databases. He has published widely on many aspects of computer law, and is co-author of a book, *Legal Protection of Computer Programs in Europe — A Guide to the EC Directive* (Butterworths, 1991).

Christopher Millard (LL.B., M.A., LL.M.) is a Partner in the Media, Computer and Communications Group at Clifford Chance (http://www.clifforchance.com). His practice is focussed on e-commerce, e-business and data protection compliance projects. He was responsible for the launch in May 1998 of NextLaw[TM], a Clifford Chance online service providing advice on data protection and related regulations in 36 jurisdictions (information about the service is available at http://www.nextlaw.com). As a Visiting Professorial Fellow of the Centre for Commercial Law Studies, he teaches on LL.M. courses in Internet Law, Information Technology Law and Telecommunications Law. He is a frequent speaker at international conferences and is a visiting lecturer at several universities. He is a past Chairman of the Society for Computers and Law and a past President of the International Federation of Computer Law Associations. He is Joint Editor of *Data Protection Laws of the World*, General Editor of the *International Journal of Law and Information Technology* (Oxford University Press) and is on the editorial boards of many IT, Internet and communications law journals.

Jeremy Newton joined the legal department of Sun Microsystems in March 2000 after ten years in private practice, most recently as a partner in the Technology Group at CMS Cameron McKenna, specialising in IT and e-commerce law. He is noted as a 'leader in the field' in *Chambers Guide to the Legal Profession* and *Euromoney Guide to the World's Leading IT Advisers*. He writes and lectures extensively on IT law and contracts.

Tim Press obtained a chemistry degree from Oxford University before qualifying as a solicitor. He joined the Bloomsbury firm of Woodham Smith and became a partner specialising in contentious and non-contentious intellectual property work, particularly patent litigation, subsequently moving to City of London firm Taylor Joynson Garrett. He then embarked upon an academic career and now teaches litigation and intellectual property at Cardiff University's Centre for Professional Legal Studies. His research interests include intellectual property, legal skills and legal practice and developing computer-based learning materials.

Dr Ian Walden is the Bird & Bird Senior Research Fellow in Information Technology Law at Centre for Commercial Law Studies, Queen Mary & Westfield College, and Director of QMW's Computer-Related Crime Research Centre. He is editor of *EDI and the Law* (1989) and joint editor of *Information Technology and the Law* (1990), *EDI Audit and Control* (1993), *Cross-border Electronic Banking* (1995), *Telecommunications Law Handbook* (1997) and Sweet & Maxwell's *Encyclopedia of Data Protection*. Ian is vice-chair of the e-centre UK's legal advisory group. Ian is a consultant to solicitors Bird & Bird, and a member of the European Commission's Legal Advisory Board.

Alison Welterveden is a senior lawyer within the IT & E-Commerce Law Group at Tite & Lewis, the associated law firm of Ernst & Young in the UK. Alison has published a number of articles on various aspects of information technology and e-commerce law, and is co-author of the chapter on 'IS Outsourcing' in the *Outsourcing Practice Manual*.

Table of Cases

Table of Statutes

Table of International Legislation

Table of Statutory Instruments and European Secondary Legislation

Introduction

Chris Reed

In about 1950 the then chairman of IBM was rumoured to have predicted that the world market for computers at the end of the century might approach one hundred machines. The degree to which his prediction fell short is a measure of how far computing technology has pervaded our lives. The result of this dramatic increase in the use of and reliance upon computing technology is that new and qualitatively different legal problems have arisen. These problems are the focus of this book.

Earlier versions of this Introduction discussed the argument that there is no need to treat computer law as a separate topic because it is no more than the application of existing principles to novel sets of facts. Today, ten years after the first edition, it has become recognised generally that computing technology does indeed give rise to novel legal problems which are not resolvable by applying existing legal principles. This is particularly apparent where transactions are carried out through the exchange of digital information rather than by human interaction. The developing law which seeks to resolve those problems is the heart of computer law.

0.1 DEFINING COMPUTER LAW

Computer law is that branch of the law which regulates the *technological* aspects of information[1] — i.e., it is the law which governs information

---

1. Thus, for example, the law of defamation is not specifically part of computer law, but those aspects of defamation which arise uniquely from information processing activities will fall to be treated under this heading, particularly if the legal principles involved are common to those applied to similar problems which would traditionally be examined under different legal headings. A particularly good example of such an issue is the question of when an Internet Service Provider is liable for the information which passes across its servers, even though it is not the author and did not originate the transmission of that information. This issue is discussed in detail in chapter 11.

processing. Information processing is the automated transformation or transmission of digital information, and the subject area extends to the information
processing aspects of the technology used. At present this primarily, though
not exclusively, means computers.[2]

The transformation in society which has been brought about by information technology has given rise to qualitatively different types of legal issue.
Traditionally, the law divided the subject matter of commerce into goods and
services and dealt with information either as an aspect of human behaviour
(e.g., negligent advice) or through intellectual property rights. Manufacturing
industry processed physical entities into other physical entities, which were
distributed under a well-defined legal framework. Services, such as advice or
labour, were essentially ephemeral matters which had no permanent existence
and could thus be regulated mainly as a question of whether the provider of
the service did so with proper care and in the proper manner. Intellectual
property was generated through human effort and ingenuity, and produced
delimited and static results (such as a book or an invention) which could be
exploited in a limited number of ways.

All these things still happen, of course, but information technology has
enabled information, formerly an ephemeral phenomenon, to be turned into
something that has a quasi-physical existence and which can be traded as if
it were a physical commodity. Thus database services sell pure information,
whilst software houses sell applied information in the form of computer
software, and much of this information is generated not by human effort but
as the result of computer-controlled processes. Fixed physical documents
turn into dynamic digital data, and are 'signed' in non-physical ways.

Some chapters of this book record the ways in which traditional divisions
of the law are adapting themselves to these new phenomena, while others
examine entirely new fields of law which are in the process of development.
Because of the constant change in the law, some of the suggestions made in
the following chapters must necessarily be speculative. Nonetheless, those
working with information technology or advising others on the legal aspects
of its use require guidance, and the authors have used their experience in their
own particular specialisms to provide the best predictions that can be made
at the moment. In an increasing number of areas there is now technology-
specific legislation, though its precise application often has yet to be decided
by the courts. Even where legislation is not forthcoming new problems still
arise, and will therefore have to be dealt with by judicial adaptation of existing
principles. This book attempts to identify those problems and suggest the
solutions likely to be adopted by the courts.

0.2 COMMON THEMES

Throughout the law relating to computers run a number of common themes,
which the reader should bear in mind.

---

2. Including related information processing devices which, nowadays, range from obvious
   devices such as mobile telephones to far more obscure machines, like electronic toasters which
   contain specially designed semiconductor chips.

0.2.1 Information or knowledge as a species of property

The law of intellectual property already recognises that certain types of knowledge should be treated to some extent as if it were private property and thus capable of 'ownership', for reasons such as the invention shown by its deviser, the creative effort put into its compilation or because it has been kept confidential. Other types of knowledge are incapable of ownership because of their nature as fundamental concepts or because they are mere ideas, and these are instead free to be used by all mankind. Thus the equation $e = mc^2$ cannot be the subject of a patent or of the law of copyright, nor can the basic concept of the internal combustion engine (though of course a specific implementation of that concept can). Because information technology concerns itself with applied information, however, it is difficult to classify it into either of these categories. Such information is normally very valuable, and in general most things which have a market value are dealt with by the law as a species of property. The law of intellectual property has developed techniques to decide which information technology products are to be treated as belonging only to one particular individual, and which are incapable of ownership and thus available to all.

0.2.2 The distribution of resources and effort

The newest challenge to intellectual property rights comes from the rise of global information networks, of which the Internet is the prime example. Copyright law, in particular, is based on the assumption that a protectable intellectual asset exists in fixed form, and thus only protects it against copying. Networks make it possible for an information resource, such a program or a digital image, to be used without copying it to a different computer, or to be incorporated in an activity in such a way that the person controlling the incorporation does not undertake any copying (e.g., linking to a resource on another's website). In other words, there are new ways of using another's intellectual property, and the question whether those uses infringe the owner's rights is still in the process of being answered.

Distribution of resources and effort is even challenging specific computer laws, such as those on data protection. Personal data is now gathered from multiple activities and sources, held in different places (which may change regularly in both location and content) and used by searching across holdings of data controlled by different persons. Data protection laws are based on the concept of a single database controlled by a single entity, and may struggle to adapt.

0.2.3 Controlling the use of personal information

The capacity which computing technology provides allows the aggregation of scattered information, and can make it available worldwide. Data which might formerly have had to be kept in a number of small collections for access to be feasible (such as an individual doctor's patient records) can now be brought together and made globally searchable (e.g., the medical records for the whole of the United Kingdom). Moreover, data can be collated across multiple data sources to produce new information about individuals and corporations — for example, it would technically be feasible to produce a detailed financial profile of any individual from his or her tax, investment and spending information, if coordinated access to the databases held by the tax authorities, credit card companies, pension funds and supermarkets were permitted.

These technical possibilities have the potential to conflict with the fundamental human right of privacy. They also question the nature of privacy itself — is it merely the right not to disclose personal information, in which case once disclosure has taken place there is no further privacy interest in that information, or does it extend to controlling the use which others make of that information? A consensus seems to have been achieved that it is the latter, but there is still no international agreement on what the use restrictions should be, and how they should be monitored and enforced. This lack of consensus raises special legal difficulties in an era in which the Internet has made all data equally accessible, regardless of the geographical location of their storage devices.

Finally, the psychological characteristics of data stored and process by computer creates legal problems, as humans still have an unjustified belief in the infallibility of computers whilst failing to recognise that the information comes, directly or indirectly (as software processing results) from fallible humans. The effects this has on their behaviour when faced with a computer's output will be of particular relevance to the law of tort.

0.2.4   Information technology as a substitute for human endeavour

In many fields of human activity information technology is used to substitute for some or all of the functions previously undertaken by humans, or to perform functions that could not previously be performed at all. This has happened before — for example, the motor car has in part substituted for walking — but in each case the mechanism has remained largely under the control of its human user. The whole point of using information technology, however, is that the machine should control itself. This raises a number of problems that the law must eventually resolve:

(a)   Where does responsibility lie when someone who, in the absence of his using a computer to perform some task would be personally responsible for loss caused to another, relies on the computer's proper operation, rather than his own expertise, to avoid causing such injury?

(b)   How are the courts to cope when the only evidence of a fact lies solely within the 'knowledge' of a machine, particularly where the machine also has the ability to alter that information? The basic evidential difficulties seem largely to have been solved, but where complex electronic transactions are carried out through largely automated processes, often crossborder, new legal issues of identity and attribution arise. Legislation is rapidly being introduced to address some of these, and the EU Directives on electronic signatures and electronic commerce introduce some important new principles of law.

(c)   The enhanced abilities of machines inevitably lead to increased expectations, and standards of performance that were acceptable before the introduction of computer technology may well now fall short of what ought to be achieved. Some readers may remember the public outcry after the 'hurricane' of 1987, when many people complained that the Meteorological Office had failed to predict the violence and extent of the storm in spite of substantial investment in information technology. It has still to be decided how far the law's allocation of responsibility (mainly in tort and contract) should reflect these increased expectations.

0.2.5 The move from products to information services

The first generation of computing technology concentrated on the electronic hardware used to process information; the second on the software which controlled that processing. Today, it is possible to identify a clear shift from these discrete products to pure trade in information services. From a user's perspective this makes a great deal of sense — what is required is the final output of the information processing process, such as a document or a set of accounts, and the precise equipment and software used to produce that output are merely means to an end.

This shift generates a further fundamental challenge to the law. Services were previously the result of human effort or skill, and the quality of service to be provided could be judged against the standards expected from other humans. Now, most information-based services are provided by computing technology, and the human input is increasingly remote from the point of service delivery. It is clearly inappropriate to judge an automated bank teller by the standards to be expected of a human, for example, and the law is still in the process of determining the new quality and liability tests which should apply to services provided in this way.

0.2.6 Trading in information products

Closely linked to the question of information as property is the legal classification of trade in information products. This is particularly relevant to the supply of computer software, information services and entertainment products and services. Initially, when the only computers were mainframe systems and software was only available from the manufacturer, it was generally accepted that the relationship between software producer and user could be classified solely as a licence of intellectual property rights and thus as a supply of services for liability purposes. Information was marketed in two forms — products, which were static (such as books), and bespoke information (such as legal advice) which was not re-usable. Entertainment either came in static form (e.g., an audio tape), or was supplied in real time in a reasonably fixed form (e.g., theatre performances or television broadcasts).

Today, we have entered into an age of mass customisation. Most software products are multifunctional, and capable of further extension and customisation by downloading additional elements. On-line delivery of information and entertainment allows the 'product' to be modified to the recipient's exact requirements. The relationship between the producer of these information products and the ultimate consumer is often remote, with new types of intermediary springing up to make information products and services available on the market. It is now far harder to say exactly what is being traded: Goods? Services? Or something entirely new which does not fit into any existing classification?

0.2.7 Paperless and people-less trading

Already in the business-to-business arena, computers are selling and buying on behalf of their owners without any human intervention or decision making. The stock control systems of supermarkets discover, through links to the tills, that a product line is running low and immediately generate an on-line order to the supplier's computer, which accepts it and puts in train the process of production and delivery. Many other industries and commercial sectors undertake automated trading. In the near future, this phenomenon will extend to the business-to-consumer market. Automated agents will scour the Internet for bargains, negotiate an agreement within the parameters set by their human principal and arrange for payment in electronic form.

These activities do not always accord with the existing legal and regulatory framework. The law of contract assumes the meeting of human minds, and requirements to undertake business transactions via written and signed documents are found in every country's laws. Major legislative reform is required to assimilate these transactions within an extended legal structure, and the most relevant proposals are examined in the applicable chapters.

0.2.8 Convergence of national laws

The information technology industry, and the dissemination and consumption of information products and services, transcends national boundaries. Differences in national treatment of these phenomena can result in major distortions of the market — for example, the current tax treatment of electronic commerce (not examined in this book) often discriminates in favour of exporters of information products and against the domestic supplier.

In the long term it is possible to detect a natural trend towards convergence[3] of national laws — indeed, countries whose laws take a different direction to the trend may be forced by the requirements of the global market to enact amending legislation. One of the earliest examples was the Australian amendment to its copyright laws following the High Court's decision that no copyright subsisted in object code,[4] and at the time of writing the United States is in negotiation with the European Commission over the transborder effect of data protection laws.[5]

---

3. 'Convergence' is used here, rather than 'harmonisation' or 'approximation', because it is a value free term which carries no connotations of a supranational legislator. Additionally, it recognises that legislators do not always set out consciously to match their laws with those of another State — in some instances (digital signature law being, perhaps, the prime example) convergence may simply happen, driven by the needs of the market rather than any legislative planning.
4. *Apple Computer Inc.* v *Computer Edge Pty Ltd* [1986] FSR 537.
5. See US Department of Commerce draft Safe Harbor Principles, 15 November 1999, at http://www.ita.doc.gov/td/ecom/Principles1199.htm.

A particularly strong force towards convergence is the Internet and the commercial and non-commercial activities it allows. These impose substantial pressure on national legislators to eradicate the differences between their own laws and those of other States. Convergence also reduces the severe difficulties of enforcing laws and regulations against an on-line actor, as compliance with the actor's home State laws is likely to mean that it is also compliant abroad. The trend is towards recognition of a basic principle that information processing activities should primarily be regulated in their home countries,[6] which in its turn requires that laws converge.

Convergence can happen in one of three ways:

(a) Through the mechanism of international conventions — normally too slow a process for computer law issues;

(b) Through harmonisation or approximation of national laws, as the result of a conscious decision of national governments to remove the differences between them. The European Union provides the classic case study for harmonisation, and where powers to enforce the adoption of new laws are lacking, approximation of national laws through bilateral or multilateral agreement is a possible alternative route;

(c) Through what might be described as accidental or fortuitous convergence, driven by pressure from information technology enterprises and influential policy organisations.

The last of these is by far the most common, and means that many of the principles of English law described in this book are likely to be replicated, now or in the future, in the laws of other countries. As a corollary, when English law changes it will often be possible to identify the inspiration for the change in another country's laws. Globalisation is a phenomenon which is not limited to trading activities — it also drives legal innovation, and computer law is more strongly affected than most areas of law.

---

6. See e.g., Directive 95/46/EC on the protection of individuals with regard to the processing of personal data and on the free movement of such data (the Data Protection Directive) art. 4; Directive 2000/31/EC on electronic commerce art. 3(2).

CHAPTER ONE

System Supply Contracts

Jeremy Newton

1.1 INTRODUCTION

1.1.1 System supply contracts

1.1.1.1 What is a 'system supply contract'? Expressions like 'system supply contracts' and 'computer contracts' cover a multitude of commercial transactions, ranging from the purchase of a single CD-ROM from a high street retailer through to multi-million pound systems or communications outsourcing projects. For historical reasons, the traditional approach to examining such contracts (and the one adopted in previous editions of this book) drew a distinction between hardware and software agreements. However, this distinction is becoming increasingly irrelevant, so the author proposes to take a more holistic line, and to look at 'system supply contracts' as a whole. A system supply contract is accordingly one under which the customer is to receive one or more of the following:

   (a)   hardware;
   (b)   software;
   (c)   other equipment (such as cabling or power supply); and
   (d)   services (such as consultancy, installation, support and maintenance).

1.1.1.2 Contract structures System supply contracts can be structured in numerous ways. One common structure is known as the 'turnkey' arrangement, whereby the supplier undertakes to supply all the elements of the system under one contract, or as prime contractor at the top of a chain of connected subcontracts. More complex structures are also possible, whereby the supplier acts effectively as a broker between the customer and third party suppliers.

1.1.2 The contract process

1.1.2.1 Function of a written contract In most commercial transactions, the terms of these contracts will be recorded in writing, and understanding the reasons for having a written contract can help the parties to negotiate it effectively. The function of a written contract is to record the terms governing the supply of goods and services. In the absence of a clear, express understanding between the parties, the law implies certain terms into the contract (discussed in more detail in section 1.2.1 below) which may run counter to the parties' actual intentions, so a written agreement gives certainty to the terms of the transaction.

1.1.2.2 Significance of the negotiation process There is also an important function to the negotiation process that leads up to signature of a written agreement. This process should help ensure that the parties understand each other's expectations about the deal in question, and to draw out differences in those expectations that can then be resolved before they lead to problems. Many IT projects fail precisely because the parties do not exercise sufficient care to ensure that the supplier's and the customer's expectations match. Ensuring that these do match is, in the opinion of this author, the key role of the legal adviser in the contract process.

1.1.2.3 Use of standard terms It is a feature of doing business in the IT sector that most suppliers will attempt to deal on their own set of standard terms. However, these are always negotiable to some degree. How far the supplier is willing to deviate from his standard terms depends mainly on the customer's bargaining power. Probably the only negotiable term in a contract for a single PC is the price, whereas a buyer who is paying several million pounds for a mainframe system will be able to negotiate most of the terms. The danger of uncritically accepting the standard terms of even the most respectable supplier can be illustrated by *Mackenzie Patten v British Olivetti* (1984) 1 CL&P 92, 95. In that case, a law firm bought an Olivetti computer system to run its accounts. They discussed their needs with the salesperson, and signed up on Olivetti's standard terms. These dealt only with the system's technical performance, but did not address certain other important issues. The system proved unsuitable for the firm's purposes; it was slow, difficult to use, and could not expand to cope with new business. None of these matters was dealt with in the contract. In the event, the court found that Olivetti was bound by the salesperson's claims that the system would be suitable for their needs, but by that stage the firm had expended time and money in the litigation, and then of course had to find a replacement system.

Put another way, standard forms are only suitable for standard transactions. No matter how comprehensive the standard contract, it will usually fail to cover some essential point envisaged by the particular parties to any particular deal.

1.1.2.4 Negotiating for the long term   There is a further reason for negotiating a detailed contract for any significant deal: unlike many sale of goods contracts, the delivery of a computer system is only the beginning of the relationship, not its culmination. Further work will be necessary to install the system and get it working properly, and the customer will usually return to the same supplier for upgrades. So although the aim of the negotiator is to get the best possible deal for the client, this should not mean gaining at the expense of the other side. The aim is to produce a mutually satisfactory contract which will provide a comprehensive basis for the continuing relationship between them.

1.1.2.5 Types of contractual provision   Any well-drawn contract will have provisions relating to three broad categories of expectation:

(a)   Contract mechanics: for example, who delivers what, and when?
(b)   Commercial highlights: for example, what is the price, who owns resulting intellectual property rights, what warranties are given in respect of the system?
(c)   Problem management: what happens if the project goes wrong, and what remedies are available?

The objective is to ensure that no essential terms are missing from the contract. Some of these are discussed in section 1.1.3 of this chapter, and others relevant to the particular circumstances should come out of the negotiations themselves. However, before looking at specific contractual provisions, this chapter will discuss some of the principal legal aspects of system supply agreements.

1.1.3 Terminology

As a general point on terminology, there are a number of expressions that may correctly be used to denote the different parties to any system supply contract. In the context of the software licensing elements, it is common to refer to 'licensor' and 'licensee'. Hardware sale agreements usually refer to 'buyers' and 'sellers'. Consultancy or software development contracts will tend to refer to 'consultant' and 'client'. However, as a system supply contract may comprise any combination of these various elements, the author refers generally in this chapter to 'supplier' and 'customer' unless there is a sound reason for using the narrower expressions (such as in the discussion of Sale of Goods legislation which specifically refers to buyers and sellers).

1.2   PRINCIPAL LEGAL ISSUES APPLICABLE TO SYSTEM
SUPPLY CONTRACTS

1.2.1   Implied terms

1.2.1.1   Background to the statutory implied terms   Certain terms may be implied into contracts (both consumer and business contracts) as a matter of statute law or common law. The main statutory implied terms arise under the Sale of Goods Act 1979 ('SGA 1979') and under the Supply of Goods and Services Act 1982 ('SGSA 1982'). These terms are generally characterised as either conditions or warranties, the distinction being that breach of a condition entitles the innocent party to terminate the contract outright, whereas breach of a warranty entitles him to sue for damages only (but he remains committed to perform his side of the deal).

1.2.1.2   Section 12(1) SGA 1979: the right to sell   Section 12(1) SGA 1979 implies a term[1] into all contracts of sale that the seller has the right to sell the goods. If the seller fails to transfer ownership, then he will be in breach of this term, and the buyer can reject the goods and recover the price, plus damages if they can be proved.[2]

1.2.1.3   Implications of s. 12(1) SGA 1979 for hardware sales   In order to satisfy s. 12(1), the buyer must receive full and unfettered rights of ownership (unless the contrary has been agreed under s. 12(3)). This means that the seller will be in breach of the condition if the goods are subject to rights belonging to a third party. The most obvious rights which exist independent of ownership are intellectual property rights (IPRs), so hardware producers risk running into difficulty if the product infringes someone else's IPR. In that eventuality, a patentee or copyright owner might prevent the buyer using any infringing equipment (or software loaded on legitimate equipment), so an innocent buyer could be prevented from using the hardware he has purchased. This is a clear breach of s. 12(1) on the seller's part, even if the IPR owner chooses not to exercise his rights.

1.2.1.4   Section 12(2) SGA 1979: quiet possession   The seller will be in breach of s. 12(1) if the third party's rights existed at the time of sale. However, some IPRs (e.g., patents and trade marks) only come into existence on registration, so it is possible that such rights might only arise *after* the sale was made. In that case, the seller is not in breach of s. 12(1), but is in breach of the term[3] in s. 12(2)(b) that the buyer will have quiet possession of the

---

1. In England, Wales and Northern Ireland, this term is a condition by virtue of s. 12(5A), added by the Sale and Supply of Goods Act 1994.
2. This is not affected by any use of the goods by the buyer. The essence of a sale of goods contract is the transfer of ownership from seller to buyer, and a failure to effect this means that there is a total failure of consideration (*Rowland* v *Divall* (1923) 2 KB 500).
3. In England, Wales and Northern Ireland a warranty by virtue of s. 12(5A), added by the Sale and Supply of Goods Act 1994.

goods.[4] This is in effect a promise by the seller that no person will in the future acquire rights over the goods and enforce them against the buyer. The warranty is broken only when the third party enforces his rights, at which point the buyer becomes entitled to claim damages from the seller (but not to reject the goods). However, if the third party prevents the buyer from using the goods, the buyer's damages will be assessed as the cost of buying a replacement, in effect returning the price.

1.2.1.5 Section 13 SGA 1979: correspondence with description Section 13 SGA 1979 provides for an implied condition that goods will correspond with their description. In general, the description of hardware will be the user requirements specification attached to the contract. However, the question arises whether any claims made by salespeople or contained in the manufacturer's publicity material amount also to a description for these purposes. The traditional test is to ask whether the words used are a term of the contract or a mere representation: this is answered by examining whether the seller intended to promise, as part of the contract, that the words were true. In practice, however, it is impossible to ascertain the seller's real intention (indeed, the seller may have had none) and what the courts appear to be asking themselves is whether the buyer got that which he was led to believe he was buying. The test would thus be whether a reasonable person in the buyer's position would have been led to believe that the seller was promising a true description of the goods. As a general rule, only if the buyer examines the goods thoroughly before he buys will the court decide that descriptive words which had no influence on his decision to buy are not part of the description of the goods for the purposes of s. 13.

1.2.1.6 Section 14 SGA 1979: quality and fitness for purpose Section 14 SGA 1979 provides for an implied condition that goods will be of satisfactory quality (s. 14(2)) and reasonably fit for their purpose (s. 14(3)). However, obligations of quality raise particular problems in relation to IT systems as it is often difficult to define a system's purposes with sufficient precision, let alone decide if it is reasonably fit. In this respect, the description[5] of the goods can be very important — in some cases, it is almost the sole determinant of the quality the buyer is entitled to expect.

1.2.1.7 Satisfactory quality 'Satisfactory quality' is defined in s. 14(2A) and (2B) (inserted into the SGA 1979 Act by the Sale and Supply of Goods Act 1994):

> (2A) For the purposes of this Act, goods are of satisfactory quality if they meet the standard that a reasonable person would regard as satisfactory, taking account of any description of the goods, the price (if relevant) and all the other relevant circumstances.

---

4. For a clear illustration of the distinction see *Microbeads AG* v *Vinhurst Road Markings Ltd* [1975] 1 WLR 218.
5. I.e., the user requirements specification, assuming one has been negotiated.

(2B)   For the purposes of this Act, the quality of goods includes their
state and condition and the following (among others) are in appropriate
cases aspects of the quality of goods—
    (a)   fitness for all the purposes for which goods of the kind in question
are commonly supplied;
    (b)   appearance and finish;
    (c)   freedom from minor defects;
    (d)   safety; and
    (e)   durability.

It will be clear from the above definition that no hard and fast rule can ever
be drawn as to whether goods fulfil the obligation of satisfactory quality.
Instead, the courts will examine the circumstances of the contract in an
attempt to decide whether a reasonable buyer would have been satisfied with
the quality of the goods.

1.2.1.8   Exceptions to s. 14(2)   The obligation set out in s. 14(2) does not
extend to defects that the seller specifically reveals, nor to those defects that
should have been discovered by the inspection (if any) that was *actually made*
by the buyer.[6] It should also be noted that it is not only the goods sold that
must be satisfactory — any goods *supplied* under the contract (e.g., manuals
or magnetic media) must also be of satisfactory quality, even if they remain
the seller's property and are to be returned to him.

1.2.1.9   Implications of s. 14(2) for system supply agreements   The problem of
ascertaining whether a system fulfils s. 14(2) is likely to turn almost exclusively on the question whether the system is fit for all its common purposes.
In this context, freedom from minor defects is probably an aspect of that
fitness, unless the defects are merely cosmetic (e.g., dents in computer cases).
The court's task is to determine what purposes systems *of the kind in question*
are commonly supplied for. This is a very difficult matter, particularly in
relation to hardware, the functioning of which is determined by the software
which runs upon it. Similarly, in relation to software, programs invariably
contain programming errors or 'bugs', and it is likely that a court will take
note of this in determining whether a program is of satisfactory quality.
Indeed, in *Saphena Computing Ltd* v *Allied Collection Agencies Ltd* [1995] FSR
616 the recorder acknowledged precisely this when he observed that 'even
programs that are reasonably fit for their purpose may contain bugs'. So the
real question to be determined is what functions the seller might reasonably
foresee the buyer as requiring. Predictably, no clear answers can be given, and
for this reason it is common in substantial computer contracts to agree a
detailed specification, listing the functions to be performed and objective
criteria for testing that performance, and then to exclude the terms implied
by s. 14(2) and (3). (Note that different considerations apply to the purchase
of commodity items such as PCs and peripherals as individual transactions,

---

6. Sale of Goods Act 1979, s. 14(2C), as amended by the Sale and Supply of Goods Act 1994.

where the contract value is too low to permit the negotiation of detailed specifications. In many such cases, it may become necessary to rely on s. 14(2).)

1.2.1.10   Fitness for the buyer's particular purpose   If the seller sells in the course of a business and the buyer expressly or impliedly makes known a particular purpose or purposes for which he intends to use the hardware, s. 14(3) implies a term[7] that it will be reasonably fit for those purposes. This condition is imposed because the buyer relies on the seller to use his expertise to select goods suitable for the buyer's needs. If the buyer produces the user requirements specification himself, this would normally suggest that he is not relying on the seller's skill and judgment to select appropriate equipment, and that s. 14(3) accordingly has no relevance. However, the seller will still be liable under that subsection in respect of matters not covered by the specification, as illustrated by *Cammell Laird & Co. Ltd* v *Manganese Bronze & Brass Co. Ltd* [1934] AC 402. In that case, the buyer entered into a contract for the supply of a ship's propeller, to be manufactured to the buyer's specification and used on a named ship. The propeller proved unsuitable for the ship because its pitch was incorrect, a matter not provided for in the specification. The court held that as this had been left to the seller's discretion it clearly showed reliance on the buyer's part. The court also made it clear that if the defect had been in the buyer's specification the seller would not have been in breach of the condition.

In the context of IT systems, standard hardware and software are not of course designed for any particular user, and will be unlikely to meet all the requirements of any user. However, where customised hardware or bespoke software is supplied, the user may more reasonably expect to receive a warranty that it will comply with his requirements: indeed, it is far from unusual for the buyer to expect the seller to check his specification, particularly where the specification has been arrived at in consultation between them. In such cases, the buyer will claim to have relied on the seller's skill and judgment.

1.2.1.11   Exceptions to s. 14(3)   The condition is not implied where it is unreasonable for the buyer to rely on the seller's expertise. This might be the case where the seller makes it clear that he cannot say whether the hardware will be suitable (e.g., where it is purchased for research purposes) or where the buyer fails to give him the information he needs to exercise his judgment properly.[8]

1.2.1.12   Section 13 SGSA 1982: reasonable care and skill   The implied terms discussed above all apply to contracts for goods. Section 13 SGSA 1982 implies a different term into contracts for services, to the effect that the services will be provided with reasonable care and skill'.

---

7. In England, Wales and Northern Ireland, this term is a condition by virtue of s. 14(6), substituted by the Sale and Supply of Goods Act 1994.
8. See *Griffiths* v *Peter Conway Ltd* [1939] 1 All ER 685.

1.2.1.13   Implications of s. 13 SGSA for system supply contracts   Although s. 13 SGSA may have little significance for contracts for hardware alone, the implied term is of course important to the supply of related services — for example, hardware maintenance, software development and support, consultancy and training. There is also a possibility that the supply of software *per se* may be viewed by the courts as a supply of services, for the reasons set out below.

1.2.1.14   Classification of software as goods or services   Until recently there did not appear to have been any cases in which the statutory implied terms had been held to apply to software, but four cases illustrate the development of judicial thinking on this point:

(a)   *Eurodynamics:* In *Eurodynamics Systems plc* v *General Automation Ltd* (6 September 1988, (unreported), Steyn J refused to decide whether software was goods, or whether the terms implied by the SGA 1979 applied to the software licence in question, as he was able to decide the case without reaching a view on these issues.

(b)   *Saphena:* By contrast, in *Saphena Computing Ltd* v *Allied Collection Agencies Ltd* [1995] FSR 616 the recorder decided that 'it was an implied term of each contract for the supply of software that the software would be reasonably fit for any purpose which had been communicated to the plaintiff [claimant]'. This decision is unsatisfactory, however, since the recorder did not explain the basis on which he found that the term was implied. He did find. however, that the software had been supplied on terms that the software might not be lent, sold or hired to any third party without the licensors consent, which might suggest a hiring rather than a sale, though this is by no means conclusive. On appeal Staughton LJ stated:

> ... it was, we are told, common ground that the law governing these contracts was precisely the same whether they were contracts for the sale of goods or the supply of services. It is therefore unnecessary to consider into which category they might come.

On the face of it that is an extraordinary statement since the law relating to goods as against services is quite different: the only term implied into a contract for services is that reasonable skill and care will be used, not that the result will be fit for any particular purpose or meet any standard of quality.

(c)   *St. Albans:* A clearer statement that the SGA 1979 applies to the supply of software appears in the obiter dictum of Scott Baker J in *St Albans City and District Council* v *International Computers Ltd* [1996] 4 All ER 481, CA. The judge concluded that although the disks or tapes on which a program is recorded certainly are goods, the program of itself is not. (The view of this author is that the distinction is more subtle than this, and should really depend on the circumstances in which the software is procured: the purchase of, say, a standard computer game should be regarded as a sale of goods irrespective of the medium by which the software is delivered; whereas a bespoke system written specially by the supplier for a particular customer necessarily entails the supply of services. Whether the terms implied by s. 13 SGSA 1982 provide adequate protection for the customer in this latter case is an argument beyond the scope of this chapter.)

(d)   *Adobe:* Against this, the Scottish decision of *Beta Computers (Europe) Ltd* v *Adobe Systems (Europe) Ltd* [1996] FSR 367, holding that a supply of 'shrink-wrapped' software was not a sale of goods, should also be noted, although the decision is only of persuasive authority in England.

1.2.1.15   Common law implied terms   It should be remembered that apart from terms implied by statute, terms may also be implied from the facts and circumstances of the particular contract. Here the courts use the 'officious bystander' and 'business efficacy' tests to determine whether the implication of a term is proper, as illustrated by *Greaves & Co. (Contractors) Ltd* v *Baynham Meikle & Partners* [1975] 1 WLR 1095. In a contract for the provision of engineering consultancy services there was an implied term that the design which was the subject of the contract should be fit for certain specific purposes. Similarly, in a software contract that is a mere contract for services (e.g., programming), it may be possible to imply a term that the software supplied should comply with particular criteria, over and above the statutory term that the work be carried out with reasonable skill and care.

1.2.2   Limitations and exclusions of liability

1.2.2.1   Introduction   It is common for system supply contracts to contain provisions excluding or limiting the supplier's liability. The most common exclusions or limitations refer to a breach of description or quality, and in particular it is common to exclude all liability for loss consequential on a breakdown or malfunction of the equipment. Such provisions need to be carefully drafted if they are to be effective, and some exclusions are not permitted by law. There are two levels of legal control over exclusion clauses — the common law, and statutory control under the Unfair Contract Terms Act 1977 ('UCTA') and the EC Directive on Unfair Terms in Consumer Contracts 1993.

1.2.2.2   Common law rules: incorporation of terms[9]   In order for an exclusion clause to protect the supplier, it must be contractually binding on the customer. This is most easily effected if it is contained in a written contract signed by the buyer. Many contracts for goods of low value, however, are made by exchange of letters, each referring to the other's standard terms, and it may be a difficult matter to decide whether the clause in question is part of the contract.[10]

1.2.2.3   Common law rules: construction and the 'contra proferentem' rule   Even if it is duly incorporated, an exclusion clause will only protect the seller if, as

---

9. See generally P.S. Atiyah, *The Sale of Goods*, 9th edn London: Pitman, 1995, ch. 13.
10. This point is too complicated for examination here, but the rules for construing such an agreement can be found in any standard work on the law of contract.

a matter of construction, it covers the breach that has occurred. The rules of construction are complicated but in general the more serious the breach of contract, the more clearly worded the clause must be if it is to exclude liability for that breach: it is interpreted against the party seeking to rely on it (the *contra proferentem* rule). A recent illustration of this principle at work can be found in *Salvage Association v CAP Financial Services Ltd* [1995] FSR 654. There, a contract to supply bespoke software contained a warranty (clause 11.1) which provided that the limitation (clause 12) applied 'if CAP fails to perform its obligations under this condition [11.1]'. The wording of clause 11.1 was sufficiently ambiguous that the official referee could construe it as meaning that the warranty did not come into effect until after acceptance by the claimant, and as the claimant's claim arose from breaches occurring prior to acceptance (which in fact never occurred because the dispute began before the contract's acceptance procedures were reached), the warranty in clause 11.1 never came into effect, and thus the exclusion in clause 12 also never came into effect. The result was that the defendant's liability for breach of contract was completely unlimited.

1.2.2.4 Unfair Contract Terms Directive: background The newest statutory control on exclusion clauses is the EC Directive on Unfair Terms in Consumer Contracts (Directive 93/13/EEC, OJ L95, 21 April 1993), implemented in the United Kingdom by the Unfair Terms in Consumer Contracts Regulations 1994 (SI 1994/3159). The Directive provides that in a contract between a seller or supplier and a consumer unfair terms shall not be enforceable against the consumer, although the remainder of the contract remains in force so far as that is feasible.

1.2.2.5 Unfair Contract Terms Directive: terms which may be regarded as 'unfair' A term is unfair for the purposes of the Directive if (i) it has not been individually negotiated, and (ii) 'contrary to the requirement of good faith, it causes a significant imbalance in the parties' rights and obligations arising under the contract, to the detriment of the consumer' (art. 3(1)). The annex to the Directive contains a list of terms which 'may be regarded as unfair' (art. 3(3)).[11] Examples from that list which are particularly relevant to computer contracts include terms:

(b) Inappropriately excluding or limiting the legal rights of the consumer ... in the event of total or partial non-performance .... .

(f) Authorising the seller or supplier to dissolve the contract on a discretionary basis where the same facility is not granted to the consumer.... .

(h) Automatically extending a contract of fixed duration where the consumer does not indicate otherwise, when the deadline fixed for the

---

11. In a consultative document, *Implementation of the EC Directive on Unfair Terms in Consumer Contracts*, London: DTI, 1993, the DTI took this wording to mean that the terms in the list may be, but are not necessarily, unfair. Other Member States may take a stronger position on this point, and in any event sellers should realise that including any of the terms in the annex is likely to give rise to a presumption of unfairness.

consumer to express this desire not to extend the contract is unreasonably early.[12]

(i) Irrevocably binding the consumer to terms with which he had no real opportunity of becoming acquainted before the conclusion of the contract.[13]

(k) Enabling the seller or supplier to alter unilaterally without a valid reason any characteristics of the product or service to be provided.

(p) Giving the seller or supplier the possibility of transferring his rights and obligations under the contract, where this may serve to reduce the guarantees for the consumer, without the latter's agreement.[14]

(q) Excluding or hindering the consumer's right to take legal action or exercise any other legal remedy, particularly by ... unduly restricting the evidence available to him or imposing on him a burden of proof which, according to the applicable law, should lie with another party to the contract.

These examples are not exhaustive — others from the annex may be applicable to particular computer contracts, and in any case the annex is purely indicative, so that terms having a similar effect are likely also to be construed as unfair.

1.2.2.6   UCTA: background   UCTA is of more general application than the Directive, as it applies to contracts between businesses as well as to those between businesses and consumers. Suppliers of IT systems to consumers will need to consider both forms of control, whereas suppliers only to businesses can ignore the Directive.

1.2.2.7   Section 6 UCTA: exclusions of liability under the SGA 1979   Section 6 of UCTA deals with attempts to exclude liability under the SGA 1979. In particular:

(a) Section 6(1) provides that it is not possible to exclude the condition that the seller has the right to sell the goods (see sections 1.2.1.2–1.2.1.4).

(b) Section 6(2) provides that where the buyer deals as a consumer, it is not possible to exclude the seller's liability for correspondence to description, quality and fitness for purposes (see sections 1.2.1.5–1.2.1.13). A buyer 'deals as a consumer' if (i) he does not buy in the course of a business, (ii) the seller sells in the course of a business, and (iii) the goods are of a type normally supplied for private use or consumption — see s. 12 UCTA.

(c) Section 6(3) provides that, where the buyer does *not* deal as a consumer, the seller's liability for correspondence to description, quality and fitness *may* be excluded, provided the exclusion clause satisfies the test of reasonableness.

---

12. Examples (f) and (h) are particularly likely to arise in maintenance contracts.
13. This is a particular problem in mail order sales, especially where the order is placed by telephone.
14. This too is a term which may be found in a maintenance contract.

1.2.2.8   Section 3 UCTA: exclusions of liability for breaches other than of the SGA 1979 implied terms   UCTA also affects clauses that attempt to exclude liability for breaches of terms other than those imposed by the SGA 1979. The most relevant section is s. 3, which provides that where the buyer deals as a consumer, or where he deals on the seller's written standard terms, the clause must satisfy the test of reasonableness to be effective. In most IT contracts, s. 3 will apply as well as s. 6, in which case the section that provides the best protection for the buyer will be applied.

1.2.2.9   When does UCTA not apply?   The only obvious case in which UCTA will be irrelevant is where the parties depart substantially from the seller's standard terms, and the breach is not of one of the implied terms. The theory is perhaps that if the parties are of such equal bargaining power that they can negotiate a non-standard contract, any exclusion clause is seen by both sides as fair. The question remains whether the entire contract needs to be in standard form, or whether it is sufficient to bring the case within s. 3 if the exclusion clause alone is the seller's standard term. These issues have been examined in some depth in three recent cases:

(a)   *Salvage Association* v *CAP*: In *Salvage Association* v *CAP Financial Services Ltd* [1995] FSR 654, which related to the supply of bespoke software, CAP had put forward its standard contract and had negotiated certain changes to it. In deciding whether s. 3 of UCTA applied to those exclusions, the official referee set out a list of factors which would be relevant:
    (i)   the degree to which the standard terms are considered by the other party;
    (ii)   the degree to which the terms are imposed on the other party;
    (iii) the respective bargaining power of the parties;
    (iv) the willingness of the party putting forward the terms to negotiate them;
    (v)   how far any alterations to the terms were agreed; and
    (vi) the extent and duration of the negotiations.
On the facts of the case, because the Salvage Association had considered various drafts and taken legal advice on them and persuaded CAP to agree to changes (though not, it is implicit, in the relevant exclusion terms), this was enough to show that the contract was not made on CAP's written standard terms. The exclusion and limitation clause therefore only fell under s. 2(2), because it limited liability for breach of the express and implied terms that reasonable care and skill would he exercised by CAP.
(b)   *St. Albans* v *ICL*: In *St Albans City and District Council* v *International Computers Ltd* [1996] 4 All ER 481, CA, ICL had developed a complex package (COMCIS) to calculate and administer the community charge or poll tax system of local taxation. St Albans used COMCIS to calculate the number of community charge payers in its area, and used that figure to set its community charge rate. The COMCIS software contained an error, so that although the St Albans database contained all the necessary details, the population figure reported was too high and, as a result, St Albans suffered a financial loss

The contract contained a clause limiting ICL's liability to the price or charge payable for the item of equipment, program or service in respect of which the liability arises or £100,000 (whichever is the lesser); and completely excluding liability for, *inter alia*, any indirect or consequential loss or loss of business or profits sustained by the customer. Liability turned on whether this clause was reasonable under s. 11 of UCTA.

ICL contested that UCTA applied at all, arguing that the contract had not been on standard terms. However, the judge held that UCTA did apply: in other words, that St Albans had contracted on ICL's written standard terms. Even though many elements of the contract were negotiated at length (e.g., delivery dates, specification), ICL's General Conditions (which contained the limitation and exclusion clauses) 'remained effectively untouched in the negotiations', and indeed were referred to by ICL staff as ICL's Standard Terms and Conditions in witness statements and letters.[15]

(c)   *South West Water* v *ICL*: In *South West Water Services Ltd* v *International Computers Ltd*, 29 June 1999 (unreported) SWW and ICL had entered into two contracts — a turnkey agreement and a project management agreement — under which ICL was to deliver a customer service system to SWW. After ICL accepted that it would be unable to deliver the system to specification and in accordance with a planned timetable, SWW sued for breach of contract, claiming that ICL had failed to deliver the system as agreed, or at all, and also for misrepresentation.

Both agreements had contained a clause based on a standard ICL contract and purporting to limit ICL's liability for any claim for loss or damage. The evidence was that, during the negotiations, SWW had originally submitted its own standard procurement conditions to ICL, and that ICL had rejected these. The question then arose whether, in these circumstances, the ICL limitations could be regarded as ICL's 'standard terms'.

Toulmin J followed the *St Albans* decision in finding that, even though SWW originally offered its own terms in negotiations, in the event ICL had dealt on ICL's own standard terms which had been only slightly adapted. The fact that one fairly predictable eventuality — failure to progress the project to a point where there was a system in place for SWW and capable of being tested — had not been addressed in the documentation also tended to suggest that the contract should be regarded as 'standard terms'.

1.2.2.10   The UCTA reasonableness test   The test of reasonableness is set out in s. 11 of, and sch. 2 to, UCTA. Section 11(1) provides that it must have been fair and reasonable to include the clause at the time the contract was

---

15. In the earlier case of *Flamar Interocean Ltd* v *Denmac Ltd* [1990] 1 Lloyd's Rep 434, the judge suggested (though did not specifically decide) that the fact that many parts of the defendant's standard terms, other than the exclusion clause, were modified in negotiations meant that s. 3 did not apply. One clear difference between that case and *St Albans* v *ICL* is that in *St Albans* there was a clear distinction between the particular terms, which were negotiated, and the General Conditions, which were not. This is consistent with the decision in *Salvage Association* v *CAP*, though it is still not clear how much negotiation will take standard terms outside the provisions of s. 3.

made. The court will take account of the matters mentioned in sch. 2, including:

(a)   The strength of the bargaining position of the parties.
(b)   Whether the buyer received some benefit (e.g., a lower price) for agreeing to the clause.
(c)   How far the buyer knew or ought to have known of the existence and extent of the clause.
(d)   If the exclusion is contingent on compliance with some condition (e.g., regular maintenance) whether it was reasonable to expect the condition to be complied with.
(e)   Whether the goods were specially made or adapted to the customer's order.

The courts have also held that the question as to which of the parties can most readily insure against the loss is a relevant consideration, and that a limitation of liability is more likely to be reasonable than a complete exclusion.[16]

1.2.2.11   The reasonableness test in practice   The three cases mentioned in section 1.2.2.9 illustrate how the reasonableness test has been applied in practice:

(a)   *Salvage Association* v *CAP*:   In *Salvage Association* v *CAP Financial Services Ltd* [1995] FSR 654, the official referee found the following factors tended to support the supplier's contention that the exclusion was reasonable: first, the parties were of equal bargaining power and, secondly, the Salvage Association had taken legal advice and advice from its insurers and auditors. Against those factors, however, were the following:
(i)   UCTA puts the burden of proof of reasonableness on CAP;
(ii)   CAP had insurance up to £5,000,000, and could thus stand a greater liability, whilst the Salvage Association could not easily obtain insurance against CAP's failure;
(iii)   the risk of CAP's failure should have been low;
(iv)   CAP assured the Salvage Association that it would succeed in constructing the software as required under the contract, and the Salvage Association had no reason to doubt this;
(v)   CAP had already decided to increase the maximum limit of its liability from £25,000 to £1,000,000, but failed to do so in this contract for unexplained reasons;
(vi)   CAP called no evidence to justify the £25,000 limit in relation to CAP's turnover or insurance, or the contract value, or the financial risk the Salvage Association was running.

---

16. *George Mitchell (Chesterhall) Ltd* v *Finney Lock Seeds Ltd* [1983] 2 AC 803. This was a case decided under the slightly different provisions of the Supply of Goods (Implied Terms) Act 1973 as its facts occurred before the 1977 Act came into force, but it was nonetheless clearly decided with at least one eye on that Act.

The official referee found that the factors in favour of the clause being unreasonable far outweighed those in favour of its reasonableness, and held the clause to be invalid so that CAP's liability for the breaches of contract was unlimited.

(b)   *St. Alban's* v *ICL*: Similarly, the judge in *St. Albans City and District Council* v *International Computers Ltd* [1996] 4 All ER 481, CA, held that the term was not fair and reasonable, and was thus ineffective to exclude or limit ICL's liability. Although St Albans knew of the limitation and had attempted to negotiate it, the following factors operated to render the clause unreasonable:

(i)   ICL had substantially more resources than St Albans;

(ii)   ICL held product liability insurance in an aggregate sum of £50 million worldwide;[17]

(iii) ICL called no evidence to show that the limitation to £100,000 was reasonable, either in relation to the potential risk or the actual loss;

(iv)   as in *Salvage Association* v *CAP Financial Services Ltd*, the contract had mistakenly been made on an outmoded version of the General Conditions. In the current version the limitation was £125,000;

(v)   local authorities are not in the same position as private sector businesses; their operations are constrained by statute and financial restraints and they cannot necessarily be expected to insure against commercial risks;[18]

(vi)   St. Albans received no inducement to agree to the limitation, and there was evidence that all ICL's competitors imposed similar limitations of liability;

(vii) when St Albans tried to negotiate the limitation, albeit at the last moment, ICL in effect said that this was not possible because it would delay the provision of the software to St Albans beyond the date for implementation of the community charge.

The judge accordingly found that ICL had not discharged its burden of proving that the term was fair and reasonable, and also that financially ICL was best placed to bear a risk of this kind through insurance and thus spread it across its customer base.

(c)   *South West Water* v *ICL*: The judge in *South West Water Services Ltd* v *International Computers Ltd*, 29 June 1999 (unreported) noted further that the extent to which a party has had discussions and has freely entered into a contract on the other party's standard terms may be relevant as an important circumstance in considering whether those terms are reasonable. ICL argued that its standard limitation clause should be treated as reasonable in this case because its terms had been subject to arm's length discussion and negotiation, but this was found not to be the case on the evidence.

---

17. It is not clear how this figure was discovered by St Albans. In *Flamar Interocean Ltd* v *Denmac Ltd* [1990] 1 Lloyd's Rep 434 the judge specifically held that details of the defendant's insurance cover did not have to be disclosed on discovery, as the relevant question under UCTA was not the specific cover that the defendant held but the availability of insurance cover in similar situations.

18. The case has received substantial criticism on this ground, which appears to reflect a somewhat idealised view of the relationship between local authorities and their suppliers. It seems unlikely to survive serious argument before another court.

The most important conclusion which can be drawn from these cases is that a clause which is devised in standard form and then used in every transaction, without considering whether it is appropriate to that transaction and modifying it as necessary, is likely to be held unreasonable by the courts. Suppliers will therefore need to examine this issue in every case, except perhaps if a category of transactions can be identified where it is appropriate for the same clause to be used each time. Suppliers point out, quite reasonably, that it is commercially impossible for them to do this, as both the time required for individual negotiation and the costs of doing so are prohibitive. The only response must be that the benefits of contracting using standard contracts carry with them the cost that, from time to time, the standard exclusions will be held unreasonable.

1.2.3 Remedies

1.2.3.1 Conditions and warranties Some of the terms of the contract of sale are defined by the SGA 1979 or by case law as *conditions*,[19] terms whose breach is considered so serious that the buyer has the right to bring the contract to an end by rejecting the goods. The buyer is not, however, required to reject: he may elect to continue with the contract and claim damages for the breach. Other terms are defined in the Act as *warranties*. Although the Act provides that breach of such terms gives rise to a claim for damages only, the position adopted by the courts is rather different. If one of these terms is broken, the buyer will still have the right to reject if the breach 'goes to the root of the contract' — i.e., is so serious that further performance is rendered pointless.[20] If the breach is not sufficiently serious to permit rejection, the buyer's only claim is for damages. This type of obligation is often known as an *innominate term*.

1.2.3.2 Rejection of goods Where the supplier is in breach of a condition of the contract, or where the breach is of an innominate term and sufficiently serious to go to the root of the contract, the customer will be entitled to reject the goods and recover the purchase price in full. It is not necessary for the customer physically to return the goods to the seller — all he is required to do by s. 36 is to inform the seller that he is rejecting and to make the goods available for collection. Rejection is a powerful remedy where the price has not yet been paid, as it forces the seller to initiate proceedings if he disputes that he is in breach. However, there are a number of reasons why the customer will find this remedy less useful than at first sight it might appear:

(a) Rejection may be undesirable because the process of specifying the system and negotiating terms has taken so long that finding an alternative supplier would result in too great a delay in the installation of replacement equipment. In such a case the buyer's only real option is to negotiate with the

---

19. Under the law of England, Wales and Northern Ireland. Scots law uses different terminology, though the effect is similar.
20. *Hong Kong Fir Shipping Co. Ltd v Kawasaki Kisen Kaisha Ltd* [1962] QB 26.

seller for the faults to be rectified and to claim damages. Indeed, the buyer may be 'locked in' to one particular supplier because the new system needs to be compatible with existing infrastructure.

(b) The right to reject can be lost, for one of three reasons: acceptance, election or waiver. These are discussed below.

1.2.3.3 Acts constituting 'acceptance' In its legal sense, 'acceptance' means that the customer has performed some act which indicates that he intends to keep the goods. The relevant provision is s. 35 of the SGA 1979, as amended by the Sale and Supply of Goods Act 1994, which essentially sets out three ways in which goods may be 'accepted':

(a) The buyer intimates to the seller that he accepts them — for example, by telling the seller that he is satisfied with them (s. 35(1)(a)).

(b) The buyer, having received the goods, does some act 'inconsistent with the seller's continued ownership' — for example, active use of the goods that goes beyond what is required merely for testing and evaluation, or physical modification of the goods such as to show that the buyer is treating them as his own (s. 35(1)(b)).

(c) The buyer retains the goods beyond a reasonable time without rejecting — a question of fact in each case, though express contractual time limits for rejection are generally accepted by the courts as the parties' view of the time that would be reasonable for the buyer to retain the goods (s. 35(4)).

1.2.3.4 Acceptance of goods comprising a 'commercial unit' One further provision to note in relation to system contracts — which will often involve delivery of numerous goods such as CPUs, monitors, printers, cabling and software media (whether all at once or over a period of time) — appears in s. 35(7). This provides that where the contract is for the sale of goods making a commercial unit (that is, a unit division of which would materially impair the value of the goods or the character of the overall unit), then a buyer accepting *any* goods in a unit is thereby deemed to have accepted *all* the goods in the unit.

1.2.3.5 Acts not amounting to acceptance Section 35 goes on to specify certain acts that do *not* amount to acceptance. These are having the goods repaired under an arrangement with the seller (such as a guarantee) (s. 35(6)(a)), and delivering the goods to a third party under a subsale or other disposition (s. 35(6)(b)). Neither of these acts *in themselves* constitutes acceptance.

1.2.3.6 Election Election involves the buyer making a choice between two remedies. Under s. 11(2) of the SGA 1979, the buyer has the right to decide not to reject the goods but to claim damages instead. If he leads the seller to believe that this is what he is doing, he has made an election and accordingly loses his right to reject. This typically occurs in the case of late delivery, where the buyer accepts delivery but reserves his right to damages. By doing so in the knowledge that the delivery is defective (i.e., late) he loses his right to reject and is relegated to a claim in damages.

1.2.3.7 Waiver Waiver is similar to election, in that it involves the buyer leading the seller to believe that he will not enforce the right to reject the goods. However, waiver entails a more complete renunciation of rights, and requires a representation that the buyer will not enforce a particular contractual right at all. The most common examples of waiver occur where the goods are not delivered on time and the buyer, instead of immediately rejecting, presses the seller to make delivery as soon as possible. This amounts to a representation by the buyer that he is not insisting on the original date, and not only does he lose his right to reject for that breach but also any claim to damages. This is not necessarily as final as it might seem, for if the seller has still to perform his obligation the buyer can reimpose the condition by giving reasonable notice.[21]

1.2.3.8 Damages payable to a buyer of goods The buyer's claim for damages will fall into one of two categories, depending on the nature of the breach of contract:

(a) Damages for failure to deliver goods (either on time or at all) — these damages are governed by s. 51 of the SGA 1979, which provides that the normal measure of damages is 'the estimated loss directly and naturally resulting, in the ordinary course of events, from the seller's breach of contract' (s. 51(2)).

(b) Damages for breach of warranty — these damages generally are governed by s. 53(2) of the SGA 1979, which is in substantially the same terms as s. 51(2). However, if the breach is of a 'warranty of quality', the statutory measure of damages will be *'prima facie* the difference between the value of the goods at the time of delivery to the buyer and the value they would have had if they had fulfilled the warranty' (s. 53(3)).

1.2.3.9 Damages payable to a seller of goods The preferred remedy of any seller will be the price of the goods, as this is what he contracted for. The basic assumption of the SGA 1979 is that he is not obliged to deliver the goods to the buyer until he has been paid, and so he has a right of lien (i.e., a right to retain possession) if payment is not forthcoming. However, if the buyer wrongfully fails or refuses to accept delivery, the seller will have a claim for damages against him. Damages are assessed under s. 50, which is in almost identical terms to s. 51, and the majority of what has already been said about that section will apply here.

1.2.3.10 Specific performance Under s. 52 of the SGA, the court has discretion to award specific performance where the contract relates to specific or ascertained goods. If the subject matter of the contract is generic — in

---

21. *Charles Rickards Ltd v Oppenhaim* [1950] 1 KB 616.

other words, it merely refers to a particular description of goods — it is generally assumed that the buyer will be able to obtain replacement goods elsewhere.[22]

1.3 COMMERCIAL AND DRAFTING ASPECTS

1.3.1 Introduction

1.3.1.1 The need for express contract terms It will be clear from the above discussion that there is no shortage of contractual terms that can be implied by law into contracts for the provision of computer systems. These implied terms will not always reflect the parties' commercial intentions, and to that extent it is preferable for the parties to set out in express terms the position they are trying to achieve. However, the contract is more than just a 'legal' document. Its function should be to record all the terms governing the supply of the system — in terms of what is being delivered, how it is paid for, what happens if the goods or services supplied are unsatisfactory, and so on. The function of the negotiation process that leads to a written contract is to ensure that the parties understand each other's expectations (and their own) about the deal in question, and to draw out differences in understanding that can then be addressed before they lead to problems. Many projects go wrong precisely because, for whatever reason — time pressure, pushy salesmen, deliberate misrepresentation — the parties do not exercise sufficient care to ensure that the supplier's and the customer's expectations match.

1.3.1.2 The role of the legal adviser As noted at 1.1.2 above, a well-drawn system supply contract will have certain features that require the parties to consider their expectations and record them. Ensuring that these expectations do match, and are properly recorded in the contract document, is the key role of the legal adviser in the contract process.

There is a common misconception in the IT industry that contract documentation is purely a matter for lawyers, and is somehow separate from the commercial realities of a transaction. As a result, the legal adviser is often left out of the early stages of negotiation, and frequently has to raise key issues such as limitations of liability at a very late stage in the process. Putting together the right team for the procurement or sale should mean involving the legal team at the outset, and using their expertise to help draft and structure the documentation generally.

1.3.2 Specification

1.3.2.1 Need for a written specification A clear specification is the foundation stone of a successful system supply contract. It defines what the supplier will provide, sets out the quality standards to be achieved, and forces both

---

22. An exception to this general rule is where a dealer has a long-term contract with a manufacturer for regular deliveries of hardware, and there is no alternative source of supply: see *Worldwide Dryers Ltd* v *Warner Howard Ltd* (1982) *The Times*, 9 December 1982.

sides to think seriously about what is really wanted, and what is achievable. In every case, the specification should address:

(a) Functionality (i.e., what the system is to do).
(b) Performance (i.e., how well it is supposed to do it).
(c) Compatibility (i.e., any software and hardware with which the system is likely to be used).

The importance of including a suitably detailed specification can be illustrated by two cases:

(a) *Micron v Wang*: In *Micron Computer Systems Ltd v Wang (UK) Ltd*, 9 May 1990, QBD, (unreported), one of Micron's complaints was that the system bought from Wang did not provide 'transaction logging'. The judge observed that 'the acknowledged absence of a transaction logging facility is not in reality a fault in the system which was sold. Micron can only complain about its absence if Micron can establish a contractual term, express or implied, or an actionable representation, to the effect that the system included such a facility. In order to make good its case on transaction logging, Micron must therefore establish that they made known to Wang that they required such a facility'. In the event, the judge found on the evidence that Micron had not made its requirement for transaction logging clear to Wang, and accordingly that part of Micron's case failed.

(b) *St Albans v ICL*: By contrast, in *St Albans City and District Council v International Computers Ltd* [1996] 4 All ER 481, CA, the local authority had made its requirements clear in its invitation to tender which had itself been expressly incorporated into the contract. When the system supplied failed to meet those requirements, the authority claimed successfully against the supplier on the basis of breach of an express term.

1.3.3 Delivery and acceptance arrangements

1.3.3.1 Delivery The arrangements for delivery should always be dealt with by express provisions in the supply contract. The contract should set out the date (or dates) on which delivery is to be made, whether all the elements of the system are to be delivered at one time or whether it is to arrive in instalments, and who has responsibility for installation and testing. From the point of view of contractual certainty, the ideal situation is for the contract to set out specific delivery dates. This may not be possible if, say, there is a lengthy development project prior to delivery, but even in that eventuality the contract should set out a timetable or project plan showing roughly how long each phase is likely to take. If no clear date is identified or identifiable, then as a matter of law the system will have to be delivered within 'a reasonable time': a position of contractual uncertainty that is unlikely to provide significant advantage to either party in the event of a dispute.

Consequences of late delivery and non-delivery What commonly happens if delivery is late is that the buyer waives the seller's obligation to achieve that date, and so loses the right to reject: for example, by continuing to request delivery after the contractual date has passed. This means that there is now *no* contractual date for delivery, and at best the seller is obliged to deliver within a reasonable time. In order to regain the right to reject, the buyer must reimpose a date by giving the seller reasonable notice that the buyer will refuse to accept that part of the system after a particular date.[23] Such notice is normally express, but it may be given impliedly (e.g., by service of a writ[24]). As an additional protection for the buyer, the contract should ideally contain an express provision permitting cancellation of the contract, with or without compensation to the buyer, if the goods are not delivered by some cut-off date. Alternatively, if the supplier does not agree to a clear target date for delivery, the contract may provide for a notice period after which the buyer can withdraw, with an appeal against the notice to a third party.[25]

1.3.3.2 Acceptance arrangements   Formal acceptance procedures are a crucial aspect of any successful system procurement. Systems are acquired in order to perform a specified set of functions, within particular performance requirements. Until the system has been tested, the buyer will not be able to assess whether what has been delivered accords with the contract.

Defining acceptance criteria   The nature of acceptance tests varies widely between projects. Where a major piece of development work is involved, the parties may negotiate and document detailed testing arrangements as part of the contract document. At the other extreme, the acceptance procedure may simply be that if the buyer uses the system 'live' for, say, 30 days without rejecting it, then it is deemed to have been accepted. The vital features of any acceptance procedure, however, are:

(a)   That it provides for an objective and measurable 'yardstick' as to the standards of performance and functionality to be demonstrated.

(b)   From the buyer's point of view, that this yardstick will demonstrate to its full satisfaction that the system meets its requirements.

(c)   That the procedure is clear as to the consequences of both the passing and failing of the acceptance test.

Consequences of acceptance   On successful completion of the testing, the system will be deemed to have been accepted. Acceptance will generally trigger payment of the whole or the final instalment of any lump sum charges, or the commencement of periodic charges, and following acceptance the buyer's remedies will be limited to a claim under the warranty provision. The contract should also provide expressly for the consequences of failure to achieve acceptance. Typically, there will be a period during which the supplier may rectify problems and then retest; but further failure will signal the premature end of the contract, with the buyer able to return the hardware and software in exchange for a refund of any moneys paid.

23. *Charles Rickards Ltd* v *Oppenhaim* [1950] 1 KB 616.
24. *Tool Metal Manufacturing Co. Ltd* v *Tungsten Electric Co. Ltd* [1955] 1 WLR 761.
25. E.g., an arbitrator, the engineer in construction contracts, etc.

1.3.4 Timetable

1.3.4.1 Need for the timetable The preparation of the specification should enable the parties to assess the likely timescale for the project and so to prepare a project plan setting out key deliverables (or 'milestones') and their expected dates. In almost all major systems implementations, staged payments will be triggered by the achievement of individual milestones. It is accordingly essential that these are identified with as much precision as possible, and reflect the terminology of the contract generally. The buyer will generally have in mind a timescale within which it wants the system provided, although the sophistication of the timetable will vary according to:

(a) The complexity of the project in question — a major development contract may include target dates for numerous stages, each of which may be divided up into smaller phases such as functional specification, systems specification. program specification, development, program testing, systems testing, debugging, retesting and acceptance.

(b) Payment arrangements — in particular, whether the price and payment arrangements are tied in to specified 'milestones', and the implications for both parties of any failure to meet target deadlines.

1.3.5 Pricing and payment

1.3.5.1 Pricing and payment structures generally From the supplier's point of view, the heart of the contract is ensuring that he gets paid for the goods or services he provides. There are as many pricing and payment structures as there are types of IT deal. For example:

(a) a single charge for the entire development and implementation project; and/or

(b) periodic charges for ongoing maintenance and support; and/or

(c) separate purchase and licence fees in respect of hardware and software elements of the system (which licence fees may themselves be periodic or a single lump sum).

As a result, there is little to be gained from making generalisations about pricing and payment terms. The one point worth making is that, where payments are tied into specific targets (such as system acceptance), the terminology and structure of the payment schedule should accurately reflect that of the timetable.

1.3.5.2 Timing of payments The time of payment will generally not be of the essence unless it is expressed as such. However, for the sake of contractual certainty, it is of course desirable to specify precisely when sums become due. This links in with delivery dates. A common practice in systems contracts is to pay by instalments as the various parts of the system are delivered, retaining a proportion of the price until the complete system has been tested.

This arrangement will incentivise the supplier to perform these obligations in accordance with the contractual timetable, while the retention of a significant proportion of the fee until acceptance will give the buyer some security for performance. Suppliers will also often seek an express right to payment of interest on overdue amounts.

In respect of periodic fees specifically, the buyer will be concerned about the supplier's rights to increase the fee, and may seek to circumscribe these in some way. For example, only one increase a year may be permitted or rises may be limited by reference to an appropriate index. The buyer may also seek to delay the first payment until after the system has been accepted.

1.3.5.3 Retention of title Where the seller gives credit to the buyer, there is always some doubt whether the seller will be paid. If the buyer is a well-established organisation this doubt is extremely small, but newer or smaller organisations may present a greater risk. For this reason, it is common for hardware suppliers to retain title in the goods they supply as security for payment. A retention of title clause is a provision in the contract that although the buyer is to be given possession of the goods, ownership is to remain with the seller until certain conditions (normally payment in full) are complied with. If the buyer fails to comply with the conditions, the seller is entitled to repossess the goods, and can then sell them to recoup his losses.

Retention of title clauses are permitted under s. 19 of the SGA 1979. It is important that the seller retains title, property or legal ownership (all these terms are equivalent).[26] As risk normally passes with property, a retention of title clause will also provide that the goods are at the buyer's risk from the moment of delivery. It should contain a clear statement of when the seller is entitled to repossess the goods, normally if payment is not made within the credit period, or if the buyer commits an act of insolvency or a receiver is appointed. It is also common to include a provision that the seller has the right to enter the buyer's premises to repossess the goods.

1.3.6 Intellectual property rights (IPRs)

1.3.6.1 The need for express treatment of IPR issues System supply contracts generally entail the transfer of information, in some form, from one party to another: for example, program specifications (in a consultancy agreement), software (in a software licence), data for processing (in a bureau services agreement) or confidential business information (in a development agreement). The lawful use of such information is dependent on compliance with the laws relating to copyright, confidentiality, database rights and other forms of intellectual property. In addition, the use of certain computer equipment may constitute an infringement of patent or similar rights if it is undertaken without the consent of the rights owner. As a result, it is essential that any system supply contract deals comprehensively with IPR issues, and in particular addresses:

---

26. Note that any drafting which amounts to a retention of equitable ownership will result in the creation of a charge which must be registered under the Companies Act 1985 or the Bills of Sale Act 1878.

(a)   ownership; and
(b)   IPR warranties and indemnities.

1.3.6.2   Ownership   The contract should specify what IPRs are to be created or used, and precisely who owns them. This is particularly important in contracts for software development or consultancy work because of s. 11 of the Copyright Designs and Patents Act 1988, which contains a common trap for the unwary: work done under a consultancy contract will normally vest in the supplier, not the customer, so a formal written assignment of copyright is needed if the aim is for the customer to own the work product outright.

1.3.6.3   Treatment of third party software   For similar reasons, where the system incorporates any third party software, the prudent customer will want an express assurance that the supplier has authority to grant the licence or sub-licence in respect of those third party rights. As a practical matter, it is essential to ensure that there is no 'hiatus' between the scope of the third party licence and the uses envisaged in respect of all other aspects of the system.

1.3.6.4   IPR warranties and indemnities   Although s. 12 of the SGA 1979 provides a remedy for the customer if the seller should turn out not to have the right to sell the products in question,[27] in practical terms, the parties are unlikely to be happy to rely on this general law position:

(a)   The customer will often impose a formal obligation to take curative action to deal with any allegations of third party' IPR infringement: this is particularly so if the system is a critical part of the customer's business and merely rejecting it and claiming back the purchase price would leave the customer in a difficult position.
(b)   Equally, the supplier may wish to reserve the right to dispute the existence or extent of the third party's claims, in order to preserve its reputation and position in the market.

As a result, most system supply contracts will contain a warranty in favour of the customer that use of the system will not infringe third party rights, and an indemnity in respect of any claims that may arise. (Similar provisions are commonplace in distribution and agency contracts, to protect the distributor/agent and its end-user customers against IPR claims brought in respect of products supplied by the principal.) The contract should set out any express warranties as to the supplier's ownership or entitlement in respect of the IPRs comprised in the system, together with a process for addressing any breach of those warranties. A clause which incorporates the following points should assist in removing some of the potential complications:

(a)   A right on the supplier's part to take over and litigate (in the customer's name) any such action by a third party, and to settle the action.

---

27. See 1.2.1.2 above.

(b)   A right for the supplier to modify the system so that it does not infringe the alleged right, provided that it still conforms with the specification.[28]

(c)   An indemnity given by the supplier against the customer's losses in the event of a successful third party claim.

1.3.6.5 Confidentiality   A further feature of the transfer of information between suppliers and customers is that provision needs to be made to ensure that the information is treated in confidence. In the context of a consultancy agreement or a bureau services contract, for example, the consultant may have access to all kinds of commercially-sensitive information about the customer's business and systems. The customer will want to ensure that this information is only used for the express, permitted purposes. Similarly, where a software house is licensing programs for use by its customer, the supplier will want to ensure that its proprietary software is not disclosed to third parties.

1.3.6.6 Access to source code   Software elements of the system will usually be delivered to the customer in object code form, with the source code being retained by the supplier. The practical consequence of this will be that, whilst the buyer is able to use the software, he will not be able to modify or maintain it. He is dependent on the supplier for software maintenance, although he may be able to protect himself against the more dire consequences of such dependence by reason of the error correction rights conferred in s. 50C of the Copyright Designs and Patents Act 1988. Again, however, the prudent customer would be unwise to rely on this general law provision, for which reason the contract should expressly provide for either:

(a)   An express right to call for and to use the source code for development or maintenance purposes (a requirement which will often be vigorously resisted by suppliers), perhaps subject to confidentiality conditions, in order to protect the supplier's legitimate interests in the secrecy of this material.

(b)   An escrow arrangement, whereby the supplier agrees to deposit a copy of the source code with an independent third party (the escrow agent) and then the supplier, customer and escrow agent enter into a tripartite agreement to govern its release. The escrow agreement will provide for the initial deposit of the source code, and for its updating with error corrections and new releases. On the happening of certain specified events (e.g., such as the supplier going into liquidation, or failing to provide maintenance services as contracted for), the escrow agent will release the source code to the customer for the purposes of maintaining the software. At least two bodies provide an escrow service along these lines, namely the National Computing Centre and the Computing Services and Software Association, and so far it would seem that the arrangements work successfully.

---

28. It must be noted that a seller cannot exclude or restrict the condition in the SGA 1979, s. 12(1) — see 1.2.1.2–3. However, until the third party has established that the right has in fact been infringed, the seller is arguably not in breach of that condition. In any event, most buyers should be satisfied with effective cure.

1.3.7 Other express warranties

1.3.7.1 The need for express warranties The existence or otherwise of implied terms in system supply contracts is, as we have seen, a matter of some uncertainty. In reality, such terms are unlikely to be of much assistance to the customer as they will be pitched in general terms, and the limited usefulness of these provisions can be illustrated by reference to two decisions:

(a) *Saphena*: In *Saphena Computing Ltd* v *Allied Collection Agencies Ltd* [1995] FSR 616, the court found that there was an implied term that software should be fit for all purposes communicated to the supplier before the contract was made, and any further purpose subsequently communicated, provided that in the latter case the supplier accepted the customer's instructions to make the relevant modification.

(b) *Micron*: *Micron Computer Systems Ltd* v *Wang (UK) Ltd*, 9 May 1990, QBD (unreported), illustrates the consequences of failing to make a requirement known. In that case, Micron failed on the evidence to show that it had made its requirement for 'transaction logging' known to Wang, and its claim that the system supplied by Wang was defective accordingly failed in that respect.

A further problem in the real world is that software licences are nearly always written, and nearly always exclude or limit the operation of all implied conditions and warranties. The efficacy of such exclusions and limitations is examined at 1.2.2 above.

1.3.7.2 Forms of warranty Express warranties given by suppliers are accordingly of considerable importance. Such express warranties normally take one of two forms:

(a) The warranty may state that the system will comply with its functional specification or user manual, or meet certain specified performance criteria, or the like: such a warranty has the advantage that compliance or breach can be objectively measured, and is usually the best form of express warranty that a licensee can obtain.

(b) The warranty may provide that defects will be corrected by the supplier or licensor, though the disadvantage here is that it begs the question of what constitutes a defect: for example, in the event of failure to perform a particular function, there may be a dispute about whether the lack of the particular function in fact amounts to a defect (which was precisely the issue in *Micron*).

1.3.7.3 Restrictions on warranties Whatever the form of warranty, it is likely to be subject to a number of restrictions:

(a) It will generally be limited to a fairly short period of time, probably between three and twelve months. After this time the system may be covered by the maintenance and support arrangements: in other words, ongoing maintenance after expiry of the warranty period has a separate price attached to it.

(b)   Some warranty clauses also state that the supplier's only liability is to correct the non-compliance or the defect. The purpose would seem to be to exclude any liability for damages. To the extent that the supplier complies with the warranty this would seem to be effective, but if he fails to remedy the non-compliance or defect, an action for damages would lie for that failure.

(c)   Warranties often state that they cease to apply if the customer makes any additions or modifications to the system. Customers would be well-advised to limit the qualification to errors or defects in the system that are actually caused by the addition or modification.

1.3.8   Limitations and exclusions of liability

1.3.8.1   Drafting effective exclusion clauses   IT suppliers generally seek to restrict their potential exposure to users resulting from breach of contract or defects in the system. This is treated by some as purely a 'legal' issue, but in fact is a major question of commercial risk assessment and allocation. This type of provision is commonplace in system supply contracts, particularly where the contract is based on the supplier's standard terms, which typically contain a limitation clause along the following lines:

(a)   The supplier does not exclude liability for death or personal injury caused by negligence (which cannot by law be excluded).

(b)   The supplier seeks to exclude liability altogether for 'special', 'indirect' or 'consequential' losses.

(c)   The supplier accepts a limited degree of liability for certain other classes of 'direct' loss.

The general legal issues as to the enforceability of limitation and exclusion clauses are discussed at 1.2.2 above. The first point in (a) above requires little further discussion: liability for death or personal injury caused by negligence *cannot* be limited, as a matter of law.[29] The second and third points in (b) and (c) are discussed below.

1.3.8.2   Consequential loss: general principles   The parties need to consider what kinds of loss might result from a system failure, and who takes the risk. The basis of the supplier's argument to exclude liability for consequential loss or loss of profits is essentially that the nature of IT products means that their uses (and thus the potential consequential losses) are not easily foreseeable at the time the contract is made, and that the potential exposure is in any case disproportionate to the contract value. Whether this is an acceptable commercial stance depends on the nature of the system and the extent of the customer's dependence on it.

---

29. UCTA 1977, s. 2(1).

1.3.8.3 Consequential loss: drafting issues However, turning that commercial position into effective (and commercially acceptable) drafting can be more problematic. There is no consensus as to the meaning of the expressions 'special', 'indirect' and 'consequential' in the context of contractual claims, and there is often a resulting lack of certainty as to the precise effect of the intended exclusion. It is not the purpose of this chapter to try to offer a definitive interpretation of these terms, but it may be helpful to summarise the semantic and philosophical problems encountered by judges and academics in trying to pin down their meanings.

1.3.8.4 Consequential loss: Hadley v Baxendale The starting point for any discussion of consequential damages is *Hadley* v *Baxendale* (1854) 9 Exch 341, which distinguished two classes of loss recoverable for breach of contract. These are:

(a) 'such [damages] as may fairly and reasonably be considered either as arising naturally, i.e., according to the usual course of things ... or such as may reasonably be supposed to have been in the contemplation of both parties at the time they made the contract as the probable result of the breach of it'; and
(b) if the parties were aware of 'special circumstances' at the time the contract was made, the damages 'which they would reasonably contemplate would be the amount of injury which would ordinarily flow from a breach under these special circumstances'.

That basic distinction has been recast on a number of occasions over the last 140 years. However, the difficulty for the draftsman is that the terminology in common usage — 'indirect' or 'consequential' loss, or 'special' damages — does not fit neatly into the *Hadley* v *Baxendale* rules, nor is it used in a consistent fashion. For example, the expression 'consequential loss' is taken by some to mean pecuniary loss consequent on physical damage. However, when used in an exclusion clause, 'consequential' means losses arising under the second rule in *Hadley* v *Baxendale*, and so does *not* preclude recovery of pecuniary losses under the first rule — see *Saint Line Ltd* v *Richardsons, Westgarth & Co.* [1940] 2 KB 99.

1.3.8.5 Consequential loss: British Sugar The most recent authoritative discussion of the meaning of 'consequential loss' is *British Sugar Plc* v *NEI Power Projects Ltd* [1998] ITCLR 118. It is also a good example of the confusion that can be caused by trying to use *Hadley* v *Baxendale* terminology to define concepts like 'direct', 'indirect' or 'consequential' loss. In the *British Sugar* case NEI supplied some defective power equipment to British Sugar, with a headline value of about £100,000. The sale contract expressly limited the seller's liability for 'consequential loss'. As a result of breakdowns, increased production costs and resulting loss of profits, British Sugar put in a claim of over £5 million. British Sugar argued for the narrowest construction of the term 'consequential loss', interpreting it to mean 'loss not resulting directly and naturally from breach of contract'; whereas NEI argued that the term meant 'all loss other than the normal loss which might be suffered as a result of the breach of contract, negligence or other breach of duty'. The Courts found for the claimant, and approved earlier authorities that consequential damages' means the damages recoverable under the second limb of *Hadley* v *Baxendale*. By this analysis, where loss of profits or loss of business (commonly regarded as typical examples of 'consequential loss') arise naturally from the breach of contract, they should be recoverable by the user: a result that may surprise many IT suppliers.

1.3.8.6   Consequential loss: defining 'indirect loss' and 'special damages'   Similar confusion applies in relation to the effect of other commonly used terms:

(a)   In relation to 'indirect loss', it used to be the case that the courts would hold a defendant liable (particularly in negligence) for all 'direct consequences' whether foreseeable or not, but they have long since ceased to try to define issues of remoteness and quantum in terms of 'direct', 'natural' or 'ordinary'. Instead, following the *Wagon Mound*[30] cases in the 1960s, the test of liability (in tort at least) is analysed simply in terms of foreseeability.

(b)   To complicate matters further, the term 'consequential' has at one point been defined simply to mean 'not direct' — see *Millar's Machinery* v *David Way* (1935) 40 Com Cas 204 — but there is also an argument, following certain observations of Lord Diplock in *P&M Kaye* v *Hosier* (1972) 1 All ER 121 that the expression 'direct' could include 'consequential' losses provided these were not too remote.

(c)   The term 'special damages' has at least four possible meanings, including (i) past (pecuniary) loss calculable as at the trial date — as opposed to all other items of unliquidated 'general damages'; and (ii) losses falling under the second rule in *Hadley* v *Baxendale* — as opposed to 'general damages' being losses recoverable under the first rule.

1.3.8.7   Consequential loss: towards a risk allocation analysis   In summary, the meanings of the terms 'indirect', 'consequential' and 'special' are at best unclear in the context of IT contracts, and it is surprising that they should continue routinely to be used. The inclusion of such imprecise terminology inevitably delays the contract process, creates uncertainty for users and suppliers alike, and reflects badly on the IT industry and its legal advisers. Instead, both suppliers and customers should focus on the specific risks associated with the particular system. The customer will generally accept that the supplier has a legitimate concern about exposure to unspecified types of liability: but the kinds of loss that will flow from a breach of an IT supply contract *can* be classified, at least in general terms. For example:

(a)   Loss of cost or salary savings, or other expected benefits.

---

30. *Overseas Tankship (UK)* v *Morts Dock and Engineering Co. (The Wagon Mound)* [1961] AC 388, [1961] 2 WLR 126 and *Overseas Tankship (UK)* v *Miller Steamship Co. Pty (The Wagon Mound (No. 2))* [1967] 1 AC 617, [1966] 3 WLR 498.

(b)   Costs of repairing or replacing the defective system.
(c)   Costs of additional IT staff and consultant required to make the system work.
(d)   Loss of profits resulting from non-performance.
(e)   Costs of wasted management time.

1.3.8.8   Consequential loss: negotiating issues   These categories of loss are not intended to be definitive: there is no 'definitive list' as such, and each customer and supplier will have its own specific concerns. However, the starting point for constructing an effective provision must be to identify what categories of loss are foreseeable and how the parties intend to allocate these risks between themselves. The aim is to avoid the (ultimately futile) job of trying to *define* 'direct' or 'consequential' loss, and instead — having regard to all the commercial circumstances of the particular transaction — to try to allocate responsibility for those *specific* types of loss that the parties might have in mind: up front, and without resorting to semantic contortions. Any unspecified types of loss will then fall to be determined by the court according to normal foreseeability principles. In any case, whether the exclusions are fully negotiated or whether they are unilaterally imposed (in the supplier's standard terms, for example), records of the negotiations in respect of exclusion clauses will clearly be of great utility in the event of a dispute, and should therefore be preserved.

1.3.8.9   Financial caps on liability   The recovery of other classes of potential loss is often limited to an agreed financial cap. It is common to place a financial cap on the supplier's liability, both for any one breach and also as a global limit (e.g., £100,000 for any breach, £500,000 in total). It is likely that any figures of this nature will be subject to negotiation, and it is clear from the limited case law under UCTA that where the parties have genuinely negotiated a limitation the court will be likely to find that limitation to be reasonable.[31] Some sellers limit liability to the contract price, though this seems to set the limits rather too low.

1.3.9   Contractual remedies

1.3.9.1   Introduction   Consideration needs to be given to the question of what happens if a contract does not go according to plan — for example, if the supplier fails to deliver a working system within the contracted time frames. The general law principles as to the remedies available for breaches of contract are set out in section 1.2.3 above. However, for the reasons discussed in that section, it is often desirable for the contract documentation to provide for specific remedies in particular situations.

---

31. *Phillips Products Ltd* v *Hyland* [1987] 1 WLR 659. See also the discussions of *Salvage Association* v *CAP Financial Services Ltd* [1995] FSR 645; *St Albans City and District Council* v *International Computers Ltd* [1996] 4 All ER 481, CA; *South West Water Services Ltd* v *International Computers Ltd*, 29 June 1999 (unreported), at 1.2.2 above, as illustrations of the consequences of failure properly to negotiate such limits.

1.3.9.2   Customer remedies: liquidated damages   One typical solution to that particular problem is to provide for payment of liquidated damages to the customer for each day or week the system is overdue. This will involve a good faith attempt to estimate the cost to the customer of such delay; and if the delay persists for a specified length of time, the customer may also want a right to terminate. The liquidated damages clause sets in advance the precise sum to be paid as compensation for certain breaches (e.g., late delivery at £X per day). Provided that sum is a *genuine preestimate* of the likely losses, and not a *penalty* to force the supplier to perform, the clause will be enforceable. This is so even if the customer's loss is in fact less than the agreed sum.

1.3.9.3   Supplier remedies: interest on late payment   Similarly, on the supplier's side, the supplier may want an express right to withhold its services or to charge interest in the event of late payment, and in the last resort to terminate the contract altogether.

1.3.10   Change control

1.3.10.1   The need for change control provisions   The successful implementation of a complex IT system imposes responsibilities not just on the supplier, but also on the customer. Unlike the supply of a simple package, a bespoke contract is more of a joint effort and, whilst the primary obligation will be on the supplier to write any software and to deliver the system, the supplier will depend on the customer providing information about his business, testing the software, providing employees to be trained and so on. Crucially, since the customer's requirements may change as the project progresses, the contract should provide a procedure for specifying and agreeing changes to the scope of work. These will involve adjustments to the functional specification, the price and probably also the timing of the project.

1.3.10.2   Documenting change procedures   The proper documentation of these changes will avoid disputes later about what the supplier's obligations actually were. The contract should accordingly include a formal 'change control' clause, setting out a mechanism whereby the customer can request (and the supplier can recommend) changes to the specification, the project plan, or any other aspect of the deal. Any such change would need to be considered from the point of view of technical feasibility and its impact on timing and pricing generally, and no change should take effect unless it has been formally agreed by both parties and documented in the manner envisaged by the change control clause.

1.3.11   Termination

Provision has to be made for termination of the contract, setting out the circumstances in which the contract may be brought to an end and the consequences of that action. These provisions will vary according to the nature of the contract and the deliverables. Apart from a general right to terminate the contract in the event of material breach or the insolvency of the other party, the following points should be considered:

(a) Hardware procurement — the customer may wish to cancel/terminate the contract before the delivery date, and in that event the contract should set out the compensation payable to the supplier.

(b) Software development — contracts for development services are typically terminable by the customer if specific time-critical milestones are significantly overdue. Provision should be made for treatment of the developed software on termination, including delivery up of all copies (and source code) and certification that no copies have been retained.

(c) Contracts for continuing services — consultancy, support and maintenance services, and bureau services should in any event be terminable on notice. The length of the notice, and the earliest dates on which it may be effective, are matters of negotiation in each case.

1.4 ADDITIONAL CONSIDERATIONS FOR SPECIFIC CONTRACTS

1.4.1 Introduction

The general legal and drafting issues discussed in sections 1 to 3 of this chapter will apply to the full range of system supply contracts. However, there are additional specific considerations that may apply to particular agreements, and these are discussed in this section.

1.4.2 Software licences

1.4.2.1 Why is software different? Software comprises the instructions which cause hardware to work in a particular way: for example, to process a company's payroll. Looked at in this way, software is intangible, and difficult to classify in legal terms. Some of the relevant case law, as to whether the supply of software comprises 'goods' or 'services', is discussed at 1.2.1 above. Equally important from the contractual point of view is the fact that software is primarily protected by the law of copyright, as a consequence of which the use of software generally requires a licence from the rights owner.

1.4.2.2 Types of software There are various distinctions that need to be kept in mind when discussing software contracts:

(a) Standard, bespoke and customised software: 'Standard' or (package) software is marketed as an off the shelf product to meet the requirements of a large number of users: commonly used business applications for example, such as Word or Excel. By contrast, 'bespoke' software is specially written to meet the requirements of the particular customer. 'Customised' software falls somewhere in between, involving the supplier altering his standard package so that it fits the customer's needs more closely. Predictably, standard

software will tend to be cheaper than bespoke, but may not reflect the way the customer's business operates, while bespoke will be more expensive but should be exactly tailored to the customer's requirements.

(b) *System software and application software*: System software organises the way in which the hardware operates, whereas application software performs the functions actually required by the user (word processing, accounts or whatever). System software is generally supplied by the manufacturer of the hardware, as a standard package, while application software might be standard, bespoke or customised.

(c) *Source code and object code*: A final distinction to be aware of is that between source code and object code. This distinction is discussed at greater length in chapter 6, but for the purposes of this chapter, 'source code' may be defined as a version of a program, using alpha-numeric symbols, which cannot be processed directly by' a computer without first being 'translated' (or 'compiled') into a machine-readable form. 'Object code' is the machine-readable form of that program, which essentially comprises long series of ones and zeroes, corresponding to the complex 'on-off' instructions used to process data. (The significance of the distinction in the context of this chapter is that it is difficult for a person to read object code, and hence access to source code is needed in order to enable a person to support or modify a computer program.)

1.4.2.3 Types of software contract   Standard software is often supplied by retailers or distributors, without the customer entering into any direct contract with the software owner. The technique of 'shrink-wrap' licensing (discussed in section 1.4.2.6 below) is commonly used to try to establish this kind of direct contractual relationship. Contracts for bespoke software tend to be entered into on a more formal basis, because of the need to agree a specification and to address other issues arising out of the development process.

1.4.2.4 Why is software licensed?   Copyright subsists in computer software, so the use of software requires the grant of a licence. Apart from legitimising the customer's use, however, the licence also enables the software owner to impose restrictions on the use of the software. For this reason, even where a copy of the software is sold without a direct agreement between the software owner and the customer, software owners still seek to impose shrink-wrap licence terms. The efficacy of such licences is discussed at 1.4.2.6 below. A further discussion of the requirement for a licence, and the extent of implied rights in relation to acts such as decompilation and error correction, appears in chapter 6.5.

1.4.2.5 The main licence clause   There is a broad range of possible licensing structures for computer software. These include, by way of illustration:

(a) the right to use the software on a single computer (sometimes identified by reference to a specific CPU number) at a single location;

(b)   the right to use the software on any number of networked or clustered computers at different sites; or any combination of numbers and sites.

Limitations on use   The use permitted is often restricted to the 'internal purposes' of the customer. This restriction is justified by the supplier on the basis that using the software for other purposes, particularly by using it to provide a bureau service for third parties, might adversely affect the supplier's ability to charge licence fees that it might otherwise receive from those third parties. The licence terms may also restrict the customer from transferring the software to any third party, again on the basis that the supplier has a right to know precisely who is using its software. Although these concerns appear reasonable, however, customers should be aware that these provisions have a number of serious implications:

(a)   Companies which are members of a corporate group may find that such wording restricts their ability to process data for their associated companies;

(b)   The restriction on assignment may be invoked by the supplier as an opportunity to charge increased fees in the event that the system has to be transferred, whether between companies in the same group (as part of a group restructuring, say) or to a third party (perhaps in the context of a business sale).

(c)   Such restrictions are also sometimes invoked by the supplier as a means to prevent the customer getting a third party in to manage the system, or as a bar to outsourcing the system to third parties. (Outsourcing is discussed in more detail in chapter 2.)

It is accordingly vital that the customer considers the business effect of licence restrictions at the very outset of its relationship with the supplier (and does so in the context of its long-term plans for its IT function and the business as a whole), and where necessary negotiates appropriate changes to the contract documentation. Failure to do so may leave the customer exposed to a claim for copyright infringement if it exceeds the scope of the permitted use, or to being charged additional licence fees for the right to do so.

Licence duration   The licence will often be expressed as perpetual, or for a long fixed term (say 99 years). In the absence of any express contractual provision, the normal rule is that an intellectual property licence is determinable by 'reasonable notice'. However, in determining what *is* reasonable (and indeed whether the licence should in fact be treated as unlimited as to duration), the court might have regard to the consequences of termination for the licensee: these consequences might be severe in the context of business-critical systems or software.

1.4.2.6   Shrink-wrap licensing

Background   Software is often mass-marketed through a distribution chain (or by mail order), in a similar manner to records or cassettes, with the result that there is no opportunity for the customer to enter into a formal licence agreement with the software owner. Many software owners have accordingly adopted the technique of the 'shrink-wrap licence': a licence agreement the terms of which are set out on the outside of the packaging, visible through clear plastic film, and the terms of which are deemed to be accepted if the packaging is opened. The shrink-wrap licence purports to be a direct contract between the software owner and the customer (quite separate from the contract of sale by which the customer acquired the software) which takes effect when the customer breaks the shrink-wrap seal in order to remove the disk.

Enforceability Although the 'headline' terms of shrink-wrap licences are broadly the same as can be found in other forms of software licence (scope of use, duration, restrictions and so on), there is a question as to whether shrink-wrap licences are actually enforceable as a matter of law, for two reasons:

(a) *Can a shrink-wrap licence embody all the elements of a contract?* Any valid contract requires three basic elements — offer, acceptance and consideration — but the shrink-wrap structure does not 'map' cleanly onto these formal legal requirements. The visible display of the licence terms clearly constitutes an offer, and consideration is given by the licensee by virtue of the promises set out in the licence. However, it is unclear whether the licensee validly accepts the offer by breaking the seal, as the usual rule is that acceptance of an offer must be communicated to the offeror.

It is of course open to the offeror to waive that requirement for communication, and a court anxious to enforce the licence against the licensor may well find that the wording on the licence constitutes such a waiver. However, when considering enforcement against the licensee, the same considerations do not apply: an offeror cannot unilaterally declare that silence will constitute consent, nor can a party impose a contract by ultimatum. In the absence of clear acceptance by words (such as by signing a user registration card) or conduct (such as returning a defective disk for replacement), the enforceability of the licence by the licensor is uncertain.

(b) *Does the doctrine of privity of contract operate to prevent enforcement of the shrink-wrap licence?* The doctrine of privity provides that a person cannot take the benefit of a contract unless he is also a party to it. This principle has historically posed problems for suppliers of shrink-wrap software in England and Wales, as it has been open to question whether they are legally entitled to enforce such licence terms in the absence of a direct contract with the customer.

This situation has now been clarified by the Contracts (Rights of Third Parties) Act 1999, which applies to all contracts entered into after 10 May 2000. A non party to a contract will henceforth be entitled to enforce a term in it where:

(i)   the contract expressly provides that he may (s. 1(1)(a)); or

(ii)   the term purports to confer a benefit on him (and it does not appear from the contract that the parties did *not* intend it to be enforceable by him) (s. 1(1)(b)).

Beta v *Adobe*   As a result of the Contracts (Rights of Third Parties) Act 1999, many of the English law concerns as to the enforceability of shrink wrap licences have evaporated. However, as noted above, the new Act only applies to contracts entered into after 10 May 2000, so there remain many contracts in respect of which the supplier will not have the benefit of the new legislation. The Scottish case of *Beta Computers (Europe) Ltd v Adobe Systems (Europe) Ltd* [1996] FSR 367, illustrates the difficulties that these legal issues can cause in practice. The customer (Adobe) had placed a telephone order with its supplier (Beta) to provide a standard package owned by a third party software house (Informix). Beta delivered a copy of the program to Adobe, which came in shrink-wrap packaging which included the statement: 'Opening the Informix software package indicates your acceptance of these conditions'. Adobe did not use the software, and sought to return the package (unopened) to Beta. Beta refused to accept it back, and sued for the price. In its defence, Adobe argued that its transaction with Beta was conditional on Adobe seeing and approving the licence terms: in other words, that there was no effective contract until Adobe had accepted the terms of the shrink-wrap licence by breaking the seal. Lord Penrose found:

(a)   That a contract for the supply of a standard package made over the telephone was not completed until the customer had seen and accepted the shrink-wrap licence terms — and since Adobe had not in fact accepted the terms and had rejected the software, there was accordingly no contract.

(b)   That if the customer *had* accepted the licence terms by opening the package, then the licensor would have been able to enforce those terms under the Scottish doctrine of *ius quaesitum tertio* (i.e., as a third party beneficiary).

(c)   That the licence terms were not in themselves capable of constituting a contract between Informix and Adobe that was discrete from the main transaction between Adobe and Beta.

However, as already noted in section 1.2.1.14, this decision is heavily dependent upon a Scottish law doctrine for which there is no English equivalent, and so is of dubious value as an authority in England.

1.4.2.7 *Specific issues applicable to bespoke software*
Contracts for bespoke software development work have many similarities to licences of standard software, but there are also important differences that arise from the fact that the bespoke software does not exist at the time the contract is made. The main differences are summarised below.

Unique specification   The essence of a bespoke software contract is that the software is written, or a package is to be tailored, to the requirements of the user. This means that the functional specification is of critical importance, just as in other system supply contracts (see sections 1.2.1 and 1.3.2 above). In the context of software development, the functional specification is best prepared by the user alone (possibly with the help of outside independent consultants) or by a combination of the user and the software house, with the user maintaining ultimate control of its contents. Indeed, where a large and complex system is proposed there may be a contract with the software house or a consultant, for the production of the specification, quite separate from the contract from the writing of the software.

Acceptance testing   Acceptance testing will also occupy a more important role in relation to bespoke software than it does in relation to a standard package.[32] If package software has been seen working at other users' sites or has been used on a trial basis by the user, the requirement for a formal acceptance test of the package may not be so important. However, in the case of completely new software, acceptance testing is clearly crucial, to determine whether or not the software house has delivered software conforming with the contract and to determine whether or not it is entitled to be paid.

IPR ownership   By contrast with contracts for the supply of standard packages, the intellectual property rights in which necessarily remain with the software supplier, a bespoke contract may vest the intellectual property rights to the software in the user. The property rights that are relevant are primarily copyright and (to a lesser extent) confidential information, although patent rights cannot be totally ignored. The general rule of English copyright law is that where a person commissions another to produce a copyright work, the copyright in that work vests in the author, and not in the commissioning party.[33] If there is no express provision as to ownership it would be open to the court to imply that notwithstanding the general rule, in equity the copyright belongs to the user, but to reach such a conclusion there would have to be some evidence that this was the intention of the parties.

All these matters should be explicitly addressed in any bespoke software contract.

1.4.3   Maintenance and support contracts

1.4.3.1   Introduction   Almost all new systems are supplied with a warranty as to functionality and performance, though this warranty will generally be of limited duration. It is quite common for the supplier, in addition to this warranty, to offer a maintenance contract which covers part or all of the expected lifetime of the system, subject to payment of additional periodic charges.

1.4.3.2   General maintenance obligations   The extent of the maintenance offered will vary according to the particular contract. It may be:

  (a)   Regular preventative maintenance.
  (b)   Repair on a time plus parts cost basis.

32. See S. Charlton, 'Product Testing: Liability, Acceptance, Contract Terms', *Computer Law and Security Report*, January–February 1989, p. 23.
33. The EC Directive, as finally enacted, is silent on this issue and therefore the general rule still applies. The first draft, however, provided that the commissioner would be entitled 'to exercise all rights in respect of the program, unless otherwise provided by contract'.

(c)   Remote diagnostics with on-site attendance where required (primarily in respect of hardware).

(d)   Full maintenance service with every fault attended to within a certain number of hours of its reporting, in accordance with a set Service Level Agreement (or 'SLA').

The precise service will depend on the customer's requirements, the supplier's ability to provide maintenance, and the charges agreed between the parties. Some important points that should be covered by any maintenance agreement are:

(a)   *Response time*: The supplier should guarantee that problems will be attended to within a specified time, with 'target' times for activities such as responding to initial calls, provision of telephone assistance, attendance on site, and time to actually fix. The shorter the response time required, the more expensive the contract. Whilst it is not possible to guarantee in advance how long any actual repair will take, the contract should be clear as to the consequences of failing to meet these target times, which may include liquidated damages in the event of late response or delayed repair.

A related point on time limits is that contractual response times to calls for assistance are often less stringent in software maintenance contracts than in hardware maintenance contracts. This is curious, since the consequences of faulty software are at least as serious as those of faulty hardware, if not more so.

(b)   *Fault classification*: Faults vary in importance, depending upon the extent to which the functionality and performance of the system is affected, and the supplier may agree to respond more quickly to more important faults. For example, a 'Level 1' fault might be one that effectively stops the customer doing business and to which an urgent fix is required; whereas a 'Level 3' fault may be some defect in the system that is trivial or annoying, but not directly harmful. There are no universally recognised classifications of fault severity, and the classifications are a frequent sticking point in contract negotiations. However, it is essential that there is a clear and effective mechanism for classifying faults quickly: leaving classification 'to be agreed at the time' is just as risky as providing that either party has the unilateral right to classify faults in its sole discretion.

(c)   *Replacement*: The contract should make it clear what is to happen if part of the system (particularly any hardware element) needs to be removed for repair or replacement, and in particular whether the supplier will provide temporary replacement equipment and within what period of time.

(d)   *Duration, increase of charges and renewal*: As the system ages, maintenance charges will necessarily increase. The contract should set out a minimum period of time for which the supplier will provide maintenance, and some way of assessing the charges that will be made in future years, for example by reference to indexation. Phrases like 'the supplier's current charges as amended from time to time' should not be acceptable, as there is no ceiling on what he might decide to charge. The agreement should also, from the customer's point of view at least, contain a right of renewal.

(e) *Transferability*: If the customer wishes to resell the system at some later date, or to transfer it intra-group, he will also need to transfer the benefit of the maintenance agreement. The contract should therefore contain a provision to this effect. The supplier might also wish to transfer the burden of the contract to another organisation, but a provision permitting this should be resisted by the customer: there is no guarantee that the new supplier will have sufficient expertise or experience of the system in question.

1.4.3.3 Specific issues relating to software maintenance: source code Software maintenance usually comprises two elements:

(a) the correction of software errors (or 'bugs'); and
(b) the provision of enhancements and updates to the software.

Software maintenance — sometimes also called 'support' — has up to now normally been provided by the supplier of the software because of the need to have access to the program source code is necessary. However, as noted in chapter 6.5.1 above, the customer has a limited right to decompile the object code to produce source code for the purpose of error correction (though not any other form of maintenance such as the development of enhancements or updates).[34] The source code may in any case be made available to the customer, either because it is the policy of the supplier to do so,[35] or because the intellectual property rights vest in the customer (under a bespoke contract, for example), or because the customer has obtained access to the source code pursuant to an escrow agreement. In such cases the customer should be able to maintain the software on its own account (or appoint a third party to do so).

1.4.3.4 Specific issues relating to software maintenance: upgrades Apart from error correction, the supplier will usually agree to supply a copy of all enhancements and updates developed by him during the term of the maintenance agreement. These fall into a number of categories:

(a) Corrections of previously reported errors.
(b) Updates necessitated by changes in the law.
(c) Variations necessitated by changes in the system software that runs on the hardware in question.
(d) Improvements or new functions.

The customer will often be obliged to accept and install the enhancements and updates, so that the whole of the maintenance company's customer base

---

34. However, the right can be excluded by contract, at least as implemented in the United Kingdom: new s. 50C of the Copyright Designs and Patents Act 1988.
35. In *Andersen Consulting* v *CHP Consulting Ltd*, 26 July 1991, Ch D, (unreported) the judge described the standard licence agreement of the claimants relating to the program in question, under which the program source code was supplied to licensees for a fee of £125,000. The judge noted that 'the result is that the plain intent of the contract was that the licensee should have the ability, the material and the right to alter and amend the programme [sic] by persons other than those who had written it'.

is using the same version of the software. For this reason, it will often be a requirement of the software licence that the licensee enters into a software maintenance agreement in the first place.

1.4.3.5 Warranties and liability Maintenance agreements are contracts for the provision of services and accordingly, by virtue of s. 13 of the Supply of Goods and Services Act 1982, there will be an implied term that the maintenance company will use reasonable skill and care in carrying out the service. It is fairly unusual to find express warranties as to the *quality* of the maintenance services, although ideally the supplier should agree to maintain system functionality and performance to the standards set out in the original system supply agreement. Suppliers will often seek to impose liability limitations similar to those in other system supply contracts, and the observations already made in that regard apply equally in this context.

1.4.4 Hardware and software leases

1.4.4.1 Introduction It is not unusual for the customer in a systems procurement to finance the transaction by entering into some form of leasing arrangement. This involves the supplier selling the system (in other words, the hardware elements and the right to use the software elements) to a third party finance company (termed the 'lessor'), which in turn leases it on to the customer to use. However, as leasing comprises a discrete (and substantial) body of law in its own right, it is not proposed to address it in this chapter, other than to make some high-level observations about two important contractual implications of the leasing structure. These are:

(a)   The ability of the customer to enforce performance and other warranties in respect of the system.

(b)   The licensing structures required in respect of software elements of the system.

1.4.4.2 Enforcement of warranties by customer The Supply of Goods and Services Act 1982 (or the Supply of Goods (Implied Terms) Act 1973 if it is a hire-purchase contract[36]) imply terms into the contract which are broadly the same as those implied by the Sale of Goods Act 1979 into a sale contract. However, as the customer's only contractual relationship (at least under a finance lease as opposed to an operating lease) is with the lessor, the question arises as to how the customer can enforce rights against the original supplier. There are three broad ways of achieving this:

(a)   *Assignment by the lessor*: the lessor agrees to assign to the customer its rights under its own contract with the supplier (or occasionally to enforce them for the customer's benefit). The problem with such a solution is that the customer's claim is limited to the damages the lessor could have recovered, which in many cases will be nothing.[37]

---

36. I.e., if it contains an option to purchase.
37. E.g. if the lease excludes liability for defects and rental is payable irrespective of such defects.

(b) *Novation*: the deal is structured initially as a direct sale between the supplier and the customer, with the 'day-to-day' obligations — such as delivery, acceptance arrangements, and payments — being subsequently novated in favour of the lessor. The intention is to leave the supplier liable to the customer in respect of matters such as warranties, although there seems to be no clear legal authority that such a partial novation is possible.

(c) *Direct collateral contract*: the deal is structured as three separate contracts, namely (i) a sale agreement between supplier and lessor, (ii) a lease agreement between lessor and customer, and (iii) a collateral contract containing the various warranties given by the supplier to the customer (the consideration for which is the customer's entering into the lease). This is thought to be the most effective of all three methods of conferring the benefit of supplier warranties on the ultimate customer, provided the supplier's warranties and the customer's remedies are drafted in the light of the terms of the lease agreement.

1.4.4.3 Software licensing structures The need to ensure that software is properly licensed gives rise to particular concerns in the context of a leasing arrangement. First, the lessor will need to ensure that the licence permits it to do any of the acts it might be required to do in connection with the financing arrangements, including (for example) assigning or sublicensing its rights to third parties in case the customer should default on its payment obligations. Secondly, the customer will want to ensure that its own licence (from the lessor) covers the full range of its intended activities in relation to the system in the same way is if it were taking a direct licence from the supplier.

1.5 CONCLUSION

The delivery of a working system which meets the customer's needs is a difficult enough task, but it is even more difficult to achieve in a contractual vacuum. In summary, there are three main advantages to a properly negotiated and well-drawn contract:

(a) Identification of the issues.
(b) Clarity as to the obligations of each party.
(c) Agreement in advance on how disagreements are to be resolved.

The overall aim is a good working relationship, leading to successful performance of the contract and the installation of an effective system. Whilst it is tempting to produce standard form contracts, particularly given the cost of negotiating individual agreements, this factor is far outweighed by the expense of sorting out the mess when things not covered by the contract go wrong.

CHAPTER TWO

Information Systems Outsourcing

Alison Welterveden

2.1 INTRODUCTION[1]

2.1.1 What is an IS outsourcing contract?

An IS outsourcing contract involves the transfer of all or a substantial part of the IS functions of a customer's business to a third party service provider. Typically, an IS outsourcing arrangement will therefore involve the transfer of assets and, frequently, staff that were previously used to support the activity or operation, to the supplier. Those assets are then used to provide a service back to the customer, to an agreed level of service. These contracts are frequently referred to as IS (information systems) outsourcing contracts or IT (information technology) outsourcing contracts.

IS outsourcing has been utilised for many years now, although IS outsourcing in its modern format has developed from the introduction of the early time sharing, facilities management and service bureau arrangements from the 1960s and 1970s. The nature of these facilities management and service bureau arrangements is described below[2]. Although facilities management and service bureau contracts are different in nature to a pure IS outsourcing, they heavily influenced its development.

It is generally agreed that the first landmark IS outsourcing contract that was signed was the contract entered into in 1989 between Eastman Kodak

---

1. Parts of this chapter are based on the chapter 'IS Outsourcing' written by Mark Lewis and Alison Welterveden and contained in the *Outsourcing Practice Manual*, London: Sweet & Maxwell, 1998.
2. See 2.1.2.

and an IBM subsidiary, Integrated Systems Solutions Corporation. Under the terms of that agreement Integrated Systems Solutions Corporation built and operated a computer centre for Kodak taking on some 300 Kodak staff in the process.[3] Since this date the IS outsourcing market has expanded rapidly as a growing number of corporate and government entities alike have rushed to jump on the outsourcing band-wagon and take advantage of the perceived benefits that an outsourced function could bring.[4]

IS functions which are now outsourced typically include one or more of the following:

(a)   data centre;
(b)   voice and data networks;
(c)   telecommunications;
(d)   applications development;
(e)   applications support and maintenance;
(f)   desktop;
(g)   project management;
(h)   contract and vendor management;
(i)   help desk and call centre;
(j)   IS training; and
(k)   disaster recovery.

IS outsourcing contracts will frequently include a bundle of functions which are transferred to the supplier, especially given the natural dependencies that exist between many different IS functions.

Although most IS functions are capable of being outsourced, the crucial decision for any business will be which elements of their IS function should be outsourced in practice. Generally, where an IS function is critical to the business (such as where a particular system enables the business to distinguish itself from its competitors) a degree of caution should be exercised before the running of that function is entrusted to a third party.

2.1.2 IS outsourcing contracts distinguished from service bureau and facilities management contracts

The early time sharing and bureaux based contracts from which the modern IS outsourcing contract has evolved were more limited in scope and did not

---

3. See Mylott, *Computer Outsourcing Managing the Transfer of Information Systems*, Englewood Cliffs, New Jersey: Prentice Hall, 1995, p. 15 and Klepper and Wendell O. Jones, *Outsourcing Information Technology Systems and Services*, Upper Saddle River, New Jersey: Prentice Hall, 1998, p. xxii.
4. Gartner Group have predicted a 16.3 per cent growth in IS outsourcing worldwide between 1997 and 2002 that will result in a $120 billion market by 2002, of which the US market will account for $51 billion (as reported in the Financial Times *FT Information Technology Survey*, 4 August 1999, at http://www.ft.com/ftsurveys). Other surveys, such as that by Wendy Currie and Leslie Willcocks in *New Strategies in IT Outsourcing*, quoted at http://www.outsourcing-academics.com/html/acad14.html/, suggest an even more rapid expansion. The future for IS outsourcing currently looks very rosy indeed.

involve the transfer of assets to the supplier. Instead, under time sharing arrangements the customer would be given a connection to enable it to access the supplier's systems at the supplier's site. The customer remained responsible for the use to which he put those systems. Similarly with service bureau arrangements, the supplier would process an application, such as payroll, using their mainframes to provide similar processes for a number of customers.

Under facilities management contracts, it is generally the customer's IS systems (whether they are owned by the customer or licensed to it from third parties) that are used by the supplier to deliver the services to the customer. Again, there is no change of ownership in the assets which traditionally remain under the ownership of the customer or are licensed to it and which remain located at the customer's premises. The supplier is merely granted access to use those IS systems necessary in order to provide the managed service.

It should, however, be borne in mind that, as with anything, the question of whether a particular arrangement is an IS outsourcing contract is really a question of degree. For example, most private finance initiative (PFI)/public private partnerships (PPP) transactions are outsourcing contracts in all but name. Although it may not be government policy to refer to these deals as outsourcing they typically involve a supplier building or supplying, owning and operating information systems and then providing a service to the government entity concerned using those systems. One of the principal conditions of PFI/PPP treatment is that the supplier owns the IT asset so that it remains on the supplier's balance sheet and thereby avoids the government taking the capital asset into its own books. So, as with IS outsourcing, assets which are owned by the supplier are used by the supplier to deliver a service back to the government customer. The structure of such a PFI/PPP contract looks very similar to that of the IS outsourcing contract.

Even where the transaction is not a pure IS outsourcing involving the transfer of assets and the related activity, and instead falls under the guise of, for example, a facilities management contract, many of the issues referred to in this chapter will still be relevant.

2.1.3 Recent trends

One thing that is certain is that the IS outsourcing market is not a static one and over the past decade a number of new variants on the traditional structure have surfaced.

Recent trends include business process outsourcing (BPO) and application service provision outsourcing (ASP). BPO, as its name suggests, involves the outsourcing of business processes (such as finance and accounting or payroll processes). It often comes hand in hand with the outsourcing of the applications that support the business processes, which would be the subject of a typical IS outsourcing contract.

The current and increasingly fashionable trend is ASP under which the power of the internet is utilised to enable the supplier to provide the customer with access to services (such as hardware platforms, applications, systems management and support) using a standard web browser. ASP contracts ironically see a return to the days of time-sharing where the customer uses a connection to access systems owned by a third party. The current focus of such ASP contracts is very much on enterprise resource planning programs and is proving popular with the smaller to medium size corporate entity who can utilise the ASP concept to gain access to more sophisticated technology than it would otherwise be able to and without the need to develop in-house resources to support it. Growth forecasts for ASP are, like most forecasts for anything to do with the '.com' economy, stratospheric.[5] Ultimately, if ASP develops into the management not just of applications but of the entire business process supported by those applications, then the ASP concept will merge into BPO.

On a slightly less glamorous note, the outsourcing of shared service centres is also often an attractive business proposition. Shared service centres typically arise from the rationalisation of a corporate entity's IS functions or on the introduction of new enterprise-wide applications that are then provided to the business. External service providers may be called in to run a shared service centre which is used by one particular corporate group or a shared service centre which is used to provide services to a number of external customers to achieve economies of scale.

2.1.4 The partnership myth

One of the common myths in outsourcing is that the relationship between the customer and supplier can be likened to a partnership. Whilst commendable on a commercial level, the legal reality is somewhat different. A true partnership involves the equal sharing of risk and reward. Suppliers may be keen to reap the benefits of the outsourcing relationship although, even then, there is no making of a 'common profit' from the outsourcing relationship — a concept at the heart of the legal definition of a partnership. Indeed, the converse is true. The supplier uses its service provision to the customer at a carefully calculated charge to make a profit from the customer. It is also virtually unheard of for the risks to be divided equally. This is evidenced most clearly in the detailed limitation of liability clauses that suppliers will seek to impose to control their risk exposure.

References to the relationship being a true partnership should therefore be avoided by the supplier and treated with a healthy dose of cynicism from the customer.[6]

The term partnership is also sometimes used in a slightly different context to refer to the creation of an ongoing relationship where it is envisaged that

---

5. Forrester Research have predicted that the global ASP market, in its pure applications rental form, would grow from virtually nothing in 1998 to $6 billion by 2001 (as reported in the Financial Times *FT Information Technology Survey*, 4 August 1999, at http://www.ft.com/ftsurveys).

6. This is not intended to belittle the outsourcing relationship. A high degree of trust and a solid working relationship will be vital to maximise the benefits that can be achieved by both parties.

a number of contracts will be awarded over time to the supplier. In these circumstances, the supplier is effectively a preferred supplier for any future outsourcing. For example, a framework agreement may be entered into governing the overall business relationship and acknowledging the intention that the supplier is a preferred one and providing certain key terms (such as pricing for any outsourced service). The terms of any such framework agreement should be negotiated carefully. The customer should not be influenced by the anticipated costs savings achievable from appointing an entity as its preferred supplier to the detriment of a well thought out contract. Any key terms specified in a framework agreement should be subject to the same, if not greater, scrutiny as a one-off outsourcing contract. Again, the relationship could not be classified as a partnership in the legal sense and any references to it being one should be avoided.

2.1.5 Reasons for outsourcing

The reasons for outsourcing are varied. The most frequently quoted incentives in the private sector are the added value that third party expertise and experience can bring and the costs benefits.[7] The added value is evidenced through the enhanced levels of service that a supplier will usually offer which, because of the experience and economies of scale available to the supplier, are often provided at a cheaper cost than that achievable in-house. Whether the first wave of outsourcing contracts entered into in the early 1990s brought the anticipated costs savings and improved service is unclear. It is apparent that at least in some cases that this was not the result.[8]

In the public sector the motivators for outsourcing are different. The nature of government bodies means that there is no need to reduce costs to increase profitability. Instead, the focus is very much on 'value for money'. This means that the public sector will typically look to increasing the quality of service for the charges paid and thereby making better use of taxpayers' money.

---

7. A recent survey carried out by the Outsourcing Institute on current and potential outsourcing end-users cited costs reduction as the primary reason and access to world class capabilities as third (as reported at http://www.outsourcing.com/howandwhy/research/surveyresults.htm). It seems that companies are, however, moving away from costs reduction as a primary reason for outsourcing and are looking at other factors (see Formation Consulting's November 1999 report at http://www.formation-consulting.co.uk/survey_questions.html and the study conducted by Lacity and Willcocks reported at http://www.outsourcing-academics.com/html/acad2.html).

8. Rudy Hirschheim, who with Mary Lacity researched IS outsourcing over a nine year period, has commented that 'many companies that have gone through large scale outsourcing exercises are finding that their flexibility is not as enhanced as they thought it would be with outsourcing, and that service levels they thought would improve have actually dropped. . . . They're beginning to find that outsourcing is not the panacea they hoped for when they initially outsourced' (see *Backsourcing: An Emerging Trend?* in Outsourcing-Academics.com at http://www/outsourcing-academics.com/html/acad1.html). Accordingly, some companies are beginning to take back in-house functions that they had previously outsourced as a result of this dissatisfaction. What this chapter should assist to establish is that a well-drafted contract can protect many of the customer's expectations as to the level of service and costs.

The technology industry is highly competitive and grows at a rapid rate as the modern economy becomes increasingly reliant on IT. Consequently, over recent years staff costs in this sector have spiralled upwards. Outsourcing obviates the need to recruit and, crucially, to retain IT staff and enables the business to focus on its core business competencies. Provided a good contract manager is appointed by the customer to oversee the operation of the contract, management will generally need to spend considerably less time in overseeing the IS function. The role required will be that of strategic input and direction, rather than managing day to day operational issues.

The outsourcing of an IS function or functions necessitates the transfer of the assets used to support and run that function to the supplier. Accordingly, responsibility for maintaining and updating those systems will also pass. The financial burden for the customer is translated from that of the costs of resources to provide an in-house service and the fluctuating costs of improving the existing, and acquiring any new, technology to a more stable regular service charge. Not only do the costs of receiving the service become more certain but the use of a third party supplier should improve access to new technology. Suppliers can acquire such technology more quickly, being able to spread the cost over a number of customers. In addition, the supplier will have the resources and skill available to evaluate and implement that new technology more rapidly than the typical corporate or government entity. The larger-scale supplier will also often be able to negotiate substantial discounts from the price of any new software or hardware. This rapid access to, and potentially lower cost of, new technology can make IS outsourcing a very attractive proposition.

These are some of the more common reasons for outsourcing. With any corporate or government customer, the business case will differ and a careful evaluation of the pros and cons of outsourcing any IS function should always be undertaken.

2.1.6   Disadvantages of outsourcing

One of the distinctions between the typical IS outsourcing contract and other computer contracts (such as software and hardware procurement or maintenance contracts) is the ongoing cooperation which will be required from the parties over the life of the contract. Without a close working relationship and an understanding of the parties obligations and responsibilities (in both the strict contractual sense and more generally) the IS outsourcing relationship may be doomed to failure.[9]

As with any business proposition, there are potential downsides to be considered. As noted above, although costs reduction is often cited as a primary motivator the much sought after savings do not always happen in practice. Indeed, with some contracts the cost to the customer has increased as a result of the contract. This is particularly the case where the service

---

9. Interestingly, a cultural 'mismatch' is often referred to as being the cause of many breakdowns in the IS outsourcing relationship.

requirements are ill-defined in the initial contract, enabling the supplier to demand additional charges through any contract change mechanism as the scope of the contract is formally increased to cover service requirements of the customer which, although always intended by the customer to form part of the outsourced function, fall outside the strict wording of the service schedule.[10]

The transfer of staff to the supplier as part of the outsourcing process[11] results in the loss of specialist skill and expertise within the business. This can be a particular problem if the business is left without any person with the technical skills required to oversee the running of the contract. Obviously, the more of the IS functions of any business which are outsourced the more likely this will be an issue. This problem can also effectively lock a customer into a relationship with a supplier. If the business lacks the technical skills required to bring the service back in-house, it may be easier to leave the service provision with an under-performing supplier rather than to expend the necessary time and management resource to locate an alternative vendor.

A decision to outsource should be treated with some sensitivity within an organisation, particularly as regards the dissemination of information to employees. Staff are not always receptive to the prospect of outsourcing and to the transfer of their employment to a third party IS supplier, although the manner in which the proposal to outsource is communicated to employees can reduce some of this negativity. An effective communications process will therefore be required to avoid negative publicity and potential strike or other employee action.[12]

Outsourcing invariably involves the transfer of a number of assets to the supplier. This may result in a lack of control over the nature of the IT infrastructure used to deliver the services — which may be a particular problem when the infrastructure is returned to the customer on the expiry or termination of the contract and the customer is left with an outdated system and with little or no knowledge as to its detailed operation. Although the essence of the IS outsourcing contract is the delivery of services to a stated level it is nevertheless therefore advisable to include provisions requiring technology refreshment on a regular basis to ensure an acceptable standard of infrastructure is maintained. An adequate flow of information throughout the duration of the contract regarding the composition of the technology architecture used by the supplier will also be essential.

One of the consequences of having part of your business function run by a third party is the security risk. In particular, there is an increased risk that others may access, and misuse, information which is confidential to the business and that the staff of the supplier may unintentionally or otherwise

---

10. The importance of the service description cannot be overstated. See 2.2.2 (in particular 2.2.2.1) below.
11. The Transfer of Undertakings (Protection of Employment) Regulations 1981 will usually apply to transfer staff associated with the function that is outsourced to the supplier. See 2.4.
12. In addition to the commercial necessity of such an effective communications process, where the Transfer of Undertakings (Protection of Employment) Regulations 1981 applies, there are legal stipulations about the consultation process which must take place. See 2.4.4.

misuse the customer's intellectual property. Detailed provisions regarding the use of, and access to, confidential information and intellectual property are the norm in IS outsourcing contracts. Suppliers should also be compelled to comply with the customer's security policies and procedures.

Rigid contracts may also prevent future expansion and growth of the customer's business. One of the inevitable consequences of the outsourcing relationship will be that the supplier's consent must be obtained before any changes can be made to the scope of the service. Contract change provisions will therefore play an important role in any contract.[13]

The constant expansion of the IS outsourcing market is testament to its popularity. The disadvantages and risks of IS outsourcing seem rarely, in practice, to outweigh the perceived benefits. For those contemplating an outsourcing contract, it will therefore be comforting to know that many of the risks outlined above can be controlled or minimised through appropriate contractual provisions.

2.1.7 The outsourcing contract

The essence of an IS outsourcing contract is a commitment by the supplier to deliver services to predefined service levels. The contract will then go on to define what happens in the event these service levels are not met. A failure to meet a particular service level will often result in the payment of service credits, a specified sum of money which becomes payable automatically in the event of a breach. Without service credits being stipulated, the customer would need to prove on each occasion that any failure to meet the service levels is a breach of contract and that they are entitled to damages from the supplier accordingly. To specify the service credits that will become payable in this way therefore gives certainty to both parties and helps to avoid protracted disputes as to whether any contract breach has occurred and, if so, whether it has caused any loss and damage to the customer which should be recoverable from the supplier. These service credit regimes differentiate the IS outsourcing contract from other IT contracts, such as system supply contracts, where such schemes are found more rarely.

The contract will contain other provisions which are key to the effective management of the ongoing relationship between the parties. IS outsourcing contracts are usually long in nature, with contracts for seven to ten year periods being relatively standard industry market practice. Flexibility will therefore be crucial, in terms of adapting the contract to reflect the customer's changing business requirements and to introduce new forms of technology and other service improvements.

This chapter will examine some of the key features of the IS outsourcing contract in turn.

2.1.8 The outsourcing process

2.1.8.1   Board/business decision   The process will begin with an evaluation by the customer of the business case for outsourcing. The evaluation process will

---

13. See 2.2.2.

review both the benefits and any disadvantages of outsourcing the particular IS function in question.[14]

The evaluation team should ideally be comprised of those who will be involved in the entire outsourcing process to ensure continuity in approach and full accountability for the outsourcing decision. The team should include those with appropriate IS technical skills and suitable management or board representation. Finance and HR managers may also need to play an important role, depending on the size and scope of the outsourcing in question.

2.1.8.2 Specifying requirements/service levels Assuming a decision to outsource is made, the customer will initially need to put together a statement of its requirements for the outsourced function. The importance of this exercise cannot be underestimated. A detailed requirements specification which clearly specifies the business need will help to attract the correct suppliers competent to provide the relevant services and avoid (or, at least, minimise) later disagreements about the scope (and consequent cost) of the service that suppliers are tendering for. Cost will be an important factor for any customer and the evaluation process should undertake a thorough review of the cost that is currently incurred in providing the service in-house and an assessment of the likely costs savings that can be achieved through outsourcing.

As well as identifying the particular function that is to be outsourced, due consideration must be given to associated issues. For example, which of the assets that are currently used by the customer to deliver the service in-house are to be transferred to the supplier? Who owns those assets and where are they located? Are there staff who are to transfer? What dependencies are there between the function to be outsourced and other functions that are to be retained in-house by the customer? Should assets used to provide the service be returned to the customer at the termination or expiry of the outsourcing arrangement? Once these, and other, questions have been considered, the customer will be in a position to go out to the market place and tender for a supplier.

Putting together the tender documentation is a skilled and time-consuming process and one in relation to which external consultants are often employed. Such consultants help draft the tender documentation, evaluate the responses, sit on the negotiation team and generally steer the client through the outsourcing process. External specialist IS outsourcing lawyers are also usually engaged from the early stages. They will define the contract requirements to be included in the tender, together with advising on associated legal issues (such as confidentiality agreements). Lawyers will also play a key role in the negotiation process, reducing the client's requirements to contractual form.

2.1.8.3 Going out to tender The tender documentation needs to include a detailed description of the services required and the service levels to which

---

14. See 2.1.5 for a description of some of the popular reasons to outsource and 2.1.6 for some of the disadvantages of outsourcing.

they should be delivered. This information is contained in either an invitation to tender (ITT) or request for proposal (RFP). The ITT or RFP will need to be sufficiently detailed to enable the supplier to provide a detailed costing. This means information regarding assets and staff to transfer, contract duration, reporting requirements and any business processes the supplier must adhere to should be included.

Whether or not the contract should be attached to the ITT is often a subject of debate. This can take the form of either the entire contract or an outline of key terms only. It enables the customer to specify the terms on which they wish to do business and compels the supplier to indicate at an early stage which of those terms are acceptable (or otherwise) to it. The supplier will therefore be reviewing and commenting on those contractual terms when their negotiating power is at their weakest and the desire to win an attractive contract may force them into making more concessions than they would otherwise do so.

In some circumstances, time constraints may mean that it is simply not feasible to include contract terms at the ITT stage, especially where the customer is new to outsourcing and has no standard contract terms in place. In any event it must also be accepted that a certain amount of negotiation will be inevitable, even where the contract was included as part of the ITT and a supplier has indicated their acceptance of its terms in their tender response.

2.1.8.4 Choosing a preferred supplier   Essentially, there are two methods that can be adopted in selecting a supplier. The first is to produce a shortlist with a number of preferred suppliers and to run negotiations in tandem with each of them. The disadvantage of such an approach is that it is very costly in terms of the management time required to participate in several negotiations at once and the associated expense of external advisers evaluating and negotiating a number of draft contracts. This acts as a considerable deterrent in smaller value contracts. The advantages can be considerable though. Suppliers who know they are in competition with others will adopt a far more flexible approach in negotiations than they would if they were the sole preferred supplier. Suppliers will inevitably end up in a 'contract race' with the first to agree acceptable terms and price winning the contract. This can assist to speed up the contract negotiation process (although this must be balanced against the management resource required to undertake negotiations with several suppliers).

An objective set of assessment criteria should be adopted against which any potential supplier is assessed, with a review of all aspects of the tender response. In addition to the obvious considerations, such as capability to provide the service and price, other factors may be relevant. The relationship between the parties will usually be a long one and it is important to ensure that there is a 'cultural' fit between the two entities. Without this, the parties may simply be unable to work together effectively.

Visits to other customer sites may also be beneficial to assess the supplier's performance in practice compared to any assurances given as part of their tender response. It also enables the customer to gain a valuable insight into the day-to-day working methods of the supplier.

2.1.8.5 Due diligence Due diligence plays an important role, enabling the supplier to verify that information provided regarding the assets and employees is correct, to ascertain the condition of any assets which are to be transferred and to consider whether the supplier believes the desired service levels can be achieved using them. Due diligence is also used to investigate any other matters which may impact on the supplier's costs model. This process helps to flush out any potential issues and, more importantly, for them to be dealt with prior to contract signature. Due diligence also helps to foster an early working relationship between the parties.

One of the aspects that will be investigated will be software and databases licensed to the customer where the supplier needs to use that software or database to continue providing the service. Many licences are drafted so as to prevent access to, or use of, that software or database by anyone other than the customer. To allow access and use by the IS outsourcing provider without obtaining the third party supplier's consent would therefore place the customer in breach of its licence terms, with the risk of that licence being terminated and a damages claim made against it.[15] In addition, the supplier may itself be making copies of such software or databases in the course of the service provision and thereby infringing the intellectual property rights of the third party owner. Some third party suppliers are renowned for the considerable fees they seek to impose for allowing access and/or use by a service provider and the allocation of these costs between the parties will often be a hotly contended issue.[16]

Due diligence is usually carried out prior to contract signature following selection of the preferred supplier. This is most desirable for both parties enabling certainty to be achieved before the contractual relationship is commenced. This is particularly the case where software is licensed to the customer and third party consent must be obtained to allow for the service provider to gain access to that software or for a new licence to be granted direct to the service provider. Identifying licences where consents must be obtained and the procedure to obtain this consent can take many months.

The alternative is for due diligence to take place in a period after the contract is entered into with an adjustment to the contract charges to take into account any inaccuracies in the information provided to the supplier which impact on the cost of providing the services. This approach can lead

---

15. For example, in October 1990 the UK press reported that Computer Associates (CA) had started legal proceedings against Hosykns, claiming alleged copyright infringement of 39 of CA's programs. This related to the use by Hoskyns of CA software that CA licensees had transferred to Hoskyns under facilities management contracts. This dispute was settled out of court.

16. Competition remedies may be available when the owner is demanding royalties, although this is at best an open question. The argument is that such a demand may be an abuse of a dominant position contrary to art. 82. Also it could be argued that the restriction on licensing can be regarded as anticompetitive contrary to art. 81(1). This would only be the case if the restriction is appreciable, which is unlikely in most outsourcing contracts.

to disputes as to whether correct information was or was not provided initially which can sour relations between the parties at a very early stage in the relationship. For this reason, it is best avoided.

2.1.8.6 Negotiating the contract   There will usually be much debate about the detailed terms of an IS outsourcing contract. These contracts are complex in nature providing a well defined service requirement whilst allowing for future change and flexibility in terms of the customer's changing business requirements and the rapid developments in the technology market.

Even where the draft contract forms part of the tender documentation, it is common to find considerable negotiation over its terms, especially where the supplier's tender indicates that the terms are acceptable in principle but subject to detailed negotiation (a commonplace, and understandable, response). This sort of response allows a 'get out' enabling the supplier to defer lengthy negotiation until after its selection as the preferred supplier.

In consequence, it can take some months to finalise the detailed contract terms and a suitable amount of time should be scheduled accordingly for this process to take place.

2.1.8.7 Public sector outsourcing   The public sector has embraced IS outsourcing with as much zeal as the private sector. The focus of such an outsourcing is different — concepts such as profitability and shareholder value which drive the private sector are irrelevant. Instead, the public sector looks for value for money in allocating outsourcing contracts.

An entity within the public sector will approach the outsourcing process in a very different manner. There are a number of laws and regulations which will impact on the procurement process, including the manner in which a tender is carried out, the negotiation process and contract award.

Various EU Directives on public procurement have been adopted which relate to procedures for the award of service contracts, supply contracts and work contracts in the public sector. Of particular importance to the outsourcing sector is the EU Services Directive[17] which was implemented into English law in 1994 by the Public Services Contract Regulations 1993[18] (the Regulations). In very simple terms these Regulations state that if a 'contracting authority' wants to award a public services contract then it must follow certain rules. The term 'contracting authority' encompasses central, regional and local government. The Regulations ensure that contracts are openly advertised and that the evaluation of bidders is carried out on a fair and open basis. There must be no unfair discrimination in the selection of suppliers. The rules apply to all such public services contracts, other than those below a minimum estimated contract value.

There are a number of requirements in the Regulations about notices which contracting authorities must publish regarding contracts to be entered into and their final award. These notices are published in the Official Journal of the European Union.

---

17. EU Directive 92/50/EC.
18. SI 1993/3228.

The Regulations provide fairly detailed procedures for contract award which must be by way of an open procedure (where all interested parties can submit tenders), a restricted procedure (where certain suppliers are invited to tender) or a negotiated procedure (where the contracting authority communicates directly with suppliers of their choice and negotiates a contract with one of them). The last type of procedure, the negotiated procedure, is particularly favoured in outsourcing projects, although the contracting authority must be able to justify its use of the negotiated procedure in accordance with the requirements of the Regulations.

In shortlisting bidders contracting authorities can only evaluate them on the basis of certain selection criteria (such as their economic and financial standing and their technical ability). Similarly, contracting authorities are also required to base their decision to award the contract to a particular bidder on the grounds of lowest price or, more flexibly, the most economically advantageous tender.

Action can be taken by third parties where the correct procurement procedure has not been followed which, where successful before the contract award, may lead to suspension of the procurement process pending a decision being made by the courts. Otherwise, damages may be awarded.

EU procurement law has recently been modified further to implement the Government Procurement Agreement, an agreement signed between the EU and non-EU countries to open up the public procurement market. This is reflected in the Directive on the coordination of procedures for the award of service contracts, supply contracts and works contracts in the public sector adopted in 1997.[19] This Directive has not been formally implemented into UK law, although UK law is already largely compliant with its terms.

2.2   THE IS OUTSOURCING CONTRACT

2.2.1   The services agreement and related documents

The central document in any outsourcing relationship will be the services agreement. This documents the services to be provided by the supplier and the service levels to which those services must be provided. It also includes other provisions relating to the ongoing management of the outsourcing relationship. There are, however, other contractual documents which may be entered into leading up to, and in the course of, the outsourcing contract.

Heads of agreement (also known as memorandums of understanding) are sometimes used to reflect the early commercial agreement reached between the parties prior to entering into the detailed outsourcing contract. For the most part, these heads of agreement simply reflect the commercial intent of the parties and are little more than an agreement to agree future detailed contract terms. As agreements to agree, they are unenforceable under English law. The exceptions to this are terms such as confidentiality and exclusivity undertakings (i.e., that during a fixed time period negotiations will not be

---

19. EU Directive 97/52/EC.

conducted with any other third parties) which will be legally binding. Their value is therefore for the most part in the commercial comfort that they give to each party that there is a mutual understanding that an outsourcing relationship will be embarked on and, very broadly, what the scope of any contract will be.

Frequently, suppliers may be asked to commence work, or may themselves suggest that certain activities should be performed, before the services agreement itself is signed. This is a reflection of the time that is usually required in order to complete the due diligence process and contract negotiations. Once a supplier has been selected as the preferred supplier it may make business sense for certain investments to be made prior to contract signature in order to minimise any period of delay once the contract is up and running. This sort of investment may include acquiring new technology or employees in order to provide the services. Suppliers will seek to cover their risk exposure during this period leading up to contract signature by obtaining from the customer its written consent to specified activities being carried out by the supplier on behalf of the customer (i.e., the acquisition of a specific piece of hardware or software) and an indemnity in favour of the supplier in respect of the costs relating to those activities (such as the price of that piece of hardware or software). Relatively informal letter agreements are frequently used to record the parties' understanding in relation to any such arrangements. The letter agreement can also formally acknowledge the customer's intention to enter into a contract with the supplier, on the assumption that suitable contract terms can be agreed.

Suppliers may seek to expand the scope of these undertakings by the customer to cover other activities and costs prior to contract signature. It should be accepted that a certain amount of time and resource should be invested by any supplier in order to achieve a successful contract. However, where there are activities which should genuinely be rewarded on a time and materials basis, the supplier should not be left out-of-pocket if the contract negotiations later fail. Any recovery under these sorts of arrangements should be on the basis of specified fee rates. In order to avoid rapidly escalating costs of which the customer is unaware, the supplier should be required to obtain the prior consent of the customer before incurring the costs. It will be in neither party's best interests for these sorts of informal arrangements to continue on an indefinite basis and it is therefore common to find time limits imposed on the expiry of which the letter agreement terminates if no outsourcing contract has been entered into by the specified date.

A consequence of the detailed discussion and disclosure process which takes place prior to contract signature is that the supplier inevitably has access to a large amount of confidential information of the customer. It will therefore be important to ensure that the supplier is required to enter into a confidentiality (or non-disclosure) agreement. This will govern the use that can be made of the confidential information (essentially, to evaluate whether a contract should be entered into) and will prevent the disclosure of that information to third parties. The supplier should also be restricted in the internal disclosures it can make of the confidential information within its own organisation — disclosure should be limited to those who are part of the bid team. This agreement should be put in place before any information or documentation, which is confidential in nature, is disclosed to the supplier. Where a letter (or other agreement) is used to cover any pre-contract investments or activities (as referred to above) these obligations can be incorporated into that letter agreement. Otherwise, a separate confidentiality agreement can be used.

As part of the outsourcing arrangement there will be a transfer of assets from the customer to the supplier. This will include third party computer programs, hardware, related contracts (such as hardware and support arrangements), software which has been developed and is owned by the customer, buildings and land and other assets, items, contracts and arrangements. The transfer of these assets can take place either within the principal services agreement or alternatively as a separate contract. In any event, the terms regarding the asset transfer will be the same.[20]

In some of the more sophisticated outsourcing arrangements, two established entities may join together in order to provide a combined service to a particular customer. This can be done by establishing a joint venture vehicle into which each of the two entities contributes staff and assets. In such circumstances, a joint venture agreement will therefore be required to record the establishment and operation of the joint venture vehicle. The customer will need to be satisfied that the joint venture company is not merely a shell company but is a substantive entity backed up by sufficient value and assets.[21] In any event, it may be appropriate to seek a finance and performance guarantee by the original two parent entities in the event of any failure to perform by the joint venture company.

2.2.2 The services agreement

As noted above, the services agreement is the principal contract between the parties governing the delivery of the services to the customer. Contracts are usually long in length reflecting the complex nature of the relationship and the need for the service provider to have a relatively long period in order to achieve the promised costs savings. Contracts for seven to ten year periods are still relatively common in the industry, although there is now a movement to shorter five-year contracts. The negotiation of the contract terms will often take many months and in light of the very commercial nature of their subject context, they will usually be highly tailored to meet any particular customer's requirements.

This section outlines some of the key provisions that will appear in any IS outsourcing contract. There will, of course, be many other terms regarding the ongoing service provision and outsourcing relationship.

2.2.2.1 Definition of the services The description of the services (and the service levels that must be attained) lies at the very heart of the outsourcing

---

20. See 2.3 for a discussion of the main elements of an asset transfer agreement.
21. Not least so that the customer can effectively pursue that company for damages claims or for service credits in the event of any failure to provide the services.

contract. It is essential to ensure that the service description captures all of the IS services to be provided by the supplier under the outsourcing arrangements. For example, where data centre operations are to be outsourced to a supplier it will not be sufficient simply to give a description of the data centre operations themselves. Other questions which should be considered by the customer will include:

(a)   What other ancillary services are to be provided by the supplier?

(b)   Who will be providing the disaster recovery service?

(c)   Who is providing the service that links the data centre to desktop and other IS environments?

(d)   How is the supplier to interact with the customer's in-house IS function and other third party service providers?

(e)   What additional services or duties should the main outsourcing supplier have, recognising the need that it should work effectively with the customer's in-house and external IS suppliers?

(f)   Are there any other services that the customer is likely to need in the future that should be covered within the scope of the services agreement?

Similar sorts of issues will be relevant to any other type of IS function to be outsourced.

The answers to these and other questions should result in the outsourcing contract listing, in addition to the core IS services to be outsourced, a number of related and ancillary services and obligations.

The value of a well defined service description cannot be underestimated. It will avoid, or at least minimise, subsequent disputes as to what is in included within the contract scope. Hastily drawn up service schedules frequently lead to a large number of contract change requests being entered into after the contract has been commenced to add in elements which have been simply overlooked during the negotiation phase, with the attendant cost increases for the customer. The service schedule should include as much detail as possible regarding the exact scope of any activity to be performed by the supplier and should be intelligible to someone who was not involved in its negotiation. Although it may be tempting to reduce the schedule to a fairly high level set of obligations it should always be borne in mind that at a later date a court, or some other third party expert or mediator, may be called on to interpret the terms of that schedule.

A distinction is sometimes drawn between services provided during an initial transition period and those fully developed services to be provided afterwards. This is usually to reflect the fact that those services provided during the initial transitional phase might be very different — in scope, duration, level of service and possibly even in the charges — than the services to be provided after that phase. Where an exception is to be made in respect of transitional services, the contract should specify very clearly which of the contract provisions they are subject to.

In some circumstances, it is not always possible for the customer to list in detail at the outset of any contract all of the services it would like to see provided in the future. It may be appropriate to include a section of additional services which the customer is entitled to require the supplier to provide at a later date on the terms of the services agreement. One advantage of such an approach will be to set out a clear fees structure which will apply to these additional services.

The services agreement will obviously need to identify the entities who are to benefit from the services provided. In a simple outsourcing arrangement there will simply be one corporate entity that will constitute the customer. In more complex arrangements, there may be an entire customer group which is to benefit and the contract therefore needs to be very clear as to whom the customer group comprises. Where there are group companies involved, it may be the case that not all of the corporate entities are to receive the services as of the commencement date. There is an increasing trend for companies to instead put in place framework contracts with outsourcing vendors under which the centralised outsourced service is provided to the holding company or principal operating vehicle, with provision to roll-out the outsourced services to other group companies as and when they decide to take those services.

Clauses which restrict the customer's ability to purchase services from other third parties or which restrict the supplier's ability to deliver services of a similar nature to other customers may infringe national or EU competition regulation. A detailed discussion of competition law is beyond the scope of this chapter and the position should be assessed on a case-by-case basis. Ultimately, issues such as the nature of the restriction and the size of each entity's market share in the relevant jurisdictions will influence whether the restrictions will be upheld. Restrictions which are prohibited by competition law are likely to be found unenforceable and fines may be imposed.

2.2.2.2 Service levels Service levels are at the core of the IS outsourcing contract, as they define the quality of the service to be provided by the supplier. Specifically, the customer will want to be assured:

(a)   That the services will be available when the customer needs them (i.e., with limited 'down time' or 'outage').

(b)   That the services will be responsive and speedy.

(c)   That they will be effective in supporting the customer's business operations.

(d)   Above all, that they will deliver the cost savings and other benefits promised by the supplier, as reflected in the services agreement.

Service levels therefore play a very important role. However, producing a defined set of service levels to be attached to the contract can often be a difficult and time-consuming process. For many customers, there will simply be no documented records as to the level of service which has been provided in-house prior to the outsourcing contract being entered into. It may be tempting to adopt the commonly used process of entering into a contract without any service levels attached, merely incorporating a contractual provision that the service levels will be reviewed and agreed during an initial stated time period. To follow this approach simply defers discussion regarding the required service levels to a stage when the customer is in a very unfavourable negotiating position which, from the customer's perspective, is a recipe for disaster.

If this approach is adopted then the contract must also deal with the issue of what should happen if the parties still can't agree service levels even after the contract has been signed and the initial review period during which agreement was to be reached has passed. In these circumstances, it would be sensible to allow the customer to terminate the agreement in respect of those services for which no service levels have been agreed with the resulting changes to be made to other provisions of the agreement through the contract change mechanism, such as a reduction in charges.

Service levels may not be attached to every type of service to be provided by the supplier as part of the services agreement. For example, there may be certain categories of service which are not seen as being a crucial part of the agreement or activities to which no objectively measurable service level can be set.

Importantly, the service level schedule needs to set out not only the service level to be attained but also how that service level will be measured (in terms of both method and frequency). In the event of any failure to achieve the service levels, service credits will usually be payable to the customer by the supplier.[22]

2.2.2.3 Customer obligations   Performance by the supplier of its obligations will, by varying degrees, depend on the customer meeting its own obligations. As a result, many contracts specify certain obligations which the customer must perform in order for the supplier to provide the services or other service dependencies. For example, any failure to transfer assets which it has been agreed by the parties should be transferred or any defects discovered in those assets which were not disclosed previously will obviously have an impact on the services that can be provided. Any obligations which are imposed on the customer should be specified clearly within the contract to avoid any later disputes.

Where the supplier will need access to the customer's premises to provide the services, standard provisions should be incorporated regarding the access to and use of those premises and other facilities.

2.2.2.4 Performance improvement   Although a customer may be prepared to accept that the contract duration should span typically five to ten years to allow the supplier to achieve the promised costs savings, in return the customer will want to ensure that they continue to receive a cost effective and high quality service for the duration of that contract. This is one of the primary reasons for the inclusion of such provisions in a typical contract.

---

22. See 2.2.2.10 for a description of how service credit regimes operate. Service credits are a valuable remedy and the 'teeth' by which the agreement is enforced.

Under performance improvement mechanisms, reviews of the service provision will be carried out by either the supplier themselves or by external third party consultants. For example, suppliers are often required to carry out annual reviews of the services to identify areas for development or improvement and to identify ways in which the services can exploit falling technology costs within the marketplace. Any changes which the parties agree should be made are then implemented through the contract change control mechanism.

In order to bring a degree of independence to the contractual arrangements, third party review procedures can be incorporated. Under such procedures external third party consultants conduct an assessment of the services to see if services of an equivalent nature can be obtained more cheaply or at increased service levels from elsewhere. These procedures are known as benchmarking procedures. Again, these benchmarking reviews usually take place on a yearly basis. In order for these reviews to take place the supplier will need to agree to allow the third party consultant access to its data, software, hardware and networks which are used in providing the services. Such third parties will, as a matter of course, be required to sign up to stringent confidentiality undertakings regarding the information and assets they have access to.

These performance mechanisms with their yearly reviews form a useful function in ensuring that the services are continually assessed and improved. However, they should not replace regular detailed reporting and meeting requirements which provide for the day-to-day review and discussion of the supplier's performance under the contract.

2.2.2.5 Reporting requirements Any IS outsourcing relationship necessitates a cooperative working relationship between the parties. The contract should formalise the discussion and reporting process without creating an unnecessary administrative burden for the supplier.

Typically, contracts will stipulate regular meetings at two levels. First, regular (such as monthly) meetings between the respective project managers of the parties to discuss day-to-day operational issues, resolve any disagreements and generally oversee the running of the contract. Secondly, meetings of representatives at a more senior level (such as Chief Information Officer or Finance Director). These need to occur less frequently (e.g., on a quarterly basis) and their purpose should be to review the overall strategic direction of the contract and the outsourcing relationship, to build the relationship at an executive level, to resolve any disputes or issues submitted to them and review any annual benchmarking survey results.

Meetings should be supplemented by a detailed reporting process. Regular reports should be submitted by the supplier regarding the performance of the services, any failures to achieve the service levels (and why this occurred) and any service credits that are paid. Reports should also be tailored to meet the specific requirements of a particular customer, for example detailing any security breaches that have occurred or on specific aspects of the services provided.

2.2.2.6 Acceptance testing In some circumstances, the supplier is required to build and supply or integrate new systems before starting to provide the outsourced services. Where the supplier is to own such a system then traditional acceptance testing is likely to be inappropriate. This is because of the nature of an IS outsourcing contract, i.e., an obligation on the supplier to deliver services to an agreed service level. How these service levels are achieved (i.e., whether or not the system conforms to any particular detailed design build and specification) is irrelevant. In this scenario, any evaluation testing is only likely to be appropriate where it enables the customer to check that the system is capable of delivering the output required to support the outsourced services.

In the event that the customer is to own the system from which the outsourced services are to be provided then it will be more appropriate to impose traditional acceptance testing. Contractual procedures will need to specify the process by which such acceptance testing is to be carried out, provide detailed obligations on the supplier to remedy or fix any defects that are located during the testing period, specify details of the tests that are to take place and provide the consequences of a failure to pass the acceptance testing procedure.

In addition, if further deliverables are to be provided by the supplier during the course of the outsourcing contract, such as new items of software or hardware, it may be appropriate to include a general acceptance testing provision governing the procedure to apply which is to be used on the delivery of any such items.

2.2.2.7 Contract change mechanisms Contract change provisions will have a particular role to play in an IS outsourcing contract. The purpose of these provisions is to allow the contract to change over its life as the scope of existing services is changed, as new services are introduced and as new forms of technology are utilised.

Contracts need to incorporate a formal process by which any changes to the contract scope will be discussed and implemented. Any changes to the scope of the contract or the services to be provided, however small, should be subjected to this procedure to enable a proper evaluation to take place. It is important to ensure that a detailed assessment is carried out by the supplier to review the impact of the change on the terms of the contract and the provision of the existing services. This then enables the customer to make an informed decision as to whether, and the basis on which, to proceed with any change. Any consequent amendments to the charges will be agreed through this procedure.

Mutual agreement is always at the core of any change control procedure, although in some contracts where the negotiating power of the customer is particularly strong, the ultimate decision as to whether or not to accept or reject the proposal for the change may lie with the customer.

2.2.2.8 The charges As in any contract, the charging structure which is to be adopted will very much be a matter of negotiation for the parties. The charges can either be fixed or variable or a combination of the two. One of the prime concerns of a customer will be how to predict and control those costs over the life of the contract, in particular to ensure that the opportunity for the supplier to introduce any increases to the charges is limited. The contract should therefore state those circumstances in which the charges may be changed.

Suppliers will naturally seek to ensure that the charges are linked to indexation with changes being made on an annual basis to reflect any change in an appropriate inflationary index. A matter which is frequently debated is the appropriate index to apply in these circumstances. The retail prices index as published by the Office for National Statistics is used in many contracts, both within the IT industry and otherwise, to govern future price increases. However, this index reflects the general rate of inflation in the economy and is based on the price of goods. It therefore fails to take into account the rather special circumstances of the technology industry and the spiralling labour costs within that market. Suppliers may therefore look to other indices specific to the IT industry as the basis on which charges should be increased. Any other changes to the charges should only be made if agreed through the contract change control mechanism.

As with any contract, provisions regarding the mechanism for payment will need to be included. Issues such as the timing of payments (i.e., whether charges are paid in arrears or in advance) and the frequency of payments must be stipulated, together with the mechanism by which any penalties under the contract, such as service credits, are to be paid. Service credits can be paid direct to the customer from the supplier or they may be deducted from invoices for the charges. Suppliers invariably favour the latter approach, not least because of the reluctance to incur costs as opposed to a loss of revenue.

As noted above, contracts will often be put in place with a certain degree of flexibility, enabling the customer to require the supplier to provide certain additional services as and when required. Ideally, the costs for any additional services which can be predicted as being a likely future requirement should be agreed at the outset and specified in the services agreement. This will not always be possible. For services that cannot be foreseen at the outset it may nevertheless be possible to specify a price formula within the contract by which the charges for any additional service will be calculated. This may be a cost-plus basis with the supplier being able to recover the cost of the new element of the services, together with an additional fixed profit element.

2.2.2.9 *Contract duration* At first sight, this may appear to be a straightforward issue. In reality, the position will be more complex. The length of the contract term will be determined by a number of factors, most of which are strategic in nature. The key factor is whether the customer and supplier will realise their respective financial returns and other benefits from the IS outsourcing over the proposed term.

A view widely held by both customers and supplier is that, because IS outsourcing contracts are difficult to enter into and exit costs need to be amortised, such contracts must necessarily be long term. So for this reason there are still many IS outsourcing contracts which are entered into for a ten year period. However, there are a number of other factors which should also be borne in mind which favour a shorter contract period. These include the fact that the customer's business changes over time and long term contracts may often be inflexible and also, that it may not always be in their best interests to enter into outsourcing contracts that will run beyond the life expectancy of the customer's technology. For these and other reasons many advisors now tend to recommend shorter contract durations, such as a three to five year term.

Contract renewal can be another contentious issue. Many customers will seek the right to extend the basic contract term for a certain time period without having to renegotiate the contract. This will be particularly important if the contract is for a shorter duration, such as a three year period. In practice, suppliers will often be happy to extend the contract term provided that an acceptable charging basis for that extension period can be agreed. The exercise of an option to extend the contract term may also be used by the supplier to renegotiate other terms which it sees as being less than favourable, such as service levels or exit arrangements. Attempts to renegotiate any terms other than those which are directly impacted by the contract extension should be firmly resisted.

2.2.2.10   Service credits and debits   If the essence of the services agreement is a commitment by the supplier to deliver services to a stated service level then the contract must define any consequences of a failure to achieve those service levels. Traditionally, service credit regimes have been adopted. Service credits are a stated monetary amount which becomes payable by the supplier to the customer on a failure to achieve a service level to which those service credits apply. They are often expressed as being a certain percentage of the monthly charges.

The advantage of such a service credit regime is that it provides the customer with an automatic financial remedy in the event of a service failure, thereby avoiding the customer being required to pursue formal legal claims for damages against the supplier. It also removes the potential for disputes between the parties as to the amount of loss and damage which has occurred in practice as a result of any service level failure and whether that loss and damage is of a type which should be recoverable from the supplier.

The imposition of service credits therefore incentivises the supplier to ensure the service levels are achieved and, in the event that they are not, provides an effective form of financial recourse to the customer.

It usually takes some time to calculate and negotiate the monetary amount which should constitute a service credit. Contracts will typically set service credits either at a relatively nominal level or at a much higher level which aims to provide true compensation for the breach of the particular service level that has occurred.

Under English law, an amount stated in a contract which operates as a penalty is not enforceable. Accordingly, service credits which are set at too high a level run the risk of being struck out. It will therefore be important to ensure that any service credits reflect a genuine pre-estimate of the likely loss and damage that will be suffered in the event of a service failure. Those involved in calculating service credits should retain records from the time of contract negotiations in the event of any later disputes as to the validity of the amounts specified.

The imposition of service credits will usually provoke a response from a supplier that the converse should also apply, i.e., that in the event that the service levels are exceeded the supplier should receive some form of compensation. For many, the idea that a supplier should be compensated for performing in excess of a level required and whilst the customer is still paying for that service is counterintuitive. If it is accepted that some form of service debit should be payable then the most frequent way of incorporating them into the contractual framework is to set up a service credit/debit bank. This requires an account, either real or notional, to be established. Service credits are then paid into the account as they are triggered. The supplier is then given the opportunity to reduce the amounts of credits payable by performing in excess of the service levels. On any over-performance, service debits will be paid into the account having the effect of reducing the balance of credits in that account. The account should then be settled on a regular basis with an appropriate payment to the customer, either direct or by a reduction against the charges which are invoiced for. Where such mechanisms are used, it is usual to ensure that service debts can only reduce the amount of credits that are payable to a zero amount and that service debits never become an amount which the customer is actually liable to pay direct to the supplier.

Service credit regimes are, of course, only one method of compensating for service level failures. Other remedies include termination rights and damages claims.[23] On a more practical note, suppliers are also usually contractually required to provide such additional resources as may be necessary to remedy the service level failure with, occasionally, the right for the customer to call on a third party to provide that failing service where the supplier has failed to remedy the situation within a specified time period.

2.2.2.11 Liability Suppliers will inevitably seek to limit their risk exposure under any IS outsourcing contract through the imposition of detailed limitation of liability clauses. Such clauses will usually impose a limit on the amount of any loss or damage, whether arising from a breach of contract, tort or otherwise, to a stated amount. Customers should also limit their own liability to the customer in the same way.

Under English law, liability for certain types of loss and damage cannot be excluded. These include, most notably, exclusions or limitations for death or personal injury caused by a party's negligence,[24] and, where the IS outsourcing contract involves the sale of goods (such as the sale of hardware from the customer to the supplier as part of the initial asset transfer), the term that the seller has the right to sell those goods.[25]

---

23. See section 2.2.2.11 below regarding the relationship between service credits and damages claims.
24. Unfair Contract Terms Act 1977, s. 2.
25 Sale of Goods Act 1979, s. 12; Supply of Goods and Services Act 1982, s. 7.

English law also provides that certain exclusions and limitations of liability must be subject to the test of reasonableness. For example, where the parties contract on the basis of one party's standard terms of business, the exclusions and limitations of liability for loss and damage in respect of any contract breach must be reasonable.[26] Although it is likely that many IS outsourcing contracts will be the subject of extensive and detailed negotiations so that the negotiated 'deal' can no longer be said to be on one party's standard terms of business, those negotiating and drafting contracts should be aware of this principle.[27]

Suppliers generally seek to exclude their liability for indirect or consequential loss and damage. This type of loss includes loss beyond the damage to the value of the property itself, such as loss of profits and loss of revenue. Suppliers who do wish to exclude their liability for consequential loss will need to draft appropriate provisions with care. Recent case law has thrown doubts over the effectiveness of the, until now, standard formulations of exclusions for 'indirect and consequential damage'.[28] See also chapter 3 for a detailed discussion of liability generally and the effectiveness of exclusion clauses.

The services agreement will include a number of provisions regarding the supplier's liability in specific circumstances. Common examples include liability in the event of an infringement of a third party's intellectual property rights, specific indemnities (for example, regarding employee transfers and the application of the Transfer of Undertakings (Protection of Employment) Regulations 1981) and in the event of a failure to achieve service levels. The services agreement must bring together all of these forms of the supplier's liability under the contract and detail how these specific liabilities are linked to the general caps on the supplier's liability for contract breaches, if at all.

The relationship between the liability provisions and the supplier's liability to pay service credits in the event of a failure to achieve a service level to which service credits relate will merit special consideration. The liability for such service credits can fall within the general cap, be subject to a separate cap or unlimited. The services agreement will need to find a balance between ensuring that the customer can recover appropriately in the event of a service

---

26. Unfair Contract Terms 1977, s. 3. Whether or not the exclusion/limitation is 'reasonable' will be assessed in light of a number of factors specified in sch. 2 to that Act.

27. Especially given the willingness of courts recently to strike out liability clauses which were in breach of the Unfair Contract Terms Act 1977, s. 3. See in particular *St Albans City and District Council* v *International Computers Ltd* [1995] FSR 686 and *South West Water Services Ltd* v *International Computers Ltd* (unreported, Technology & Construction Court, 29 June 1999), although both of these cases involved rather specific facts which may well enable courts to later distinguish from them in future judgments.

28. The Court of Appeal judgment in *British Sugar* v *NEI Power Projects Ltd* (1998) 87 BLR 42 suggested that the meaning of the word consequential was loss which flows from special circumstances and therefore within the second limb of the *Hadley* v *Baxendale* (1854) 9 Ech 341 damages test. This reasoning contradicts the opinion of many that certain types of consequential loss can constitute direct loss and therefore loss within the first limb of *Hadley* v *Baxendale*. However, until further guidance is received from the courts those drafting contracts have to navigate the rather confusing judgement of the British Sugar case as best they can.

failure (bearing in mind that including service credits within a general liability cap of, say, the total contract price, may not provide adequate compensation to the customer or incentive to the supplier to avoid breaches) against the supplier's understandable desire to limit its total liability exposure.

The services agreement will typically include some specific remedies which are available to the customer in the event of a contract breach. A good example comes from provisions stipulating what will happen in the event that any of the customer's data is lost or corrupted. This loss of data is a consequential loss and one which typically (as noted above) the supplier will seek to exclude its liability for. However, to leave a customer with no remedy in these circumstances where the potential for damage to the customer's business as a result of that loss is so great, would be unacceptable. Services agreements therefore often require the supplier to restore or procure the restoration of any data that has been lost or corrupted to the last transaction processed. This data recovery is carried out at the supplier's cost.

2.2.2.12 Warranties The services agreement will need to incorporate a number of warranties to deal both with the status and performance of the supplier generally and then to cover a number of specific issues arising in relation to IS outsourcing contracts.

English law will imply certain terms into any contract. In relation to a contract for the provision of services, as an IS outsourcing contract will be, the supplier will be required to use reasonable care in the provision of the services.[29] In practice, this implied warranty will usually be replaced by detailed contractual assurances regarding the nature of the services to be provided. Accordingly, the application of implied terms is often expressly excluded.[30]

Assuming that the contract will therefore replace warranties implied by law with express warranties, general warranties to be included regarding service performance will include those regarding the performance by the supplier of its obligations in accordance with all applicable laws, the use of skilled and experienced personal and performance of obligations in accordance with good industry practice. Warranties are also included regarding the general standing of the supplier at the time the contract is entered into, such as warranties that the supplier has full capacity and all necessary consents and licences to enter into the contract, that it is not subject to insolvency (or similar) proceedings and that there is no material litigation pending to which the supplier is a party.

Equivalent warranties may also be sought regarding the general standing of the customer at the time the contract is entered into.

Specific issues to be covered will include Year 2000 compliance, euro compliance and the absence of any viruses in systems provided or used.

Year 2000 compliance was not just a problem in relation to the date 1 January 2000. There are a considerable number of other dates throughout the

---

29. Supply of Goods and Services Act 1982, s. 13. Where goods are supplied, the Sale of Goods Act 1979, ss. 14, 15 requires them to be of satisfactory quality and fit for their purpose.
30. As with any exclusion or limitation of liability, caution must be exercised to ensure the Unfair Contract Terms Act 1977 (and, in particular, ss. 2(2), 3 is adhered to.

year 2000 which may impact on a system's ability to handle and recognise date related data.[31] In addition, the requirement for systems to recognise and deal with historical data containing the millennium date means that Year 2000 compliance will remain a relevant issue in IS outsourcing for some time yet. For both of these reasons it is therefore advisable to include an express warranty within the services agreement. Year 2000 warranties are often based on the definition published by the British Standards Institute[32] although other formulations can be used.

The terms of Year 2000 assurances should be considered carefully. It may be necessary or, from the supplier's perspective, highly desirable to carve out from the supplier's liability any Year 2000 failure which is caused by the failure of any other software and hardware with which the system or item in question interfaces or operates and for which the supplier is not responsible. The terms of the warranty may also exclude items of hardware, software or other equipment that a supplier inherits from the customer or in relation to any other items that the customer expressly requires the supplier to provide the services with.

Similar assurances should also be obtained regarding euro compliance where any IT system provided or used by the supplier needs to recognise and deal in euros. Legal requirements relating to the euro are currently contained within two Council Regulations[33] and the definition of euro compliance traditionally is based on the system in question performing in accordance with them.

As noted above, the position regarding viruses should also be considered. Where software is provided by a supplier, contractual assurances may be obtained acknowledging that the software does not contain any virus or lock or any other device which enables the supplier to prevent its continued operation. For example, if the customer fails to make payment the software is then disabled by the supplier activating such a device. Such locks and time bombs will be illegal under the terms of the Computer Misuse Act 1990 unless the supplier has notified the customer in advance of its intention to use such devices in the software and their effect.

2.2.2.13 Data and data protection Most IS outsourcing contracts will involve the supplier handling a considerable volume of the customer's data, either where the supplier generates data using systems which are utilised by the supplier as part of the services or data which the supplier themselves directly generates in the course of performing the services.

---

31. Other potential trigger dates are 10 October 2000 (the first date in 2000 with 8 digits) and 2020 (as a result of a fairly widespread fix used previously to cure the millennium bug where computers were instructed to add 19 before numbers of 20 or more so, e.g., 2020 would become 1920).
32. Reference DISC PD 2000-1.
33. Council Regulation (EC) No. 1103/97 dated 17 June 1997 and Council Regulation (EC) No. 974/98 dated 3 May 1998. These Regulations cover conversion (from ecu and national currencies to the euro) and rounding requirements, together with a number of other legal issues.

Customers should therefore ensure that they own all of the rights in their data and that appropriate assignments are obtained from the supplier of the intellectual property rights in the data.

Data protection law will also have a considerable impact on outsourcing activities. Data protection law has recently undergone some important changes with the introduction in the United Kingdom of the Data Protection Act 1998. Despite its title, the Act was effective as of 1 March 2000. It has been implemented as a result of an EU Directive on data protection[34] and applies to any data relating to a living individual and from which the individual can be identified.

The Act replaces the earlier provisions relating to computer service bureaux which were contained in the predecessor to the 1998 Act, the Data Protection Act 1984, with the concept of the data processor.

A data processor is someone who carries out the processing of personal data on behalf of a data controller. The data controller is an entity which (either alone or jointly or in common with other persons) determines the purposes for which, and the manner in which, any personal data are processed. In a standard outsourcing contract the customer will usually take the role of the data controller and the supplier the role of a data processor.

The Act requires that a data controller should impose certain obligations on any data processor that it appoints. Data processors must be appointed under a written contract (unlikely to be difficult to satisfy!) and must carry out any processing activities only on the instructions of the data controller. Importantly, the data controller must choose a data processor with sufficient guarantees in respect of the security measures they take to protect the data processed against unlawful or accidental loss or destruction.

One of the further changes arising from the new data protection legislation is the introduction of the much publicised eighth principle under Schedule 1 to the Act. Schedule 1 lists a number of principles with which a data controller must comply. This eighth principle states that personal data cannot be transferred to a country outside of the European Economic Area unless that third country offers an adequate level of protection for the data concerned. With the increasingly global nature of business, today's modern IT systems will invariably involve the transfer of personal data between a number of countries. Businesses therefore need to be aware of the eighth principle and that further steps may need to be taken to ensure compliance with it.

2.2.2.14 Termination As with any IT contract, a number of standard termination rights should be incorporated. These should include rights of termination in the event that the other party to the contract breaches one of its terms or becomes insolvent.

More specific termination rights should then be catered for. These will often include defining a minimum service level and providing that if the service drops below this minimum level then the customer has a right of immediate termination. Defining a minimum service level in this way

---

34. EU Directive 95/46/EC.

effectively defines what the parties consider amounts to a material breach and avoids protracted disputes about whether any particular service level failure is of sufficient impact to otherwise entitle the customer to terminate under standard material breach provisions.

It is not only one-off breaches of the service levels that should be considered for specific treatment within the termination provisions but also persistent, albeit more minor, breaches of service levels. It may be unacceptable for the parties to be locked into a contract indefinitely where there are repeated more minor breaches (even where this triggers service credits) and it may therefore be useful to define further termination rights as existing after there have been a specified number of these more minor breaches within any fixed time period.

Under many IS outsourcing contracts there is a mix of a different number of services which are provided by the suppliers. For this reason, rights to partial termination may be appropriate, and highly desirable, enabling the customer to retain a high degree of flexibility as to how its business develops in the future. In each circumstance, those drafting a contract will need to consider the extent to which the services are bundled together and whether they can be easily separated. If it is possible to separate the services, or part of a service, partial termination rights may be appropriate. In practice, any partial termination rights are likely to be resisted heavily by the supplier. Where the services are partially terminated there will inevitably be an impact on the remaining provisions of the contract (such as the other services being provided, the service levels and the charges). Accordingly, any necessary changes to the remaining contract terms should be made through the contract change provisions.

Break options are also a popular remedy, entitling the customer to terminate a contract at will after a number of years. The customer therefore does not need to prove any breach by the supplier or any other cause entitling them to terminate. Many suppliers will calculate their cost models on the basis of recovery of various investment costs over a relatively long period and to allow termination in this way would potentially leave a supplier seriously out of pocket. For this reason, break options are usually accompanied by large financial penalties under which the supplier seeks to recoup this type of investment cost.

As has been seen, IS outsourcing contracts require a close working relationship to be established between the parties and a number of the customer's assets will have transferred to the supplier at the beginning of that relationship. The exercise of termination rights can therefore pose difficult issues for the customer. It is not a relationship from which the customer is likely to be able to extricate itself in a number of weeks. Assets will need to be transferred back to the customer or to a replacement service provider to enable the customer to continue to receive the service. There will need to be a flow of information and assistance between the parties. Consequently, exit provisions dealing with the handover of assets and information and ensuring ongoing service provision whilst the customer or its replacement service provider take over the service provision will be vital to ensure a seamless transition of the services. The importance and nature of exit provisions are discussed in more detail at 2.5 below.

2.2.2.15 Dispute resolution It is being increasingly common to formalise escalation procedures within a contract providing for stated levels within each entity to which any dispute will be escalated (within fixed timescales) before the matter can be referred to the courts. For example, project managers may initially be required to resolve any dispute and, on their failing to do so within a specified time, the issue is referred to the finance directors of each organisation. The purpose of these provisions is to encourage settlement of any dispute at an early stage.

There are a number of matters which should be excluded from the scope of these escalation procedures as there are some circumstances in which it will not be appropriate to follow this type of process before being free to pursue legal action. For example, where one party has committed a material breach of the contract the other party will want the immediate right to terminate and to pursue any other legal remedies (such as a damages claim) without being required to first discuss the dispute with the other party. Also, if one party suspects that its intellectual property rights have been, or are about to be, infringed or if it thinks that its confidential information has been, or is or is about to be, disclosed then immediate action will be required (for example through seeking an injunction) to protect the rights of that party.

Contracts may also provide for other forms of dispute resolution in the event that the internal escalation process does not resolve the matter. This is particularly the case given an increasing reluctance to refer matters to the court due to the fact that the costs of court action can be extremely high and the length of time that court proceedings can take. In addition, disputes arising out of IS outsourcing contracts can often be of a highly technical nature meaning that it may be more appropriate to refer the issue to an expert with suitable knowledge and understanding rather than to the courts.

Third party experts may therefore be used for disputes of a technical nature. The contract will need to specify the processes the expert will adhere to and how that expert is appointed. Experts' decisions are usually expressed as being binding. Mediation is often used to resolve other disputes (i.e., those of a non-technical nature) and the contract will need to specify a body which, in the event of a failure by the parties to agree on the identity of a mediator, will be required to appoint one. The Centre for Dispute Resolution is often used in this context. Again, the contract will need to specify the process which will be adopted where mediation is used.

The use of such dispute resolution mechanisms in any contract also reflects the increasing trend to consider appropriate forms of alternative dispute resolution as a result of the Woolf reforms to the UK litigation process. Litigants are now asked whether they considered or participated in other dispute resolution mechanisms before resorting to the courts. For those who have not, there are significant costs implications.

2.3 SALE AGREEMENTS

2.3.1 Purpose of sale agreement

One of the features of an IS outsourcing contract is the transfer of assets from the customer to the supplier. A formal document of transfer will be required to identify those assets which are to be transferred, the mechanism by which they are to be transferred and the price which the supplier is to pay for them.

Provisions can be incorporated into the principal services agreement dealing with the assets transfer. It may, however, be easier to use a separate sale agreement to document the provisions regarding the one-off transfer of assets. This is particularly likely to be the case where there are a considerable number of assets to be transferred.

2.3.2 Identification of assets

Early in the outsourcing process the customer should identify the assets which are currently used by it to deliver the service in-house. This should include a listing of the assets themselves and any related contracts. Ultimately, this information will need to be attached as a schedule to the sale agreement. It is important not to underestimate the length of time that will be required to compile this listing. Unfortunately, it is often found to be the case that customers have poorly documented the systems that are used in providing services in-house, especially regarding pieces of software which are developed on a fairly ad hoc basis for use by the company. It can therefore be a difficult and time-consuming task to piece together the relevant information.

The types of assets which are likely to have been used by the customer and which the supplier may require will include software and hardware and their related support arrangements, together with other items such as premises, equipment and other items and contracts. In respect of items of software, hardware or other equipment which are owned by the customer the position will be relatively straightforward. A decision will need to be taken whether these assets are to be transferred to the supplier for an appropriate payment or whether a lease or licence of them will be provided and, if so, the terms of that lease or licence.

Items of software or hardware that are owned by third parties and leased or licensed to the business may cause more difficulties. Often the terms of those contracts will prevent the use of that item by a third party, even where the third party is acting on behalf of the customer, let alone an outright transfer of it to the supplier. Any use by a supplier of those items will therefore be in breach of the contract provisions exposing the customer to a damages claim and to termination of the contract for material breach of its terms. In addition, such unauthorised use will infringe the intellectual property rights (usually copyright) of the third party and the supplier may therefore be liable accordingly.

The third parties who provide those items of software, hardware or other equipment will therefore need to be approached to give their consent to the transfer of the relevant item by the third party supplier. If this consent cannot be obtained then the primary alternative will be to seek a licence in favour of the supplier from the third party owner of the item involved. Obviously, the consequences of either of these two methods is the sum of money which the third party imposes on the supplier to provide its consent or provide the licence. Traditionally, the customer is forced to bear the costs associated with obtaining any necessary consents from third parties. This will, however, very much depend on the negotiating power of the parties. Also, it should be noted that the process for approaching those third parties and obtaining consents from them can be a lengthy one and it should therefore be started well in advance of the anticipated contract commencement date.

The contract should also specify the consequences if relevant third party consents cannot be procured. It may be that an alternative item can be found or that the customer continues to operate the item of software or hardware that cannot be transferred. This is discussed in more detail in 2.3.3 below.

2.3.3 The sale agreement

The sale agreement will thus identify all of the assets which are to transfer to the supplier and will specify the date on which this is to take effect. As the supplier will usually take over the obligations and liabilities in relation to third party items after the transfer date, the customer will usually warrant that it has fulfilled all of those obligations and liabilities up to that date.

The supplier will be in control of those third party items after the transfer date, so the customer will want to have assurance that, if there are any problems that arise after that date, the supplier will be legally responsible for them. It is therefore usual for the customer to seek an indemnity from the supplier in respect of any claims and expenses arising after the transfer date. Often, the supplier then seeks a counter indemnity from the customer in respect of the fulfilment of the customer's obligations in relation to the third party items prior to the transfer date.

The supplier may seek warranties from the customer regarding the performance and quality of assets which are to be transferred to it. Whether these warranties are ultimately incorporated into the sale agreement will be a question of the respective bargaining power of the parties. Where, as is usually the case, the supplier undertakes a detailed due diligence process prior to entering into the contract,[35] then one of the primary purposes of this due diligence exercise will have been for the supplier to ascertain the quality and condition of the assets and for this to be reflected in the purchase price accordingly. On this basis, warranties should be resisted. Where no, or little, due diligence has taken place prior to entering into the contract it may be necessary to incorporate some limited warranties for the benefit of the supplier.

A great deal of cooperation will be required between the customer and the supplier to ensure the smooth transition of the assets to the supplier. As

---

35. See 2.1.8.5.

mentioned above, it should be accepted that there may be some items where consent simply cannot be obtained from the relevant third party prior to the commencement of the services agreement. In this circumstance, it will be necessary to consider other options in order to ensure that the services can nevertheless still be provided by the supplier. Contracts may therefore need to build in a mechanism to deal with this scenario, including, for example, removing those third party items from the scope of the outsourcing or for the third party vendor to simply manage those contracts on behalf of the customer until such time as the third party consents to the transfer.[36]

In relation to any particular IS function that is being outsourced, there may well be assets which although related to the function are not to be transferred and will be retained by the customer. For the sake of clarity, contracts may also need to identify the assets and contracts which are to be retained by the customer in this way and which are therefore outside the scope of the sale agreement.

As far as the transfer of third party contracts is concerned, the most effective form of legal transfer will be novation. The legal effect of novating a contract is to terminate the existing legal arrangement between the customer and third party and to create a new legal arrangement (on the same terms as the previous contract) between the supplier and the third party. The other method of transfer which may be referred to is an assignment. However, generally, an assignment can only transfer benefits and not burdens.[37]

Where property is involved, the supplier may need to be sold or leased premises, or a sublease may need to be granted. Where the customer is granting a sublease of property, it will need to get the owner's consent. As with other third party assets that are transferred, there are likely to be costs implications in obtaining these consents and other conditions may be imposed. The sale or leasing of property will also raise issues of property law (which are beyond the scope of this publication) and specialist advice should be obtained in this regard.

Staff may also transfer to the supplier, together with the valuable body of knowledge that each staff member will have built up regarding the IS systems and generally, in relation to the business operations of the customer.

2.4   STAFF

2.4.1   TUPE and the Acquired Rights Directive

The impact on the customer's staff will need to be considered carefully in any potential IS outsourcing. The law gives considerable rights to employees to

---

36. Note that these arrangements too can be problematic as many third party contracts will contain standard provisions preventing or restricting the customer's ability to assign, transfer or otherwise dispose of its rights under that contract. Also, there are often confidentiality obligations imposed on the parties to such contracts which will effectively prevent the access to, and use of, that item by a third party. The management option may therefore not always be a viable option.

37. So, where the customer has obligations to perform, as in a standard software licence, novation is the more effective and complete way of transferring that licence.

ensure that they are fully protected where they undergo a change of employer which results from a transfer of the undertaking that they work for.

The Transfer of Undertakings (Protection of Employment) Regulations 1981 (TUPE) give effect to the earlier European Acquired Rights Directive[38] in the United Kingdom. TUPE will apply on any relevant transfer of an undertaking. An undertaking is defined in TUPE as including any 'trade or business' and will include a self contained, separate or separable part of the business capable of operating as a going concern.

For the purposes of TUPE, a transfer can be exercised by a sale of that undertaking (or part of it) or, of perhaps more importance in the outsourcing scenario, on an alternative form of disposition.

The application of TUPE encompasses the scenario of an outsourcing of an undertaking's business and a change in the contractors carrying out the business of an undertaking. It does not matter that the legal ownership of the undertaking is consistent pre- and post-transfer. What will be key will be that there is an undertaking which retains its pre-transfer identity at the post-transfer stage — see *Spijkers* v *Gebroeders Benedik Abattoir* (Case 24/85) [1996] ECR 119).[39]

Importantly, later cases have emphasised the need for there to be an accompanying assets transfer and that the transfer of an activity alone would not be sufficient to trigger the application of the legislation. To date, these cases have been confined to the re-tendering of contracts on their expiry or termination. They are discussed in detail at 2.4.3 below. There is no reason why some of their logic should not be applied to the initial grant of a contract, although further clarification from the courts is awaited on this issue.[40]

In relation to IS outsourcing, one of the difficult issues will be to determine which employees 'belong' to the undertaking (or part of it) that is being transferred. Where only part of the IS function is being outsourced and where employees previously carried out duties both in relation to the functions being outsourced and those being retained, it is not always apparent whether or not they will transfer. There are no clear rules on this and ultimately it is a question of fact to be determined by looking at all the relevant circumstances. Relevant considerations will be the proportion of time allocated to the undertaking that is being transferred by each employee and the description of their duties contained in their employment contract.

The application of TUPE has caused some uncertainty in the United Kingdom. For example, it was unclear for many years whether TUPE would always apply to an outsourcing in the public sector — indeed it was not until

---

38. EU Directive 77/187/EC.
39. In determining the issue the Court of Justice laid down a helpful set of factors to be taken into account when determining whether the undertaking remains the same, although subsequent case law has established that these factors cannot be considered in isolation and the overriding criteria will be whether or not there is an economic entity which retains its identity.
40. In the *Suzen* case referred to in 2.4.3 there was some suggestion that the case was clarifying some of the earlier case law and from this it may therefore be possible to predict that the courts will take a similar approach when looking at the initial grant of the contract as they will on its subsequent re-tender.

1993 that this issue was finally resolved.[41] Fortunately, case-law (on a European and national basis) has assisted to clarify a number of issues, although there are still areas where the potential effect of the legislation is not yet fully understood.

2.4.2 Effects of TUPE

In circumstances where TUPE applies, there will be a transfer of the existing employment contracts of employees connected to the undertaking on the transfer of that undertaking. This means that the supplier will become responsible for those employees and any associated liabilities arising from their employment from the date of the transfer. Consequently, the customer will relinquish all liability (except in relation to any occupational pension scheme which the employee may belong to — TUPE does not apply to transfer these).

TUPE also operates to protect employees from being dismissed merely as a result of the transfer of the relevant undertaking. In relation to employees that are dismissed prior to the transfer of the undertaking for reasons unconnected to the transfer then those employees will remain the responsibility of the transferor. TUPE will, however, apply to employees who are dismissed prior to the transfer for a reason connected to the transfer (*Lister* v *Forth Dry Dock & Engineering Co.* [1989] IRLR 161).

Employees who lose their jobs as a result of the transfer will automatically be considered to be unfairly dismissed[42] unless there are economic, technical or organisational reasons justifying the job loss. Even where there are apparently justifiable reasons for that job loss an employee of the transferred undertaking can claim for constructive dismissal.

In practice, the services agreement will normally incorporate allocations of liability between the customer and the supplier relating to the potential liabilities attached to the customer's staff who will transfer. For example, the customer may be required to indemnify the supplier in relation to any such liabilities which have arisen due to acts of the customer prior to the contract commencement date with a reciprocal indemnity from the supplier in favour of the customer for the period thereafter.

As a result of the transfer, the employee will be shown to have a continuous record of employment and his or her time spent with the undertaking pre- and post-transfer will therefore be treated as a continuous period of employment.

Agreements reached between the transferor (i.e., the customer on the grant of the outsourcing contract) and a trade union representing the transferor's employees will also transfer to the transferee.

---

41. Through a combination of the Trade Union Reform and Employment Rights Act 1993 (which removed the previous exclusion from TUPE of undertakings that were 'not in the nature of a commercial venture') and *Wren* v *Eastbourne Borough Council* [1993] IRCL 425 it became apparent that TUPE would apply to public sector outsourcings.
42. Provided they have had two years' continuous employment before the effective date of termination.

2.4.3 Effect of TUPE on expiry or termination of the services agreement

There has previously been some debate as to the extent to which TUPE would apply on the expiry or termination of an outsourcing contract to automatically transfer employees engaged in the service provision either back in-house to the customer or to a third party replacement service provider. Recent case law has shed some light upon this issue.

In *Suzen* v *Zehnacker Gebaudereinigung GmbH Krankenhausservice* Case 13/95 [1997] ECR 1259 it was found that the Acquired Rights Directive did not apply to a situation in which a person who had entrusted the cleaning of premises to a first undertaking terminates their contract with that undertaking and, for the performance of similar work, enters into a new contract with a second undertaking if there is no accompanying transfer from the first undertaking to the second of a significant amount of tangible or intangible assets or by taking over a major part of the workforce, in terms of their number and skill, assigned by the previous undertaking to the performance of the contract.

The *Suzen* case therefore establishes that whether or not TUPE will apply on the termination or expiry of an outsourcing contract will depend on the extent to which there is a transfer of associated assets.

The findings of the *Suzen* case have subsequently been applied by the Court of Appeal in *Betts* v *Brintel Helicopters* [1997] IRLR 361. Again, in the *Betts* case it was held that there was no relevant transfer for the purposes of the directive and TUPE where a replacement contractor did not take on any of the initial contractor's employees or assets.

This has subsequently lead to some concern that replacement contractors may try to avoid the effect of TUPE by not employing any of the employees following the transfer. The courts have gone some way to rectify this and in the case of *ECM (Vehicle Delivery Services) Ltd* v *Cox* [1998] IRLR 416, the courts stressed the importance of looking at why employees were not taken on by a new contractor so as to prevent transferors being able to circumvent the application of TUPE.

2.4.4 Consultation

As good commercial practice, many employers will wish to embark on a full consultation process with their employees well in advance of any IS outsourcing. For many employees, the prospect of transferring their employment to a specialist IT firm will be viewed as an exciting one with the new career development opportunities it brings. The way in which the possibility, or decision, to outsource is notified to employees will be very influential in determining whether it is seen in a positive light or not.

Aside from this, TUPE imposes obligations on employers to notify and consult with employees. The notification and consultation process should relate to the transfer and also as to any redundancies. Employees must be informed about the transfer, its implications for them and any measures that the employer anticipates he will take in relation to affected employees. Where there are proposed redundancies, the notification obligations will vary dependent on the number of employees who will be affected.

2.5 EXIT ISSUES

2.5.1 Importance of service continuity

Many customers find it difficult to tackle the issue of exit provisions with the supplier during negotiation for the services agreement. To contemplate the end of the relationship before it has begun can seem at best like being overly detailed and, at worst, a damning indictment of the future partnership between customer and supplier. However, detailed provisions which specify the rights and obligations of the parties on any termination or expiry of the contract will be important to ensure that the customer is able to exit from the relationship without undue disruption to its business and to ensure a seamless transition of the services either back in-house to the customer or to a replacement third party service provider.

Just as the services agreement (or, in some cases, the sales agreement) incorporates detailed provisions regarding the transfer of assets from the customer to the supplier on the commencement of the contract, the contractual documentation should also specify how relevant assets will be transferred to the customer or the replacement service provider on the termination or expiry of the relationship. Obviously, the customer will be in a far better position to negotiate favourable exit provisions prior to entering into the original outsourcing contract when the supplier is anxious to win the business rather than at the time of termination when the relationship has broken down and any goodwill between the parties may be limited or non-existent.

Typically, these provisions will be incorporated into a separate schedule of the services agreement specifying the consequences of any termination or expiry.

2.5.2 Exit provisions

The contract will need to deal with a number of issues relating to the transfer of information and assets from the supplier to the customer. Some of the principal provisions are outlined below in this section. There will, of course, be other ancillary obligations which any contract will need to deal with.

2.5.2.1 Assets register   In order for the customer to continue to itself provide the service or to engage a third party to do so on its behalf, it will need to have knowledge of the assets used by the supplier during the term of the services agreement. Many customers seek the option to choose the particular assets they wish to have transferred from the supplier rather than being under any general obligation to take over all the relevant assets used.

The supplier should therefore be required to maintain on a regular basis an inventory record which lists all of the assets used by the supplier to provide the services, such as any software, hardware, data, documentation, manuals and details of licenses, leases, or other arrangements relating to the services provided. A customer should have access to or receive copies of this inventory on a regular basis and should be provided with a copy of it on any expiry or termination. The customer will then be able to select which items it wishes to acquire from the supplier on the expiry or termination of the contract. The issues regarding the transfer of such assets are discussed in more detail below.

2.5.2.2 Ongoing service provision The typical IS outsourcing contract will take a number of months from selection of a preferred supplier to the go live date from which services are provided. This should serve as an indication of the complexity of exiting from an existing outsourcing relationship. For the services to be discontinued immediately by the supplier on the service of a notice of termination will be unacceptable to the customer as it will find itself without crucial services for a potentially significant time period until it is able to identify a replacement service provider and enter into a suitable contract with it for the new service provision. It is therefore typical to include provisions which require the supplier to continue providing the services, at the customer's option, for specified blocks of time. For example, it may be that a customer has a right to buy chunks of service from the supplier for three month periods up to a total period of one year.

During the period for which such run off services are provided, services should be delivered in accordance with all the existing terms of the contractual arrangements, including as to the charges and to service levels. The supplier may wish to carve out certain provisions which are not to apply, such as the performance improvement provisions.

2.5.2.3 Assets transfer Provisions should be incorporated regarding the transfer of assets from the supplier back to the customer.

The supplier should return copies of any of the customer's proprietary software, including copies of any modifications that are to be made to that software.

In relation to third party items, such as software, hardware and related support arrangements, the supplier should novate such licences and other agreements to the customer.

It is also quite likely that the supplier may have used some of its own proprietary software for the purpose of providing the services. Customers may therefore also seek a licence to use this proprietary software as a minimum during the exit period for which any ongoing services are provided and, quite possibly, beyond the expiry of that time. Licence fees will obviously need to be negotiated for any ongoing licences which are granted.

Where the supplier has used its own premises to provide the services which the customer requires further access to on termination, it may be possible to obtain a lease to use part (or all) of those premises from the supplier. Where the premises are leased to the supplier from a third party, this will usually be done by granting a sublease to the customer for the appropriate areas of the premises. The terms of the sublease will generally need to mirror those of the head lease. Consents may well be required from the original head lessor to any sublease and, in addition, the head lease may stipulate terms which must be incorporated into a sublease.

In addition to the tangible and intangible assets that may be required by the customer, there will also be a considerable amount of knowledge obtained by the supplier's personnel regarding the operation and use of any IS systems and other procedures involved. Exit provisions should therefore also provide for a transfer of knowledge from the technical staff of the supplier to the customer through the provision of general information and assistance, as required by the customer. Access should also be given to the supplier's premises and equipment used to provide the services and to staff deployed in the provision of the services.

The Transfer of Undertakings (Protection of Employment) Regulations 1981 might apply at the expiry of the IS outsourcing contract to transfer the staff of the supplier who have been substantially employed in providing the services to the customer (or the replacement contractor), although whether TUPE does apply is likely to depend on the extent of any related asset transfer.[43]

2.5.2.4 Exit plans Although the contractual provisions should specify as much detail as possible regarding the respective rights and obligations of the parties, it will be impossible to stipulate every act that should take place on termination at the time that the services agreement is entered into. It is therefore common to include general provisions requiring the supplier to draw up an exit plan on any exit or termination. The exit plan will then specify in detail how all of the exit obligations are to be carried out.

The overall purpose of the exit plan is to ensure the smooth transition of services from the supplier either back in-house to the customer or to its replacement third party service provider. Contractual assurances should be obtained so that the exit plan will achieve this if it is followed by both parties.

2.5.2.5 Costs issues There will always be a considerable amount of negotiation over the extent to which the supplier is permitted to charge in respect of performing its obligations under the exit provisions. As part of the exit provisions and as noted above, the customer should have the right to buy further periods of service provision up to a maximum specified time period. Obviously, the charging provisions will continue to apply and the supplier will therefore be paid in respect of the base service provision. There are, however, likely to be a number of additional costs arising as a result of the exit provisions, including the costs of obtaining any necessary third party consents and the additional resource costs of drawing up and implementing the exit plan. Suppliers are therefore likely to seek payment on a time and materials basis for any assistance provided under the exit provisions. Ultimately, the contract should specify which types of obligations the supplier is entitled to recover additional amounts for and those which the supplier is expected to bear as part of its internal costs.

---

43. See 2.4.3.

CHAPTER THREE

Liability

Chris Reed and Alison Welterveden

It is probably impossible to live a day in the developed world without at some point becoming involved with a computer-controlled process, although it may not be obvious that this is happening. Everyday objects such as washing machines and toasters are now microprocessor-controlled, the telephone system is fully computerised, and a high proportion of employees now use computers as part of their normal work activities. If a computer-controlled process does not function properly, loss may arise and thus potential liability.

Losses can be caused by three basic types of malfunction:

(a)   Hardware malfunctions, e.g., a computer catches fire.
(b)   Software produces incorrect information which feeds directly into a physical process, e.g., in a car's anti-lock braking system, or a bank ATM dispensing currency notes.
(c)   Software produces incorrect information which is relied on by a human mind, e.g., computer-controlled traffic signals, reliance on spreadsheet calculations to build a bridge or calculate tax liability.

This apparently simple classification is complicated by the fact that hardware and software interact. Deciding whether a malfunction is caused by hardware or software defects, or by a combination of both, often requires expert evaluation. This interaction also means that defectiveness may be a relative, rather than an absolute, concept as the software in question might run perfectly on a different hardware platform, and the hardware platform operate correctly if different software is running.

Liability claims may be based on a number of different causes of action:

(a) Breach of contract, which can be subdivided into:
  (i)   contracts of sale or supply;
  (ii)   contracts to provide services; and
  (iii) licence contracts.
(b) Product liability, for physical injury or property damage caused by a defective product.
(c) Negligence claims for physical injury or property damage.
(d) Negligence claims for financial loss, divided into:
  (i)   consequential losses because the software is unusable; and
  (ii)   losses caused by reliance on information, produced by the software and addressed to the human mind.

Additionally, a claim in negligence or contract may be made on the basis that the defendant has *acted* negligently, either in the way the software was used or by failing to use appropriate software.

This chapter will concentrate on liability in respect of defective software. Software is important because its whole purpose is to produce results — instructions for process control, financial or other information, and even advice — which will be acted upon. These results will almost always be uncheckable (in practice if not in theory) or there would be little point in employing a computer to produce them. Reliance on those results where the results, or the action taken upon them, are in some way defective gives rise to questions of liability. How far is the producer or user of computer software to be held responsible for losses caused by his production or use?

Once it is accepted that liability for losses caused by software requires particular investigation, it should also be clear that the most relevant areas of the law will be contract and negligence. However, European legislation has imposed strict liability on the producers of products, and it is necessary also to examine that area of liability. It is also important to remember that where there is contractual liability for defective software, the position will be very similar to that in negligence except where this liability arises from the express terms of the contract or the terms implied into contracts for the supply of goods.

3.1 CONTRACTUAL LIABILITY

In liability terms it is important to distinguish between the two different elements of software supply; the licence of intellectual property and the development and/or supply of a copy of the software. So far as licensing is concerned, the only real *contractual* risk is that a third party may possess intellectual property rights which are superior to those of the licensee. The nature and extent of this risk is quite clear, and the drafting of suitable provisions to control it is a comparatively simple matter. By contrast, the development of software under a contract with the user, or the supply of a copy of a package, gives rise to potential contractual liability which is less certain in scope. Liability will arise either from the express terms of the contract or from those implied by law, and the terms in development contracts will be quite different from those in supply contracts.

Liability under more complex service based contracts will primarily arise in relation to the quality of the service delivered. Although implied terms have a role to play, it will become apparent that express contractual terms will be at the heart of any such contract.

3.1.1 Software development contracts

If a client commissions a software house to write an application, this will certainly create a contract between them. In almost every case this contract will be in writing, and will normally contain clauses excluding the software house's liability; but what is this liability?

The answer is that the software house has contracted to provide a service — the production of software to the client's specific requirements. Subject to any express contractual provisions setting out the software house's obligations more fully, its liability to the client is governed by s. 13 of the Supply of Goods and Services Act 1982. This section implies into the contract a term that the provider of the service will take reasonable care in its provision.[1] In the context of software production contracts, the obligation is to take reasonable care to ensure that the software performs the functions specified by the client, together with any other functions which a reasonable software producer would realise to be necessary if the software is to work effectively. For software supplied prior to 1 January 2000 this might have obliged the software house to use all reasonable skill and care to ensure that the software is Year 2000 compliant, although this will very much depend on the time at which the software is developed and the anticipated life span of the product at the time of development. This duty should be distinguished from the stricter liability placed on the supplier of goods by ss. 13 and 14 of the Sale of Goods Act 1979. Although that obligation is not absolute, in the sense that goods need only be *reasonably* fit for their common or specified purposes, the supplier is not excused by reason of the fact that he took all reasonable precautions to ensure that the goods were reasonably fit. However, if in our example the software house wrote an application that totally failed to perform, it would not be liable unless it could be proved that the cause of that failure was a lack of care on the part of the software house. The fact of making a contract establishes the duty to take reasonable care. The defendant will be in breach if he has failed to take as much care in producing his software as a reasonable man in the same position, professing the same expertise, would have done. An attempt to prove that the defendant did not take sufficient care may run into a number of difficulties.

First, the fault may not be self-contained, but due to interaction with the hardware. If the fault is caused by a feature of the hardware which a reasonable software producer would not have expected, then he will not be in breach of his duty. For example, many of the programs written to run on the PC family of computers use functions provided by the machine's BIOS

---

1. *Salvage Association* v *CAP Financial Services Ltd* [1995] FSR 654. The review of the evidence in the transcript of this case, which unfortunately is omitted from the published report, is a splendid case study of the ways in which a software development contract can go wrong.

chip, but some BIOSs do not implement all functions in a standard manner. In some cases the result is that the software fails to recognise the machine, often part-way through execution of the program, and the results can be unpredictable. If the producer should have recognised and dealt with the incompatibility he will be in breach, but in many cases this will be hard to demonstrate, particularly if the hardware in question was not commercially available when the software was designed. The burden of proving breach is on the claimant — clearly in some cases it will be difficult to discharge this burden. Of course, the problem will sometimes be entirely due to malfunction of the hardware, but it may be impossible to decide whether this is the case if the fault is one-off or intermittent.

Second, much software is, or could be claimed to be, of an experimental nature. Software released as version X.0 is generally updated within a few months as faults are discovered and corrected, and new versions appear on a regular basis. As the duty is to take such care as other reasonable producers would take, it is arguable that, in the current state of the art, the production of software which works perfectly is impracticable. It may not be careless to release slightly defective software. Again, it will be for the claimant to show that the defects are such that a reasonable producer would not have released that version.

Third, the output of the system is in most cases produced by the interaction of the software with data or instructions provided by the user. Before it can be shown that the software is defective, its workings must be disentangled from the data — this will not normally be easy. The problem may arise from a particular combination of circumstances with which the software could not cope — again, should a reasonable producer have foreseen this possibility? It is also conceivable that the use to which the software has been put is not a use that the producer had expected. Should he then be liable? Again, it depends on the foresight of a reasonable producer.

Given these uncertainties, it is essential to establish clearly in the contract the quality standards to be attained, rather than relying on the term implied by the Supply of Goods and Services Act 1982. This can only be done through a combination of careful specification and clear provisions for acceptance testing against that specification. A properly drafted software development contract would contain an express warranty of quality linked to a detailed specification of what is to be achieved, along the same lines as a system supply contract (see sections 1.3.2, 1.3.7). Where the developer has produced similar software in the past, he may give an absolute warranty that the system will perform as specified. In other instances, though, the parties may recognise that achieving all the functions in the specification is not feasible, or not feasible at an acceptable price. In that case the warranty is likely to be that the developer will use reasonable care and skill to achieve the initial specification, together with a procedure for modifying the specification and price as the development proceeds. This will be coupled with a further warranty that the software will comply with the final agreed specification.

Although express warranties of quality are clearly desirable and will be found in most bespoke software contracts, the term implied by s. 13 of the

1982 Act will still be important. Any term which reduces the rights the client would have had under that Act is an exclusion clause,[2] and thus subject to the test of reasonableness by virtue of s. 2(2) or s. 3 of the Unfair Contract Terms Act 1977.[3]

The foregoing only applies, however, to those software development contracts which can be classified as contracts for the provision of services. In most case bespoke or custom software contracts will normally fall into this category as any physical component, such as the manuals or even the media on which the software is supplied, is clearly subsidiary to the main purpose of the contract, which is the design and writing of a unique software package. Problems with the classification of bespoke software will arise, however, where what is contracted for is not a completely new package but one which has already been created and which is modified to meet the customer's requirements. If the modifications are not substantial the main purpose of the contract is the provision of the basic package, and if this is supplied on physical media the contract might well be construed as one for the sale of goods.[4] This point will be increasingly relevant as modular software engineering methods become more common. If all that the software house is doing is combining standard program modules from its library, it will be difficult to discern the same 'service' element as in a complete rewrite.[5] As Hilbery J said, referring to the manufacture of a fur coat:

> I cannot uncover anything to distinguish this from the case of any article which it is part of someone's business to supply and which he makes up to special measurements for the customer. It requires skill, labour and materials to make it but the purpose of the transaction is the supply of the complete article and the receipt of the price.[6]

3.1.2 The supply of software packages

The legal classification of software is likely to bear little relation to commercial classifications. English law essentially divides the subject matter of commerce into real property, choses in action, goods and services. Only the last two categories are potentially appropriate for software. The legal regime governing the contract to supply software is thus dependent on which of these categories best fits the software in question. The establishment of the

---

2. *Smith v Eric Bush* [1990] 1 AC 831.
3. See section 1.2.2 above and section 3.2 below.
4. By analogy with the 'work and materials' cases such as *Robinson v Graves* [1935] 1 KB 579 and *Marcel (Furriers) Ltd v Tapper* [1953] 1 WLR 49. See further section 1.2.1 above and section 3.1.2 below.
5. To take an example from a different part of the IT industry, the DEC VAX computer used to be individually configured to the customer's requirements from standard DEC components. There were many thousands of possible configurations — so many that DEC used an expert system, XCON, to design each VAX. Nonetheless, it would be a brave lawyer who was prepared to argue that the supply of a VAX was a contract for services rather than a sale of goods.
6. *Marcel (Furriers) Ltd v Tapper* [1953] 1 WLR 49 at 51.

appropriate legal regime is important as it defines the default set of obligations which are modified by the express contract. We have already seen that bespoke or custom software will usually be classified as services. Package software will normally be goods, as it is supplied on physical media in multiple copies. However, 'telesoftware', downloaded from websites or similar sources, will probably be treated as services, or perhaps *sui generis* because it has no tangible component.

This classification of software into goods and services is completely illogical, if the normal rules for classifying the products of commerce are followed. These rules are based not on the software's purpose or its format, but on how it is supplied. Goods are defined in s. 61 of the Sale of Goods Act 1979 as personal chattels, which requires them to possess some tangible or corporeal element, so it is clear that pure information cannot be goods.[7] Nonetheless, a supplier of standard, packaged software will normally be selling goods. The supply of software is, in part at least, a sale of goods if the main purpose of the transaction is that the purchaser will become the owner of some tangible property containing the software, i.e., the medium on which it is supplied, usually a CD-ROM or a series of floppy disks. Software which is installed by copying it onto the purchaser's system from a medium that remains the property of the supplier will lack the necessary tangibility.

Software producers might attempt to argue that, even though some tangible medium is supplied, it is only that medium that is goods, so that the software recorded on it is merely information and thus not covered by the Sale of Goods Act 1979. The argument is that, because the value of packaged software subsists mainly in the intellectual property element which is licensed rather than 'sold' to the user, what is supplied is a service and thus subject only to standards of reasonable care. This argument fails to distinguish between the contract *supplying* the package, which is between the dealer and the user and could well be a sale, and the licence of intellectual property rights granted by the *software house* which is clearly not a sale.[8] It is analogous to the seller of a pre-recorded cassette tape arguing that the tape is not defective because the only fault is that the music is distorted whilst the tape itself is perfect. The reason that the purchaser pays more for a pre-recorded than a blank tape is precisely because it has information (music) on it. This point appears to have been recognised in *Cox v Riley* (1986) 83 Cr App R 54[9] where the defendant was charged with criminal damage. He had erased the programs from a magnetic card that controlled a programmable saw, rendering the card almost valueless. In spite of his argument that he had not damaged the card itself he was convicted, on the ground that he had damaged the 'card as programmed', which was property for the purposes of the Criminal Damage Act 1971.

This rather technical approach may turn out to be unnecessary, as in *St Albans City and District Council v International Computers Ltd* [1995] FSR 686,

---

7. *Oxford* v *Moss* (1978) 68 Cr App Rep 183.
8. This argument has been accepted in Sir Ian Glidewell's judgment in *St Albans City and District Council* v *International Computers Ltd* [1995] FSR 686.
9. See also *R* v *Whiteley* (1991) 93 Cr App R 25. This issue is discussed in greater depth in section 9.2.2 below.

[1997] FSR 251 (CA) the first instance judge was firmly of the view that software is goods (at pp. 698–9), although a final determination on that point was not necessary for the decision in the case. The software in question was a substantial package, for which the council was to pay £1.3 million over five years, and it is unlikely that it was supplied on a tangible medium ownership of which was to pass to the council. A strongly influential factor in forming the judge's opinion was his finding that, if software were not goods, it would fall entirely outside any regime of statutorily implied terms. However, in the Court of Appeal Sir Ian Glidewell held that the contract was not a sale of goods, because property in the tangible medium of a disk had not been transferred, but that nevertheless:

> In the absence of any express term to the contrary, such a contract is subject to an implied term that the program will be reasonably fit for, i.e., reasonably capable of achieving, the intended purpose. ([1997] FSR 251, 256.)

Although the difference between the first-instance and Court of Appeal judgments is of theoretical importance, in practical terms the result is identical.

If package software *is* goods, the seller is obliged under s. 14 of the Sale of Goods Act 1979 to supply software that is of satisfactory quality and reasonably fit for the purposes the buyer has made known to him. This is assessed in relation either to the common purposes for which software of that type is purchased or by reference to the purpose that the buyer has made known. Software, however, does not have the same degree of homogeneity within its various categories as, say, motor cars. Different word processing or database systems may go about the task in entirely different ways, and prove more or less suitable for entirely different tasks. It is likely that the only clear guidance available to the court will be the claims the producer has made in his advertising and promotional material. This may amount to a description of the goods, or may be some other relevant factor the courts may take into account in deciding if the software is of adequate quality. Depending on the time of supply of the software package and the nature of the software, Year 2000 compliance might have been a typical requirement which the courts could consider to determine whether that software package is of satisfactory quality. Suppliers often incorporated express provisions into their contracts regarding Year 2000 compliance (and, in particular, their liability for non compliance and any steps they would take to remedy a failure to comply) rather than risk more general implied terms being applied.

It is obviously possible to overcome some of these classification problems by including express provisions as to quality etc. in the contract and providing that these are in substitution for all other rights. However, it must be remembered that if these provisions impose lower obligations on the seller than would be the case under e.g., the Sale of Goods Act 1979, the term will amount to an exclusion clause and be potentially subject to attack under the Unfair Contract Terms Act 1977.[10]

3.1.3 Service contracts

Service based contracts are frequently used in the IT industry, whether they relate to the development of a bespoke software package or the provision of consultancy services to more complex projects, such as outsourcing or facilities management arrangements. The position in relation to software development contracts has already been dealt with at 3.1.1 above.

As noted at 3.1.1 above, s. 13 of the Supply of Goods and Services Act 1982 will apply to imply into service contracts a term that the service provider will take reasonable skill and care in the service provision. However, customers (and service providers) under service based contracts will rarely want to rely on this general term and instead will want to agree more detailed provisions regarding the scope of the obligation. In such contracts it is the quality of the supplier's personnel which will be key. A relatively simple consultancy services contract will therefore typically include warranties by the consultancy firm regarding the use of appropriately experienced personnel and the use of good industry practice (or similar standards).

Customers under more complex outsourcing and facilities management contracts are likely to seek detailed warranties specifying (in addition to those regarding experienced personnel and the use of good industry practice) that services will be provided in accordance with applicable laws and with any relevant policies and procedures. The services will usually also be provided to stated service levels. Failure to achieve those service levels will usually expose the supplier to contractually pre-determined financial penalties, such as service credits or liquidated damages. Reliance on the basic provisions under the Supply of Goods and Services Act 1982 alone is of little use in these more complex high value transactions. Indeed, its application is frequently expressly excluded in the business to business context although care must be taken in doing so to avoid breaching the provisions of the Unfair Contract Terms Act 1977, in particular s. 2(2) and s. 3.

3.2 EXCLUSION CLAUSES

It is by no means uncommon to find a clause in contracts of US origin that provides (a) that the software house warrants only that the media on which the software is supplied are free from defects in normal use, (b) that this warranty is in lieu of all other liabilities, express or implied, whether by statute or otherwise, (c) that liability for breach is limited to rectification of defects in or replacement of the media, and (d) that no liability is accepted for consequential loss.

In the light of the Unfair Contract Terms Act 1977 such a clause is almost worse than useless. If the software is goods, the terms that the seller or

---

10. Although sch. 2 to the Unfair Contract Terms Act 1977 excludes from the operation of the Act contracts creating or transferring intellectual property rights, the consensus interpretation is that the Act still applies to other parts of the contract, e.g., obligations of quality, delivery dates etc.

supplier has the right to sell[11] or supply[12] cannot be excluded at all, and the implied terms as to description and quality cannot be excluded at all if it is a consumer sale or supply, and only subject to the test of reasonableness if not.[13] In the case of bespoke software, the term as to reasonable care under s. 13 of the Supply of Goods and Services Act 1982 can only be excluded subject to the test of reasonableness,[14] and exclusion of liability for breach of other terms in the software house's standard form contract are subjected to the same test by s. 3 of the Unfair Contract Terms Act 1977.

The test of reasonableness is set out in s. 11 of the Unfair Contract Terms Act 1977, which provides that it must have been fair and reasonable to include the clause at the time the contract was made. Schedule 2[15] sets out a number of factors for the court to take into account — the strength of bargaining position of the parties; whether the party bound by the clause received some benefit (e.g., a lower price) for agreeing to it; how far he knew or ought to have known of the existence and extent of the clause; if the exclusion is contingent on compliance with some condition (e.g., informing the software house of defects in the software within 28 days of the end of acceptance testing) whether it was reasonable to expect the condition to be complied with; and, in a sale of goods contract, whether the goods were specially made or adapted to the customer's order. The courts have also held that the question as to which of the parties can most readily insure against the loss is a relevant consideration.[16]

The principles which will be applied by the courts in determining whether an exclusion clause satisfies the test of reasonableness have already been examined in chapter 1.2.2. The cases make it clear that to pass the test there should have been a proper assessment of the potential consequences of breach, and the clause should allocate these risks in accordance with the financial strengths of the parties and their respective abilities to insure.

In the United Kingdom, the Court of Appeal judgment in *St Albans City and District Council* v *International Computers Ltd* [1995] FSR 686 has caused some concern and, consequently, it may indicate the beginning of a stricter approach to exclusion and limitation clauses by the English courts. In that case the court considered that a clause limiting liability to the price payable for the item of equipment, program or service in respect of which the liability arose or £100,000 (whichever was the lesser) was found not to be reasonable within the terms of the Unfair Contract Terms Act 1977 and was struck out. However the very specific facts of *St Albans*, most notably the existence of a

---

11. Sale of Goods Act, s. 12.
12. Supply of Goods and Services Act, s. 7.
13. Unfair Contract Terms Act 1977, ss. 6, 7.
14. Unfair Contract Terms Act 1977, s. 2.
15. In theory sch. 2 applies only to contracts where the possession of goods is transferred; in practice, however, the courts are likely to take its provisions into account when deciding on the reasonableness of other exclusion clauses.
16. At present the insurance market has limited experience of the software industry, and insurance may be difficult to obtain on reasonable terms. This fact may make limitations of liability more likely to satisfy the s. 11 test. However, as the claims record of the industry becomes clearer, this position is likely to change.

relatively unsophisticated local authority as a contracting party, the low value of the liability cap (£100,000) compared to the overall contract value (£1,300,000) and the availability of resources and insurance cover to meet the claim, means that it is perhaps unlikely to be applied widely.[17]

Similar points apply to the earlier case of *The Salvage Association* v *Cap Financial Services Ltd* [1995] FSR 654. Obiter comments were made by Judge Thayne Forbes regarding the reasonableness of a limitation clause to £25,000. The availability of insurance cover for Cap's financial exposure and the fact that Cap's standard contract was being revised to increase (significantly) the amount Cap would be liable for were strong factors in the judge's reasoning that the liability limitation was not reasonable. Again, the specific facts mean the case can be distinguished.

In the United Kingdom, a common approach in IT contracts is the limitation of a supplier's liability in direct damages to the overall value of the contract or the price paid over a twelve month period prior to the breach. It remains to be seen whether such limitations would be held to be reasonable, if and when challenged before the English courts. In any event, suppliers should be careful to record and keep written calculations of how liability limits have been arrived at, rather than relying on arbitrary figures. Suppliers should also reconsider the standard approach when contracting under larger contracts, such as outsourcing arrangements. Arguably, in such contracts the fees paid by the customer may be less relevant to the question of reasonableness than the importance and value to the customer of the contract and IT systems being outsourced, and liability limits may need to be reconsidered accordingly.

It has been common practice for suppliers in the United Kingdom to draft exclusion clauses to exclude their liability for indirect or consequential loss. The phrase is generally used to encompass loss beyond the damage to the value of the property itself, such as loss of profits and loss of revenue. The Court of Appeal decision in *British Sugar* v *NEI Power Projects Ltd and Another* (1998) 87 BLR 42 suggests that such clauses may no longer be sufficient to exclude the supplier's liability as desired. In this case the defendant was relying on a clause limiting liability for consequential loss to a maximum of the value of the contract in question. Lord Justice Waller approved Parker J's earlier judgment that the word 'consequential' does not 'cover any loss which directly and naturally results in the ordinary course of events'[18] and went on to state that such consequential loss therefore equated to loss which is not direct, such as damage flowing from special circumstances within the second limb of *Hadley* v *Baxendale* (1854) 9 Exch 341. This contradicts the long

---

17. See also the rather specific facts of *South West Water Services Ltd* v *International Computers Ltd* (unreported, Technology & Construction Court, 29 June 1999) where it was held that South West Water Services Ltd had entered into contracts made on ICL's standard terms of business and that, under s. 3 and s. 11(1) of the Unfair Contract Terms Act 1977, the exclusion clauses were manifestly unreasonable and so unenforceable. The case concerned a system which, following a series of project delays, failed to even reach acceptance testing and the effect of the exclusion clauses would have meant that South West Water Services Ltd would have been in a far worse position than if the system failed after acceptance testing.

18. *British Sugar* v *NEI Power Projects Ltd and Another* (1998) 87 BLR 50.

standing view of many commentators[19] that direct loss (i.e., that under the first limb of *Hadley* v *Baxendale*) can include some types of financial (consequential) loss and introduces a confusing link between the definition of consequential loss and the rules for remoteness of damage. For example, in circumstances where a supplier has been made aware of further contracts the customer intends to enter into and the customer's reliance on the supplier for that purpose, it was generally thought that the loss of profits on those further contracts would be capable of being recovered under the first limb of *Hadley* v *Baxendale*. Following the approach of British Sugar, this would no longer be the case.

The effect of the British Sugar case is to render unclear the meaning of the phrase 'consequential loss' and when such loss is recoverable. Those drafting exclusion clauses would therefore be prudent to define exactly what is meant by the phrase and to state precisely what a supplier is liable for and what types of liability are excluded. This needs to be done in the context of the restrictions and test of reasonableness imposed by the Unfair Contract Terms Act 1977 with an appropriate allocation of risk accordingly.

Whilst it may be tempting to exclude as much liability as possible, the danger of this approach is that the software house supplier will be left completely unprotected against claims if a court finds the clause unreasonable. It should also be apparent that there is no point in merely copying a clause used by one's competitors, particularly if (as is often the case) it was drafted with US law in mind. Conversely, when contracting with a US or other foreign client it is essential to take advice on the effect of any standard exclusions under the client's domestic law. Although a clause providing that the contract is to be governed by English law and adjudicated in England may be effective, it may not be so where the contract is to be performed primarily abroad. Again, advice should be taken on the specific circumstances.

3.3   THIRD PARTY RIGHTS

The Contracts (Rights of Third Parties) Act 1999 heralds an important change to the long standing rule of privity of contract (i.e., that only the parties to a contract can sue in relation to its terms). The Act came into force on 11 November 1999, but will apply only to contracts entered into following the expiry of six months after that date.

The Act gives third parties rights in two circumstances, set out in s. 1(1). A contract can provide expressly for a benefit to be conferred upon a third party. Alternatively, a contract can expressly provide that a third party is entitled to enforce its provisions. In either circumstance the third party is entitled to enforce that contract against the other parties to it. Given the frequent use of three (or other multi) way relationships in the IT industry (e.g., customer-licensor-reseller relationships and licensor-licensee licences for the benefit of a number of licensee group companies) liability provisions and contractual provisions will need to be reassessed to ensure that liability to third parties is provided for and excluded, where appropriate.

---

19. See, e.g., *McGregor on Damages* (16th edn, London: Sweet & Maxwell, 1997) p. 25.

Contracts will, under the new legislation, only be able to provide for a benefit to a third party. They cannot impose a burden. Any exclusions or limitations of liability contained in the contract will also be effective as against the third party seeking to enforce its rights. Generally, the third party is afforded the remedies the contracting party would have had. It should be noted though that s. 2(2) of the Unfair Contract Terms Act 1977 does not apply regarding negligence consisting of the breach of an obligation arising from a term of the contract and where it is the third party seeking to enforce that contract term.

3.4   STRICT LIABILITY — THE CONSUMER PROTECTION ACT 1987

Following the EC Directive on Product Liability (85/374), the Consumer Protection Act 1987 came into force on 1 March 1988. The essence of the Act is that producers or suppliers of products in the course of a business[20] should be liable to anyone who suffers personal injury or property damage caused by a defect in that product, irrespective of any fault on the producer's part. As we shall see, however, the effect of the 'state of the art' defence (included largely at the request of the pharmaceutical industry) is to retain the requirement of fault though placing the burden of disproof on the producer.

The main requirements for liability are set out in s. 2(1), which provides that subject to the remaining provisions of the Act:

> where any damage is caused wholly or partly by a defect in a product, every person to whom subsection (2) below applies shall be liable for the damage.

The obvious question raised by this subsection is whether computer software is a 'product', for if it is not the Act is irrelevant to our discussion. 'Product' is defined in s. 1(2) as 'any goods or electricity' including components. 'Goods' are defined in s. 45 as including (amongst other things such as crops and aircraft which clearly do not cover software) 'substances', and the same section defines 'substance' as 'any natural or artificial substance . . .'. In spite of the circularity of this definition, it is clear that computer software will only qualify as a product if it is a 'substance', which suggests that it must have the tangible quality normally associated with goods. This is supported by the text of the Directive which defines 'product' as any moveable. It seems likely, therefore, that the Act applies only to software which is marketed on some form of tangible medium (e.g., a tape or disk) ownership of which is transferred to the purchaser. Software which is installed by copying it onto the purchaser's system from a medium that remains the property of the supplier will lack the necessary tangibility to fall within the definition. The Act is to be interpreted in accordance with EEC law and the Directive, and

---

20. Section 4(1)(c).

it has been held that television programmes, which similarly consist of information transmitted as electric signals, are not goods but services.[21]

The Act also limits liability to death or personal injury[22] or damage to property (including land) which is ordinarily intended for private use or consumption and was so intended to be used by the claimant.[23] It does not cover damage to the product itself or to any product containing the defective product[24] and the damage must exceed £275.[25] Thus where software is purchased by a business and used solely within the business, claims can only be expected from outsiders who are injured by the business's activities where the cause was a defect in the software. The most obvious case where the Act might otherwise apply, air traffic control, will not be covered as the software in question is unlikely to be a product. Even so there are a number of situations which will at present fall within the Act — computer-controlled lifts, chips in washing machines, etc. — and with the growth in the number of computers in the home, the Act will become increasingly important.

Section 2(1) requires that the damage be caused by a 'defect' in the product, and this is defined in s. 3. A product is defective if it does not provide the level of safety (in respect of property as well as the person) that persons generally are entitled to expect. This raises no problems so far as manufacturing defects are concerned, but if the defect is in the design of the product it is suggested that this test is little more than the existing test for negligence. The courts are required to consider such matters as the manner of marketing, instructions and warnings, what the producer might reasonably expect to be done with the product, and the time at which it was supplied. This is the kind of risk/utility balancing that is used to decide liability in negligence, and it may well be the case that a manufacturer who would not be liable in negligence will escape liability under the Act as well.[26]

Once the claimant has established that he has suffered damage through a defective product, he has a choice of defendants. The obvious person against whom to claim is the producer (defined in s. 1(2)), but he may also claim against any person who holds himself out as the producer or against the importer of the product into the EEC if it is produced outside.[27] In some cases, however, it may not be obvious who the producer is, and so the claimant is given a right of action against the supplier under s. 2(3). The

21. *Italy* v *Saachi* [1974] ECR 409. Note though that this finding was in the context of the Treaty of Rome provisions on the free movement of goods — whether the same is true in the context of the product liability Directive is a matter of some doubt. It has been argued that some non-UK jurisdictions may take a purposive approach to the definition of 'product', and decide the issue on whether the item in question is effectively mass-marketed or produced only on a one-off basis — see J. Herschbaeck, 'Is Software a Product?' (1989) 5 *Computer Law & Practice* 154. See also *St Albans City and District Council* v *International Computers Ltd* [1995] FSR 686, discussed at 3.1.2 above, which suggests that the English courts might adopt a similar approach.
22. Section 5(1).
23. Section 5(1) and (3).
24. Section 5(2).
25. Section 5(4).
26. See, e.g., *Evans* v *Triplex Safety Glass Co. Ltd* [1936] 1 All ER 283.
27. Section 2(2).

supplier is only liable, however, if the claimant requests from him the name of the producer or importer and the supplier fails to give that name within a reasonable time.

Finally, mention should be made of the 'state of the art' defence. Whilst s. 4 contains a number of defences, some of which might be useful to a software producer, the most relevant by far is that contained in s. 4(1)(e). This provides that the producer can escape liability if he can show that the defect is such that a reasonable producer would not, in the current state of the art in that industry, have discovered the defect. The practice in the software industry is to release software that is not entirely 'bug'-free, on the not unreasonable ground that the use made of the software is not totally predictable and thus exhaustive testing is, commercially at least, impracticable. It has even been suggested that it is impossible to produce bug-free software, though this proposition appears to depend on the logical proof that it is impossible to write a program that can be guaranteed to debug another program. Given this practice, it is arguable that a software producer who failed to discover even a quite serious defect in his software would nevertheless be able to take advantage of the defence, so long as the defect is not in an area of the program that would be tested as a matter of course by others in the industry. If this is so, the effect of the defence is merely to permit the producer to *disprove* negligence, a very different matter from the strict liability that the Act apparently introduces.

As the application of the Consumer Protection Act 1987 is so limited in scope and the majority of claims in respect of software will be for financial loss, it seems likely that the Act will have a comparatively small impact on the liability of software producers. Nonetheless, where the claim is for physical injury or property damage the evidential burdens placed on the claimant are much lighter than in negligence, and the Act would be the obvious first line of attack. For most claims, however, the common law of negligence will remain the most fruitful hope of recovery.

3.5 NEGLIGENCE

Although the general heading 'tort' covers a wide range of legal wrongs, it becomes clear on closer examination that the only real tortious problems posed by information technology arise in the field of negligence. It is quite possible to imagine situations where a computer might play a part in the commission of another tort, but almost certainly some question of negligence would be involved. Thus in the American case of *Scott* v *District of Columbia* (1985) 493 A 2d 319, where the claimant alleged false arrest and wrongful imprisonment against the police, who had relied on a warrant erroneously issued by a computer system, her suit failed because the officers who arrested her had not been negligent in relying on the computer. In other false arrest cases, if there were no question of carelessness in the use of the computer, it would be legally irrelevant that a computer was somehow involved. This is true for other torts — e.g., where the noise from a computer printer constituted a nuisance or an information retrieval system contained defamatory material. These cases would normally raise the same legal problems as noise from a typewriter or defamation in a book, except for the special case of intermediary liability — see chapter 11.

Before going any further, it is necessary to recognise that the question of liability may be affected by the type of damage suffered by the claimant. If this is physical injury or property damage few problems will arise; the test for the existence of a duty of care will be that in *Donoghue* v *Stevenson* [1932] AC 562, and breach and causation will be dealt with as in any other negligence action. The real problems arise when the claimant's losses, as is likely to be the case almost every time, are purely economic. If this is so, the question of whether the defendant owes him a duty of care will depend to a large degree on the type of damage that was sustained.

3.5.1 Loss of use of the software

Any producer of software will, to some degree, be aware of the potential that his product has for causing loss to someone who makes use of it. If he fails to take sufficient care when designing the product, and so causes loss to users, his commercial interests will suffer. This does not necessarily mean that he is under a legal duty to take such care. The general principle laid down in *Donoghue* v *Stevenson* [1932] AC 562 that one person owes a duty of care to another if he ought reasonably to have foreseen that his actions or inaction will cause harm to that other, expresses the duty very widely. It might therefore be thought that the producer of software is in the same position as, say, the producer of electric toasters, who clearly owes a duty of care to any person who uses the toaster. In such a case the duty is to design the toaster so as to avoid injuring the user or damaging the user's property. In the case of a software designer the position is rather different. It is unlikely that defective software will cause any loss that is not purely financial,[28] and the attitude of the law towards financial losses is less favourable than towards physical or property damage.

For many years the position appeared to be settled that a claimant could only recover for economic loss if it was consequent on physical injury or damage to property[29] or caused by reliance on a negligent misstatement. However, in *Junior Books Ltd* v *Veitchi Co. Ltd* [1983] 1 AC 520 the possibility of a more relaxed attitude to pure economic loss was recognised. In that case the defendants were building subcontractors who laid a floor at the claimants' premises. The floor quickly proved defective and unsuitable for use. The claimants successfully claimed the cost of replacing the floor and lost profits while this was done, in spite of the defendants' argument that these losses were purely financial and thus not recoverable. The House of Lords held that

---

28. Though we should note that common physical processes are increasingly becoming computerised — for example, Honda has produced a four-wheel steering system which replaces the physical link between the steering wheel and the road wheels with a computerised link, and 'fly-by-wire' airliners are now commonplace. These types of applications, which include anti-lock braking systems and such mundane things as washing machines, are generally implemented by turning the software into an application specific integrated circuit, i.e., a physical microchip, which is clearly both goods and a product.
29. *Spartan Steel and Alloys Ltd* v *Martin* [1973] QB 27.

a duty to take care to avoid financial losses could be owed if there was sufficient proximity between claimant and defendant, and that in this case, the defendants having been nominated as subcontractor by the claimants, a sufficiently close relationship did exist.

However, *Junior Books* has proved a source of worry to the courts, for the fear of opening the floodgates is ever-present. In *Muirhead* v *Industrial Tank Specialties Ltd* [1986] QB 507 the Court of Appeal distinguished it, holding that in that case the claimant and defendant (the supplier of a defective pump to the builder of a tank for the claimant's lobsters) were not in a sufficiently proximate relationship for the defendant to owe the claimant a duty to take care to avoid causing financial loss. Robert Goff LJ explained *Junior Books* as deciding that such a relationship would only arise if the claimant relied on the defendant to avoid such losses, and if the defendant could be seen as undertaking responsibility to do so. Similarly in *Simaan General Contracting Co.* v *Pilkington Glass Ltd* [1988] QB 758 the Court of Appeal held that the defendants, who supplied glass to a subcontractor of the claimants, owed no duty to the claimants to supply glass that was of a consistent colour. There was no reliance on the defendants' expertise and no discussion with them as to the nature of the glass to be supplied. Any remedy the claimants might have would be in contract against the subcontractor. Finally in *D & F Estates* v *Church Commissioners* [1989] AC 177, a case almost identical to *Junior Books* except for the fact that the subcontractor was not nominated by the claimant, the House of Lords refused to follow that case and held that it was a case which turned on its own special facts, although the following year the House of Lords refused to disapprove *Junior Books*, recognising that in a few special cases there would be sufficient proximity to give rise to a duty of care in respect of pure economic loss.[30]

More recently, a series of House of Lords cases has re-examined the circumstances in which a duty to avoid causing economic loss will arise, whilst carefully avoiding a re-examination of *Junior Books*. The basic principle adopted is that laid down in *Caparo Industries plc* v *Dickman* [1990] 2 AC 605, a negligent misstatement case, that liability is based on the defendant's undertaking of responsibility for achieving a particular result where economic loss is a foreseeable result of failure to meet that responsibility.[31] This is perhaps most clearly explained in *Marc Rich & Co. AG* v *Bishops Rock Marine Co. Ltd* [1996] AC 211. A bulk carrier vessel developed faults and the surveyor acting for the ship's classification society recommended that it could proceed to its next scheduled port for repairs. The following day, the ship sank with a total loss of cargo. The cargo owners claimed in negligence against the classification society. The House of Lords held that the same test should apply to physical and financial losses. The question of whether there

---

30. *Murphy* v *Brentwood District Council* [1990] 2 All ER 908.
31. In negligent misstatement cases an additional requirement, that of reliance on the statement, is also imposed, but *White* v *Jones* [1995] 2 AC 207, a case in which a solicitor failed to draft a will in time to ensure that the claimant beneficiary received a legacy, shows that the requirement of reliance is not essential in non-misstatement cases, as its purpose is to show a causal link between the negligent misstatement and the loss.

was sufficient proximity between claimant and defendant, which in physical damage cases is normally determined almost exclusively by foreseeability of the likelihood of harm, is decided in economic loss cases by seeking the relevant undertaking of responsibility.[32]

However, even on the assumption that there was sufficient proximity between the cargo owners and the surveyor, the court also held that on the facts it was not fair, just and reasonable to impose a duty of care because of the agreed contractual structure adopted in the shipping industry which allocates losses of this type between shipowners and cargo owners. This recognition that the imposition of a duty of care can upset carefully crafted contractual arrangements is also found in Lord Nolan's judgment in *White* v *Jones* [1995] 2 AC 207, in which he said:

> I would for my part leave open the question whether ... the defendant who engages in the relevant activity pursuant to a contract can exclude or limit his liability to third parties by some provision in the contract. I would prefer to say that the existence and terms of the contract may be relevant in determining what the law of tort may reasonably require of the defendant in all the circumstances.

It appears from these cases that the kind of circumstances in which a duty of care to avoid economic losses will arise would be where one software producer is employed to devise software specifically for the user, and subcontracts some or all of the work to another software house. In such a case, provided there is evidence that it is the subcontractor rather than the main contractor who is undertaking responsibility for that part of the work, which is likely to require there to have been sufficient discussion between user and subcontractor to show that the user is relying on the subcontractor's expertise, the user will have an arguable case in tort for the cost of replacement or repair. However, the role of contracts in determining whether it is just and reasonable to impose a duty of care will need to be examined, if, as is quite likely, the subcontractor has effectively[33] limited his liability to the main contractor, the fact that imposing direct tortious liability would evade that limit might be sufficient to persuade a court that it would not be fair, just and reasonable to impose a duty.

3.5.2 Consequential losses caused by reliance on the output of the software

In a standard negligence action, the question whether economic loss can be recovered at all is dealt with as a matter of the scope of the defendant's duty,

---

32. See also *Henderson* v *Merrett Syndicates Ltd* [1995] 2 AC 145; *White* v *Jones* [1995] 2 AC 207; *Spring* v *Guardian Assurance plc* [1995] 2 AC 296, all of which stress assumption of responsibility as the test for proximity.

33. If the subcontractor's limitation of liability were ineffective, it would clearly not for that reason be unfair, unjust or unreasonable to impose a duty of care on him. This raises the interesting spectacle of a court being required to give judgment on the effectiveness of a contract term which is not actually in dispute.

as explained above. It is arguable, however, that if the loss is consequential on reliance on the output of the software a less stringent test should be imposed, a test similar to that used in the cases on negligent misstatements. The results produced by the software are similar to (and in many cases treated by the user as) statements of fact. If reliance on those statements is foreseeable it would seem reasonable to assume that the considerations influencing the courts in negligent misstatement cases will also be relevant in deciding the extent of the duty owed by a software producer.

In 1998 a similar argument was applied by the courts in deciding whether a software package which assisted users to decide which stocks and shares to buy constituted the giving of investment advice under the Financial Services Act 1976.[34] In *Re Market Wizard Systems (UK) Ltd*, *The Times*, 31 July 1998, the Secretary of State petitioned for the compulsory winding up of the company on the ground that it was engaged in an unlawful activity, the carrying on of an investment business without authorisation contrary to s. 3 of the Act. The company's business consisted of supplying computer software to end users. The software required users to enter share prices and other information about a selected set of securities on a daily basis, and then calculated the financial futures positions which the user should hold in respect of those stocks. The software was advertised on the basis that users could expect to make substantial profits if they followed its recommendations. The user manual described the Market Wizard program as a 'computerised trading tool' which 'generates detailed trading advice for a specific range of exchange traded securities'.

Carnwath J, holding that the company should be wound up, made two findings which are relevant here:

(a)   That the output of the Market Wizard program constituted advice:

I have no doubt that the signals generated by the use of the system constitute the kind of advice with which para. 15 [of the Financial Services Act 1976] is concerned. The signals provide guidance as to the course of action which the user should take in relation to the buying or selling of the investments. Such guidance, in the ordinary use of English, is 'advice on the merits' of purchasing those investments. It matters not that the user is free to follow or disregard the advice; nor that he may receive further advice from his broker before making a final decision.

(b)   That the company was responsible for that output, and was therefore giving investment advice to users through the medium of the program's output:

---

34. Activities which require authorisation under s. 3 of the Act include:

Giving, or offering or agreeing to give, to persons in their capacity as investors or potential investors advice on the merits of their purchasing, selling, subscribing for or underwriting an investment, or exercising any right conferred by an investment to acquire, dispose of, underwrite or convert an investment: Financial Services Act 1976, sch. 1, pt. II, para. 15.

The question is whether the company is carrying on the business of giving advice. It is not necessary to identify a particular point in time at which the advice is given. It is enough, in my view, that it is providing the customer with a medium by which its purported expertise in the analysis of historical trading patterns is communicated in the form of advice related to a particular investment. If the programme were being operated by the company itself to produce the signals, in response to specific requests from customers, there would be no doubt that it was the company which was providing the advice. The fact that it is the customer who is operating the programme does not change the nature of the advice or its source.[35]

This judgment is the first acceptance by the English courts that the output of software might constitute advice, although it must be recognised that there were a number of special factors in this case which led to that finding, in particular the way in which the company advertised the software. Nonetheless, the decision in *Re Market Wizard* is strongly supportive of the argument that non-contractual liability for defects in the output of a program should be dealt with on the basis that they are, or are closely analogous to, negligent misstatements.

Software may cause reliance losses in a number of different ways, and the potential causes of action may be classified as follows:

(a) Negligence in designing the system.
(b) Negligence in operating the system.
(c) Negligence in relying on the output of the system.
(d) Failure to use a computer system.

3.5.2.1 Negligent design The greatest difficulty that a defendant will have in suing a software producer for losses caused by a negligently designed piece of software is establishing that the producer owed him a duty of care.[36] If, as the decision in *Re Market Wizard Systems (UK) Ltd, The Times,* 31 July 1998 suggests, the relevant test[37] will be based on the same principles as are used in establishing liability for negligent misstatements, those principles need to be examined here. In *Hedley Byrne & Co. Ltd* v *Heller & Partners* [1964] AC 465 the claimant suffered loss when he gave credit to a firm called Easipower in reliance on a reference given by the defendant bank. The court held that because the claimant and the defendant were in such a close relationship, the defendant owed a duty to take care in giving the reference. This case

---

35. The link between the company and the advice was, in the judge's opinion, reinforced by a requirement to update the software on a daily basis via the Internet from the company's website.
36. The House of Lords in *IBA* v *EMI and BICC* (1980) 14 Build LR 1 has recognised that the designer (in this case of a building) can owe a duty to take reasonable care in making the design.
37. For an alternative approach based on the liability of professionals for careless advice, which nonetheless also examines the misstatement cases, see D. Rowland, 'Negligence, Professional Competence and Computer Systems', (1999) 2 *The Journal of Information, Law and Technology (JILT)*, at http://www.law.warwick.ac.uk/jilt/99-2/rowland.html.

established the possibility of claiming for negligent misstatements. The problem that troubled the court most was the danger of 'opening the floodgates' to litigation. The difficulty with careless words as opposed to careless actions is that the range of those affected is potentially very large indeed. The example given by Denning LJ in *Candler* v *Crane Christmas & Co.* [1951] 2 KB 164 of the marine hydrographer is instructive: we are asked to envisage that the hydrographer, in drawing up a chart of a particular part of the oceans, negligently fails to mark in a reef that is a danger to shipping. The chart is published, and is used by the masters of ships sailing in those waters. One or more ships run on the reef, entirely due to the fact that it is not marked on the chart. Should the hydrographer be liable to compensate the master of the ship, the ship-owners, and any passengers or cargo owners, all of whom will suffer loss because of his carelessness? Clearly the hydrographer satisfies the test of foreseeability laid down in *Donoghue* v *Stevenson* [1932] AC 562. Clearly, also, his liability is potentially so wide, and extends so far in time (the charts might well be used for many years) that it seems wrong to say that he ought to be held liable.

The solution adopted in *Hedley Byrne & Co. Ltd* v *Heller & Partners Ltd* was to limit the duty of care to those who were in a 'special relationship' with the maker of the statement. This special relationship was variously defined as being 'equivalent to contract' (per Lord Devlin), a voluntary undertaking given to the claimant to undertake skill and care (per Lords Morris and Hodson), or knowledge by the defendant that the claimant would rely on the statement (per Lord Reid). In any event, it was clear that the mere fact that it was foreseeable that some person in the defendant's position *might* rely on the statement would not be enough to establish a duty of care.

The position has been somewhat clarified in *J.E.B. Fasteners* v *Marks, Bloom & Co.* [1983] 1 All ER 583, where the defendant accountants negligently overvalued a company's assets in a report prepared for the company. As the defendants knew, the report was intended to be shown to prospective investors in the company. The claimants, who were the eventual purchasers, brought an action against the defendants based on the negligent misstatement in the report. The court held that although the defendants did not specifically know that the report was to be shown to the claimants, they did know that the report would be shown to, and relied on by, the class of intending purchasers, a class of which the claimants were a member. There was, therefore, sufficient proximity for the defendants to owe the claimants a duty of care, though in the event their action failed as they had not relied on that statement in deciding to purchase the company.[38] An important element in deciding the proximity question appears to be the purpose for which the advice was produced. In *Caparo Industries plc* v *Dickman* [1990] 2 AC 605 the House of Lords held that a company's auditors owed no duty of care to the shareholders in respect of the accounts because the accounts were not produced for the purpose of being relied on when making investments (even though it was *foreseeable* that they would be relied on[39]). This question is likely

---

38. See also *Haig* v *Bamford* (1977) 72 DLR (3d) 68 (Canada).
39. See the judgment of the Court of Appeal.

to be answered in the affirmative in the case of most software producers — if the output of the software is not intended to be relied on, it is difficult to see why the user bought it.

Applying these principles to the question of whether a software producer owes a duty of care to the ultimate user, the following position seems a likely one:

(a)   If the software was commissioned by, or modified for, the user, the producer will owe him a duty of care. This appears to follow from *Hedley Byrne* and is supported by *Junior Books Ltd* v *Veitchi Co. Ltd* [1983] 1 AC 520.

(b)   If the software was produced for use by a limited class of users, e.g., for a trade organisation which would market the software to its members, then a duty of care would seem to exist following *J.E.B. Fasteners* v *Marks, Bloom & Co.*, provided it was intended to be used and relied on by that group.

(c)   If the software was produced for release to the general public, then it appears unlikely that the producer owes a duty of care to the user, as the class of users is too indeterminate to satisfy the tests laid down in *Hedley Byrne* and *J.E.B. Fasteners*. It is still the case, however, that the user might have a contractual claim against his supplier.

It should also be recognised that even if the designer of the system does not owe a duty of care in the design itself, if defects become apparent he, or the manufacturer or distributor, may well then owe a duty to users to warn them of the defect. This is well-illustrated by the case of *Walton* v *British Leyland* (1980) Product Liability International 156. Here the claimants were injured when a wheel came off their Austin Allegro car. The defendants had known of this danger for some time, but instead of recalling the model and publicising the danger, they simply instructed their dealers to deal with the problem as the cars came into the dealers' garages. The claimants' car had been purchased from, and was serviced by, a non-Leyland dealer, so it was never modified. The court held that the defendants were liable in negligence, on the ground that once the danger became apparent they were under a duty to warn users, and they had failed to carry out this duty.

Even if a duty of care can be established, it is still necessary for the claimant to prove that the defendant was in breach of that duty, and that there is a sufficient causal connection between the breach and the loss that the claimant has suffered. The defendant will be in breach if he has failed to take as much care in producing his software as a reasonable man in the same position, professing the same expertise, would have done. The questions which arise here are the same as when a breach of a contractual duty of care is alleged, and have already been examined in section 3.1 above.

The requirement that there be a sufficient causal link between breach and loss may also raise problems. The test for sufficiency is a simple one — is the loss a foreseeable result of the breach? This test was laid down in *The Wagon Mound (No. 1)* [1961] AC 388, where oil that had carelessly been discharged from the defendants' ship was ignited by sparks from the claimants' welding operations and burnt down the claimants' wharf. On the evidence before it, the court held that fire damage was not a foreseeable consequence of the discharge, and thus the claimants' case failed.

More recent cases such as *Anns* v *Merton London Borough Council* [1978] AC 728 and *Junior Books Ltd* v *Veitchi Co. Ltd* [1983] 1 AC 520 have emphasised the close connection between duty and causation. The test for a duty of care is, in part at least, whether the defendant ought to have foreseen that damage of that type might occur? Nevertheless, it is possible to envisage situations where a duty of care is owed but the loss is an unforeseeable consequence of the breach of duty. Let us imagine that, owing to a defect in its design, an accounting program destroys all its data, and that for some reason the user has failed to take back-up copies of the data. Assuming the designer of the program owes the user a duty of care (e.g., the program was specially modified for the user) then it is clear that some loss of data is foreseeable. Nevertheless, it is not foreseeable that all data would be lost, as it is standard practice to take regular back-ups. It follows that further consequential losses — perhaps loss of business, penalties imposed by the Inland Revenue, etc. — will also be unforeseeable consequences of the breach.

One final point that should be considered here is that many users of software, in addition to their contract with the supplier, are bound by a licensing agreement entered into between the producer and themselves. This licence operates as a collateral contract,[40] and in many cases will contain clauses excluding the producer's liability for negligent design. It is quite likely that such a clause, insofar as it amounts to a promise by the user not to sue in negligence, will be caught by s. 2(2) or s. 3 of the Unfair Contract Terms Act 1977 and thus fail to protect the producer unless it satisfies the test of reasonableness. The question of whether a clause does satisfy this test can, of course, only be decided by reference to the particular facts of the case, though relevant factors are likely to be the price of the software, how clearly its limitations are spelt out in the documentation, and whether the function performed is innovative or commonplace.[41] Even if the clause fails the test, it may still have a residual importance as a warning to the user of the reliance he may safely put on the results of the software. In *Hedley Byrne & Co. Ltd* v *Heller & Partners* [1964] AC 465 the bank was in the end held not liable in negligence to the claimant because it had issued its reference 'without responsibility', thus making it clear to the claimant that reliance could not be placed upon it.

3.5.2.2 Negligent operation The allegation that the claimant's loss was caused by the defendant's negligent operation of his computer system will generally give rise to few special legal problems. In most, if not all cases, the defendant will be performing some function affecting the claimant, and the

---

40. If it operates at all when the software is mass-marketed — see section 1.4.2.2 above; G. Smith, '*"Tear-open licences"* — *are they enforceable in England*' (1986) 2 *CL&P* 128; C. Millard, '*Shrink Wrap Licensing*' (1987) 3 Computer Law and Security Report 8.
41. See section 3.2 above.

computer will merely be the means by which he performs the function — for example, an air traffic controller. The question, 'did he take sufficient care in operating the computer?' is really part of the larger question, 'did he take sufficient care in performing that function?'

The problem of duty of care was considered in the American case of *Independent School District No. 454, Fairmont, Minnesota v Statistical Tabulating Corporation* (1973) 359 F Supp 1095. In that case, a firm of surveyors had been employed by the claimant school to value its buildings for insurance purposes. The surveyors employed the defendants to carry out the computational work on their measurements. Unfortunately this work was performed carelessly, with the result that the school was under-insured and suffered losses when buildings caught fire. There was no point in bringing an action against the surveyors as they had performed their work with care and skill, so the school brought an action against the defendants. The court held that the defendants did owe a duty of care to the claimants, as they knew that the school would rely on their work in insuring the buildings, and the class of potential claimants was small (in this case, one member). It can be seen that the approach here is similar to that adopted in *Junior Books Ltd v Veitchi Co. Ltd* [1983] 1 AC 520, probably because in both cases the losses caused by the negligence were purely financial.

However, it seems fair to say that the courts will be less reluctant to find a duty to take care in operating a computer system than in designing one precisely because the class of claimants will, in the end, be small. The analogy may be drawn with road works; although the number of people at risk is potentially very large, in the end only one or two are likely to fall into the hole. Similarly, a negligently *operated* computerised accounting system is likely to cause loss to a few clients only. A negligently *designed* accounting system may cause loss to *all* those potentially at risk (its users) and for this reason a duty of care may be held not to exist.

With regard to the question whether the defendant was in breach of his duty of care, that is whether he took sufficient care in performing that function, it should be recognised that the introduction of new technology will have an effect on the required standard of performance. The fact that a computer has been used may lead those who are affected by the defendant's performance of his function to expect a higher standard of performance than they would be entitled to expect if a computer had not been used. A failure to perform at this standard may well be evidence of negligence, precisely because proper operation of the computer would produce a higher standard. Thus in the American case of *Southwestern Bell Telephone Co. v Ray P. Reeves* (1979) 578 SW 2d 795, in which the telephone company failed for a year to re-route the claimant lawyer's telephone calls to his new number, the jury inferred negligence on the telephone company's part from the fact that the only reasonable explanation was some malfunctioning of the computer or other equipment involved, all of which were under the company's control. The First Court of Civil Appeals, Houston, refused to hold that there was insufficient evidence on which to base this inference.[42]

---

42. See also *County Trust Co. v Pascack Valley Bank* (1966) 225 A 2d 605.

Nevertheless, it is reasonable to expect 'teething problems' in the introduction of any new technology, and the fact that these problems are foreseeable does not mean that it will be negligent to introduce the new system. The question is whether the new system will, in the end, produce an improvement, and of course whether sufficient care was taken in its introduction and operation, and in curing the initial difficulties. It was for this reason that in the American case of *Gosney* v *State of California* (1970) 89 Cal Rptr 390 the court refused to grant an injunction to force the state to operate its new computerised system of social security payments properly and to introduce new checks and 'fail-safe' procedures. Overall the new system reduced the number of errors; the question of negligence in respect of individual cases could be left to trial of those actions.

3.5.2.3   Negligence in relying on the system's output   We have already seen that a person who relies on the output of a computer system that has been negligently designed or operated may have a claim against the designer or operator. Is it possible, though, that the very act of relying on the system might be negligent?

Clearly the answer to this question must be yes if the defendant who relied on the system knew, or ought to have known, that the system was defective in design or operation. Generally, however, the defendant's reliance will not be negligent if he had no reason to suppose that the output was defective and had acted reasonably in choosing to rely on it. Thus in the *Independent School District No. 454* case discussed in 3.5.2.2 it is clear that the surveyors were not negligent as they had no reason to suspect that the data had been carelessly processed, and had chosen an apparently competent firm to undertake the work. Similarly in *Scott* v *District of Columbia* (1985) 493 A 2d 319 (see 3.5) the police officer who arrested the claimant on the erroneous warrant had not been negligent because '[the claimant's] protests gave [the officer] no factual basis for questioning the accuracy of a computer system regularly relied on by officers throughout the metropolitan area'. Once there is evidence, however, that the system has produced an incorrect output, reliance on that output will be a breach of duty. This is similar to *Prendergast* v *Sam & Dee Ltd*, *The Times*, 24 March 1988, where a pharmacist misread a doctor's writing on a prescription form and as a result supplied drugs to the claimant which caused him to suffer brain damage. The court held that, even on the misreading made by the pharmacist, the prescription was clearly defective (the drug he thought had been prescribed was not made in the strength stipulated on the prescription) and thus the pharmacist was under a duty to check the prescription with the doctor before he dispensed it. His failure to do so was therefore negligent.

It should also be recognised that where a computer system is under the defendant's control the fact that it produced incorrect results may suggest so strongly that the work was undertaken negligently that the doctrine of *res ipsa loquitur* comes into operation. It will then be for the defendant to show that the system of work was sufficiently well-planned and designed that it was reasonable for him to rely on the results. The position is similar to that in

Henderson v *Henry E. Jenkins & Sons* [1970] AC 282 where a lorry's brakes failed when a brake pipe fractured, injuring the claimant. The defendants showed that they operated a safe system of inspection, and argued that this demonstrated that they had taken sufficient care. However, they failed to show that they had no knowledge of special facts that might render their system inadequate (for example that the brake pipe had been exposed to corrosive agents such as salt water) and as a result were held liable.[43]

It is quite possible to imagine situations where it might be insufficiently careful to rely on the output of the system even though there is no particular reason to suspect that the system has worked incorrectly, because the general possibility of its inaccuracy ought to be in the defendant's mind. One example was suggested in 'Computer Horizons' in *The Times* of 1 October 1987, where it was pointed out that auditors of a company's accounts may well be negligent in declaring the accounts to be a 'true and fair' picture of the financial position of the company precisely *because* the accounting system runs on a computer. The dynamic nature of a 'real-time' system, where the information is constantly changing, and the fact that data can simply and untraceably be altered, means that the auditor cannot be certain that the information on which he bases his audit is accurate.

In America, this point has been considered in *Chernick* v *Fasig-Tipton Kentucky Inc.*, 1986 (unreported). In that case, the defendants were inter-mediaries in the sale of race horses. They sold a horse belonging to the claimants to Cloverfield Farm Inc., who intervened in the action. The horse was described in the sale catalogue as 'barren and free from infection', which suggested that the horse would be suitable for breeding purposes. In fact the horse, a mare, had twice spontaneously aborted foals, a fact which substan-tially affected the horse's value. When Cloverfield discovered this, they complained to the defendants, and eventually a case came to trial in which the claimant sellers sued the defendants for the purchase money (which the defendants had refused to hand over) and Cloverfield sued both the claimants and the defendants. It is the action by Cloverfield against the defendants that concerns us here. The defendants had prepared their sale catalogue from information supplied by the claimants, and from information on the Jockey Club computer. It was well-known that the information on the computer was likely to be inaccurate. Nevertheless, the defendants relied on this informa-tion to check the claimants' assertions. Not surprisingly, the court at first instance held that the defendants had been negligent, and the Court of Appeals of Kentucky agreed. Unfortunately for Cloverfield, in spite of this negligence their action against the defendants failed on a technicality.

A similar point was made in *Brown* v *United States* (1984) 599 F Supp 877 where two fishing boats had been lost at sea due to an inaccurate weather forecast. The National Oceanographic and Atmospheric Administration, which produced the forecast, knew that the relevant weather buoy was out of action but nevertheless issued the forecast without adding a warning that it

---

43. See also *C.K. Security Systems Inc.* v *Hartford Accident and Indemnity* (1976) *Co.* 137 Ga App 159.

was potentially inaccurate. It was held that this amounted to negligence, and thus the claimant's case succeeded.

Another reason why relying on the output of the system might be negligent is that, although the output is accurate, it is not sufficient on its own to justify the reliance that was placed on it. In *The Lady Gwendolen* [1965] P 294 a ship was fitted with the new technology of radar to assist the master in avoiding collisions at sea. In fact, the radar induced the master of the ship to travel at high speeds, even in fog. At the time he collided with another ship, in dense fog and in the restricted channel of the Mersey, he was not only travelling at top speed, but was operating the radar incorrectly. The court was clear that even if the master had operated the radar properly, he would still have been negligent because the radar did not give sufficient warning of other shipping to allow him to proceed at such a speed. Similarly in *Central Maine Power Co. v Foster Wheeler Corporation*, 1988 (unreported) a power company brought an action in negligence against the designer of a condenser which leaked and damaged other parts of the plant. It was held that the power company was contributorily negligent as its employees had relied solely on the computer system to bring any alarms to their notice, though at the time it was not programmed to do so, and thus failed to prevent the damage.

Problems in this area will often arise when professionals give advice which is based on the output of a computer program. For example, if a solicitor were to undertake a LEXIS search in an attempt to discover the answer to his client's problem, and, having discovered an apparently relevant case, based his advice entirely on the results of the search, he would undoubtedly be liable in negligence if it transpired that the case had been overruled or superseded by statute.

3.5.3 Failure to use a computer system

The question of when failure to use a computer system might amount to a failure to be sufficiently careful, and thus a breach of duty, will always depend on the particular circumstances of the case. The mere fact that use of a computer would have prevented harm to the claimant is not, in itself, proof of negligence, though it must be proved in order to establish the necessary element of causation. If non-use did cause the claimant's loss the question will then be whether a reasonable man in the defendant's position would have used the computer so as to avoid the loss. This will be decided by reference, amongst other things, to the 'state of the art' in that particular field.

If the possibility of harm through non-use of the computer is not known at the time of the loss, then it cannot be negligent to fail to use one. For example, it is obvious that a solicitor who advises his client wrongly will cause the client loss. At the time of writing, however, expert systems that might prevent this happening have not been developed to the stage of commercial availability, with the result that it cannot be negligent not to use them. If such systems are developed and prove successful, it will in the end be negligent not to use them, provided that they are sufficiently cheap and easy to use that a reasonable solicitor would provide himself with them. Once the 'state of the art' both recognises the problem and produces usable solutions, it will be negligent not to adopt those solutions even if the custom in that area is not to use them. In the American case of *The T.J. Hooper* (1932) 60 F 2d 737 the claimant's barges were lost in a storm at sea whilst being towed by the defendant's tugs. If the tugs had been fitted with radios, they could have received warning of the storm and taken shelter, thus avoiding the loss of the barges. In spite of the fact that it was not common practice to fit radios to tugs, the court held that the defendant was negligent — the technology was easily available, comparatively cheap, and its utility was clear. More recently in *United States Fire Insurance Co.* v *United States* (1986) 806 F 2d 1529 it was held that the action of the Coast Guard in calculating the site of a navigation beacon by manual rather than computerised means, when the computer system was both available and known to be many times more accurate, was potentially negligent and thus an issue to be decided by the jury at the trial. Similarly, in *Chandler* v *United States* (1988) 687 F Supp 1515 the claimant was awarded $1000 for negligent disclosure of tax return information. The disclosure took place when the IRS instructed Ms Chandler's employers to deduct arrears of tax from her salary, although a computer search (which was not made) would have revealed that the arrears had already been paid. This was held to be negligent.

The position is much the same in English law. In *General Cleaning Contractors* v *Christmas* [1953] AC 180 the claimant was a window cleaner who was injured when the lower sash of a window suddenly fell. He claimed that his employers had been negligent in not instituting a system of precautions to prevent this from happening. The defence put forward by the employers was that the trade took no such precautions. Lord Reid said: 'even if it were proved that it is the general practice to neglect this danger, I would hold that it ought not to be neglected and that precautions should be taken' because the danger was so obvious, and because although it was not clear exactly what precautions could be taken, it was apparent that the problem could very easily be solved, e.g., by wedging the window.

It follows from *General Cleaning Contractors* v *Christmas* that there is scope for a court to decide that failure to use also encompasses failure to invent or modify a computer system to prevent harm might amount to negligence if the invention or modification would be simple to effect. In order to decide whether a reasonable man would make such an invention or modification, it is necessary to balance the seriousness of the potential loss, the likelihood of its occurrence, and the expense of invention or modification. It should, however, be noted that in the cases that establish this principle[44] there was in each case a precaution that could have been taken that would *certainly* have prevented the claimant's loss. Whether the courts would be prepared to hold that a failure to innovate a system which *might* prevent loss (e.g., an expert system) amounts to negligence remains a matter for speculation.[45]

In areas where the new technology has already provided some new service, the question of whether a failure to use it amounts to negligence is greatly

---

44. E.g. *Paris* v *Stepney Borough Council* [1951] AC 367; *Bolton* v *Stone* [1951] AC 850.
45. See further *Midgen* v *Chase Manhattan Bank* (1981) 32 UCC Rep 937.

exercising the minds of practitioners. For example, is it negligent for a solicitor not to use a legal database when advising a client? The answer to this question is probably 'no', if the matter is a straightforward one. If the matter is complex, or is in an area where the law is constantly being modified, then it would seem likely that a solicitor would be negligent if he did not either use a database or take counsel's opinion. This again must remain a matter for speculation until the courts have pronounced on it. It is, however, known that many firms of solicitors are insisting that work is checked in this way before it goes out to clients.

3.6 CONCLUSION

As yet the English courts have not been called upon to decide the negligence issues raised in this chapter. The problems, however, lie not so much in the technology as in the application of existing principles to facts that are entirely novel and which have few conceptual similarities with the kind of facts the judiciary is accustomed to encounter. This need not be an insoluble problem; its solution requires the education of the legal profession not merely in how to use the new technology but also in how it works. A lawyer who is entirely ignorant of the processes involved in the creation and running of software can hardly be expected to understand how the principles of negligence, or indeed any other rules of law, should be applied to it. In *Ministry of Housing* v *Sharp* [1970] 2 QB 223 Salmon LJ referring to a proposal to computerise the Land Registry, said, 'Computers might produce an inaccurate certificate without negligence on the part of anyone'. As we have seen, this proposition is unlikely to be true, and the number of judges who would support it is significantly smaller than in 1970.

CHAPTER FOUR

Patent Protection for Computer-Related Inventions

Tim Press

4.1 AN OVERVIEW OF THE PATENT SYSTEM

4.1.1 The United Kingdom and European legal framework

Patent protection in the United Kingdom is governed by the Patents Act 1977 and rules made under it relating to the procedure for obtaining patents.

The Patents Act 1977 was passed in order to implement the European Patent Convention (the 'EPC'), to which the United Kingdom and most major European countries, including all the then members of the EEC, were signatories. The Convention provides for harmonisation of all major aspects of domestic patent law of the signatory States and also provides for the setting up of the European Patent Office (the 'EPO') to grant European patents. The national systems of granting patents via national patent offices remained in force, although patents granted at the national level were subject to the newly harmonised patent laws.

The EPO is concerned solely with the granting of patents. An applicant makes an application to the EPO (via a national patent office) indicating which convention States protection is desired in (the fees are lower if fewer States are designated). The application is examined within the EPO, and EPO examiners decide whether a patent should issue. But any patent that is eventually granted takes effect as if it were a bundle of national patents granted by the domestic patent offices of each of the designated States. So proceedings to restrain acts of infringement would be commenced before the

German courts if the acts were committed in Bonn and the English courts if the acts were committed in Liverpool. Any remedy would only cover the territory of that court, so the English injunction would only operate within the United Kingdom and any enquiry as to damages ordered by the UK court would only cover acts of infringement carried out within the UK.[1]

The UK part of a patent granted by the EPO and designating the United Kingdom is referred to as a European patent (UK). After grant, subject to a nine-month opposition period, all influence of the EPO over a patent ceases and this applies to challenges to the validity of or applications to amend patents after grant, which are decided by national courts or patent offices just as they would be for domestically granted patents, as well as to issues of infringement. It is possible for the UK part of a European patent to be revoked whilst the Swedish or Spanish parts remain in force and perfectly enforceable in those jurisdictions. Of course, the basis for granting and revoking the domestic patents will be the same as that applied by the EPO because the provisions of the Treaty provide for harmonisation of the key principles.

Thus in theory, when matters relating to the validity or infringement of the German part of a European patent are considered by the German courts, the same considerations will be applied as when the same matters are considered in relation to the UK part of the same European patent by the English (or Northern Irish or Scottish) courts or the UK Patent Office. In practice there is not as much consistency as might be desired. Not only are the procedures whereby validity and infringement are considered (for example, rules relating to evidence and disclosure of documents) very different in the different States, but the respective histories of national patent law against which the Treaty-inspired current domestic legal provisions are construed are quite different.

In the case of issues of validity, there is a source of moderation between the EPC States in the decisions arising from the appeals procedure of the EPO. The Patents Act 1977 expressly allows reference to be made to the EPC in matters of interpretation and the courts have shown themselves quite willing to pay careful heed to decisions of the Technical Boards of Appeal of the EPO when the validity of UK patents or European patents (UK) is in issue. However, in the case of issues of infringement, although the EPC lays down a general definition there is no supranational body with jurisdiction to decide issues of infringement or review domestic decisions. There has indeed been considerable debate concerning whether the provisions of the Patents Act 1977 relating to infringement as interpreted by the UK courts comply with

---

1. Pursuant to the European Convention on Judgments and Jurisdiction, there are limited circumstances where issues of infringement of a national patent forming part of a European patent granted in one country can be litigated in another. Specifically, these are, firstly, where a summary remedy can be granted and, secondly, where the dispute between the parties concerns more than one of the national patents granted pursuant to a European patent and the infringing articles are the same. Issues of validity must always be litigated in the national courts of the country for the relevant part of the European patent. This has lead to great difficulties — see *Expandable Grafts Partnership and ors* v *Boston Scientific BV and ors* (CA, The Hague) [1999] FSR 352 and *Coin Controls Ltd* v *Suzo International (UK) Ltd and ors* [1997] FSR 660.

the EPC. Decisions from other States (notably Germany) have been considered by the UK courts in relation to this issue, but German decisions are no more authoritative than French or Swedish ones in this regard, so there is no authority to say which EPC State has 'got it right'.

It must be stressed that the EPO is not a creature of the EC and decisions of its tribunals do not have the same force as decisions of the European Court of Justice. Nevertheless decisions from the EPO will be referred to in this chapter and are of great weight in practice. The legislative outline is in place (in the EPC and the Act) to enable the creation of genuine European patents covering the whole of the EC ('Community patents') but the scheme has not been implemented.[2]

4.1.2   International considerations

Beyond the European system noted above, there is a system of international conventions in the field of patents covering essentially all the industrialised countries of the world.

(a)   The Paris Convention[3] allows for the nationals of one Convention country to be granted patent protection in any other. Most importantly, it provides for an application filed in one State to give priority to subsequent applications, based on that first filing, made in any Convention country provided the subsequent applications are made within one year from the first.

(b)   The Patent Co-Operation Treaty allows for an 'international application' to be made at a 'receiving office' which will generally be the applicant's national patent office. An applicant can ask for an 'international search' to be carried out in respect of an application, the results of which will be used in subsequent prosecution proceedings in the various jurisdictions.

These provisions are of course of immense importance in enabling effective worldwide protection to be obtained without excessive costs having to be incurred at an early stage when an invention's true value may not be apparent. Patent applications will still ultimately have to be prosecuted in all States (or supranational granting bodies such as the EPO) where protection is required, but the inventor has a year to decide whether the invention is of value and where protection should be sought, and search fees may be reduced.

This chapter will also consider aspects of the law relating specifically to computer-related inventions from the United States. The US and European practices represent two different approaches, and other patent laws often tend to follow one or other model. It should further be noted that, whilst differences within the problem areas (and computer-related inventions are a problem area) between patent laws are interesting, patent law is an area where there is considerable congruence at the level of general principles between the laws of the countries of the world.

---

2. This lack of a genuinely unified European patent system is generally regarded as unsatisfactory and change may be on the horizon — see 'The Future', at 4.5.
3. The International Convention for the Protection of Industrial Property.

4.1.3   The nature of patentable inventions

Patents granted by most countries or bodies now follow a similar form. First, they set out information about the inventor, the owner and the history of applications and dates leading up to the grant of the patent. There will then be a descriptive part forming the bulk of the patent in which the invention is explained. Lastly, there will be the numbered claims where the inventor sets out precisely what the monopoly covers. In deciding whether a patent is infringed, one looks at the claims and asks the question 'does what is complained of fall within the scope of what is described in the claims'. The description can be used to provide definition to or resolve ambiguities in the claims. The precise latitude allowed in interpreting the scope of the claims varies from jurisdiction to jurisdiction.

The claims and their precise wording are thus central to the patent system. In many cases where an inventor disagrees with the decision of a patent office, the disagreement is not about whether a patent should be granted but about the precise scope of the claims that should be allowed. Patent examiners are naturally concerned that the monopoly granted should not be wider than the law permits, whereas from the inventor's point of view, the broader the claims the better.

Claims may describe machines, articles, materials or processes for doing or making things. The claims to patents are arranged in series (normally only one or two of them), each headed by an 'independent claim'. All non-independent claims in a series incorporate by reference the description of a product, process or whatever from an earlier claim in the series and add further elements which serve to narrow down the scope of the claim. Thus, for example, claim 2 of a (hypothetical) patent might be worded thus: 'A cigarette rolling machine according to claim 1 in which the main shaft rotates at above 2,000 rpm'.

The purpose of the explanatory part is to enable the invention (as claimed in the claims) to be carried out by any person reasonably skilled in the area of technology in question — to teach how to do it. This teaching is considered part of the quid pro quo for the granting of the patent monopoly: an inventor can either try to keep his technology secret or apply for a patent, but if the latter course is adopted the invention must be explained. The explanation is assumed to be of benefit to society by advancing the general corpus of knowledge available to other researchers who may use it to make further advances. It appears beyond doubt that the pace of technological development is hastened in some instances by the publication of matter in patent specifications. Whether the public benefit in each case justifies the monopoly granted is of course another matter.

The need for teaching in a patent is enforced by virtue of a rule in most jurisdictions (including Europe and the United States) that any claim in a patent that is not sufficiently well taught is invalid. Lack of adequate teaching is a not uncommon ground for objection to a patent. Apart from this issue of 'internal validity', for a patent to be granted the invention claimed in the claims has to be:

(a) a patentable invention;

(b) new; and

(c) not obvious, that is containing an inventive step.

These concepts will be discussed below, particularly the concept of patentable inventions, in which area the status of computer-related inventions has been a cause of much debate.

4.2 PATENTS FOR COMPUTER-RELATED INVENTIONS IN DETAIL

4.2.1 An overview of the problem

The precise scope of what is a patentable invention is an important issue because, traditionally, patents have been granted for industrially useful things such as new machines, chemical compounds and materials and processes for making such things or otherwise achieving a useful result. A computer program of itself is not, to many minds, such a thing. We tend to use the term 'computer program' to describe a sequence of instructions to a computer in the abstract sense, much as we talk of a novel or play as an abstract entity which is separate from the book (disk) it is recorded on or any particular performance (reading, running) of it. The example below illustrates a computer-related invention, and the distinction between that and a computer program.

In 1970 Albert and John Carter invented the 'nudge' feature on fruit machines.[4] Claim 1 of their patent read:

A coin-operated ... gaming machine ..., wherein at least one drum ... displays at least two symbols and this or each such drum has associated therewith ... an adjustment button or mechanism the operation of which after the machine has been played, causes the respective drum ... to be indexed to display on the combination line another symbol which was previously visible to the player but not on the combination line and which thereby completes or contributes to a winning combination.

Note that this claim specifies a machine with reference to what it does rather than how it does it. The body of the patent sets out a method of achieving this using electromechanical means (switches, relays and so on). By the time the patent expired, fruit machines operated under microprocessor control. In such machines the nudge was achieved by the nudge button sending a message to the microprocessor which arranged for signals to be sent to the stepping electric motor for the relevant reel which turned so as to rotate the reel by exactly one position. Such computerised machines still infringed the patent and their manufacturers paid royalties under it.

The nudge feature is an example of an invention that can be achieved by computer or mechanical means. Apart from the provision of a nudge button

---

4. UK patent 1,292,712.

and suitable information on the machine, in modern machines the nudge feature is contained solely in the program that runs on the microprocessor, whereas at the time of its invention it was hard-wired by the use of conventional electromechanical components. This patent also provides a good example of the importance of careful claim drafting in ensuring that economically useful protection will last for the legal duration of the patent.

There is generally no problem with claims of the above type, that is claims to machines or processes that happen to be implemented with the aid of a suitably programmed computer. The important point to such inventions is generally not the development of the program but the realisation that a better (more useful, cheaper to make, etc.) machine results from making the machine behave in that particular way. All the program does is take a series of inputs (numbers), operate upon them in a certain way and produce an output (different numbers). Consider a program used to control, say, a welding arc by relating the voltage to various measured parameters of the arc. If the method of controlling the arc was new, a patent would be granted. The same program could be used to operate a food processor or toy car if the same mathematical relationship was useful in those areas, but the patent wouldn't cover those uses nor would previous uses in food processors or toy cars invalidate the welding equipment patent.

In fact a program on its own is nothing more than a representation, in the form of instructions how to carry it out, of a mathematical formula or relationship[5] — which could be applied in any number of ways. Such descriptions of processes are also referred to as 'algorithms' and this term has formed a central feature of discussions of patentability of computer-related inventions. Prior to the invention of computers it had always been held that scientific discoveries, laws of nature, mathematical formulae and the like were not suitable subject matter for patents — the formula or discovery had to be applied and only the particular application developed could be patented.

Broadly speaking it is still the position that mathematical formulae and so on are not patentable, but great difficulties have been experienced in applying this apparently simple concept in the field of many computer-related inventions. In the examples given above the distinction between the program/ algorithm and its application is quite clear. But cases arise where the distinctions are more blurred and this is particularly so where the subject matter of the invention is not an obvious industrial process such as welding but is itself of a more abstract nature, such as methods of analysing electronic data, or an aspect of computer design, architecture or organisation. The distinction between a fruit machine and the mathematical relationships underpinning its operation is clear. The distinction between a computer and the logical and mathematical rules by which it operates is altogether more tricky. What is a computer other than an assembly of things obeying logical (mathematical) relationships? Yet patents are granted for developments in computer technology.

---

5. It must be understood that this term is used in a broad sense to cover matters of logic as well as arithmetic. Many modern programs are far too complex for a precise mathematical description of their operation to be written down, but at least in theory one does exist.

4.2.2   The European position

4.2.2.1   The basic provisions of the EPC   The fundamental provisions of the EPC are found in art. 52(1), which states that 'European patents shall be granted for any inventions which are susceptible of industrial application, which are new and which involve an inventive step'. Article 57 further states that 'An invention shall be considered as susceptible of industrial application if it can be made or used in any kind of industry, including agriculture'.

Article 52(2) provides exclusions to patentability:

> The following in particular shall not be regarded as inventions within the meaning of paragraph 1:
>   (a)   discoveries, scientific theories and mathematical methods;
>   (b)   aesthetic creations;
>   (c)   schemes, rules and methods for performing mental acts, playing games or doing business, and programs for computers;
>   (d)   presentations of information.

The scope of the exclusions is explained (not as helpfully as might have been hoped) by art. 52(3):

> The provisions of paragraph 2 shall exclude patentability of the subject-matter or activities referred to in that provision only to the extent to which a European patent application or a European patent relates to such subject-matter or activities as such.

It had been suggested that anything was capable of being an 'invention' for the purposes of art. 52(1) EPC (although the exclusions of art. 52(2) would then have to be applied). The case of *Genentech Inc's Patent* [1989] RPC 147, CA, stated that this was not so, it being held that the word invention' in the similar provisions of s. 1 of the Patents Act 1977 had to be given a meaning and that some things were not 'inventions' even though they fell outside the scope of the art. 52(2) exclusions.[6]

The EPC does not elucidate on what a claim for a computer program is or indeed define a 'computer program' at all. It can be seen, however, that the restriction applies only to programs, not software in the more general sense. As will be seen, the specific 'computer program as such' exclusion is by no

---

6. The court were concerned not to allow a claim drafted so as to cover a wide field of which the innovation actually made by the inventor was only a small part. It was no doubt influenced by concern (not so prominent following *Biogen Inc. v Medeva plc* [1997] RPC 1) that in the EPC and the UK Act the provisions which require claims to be 'supported by' the description cannot found applications to revoke after grant. The claim was for a known product when made by any process of genetic engineering, the inventors having been the first to find a way to make the product by a genetic engineering process. The majority held that the applicant had not 'invented' everything within the scope of these wide claims, so they were not for 'inventions' at all. It has also been held in the EPO decision *Christian Franceries/Traffic regulation* [1988] 2 EPOR 65, that the list of what is not an invention in art. 52(2) is not exhaustive.

means the only hurdle in the way of protection for computer-related inventions.

4.2.2.2 The EPO Guidelines The EPO issues guidelines to its examiners which set out the practice adopted on the examination of claims. These discuss the exclusions to patentability in chapter IV section 2 and are summarised below.

(a) It is observed that:

... the exclusions [of art. 52(2)] are either abstract (discoveries, scientific theories etc.) or non-technical (e.g., aesthetic creations or presentations of information).[7]

... an invention within the meaning of art. 52(1) must be both of a concrete and a technical character.

(b) When considering whether the subject matter of an application is an invention within the meaning of art. 52(1) the form of the claims should be disregarded. The examiner should identify what the 'real contribution to the art' made by the invention is, and if this 'is not of a technical character' there is no invention. The example given is of a known thing with a new painted design on it which serves only an aesthetic purpose, which would be non-patentable as making only an aesthetic contribution, although the article as a whole might be industrially useful.

(c) The basic test of whether there is an invention within the meaning of art. 52(1) is separate and distinct from the questions of industrial applicability, novelty or inventiveness.

(d) Mathematical methods are not patentable. However, a machine that operates in accordance with such methods may be patentable provided it has 'a novel technical feature to which a product claim can be directed'.[8]

(e) Aesthetic creations are by definition articles having aspects which are other than technical and the appreciation of which is essentially subjective. If an aesthetic effect is obtained by a technical structure or other technical means, the means of obtaining it may be patentable. A book characterised by a technical feature of the binding may be patentable, as may a substance characterised by technical features serving to produce a special effect with regard to scent or flavour.

(f) The 'computer program' exclusion should be dealt with in exactly the same way as the other exclusions and no distinction should be made between data processing operations carried out by means of a computer program and those carried out by means of special circuits. An example is given of a method of organising fast and slow memories in a computer so as to increase

---

7. The case of *Bosch/Electronic computer components* [1995] EPOR 587 (discussed at 4.2.2.4) has modified this position somewhat.

8. It can be seen that this appears to breach the admonition to consider novelty separately. It is submitted that to comply with the spirit of the guidelines as a whole, the 'real contribution to the art' should be considered for technical content, not what is novel.

working memory whilst maintaining speed, i.e., virtual memory. This might be patentable as having a technical effect.

It can be seen that the concept of technical methods or a technical effect has been abstracted from the EPC and used as the basis for the whole approach. The EPC itself does not refer to the need for technical content. It is not clear from the decisions (see 4.2.2.3 below) whether the technical content test is interpreted so as to conform to relevant terms of the EPC or vice versa. The operation of this scheme is illustrated in the cases heard by the Technical Boards of Appeal and Enlarged Board of Appeal. It should be noted that these bodies do not operate the same system of binding precedent that English or US courts do. Rather they develop an interpretation of the EPC and interpret the facts of each case in accordance with that. The reasoned decisions can therefore seem rather declaratory in tone, although they are commendably short.

The Guidelines are prepared to assist examiners in assessing claims for patentability. They represent a synthesis of the decided cases of the Technical Boards of Appeal, but tend to lag behind more recent developments. In particular, the Guidelines current at the time of going to press (July 2000) do not take into account the decision in *IBM's Application* [1999] RPC 563, discussed at 4.2.2.3 below. It is in any event necessary to look at the cases in some detail.

4.2.2.3   The basic approach — 'technical content' needed   The discussion of patents for computer-related inventions before the EPO has largely concentrated on the concept that patentable inventions must be 'technical'. This concept is difficult to explain, but the first clear explanation of the requirement for technical content was given in *IBM/Document abstracting and retrieving* [1990] EPOR 99:

> Whatever their differences [they being the things excluded under art. 52(2) EPC] these exclusions have in common that they refer to activities which do not aim at any direct technical result but are rather of an abstract and intellectual character.

The decision goes on to point out that the Rules of the EPC require a claim to have 'technical features' and therefore that the EPC requires inventions to have a 'technical character. Reference to the patent law histories of the contracting States is made, apparently to assist in construing a technical character as being a fundamental principle underlying the concept of what is an invention and the exclusions of art. 52(2).

The EPO generally approaches the problem of technical content by deciding whether or not the real contribution to the art of the alleged invention falls in any of the excluded areas, but has also found technical content by analogy with products, processes or areas of industry which have previously been established as of a technical nature, or which are felt to be clearly of a technical nature.

Vicom/Computer-related invention [1987] EPOR 74, is the leading decision in the area of computer-related inventions. The claims concerned a general method and apparatus for processing digitised images within a computer in particular ways. The process consisted of operating on the data representing an image mathematically so as to alter the nature of the image in some way, for example sharpening or smoothing out edges. It was accepted that the process could be carried out by suitably programming a known computer. The Examining Division rejected the claims but the Technical Board of Appeal remitted them for further consideration. It was held that:

(a)   Manipulating an image was an industrial process, which could be used, for example, in the design field.

(b)   Just because the claims might be drafted in terms of an algorithm, that did not make them unpatentable if the invention related to a *technical process*. The distinction was drawn between claims for 'a method for digitally filtering data' (which would be unpatentable as being merely for a mathematical method), and the invention as claimed. In the former case, no physical entity is represented by the data whereas in the latter it is (an image).

(c)   Similarly, a claim to a *technical process* carried out under the control of a computer program is not a claim to a computer program *as such*.

(d)   A known computer which is set up to operate a new computer program cannot be said to form part of the state of the art (i.e., lack novelty).

(e)   It would not be appropriate to draw a distinction between an invention when carried out in hardware and the same invention when carried out in software when the choice between the two ways of doing it would be based on technical and economic considerations unrelated to the inventive concept as such.

In *Koch and Sterzel/X-ray apparatus* [1988] 2 EPOR 72, there was no problem in finding a link with a real world object of a technical character, but the question arose of how any technical features should be related to the teaching of the invention. The claim was for standard X-ray apparatus which was linked to and controlled by a data processing unit. This unit stored information about different exposure parameters and used that information to set the tube voltages so as to obtain the optimum desired exposure. Clearly an X-ray apparatus is a technical thing, but the opponents to the patent cited German authority to the effect that the main area of the teaching of the patent had to be of a technical nature (i.e., not relate to unpatentable matter such as computer programs or mathematical methods). They argued that in this case no technical effect was achieved because any technical effect occurred after the operation of the program. The opponents also argued that *Vicom/Computer-related invention* [1987] EPOR 74 was wrong and effectively allowed any computer when programmed to evade the exclusion of computer programs. The Technical Board of Appeal held that:

(a)   The German approach did not conform with the EPC and was fraught with the difficulty of identifying what the essential contribution to the invention's success is. If the invention defined in a claim 'uses technical means' it is not a claim to a computer program 'as such', regardless of whether it also contains non-patentable matter such as computer programs.

(b)   When the technical effect occurs is irrelevant, so long as the invention does produce a technical effect.[9]

(c)   A program used in a general purpose computer is a computer program as such. But if the program controls the operation of the computer 'so as to technically alter its functioning', the unit consisting of the program and computer combined may be a patentable invention. In the present case, the technical effect was the manner of operation of the X-ray apparatus.

(d)   The invention claimed was patentable whether or not the apparatus without the program formed part of the state of the art.

This case illustrates the difference between deciding whether what is new about the alleged invention is excluded (not the correct test under the guidelines) and looking at the invention as a whole (the 'real contribution to the art' of the guidelines). In a narrow sense the novelty resided in a computer program, but the real contribution to the art was a way of operating an X-ray machine. In the language of the decision, the program altered the functioning of the computer technically. One can attempt to give an everyday language explanation of the 'real contribution to the art' as 'the thing people got from the invention that they didn't have before and that was ultimately useful to them', although this should not be taken as a strict statement of the law.

Until the 1999 case of *IBM's Application* [1999] RPC 563, it was the position that claims relating to computer programs were only allowed when cast in the form of a claim to a computer or a method of doing something using a computer. It was held that claims to the program itself, or the program when recorded on a 'carrier' (i.e. a disk or memory chip) were claims to computer programs 'as such' and therefore not patentable. In this decision the Technical Board found that it was not consistent with the reasoning in cases such as *Vicom* and *Koch and Sterzel* to limit claims to computer programs in this way. The Board's position on this point is set out below:

> In the view of the Board, a computer program claimed by itself is not excluded from patentability if the program, when running on a computer or loaded into a computer, brings about, or is capable of bringing about, a technical effect which goes beyond the 'normal' physical interactions between the program (software) and the computer (hardware) on which it is run.
>
> 'Running on a computer' means that the system comprising the computer program plus the computer carries out a method (or process) which may be of the kind according to claim 1.[10]

---

9. A very similar problem caused somewhat more difficulty in the United States — see the discussion of *Parker* v *Flook* (1978) 473 US 584 in 4.2.3.2.
10. The claims related to a system for use in a windowing environment which re-arranged the information on underlying windows so that it could all be seen in the part of the underlying window still visible. Claim 1 was for 'A method in a data processing system for displaying information, wherein . . .'.

'Loaded into a computer' means that the computer programmed in this way is capable of or adapted to carrying out a method which may be of the kind according to claim 1 and thus constitutes a system (or device or apparatus) which may be of the kind according to claim 5.[11]

. . . Furthermore, the Board is of the opinion that with regard to the exclusion under Article 52(2) and (3) of the EPC, it does not make any difference whether a computer program is claimed by itself or as a record on a carrier (following decision T 163/85 BBC/Colour television signal, as cited above).

The main claim which the Examiner had objected to read:

8.   A computer program element comprising: computer program code means to make the computer execute procedure to display information within a first window in a display; and responsive to the obstruction of a portion of said first window information by a second window, to display in said first window said portion of said information that had been obscured by said second window, including moving said portion of said information that had been obscured by said second window to a location within said first window that is not obscured by said second window.

9.   A computer program element as claimed in claim 8 embodied on a computer readable medium.

The other EPO cases that are referred to in this chapter should be read with *IBM's Application* (1999) in mind. The patent claims involved will have been framed so as not to offend the erstwhile requirement that program-related claims be drafted as claims to computers which operate in a specific way. But the relaxing of this requirement has not changed the underlying principle by which technical content is assessed: the program itself still has to have a technical character[12] and be capable of being run on a machine so as to achieve that effect. Thus the Technical Board observed:

9.6   A computer program product which (implicitly) comprises all the features of a patentable method (for operating a computer, for instance) is therefore in principle considered as not being excluded from patentability under Article 52(2) and (3) of the EPC.

It is self-evident that a claim to such a computer program product must comprise all the features which assure the patentability of the method it is intended to carry out when being run on a computer. When this computer program product is loaded into a computer, the programmed computer constitutes an apparatus which in turn is able to carry out the said method.

The main effect of this decision is thus on the way in which claims to inventions can be drawn, rather than on the inventions for which protection

---

11. Claim 5 was for 'A data processing system for displaying information, wherein . . .'.
12. In this case the technical content was an effect on a computer's display.

in some form can be achieved. This is not insignificant, as it will affect the scope of activities that will infringe the patent granted. But a claim for a program which is expressed purely in terms of abstract numerical or logical inputs and outputs will still fail as having no technical character, even if a program having that effect could be incorporated into a system which did have a technical character.

It should follow from this decision that claims to data structures can similarly be made. Such claims would not have to refer to a machine or method which operates on the data, provided that the data structure is adapted to be useful in a technical way when operated on by a known computer. So far, claims that have been pursued before the Technical Boards have addressed machines or methods that make use of a data structure, rather than the data structure itself. The door would now appear to be open for technically useful data structures to be claimed as such in Europe. Data structures have been patented in the US — see 4.2.3.5 below.

The precise limits of the requirement for technical content are discussed below. The concept of 'technically altering the functioning' of a computer is (relatively) easy to apply where the properties claimed for the computer/ program combination relate to the effect of the combination on the outside world, for example the exposure times of the X-ray tubes in the above invention. But where the claimed properties of the combination are matters of the internal working of the computer, the 'technical effect' test is more difficult to apply. Which aspects of computer technology are to be considered 'technical' and which are not?

4.2.2.4 The internal operation of computers In *IBM/Data processor network* [1990] EPOR 91, the claim concerned a data processing system comprising a number of data processors forming the nodes of a communications network. In the invention claimed the processors are so arranged that a transaction request originating at one node may be split up and part or parts of the transaction carried out at another node. The claims specified in general terms a method of carrying this out but did not give any detail of the computer programming structures used to achieve the method. The Technical Board of Appeal decided that 'the coordination and control of the internal communication between programs and data files held at different processors in a data processing system ... is to be regarded as solving a problem which is essentially technical'. Again no attempt was made in the decision to state any general rule defining what is and isn't 'technical', which was treated as simply a matter of fact to be decided in each instance.

In *Bosch/Electronic Computer Components* [1995] EPOR 587 the claims covered a 'device for monitoring computer components' which was capable of re-setting the computer's processor. The contents of the computer's volatile memories were compared with a pattern contained in non-volatile memory to establish whether, when the computer's processor had been re-set, it was the result of the device or an operation of the manual re-set circuit. On the basis of this decision, the re-set procedure could be made significantly shorter than would otherwise be possible because it would not be necessary to re-load all programs into memory. This process was held to have the necessary technical content by applying the reasoning of *Vicom*.[13]

It is comparatively easy to understand why the Board was prepared to classify both of the above inventions as having a technical character, although difficult to define a clear dividing line between such 'hardware' inventions and programs as such which effect the operation of a computer. In *IBM/Computer-related invention* [1990] EPOR 107, the claim was for a method of displaying one of a set of predetermined messages in response to events occurring to or within the computer. The method is achieved on a known computer, and involves using tables containing words used in the messages from which each message is built up by a 'message build program'. The problem of extracting any theoretical basis from EPO decisions is illustrated by quoting from the Board's reasons:

> Generally the Board takes the view that giving visual indications automatically about conditions prevailing in an apparatus or system is basically a technical problem.

It was held that IBM's claim, in claiming one way of overcoming such a technical problem, was not to a computer program as such even though the basic idea resides in a computer program.[14]

4.2.2.5 Data processing and data structures As with *IBM/Computer-related invention* [1990] EPOR 107, where data manipulation is concerned the approach has been to cast around for some real-world, non-digital analogies in looking for technical content.

In *Vicom/Computer-related invention* [1987] EPOR 74, the claim dealt with the manipulation of digital images. Although the Board talks of an image as a 'physical entity' and as a 'real world object', it is made clear that an image stored in any form, hard copy or electronic, will be regarded as a physical entity. The crux of the decision was the finding that images could be used in the design field, which was an industrial area. It was this point which enabled the Board to find the necessary technical content. It appears that the fact that images could be used in the *industrial* design field was important to this finding, although of course the invention would be equally applicable to images whose sole purpose was aesthetic.

In the light of subsequent cases, the 'real world' test needs elucidating. The reference to the 'real world' is in the context of distinguishing between digital

---

13. In *Bosch* it was also held that notwithstanding the provisions of the Patent Co-Operation Treaty which relieve the requirement to search in the field of computer programs, if an office was equipped (i.e., had the necessary personnel) to search or examine against computer programs then it should do so. This illustrates an acceptance that computer programs can lie at the heart of inventions that are nevertheless potentially patentable.

14. The finding on the facts of this relatively early case can be criticised. In subsequent decisions less reliance is placed upon drawing analogies with non-computer things that have been found before to be technical. If the rules are applied to these facts, it can be seen that numerical error messages, where the operator has to look the number up in a manual to find out the error, were known. The real contribution is an automated way of performing this looking-up operation, which is a mental process — an excluded thing.

data which represent numbers with no meaning (clearly not technical things) and data which represent numbers which represent something more, something outside the confines of the purely theoretical. It is clear that real world content is not enough: in addition the real world impact of the invention must have a technical character.

In *Sohei/General purpose management system* [1996] EPOR 253 Claim 1 was directed to 'A computer system for plural types of independent management including at least financial and inventory management ...'. A common 'transfer slip' is displayed on a screen from which entries can be made affecting all of the different 'types of management', a 'memory' is provided for which holds data in various 'files' and 'processing means' are provided for which operate on inputs, outputs and data. Claim 2 was directed to a 'method for operating a general-purpose computer management system' along very similar lines.

The reasoning of the Board in finding (as they did) technical content in *Sohei* is at times impenetrable. Firstly, they did not regard the requirement for financial and inventory elements as restricting the claims to just those elements, and therefore when considering technical content considered the claims as covering different types of generalised management. This assisted them in not raising an objection on the grounds that the claims were directed to a method of doing business. The crux of this part of the decision is that if an invention can cover a number of fields, some of which are excluded and some not, it is a patentable invention. The example of management of construction work and workers is given as comparable with managing manufacturing processes (technical), whereas other kinds of management would be of a more abstract character and therefore excluded as business methods. This echoes the reasoning in *Vicom* where the fact that images could serve technical as well as non-technical purposes was significant.

The Board also had to deal with the 'computer program as such' exclusion. The basis of its decision here was that the 'transfer slip' amounted to a 'user interface' and as such was patentable as having technical content. They held that the provision of this 'interface' constituted neither only presentation of information nor only computer programs as such, because it allowed two kinds of systems to be combined by a common input device.

> ... it is noted that programming may be implied also in the subject matter as presently claimed. Mere programming as such would ... also be excluded from patentability by virtue of the fact that it is an activity which essentially involves mental acts. ... However, the implementation ... of the said 'interface' ... is not merely an act of programming but rather concerns a stage of activities involving technical considerations to be carried out before programming can start.

Presumably, 'before' is not to be taken literally so as to require program 'front ends' to be created before their 'back ends'. The interesting point here is that the Board held that the technical content would arise from the implementation of the user interface, in other words it was implicit in the

invention, rather than being explicitly taught in the specification. They held
that this did not matter, the result was still a technical contribution to the art.

4.2.2.6 Text processing decisions   The requirement for the real contribution
to the art to have a technical effect has been developed in a number of cases
involving text manipulation. Almost by definition, text is a set of symbols
(alphanumeric characters) whose combination as words is addressed to the
human mind, and processed by that mind in a non-technical way. The
Technical Boards have been ready to find in such cases that the real
contribution to the art lies not in any technical area but in areas such as
semantics which are the same thing as (or analogous to) a series of mental
steps.

In *IBM/Document abstracting and retrieving* [1990] EPOR 99,[15] the claim
was for a system for automatically abstracting a document and storing the
resulting abstract. The system involves comparing the words used in a
document with a dictionary held on a computer, thereby noting proper names
and the occurrence of other words which would be of assistance in charac-
terising the document, and incorporating these words in the abstract. This
information is used to assist in identifying documents in response to enquiries. It was held that (*inter alia*):

(a)   The claims were unpatentable by reason of lack of a technical
character and 'more particularly as falling within the category of schemes,
rules and methods for performing mental acts'.
(b)   The fact that technical means were used in carrying out the abstracting process did not make the process patentable, because the contribution
made to the art by the invention was not technical but purely associated with
the set of rules whereby the abstracting process was carried out.
(c)   There were no changes to the documents themselves as 'technical
entities', only changes in the electrical signals representing the information
stored. By contrast, in *Vicom* there had been a change in the image.

The last point is not made with great clarity. It appears to build upon the
finding that the abstracting process itself is not patentable as lacking technical
content by affirming that the body of documents themselves, whilst changed
as digital files by the addition of the abstracting information, are not changed
in any other way and therefore not in any technical way.

An IBM application refused for essentially the same reasons was *IBM/Text
clarity processing* [1990] EPOR 607. The invention claimed was a method of
identifying expressions in a text processing system which fell below a
determined level of 'understandability' and replacing them with more 'understandable' expressions. It was held that evaluating understandability was a
series of mental acts and that once this was given, it would have been obvious
to any skilled programmer how to instruct a computer to do it, so the real
contribution to the art was not in a technical field.

---

15. See 4.2.2.3.

Similarly in *IBM/Semantically-related expressions* [1989] 8 EPOR 454, the claim concerned a system for automatically generating a list of expressions semantically related to an input linguistic expression. It was held, as a matter of fact, that matters of semantic relationship are not technical matters. Reference to the excluded matters under art. 52 of the Convention was made by pointing out that a semantic relationship can only be found by performing mental acts. Again it was stressed that these claims were refused because the contribution to the art was found not to stray beyond the matter of identifying semantically related expressions, and that an invention directed to semantic relationships might be patentable provided a contribution was made outside the range of excluded things.

The refusals of the latter two cases are perhaps not surprising. A case which causes more difficulty is *Siemens/Character form* [1992] EPOR 69. This concerned a process for displaying on a VDU screen characters which have different forms depending on whether they are used in isolation, or at the beginning, middle or end of words, such as occur in Arabic. The process involved initially choosing the most likely form and subsequently altering the form if necessary depending on the following character. The application was initially rejected (perhaps unsurprisingly) for lack of inventive step. On appeal, the Technical Board of Appeal rejected the application on the grounds that the invention lacked technical content. *Koch and Sterzel/X-ray apparatus* [1988] 2 EPOR 72[16] was distinguished on the basis that there no technical means were used but the effect was technical.

Here, the problem of identifying technical content is split into two parts: are technical means used to achieve a result, and if not, is the result to be achieved a technical one? On applying these tests it was held that the claim was directed to a non-technical procedure in that all that was achieved by the program was the retrieval of a character in one form and its replacement in another form. These two pieces of data were held to differ 'only in the information they contain, not technically'. Furthermore, the purpose of the procedure (the problem to be overcome) was of a non-technical nature as it related to improving the 'mental registering of the character' by the viewer of the VDU.

In contrast to these decisions where the text processing application was rejected, the application in *IBM/Editable document form* [1995] EPOR 185 succeeded before the Technical Board. The application claimed a method of transforming text stored in one editable form to another (basically, translating word processing formats). On appeal the claim was amended to restrict its scope to documents stored as digital data and was allowed. The technical features of text processing were said to include 'printer control items' and so transforming these from one system to another was a method having a technical character. The objection overcome had been that the method for transforming the documents was no more than a mental act.

This decision apparently allowed a claim for a method of conversion between word processor file formats. But the types of text file referred to are

---

16. See 4.2.2.3.

said to contain formatting information that substantially overlaps with the printer control codes which would be used to direct a line or character type. of printer (as opposed to a page printer such as a laser printer). It was this close relationship with the control of a piece of everyday hardware that made the claims allowable.

An analysis of these text processing decisions reveals that the reasons (or possible reasons) for rejection were related to the 'mental acts' exclusion. The exception is *Siemens/Character form* [1992] EPOR 69 from which it is not entirely clear whether the ground for rejection was non-technicality as a mental act or because the claim was for a computer program as such (the Technical Board described claim 1 as being for 'an idea for a program').[17] It can be seen that the Technical Boards have developed a more sophisticated means for finding 'technical content' (or perhaps seeking out the lack of it) than that used in *Vicom/Computer-related invention* [1987] EPOR 74. In *Vicom* the usefulness of the images in a technical area (industrial design) appeared determinative. Documents are of course useful in all technical and non-technical industries, as are images, but that has not been sufficient.

4.2.2.7 Inventions relating to programming itself Many Decisions of the EPO have referred to the possibility that computer programs may have technical content. In all of them, it appears that the Board concerned was referring to the fact that the computer program might, when run on a computer, have a technical effect in the outside world or on the operation of the computer itself. This begs the question of whether developments in the field of computer programming itself can be patented.

In *IBM's Application* [1999] RPC 563 the Board affirmed the unreported decision *ATT/System for generating software source code*, case T 204/93. They identified its real reasoning as being that the activity of programming a computer was essentially a 'mental act'. (They needed to over-rule the decision to the extent that it relied upon the rule that computer programs, even if they had a technical character, could not be patented as such.)

The Board in *IBM* did not directly address the question of whether inventions which relate solely to the field of computer programming itself are patentable. But taking the Board's discussion of *ATT* overall, it appears that the *IBM* Board would exclude inventions which did not go outside the field of computer programming as mental acts which lack any technical character. Claims to such inventions would be refused whether they were directed to computer programs or to computer devices operating under the control of such a program.

This does not mean that claims to all aspects of programming will be unpatentable. As in *Bosch/Electronic Computer Components*,[18] programs which enhance the operation of a computer in a technical way are patentable.

---

17. In the United Kingdom, Laddie J has described the distinction between the 'mental acts' and 'computer program' exclusions as a mere matter of semantics — see the discussion of the *Fujitsu* case at 4.2.2.8.
18. See 4.2.2.4 above.

Inventions which apparently concern programming may be patentable if some technical content can be found for them.

4.2.2.8   Analysis of the EPO cases   Two routes for finding technical content in the real contribution to the art are now used:

   (a)   Are technical means used to produce a result or solve a problem? Or, alternatively,
   (b)   Does the invention produce a technical result? Applying this test to the language of *Vicom/Computer-related invention* [1987] EPOR 74 results in: Does the invention produce a technical change in the characteristics of a 'real world object'?

   And (following *Sohei/General purpose management system* [1996] EPOR 253[19]) the technical means of solution or technical problem to be overcome may be implicit, in the sense that they only occur in the implementation of the invention and may not be apparent from the invention as claimed.
   It is difficult to derive from the cases any satisfying general test for what is and is not technical content or effect. In the case of text processing it can be tentatively proposed that ways of manipulating the bytes of a text file on a mechanical basis would be patentable by analogy with the ways of manipulating the images of *Vicom*,[20] but that ways of manipulation that are based on the meaning of the text will not if there is no invention at the byte-swapping level (e.g., *IBM/Text clarity processing* [1990] EPOR 607[21]).
   This principle can be used to distinguish the finding in *Siemens/Character form* [1992] EPOR 69[22] from that in *Vicom*. Both these cases claimed processes for altering digital files, *inter alia*, to make them easier for humans to perceive. But no specific industrial use for the documents made up by the characters of *Siemens* was identified. Also, the *Siemens* invention was based upon rules of writing and depended on the characters forming words having meaning, it would be irrelevant to random text; by contrast the invention of *Vicom* could apply to any image, even an abstract one and was independent of the meaning of the image.[23] Presumably ways of manipulating images that altered the meaning of what was represented, for example by detecting grimaces and replacing them with smiles, would not be patentable as smile detection would be considered a series of mental steps based on the theories

---

19. See 4.2.2.5.
20. See 4.2.2.3.
21. See 4.2.2.6.
22. See 4.2.2.6.
23. One can also make the distinction in terms of the type of human perception required to receive the benefit of the invention. The appreciation of the lines and edges in images operated on by the *Vicom* invention is a lower-level, more fundamental human ability than the deciphering of text, which is a socially or culturally developed ability. One can extend an analogy to inventions affecting the internal operation of computers (mechanical minds), where it appears that low-level, basic features stand a greater chance of forming the subject of patentable inventions.

of human behaviour and perception.[24] To put it simply, making images or text meaningful to humans is not considered technical, whereas making them intelligible to printers (*IBM/Editable document form* [1995] EPOR 185[25]), is. Of course, both tasks can be frustratingly difficult.

In the field of computer internal operation, the reasoning discussed above is not helpful as there is no connection with the non-computer world. Any information will only have meaning to a computer and the invention will only be useful to a computer. The result of the invention will clearly be a computer, a technical thing. But the problem of identifying a technical change in it, or technical means in its achievement, remains peculiarly difficult. The most that can be said is that it appears that the problem addressed has to be a low level one, close to the hardware. Thus, the method of generating messages in response to events of *IBM/Computer related invention* [1990] EPOR 107[26] would be of general usefulness, yet its patentability was based on its use to monitor hardware-related events. (It has been noted that on its facts this decision might well go the other way if decided in recent times.) By contrast the method of generating a data file of abstracting information (a high level concept clearly in the software domain) in *IBM/Document abstracting and retrieving* [1990] EPOR 99 was not technical.

It is a fact that all manners of computer operation are the result of logical relationships between things that could be defined in terms of mathematics and carried out as a series of mental processes by a human (and should perhaps thus be excluded). Of course some things are too complex or difficult for any human to model mathematically or carry out in person. In the United Kingdom, *Fujitsu*[27] has said expressly that this is an irrelevant consideration. EPO cases such as *Sohei*, which involved computerisation of a task that could clearly have been carried out on pencil and paper, indicate that this is not a useful approach.

Sohei perhaps illustrates either a general softening of approach, or a more liberal approach in cases involving the use of computers to operate on data other than text. The lengths gone to by the Technical Board to identify technical content in that case, even looking outside the words of the patent, make a clear contrast with the text processing decisions. But the EPO still takes the (computer program as such) exclusion seriously: it will not generally concern itself with detail relating to the programming of computers, however innovative that might be, because such efforts will either make a non-technical contribution or a technical contribution to the art of computer programming, which is excluded. The reasoning in all cases involving the

---

24. Subject always to the caveat that if 'technical means' are used in the process then they may be patentable if they form part of the real contribution to the art of the invention. But general programming means do not generally form part of the real contribution to the art of a computer-related invention, see for example *Koch and Sterzel*, at 4.2.2.3, above. And if the real contribution to the art did lie in matters of programming, the claim would fail as being for a computer program or series of mental steps.
25. See 4.2.2.6.
26. See 4.2.2.4.
27. See 4.2.2.9.

application, rather than the operation, of computers tends to focus on non-computer arguments, on the real-world uses to which the data can be put. It is thus informative to look more generally at how the EPO deals with inventions for excluded things.

To give further examples not specifically related to computers, the following have been held to represent non-technical subject matter: methods of directing traffic-flow ('economic activity' according to the French text of the EPC);[28] methods of marking sound recording carriers and their packaging to avoid counterfeiting (business method);[29] a marker for facilitating the reading and playing of music (teaching method which was a method for performing mental acts);[30] a coloured jacket for flexible disks which was claimed to be writeable on, easily distinguished and to resist fingerprints (aesthetic creation and a presentation of information);[31] an automatic self-service machine in which the user could use any machine-readable card he possessed once that card had been recognised by the machine (method of doing business).[32] By way of contrast, a television signal has been held to constitute technical subject matter,[33] as has a system (incidentally, computer controlled) for controlling a queue sequence for serving customers at a number of service points.[34]

4.2.2.9 The UK perspective The terms of the EPC are directly reflected, so far as patentable inventions are concerned, in the Patents Act 1977. Section 1(2) of the Act sets out, essentially verbatim, the exclusions of art. 52(2) EPC and the 'as such' caveat of art. 52(3). The most directly relevant authorities on the interpretation of the Act are decisions from the UK courts.

There are a number of situations when UK courts are required to decide issues of the validity of patents and interpret the legislation:

(a) The validity of a patent can be put in issue in infringement proceedings.

(b) Petitions to revoke patents after grant can be made to the courts.

(c) Appeals lie to the courts from decisions of the Patent Office made during the prosecution of UK patents.

In addition to handling applications for UK patents, the Patent Office can hear applications to revoke UK patents and European patents (UK).

The UK legislative tradition in the field of patents is somewhat different from that of most other EPC countries, and in particular the concept of 'technical content' is alien to UK patent lawyers and judges. A certain

---

28. *Christian Franceries/Traffic Regulation* [1988] 2 EPOR 65, agreed with by Aldous J in *Lux Traffic Controls Ltd* v *Pike Signals Ltd* [1993] RPC 107.
29. *Stockburger/Coded distinctive mark* [1986] 5 EPOR 229.
30. *Beattie/Marker* [1992] EPOR 221.
31. *Fuji/Coloured disk jacket* [1990] EPOR 615.
32. *IBM/Card reader* [1994] EPOR 89.
33. *BBC/Colour television signal* [1990] EPOR 599.
34. *Pettersson/Queuing system* [1996] EPOR 3, where the ground of objection considered was 'scheme, rule or method of doing business'.

difficulty in understanding and applying this concept is often expressed in the judgments, although the UK courts have sought to reach decisions in conformity with those from the EPO.

In *Merrill Lynch's Application* [1989] RPC 561, the claim was for a computerised method of setting up a trading market in securities, using a known computer which could be suitably programmed by known techniques. It was held by the Court of Appeal (in accordance with the decision in *Genentech Inc's Patent* [1989] RPC 147, CA[35]) that an invention was not excluded simply because the novelty lay in an excluded thing (namely a computer program)[36] and that the claim had to be looked at as a whole. However, because *Vicom/Computer-related invention* [1987] EPOR 74[37] was followed the Court of Appeal also held that the contribution to the prior art must not itself be excluded, and in this case the result of the claimed invention was a method for doing business. Fox LJ postulated that a 'technical advance on the prior art' could nevertheless be excluded as a business method. This last comment must be qualified. In the terminology used by the EPO, as subsequently made clear in *IBM/Document abstracting and retrieving* [1990] EPOR 99,[38] advances in the field of business are not considered technical advances.

In *Gales Application* [1991] RPC 305 Aldous J held that a computer program held on a ROM chip was patentable although the program itself did nothing more than provide the computer in which it was installed with a new method of calculating square roots. The Court of Appeal reversed this, holding that differences in the physical structures holding the program were not material and that the program did not produce a novel technical effect. The approach of *IBM/Document abstracting and retrieving* was followed and it was held that the instructions embodied in the program did not represent a technical process outside the computer or a solution to a technical problem inside the computer. It was accepted that a new method for finding square roots had been discovered.

In *Wang Laboratories Inc's Application* [1991] RPC 463 the approach of the EPO was also approved of and followed, albeit in a characteristically English way.[39] There the claim was for an 'expert system' program, but was phrased to include programming a conventional computer with the program. It was held that the contribution made to the art was by the program and nothing more. In this case Aldous J complained that the meaning to be attributed to

---

35. See 4.2.2.1.
36. This had been the approach at first instance, reported at [1988] RPC 1. A similarly erroneous approach was taken and overruled in the US case of *In re Abele* discussed at 4.2.3.3.
37. See 4.2.2.3.
38. See 4.2.2.3.
39. In many aspects of patent law, the UK courts have found that the tests they apply under the Patents Act 1977 are effectively the same as those applied by the EPO and other EPC States under equivalent provisions although the words used to define the test seem starkly at variance. See for example the debate over the construction of claims addressed by Aldous J (as he then was) in *Assidoman Multipack* v *The Mead Corporation* [1995] RPC 321 and in *Kastner* v *Rizla* [1995] RPC 585, CA.

the word technical in all the various ways it was used in the EPO decisions was unclear. In his judgment he therefore avoids reliance on this concept:

The machine, the computer, remains the same even when programmed. The computer and the program do not combine together to produce a 'new computer'. They remain separate and amount to a collocation rather than a combination making a different whole. The contribution is, to my mind, made by the program and nothing more.

This attempt to Anglicise the EPO's formula was not entirely successful, the concept of a new computer' being every bit as intractable as that of a 'technical alteration of behaviour'. Whenever a computer is operating a unique program it exists in a unique electrical configuration that could in theory be measured with physical apparatus. Yet the distinction cannot be between permanent and temporary changes because that would be contrary to the sensible and necessary *Gale* test. The problem is to distinguish those aspects of computer configuration (whether permanent or temporary, 'hardware' or 'software') in which developments are deemed patentable from those that are not.

The most recent UK case is *Fujitsu Ltd's Application* [1997] RPC 608 where we see a continued divergence of interpretation between the UK courts and the Technical Boards of Appeal. The invention was for a method of generating and manipulating graphical representations of the crystal structures of known chemicals on a computer monitor to assist chemical engineers in developing new compounds with a desired functionality. The claims were refused, and this demanded comparison with *Vicom*. Whilst it is unclear what the *Vicom* board would have made of the Fujitsu claim, it is arguable that the EPO would now also refuse it. The somewhat unsophisticated finding in *Vicom* that 'manipulating images is technical' is not binding as a general principle and the EPO interpretation of technical content has progressed since that case.[40]

Aldous LJ sought to explain *Vicom* by saying that the technical contribution there was the way that the image was reproduced and that it did not mean that anything to do with image manipulation was patentable. The requirement for a 'technical contribution' as the defining ingredient of a patentable invention was difficult to reconcile with ss. 1(2)(a) and (d) of the Patents Act 1977. At first instance Laddie J had stated that whether the claims were refused as being for a 'computer program' or a 'method for performing a mental act' was a matter of mere semantics. Aldous LJ effectively approved this view by identifying the key question as 'whether the application consists of a program for a computer as such or whether it is a program for a computer

---

40. The argument would be that, assuming no technical contribution in the basic fields of crystal structure generation and image production and manipulation, what is left is the mental process of manipulating and comparing shapes one with another, which could in theory be carried out with physical models or by manual calculation. This can be seen as a higher level of processing of information derived from images than that addressed by *Vicom* — see note 23, above.

with a technical contribution' (implicitly, that a technical contribution will always mean patentability). Following *IBM's Application* [1999] RPC 563, the EPO are now *ad idem* with the Court of Appeal on this issue.

Aldous LJ also considered the 'Method for performing a mental act' exclusion, and in this respect he was at one with the Technical Boards in finding that 'Methods for performing mental acts, which means methods of the type performed mentally, are unpatentable. unless some concept of technical contribution is present' (*Fujitsu Ltd's Application* [1997] RPC 608, at 621). In the same passage Aldous LJ rejected arguments that the mental acts exclusion should only apply to acts which were actually carried out by human minds: 'A claim to a method of carrying out a calculation (a method of performing a mental act) is no more patentable when claimed as being done by a computer than when done on a piece of paper.'

As can be seen, the words used by UK judges can if closely analysed lead to a conclusion that the test applied is different from that used by the EPO. Such conclusions are to be viewed with caution in view of the frequently expressed opinion that the courts are in fact applying the same doctrine. It is submitted that the courts are doing their best to achieve results in conformity with those of the EPO whilst working within a different procedural framework and legal tradition. It is not clear that there are material differences.

The position under the 1949 Patents Act which the UK courts had to adapt from had developed along different lines. Claims for computers when programmed to perform specified functions were allowed on the basis that a computer programmed to perform a task was a machine and if that machine was novel and inventive then a patent should be granted.[41] The 1949 Act contained no specific exclusions so the courts based their reasoning upon general considerations of what an invention was. In some respects it can be seen that this approach persisted in decisions under the 1977 Act.[42] In the United States the statutory framework remains more similar to the 1949 Act and, as is demonstrated below, the US Patent and Trademark Office and Federal courts have in effect continued to develop (not always in the same direction) this type of approach.

4.2.3 The US position

4.2.3.1 The statutory provisions   The US Constitution grants Congress the power 'to promote the progress of ... useful arts, by securing for limited times to ... inventors the exclusive right to their respective ... discoveries'. Cases have interpreted 'the useful arts' to mean 'the technological arts', but not in a limiting way. Indeed, anything useful (as opposed to only of artistic or intellectual value) is considered part of the 'technological arts'.[43] This power is currently exercised by Congress in the form of the Patent Act of 1952, Title

---

41. See, e.g., *IBM Corporation's Application* [1980] FSR 564.

42. Which Act applies depends broadly upon when the patent was applied for, the provisions of the 1977 Act applying to applications made on or after 1 January 1978.

43. In *Re Musgrave* 431 F 2d 882 (1970), where the claims essentially related to a method of analysing seismic data and were held to form part of the technological arts.

35 USC. The section of particular interest from the point of view of computer-related inventions is s. 101 which states:

> Whoever invents or discovers any new and useful process, machine, manufacture, or composition of matter, or any new and useful improvement thereof, may obtain a patent therefor, subject to the conditions and requirements of this title.

The US statutory regime contains no reference to computer programs; indeed, there is no list of excluded things comparable to that contained in art. 52(2) EPC. The approach to computer programs taken by the US Patent and Trademark Office and the US Federal courts has fluctuated somewhat over the years, but has generally been to exclude fewer computer-related inventions than would be excluded under the EPC. The current position in the United States is to exclude only a narrow range of claims from patentability. It is worth considering how this position was arrived at because the arguments are of general relevance and cast an interesting sidelight in the European position.

The words of s. 101 are taken to limit what may be patented to:

(a) processes;
(b) machines;
(c) manufactures; and
(d) compositions of matter,

provided they are new and useful. In decided cases, judges and examiners do not always trouble to identify clearly which of the four headings an invention falls under, preferring instead to concentrate on whether the invention falls into a general category of things outside those allowed. This judge-defined excluded category includes mental acts and thus, by reason of arguments that should now be familiar, may exclude some computer-related inventions. It must be borne in mind that in the United States there are no statutory exclusions to worry about, let alone one for computer programs. This is probably the main reason why the scope of what is patentable in the United States is wider in many respects than that in Europe.

4.2.3.2 Early case law — a liberal approach   It has been held that a process is:

> a mode of treatment of certain materials to produce a given result. It is an act, or a series of acts, performed upon the subject matter to be transformed and reduced to a different state or thing.

These words have been explained in the light of technological developments so that the matter to be transformed may form electrical signals representing data about something.[44]

---

44. Ibid.

Gottschalk v *Benson* (1972) 409 US 63 specifically identified ideas, mental steps and discoveries of physical phenomena or laws of nature as not falling within the scope of what was patentable. Thus it was held that if a patent claim wholly pre-empts a mathematical formula used in a general purpose digital computer, then the patent is directed to the formula and therefore does not define patentable subject matter under s. 101. This decision was based upon the proposition that the formula was not patentable as a law of nature and therefore should be free for anybody to use in a computer. It was held:

The mathematical formula involved here has no substantial practical application except in connection with a digital computer, which means that if the judgment below is affirmed, the patent would wholly pre-empt the mathematical formula and in practical effect would be a patent on the algorithm itself.[45]

Gottschalk v *Benson* used the term 'algorithm' synonymously with 'mathematical formula' and defined it as a 'procedure for solving a given type of mathematical problem'.[46] Among the concerns expressed about allowing such patents was the reported incapability of the USPTO to search the literature on programs so as to discover the prior art. This concern seems to have fallen away in later cases. The Guidelines for Examination[47] in respect of computer-related inventions issued by the USPTO in February 1996 now envisage searching computer program material when assessing computer-related claims.

In *Parker* v *Flook* (1978) 437 US 584 the claim concerned a process for updating alarm limits in a chemical process involving a programmed computer.[48] However, despite stressing that the claim is to be looked at as a whole, the court decided that since the only novel thing about the invention was a formula, the claim viewed as a whole contained no patentable

---

45. The claims were directed to a process of mathematical or logical steps for converting numbers between two common formats for storing them in the binary forms used in computers, 'binary coded decimal' and 'pure binary'. Claim 8 commenced 'The method of converting signals from binary coded decimal form...'. The claims would have prevented the use of the process on any digital computer whether electrical or mechanical, but not by a human using pencil and paper.
46. Subsequent cases have favoured more general definitions and stressed that numbers in the mathematical sense are not necessary, for example quoting *Webster's New College Dictionary*: 'a step-by step procedure for solving a problem or accomplishing some end' (*In Re Iwahashi* (1989) 888 F 2d 1370), discussed further at 4.2.3.3).
47. Discussed further at 4.2.3.6.
48. In the catalytic conversion of hydrocarbons, various parameters such as temperature, pressure and flow rates are monitored and if they exceed predetermined limits an alarm is triggered. It was known that to take care of transient conditions, these 'alarm limits' required constant monitoring and sometimes updating. The process of automatically monitoring the parameters and generating alarms was also known and the court assumed that the mathematical formula used was known. What appears to have been new was the use of that particular formula for the purpose of alarm limit updating. The court was concerned that the formula contained variables yet the patent did not teach how to select any of them. An example of using a finding of non-patentable subject matter to disallow claims that appear too wide or vague?

invention. It was held that a new use of a known mathematical formula may be patented, and the discovery of a new mathematical formula cannot support a patent unless there is some other inventive concept involved in applying it. In this case use of the formula could not be said to have been totally 'pre-empted' but the claim failed nevertheless. The court expressed concern that skilful claim drafting could allow any formula to be patented by including irrelevant 'post-solution activity' in a process claim.

Diamond v Diehr (1981) 450 US 175 followed the 'claim as a whole' approach whilst allowing the claim to proceed. The claims covered a process for curing rubber moulded products. The cure has to take place at an elevated temperature and for a time which depends on the precise temperature-time history. Known methods involved measuring the temperature and making calculations, but these were not completely accurate because temperature wasn't constantly monitored. In the claimed process, temperature was continually monitored and the expected cure time recalculated using a computer so the mould could be opened at precisely the right time. The computer automatically caused the mould to open after the correct curing time. It was held that the claims here were for a new method of curing moulded rubber products, which was clearly a patentable process, and not merely claims for a process of calculating a formula. *Gottschalk v Benson* and *Parker v Flook* were distinguished on the grounds that the claims were not seeking to patent or pre-empt a formula. The warning against irrelevant 'post-solution activity' was repeated.

4.2.3.3   A restrictive approach to algorithms — Freeman-Walter-Abele   After *Gottschalk v Benson* (1972) 409 US 63, the courts applied a two-part test for establishing whether process claims were 'drawn to statutory subject matter' (i.e., whether they claimed patentable inventions). This was developed after *Diamond v Diehr* (1981) 450 US 175 into the *'Freeman-Walter-Abele'* test. The two parts of the test were set out in *In Re Abele* (1982) 684 F 2d 902 as:

1.   *(first part)*
do the claims directly or indirectly recite an algorithm, if so
2.   *(second part)*
2.1   is the algorithm applied in any manner to physical elements or process steps; and
2.2   is this application circumscribed by more than a field of use limitation or non-essential post-solution activity?

It can be seen that claims to processes are particularly liable to objection on the 'algorithm' ground in a way that claims to physical things ('machines' or 'manufactures' in the language of s. 101) are not. But many claims relating to computer-related inventions are addressed to 'machines' but delimited solely or mainly with reference to the processes carried out by the machine (for machine read computer). This contrasts with ways of claiming machines which describe the physical nature of the elements of the machine and their interconnections. A claim to a computer-related invention in the former form would be largely hardware and software independent, whereas a claim in the latter form would be limited in its scope to only certain hardware and/or software configurations. Concerns were raised at the prospect of claims to machines being drawn which did no more than implement otherwise unpatentable processes.

Prompted by such concerns, 'means plus function'[49] (also known as 'means for') claims were included within the ambit of the test.[50] This led to many computer-related inventions being refused protection because they were considered to amount to no more than mathematical processes notwithstanding that the claims were directed generally to apparatus involving computers.

In *Abele* itself the invention involved a system of computerised tomography (CAT scanning). Claim 5 (which was rejected) claimed simply a method of manipulating data followed by the display of that data. Claim 6 (accepted) was in essence claim 5 when the data concerned were X-ray attenuation data. The interpretation of *Parker v Flook* (1978) 437 US 584 made by the examiner, who held that the non-algorithm part of the claim must itself be novel and unobvious, was held to be erroneous. It was held, comparing with *Diamond v Diehr*, that 'The improvement in either case resides in the application of a mathematical formula within the context of a process which encompasses significantly more than the algorithm alone'.

In *In Re Iwahashi* (1989) 888 F 2d 1370, Rich J sought to overturn the rule that 'means for' claims should be interpreted widely for the purposes of examination.[51] The result was that a claim addressed to an 'autocorrelation unit' for use in pattern recognition (for example speech recognition) was allowable, despite the fact that the invention could have been achieved purely by programming a general purpose computer. However the claims, whilst containing a large number of 'means for' elements, also contained reference to specific hardware elements, namely ROM and RAM, in which the program was stored.

---

49. *In Re Walter* (1980) 618 F 2d 758. Section 112 ¶6 of the US Patent Act deals expressly with such claims. For the purpose of infringement, such claims only cover the actual means taught in the body of the patent and its 'reasonable equivalents', not any means that achieve the desired function, even though the wording of the claim contains no such limitation. *In Re Walter* held that this claim interpretation rule did not apply when considering claims for validity, thus widening the scope of claims and rendering them more likely to a s. 101 objection. Such claims are frequently used when claiming computer-related inventions. The EPC contains no such interpretative provision, and 'means for' claims will be interpreted as including any means suitable for the specified function. Widely-drawn claims may be held not to be 'supported by' the specification under art. 84 EPC: see e.g. *General Electric/ Disclosure of computer-related apparatus* [1992] EPOR 446.

50. The USPTO and courts have had more problems with basing their rules on matters of claim form rather than substance than the EPO has. In Europe the 'real contribution to the art' concept allows examiners to look at the process underlying a claim to an article or apparatus if that is the important development. The recent case of *In Re Alappat* (discussed at 4.2.3.4) may have signalled a move towards a more overall view of what a patent claims, similar to the European approach.

51. The claim was for a new method of calculating autocorrelation coefficients used in pattern recognition that involved calculations that were simpler to implement on a computer. A ROM was specified to store squares of numbers that would be used in calculations. It should be noted that the claims apply to apparatus for comparing stored signal samples generally and are not limited to voice recognition.

Iwahashi was viewed as allowing great freedom in patenting computer-based processes and machines for carrying them out, but there was still the question of the extent to which it was necessary to specify physical hardware elements as part of the claims, which had been done in that case. The *Freeman-Walter-Abele* test was still criticised for deviating from the simple 'claim as a whole' test of *Diamond v Diehr* and losing sight of s. 101.

4.2.3.4 In Re Alappat — Judge Rich removes the restrictions In Re *Alappat* (1994) 33 F 3d 1526 can be viewed in part as a return to the *Diamond v Diehr* (1981) 450 US 175 test. The claim involved a scheme for displaying a smooth waveform on a digital oscilloscope.[52] In a digital oscilloscope, the input signal is sampled and digitised. The numerical values are then portrayed by illuminating the pixels at the appropriate position on the screen in accordance with the value of the signal and its position in the waveform. A problem was experienced with this type of machine in the form of momentary aberrant signal values which made rapidly rising or falling sections of the waveform appear discontinuous. The invention used an anti-aliasing system to illuminate each pixel along the waveform differently so as to give the appearance of smoothness.

The majority opinion of Rich J in *Alappat* amounted to a direct attack on the *Freeman-Walter-Abele* test as applied by the USPTO and a complete re-evaluation of s. 101, *Gottschalk v Benson* (1972) 409 US 63, *Parker v Flook* (1978) 437 US 584 and *Diamond v Diehr*. Among his conclusions were:

(a)   When considering a 'means plus function' claim for patentability, the same rule of interpretation should be used as when considering 'means plus function' claims for infringement, i.e., the claim should be taken to be limited to the actual 'means' taught in the patent and its 'reasonable equivalents'[53] (relying on an earlier opinion delivered by Rich J in *In Re Donaldson* (1994) 16 F 3d 1189). Construing the claim in issue in this way, the claim was held to cover patentable material, that is, a 'machine'. The USPTO in this case had ignored Judge Rich's comments to this effect in *In Re Iwahashi* (1989) 888 F 2d 137 as being *obiter dicta*. Rich J approved the findings in *Abele* and other cases but sought to distinguish them by pointing out that in those cases there had been no specific teaching of how to achieve the means in the specification.

(b)   A machine must perform a function that the laws were designed to protect (e.g., transforming or reducing an article to a different state or thing). But in the instant case the invention claimed calculations to transform digitised waveforms into anti-aliased pixel illumination data and that was sufficient.[54]

---

52. An oscilloscope displays a signal representing something that fluctuates regularly with time, such as the sound pressure in the vicinity of a musical instrument or the electrical signal given off by a human heart, as a static waveform on a television screen.

53. US Patent Act, s. 106; see note 50, above.

54. The comparison between this case and the European case *Vicom/Computer-related invention* [1987] EPOR 74 (discussed at 4.2.2.3) is instructive In *Alappat* the waveform display is held to be a thing forming suitable subject matter for an invention in a very similar fashion to the

(c) It was accepted that the 'mathematical algorithm' exception could apply to genuine machine claims, but s. 101 should be given its widest interpretation. Thus if a machine produced a 'useful, concrete and tangible result' it was patentable and to be contrasted with a disembodied mathematical concept.

(d) A general purpose computer when programmed in a particular way amounted to a 'machine' which would be patentable if the other requirements for patentability were met.[55]

Apart from reversing the claim interpretation rule of *Freeman-Walter-Abele* and effectively confining the application of the rule to genuine process claims, the important contribution of this decision is in the approach adopted in analysing a claim. The accent has shifted back to looking at the claim as a whole to see whether it is for a patentable thing (machine, manufacture, process etc.) rather than on searching out algorithms in the claim and then seeing if the claim goes beyond that (the *Freeman-Walter-Abele* approach).

4.2.3.5 Post Alappat — programmed computers are 'machines' and data structures in a memory are 'manufactures' Whilst many computer-related inventions are apt to be claimed as processes or the means for carrying them out, things such as computer memories or disks can also form the basis of claims. In *In Re Lowry* (1994) 32 F 3d 1579, the claim was for a computer memory organised in accordance with the 'attributive data model'. This comprised a way of organising data into primitive data objects which were arranged in a hierarchy whilst also providing links between objects separate from the hierarchy. Improved data access when such structures were used in combination with programs running on the computer was claimed. The USPTO Appeals Board had allowed the claims under s. 101, holding that a computer memory was an 'article of manufacture' (and this was confirmed by the Federal Circuit). However, the Appeals Board had held the claims not novel, relying on a line of cases relating to printed matter and holding that the only novelty rested in the information content and so didn't count.

The Federal Circuit cautioned against over-zealous use of the printed matter exception and held that the proper test was simply, 'is the article [i.e.,

---

continued
way images were held to be 'real world objects' in *Vicom*. *Alappat* talks in more down to earth terms of electrical signals, no doubt influenced by the need to read the facts on to the well-established definition of a 'process' (see 4.2.3.2), but the basic reasoning is similar. The important difference between the two cases is that in *Alappat* the transformation had merely to be found 'useful' to found patentability. In *Vicom* it was necessary to find 'technical content'. It seems likely that a suitable claim to the invention of *Alappat* would issue in the EPO without problems over the patentable nature of the invention because of the clear technical nature of the subject matter — an illustration that whilst the European approach may be overall more restrictive, the 'real contribution to the art' concept can operate in favour of inventors as well as against them.

55. It can be seen that this position is now the same as that which the UK courts were working towards under the 1949 Patents Act (see the discussion at 4.2.2.8).

the computer memory] useful [in the technological sense identified above]'. On this basis the claim defined a functional thing with new attributes. These were not simply the data themselves, but the organisation of those data. The fact that the claims specified no particular physical organisation for the data structure, only a set of logical relationships, was not material; the data structure was represented by physical (electrical or magnetic) structures. The Federal Circuit were careful to point out that the attributive data model was not being patented in the abstract.

In Re Warmerdam (1994) 33 F 3d 1361 concerned an improved method for navigating robotic machines which avoided collisions by using 'bubbles', imaginary spherical objects encompassing real objects to be avoided. The basic bubble idea was known, but the invention added a layer of sophistication by using a 'bubble hierarchy' whereby once a bubble was violated it was replaced with a set of smaller bubbles and so on. A technique of collision avoidance known as 'bubble bursting' is provided. Claims 1–4 were for 'A method for generating a data structure which represents the shape of physical object [sic]...'. Claim 5 was for a machine but did not use any 'means for' language. In fact the function of the machine was not referred to in any way and the only features claimed for the machine were the presence and contents of memory. It read: 'A machine having a memory which contains data representing a bubble hierarchy generated by ... the method of claims 1–4'. Claim 6 was for a data structure generated by the method of claims 1–4. The Board of Appeals rejected claims 1–4 and 6 under s. 101 and claim 5 for indefiniteness under s. 112.

In *Warmerdam* the USPTO had applied *Freeman-Walter-Abele* to claims 1–4. When the case came before the court *In Re Alappat* (1994) 33 F 3d 1526 had recently been decided and the court did not feel constrained to follow the two-part test precisely. It held that in this case the crucial question in relation to s. 101 was whether the claim went beyond simply manipulating 'abstract ideas' or 'natural phenomena'. The court affirmed the rejection of these claims and rejected the applicant's arguments that one first had to measure real objects to apply the process because the claims themselves did not require this, nor would such a limitation be implied into them. The court also upheld the rejection of claim 6. This was on the basis that the structure as described 'is nothing more than another way of describing the manipulation of ideas contained in claims 1–4' and so had to stand or fall with them.

However, claim 5 was allowed by the court as sufficiently claiming a 'machine'. It was held that a person skilled in the art would have no problems identifying whether a machine fell within the claims because 'the ideas expressed in claims 1–4 are well-known mathematical constructs'. It should be pointed out as a note of caution that the question of the utility of the invention of claim 5 was not in issue in the appeal. The USPTO had not applied *Freeman-Walter-Abele* to claim 5 (it had not rejected under s. 101) and the court did not apply it either. Although considering the claim under s. 101 and acknowledging that it contained process elements, the court did not look at the claim from the point of view of the underlying process to be carried out by the machine.

Subsequent cases[56] reaching the Court of Appeals for the Federal Circuit have confirmed that *Alappat* should be regarded as the leading authority in relation to application of the 'mathematical method' exclusion. In *State Street* v *Signature* (1998) 149 F 3d 1368 the court re-examined the 'mathematical algorithm' exclusion and explained the effect of its earlier decisions in cases such as *Alappat* and *In Re Iwahashi* (1989) 888 F 2d 1370. Rich J again delivered the judgment, and some of his comments are worthy of note:

> ... the mere fact that a claimed invention involves inputting numbers, calculating numbers, outputting numbers, and storing numbers, in and of itself, would not render it nonstatutory subject matter unless, of course, its operation does not produce a useful, concrete and tangible result.
>
> ... The question of whether a claim encompasses statutory subject matter should not focus on *which* of the four categories of subject matter a claim is directed to — process, machine, manufacture, or composition of matter — but rather on the essential characteristics of the subject matter, in particular, its practical utility.

Rich J also pointed out that every step-by-step process involves an algorithm in the broad sense of the term, and discouraged any use of *Freeman-Walter-Abele*.[57] In *State Street* the claim was essentially for a general purpose programmable computer programmed with so-called 'hub and spoke' software for use in assisting the management of State Street's business of an administrator and accounting agent for mutual funds. Such claims were allowed, and in allowing them Rich J buried the 'Business Method Exception' so far as the United States was concerned: 'Whether the claims are directed to subject matter within s. 101 should not turn on whether the claimed subject matter does 'business' instead of something else'.

4.2.3.6 Current US practice As a result of the recent case law developments, in which USPTO policy has been criticised as lagging behind judicial pronouncement, the USPTO has issued revised guidelines[58] to examiners. These may be slightly inconsistent with the most recent *State Street* v *Signature* approach, but the current position can be summarised as follows:

(a) Examiners should look at the claim and specification as a whole to decide what the alleged invention is.

(b) The subject matter so identified must have practical utility.

(c) A computer, even a known general purpose computer when programmed in a particular way, will be patentable if it has practical utility.

(d) A known type of computer memory (disk, ROM, whatever) that carries information in a particular form is patentable if it has practical utility.

---

56. *State Street* v *Signature* (1998) 149 F 3d 1368 and *AT&T* v *Excel Communications*, case 98-1338, which followed.
57. It was arguably still an optional method of analysis, and is still permitted by the revised USPTO guidelines (below), which were issued after *Alappat* but before *State Street*.
58. 61 Fed Reg 7478 (28 February 1996).

(e)   A claim which only covers a mathematical algorithm and cannot be construed so as to cover something of practical utility is not patentable.

The guidelines were issued after a period of consultation. The preamble discusses some of the proposals made during that process that were not adopted. These include:

(a)   Allowing claims for data structures and computer programs *per se*.
(b)   Allowing claims for 'non-functional descriptive material' embodied on computer-readable media.
(c)   Allowing claims which only infer (sic) that 'functional descriptive material' is embodied on a computer-readable medium.

The distinction between functional and non-functional descriptive material is interesting. To be functional, material must 'exhibit a functional inter-relationship with the way in which computing processes are performed'. It is easily seen that the memories of *Re Warmerdam* (1994) 33 F 3d 1361 and *Re Lowry* (1994) 32 F 3d 1579 would satisfy this test whereas plain text or music files would not.[59] The use of this definition neatly side-steps the somewhat arbitrary distinction between what is considered 'a program' and what is considered mere data. As a matter of strict theory, all computer-readable information consists of binary numbers which are capable of influencing the sequence of instructions performed by a computer, whether those numbers were intended as instructions to the computer's processor or not.

4.2.3.7   Everything under the sun? It can be seen that, after a period of fluctuation, US law has now adopted a very liberal position on the patentability of computer-related and other inventions whose subject matter is essentially the manipulation of numbers: the 'algorithm' exclusion still holds, but it has shrunk to an essentially literal interpretation. Claims to any new and useful machine or article will be allowed protection regardless of any fears that an algorithm is being patented by the back door. It is instructive to consider earlier refused claims from cases such as *Gottschalk* v *Benson* (1972) 409 US 63 and *Parker* v *Flook* (1978) 437 US 584. They would appear to stand a good chance of acceptance post *Re Alappat* (1994) 33 F 3d 1526, perhaps after casting into forms similar to those used in *Re Warmerdam* (1994) 33 F 3d 1361 or *Re Lowry* (1994) 32 F 3d 1579.

These cases and *Alappat* also illustrate the lack of zeal on the part of US examiners and judges, when compared to their European counterparts, for

---

59. Assuming the invention claimed lay in the words or music content rather than the data structure in which they were recorded. The data structure could found an invention if it assisted in the playing, display or manipulation of the words or music on a computer. The requirement of 'usefulness' of *Alappat* must (and clearly would) be construed as meaning useful other than for the reason that you can sell the disk at a healthy profit margin because people will enjoy experiencing the data recorded on it. This would be consistent with the direction in *Diehr* that 'laws of nature, natural phenomena, and abstract ideas' are not patentable.

digging for the essence of an invention in order to find that it addresses non-patentable matter. In *Warmerdam* the examination stopped at a relatively superficial level in finding that a machine was claimed: there was no further investigation of what that machine did. *Alappat* has also had the effect that claims for processes, machines as processes and articles of manufacture will be looked at in accordance with broadly the same overall test in mind. The claims in *Lowry* and *Warmerdam* may have been drafted to avoid 'means for' language so as to avoid the effects of *Freeman-Walter-Abele* (and were successful in this). Now the issue of the form of a claim, which was important when the Freeman-Walter-Abele test held sway, will no longer be of such significance.

Nevertheless it remains the case that a claim to a computer program (dare we say 'as such') will be refused in the United States on the grounds that it is not a manufacture, machine or process. A mathematical process will not be patentable, but should there be any practical application of it, claims to computers or memories to carry out the process or embody it will be allowed.

4.2.4 A comparison and discussion of the two approaches

The European approach to patentability of computer-related inventions is based around the requirement for a technical contribution to the art. This has resulted in a wide interpretation of the exclusions from patentability set out in art. 52(2) EPC. It appears that claims draftspersons have become adept at framing claims that address machinery or processes for achieving specified ends in technical fields rather than computer programs, so few claims are refused on the 'computer program' ground. However, the real contribution to the art test tends to result in computer-related inventions being refused protection under art. 52(2) because they fall within the 'methods for performing mental acts' exclusion. It is thus not the 'computer program' exclusion that causes the problems but a similar objection to that upheld in the United States that a patent should not be granted for an algorithm. But in Europe, the interpretation of when a claim is directed to an algorithm is much stricter, influenced no doubt by the presence of express restrictions in art. 52(2).

The genesis of the 'technical content' test and its explanation through the cases has already been analysed. It is submitted that it is equally possible to construe the EPC without elevating technical content to the status of a fundamental principle. 'Technical' and related words when used in the Rules could be taken as having to be interpreted in accordance with the Articles of the Convention (which logically ought to take precedence over the Rules) rather than the other way round.

It is also questionable whether the requirement for the 'real contribution to the art' to have technical content sufficiently takes into account the apparent intent of the 'as such' caveat of art. 52(3). The test applied in the EPO can be stated as 'does the invention claimed have as its real contribution to the art any excluded things?' Whatever this, or any similar formulation of the question one might choose means, it is not the same thing as 'does the invention claim an excluded thing as such?' It is likely to exclude more. The test as applied certainly excludes excluded things as such (for example a mental process for finding documents by preparing abstracts using key words, as in *IBM/Document abstracting and retrieving* [1990] EPOR 99). But it also excludes excluded things as other things (for example a computer programmed to carry out the same process so documents on it are easy to find).

A superficial reading of *IBM's Application* [1999] RPC 563 might suggest that the European position is now more liberal than that in the US since programs can be claimed without reference to any medium for carrying them. But the Technical Board's reason for not making a distinction between the program and the medium on which it is stored was that there is no point in making such a distinction. Current scientific theory holds that information is incapable of existing other than as a result of a particular physical state of matter. So it is impossible to infringe a claim to a computer program without having it stored on a data storage medium, because the program will not exist otherwise. Thus claims for 'computer programs . . .' are not practically any more useful than US-style claims to the storage medium as a 'useful manufacture'. *IBM* (1999) made no changes to the requirement for technical content, which remains the main difference between the two systems.

The cautious approach taken by the EPO can be defended in that the exclusions set out in the EPC have to be given an interpretation that gives them teeth and doesn't allow them to be side-stepped by irrelevant claim drafting. On the other hand, the requirement for technical content tends to exclude from consideration many important areas of technological (in the general sense of the word) development. We are constantly told that information will form the raw material and currency of the industries and societies of tomorrow. To place limitations on the patentability of inventions that operate upon information at the same level as humans do (as opposed to merely manipulating bits) may be thought artificial, but that appears to be the approach of the EPO. An illustration of how the two systems differ is given below in relation to the *Warmerdam* invention.

In *In Re Warmerdam* (1994) 33 F 3d 1361[60] claims were allowed in the United States essentially for a computer as programmed and for a memory carrying data in a particular structure. It seems unlikely that any such general claims would succeed in the EPO. The contribution to the art would be the mental process of constructing the hierarchy of bubbles and then using the 'bubble bursting' technique on it. Once this is proposed, the programming and hardware means for putting it into effect as a computer or memory (which might well have a 'technical' character) are known and do not form part of the contribution to the art of the invention claimed. To comply with the requirement for technical content, any claims to the Warmerdam invention would have to be directed to a machine with an identifiable real-world use, such as a robot. After *IBM's Application* (1999), such claims could be addressed to a computer program or perhaps even a data structure without the need for a reference to a carrier. But they would only cover such a program or data structure to the extent that it was adapted to operate in a

---

60. See 4.2.3.5.

computer so as to achieve a technical effect. Such claims might well issue in Europe following the reasoning of *Sohei/General purpose management system* [1996] EPOR 253.[61] Whilst it might be thought that such matters of claim drafting are mere technicalities, this is not so. Claims in the general *Warmerdam* form will afford significantly greater protection to the patentee, which might well be of economic value.

Even accepting that the EPC dictates a degree of exclusion, one can nevertheless question the way in which the exclusion operates in practice. An impression can sometimes arise when reading the decisions of the EPO that the classification of what is 'technical' is not receptive to new technology and the new types of activity that have come with it. It certainly seems from the decisions that patents which relate in some way to physical objects (X-ray machines, industrial designs albeit electronically recorded ones, printed matter, the internal hardware of a computer) are allowed, whereas those that relate to less tangible things such as the display of characters and ways of recording information about documents to make them automatically retrievable are not. As the EU Commission have noted,[62] and as is readily apparent from this chapter, predicting whether a particular computer-related invention will be patentable, and in what form claims will be allowed, is not an easy process. The current US position, by contrast, has achieved considerable predictability.

4.3 OTHER ASPECTS OF PATENT LAW

Under this heading an outline of the UK interpretation of the position under the EPC (in the form of the Patents Act 1977 as interpreted by the courts) will be given. A detailed treatment of these matters, which are largely independent of the nature of the subject matter of the invention, is beyond the scope of this chapter and readers should consult relevant works on patent law.[63] The position in other jurisdictions is likely to be broadly similar as to the general principles concerned, although differing in matters of detail.

4.3.1 Novelty

Article 54 EPC (Patents Act 1977, s. 1(1)) states that an invention is novel if it 'does not form part of the state of the art'. The state of the art is defined in art. 54(2) (s. 1(2)) as 'comprising everything made available to the public by means of a written or oral description, by use, or in any other way'. The date on which the state of the art is considered is the priority date of the claim in question, which will be the date of the application for the patent or a date within one year previous to that on which another document was filed from which priority is claimed. US readers should note this (the 'first to file'

---

61. See 4.2.2.5.
62. See 4.5.
63. See for example Young et al, *Terrell on the Law of Patents*, London: Sweet & Maxwell 1994 and Reid, Brian C., *A Practical Approach to Patent Law*, 3rd edn, London: Sweet & Maxwell, 1999.

system) most particularly. The US system of 'first to invent' means that a disclosure by the inventor of their invention cannot invalidate any patent that is subsequently duly applied for within a year of the date the invention was made. In Europe and many other jurisdictions it can, and frequently does (and US inventors are often the culprits).

It is established law that the phrase 'made available to the public' means that any disclosure will only contribute to the art that which it 'enables'. In respect of any particular invention, an enabling disclosure is one which would enable the skilled man, using only his general knowledge in his field and not having to exercise any inventive capacity, to achieve the invention, that is make the product or carry out the process claimed. There are several important points that follow from this:

(a)   The skilled man is a hypothetical person who was skilled in the relevant areas of technology as at the priority date. The relevant areas are those which are relevant to a particular claim of a patent whose novelty might be under consideration. It is thus not strictly relevant to consider a disclosure in a vacuum — there has to be an invention in mind to focus attention on a particular recipient of the information and what that recipient is enabled to do.

(b)   'Mosaicing' is not allowed. That is, different disclosures cannot be combined to add up to an enabling disclosure, each disclosure must be looked at separately.[64] A combination of disclosures might render the patent obvious, but that is a separate ground of invalidity.

(c)   Disclosures made under conditions whereby all recipients of information were under duties of confidence make nothing available to the public and are disregarded. In English legal terms, the recipient has to be 'free in law and equity' to do what they will with whatever is gleaned from the disclosure. There are savings for information published in breach of duties of confidence.

(d)   The fact that nothing actually was disclosed to anybody is irrelevant, what matters is availability. If nobody ever read an article in a journal that was published, matter would still be available to the public. (And since this is a work on computer law, it should be pointed out that publication by placing information on a computer to which there is unrestricted dial-up or Internet access makes matter available to the public.)

(e)   In the case of public demonstrations, the use of machines in public places and the distribution to the public of objects or substances, the scope of disclosure is determined by considering what the skilled man could have gleaned by inspecting the material had he got his hands on it (again it is irrelevant that no recipient of the object actually had the relevant skill).

(f)   There are complex rules governing the situations that arise when a patent application anticipating a later application is not actually published (made available to the public) before the priority date of the later application.

Thus where the use on a public road of traffic control apparatus would have revealed the claimed manner of operation to a passing skilled man had he

---

64. There are exceptions where, for example, two documents cross-refer.

simply observed the operation of the system, the claim was held to lack novelty.[65] In the case of computer-related inventions it will normally be the case that public distribution of computers or disks containing all the relevant software will make available all relevant matter to the skilled man (a complete decompilation and understanding of the code may not be necessary to understand the alleged invention sufficiently to reproduce it). If development products are to be distributed, this must either be done after any patent filing or conditions of confidence must be imposed on all recipients.

Generally novelty can reside in a new thing or a new process, which can include a new use for an old thing. The case of *Mobil Oil/Friction reducing additive* [1990] EPOR 514 represents a high point in this area. Mobil found that a certain chemical additive to engine oil reduced friction in the engine. The identical compound had been known and used as a wear reducing agent in engine oil but it had not been realised that it reduced friction. The enlarged Technical Board of Appeals held that a claim to use of the additive 'as a friction reducing additive' was novel. This has been criticised as effectively allowing claims to old uses of old products for new purposes, although the Board held that the use was new.[66] Subsequent patentees do not appear to have sought claims in precisely these circumstances and generally it will be possible to find some physical distinction in the product or the use over the prior art.

4.3.2 Obviousness

The requirement for an inventive step is set out in art. 52(1) EPC (Patents Act 1977 s. 1(1)). Article 56 (s. 3) defines an invention as having an 'inventive step' if the invention would not have been obvious to a person skilled in the art having regard to the state of the art. Whilst the basic idea of obviousness is clear and similar across the jurisdictions, as a practical matter it is the most difficult fact to address in any judicial process and a number of principles and approaches have emerged from courts and patent offices around the world. It is generally thought that the UK courts are more ready to find a patent obvious than the EPO or some European courts. This may be related to the different procedures, particularly the reliance on live expert evidence in the United Kingdom compared with a more paper-based approach elsewhere. It should also be pointed out that it is difficult for patent

---

65. *Lux Traffic Controls Ltd* v *Pike Signals Ltd* [1993] RPC 107.
66. The Board held that since the friction reducing properties were not known to the public the invention was not made available. But the friction reducing properties were available in the practical sense in every motor car using the prior additive. In the English courts at least, the claim appears unenforceable because the only difference between the prior use of the additive (which, it is axiomatic, the public can carry out as well after the patent as before) and the claim is effectively the purpose for which the additive is used, a wholly mental distinction. To find infringement one would have to postulate a mental element to the tort of patent infringement. The 'Gillette' defence which may be paraphrased as 'I am only doing what is disclosed in the prior art so either the claim doesn't cover what I am doing or it is not novel (and I don't care which)' would appear to be applicable in all cases unless a mental element is postulated.

offices to deal with the issue of obviousness at the examination stage in the same way as a civil court would do on hearing an opposition to the patent. Many successful post-grant oppositions are based on obviousness.

The basic principles applied in Europe are that the skilled man is assumed to possess common general knowledge and is also assumed to know of each piece of prior art (but no subsequent disclosure). He is therefore a highly theoretical construction. Commonly, expert testimony is led on this issue and the expert is asked to put herself in the position of the hypothetical skilled man. An example of an obvious invention is the English 'sausage machine case'.[67] It was held that there was no inventiveness in combining a known machine for making sausage filling with a known machine for filling sausages since there was no difficulty in making the connection and it was obvious that the elements could be combined to produce an all-in-one machine if such was desired.

The approaches of the UK courts and the EPO to this issue have differed. The UK approach is summarised in the test postulated in the *Windsurfing*[68] case:

(a) First the court identifies the inventive concept in the claim in suit.

(b) Next the court will assume the mantle of the normally skilled but unimaginative addressee in the art at the relevant date and will impute to him what was, at that date, common general knowledge.

(c) The court should then identify what, if any, differences exist between the matters cited as being known or used and the alleged invention.

(d) Finally the court has to decide whether, viewed without any knowledge of the alleged invention, those differences constitute steps which would have been obvious to the skilled man or whether they required any degree of invention.

The approach of the EPO has been to identify the technical problem to be overcome and consider the possibility of moving to a solution from the 'closest' piece of prior art. However, the Technical Board of Appeal has recognised that this approach is not appropriate in all cases, especially where there is no obvious closest piece of prior art, and that the EPC does not specify any method of finding obviousness (which is ultimately a question of fact). In *Alcan/Aluminium alloys* [1995] EPOR 501 it was pointed out that the problem and solution approach led to a step-by-step analysis that was based on hindsight and unreliable, although most EPO cases still use it. Cases on obviousness are strewn with admonitions about the care that must be taken to avoid hindsight and rejections of step-by-step arguments whereby each step on the road to the invention is painted as obvious whilst losing sight of the overall inventive contribution. Obviousness is and will remain a difficult question of fact to decide whatever theoretical frameworks it is placed into.

In *Bosch/Electronic computer components* [1995] EPOR 587 the audacious claim was made by an applicant that since prior documents cited against the

---

67. *Williams* v *Nye* (1890) 7 RPC 62.
68. *Windsurfing International* v *Tabur Marine (Great Britain) Ltd* [1985] RPC 59 at 73–74.

application were written partly in program code and not 'ordinary language', the code listings therein should be ignored when considering obviousness. Thankfully for the sanity of commentators, this claim was rejected on the basis that the skilled man in that case would have been or have had access to a sufficiently skilled programmer to understand the prior citations. It was also held that the skilled man could in fact comprise a team of mixed skills.

The test is objective, and is sometimes stated as looking at what *could* the skilled man have done rather than *would* he have decided to do.[69] The inventiveness must also be of a technical nature. Where the inventor spotted a previously unfulfilled market need for an improved corkscrew but, given the task of developing such a product, it would have been obvious how to achieve it from a technical point of view, the invention was obvious.[70]

It is the test of obviousness that ensures that mere clever programming will not found an invention. The skilled man is deemed to be a clever programmer, he is just not inventive — a different matter. This is why the patent claims discussed in this chapter have been addressed to principles of operation and organisation of computers and data structures and have not recited detailed code. In a trivial sense many original programs are likely to be new, in that nothing identical has been written before, but few will be inventive.

In general, applications written by software houses for clients or for general sale are unlikely to involve anything patentable for reasons of obviousness. Inventive data structures or modes of operation may be involved in the programming tools used to create the products (for example database 'engines' or image manipulation tools) but any patents to those will belong to the owner of the tools not the writer of the end product. For most software developers therefore, limiting access to source code and enforcement of copyright are likely to be the main avenues for protection of their investment in production.

4.3.3 The need for disclosure

In return for the monopoly granted by the patent (see 4.3.4 below), the applicant is required to disclose how the invention works. The specification must describe the invention claimed clearly and completely enough to enable the skilled man to put it into effect (art. EPC; Patents Act 1977, s. 14(3)). It does not have to do more, so detailed design issues need not be addressed. One reason why the drawings to patent specifications can appear old-fashioned and unworkable is because they are there to teach principles, not to give away detailed designs.

In the case of computer-related inventions, what this means is that full code listings for programs may not need to be given. Schematics or flow diagrams

---

69. In *Perkins/Piston* [1996] EPOR 449, 'would' is preferred over 'could', but on the basis that the skilled man is already assumed to be looking to improve the technology.
70. *Hallen Company and anor* v *Brabantia (UK) Ltd, The Financial Times*, 24 October 1990, CA, approving first instance judgment of Aldous J reported at [1989] RPC 307. This approach was also taken in *Esswein/Automatic programmer* [1991] EPOR 121, where the 'invention' consisted of the appreciation that many consumers only required three programmes on their washing machines!

may suffice to teach the principles involved. The comments made about what is assumed of the relevant skilled man in relation to obviousness apply equally here.

4.3.4 The rights granted by a patent

Article 64 EPC states that holders of European patents should have the same rights as holders of national patents. A patent grants the exclusive rights to the commercial exploitation of the invention claimed. Thus the manufacture, importation, sale or use in the course of trade of products falling within the claims of a patent may be prevented by the patent owner.[71] In the case of patents for processes, it is an infringement to use the process or to dispose of, use or import any product obtained directly by means of the process. A detailed description of the various ways of infringing a UK patent is set out in s. 60 of the Patents Act 1977.

Two immediate contrasts can be drawn with the remedy for breach of copyright:

(a)   Copying is irrelevant, as is knowledge of the patent (although absence of the latter can provide a seller with a defence to a claim for damages): the monopoly is in this sense absolute.

(b)   Private and experimental use is permitted[72] so end-users of products who do not use them in the course of a trade (i.e., consumers) cannot infringe patents — not even when purchasing the product from a retailer (who would be an infringer). But note that where there is dual purpose use, that will infringe.

It is necessary to provide a word of warning concerning use in the course of trade versus private or experimental use. It has been held[73] that experiments may have an ultimate commercial end in view and still fall within the exception, but that experiments to obtain regulatory approval or to demonstrate to a third party that a product works are not covered by the exception. It is clear from this that if a product or software forming part of an invention is investigated to find out how it works, for example by disassembling program code, that will not infringe any patent (compare the position under copyright law — see chapter 6). But as steps are made towards a commercial product, infringement is likely to occur prior to launch or Beta-testing.

It is also an infringement for a person to supply or offer to supply 'any of the means, relating to an essential element of the invention, for putting the invention into effect when he knows, or it is obvious to a reasonable person in the circumstances, that those means are suitable for putting, and are intended to put, the invention into effect in the United Kingdom'.[74] This is known as 'indirect infringement' and may be of considerable relevance to

---

71. Patents Act 1977, s. 60(1).
72. Ibid., s. 60(5).
73. *Monsanto Co. v Stauffer Chemical Co.* [1985] RPC 515.
74. Patents Act 1977 s. 60(2).

computer-related inventions. If a patent doesn't cover a program as such or in the form of a recorded medium such as a disk, suppliers of disks (or providers of services from which the code may be downloaded) may nevertheless be liable if the code or data on the disk forms an essential element of the invention. A possible let-out is that if the means supplied is a 'staple commercial product' then for there to be infringement the supply must be for the purpose of inducing the person supplied to do an infringing act.[75] 'Staple commercial product' is not defined but it is submitted that whereas it would include a blank disk or ROM, it would not include one on which a particular program or data had been recorded.

This still leaves the question of how to decide when a product or process falls within the scope of a claim of a patent. This is the problem of construing the claims of a patent. Article 69 EPC and the protocol thereto provide a general test to be applied, but from this apparently very different tests have grown. In the United Kingdom the approach of purposive construction originally applied under the 1949 Patents Act has been used under the 1977 Act as well, and has been held (by the UK courts) to comply with the EPC. Other EPC countries adopt what is known as the 'doctrine of equivalents'. The former is based on an analysis of what the patentee intended to claim (and not to claim) as disclosed in the whole specification, whereas in the latter test the invention is identified and its equivalents may be considered infringing even if on a strict analysis of the wording of the claims there would be no infringement. There has been much debate concerning whether the UK approach really does comply with the EPC and how different in practice the two tests are (despite coming at the problem from different angles, they do seem to converge on detailed analysis).[76] Whatever test is adopted, it does not alter the fact that careful claim drafting is the key to obtaining a commercially useful, easily enforceable patent.

The remedies for infringement of patent are similar to those available for other intellectual property rights, that is damages (based on lost profits) or an account of profits earned by the infringer, an injunction to restrain further infringement and delivery up of infringing items. The full range of preemptive interlocutory remedies (early injunctions, search orders and so on) are available in patent actions in accordance with the normal principles. A detailed consideration of these is beyond the scope of this chapter.

4.3.5 Duration, revocation and amendment

Under the EPC patents last for 20 years from the date of the full application, although priority can be claimed from a filing made up to a year prior to that. In the case of US patents tiled prior to 8 June 1995 the term ran from the date of issue of the patent but was for 17 years. For subsequently filed applications the position is the same as the European position. This was necessary to take account of the TRIPS agreement[77] which provides for a degree of uniformity between patent laws.

---

75. Ibid., s. 60(3).
76. See the *Assidoman* and *Kastner* cases, note 39 above.
77. Part of the GATT, discussed further at 4.5.

The validity of patents can generally be challenged after grant in the course of infringement proceedings or upon application by an opponent. In the United Kingdom the court hears such applications in the course of infringement proceedings, although in some jurisdictions matters of validity are considered by the Patent Office in separate proceedings. In the United Kingdom a patentee can apply to amend a patent after grant subject to certain safeguards. This is generally undertaken so as to narrow down the patent to give it a better chance of survival in the face of an opposition to validity.

4.3.6 Ownership, transmission and employee inventions

The EPC states that the inventor should be the first owner of any patent, but leaves the ownership of employee inventions up to the laws of the EPC State in which the invention is made. In the United Kingdom the basic rule is that inventions made in the course of employment belong to the employer,[78] although there are provisions for compensation to be provided to employee inventors.[79]

UK employers should note the following potential pitfalls:

(a)   If an employee whose normal duties do not include programming or computer-related developments and who has not been specifically assigned a computer-related task makes a computer related invention, the employer may not own it.

(b)   Workers who are on contract, not employees in the employment law sense, will own any inventions they make pursuant to a contract unless the contract specifically provides, by express or implied term, for ownership of inventions (which of course it should!)

Patents can be assigned and licensed like any other right, but assignments are only effective if in writing. The national patent offices of the EPC States have systems for the registration of transfers of ownership and generally registration is necessary for an assignment to be fully effective. After grant, a European patent is no different from a portfolio of national patents and the administrative requirements of each national system must be complied with. The separate national patents can be disposed of or licensed separately.

4.4   WHY EXCLUDE ANYTHING FROM PATENTABILITY?

A great deal of intellectual effort has been expended in addressing the more theoretical aspects of the issue of intellectual property protection for computer software. Some of the main arguments that are put forward in relation to patentability are discussed below.

---

78. Patents Act 1977, s. 39.
79. Ibid., ss. 40–43.

4.4.1   Which form of protection?

It has been questioned whether patent protection (as opposed to copyright protection, some other protection or no protection at all) is the right form of protection for computer programs or computer software.

It will be noted that this chapter has tended to use the rather cumbersome expression 'computer-related inventions'. The reason for this is that by their nature patents tend to protect matters of fundamental structure and functional features rather than the details of how things are written, and thus will only protect some aspects of software.[80] By contrast, copyright tends to protect the actual way a program is written and the actual data recorded in a data structure (as well as only preventing copying). This is not to say that there can be no overlap. There is no rule which says that a description of the function of a program that is sufficiently brief and general to form the substance of a patent claim would not amount to a substantial part of that program for the purposes of copyright infringement.[81] But if there is overlap it will be at the margins.

The distinction between patent and copyright protection is easily illustrated by the following example. A document setting out a novel chemical process would attract copyright protection, but that protection would protect the document against copying, not the process from being carried out. A patent for the process would prevent it from being carried out but not from being written about or broadcast. Here there is no difficulty in separating the creative literary content from the inventive technical content. In general, prior to the introduction of computers and digital methods of recording data, literary and artistic works were easily identifiable, as were technical inventions, and problems in classifying something as one or the other were rare (although they did arise).

The work of the programmer or computer technologist can fall into both the 'technical' and 'creative' camps. Whilst the chemist of the preceding paragraph clearly utilised artistic literary skill to write out the instructions and technical skill to develop the process, in programming the separation of the two is more problematical (indeed it is a similar problem to that addressed by the EPO when it looks for 'technical content'). Programming clearly involves an understanding of numbers and logic and some sympathy with the technical restraints imposed by the physical apparatus on which the program is to run, which are abilities we associate with the technologist. Yet it may also require the creation of things whose performance cannot be accurately measured and an understanding of the psychology and reactions, likes and dislikes of the user of the computer on which the program will eventually run. These are abilities we associate with people in the creative trades such as copy-writing, design and publishing.

---

80. Because, as we have seen, the detailed working out of the principles may be difficult or time-consuming, but is unlikely to be inventive.
81. This is to apply the UK concept of copyright infringement. Perhaps the idea/expression test favoured in the US is more likely to preclude the taking of this type of feature from ever amounting to copyright infringement. See further chapter 6.

Separating the 'technical' aspects of a piece of program code from its 'artistic' elements may not be an easy or even meaningful process. Nevertheless the patent system allows for principles to be extracted and afforded one form of protection whereas the copyright system gives protection to other aspects of the programmer's work. It is not sensible to take any area of human creative endeavour and arbitrarily say 'this should be protected by patents not copyright' or vice versa. In appropriate circumstances both a patent and copyright will protect different aspects of a computer programmer's work.

4.4.2 Upholding the basic principles of patent law

The 'bargain' theory of patent protection has already been mentioned. The purpose of patent protection in accordance with this theory is to grant a monopoly which will be commercially useful to the patentee whilst making available practically useful things and processes to society at large. Theories, scientific discoveries, mathematical formulae and artistic works are not useful in this practical sense although their consideration might affect our quality of life in the spiritual or intellectual sense.

The notion that the scope of patent protection granted should in some way reflect the scope of what the patent teaches people to do (referred to above) satisfies a basic consideration of fairness yet is inconsistent with allowing patent protection for mere discoveries. If a discovery or mathematical relationship were to be patentable in some way, then all industrial developments building on it (whether foreseen by the original 'inventor' or totally unexpected) would be covered by the scope of the claim. There are obvious moral and economic arguments to be mounted against the grant of excessively wide monopolies of this type. The general rule has emerged therefore that a principle or discovery must be applied to a practical purpose in some way for patent protection to be possible, and reasonable protection will be given to that particular application. Thus useful things, machines or processes designed to exploit scientific discoveries or mathematical relationships are patentable provided they satisfy the various other tests for patentability.

It is not clear that the above principle is violated by the US approach to patenting computer-related inventions, even though that approach is apparently very liberal. It must be remembered that patents do not prevent private or experimental use of a product or process, so no patent can remove an individual's freedom to enjoy the intellectual aspects of an invention. The restriction to useful manufactures etc. ensures that, for example, a human is free to choose to avoid painful contact with fixtures and fittings by using a bubble hierarchy, paper and pencil if he so wishes: it is the programming of a machine to carry out the task that would be prevented by any patent.

It is also arguable that the requirements of novelty, unobviousness and sufficiency of teaching will be adequate to ensure that unwarranted and restrictive monopolies are not granted pursuant to a US-style approach.

To take the alleged invention from *IBM/Document abstracting and retrieving* [1990] EPOR 99,[82] if the idea of generating an abstract in that way was

---

82. See 4.2.2.3.

obvious and it was obvious how to automate it then the patent would fail. If either of those things was not obvious then there would appear to be no harm in allowing the patent. It is true that in the early days of microprocessor and computer use many patent applications were filed (and some patents granted) for what amounted to simple digital automation of previously known manual or electro-mechanical systems. Had a wide range of computer-related matter been patentable some patents for basic concepts might have been granted wrongly, thereby restricting technical development and competition. But the computer industry is now mature and the technology well documented. Apparently both the USPTO and EPO accept that they must search in relation to programs.[83] It should not be possible to obtain a patent simply by deciding to computerise a known or obvious mental or other process using standard programming techniques and hardware.

4.4.3   Scientific consistency

Against a restrictive approach can be ranged arguments based upon consider-ations of the technical reality of the situation. According to these, the problem with trying to exclude programs from patentability is that a sharp dividing line is sought where none exists. Most involved in the computer industry would say they knew what was a program and what wasn't, but a computer program is a disembodied concept, whereas a patent claim must define the scope of an industrially useful monopoly. Knowing what a program is doesn't help in defining the limits of patentability.

When a computer runs a program, all or parts of the program code are copied from the computer's hard disk and stored in the computer's temporary memory. As the program runs, instructions are fetched from the memory and executed by the processor, and the computer then goes on to execute further instructions. Execution of instructions may involve the creation or transposi-tion of data in the computer's memory or the performance of input/output operations to the screen, a printer or a hard disk. All these operations occur inside the computer's integrated circuits as changes in the electrical values at various points. Data pathways are physically opened and closed and electrical circuits re-configured by the act of running the program.

Instead of being loaded into temporary memory from a disk, some programs are permanently held in ROM chips on the computer's circuit boards. They stay in place and are readable even when the computer is turned off. These programs are often low-level routines dealing with matters of the internal operation of the computer. Some program routines may be stored on the processor chip itself and built into it at the time of manufacture, so that they are embodied in the way the circuit elements of the chip are arranged and interconnected. These would deal with complex arithmetical instructions such as division and so on. The distinction between 'hardware' and 'software' is not sharp, there is a continuum. And however a program is executed, it

---

83. See the current guidelines for examination in the USPTO, 4.2.3.6 above, and *Bosch/ Electronic computer components* [1995] EPOR 587, at 4.2.2.4 above.

results in a computer that is physically, electrically configured in a special way so as to operate that program.[84] So, the argument goes, there is no scientific basis for distinguishing computer-related inventions from those relating to bits of bent metal and plastic.

But it can also be argued that a solely scientifically driven view misses the point about patents. Patents are about monopolies for inventions that are useful to people. The EPO has recognised that running a computer program produces a physical change in a computer, but regards that issue as neither here nor there. The focus in Europe is on what those changes actually produce in terms of a technical contribution. That question may be fraught with difficulties and illogicalities, but it is surely not illogical to look at the practical contribution of an invention to society, rather than at its technological building-blocks, to decide whether (and over what) a monopoly should be granted.

4.4.4 Economic and social expedience

Perhaps the most sensible basis for deciding these issues is to simply ask 'what do we actually want'. There is a body of opinion that all software should be free from intellectual property restraints (understandably, many computer users subscribe to this view). Yet the software industry is an industry like any other and if intellectual property rights are deemed desirable to reward invention and protect creative skill and labour in other industries, why make exceptions?

Having said that, it is not clear to what extent patents are a real commercial force in the computer industry (other than in relation to definite hardware elements) in the way that they are in some other industries. The pace of technological development will clearly affect the commercial lifetime of many computer-related inventions and the time involved in obtaining a patent may make it commercially pointless to apply. It is also worth repeating that patent protection will not be relevant to most new computer programs regardless of which patent system protection is sought under.

A study carried out in the United States[85] has come to the conclusion that a *sui generis* right to protect computer programs should be introduced. Discussion of this is beyond the scope of this chapter, but it should be pointed out that the introduction of such a right will not remove the problems of defining the limits of patent protection. Indeed, the current inclusive US approach is perhaps easier to understand and apply than the exclusionary European approach.

---

84. It is interesting to note that this congruity between program and circuit is mirrored in the field of UK copyright law, where electrical circuit diagrams have been viewed as literary works (*Anacon Corporation Ltd v Environmental Research Technology Ltd* [1994] FSR 659), just as programs are. But this does not suggest that excluding 'electrical circuits' from patentability would provide an answer to the problems discussed. Indeed one can see that precisely the same problems of what amounts to an electric circuit 'as such', and whether in any event the claim really relates to a mental process will present themselves.

85. P. Samuelson, R. Davis, M. Kapor and J. Reichman, 'A manifesto concerning the legal protection of computer programs' 94 Colum L Rev 2308.

As noted below, considerations of competitiveness between trade areas can also influence intellectual property policy. The perception of such pressures is often that they dictate strong IP rights, although in some areas of business and industry a loose regime is more conducive to innovation and wealth creation.

4.5 THE FUTURE

After a flurry of activity occurring largely between the second and third editions of this book, the position of computer-related inventions under US law has stabilised at what might be viewed as an extreme position. The difference of approach in Europe has caused concern amongst European commentators and legislators. In 1997 the European Commission published its 'Green Paper on the Community patent and the patent system in Europe'.[86] This sought wide-ranging comment, including on how or whether to proceed with a Community Patent and on the issue of patent protection for computer-related inventions.

Following the consultation period, the Commission has issued a Communication[87] indicating its intended follow-up measures. These include:

(a)   There is a real need for a Community Patent. This is to be implemented by a Regulation, not under the existing treaty provisions, which it now appears will never be implemented.

(b)   The consultation process revealed that the current position concerning legal protection for computer programs 'did not provide sufficient transparency', and that there were national differences in interpretation within the EPC area. The Commission has concluded that the difficulties in obtaining protection for some computer-related inventions in Europe when compared to the United States is damaging to European economic interests, and a more liberal regime should be put in place. It will issue a draft Directive on the patentability of computer programs (which all EU States will have to comply with) and has recognised that art. 52(2)(c)[88] of the EPC will have to be 'modified' so that the EPC does not conflict with States' duty to comply with the Directive.

(c)   The Commission also concluded that Europeans' perception is that European patent protection for computer-related inventions is less widely available than is actually the case. According to their statistics, the bulk of what they refer to as 'software patents' in Europe are held by non-Europeans.

---

86. COM (97) 314 Final.
87. 'Communication from the Commission dated 5 February 1999 to the Council, the European Parliament and the Economic and Social Committee — Promoting innovation through patents — the follow-up to the Green Paper on the Community Patent and the Patent System in Europe' COM (99) 42, also published at EPO 01 4/1999 201.
88. This is what excludes from protection 'schemes . . . and programs for computers'. In fact, art. 52(2)(a), which excludes mathematical methods, could also prove a stumbling block. As we have seen, the amendments will have to make it clear that a requirement for a 'technical contribution' is not necessary if the position under the EPC is to approximate to that in the US. This will involve following 35 USC s. 101 and defining what *is* patentable rather than what is not.

The European Commission has published a Green Paper[89] regarding Utility Models. Some EC States grant these, which are similar to patents but with sometimes less stringent novelty and obviousness criteria. In some States they apply only to three-dimensional forms. The intention is apparently to introduce a Directive harmonising such rights across the EC. The preferred approach is a patent-like system with a similar range of excluded areas to that of the EPC, a ten-year term, a lower inventiveness threshold and with Community-wide novelty. It is therefore possible that many computer-related developments would become registrable under the rights introduced or amended pursuant to any eventual Directive.

Under the Agreement on Trade-Related Aspects of Intellectual Property Rights, part of the GATT, (the TRIPS agreement) broad harmonisation of the scope of patent rights is provided for. Article 27.1 states that '. . . patents shall be available for any inventions, whether products or processes, in all fields of technology, provided that they are new, involve an inventive step and are capable of industrial application . . . patents shall be available and patent rights enjoyable without discrimination as to the field of technology'. 'Capable of industrial application' may be taken to mean the same as 'useful'. The EC and United States, among many others, are signatories to this agreement.

The recent decision in *IBM's Application* [1999] RPC 563 has recognised the possibility of conflict with the TRIPS agreement. Whilst finding that it was not possible for the EPC to be re-interpreted in the light of TRIPS, the Technical Board in that case did arrive at an interpretation of the EPC which is much more in accordance with TRIPS than the previous position. In addition, the Technical Board in that case appears to have accepted the Commission's view that the European patent system must compete on the world patent stage. The following extract from the decision indicates, perhaps, the dawn of a more flexible approach which is responsive to the rapid changes in technology:

2.5 The appellant also referred to current practice in the U.S. and Japanese patent offices. The Board has taken due notice of these developments, but wishes to emphasise that the situation under these two legal systems (U.S., JP) differs greatly from that under the EPC in that it is only the EPC which contains an exclusion such as the one in Article 52(2) and (3).

2.6 Nevertheless these developments represent a useful indication of modem trends. In the Board's opinion they may contribute to the further highly desirable (world-wide) harmonisation of patent law.

---

89. COM (95) 370 final.

CHAPTER FIVE

Design Right and Semiconductor Chip Protection

Robert Hart and Chris Reed

Prior to the Copyright, Designs and Patents Act 1988 (the 1988 Act), industrial designs were protected by a complex set of interacting legislative provisions.[1]

The 1988 Act set out to reform the law by introducing a new design right to replace several aspects of the pre-existing regime of protection. The system of rights in designs is now rather simpler, though several different types of right are still involved:

(a) If the design is for an artistic work, it is primarily protected by copyright.

(b) If the design is non-functional (i.e., appealing solely to the eye and not dictated by the functions the article made to the design is to perform) it is registrable under the Registered Designs Act 1949. This gives the proprietor of the right a monopoly protection of the design for a term extended to 25 years by the 1988 Act.

(c) If the design is to be used for manufacturing functional items, the design itself (i.e., the drawing plus any associated text) will still attract copyright as an artistic or literary work, so that directly copying it will be an infringement. However, under s. 51 of the 1988 Act copyright in that design is not infringed by manufacturing items to the design. Instead, protection is

---

1. For a brief description of the position before the 1988 Act see G. Dworkin and R. Taylor, *Blackstone's Guide to the Copyright, Designs and Patents Act 1988* (London: Blackstone Press, 1989), pp.138–45.

given by means of the new design right (see 5.1). Design right can subsist in parallel with registration of the design.

So far as the computer industry is concerned, the new design right is likely to be the most important method of protecting designs. It would potentially cover such matters as the layout of circuit boards, component designs, designs for paper paths in laser printers etc. The area in which it will have the greatest impact, however, is in the design and manufacture of semiconductor chips. These were previously protected under a *sui generis* topography right, but for chips designed after 1 August 1989 this right disappeared and protection now subsists under an amended version of design right.

5.1 DESIGN RIGHT

This is a property right which, under s. 213(1) of the 1988 Act, subsists in original designs. 'Design' is defined in s. 213(2) as: 'the design of any aspect of the shape or configuration (whether internal or external) of the whole or part of an article'.

'Originality' has a somewhat more restricted meaning than for copyright, and not only must the design not be copied, but it must not be commonplace in the design field in question when it was created (s. 213(4)).

There are three aspects of designs in which by virtue of s. 213(3) no design right can subsist:

(a) A method or principle of construction.

(b) What have been described as the must-fit/must-match exceptions. It is not an infringement to copy aspects of the design which are essential to ensure that another article will connect with or fit against the original article, or which are dependent on the appearance of the original article where the new article is intended to form an integral part of it. A good example of the working of this exception would be the design of a paper output tray to attach to a printer. Here, it must fit to the printer and so can copy features of the printer's design which are essential for that purpose, and as it is intended to become an integral part of the printer it can copy design features which allow it to match the printer's appearance.

(c) Surface decoration (this is potentially registrable under the 1949 Act).

Design right comes into existence at the moment the design is recorded in a design document by a qualified person,[2] and normally belongs to the designer. However, if the design is made in the course of employment it belongs to the employer, or if it is commissioned then, unlike the position in relation to copyright, the commissioner is the proprietor (s. 215). In each case, though, this is subject to any agreement in writing to the contrary.[3] If

---

2. Who is a qualified person is defined in orders made under s. 221, but it is essentially the same as for copyright.
3. Design Right (Semiconductor Topographies) Regulations 1989, reg. 5, amending s. 215 of the 1988 Act.

the design is computer-created, the designer is the person who made the arrangements necessary for its creation (s. 214(2)).

Design right has a shorter term than copyright. Under s. 216 it lasts for 15 years from the end of the year of creation or 10 years from the end of the year in which articles made to the design are made available for sale or hire, whichever is the shorter period. The right may be assigned in the same way as copyright, except that licences of right are available during the last five years of the term (s. 237).

Infringement is dealt with in ss. 226 to 228 of the 1988 Act. These provide that the owner of the design has the exclusive right to reproduce it for commercial purposes, which means:

(a)   to make articles to the design, or
(b)   to make a design document for the purpose of enabling such articles to be made.

Secondary infringement is essentially the same as for copyright, by importing, possessing for commercial purposes or trading in infringing articles (i.e., articles manufactured to the design). However, even though the unauthorised making of a design document is an infringement, importation of or commercial dealing with such a document is not (s. 228(6)). The remedies available to the proprietor of the right are also similar, and in addition to injunctions, damages or an account of profits, the owner of the right can also apply for an order for delivery up of infringing articles and for orders for their destruction (ss. 229 to 235).

Although these general principles of design right will apply to many aspects of computer technology, it is important to note that their application to semiconductor chip designs is substantially different. The regime of semiconductor chip protection will be examined in 5.2 in some detail, highlighting these differences.

5.2   SEMICONDUCTOR CHIP PROTECTION

Semiconductor chips are formed from layers of semiconductor material such as silicon, germanium or gallium arsenide, with insulators of various compositions that combine to form the components required to make up an electronic circuit. The layers are 'doped' in predetermined places with traces of other elements, and sandwiched together with insulating and metallic layers to form the chip. The configuration of these layers is determined by directing a pattern of light on to a photosensitive surface, either through a physical 'mask' or via a computer-controlled light beam which traces out the circuit, and it is the circuit thus produced which determines the chip's functionality. The investment in establishing these configurations is extremely high, and the development of a new family of semiconductor chips can cost over £10 million. A chip can be copied, however, for less than £100,000, as the physical technology is in most cases standard in the industry. It is thus clear that the aspect of semiconductor chips which requires protection from unauthorised copying is their design.

Until recently, no country's intellectual property regime provided specific protection for semiconductor products. Although it was generally thought that designs for chips received some protection under the intellectual property laws of the UK,[4] the position was never very clear. In 1984, however, the US passed the Semiconductor Chip Protection Act (the US Act) which introduced a new form of protection for 'mask works'. These are defined in s. 901(a)(2)(A) as:

a series of related images, however fixed or embodied, having or representing the predetermined three-dimensional pattern of metallic, insulating or semiconductor material present or removed from the layers of a semiconductor chip product.

If the work is original (i.e., not staple, commonplace or familiar in the industry: s. 902(b)) and first exploited in the US or exploited elsewhere by a US national or domiciliary, the designer of the mask work receives the exclusive right to reproduce or to import or distribute the work or products containing the work (s. 905). This right lasts for 10 years from the earlier of the mask work's registration or its first commercial exploitation (s. 904(b)).

The US Act also provides that reverse engineering will not be an infringement if the work produced by such engineering is itself original, not substantially similar to the first work, and involves significant toil and investment (s. 906(a)). When considering the acts which are permitted under 'reverse engineering' it is important to recognise that the US legislators attempted to codify so-called established industry practice, so that a second chip designer could reproduce and use the designs of a protected chip for the purposes of research and development, resulting in the design of a second chip with the same electrical and physical performance characteristics as the protected chip. During the House debate on the US Act this was identified as achieving 'form, fit and function' compatibility.

The intention of the reverse engineering exception was to permit the making of improvements on or alternatives to existing chips by incorporating substantial parts of the first design into the second chip. If the second chip is the result of substantial study and analysis and not the result of simple plagiarism, the creation of a second mask work whose layout is 'in substantial part similar to the protected mask work' is permitted.

In addition to the originality requirement, the existence of a 'paper trail', which will substantiate the level of study and analysis embarked on by the reverse engineer, is important in separating the pirate from the legitimate engineer. In *Brooktree Corporation* v *Advanced Micro Devices Inc.* (1988) No. 88-1750-E (cm) (SD Cal 13 December 1988), the court noted that both parties agreed that if the defendant could produce an adequate paper trail establishing reverse engineering the appropriate standard for infringement would be that the two masks were 'substantially identical'; if no independent

---

4. See R. Hart, 'Questions Raised on Legally Protecting Semiconductor Chips' (1986) 2 YLCT 93.

creation through reverse engineering was established, the appropriate standard would be that the two mask works were 'substantially similar'. However, the US Court of Appeals for the Federal Circuit in this case held that a 'paper trail' does not conclusively prove a reverse engineering defence under the US Act. The court explained that the statute does not excuse copying where the alleged infringer first tried and failed to reverse engineer a chip without copying. The court rejected the claim that the reverse engineering defence can be established by the sheer volume of paper, pointing out that the paper trail is evidence of independent effort but not incontrovertible proof of either the originality of the end product or the absence of copying.

The importance of this Act outside the US lies in its reciprocity provisions, for s. 902 provides that mask works from countries outside the US are only protected within the US if that country has signed a mask work protection treaty with the US and provides equivalent protection for mask works in its own domestic legislation. As a result, many developed countries have introduced legislation along the lines of the US Act, and the Council of the EEC issued Directive 87/54/EEC[5] (the Directive) to ensure that member States amended their legislation to qualify for reciprocal protection. Initially this was done in the UK by the Semiconductor Products (Protection of Topography) Regulations 1987 (SI 1987 1497, the 1987 Regulations).

The 1987 Regulations differed somewhat from the US Act by creating a new intellectual property right, 'topography right', which was the exclusive right to reproduce the whole or a substantial part of an original topography, or to deal in a reproduction of it or in a semiconductor product incorporating such a reproduction (reg. 4(1)). 'Topography' was defined as the design of the pattern fixed or intended to be fixed on a layer of a semiconductor product, or on a layer of other material (e.g., a mask) to be used in the manufacture of such a product, and included the arrangement of the layers of semiconductor product.[6] To satisfy the requirement of originality, reg. 3(3) provided that the topography must be the result of the creator's (or creators') intellectual efforts, and must not be commonplace amongst creators or manufacturers of topographies and semiconductors. However, a work that consisted of non-original elements would still be original if the *combination* of those elements satisfied the two-part test of originality.

Topography right is now replaced by a modified version of design right, implemented by the Design Right (Semiconductor Topographies) Regulations 1989 (SI 1989 1497, the 1989 Regulations). These regulations amend and extend the 1988 Act's application to semiconductor products, and references in this chapter to the 1988 Act are to the Act as amended. It is worth saying at the outset that the overall reaction of the semiconductor industry is that, as so much adaptation was required to make design right conform with the Directive, it would have been better to remove semiconductor topographies from design right altogether and to re-enact the 1987 Regulations. However, the industry has always been seriously concerned that

---

5. OJ L24, 27 January 1987, p. 36.
6. 1987 Regulations, reg. 2(1). This regulation also defines the term 'semiconductor product'.

the 1987 Regulations had major flaws, and some of these are overcome in the 1989 Regulations.

5.2.1 Creation and subsistence of the right

Regulation 2(2) of the 1987 Regulations provided that 'the creation of a topography occurs upon its first expression in a form from which it can be reproduced'. This complied with art. 7(1)(c) of the Directive. Although the US Act only provides protection for 'mask works fixed in a semiconductor chip product' the effect is much the same, as that Act's definition of 'fixed' includes the requirement that 'its embodiment in the product is sufficiently permanent or stable to permit the mask work to be perceived or reproduced from the product'.

Regulation 2(1) of the 1989 Regulations defines a 'semiconductor topography' to be a design falling within s. 213 of the 1988 Act which is a design of either of the following:

(a) the pattern fixed, or intended to be fixed, in or upon—
  (i) a layer of a semiconductor product, or
  (ii) a layer of material in the course of and for the purpose of the manufacture of a semiconductor product, or
(b) the arrangement of the patterns fixed, or intended to be fixed, in or upon the layers of a semiconductor product in relation to one another.

Even though a design has been made, s. 213(6) of the 1988 Act provides that design right 'does not subsist unless and until the design has been recorded in a design document or an article has been made to the design'. A design document is 'any record of a design, whether in the form of a drawing, a written description, a photograph, data stored in a computer or otherwise' (s. 263(1)). Design documents for topographies are given more protection than other design documents, as their importation or commercial dealing is a secondary infringement (see 5.2.2).

It would seem, therefore, that a design document for a semiconductor product is defined much more broadly than a mask work under the US Act or a topography under the Directive. Both of these latter definitions include the requirement that it be a series of related images which represent the three-dimensional pattern of the product's layers. Contrast this with the definition of a design document above. This does not restrict protection to a series of related images, and so a list of the functional requirements of a complex application-specific integrated circuit (ASIC) held in a computer which operates a chip design program would probably qualify as a design document.

5.2.2 Infringement

If a competitor wants to emulate the original ASIC, and his analysis and evaluation produces a similar list of functions and requirements, this would potentially be an infringement of design right in the original list. However, the competitor is relieved of liability by reg. 8(1) and (4) of the 1989 Regulations. Paragraph (1) of reg. 8 provides that the design right owner's rights are not infringed by reproducing the design privately for non-commercial aims, or by reproducing it for the purpose of analysing or evaluating the design, or for analysing, evaluating or teaching the concepts, processes, systems or techniques which are embodied in it. This permits direct copying of the topography for those limited purposes only. Indirect copying by *using* the analysis to create a *new* design is excused by reg. 8(4), so that it is not an infringement to:

(a)   create another original semiconductor topography as a result of an analysis or evaluation of the first topography or of the concepts, processes, systems or techniques embodied in it, or

(b)   reproduce that *other* topography. (Emphasis added.)

The important thing to note is that the US Act and the Directive only provide protection against the unauthorised reproduction etc. of mask works and topographies. 'Reverse engineering' is expressly permitted, and incidental copying in the reverse engineering process is not an infringement of design right.

A significant amendment to the 1988 Act is the removal of the words 'for commercial purposes' from s. 226(1) so far as topographies are concerned. As a result, the owner of design right in a topography has the exclusive right to make chips to the design, or to make a design document recording the topography, for both commercial and non-commercial purposes. This is, of course, subject to the exceptions contained in reg. 8(1) and (4) of the 1989 Regulations. The net effect is that non-commercial manufacture of chips to the design is forbidden, whilst copying for the purpose of reverse engineering is permitted. This overcomes the problem that manufacture for in-house use would otherwise not have been an infringement, since s. 263(3) of the 1988 Act defines an act done for 'commercial purposes' as an act done with a view to the article being sold or hired in the course of business.

Indirect infringement of design right under s. 227 of the 1988 Act occurs when an infringing article is imported into the UK for commercial purposes, or where a person has an infringing article in his possession for commercial purposes or, in the course of a business, sells or lets it for hire or exposes it for sale or hire. When the Directive was drafted the Commission was keen to ensure that protection was given to the topography itself, so that design houses producing topographies would be provided with protection for those products separate from their incorporation in a chip product. For this reason, s. 228(6) does not apply to semiconductor topographies, thus indirectly including topography design documents in the definition of infringing articles.[7] This is clearly an important issue, as already design houses are providing an ASIC design service which will produce for a customer the

---

7. 1989 Regulations, reg. 8(3).

design information (i.e., masks) which can then be used by a separate silicon fabrication house to produce the ASIC.

It should also be noted that under reg. 8(5) of the 1989 Regulations any of the above acts will amount to an infringement if done in relation to a *substantial part* of the topography as well as in relation to the whole. It is not clear whether this adds anything to s. 213(2) of the 1988 Act, under which 'design' means the design of the whole or part of an article. Both these provisions apply to topography designs, and s. 213(2) may be broader in scope than reg. 8(5).

Because topography protection is subject to EC law, the doctrine of exhaustion of rights applies. Once the article in question has been lawfully sold or hired within the EC, its further importation into or dealing in the UK is not prohibited by s. 227.[8]

5.2.3   Originality

The Directive calls for 'the creator's own intellectual effort', though this may be shown by the original combination of elements of the design which are not themselves original. This restrictive definition of originality was included in the 1987 Regulations, but is *not* found in the 1988 Act. The only qualification is that a topography design will not be original if it is commonplace in the design field (s. 213(4)), and a similar qualification is found in the US Act. This is an important issue for semiconductor topographies as they are, in the vast majority of cases, new compilations of well-known (i.e., commonplace) elements. A topography will be protected by design right if the combination is not commonplace, and there will be no need to show 'intellectual effort' (which might be difficult given the use of design teams, and the fact that the principles of assembling the elements of a design are fairly well-established, though the effort involved in successfully doing so might be substantial). The inclusion of computer-generated designs in the scope of design right is particularly important, especially in respect of ASICs produced by computer–aided design techniques.

5.2.4   Design right exclusions

Neither the US Act nor the Directive contain provisions equivalent to s. 213(3) of the 1988 Act (see 5.1). These exclusions from the protection of design right have the potential to limit substantially the protection offered to semiconductor topographies. It seems probable that the configuration of the interfacing area of the topography of a semiconductor chip would fall within the 'must-fit' exclusion of s. 213(3)(b)(i), which may seriously restrict the protection provided for the topography of an integrated circuit under the design right.

The layout of the pins of an integrated circuit has to be copied when producing, for example, a form, fit and function compatible replacement

---

8. 1989 Regulations, reg. 8(2).

device. The location of the pins may dictate to a large extent the circuit layout of the power rails and the input and output signal carrying sections of the device. Similarly, high-power or frequency-sensitive circuit elements must be located so as to minimise interference with the rest of the circuit and the input and output paths. These design features may, therefore, reduce the layout options available to the producer of a replacement chip. It could be argued that the must-fit exception not only permits the copying of the pin layout but also has an influence on the copying of that part of the layout which is a consequence of the pin layout. All of these requirements, if considered as 'must-fit' features, would be excluded from the design right protection provided for the original integrated circuit layouts and are, therefore, available to be copied without infringement for use in a form, fit and function compatible integrated circuit layout.

More serious is the exclusion in s. 213(3)(a) of a 'method or principle of construction', since it is arguable that the topography, when held in electronic form, defines the principles of the construction of the chip and may well also define the method (i.e., doping requirements) to be used to create the chip. If this is so, much of the protection which the 1989 Regulations were intended to provide will be lost under this exception. It is possible that we might find ourselves in a position where advances in technology outstrip the law's provisions (in this case before they came into force!) as older methods of chip production such as physical masks will attract protection whereas computer-controlled light or electron beam scanning may well fall within this exception.

5.2.5 Duration of the right

Design right normally subsists for 15 years from the end of the year in which the design was first recorded in a design document or in which articles were first made to the design, or 10 years from the end of the year in which articles made to the design were first made available for sale or hire, whichever is the shorter period. Design right in a topography is capable of subsisting for nearly 26 years. This is because s. 216 of the 1988 Act as amended by reg. 6(1) of the 1989 Regulations follows the Directive, which does not limit the subsistence of the right to the shorter of these two periods. Thus if a topography were created on 1 January 1989 but not commercially exploited, under the amended s. 216(b) the right would not expire until midnight on 31 December 2004. If it was first made available for sale or hire on that date, the right would continue under s. 216(a) until 31 December 2014. Design right in topographies also differs from other design rights in that there is no provision for compulsory licences of right in the last five years of the term, as reg. 9 of the 1989 Regulations provides that s. 237 of the 1988 Act does not apply to semiconductor topographies.

5.3 THE WIPO TREATY

The WIPO Treaty concerning integrated circuit design protection was adopted by WIPO at a diplomatic conference in Washington on 26 May 1989.

Articles 2 to 8 deal with the issue of protection for integrated circuit designs, whilst arts. 9 to 20 deal with administrative issues; only the former are examined in this chapter.

5.3.1 Definitions

The Treaty provides definitions in art. 2 for 'integrated circuit' and 'layout-design (topography)'. It also defines who is the holder of the right and the requirements for a layout-design to be protected.

The definition of integrated circuit differs from that used in the US Act and the Directive, but the essence is a layout-design (topography) which has been integrally formed in or on a piece of material and is capable of an electronic function. It should be noted that the definition envisages only one active element, and it may well be that protection for discrete components of a design could be included under a law which conforms with the Treaty.

The definition of 'layout-design (topography)' also differs from the equivalent definitions in the US Act and the EC Directive. It is defined as: 'the three-dimensional disposition, however expressed, of the elements, at least one of which is an active element, and some or all of the interconnections of an integrated circuit'. Because the definition includes the words 'however expressed', computer-held information will fall within the scope of the definition. It should also be noted that there is no need for the design to have been implemented in physical form as the words 'or such a three-dimensional disposition prepared for an integrated circuit intended for manufacture' have also been included in the definition. This is an important issue since, in Europe at least, there are specialist design houses which will prepare the layout design or topography of an ASIC for a customer, the topography being implemented by a separate semiconductor foundry. Clearly it is important for the design to be protected at this stage, and not merely after its implementation in a semiconductor chip product as is the case under s. 902(a)(1) of the US Act.

5.3.2 Subject matter

Article 3(1) of the WIPO Treaty obliges each contracting State to secure intellectual property protection in respect of layout-designs which meet the requirements of art. 3(2), i.e., if they are the result of the creator's own intellectual efforts and are not commonplace. This is very similar to art. 2(2) of the EC Directive. It should be noted that the question of whether computer-generated designs satisfy these requirements has been left open.

5.3.3 Scope of protection

Article 6(1) of the WIPO Treaty identifies two acts which are unlawful if performed without the authorisation of the rightholder:

(a)   Reproducing, whether by incorporating in an integrated circuit or otherwise, the whole or any part of a protected layout-design.

(b) Importing, selling or otherwise distributing for commercial purposes a protected layout-design or an integrated circuit incorporating the protected layout-design.

Only the second of these acts is prohibited under the US Act and the Directive, though of course the manufacture of a chip inevitably requires the reproduction of its design. The question of whether innocent infringement (i.e., performance of one of the prohibited acts by a person who does not know or have reasonable grounds for knowing that a right subsists in the design) should be unlawful is left to be decided by each signatory (art. 6(4)).

Article 6(2) contains exceptions for teaching and research, and more importantly a reverse engineering exception, reproduction for the sole purpose of evaluation, analysis and research. The reverse engineering exception also permits the creation of a second layout-design, if it complies with the originality requirements of art. 3(2), on the basis of evaluation or analysis of a protected layout-design.

The Treaty also permits signatories to provide for compulsory non-exclusive licences (art. 6(3)) and for the exhaustion of rights (art. 6(5)). The compulsory licensing provision was one of the main reasons why the US and Japan voted against adoption of the Treaty.

5.3.4 Duration of protection

Under art. 8 of the WIPO Treaty protection is to last for at least eight years. As most existing legislation sets a longer period (usually 10 years) for protection and contains reciprocity provisions, it is likely that any signatory which wishes to obtain effective international protection for its nationals' designs will adopt a 10-year period. However, the adoption of norms in an international treaty of this type might eventually lead to international pressure to reduce the length of protection in countries which already have semiconductor chip protection legislation, and this provision was also objected to by the US and Japanese delegations.

5.3.5 Adoption and ratification

The Treaty was adopted by 49 votes to two (US and Japan) with five abstentions. The Treaty has been signed by eight states (China, Egypt, Ghana, Guatemala, India, Liberia, Yugoslavia and Zambia) but so far only ratified by Egypt. Under art. 16(1) five ratifications are necessary for the Treaty to enter into force.

5.4 CONCLUSIONS

Although the UK regime of protection for semiconductor topographies is in theory just a special case of design right, in practice it will be best to treat it as a separate type of intellectual property right. Because of the Directive, any decision of the European Court will be binding on UK courts, and the 1989

Regulations will need to be interpreted in the light of EC law. It should also be noted that because the right was devised in response to US legislation, any changes in the US Act are likely to be implemented in this country and the other EC member States.

So far as other computer products are concerned, design right will in some circumstances provide a useful form of protection for hardware manufacturers. This right, together with other forms of protection such as registered designs, trade marks and the tort of passing off, offers manufacturers some protection for their efforts in entering or creating new markets. The pace of innovation in the computer industry is so great, however, that the protection offered is likely to be of short duration in practical terms. The best form of protection of one's competitive position, as the most successful manufacturers have demonstrated, is the quality of the product and its technical excellence.

CHAPTER SIX

Copyright

Christopher Millard

6.1 INTRODUCTION

6.1.1 The nature of copyright

Notwithstanding its considerable and ever-increasing significance to business, intellectual property continues to be one of the law's more obscure and esoteric fields. In popular parlance, confusion often reigns and talk of copyrighting an invention or patenting a trade mark is not uncommon. Such misunderstandings are, perhaps, not surprising given the highly technical nature of much of the law in this area and the scope for overlaps and conflicts between the various rights.

Nevertheless, the effective protection and exploitation of intellectual property rights is crucial to the success, and in some cases the survival, of a growing number of businesses. Nowhere is this more strikingly the case than in the computer industry. For example, the right to manufacture, sell, buy or use a complex product such as a computer system comprising hardware and software may depend on licences of any or all of patents, copyrights, design rights, know-how and trade marks. Similarly, the primary assets of a software house will usually be its copyright works. The focus of this chapter will be on copyright. Other intellectual property rights are covered elsewhere in this book.

What then is copyright? Copyright is, in essence, a right given to authors or creators of 'works', such as books, films or computer programs, to control the copying or other exploitation of such works. In marked contrast to patent rights, copyright begins automatically on the creation of a 'work' without the need for compliance with any formalities. The only prerequisites for protection, which apply to all works, are that the work must be of a type in which copyright can subsist, and that either the author is a 'qualifying person', or the work has been published or broadcast in an appropriate manner. In the case of certain types of works, including literary works such as books and computer programs, the work must also be 'original' and it must be 'recorded' in some form (e.g., written down or stored in computer memory).

In addition to controlling the making of copies, the owner of copyright in a work has the exclusive right to control publication, performance, broadcasting and the making of adaptations of the work. In certain cases, the author, director or commissioner of a work may be entitled to exercise certain 'moral rights' which may include the right to be identified with a work and to object to distortion or unjustified treatment of the work.

Where any of the various exclusive rights that collectively make up copyright in a work have been exercised without permission, civil remedies may be available to the owner or author. In certain cases criminal sanctions may also be brought to bear, principally where copyright is being infringed with a view to commercial gain. Most of these concepts and terms are discussed in more detail in the rest of this chapter.

6.1.2 Evolution of UK copyright law

English copyright law has a history going back five centuries and has been regulated by statute for almost three.[1] The first modern copyright law, the Copyright Act 1709, was an attempt to balance the interests of authors and publishers in the case of the leading-edge technology of the day, the printing press. Technology has since moved on and so has the law. The two have not, however, always been in step. Notwithstanding regular piecemeal amendment of the law, the gap between copyright law and new media has periodically had to be closed, or at least narrowed, by means of a radical overhaul of the law. Increased sophistication in the means for commercial exploitation of the economic value of copyright has been a particularly powerful catalyst for change. Cable and satellite broadcasting of films and other works, and the distribution of computer programs and other works in digital form are examples.

A major realignment occurred with the enactment of the Copyright, Designs and Patents Act 1988 ('the 1988 Act').[2] Its predecessor in the copyright field, the Copyright Act 1956 ('the 1956 Act'), had been the subject both of detailed reform discussions[3] and temporary piecemeal

---

1. For an interesting historical review see Breyer, 'The Uneasy Case for Copyright: A Study of Copyright in Books, Photocopies and Computer Programs' (1970) 84 *Harv L Rev* 281.
2. Royal assent 15 November 1988.
3. A committee set up in 1973 under the chairmanship of Mr Justice Whitford reported in 1977 that the time had come for a general revision of the 1956 Act: *Copyright and Designs Law: Report of the Committee to Consider the Law on Copyright and Designs* (Cmnd 6732), London: HMSO, 1977. This was followed by two Green Papers which did little to advance the reform process: *Reform of the Law Relating to Copyright, Designs and Performers' Protection* (Cmnd 8302), London: HMSO, 1981, and *Intellectual Property Rights and Innovation* (Cmnd 9117), London: HMSO, 1983. The publication in 1986 of a White Paper entitled *Intellectual*

amendments[4] for half of its time on the statute book. The 1988 Act, most of the provisions of which came into force on 1 August 1989,[5] represents an attempt to start again with a clean slate. On this slate are written both a restatement of the general principles of copyright, and also various sets of rules to deal with specific types of copyright work and their commercial exploitation. Although there is considerable scope for criticising the 1988 Act at a detailed level, on the whole it is a far more coherent, comprehensive and accessible statement of the law than the statutes that it replaced.

6.1.3 The Copyright, Designs and Patents Act 1988

The Copyright, Designs and Patents Act 1988, as its name suggests, does not deal solely with copyright. It established a significant new property right, known as 'design right'; the law relating to registered designs was changed; changes were made to patent and trade mark law; and the law relating to performers' protection was reformed and restated.[6] Unless otherwise indicated, references to sections are to those of the 1988 Act.

Although judges have provided some guidance on interpreting the 1988 Act, there remain many areas that have not yet been considered by the courts. In the meantime, some pointers can be obtained from court decisions based on the 1956 Act (as amended), and indeed on earlier statutes, such as the Copyright Act 1911. The extent to which reliance can be placed on such old decisions is, unfortunately, not at all clear. This is because s. 172 of the 1988 Act, given the marginal note 'General provisions as to construction', provides:

(1)   This Part restates and amends the law of copyright, that is, the provisions of the Copyright Act 1956, as amended.

(2)   A provision of this Part which corresponds to a provision of the previous law shall not be construed as departing from the previous law merely because of a change of expression.

(3)   Decisions under the previous law may be referred to for the purpose of establishing whether a provision of this Part departs from the previous law, or otherwise for establishing the true construction of this Part.

Each part of this section seems to introduce a layer of confusion. The first subsection states that the 1988 Act is both a restatement and an amendment

---

continued

   Property and Innovation (Cmnd 9712), London: HMSO, 1986, set the stage for a general overhaul of the law.

4. Design Copyright Act 1968; Copyright Act 1956 (Amendment) Act 1982; Copyright (Amendment) Act 1983; Cable and Broadcasting Act 1984; Copyright (Computer Software) Amendment Act 1985.

5. The Copyright, Designs and Patents Act 1988 (Commencement No. 1) Order 1989 (SI 1989/816).

6. For a helpful introduction to the Act as a whole, which incorporates the full text of the statute, see Gerald Dworkin and Richard D. Taylor, *Blackstone's Guide to the Copyright, Designs and Patents Act 1988*, London: Blackstone Press, 1996. For a more detailed analysis see Hugh Laddie, Peter Prescott and Mary Vitoria, *The Modern Law of Copyright and Designs*, 3rd edn, London: Butterworths, 2000.

of the old law. The second provides that a change in language does not necessarily indicate a change in meaning although, by implication, it may do. The third suggests that we look to court decisions based on the 1956 Act to see whether there has in fact been a change in meaning and generally to assist in understanding the new Act. Thus, even if it can be shown that a particular provision of the 1988 Act 'corresponds' to a provision of the 1956 Act, the fact that the provision has been redrafted in different language may or may not indicate anything about its meaning. It is particularly difficult to see how cases decided under the 1956 Act could illuminate Parliament's intentions in 1988 in including, excluding or substituting specific words in the 1988 Act. There is no reference to the status, if any, of cases decided under older statutes such as the Copyright Act 1911. Taken as a whole, s. 172 should give advocates plenty of scope for argument over semantics, and leave courts with considerable discretion as to whether to rely on or disregard particular precedents as they seek to interpret and apply the new law.

6.1.4   EU Directives and their implementation in the UK

Differences in the nature and scope of the intellectual property rights available in the 15 EU Member States have frequently given rise to trade barriers. In seeking to limit the effects of such restrictions, the European Commission and the European Court have drawn distinctions between the existence and the exercise of intellectual property rights. Ownership of an intellectual property right is not inherently anticompetitive, indeed the Treaty of Rome sanctions import and export restrictions that can be justified as being 'for the protection of industrial or commercial property'.[7] However, attempts to use intellectual property rights as a means of carving up the internal market are vulnerable to challenge under the Treaty. According to the 'exhaustion of rights' doctrine developed by the European Court, goods that have been put on the market lawfully in one of the Member States by or with the consent of the owner, must be permitted to circulate freely throughout the European Union (EU). Of particular significance to the computer industry is the availability and scope of copyright protection for software products. In June 1988 the Commission published a Green Paper entitled *Copyright and the Challenge of Technology*.[8] In that discussion document the Commission inclined towards the view that copyright is the most appropriate form of protection for computer programs and should provide the foundation for a Directive on software protection. Comments were, however, invited on a number of issues relating to the precise nature and scope of the exclusive rights that Member States should be required to grant software owners.

Following a period of consultation that ended in December 1988, a Directive on the Legal Protection of Computer Programs ('the Software Directive') was adopted by the Council of Ministers on 14 May 1991.[9] Legislation to implement the Software Directive in the UK the Copyright

---

7. Treaty of Rome, art. 30.
8. Green Paper on Copyright and the Challenge of Technology: Copyright Issues Requiring Immediate Action COM (88) 172, final.
9. 91/250/EEC, OJ L122, 17 May 1991, p. 42.

(Computer Programs) Regulations 1992,[10] was enacted in time for the implementation deadline of 1 January 1993. Specific aspects of the Software Directive and UK implementing legislation are discussed later in the chapter. The EU has adopted a Directive on the Legal Protection of Databases.[11] The copyright provisions in the Directive only deal with the structure of databases (recital 15 and art. 5) and not the contents of databases.[12] The contents of databases remain governed by national copyright laws and a novel and separate property right introduced by the Directive, the so-called '*sui generis*' or database right, which exists independent of any copyright (art. 7(4)) (see chapter 7). The Directive effectively creates three tiers of protection; databases may contain contents that are copyrighted, the contents may also attract the *sui generis* protection and the database itself may also be protected. The Copyright and Rights in Databases Regulations 1997[13] implemented the Directive in the UK by amending the 1988 Act to include a new test of originality for copyright databases[14] and introducing the *sui generis* database right.

A proposal for a directive on copyright and related rights in the Information Society was presented by the European Commission on 10 December 1997[15] and an amended proposal was submitted on 21 May 1999.[16] The proposed directive would alter as well as add to the existing EU framework on copyright and related rights in order to: ensure that copyright-protected works enjoy adequate protection across the Member States thereby responding to the challenges of new technology and the Information Society; facilitate cross-border trade in copyrighted goods and services relevant to the Information Society, including on-line and physical carriers (e.g., CDs); and ratify international treaties on the protection of authors, performers and phonogram producers, agreed in December 1996 by the World Intellectual Property Organisation (WIPO) (see 6.1.5).[17]

The 'Conditional Access' Directive,[18] which is due to be implemented by 28 May 2000, requires Member States to prohibit the supply of devices (including software) for circumventing technical means for limiting entry to protected, and other conditional access, services.

6.1.5 International copyright conventions

There are several international copyright conventions that have had significant effects upon the development of copyright law. The Universal Copyright

---

10. (SI 1992/3233).
11. 96/9/EC (OJ L77, 27 March 1996).
12. See Art. 2(5) of the Berne Convention.
13. (SI 1997/3032), entry into force 1 January 1998.
14. By reason of the selection or arrangement it must be its author's 'own intellectual creation' (reg. 6 inserting s. 3A(1)). See further 6.2.1.3.
15. COM (97) 628 final, which was commented on by the European Parliament in its February 1999 Opinion.
16. COM (1999) 250 final, 21 May 1999.
17. See further Stephen Saxby, 'CLSR Briefing', *Computer Law and Security Report*, vol. 15, no. 5 (September–October 1999), p. 355.
18. 98/84/EC, adopted 20 November 1998.

Convention[19] and the Berne Convention for the Protection of Literary and Artistic Works[20] oblige Member States to provide the same rights to nationals of another Member State as they provide to their own authors (the so-called 'national treatment' rule). The TRIPS Agreement[21] provides for national treatment[22] and most-favoured-nation treatment. The latter requires Member States to apply immediately and unconditionally any advantage, favour, privilege or immunity granted by a Member State to nationals of any other country.

The TRIPS Agreement provides that, under the Berne Convention, the object and source codes of a computer program are to be protected as literary works (art. 10 TRIPS). Specific rights are provided for under TRIPS, such as the author's right to authorise and prohibit the commercial rental of a computer program, except where the computer program is not the 'essential object' of the rental (art. 11 TRIPS). The TRIPS Agreement provides that, in accordance with the Washington Treaty (1989) on the protection of integrated circuits, semiconductor chips are to be protected (art. 36 TRIPS). Infringement of integrated circuits, the term of copyright protection, compulsory licensing and the treatment of innocent infringers were also dealt with (arts. 37 and 38 TRIPS). In relation to databases, the compilation of these works is to be protected by copyright provided that it constitutes an 'intellectual creation' (art. 10(2) TRIPS).[23] This contrasts with the position in the United Kingdom up to 31 December 1997 (prior to the Copyright and Rights in Databases Regulations 1997), in that 'originality' was sufficient to establish copyright protection (see 6.2.1.3).

The WIPO Copyright Treaty supplements the Berne Convention (see art. 1) and applies the following 'traditional' copyright rules to the digital environment: the reproduction right (as set out in art. 9 of the Berne Convention),[24] particularly in the context of the use and storage of works in digital form; the fair use principle for on-line communications, whereby the making of a limited number of copies of the protected work is permitted provided the 'legitimate interests' of the copyright owner are not harmed (which is generally limited to use of a non-commercial nature);[25] and the right of making available to the public, which rests with the right holder. The

---

19. 6 September 1952, 6 UST 2713 (1955), TIAS No. 3324, 216 UNTS 132 (effective September 16 1955) (Geneva Act); revised July 24 1971, 25 UST 1341 (1974), TIAS No. 7868, 943 UNTS 178 (effective July 10 1971) (Paris Act); which requires contracting States to give adequate and effective protection to the rights of authors and other copyright proprietors of literary, scientific and artistic work (art. 1).
20. 9 September 1886; Paris Act of 24 July 1971, as amended on 28 September 1979.
21. Trade Related Aspects of Intellectual Property Rights, concluded under the Uruguay Round of the General Agreement on Tariffs and Trade, Final Act Embodying the Results of the Uruguay Round of Trade Negotiations, Marrakech, 15 April 1994.
22. Subject to the exceptions under the Paris Convention (1967) on industrial property, the Berne Convention (1971), the Rome Convention (1961) on sound recordings, producers and performers and the Washington Treaty (1989) on integrated circuits.
23. See further Louwers & Prins, *International Computer Law*, USA: Matthew Bender, Chapter 8.
24. This is by way of an 'Agreed Statement' in the Treaty.
25. Article 10(2).

WIPO Copyright Treaty provides for protection against the circumvention of technological protection devices for controlled access to copyrighted material (art. 11) and against the removal of electronic rights management information without authorisation (art. 12). The following provisions of the TRIPS Agreement are restated: computer programs are to be protected as literary works within the meaning of art. 2 of the Berne Convention;[26] and compilations of data or other material may be protected by copyright where they are intellectual creations[27] (but the protection does not extend to the material contained in the database[28]).

The treaty on intellectual property in databases initially proposed as part of the WIPO Diplomatic Conference of 20 December 1996, which was to include the *sui generis* right for data contained in databases, was not adopted. However, art. 5 of the WIPO Copyright Treaty seems to allow for the possibility of such a right in providing that:

> Compilations of data or other material, in any form, which by reason of the selection or arrangement of their contents constitute intellectual creations, are protected as such. This protection does not extend to the data or the material itself and is without prejudice to any copyright subsisting in the data or material in the compilation.

The database right created by the EU Database Directive appears to be consistent with art. 5 of the WIPO Copyright Treaty. The question of adopting a *sui generis* right, similar to that of the Database Directive, was again discussed by WIPO at a meeting on database protection between 17 and 19 September 1997, but any action at an international level seems to have been postponed indefinitely.[29]

6.2   IN WHAT CAN COPYRIGHT SUBSIST?

6.2.1   General criteria for protection

6.2.1.1   Works   Section 1 of the Copyright, Designs and Patents Act 1988 provides that:

> (1)   Copyright is a property right which subsists in accordance with this Part in the following descriptions of work—
> (a)   original literary, dramatic, musical or artistic works,
> (b)   sound recordings, films, broadcasts or cable programmes, and
> (c)   the typographical arrangement of published editions.
> (2)   In this Part 'copyright work' means a work of any of those descriptions in which copyright subsists.

---

26. The Agreed Statement to art. 4 notes this restatement of the TRIPS Agreement.
27. The Agreed Statement to art. 5 notes this restatement of the TRIPS Agreement.
28. Compare the EU Database Directive; op cit., note 11 and chapter 7.
29. For further discussion of international copyright conventions, see Christopher Rees & Simon Chalton, *Database Law*, London: Jordans, 1998.

Many products that are protected by copyright do not fit neatly into any single category from this list. On the contrary, by the time they are brought to market, most films, books, software packages, multimedia products and other composite works comprise a complex bundle of discrete copyright works. Most of the categories of work listed above are of relevance in the computer context. For example, a software product such as a word processing package could be analysed as a collection of copyright works as follows:

(a) The program code which, when run on a computer system, provides word processing functions would be a literary work: s. 3(1) of the 1988 Act defines 'literary work' as including 'a computer program' (s. 3(1)(b)).

(b) The preparatory design material for the computer program would itself be a literary work (s. 3(1)(c)).[30]

(c) Any documentation or other written materials supplied with the package would be one or more conventional literary works.

(d) Any built-in dictionary, thesaurus, or help-screen files would be literary works, but would probably not be computer programs.

(e) Artwork included on packaging or in documentation would be one or more artistic works (s. 4).

(f) Graphic works or photographs used to produce screen images would be artistic works (s. 4(1)(a)).

(g) Copyright would subsist in the typographical arrangement of the documentation supplied with the package: s. 1(1) defines 'the typographical arrangement of published editions' as a separate category of copyright work (s. 1(1)(c)).

In addition to these seven categories of work, three other types of work may be embodied in an audiovisual product such as a video game:

(h) The sounds which are produced when the game is run or played might include a recording of one or more musical works: s. 3(1) defines 'musical work' as 'a work consisting of music exclusive of any words or action intended to be sung, spoken or performed with the music'.

(i) The code producing the sounds would itself be a sound recording: s. 5A(1)[31] defines 'sound recording' as '(a) a recording of sounds, from which the sounds may be reproduced, or (b) a recording of the whole or any part of a literary, dramatic or musical work, from which sounds reproducing the work or part may be produced regardless of the medium on which the recording is made or the method by which the sounds are reproduced or produced'.

(j) Any set sequence of images that is produced when the program is run would be a film: s. 5B(1)[32] defines 'film' as meaning 'a recording on any medium from which a moving image may by any means be produced'.

---

30. Inserted by Copyright (Computer Programs) Regulations 1992 (SI 1992/3233), reg. 3, in force 1 January 1993.
31. Substituted by the Duration of Copyright and Rights in Performances Regulations 1995 (SI 1995/3297), reg. 9, subject to transitional and savings provisions specified in regs. 12–35.
32. Ibid.

A further four bases for protection may be relevant in relation to a database[33] or multimedia product:

(k)   A database itself may attract copyright protection: s. 3(1) defines 'literary work' as including a database (s. 3(1)(d)).[34] A database will fall within the scope of the 1988 Act, as amended, if it consists of a collection of independent works, data or other materials arranged in a systematic or methodical way and individually accessible by electronic or other means.[35] Databases are to be protected by copyright only so far as they are original by reason of their 'selection or arrangement' and if they constitute the 'author's own intellectual creation'.[36] Therefore, a computer-generated database would not be protected by copyright as a database.

(l)   A computer program used in the making or operation of a database would be a literary work (s. 3(1)(b))[37] and may also comprise preparatory design material (s. 3(1)(c)).

(m)   Some or all of the items comprised in the product may be protected separately as literary, dramatic, musical or artistic works or as sound recordings or films.

(n)   If made available to subscribers to a broadcast videotext or cable service, the product would be a broadcast or cable programme: see definitions of 'broadcast' in s. 6(1) and of 'cable programme service' in s. 7(1).

While it is clear that compilations attract copyright protection,[38] the fact that, for example, a software product is not a single work for copyright purposes has a number of significant consequences. First, many different authors, graphic designers, programmers, publishers etc. may be involved in the production and marketing of the product and, as individual authors, may have separate claims to copyright in their respective contributions (see 6.3.1). Secondly, copyright protection will expire at different times in respect of different component parts of the product (see 6.3.3). Thirdly, the scope of copyright protection will not be the same for all of the works that make up a package. For example, unauthorised adaptation of the program code would infringe copyright, whereas there would be no copyright restriction on

---

33. Note that the contents of a database may also attract a *sui generis* right, which protects the investment made by database makers rather than the author's creativity in the selection or arrangement of the contents of databases, as is the case with copyright.

34. Inserted by the Copyright and Rights in Databases Regulations 1997 (SI 1997/3032), reg. 5, in force 1 January 1998.

35. Section 3A(1), inserted by the Copyright and Rights in Databases Regulations 1997 (SI 1997/3032). Presumably databases where the contents are automatically calculated using other data in the database, for example, would be excluded.

36. Section 3A(2), inserted by the Copyright and Rights in Databases Regulations 1997 (SI 1997/3032).

37. Such programs are excluded from protection as a database (see art. 1(3) of the Directive on the legal protection of databases 96/9/EC).

38. See, for example, *Exchange Telegraph* v *Gregory* [1896] 1 QB 147, concerning the unauthorised dissemination of lists of London Stock Exchange price data; and *Waterlow Directories Ltd* v *Reed Information Services Ltd* [1992] FSR 409, concerning a compilation of practising solicitors in the UK.

adaptation of the various artistic works, provided it did not amount to copying or some other restricted act (see 6.4.2.1 and 6.5.2). Fourthly, an author of the text or designer of artwork included in the documentation might be able to exercise moral rights in respect of the works he or she contributed, whereas a programmer could never make such a claim in respect of the program code (see 6.6).

6.2.1.2 Recording There can be no copyright in a literary, dramatic or musical work 'unless and until it is recorded, in writing or otherwise'. The term of copyright starts to run from the time of such recording (1988 Act, s. 3(2)). 'Writing' is given an expansive definition in the 1988 Act as including 'any form of notation or code, whether by hand or otherwise and regardless of the method by which, or medium in or on which, it is recorded, and 'written' shall be construed accordingly' (1988 Act, s. 178). Storage in any form of machine-readable media would thus appear to qualify as 'writing'. The words 'or otherwise' would cover fixation in the form of, for example, an analogue recording of sounds or spoken words.

The 1988 Act does not contain a definition of 'recording' as such. It is not clear whether a degree of permanence is implied. By analogy with 'sound recording', which is defined, the essence of the concept of recording of a work is probably that there is something from which the work, or part of it, can be reproduced. Presumably, once a work has been fixed in such a form, copyright will continue to subsist in the work notwithstanding the subsequent destruction of the original recording of the work, even where no copy has ever been made in a material form. This issue might be significant if a substantial part of a program, or other work, were to be reproduced from human memory after the author had accidentally or deliberately deleted the original from the memory of the computer on which it was created.

6.2.1.3 Originality Literary, dramatic, musical or artistic works are only protected under the 1988 Act if they are original (1988 Act, s. 1(1)(a)). There is no definition or explanation of the concept of originality. However, the word 'original' was used in both the 1911 and 1956 Copyright Acts and, almost invariably, was interpreted by the courts as relating essentially to origin rather than to substantive considerations such as novelty. Thus, a work will usually be original provided merely that it originates with the author or creator and has not been copied. In many cases originality has been found to exist where the work was created either independently or by the exercise of the author's own skill, knowledge, mental labour or judgment. While one (or more) of these attributes is usually required in order to secure copyright protection, courts have tended to resist arguments that the originality requirement should be interpreted as importing connotations of aesthetic quality or innovation.[39]

---

39. See, for example, *Victoria Park Racing & Recreation Grounds Co. Ltd* v *Taylor* (1937) 58 CLR 479; *Football League Ltd* v *Littlewoods Pools Ltd* [1959] Ch 637; *Ladbroke (Football) Ltd* v *William Hill (Football) Ltd* [1964] 1 WLR 273; applied *John Richardson Computers Ltd* v *Flanders* [1993] FSR 497, Ferris J.

The low level at which the originality threshold has tended to be fixed by the courts means that even relatively simple and utterly mundane works can be protected by copyright. This is very important in the computer context where programs and other functional works may lack aesthetic appeal and display little creativity yet be of tremendous commercial value. Were a higher threshold to be set for the originality test, it is probable that much computer software and data would fall completely outside copyright.[40] The one area where, under the 1956 Copyright Act, the originality criterion was a particular cause for concern for the UK computer industry, computer-generated works, was specifically addressed in the 1988 Act and is discussed in 6.2.2.2.

Since 1 January 1998, subject to transitional provisions, a collection within the definition of a 'database' (that is, a literary work consisting of a database) will not qualify for copyright protection unless it achieves a certain level of originality. The requisite standard is that, by reason of the selection or arrangement of the contents of the database, the database constitutes the author's own intellectual creation.[41] The standard of originality for a literary work consisting of a database remains, at this stage, untested before the courts. It could be argued that the standard is higher than that required for other literary, dramatic, musical or artistic works, because of the inherent difficulties associated with gauging intellect and/or requisite mental effort. Note, however, that while the 'own intellectual creation' test was contained in the Software Directive,[42] the implementing legislation for that Directive did not alter the basic 'originality' test, which suggests that the new standard was not seen to be significantly different from the old. Irrespective, this will not prevent such a database from being protected by the Database Directive's *sui generis* right (the database right under the Database Regulations), provided sufficiently substantial investment in the obtaining, verification or presentation of the database's contents can be demonstrated (art. 7 and reg. 13(1)). The database right will be infringed by the extraction or re-utilisation of all or a substantial part of the contents of the database (see chapter 7).

6.2.1.4 Qualification Copyright will not subsist in any work unless certain 'qualification requirements' are met. The rules, which are set out in Part IX of the 1988 Act (ss. 153–162), are complex. For most types of work, however, the general rule is that either the author must be a 'qualifying person' at the time the work is made or, alternatively, the work must be first published in the UK or some other country to which the Act extends. An author will be a qualifying person if he or she is a citizen of, or domiciled or resident in, the UK or some other country to which the Act extends. The qualification requirements will also be satisfied if the author is a citizen of, or domiciled or resident in, or first publication is in, a country to which the Act has been 'applied'.

---

40. As was the case, for example, in West Germany prior to implementation of the Software Directive. See Moritz Röttinger, 'The legal protection of computer programs in Germany: renunciation of copyrights?' (1987) 4 CL&P 34.
41. Section 3A(2) of the 1988 Act, inserted by the Copyright and Rights in Databases Regulations 1997 (SI 1997/3032).
42. See note 9.

By virtue of a statutory instrument that came into force along with most of the provisions of the 1988 Act on 1 August 1989, Part I of the Act has been applied to works of different types originating in over 100 specified countries.[43] Special rules apply to certain countries which are not members of either the Berne Copyright Convention or the Universal Copyright Convention but in which the UK government is satisfied that there exists adequate protection for copyright. An order has also been made applying Part I of the Act to works made by officers or employees of the United Nations and certain other international organisations that would otherwise not qualify for protection.[44]

6.2.2 Protection of programs and computer-generated works

6.2.2.1 Computer Programs Whereas, in its original form, the Copyright Act 1956 contained no reference whatsoever to computers or computing, in the Copyright, Designs and Patents Act 1988 computers make their first appearance in s. 3. Further direct and indirect references are scattered throughout the Act. Section 3(1) of the 1988 Act defines 'literary work' as including:

(a) a table or compilation other than a database;
(b) a computer program;
(c) preparatory design material for a computer program; and
(d) a database.

This form of words has made it completely clear that programs are literary works and not merely to be protected as though they were literary works.[45]

What remains unclear is the scope of the term 'computer program', which has still not been defined. Foreign legislatures and international organisations that have defined the term have tended to characterise programs in terms of their information-processing capabilities, with specific emphasis on their ability to cause hardware to perform functions.[46] We have already seen that a software package such as a video game is in fact a complex collection of

---

43. The Copyright (Application to Other Countries) Order 1989 (No. 2) (SI 1989/1293). This was replaced by a statutory instrument in similar terms, which came into force on 4 May 1993, entitled The Copyright (Application to Other Countries) Order 1993 (SI 1993/942) and this was in turn replaced by The Copyright (Application to Other Countries) Order 1999 (SI 1999/1751) which came into force on 22 July 1999.
44. The Copyright (International Organisations) Order 1989 (SI 1989/989). In force, 1 August 1989.
45. As was the case under the 1956 Act, as amended by s. 1 of the Copyright (Computer Software) Amendment Act 1985.
46. For example, 'A "computer program" is a set of statements or instructions to be used directly or indirectly in a computer in order to bring about a certain result' (United States Copyright Act 1976, 17 USC s. 101); 'A "computer program" is a set of instructions expressed in words, codes, schemes or in any other form, which is capable, when incorporated in a machine-readable medium, of causing a "computer" — an electronic or similar device having information-processing capabilities — to perform or achieve a particular task or result' (World Intellectual Property Organisation, Model Provisions on the Protection of Computer Software, 1978, restated in Memorandum on a Possible Protocol to the Berne Convention, 1991).

separate copyright works. Only some of the works will be computer programs. To take another example, most of the material supplied in printed or electronic form in a word processing package will not be 'programs' in the sense of computer code that will cause a computer to process information. The printed materials will be conventional literary and other works. Moreover a great deal of the material supplied in electronic form will be digital versions of a dictionary, a thesaurus, and help-screen information, all of which, again, will be conventional literary and possibly artistic works.

The existence of special provisions in the 1988 Act that apply to computer programs but not to literary works in general means that the two terms are certainly not coextensive. Moreover, the inclusion in the Act of many provisions that deal with the use and distribution of conventional works in electronic form makes it clear that a work is not a program just because it is stored digitally.

Neither the Software Directive nor the Copyright (Computer Programs) Regulations 1992 shed much light on the definitional issue. The preamble (recitals) to the Directive merely includes a statement that 'the function of a computer program is to communicate and work together with other components of a computer system'. Article 1(1) is a little more explicit in stating that 'for the purpose of this Directive, the term "computer programs" shall include their preparatory design material'. The Copyright (Computer Programs) Regulations 1992 contain no reference to the meaning of the term 'computer program' except to restate that 'preparatory design material for a computer program' shall be protected (see also s. 3(1)(c) of the 1998 Act).

6.2.2.2 Computer-generated works As already noted (see 6.2.1.4, above) for copyright to subsist in a work, certain qualification requirements must be met. In most cases, the criterion will be whether the author of a work was 'a qualifying person' at the time the work was made. With the widespread use of programming 'tools' and automated processes for collecting, processing and compiling data, it is likely that an increasing number of works, including computer programs and databases, will have no identifiable human author or authors. Prior to the 1988 Act, there was considerable doubt as to whether such works were eligible for copyright protection.[47]

To ensure that substantial categories of works did not gradually fall out of the realm of copyright, provisions were included in the 1988 Act to enable copyright to subsist in a literary, dramatic, musical or artistic work 'generated by a computer in circumstances such that there is no human author of the work' (ss. 9(3) and 178). The author of such a 'computer-generated' work 'shall be taken to be the person by whom the arrangements necessary for the creation of the work are undertaken' (s. 9(3)). Whilst providing a welcome safety net for useful and valuable works that would otherwise fall outside copyright law, determining whether these new provisions apply to a particular work will still require a careful analysis of the facts.

---

47. See C.J. Millard, *Legal Protection of Computer Programs and Data*, London: Sweet & Maxwell, 1985, pp. 25–30.

In particular, care should be taken to distinguish between 'computer-generated' and 'computer-assisted' (or 'computer-aided' works). The latter type of work does not receive special treatment under the 1988 Act. The availability of copyright protection for such works was in effect recognised in a decision under the 1956 Act. In pre-trial proceedings in *Express Newspapers plc* v *Liverpool Daily Post & Echo plc* [1985] 1 WLR 1089, the court ruled that grids of letters produced with the aid of a computer for use in prize draws were authored by the programmer who wrote the relevant software. Rejecting an argument to the contrary advanced by counsel for the defendants, Whitford J stated:[48]

> I reject this submission. The computer was no more than the tool by which the varying grids of five-letter sequences were produced to the instructions, via the computer, of Mr Ertel. It is as unrealistic as it would be to suggest that, if you write your work with a pen, it is the pen which is the author of the work rather than the person who drives the pen.

It was perhaps convenient for the court in the *Express Newspapers* case that the programmer was also the person who ran the program on the particular occasion in question and checked the results. The nexus between one person and the finished work was thus very close. It is not clear how the court would have resolved conflicting claims between several programmers, data providers, system operators and so on.

In cases where the association between any individual or individuals and a finished work is so remote that it can fairly be said the work has been created without a human author, there is now the possibility that it will qualify for copyright as a computer-generated work. However, it is unlikely that the 1988 Act provisions will be dispositive of all doubts as to the subsistence and ownership of copyright in computer output. Disputes may still arise where a number of competing individuals claim to have made the 'arrangements necessary for the creation of the work'. Would, for example, a person using a mass-marketed program generator be entitled to copyright in all such output? Would the author of the underlying software have any claim to copyright in the output? Would two or more identical works produced by different individuals using the same program generator all qualify for protection as original literary works?[49]

6.3 OWNERSHIP AND DURATION OF COPYRIGHT

6.3.1 First ownership

The first owner of copyright in a work is usually the author of the work (Copyright, Designs and Patents Act 1988, s. 11(1)). This is the case

---

48. This passage echoes a statement in para. 514 of the Whitford Committee Report (see note 3) in which it was stated that a computer used in the creation of a copyright work was a 'mere tool in much the same way as a slide-rule or even, in a simple sense, a paintbrush'.
49. For further discussion, see J.A.L. Sterling, 'The Copyright, Designs and Patents Bill 1987', *Computer Law and Security Report*, vol. 3, no. 5 (January–February 1988), p. 2.

regardless of whose ideas underlie the work and of who commissions or pays for the work. This general rule is, however, subject to several significant exceptions. Of widest importance is the special rule that, subject to contrary agreement, the first owner of copyright in a work created by an employee during the course of his or her employment is the employer, not the employee (s. 11(2)).[50] Whilst this rule seems straightforward in principle, in practice its consequences are frequently overlooked.

The most common difficulty arises where a software house or freelance programmer is commissioned to write software under a contract *for* services (as distinct from a contract *of* service, i.e., an employment agreement). Such scenarios are often complicated where contributions to the program development process are made by employees of the company that has commissioned the work and possibly also by independent consultants. The automatic operation of the rules as to first ownership may produce results that are contrary to the reasonable commercial expectations of one or more of the parties. For example, the commissioning party may contribute a brilliant original concept and pay all the costs of its subsequent development and implementation, yet end up with no legal rights of ownership in the final product. Even if it had been understood from the start, and possibly even agreed orally, that the commissioner would in all respects 'own' the product, this will not be sufficient to alter the operation of the first ownership rules. This is because, as will be discussed below, assignments of copyright and agreements as to future ownership of copyright will only be enforceable if they are evidenced in writing (1988 Act, ss. 90(3) and 91(1); see 6.3.2). It is possible in such a case that the commissioner will be able to persuade a court of equity to order the developer to execute an assignment of copyright. This might be justified on the basis that such an assignment was an implied term of an agreement between the parties.[51] The mere fact that the commissioner paid for the work would not normally be sufficient grounds for inferring such a term, although such an arrangement may be evidence of an implied licence to use the work for the purpose for which it was commissioned.[52]

Further potential for dispute arises where there is joint authorship and/or joint ownership of copyright. In the computer industry it is common for several people, sometimes a large number, to be involved in the initial development of a software package. Thereafter, still more people may be involved in the preparation of revised versions and updates. Multiple authorship and divided ownership are, however, by no means uncommon in the copyright field. Section 10(1) of the 1988 Act defines a 'work of joint authorship' as 'a work produced by the collaboration of two or more distinct

---

50. The other exceptions to the rule relate to Crown and Parliamentary copyright, and the copyright of certain international organisations (1988 Act, s. 11(3)).
51. See, for example, *Merchant Adventurers Ltd* v *M. Grew & Co. Ltd* [1973] RPC 1. The ruling is probably limited to the special facts of that case, however. Where ownership is disputed, a court would be most unlikely to upset the automatic operation of the statutory ownership rules.
52. For judicial discussion on this point see *John Richardson Computers Ltd* v *Flanders* [1993] FSR 497 at p. 516 and *Ibcos Computers Ltd* v *Barclays Mercantile Highland Finance Ltd* [1994] FSR 275 at p. 293.

authors in which the contribution of each author is not distinct from that of the other author or authors'. Thus, where the development of a program really is a joint effort copyright will, subject to the rules governing employee works just discussed, vest in the various contributors jointly. This scenario must be distinguished, however, from that in which a number of people have made separate contributions to a software development project each of which can be identified as such. It may well be that in the latter case there will be a number of quite distinct copyrights in a program or package.

An example of the potential problems associated with divided ownership is where a software house or contractor writes software code for a specific customer. In such an instance, there is often a great deal of collaboration with the customer or third party with resulting issues of joint authorship or implied licence to exploit the software. The degree and kind of collaboration necessary to support a claim of joint authorship or warrant an implied licence to exploit the software was dealt with by the Chancery Division of the High Court in *Flyde Microsystems* v *Key Radio Systems Limited* [1998] FSR 449. Laddie J found that while the defendant, who cooperated in the design of software to be used in a new generation of radios to be sold by the defendant, did in fact improve the software program by ironing out 'bugs' this was more akin to the skill exhibited by a proof reader not an author. As a result, it was held that the level of 'creative' skill was not sufficient to evidence copyright ownership or give rise to an implied licence to exploit the software. In *Robin Ray* v *Classic FM plc*, 18 March 1998 (unreported), Lightman J found that to establish joint authorship, it was necessary to show that: there was a direct responsibility for the work by providing a creative contribution that was not distinct from that of the author (ss. 9 and 10 of the 1988 Act); there was more than a mere contribution of ideas to the author or some division of labour in the creation of the copyright work; and there was no employment contract whereby copyright would be legally owned by the defendant. Further, if joint authorship did in fact exist, the consent of the other joint author to the exploitation of the work would need to be obtained (ss. 16 and 173). It was also found that an implied licence to exploit copyright material would only arise where strictly necessary to make sense of the relevant commercial arrangements.[53]

Serious difficulties may arise at the exploitation stage where a software package either has a number of joint owners, or is made up of a number of programs or modules each separately owned. In either case, infringement of copyright will occur if any of the owners seeks to exploit the package as a whole without the consent of all the others. Where the various owners have quite distinct copyrights and one owner refuses to cooperate with the rest, the others may choose to rewrite the relevant part of the package and proceed to market the software without the objecting contributor being involved. This solution will not, however, be available in the case of a single work if various people are joint owners of the whole of it. Unless the rights of the un-

---

53. See further John Warchus, 'CSLR Briefing', *Computer Law and Security Report*, vol. 14, no. 6 (November–December 1998), p. 424.

cooperative party or parties can somehow be severed, attempts to exploit the package may be thwarted permanently.

There are thus many circumstances in which there is a possibility of more than one party claiming copyright and of disagreements about how multiple owners should exercise their rights. Such issues may arise where there is a misunderstanding about ownership of a work that has been commissioned; where a work has been or is likely to be computer-generated; where there are multiple authors; and where ownership is divided. In all such cases, the most satisfactory arrangement for all concerned will usually be for agreement about ownership and exploitation of any rights to be reached in advance and be evidenced in writing. Where the potential for disputes has not been success-fully pre-empted, assignments or confirmatory assignments of copyright may be appropriate to resolve doubts about rights in existing works.

6.3.2 Assignments and licences

A copyright can be given away, be bought and sold, or be left as an inheritance under a will as personal or movable property (1988 Act, s. 90(1)). An assignment, or other transfer, of copyright may be outright or may relate only to certain of the exclusive rights enjoyed by the owner. Thus, for example, an assignee may be given the right solely to translate a software package into a particular language. A transfer may also be limited to any part of the remaining term of the copyright (1988 Act, s. 90(2)). In practice, limited rights, such as to convert a program for use with a particular operating system or for foreign language users, are more often granted by way of licence than by partial assignment. Where such a licence is 'exclusive', the licensee will in effect be treated as the owner in terms of rights and remedies and the distinction between such a licence and a corresponding assignment will, for most purposes, be academic.[54] Assignments of copyright and of 'future copyright' (that is, copyright which will or may come into existence in the future, e.g., in a commissioned work) will only be effective if made in writing and signed by or on behalf of the assignor (1988 Act, ss. 90(3) and 91(1)).

Licences other than exclusive licences can be made informally without being evidenced in writing. Indeed, they may even be inferred from the circumstances of a transaction or the general or specific conduct of the parties. Licences relating to the use of software are generally recorded in a written statement of terms, though frequently there is no signed agreement or contract as such.[55] The 1988 Act provides, in limited circumstances, for deemed licences to use second-hand copies of programs and other works distributed in electronic form (see 6.5.9).

The circumstances in which a copyright owner has the right to refuse to grant a licence were at issue in the European Court of Justice case of *Radio Telefís Eireann* v *Commission* (cases C-241 and 242/91) [1995] ECR I-743.

---

54. Section 101(1) of the 1988 Act provides that 'An exclusive licensee has, except against the copyright owner, the same rights and remedies in respect of matters occurring after the grant of the licence as if the licence had been an assignment'.
55. See C.J. Millard, 'Shrink-wrap Licensing' (1987) 4 *CLSR* 8.

The case concerned the attempted production of a weekly television guide by Magill TV Guide Ltd covering programmes broadcast by the BBC, ITV and the Irish network RTE. The networks obtained an injunction against Magill on the basis that they were entitled to refuse to grant licences of copyright. The case was then taken to the Commission where it was decided that each of the networks had abused a dominant position contrary to art. 86 of the EC Treaty.[56] This decision was later upheld in the Court of First Instance.[57] Despite an opinion of the Advocate General proposing that the Court of Justice set aside the judgments of the Court of First Instance, the final judgment of the Court upheld the first instance judgment. This ruling has left considerable uncertainty amongst copyright owners as to the circumstances in which they are entitled to refuse to grant licences. Although the case only impacts upon copyright owners in a dominant position, the ability of Community authorities to invoke competition principles to curtail the rights of copyright owners may in future have significant consequences for the computer industry.

6.3.3   Term of protection

The term of protection afforded to various forms of copyright has been modified by the Duration of Copyright and Rights in Performances Regulations 1995[58] and the Copyright and Related Rights Regulations 1996.[59] These Regulations implemented an EU Directive on the subject, which aimed to make copyright coterminous in all Member States.[60] The 1988 Act originally stipulated, subject to certain exceptions, a period of 50 years from the end of the year in which the author dies for literary, dramatic, musical or artistic works (s. 12(1)). This was extended for those works to a period of 70 years from the author's death by the 1995 Regulation (SI 1995/3297). In the case of films, the duration of copyright was extended by the 1995 Regulations from 50 years from the making or release of the film to a period of 70 years from the death of the last to die of the principal director and the author of the screenplay, dialogue or music. The 1996 Regulations (SI 1996/2967) introduce an innovative new right, known as the 'publication right' — reg. 16 provides that a person who publishes a previously unpublished work after the expiry of copyright protection will be entitled to a period of 25 years of protection from the end of the year of first publication. This right is described as a property right equivalent to copyright and is intended to cover, for example, the publication of freshly discovered works of well-known authors. The 1988 Act provides, unamended by the 1995 Regulations and 1996

56. *Magill TV Guide/ITP* OJ 1989 L78/43 1989. Note that the relevant article of the EC Treaty is now art. 82.
57. *Radio Telefis Eireann* v *Commission* (case T-69/89) [1991] ECR II-485 and *Independent Television Publications Ltd* v *Commission* (case T-76/89) [1991] ECR II-575.
58. SI 1995/3297, which came into force on 1 January 1996.
59. SI 1996/2967, which came into force on 1 December 1996.
60. Council Directive of 29 October 1993 harmonising the term of protection of copyright and certain related rights (93/98/EEC), OJ L290, 24 November 1993.

Regulations, that, in the case of computer-generated work, copyright expires after 50 years from the end of the year in which the work was made (1988 Act, s. 12(3)). This latter rule is similar to the rules applying to sound recordings, broadcasts and cable programmes (ss. 13 and 14). The typographical arrangement of a published edition, which is itself a work for copyright purposes, is protected for a still shorter term of 25 years from the end of the year of first publication (s. 15). Thus, in the case of a product such as a software package comprising multiple works, copyright in the various component parts will run out on a number of different dates. Duration of copyright may depend, for example, on the life expectancy of various human contributors, the year in which any computer-generated works were made, and the year of first publication of the documentation.

The recent lengthening of the term of protection of various forms of copyright has two consequences, which further complicate matters in relation to those types of works. One is the extension of copyright in works whose protection in the UK would have expired under the provisions of the 1988 Act and the other is the revival of copyright in works whose protection has expired in the UK within the last 20 years. In respect of copyright extension, reg. 21 of the 1995 Regulations provides that copyright licences which subsisted immediately before 1 January 1996 and were not to expire before the end of the copyright period as it was under the 1988 Act shall continue to have effect during the period of any extended copyright. In cases of copyright revival, reg. 22 provides that any waiver or assertion of moral rights, which subsisted immediately before the expiry of copyright, shall continue to have effect during the period of revived copyright. In addition, by reg. 23, no act done before 1 January 1996 shall be regarded as infringing revived copyright in a work and, by reg. 24, where revived copyright subsists, any acts restricted by copyright shall be treated as licensed by the copyright owner, subject to the payment of a reasonably royalty, to be determined, in case of dispute, by the Copyright Tribunal. By reg. 16, the revival provisions will apply to works in which copyright has expired, but which were, on 1 July 1995, protected in another EEA State.

The provisions of the 1988 Act dealing with the duration of copyright (ss. 12–14, which apply respectively to literary, dramatic, musical or artistic works, to sound recordings, to films and to broadcasts or cable programmes) require that, in circumstances where the country of origin or the nationality of an author is not an EEA State, the duration of copyright is that to which the work is entitled in the country of origin, provided the period does not exceed that provided for under the 1998 Act. Section 15A of the 1998 Act[61] provides that in respect of the duration of copyright protection, the country of origin is: the country of first publication if it is a Berne Convention country (s. 15A(2)); a Berne Convention country if the work is simultaneously published in a non-Berne Convention country (s. 15A(3)); or an EEA State or otherwise the Berne Convention country that grants the shortest period of

---

61. Inserted by the Duration of Copyright and Rights in Performances Regulations 1995, reg. 8(1), which came into force on 1 January 1996.

protection (s. 15A(4)). Quite what the overall consequences of the extension and revival provisions may turn out to be in terms of extra costs is a matter of some concern to industry, especially as those costs will have been wholly unforeseen in some cases. For example, a multimedia product may contain materials selected on the basis that the relevant copyrights had expired. A subsequent requirement to pay royalties in respect of revived copyrights might undermine the financial viability of the product.

6.4 INFRINGEMENT OF COPYRIGHT

6.4.1 Types of infringing act

Space does not permit a full discussion of all of the acts that can constitute infringement of the copyright in a work. Instead, the focus will be on the principal acts of so-called 'primary infringement' with reference also being made to the various acts of 'secondary infringement'. A primary infringement occurs where a person directly commits an infringing act or authorises someone else to do so. Secondary infringers, as their name suggests, are generally one stage removed from the relevant primary infringing acts, but may be implicated by, for example, importing or distributing infringing copies without the consent of the copyright owner. A crucial distinction between primary infringers and secondary infringers is that those in the former category can be liable for infringing copyright whether or not they realise they are doing so, whereas those in the latter category are only liable if they know, or have reason to believe, that they are committing an act of secondary infringement. Three of the most relevant primary infringing acts (copying, adaptation, and issuing copies to the public) are discussed in 6.4.2 and the various acts of secondary infringement are outlined in 6.4.3.

6.4.2 Primary infringement

6.4.2.1 Copying Whereas the 1956 Act gave the owner of copyright in a work control over the act of 'reproducing the work in any material form' (s. 2(5)(a)), the Copyright, Designs and Patents Act 1988 contains the much simpler statement that a copyright owner has the exclusive right 'to copy the work' and to authorise anyone else to do so (s. 16(1)(a) and (2)). The 1988 Act provides that control over copying applies in relation to the whole or any substantial part of a work, and regardless of whether copying occurs directly or indirectly (s. 16(3)). As will be seen in 6.5, it may be difficult to establish whether the reproduction of certain structural or other characteristics of a computer program will constitute either direct or indirect copying of a substantial part of the program.

Section 17(2) of the 1988 Act defines copying, in relation to a literary, dramatic, musical or artistic work, as 'reproducing the work in a material form' including 'storing the work in any medium by electronic means'. This provision is reinforced by s. 17(6) which provides that 'Copying in relation to any description of work includes the making of copies which are transient or are incidental to some other use of the work'. As will be seen in 6.5.2, these provisions have significant consequences when applied to computer programs and other works distributed in electronic form.

6.4.2.2 Making adaptations Section 21(1) of the 1988 Act restricts the making of an adaptation of a literary, dramatic or musical work. 'Adaptation' means, amongst other things, making a translation of a literary work, and 'in relation to a computer program a "translation" includes a version of the program in which it is converted into or out of a computer language or code or into a different computer language or code' (s. 21(3) and (4) as amended by the Copyright (Computer Programs) Regulations 1992, reg. 5). In relation to a computer program 'adaptation' means an arrangement or altered version of the program or a translation of it (s. 21(3)(ab))[62] and in relation to a database 'adaptation' means an arrangement or altered version of the database or a translation of it (s. 21(3)(ac)).[63] The possible implications of s. 21 for the scope of a program copyright owner's control over simple 'use' of software are discussed in 6.5.2, below.

6.4.2.3 Issuing copies to the public Section 18(1) of the 1988 Act provides that 'the issue to the public of copies of the work is an act restricted by copyright in every description of copyright work'. The issuing of copies of a work includes the issue of the original (s. 18(4)).[64] The act of issuing copies of a work to the public is defined in terms of 'putting into circulation in the EEA copies not previously put into circulation in the EEA by or with the consent of the copyright owner' (s. 18(2)(a)) or 'putting into circulation outside the EEA copies not previously put into circulation in the EEA or elsewhere' (s. 18(2)(b)). Broadly speaking, this gives the owner of copyright in a work control over publication of the work. Specifically excluded, however, from the ambit of s. 18 are distribution, sale, hiring, loan, or importation into the United Kingdom of copies that have lawfully been issued to the public anywhere in the world (s. 18(3)). Previously this exclusion was, in turn, qualified in a most significant respect with the words 'except that in relation to sound recordings, films and computer programs the restricted act of issuing copies to the public includes any rental of copies to the public'.

This restriction on the rental of copies of certain categories of works, including computer programs, was an innovative feature of the 1988 Act. Prior to the 1988 Act no such automatic restriction existed. Copyright owners were, of course, able to restrict rental of their works by agreement and, in addition, the absence of a restriction on rental did not give a person who rented a copy any right to make a further copy. In practice, however, copies of works are often distributed in circumstances such that it is not feasible for

---

62. Inserted by the Copyright (Computer Programs) Regulations 1992, reg. 5(2), which came into force on 1 January 1993.
63. Inserted by the Copyright and Rights in Databases Regulations 1997, reg. 7(b), which came into force on 1 January 1998.
64. Inserted by the Copyright and Related Rights Regulations 1996, reg. 9(3), which came into force 1 December 1996.

appropriate restrictions to be imposed in that way. An obvious example is mass-market distribution of 'shrink-wrapped' software packages.[65] Moreover, a theoretical right to restrict the making of further copies from a rented copy is of limited efficacy in the face of widespread private copying of works such as compact discs, videos and software packages. Of far greater use to copyright owners was the new right to prevent, or regulate at source, the rental of copies of such works to the public.

In response to an EU Directive on rental and lending rights adopted in 1992 ('the Rental Directive')[66] and one concerning satellite broadcasting and cable retransmission in 1993 ('the Satellite Directive'),[67] the Copyright and Related Rights Regulations 1996[68] were issued. The regulations amend the definition of 'rental' in the 1988 Act[69] and add a new definition of 'lending'.[70] Section 18A(2) of the 1998 Act defines 'rental' as 'making a copy of the work available for use, on terms that it will or may be returned, for direct or indirect commercial advantage' (s. 18A(2)(a)) and 'lending' as 'making a copy of the work available for use, on terms that it will or may be returned, otherwise than for direct or indirect economic or commercial advantage' by means accessible to the public (s. 18A(2)(b)). These definitions exclude any arrangement by which copies are made available for the purpose of public performance, exhibition or for on-the-spot referencing (s. 18A(3)). The Regulations also provide for an extension of rental rights to all literary, musical and dramatic works and most artistic ones.[71] The rental right is the right of the owner of copyright to authorise or prohibit the rental or copies of the work, which are deemed to be restricted acts under s. 18A (s. 179). As a result of the changes brought about by the Regulations, performers are accorded some additional rights, including rental, lending and distribution rights and rights to income for performances in films and sound recordings. The Rental Directive provides that Member States must implement a right to authorise or prohibit the rental and lending of originals and copies of copyright works,[72] but derogations may be made in respect of the grant of exclusive lending rights provided authors, at least, are remunerated for lending. A derogation is made to cover films and sound recordings in the Regulations. In addition, certain exemptions apply to libraries and education-

65. See C.J. Millard, 'Shrink-wrap Licensing' (1987) 4 *CLSR* 8.
66. Council Directive of 19 November 1992 on rental right and lending right and certain rights related to copyright in the field of intellectual property (92/100/EEC). OJ L346, 27 November 1992.
67. Council Directive of 27 September 1993 on the coordination of certain rules concerning copyright and rights related to copyright applicable to satellite broadcasting and cable retransmission (93/83/EEC), OJ L248, 6 October 1993.
68. SI 1996/2967, entry into force 1 December 1996.
69. Substituted by the Copyright and Related Rights Regulations 1996, reg. 10(4), in force 1 December 1996. See ss. 179 and 18A(2)–(6).
70. Inserted by the Copyright and Related Rights Regulations 1996, reg. 10(4), in force 1 December 1996. See ss. 179 and 18A(2)–(6).
71. Inserted by the Copyright and Related Rights Regulations 1996, reg. 10(4), in force 1 December 1996. See s. 178.
72. Article 1(1). By art. 2(1) the right is granted, in special circumstances, to authors, performers and phonogram and film producers. See s. 18A(1) and (6).

al establishments. The Regulations also cover the requirements of the Satellite Directive and contain provisions to determine applicable law where broadcasts are made within or outside the EEA and received in more than one Member State. They also address cable retransmission, requiring the exercise of rights by persons other than broadcasting organisations to be exercised through a licensing body.

6.4.3 Secondary infringement

6.4.3.1 Dealing in infringing copies   Secondary infringement occurs where, without the consent of the copyright owner, a person 'imports into the United Kingdom, otherwise than for his own private and domestic use, an article which is, and which he knows or has reason to believe is, an infringing copy of the work' (Copyright, Designs and Patents Act 1988, s. 22). Infringement also occurs where a person, again without consent, 'possesses in the course of a business' or deals in articles which he knows or has reason to believe are infringing copies. Relevant dealings are selling, hiring, offering for sale or hire, commercial exhibition or distribution of copies of the work, and any other distribution 'otherwise than in the course of business to such an extent as to affect prejudicially the owner of the copyright' (s. 23).

6.4.3.2 Providing articles for making infringing copies   Copyright in a work is infringed where, without the consent of the copyright owner, 'an article specifically designed or adapted for making copies of that work' is manufactured, imported or commercially dealt in by a person who knows or has reason to believe that it will be used for that purpose (1988 Act, s. 24(1)). The scope of this infringing act is not clear. It is not necessary that an article be intended specifically for use in making *infringing* copies, merely that the article is 'specifically designed or adapted' for making copies and that such copies may infringe copyright. Thus, at its broadest, the provision arguably could be construed as covering commonplace articles such as photocopiers, tape recorders, and personal computers which every importer, manufacturer, or dealer should suspect may be used to make infringing copies of works. Such a construction of the section would, however, be absurd. An extremely limited interpretation would probably be nearer the mark. The basis for a narrow construction is the reference to the making of copies of *that* work, meaning that the device in question must have been specifically designed or adapted to make copies of a particular work owned by a particular person, and not merely for making copies of works generally.

6.4.3.3 Facilitating infringement by transmission   As where a copy of a work is rented out and copied by the renter, where a copy of a work is made available by transmission over a telecommunications system, there may in theory be a cause of action against each recipient who stores, and thus copies, the work on reception. However, the practical difficulties inherent in enforcing this right to sue each ultimate infringer render it of little practical use to copyright owners. Section 24(2) of the 1988 Act provides copyright owners with a basis for regulating such dissemination of a work at source, as follows:

Copyright in a work is infringed by a person who without the licence of the copyright owner transmits the work by means of a telecommunications system (otherwise than by broadcasting or inclusion in a cable programme service), knowing or having reason to believe that infringing copies of the work will be made by means of the reception of the transmission in the United Kingdom or elsewhere.

Accordingly, a supply down a telephone line of software, data, or any other work protected by copyright, may be an act of secondary infringement if done without an appropriate licence.

6.4.3.4 Circumvention of copy-protection A further area in which the 1988 Act strengthened the right of owners of works distributed in electronic form relates to devices or information intended to facilitate the circumvention of copy-protection measures. The relevant provision is not grouped with the other sections that deal with secondary infringement but appears quite separately in Part VII of the Act under the heading 'Miscellaneous and general'. Section 296 provides that a copyright owner who issues a work in copy-protected electronic form has the same rights against a person who, with intent, makes available any device or means designed or adapted to circumvent the copy-protection as would be available against a copyright infringer. 'Copy protection' is defined as including 'any device or means intended to prevent or restrict copying of a work or to impair the quality of copies made' (s. 296(4)).

As with the discussion of the restriction on providing articles to be used for making infringing copies (see 6.4.3.2), it is not clear how broadly the circumvention of copy-protection provision will be interpreted by the courts. At its widest, s. 296 could be construed as encompassing any hardware, software, or information intended to facilitate copying of, or access to, encrypted files, or even recovery of corrupted data. Thus, suppliers of bit-copiers and utilities designed to restore garbled or incomplete data might be vulnerable to attack under the provision. Similarly, distributors of hardware devices such as 'ROM blowers', which are designed for copying data from one chip to another, might be caught. However, as with our earlier conclusions regarding secondary infringement, it is likely that a much more restricted analysis would prevail. Thus, a court would probably look for some specific evidence, perhaps based on a special configuration of a device or perhaps based on provocative advertising to suggest that the manufacturer, importer or dealer intended the device or information in question to be used to circumvent copy-protection. Where a device has multiple potential uses, at least some of which are legitimate, it seems unlikely that s. 296 will be applicable.

6.4.4   Copyright infringement via the Internet[73]

The law of copyright, as has been seen, has sometimes been hard pressed to keep pace with the legal implications of technological advances. Probably the most difficult challenge to legislators and courts to date has been regulating the use and abuse of copyright material accessed via the Internet.

Three of the most fundamental questions are these. First, who may be liable for copyright infringement? Secondly, what is the appropriate law and jurisdiction? Thirdly, what acts of infringement may have been committed under the relevant law? Possible infringers fall into three main categories: originators of material, recipients of it and network operators. Some of the ways in which they could find themselves liable under English law are as follows.

An originator who transmits infringing material via the Internet may, by the act of transmission, be infringing copyright. The originator may also infringe if he or she is regarded variously as performing, displaying, showing, playing or broadcasting[74] the material. This is because the act of sending a message containing infringing material in the knowledge that it will necessarily be copied along the way may constitute infringement of copyright by trans-mission. It may also be the case that the originator will be liable for merely making material available on his or her computer to be browsed or copied by means of an instruction by another computer to send the material to it (for example, via the World Wide Web or File Transfer Protocol). However, in the case of piracy at least, the greatest problem may not be in identifying whether or not an originator of material has infringed copyright, but in identifying who and where the originator is. Sophisticated techniques exist for ensuring the anonymity of persons making material available via the Internet.[75]

Likewise, the recipient of material may be infringing copyright if he or she receives material which infringed copyright at the time of sending,[76] and someone who browses material on a web site, or accesses it by instructing the originator's computer to send the material, may infringe copyright. Material may be downloaded deliberately or a copy of part or all of a file held on a remote web site may be made automatically by a process known as 'caching' whereby material is copied on to a user's PC to speed up future access to a web site.

Network operators that carry bits of data containing infringing material, and there may be several such operators in different jurisdictions along the

---

73. See also section 11.6.1 below in relation to the liability of Internet Service Providers for third party activities which infringe copyright.

74. See, for example, *Shetland Times Ltd v Dr Jonathan Wills and Another* [1998] Masons CLR 159, where, in finding that the balance of convenience fell in favour of awarding an interim injunction against the use of a website containing headlines of the pursuer, Lord Hamilton accepted the argument that there was a *prima facie* case of infringement of a cable broadcast service in that the information was conveyed to the user's site, and that constituted sending within the meaning of s. 20 of the 1988 Act.

75. For example, 'spoofing', which involves obtaining a false Internet protocol address, or the use of anonymous remailers.

76. This would be the case if the recipient were in possession of the infringing copies in the course of a business and had the requisite *mens rea*.

route of transmission, may be liable for infringement of copyright by the fact of having copied the material en route, even though copying may be automatic and though the network operator may never 'see' the material in question. This would mean that, subject to express or implied licences, network operators would be infringing copyright *whenever* they transmitted a message protected by copyright, whether or not the message infringed copyright when it left the sender. Similarly, they may be caught by the various displays and performance provisions referred to above in relation to originators.

However, under the law as it stands, network operators are most likely to infringe by transmission. The question is what degree of knowledge would be necessary for them to fulfil the *mens rea* required for secondary infringement? Would it be sufficient for a software house to issue a letter to, say, a public network operator such as BT, stating that, in all probability, that operator's network was being used for the purpose of creating infringing copies? Would it be sufficient to produce evidence that a specific customer was using the network in this manner? Would it be sufficient that the network operator knew that the material being transmitted was sourced from a copy of the material on a neighbouring network, which was unlikely to have received explicit permission to copy the work? The answers to such questions are unknown at this point, but network operators would probably not be held to have the requisite knowledge unless they had received very specific and detailed information concerning the activities of a specific customer. Even at that point, there are good policy reasons not to hold network operators liable for secondary infringement, many of which have actively been drawn to the attention of legislators by network operators themselves.[77]

As yet, there has been no English court decision concerning the potential liability of network operators for copyright infringement via the Internet. In the United States, however, there have been several cases already, of which we shall look briefly at two. In *Playboy Enterprises Inc.* v *Frena* (1993) 4 CCH Computer Cases 47,020 it was held that there had been infringement of the claimant's right publicly to distribute and display copyrighted photographs by the defendant, on whose bulletin board the photographs had been posted by some of the defendant's subscribers without his knowledge. A different conclusion was reached in the more recent case of *Religious Technology Center* v *Netcom Online Communications Services* (1995) CCH Computer Cases 47,411 which may have signalled a move away from the imposition of liability for direct infringement upon service providers despite strict liability under the Copyright Act 1976 (17 USC, s. 501). In the *Netcom* case the District Court of the Northern District of California held that 'it does not make sense to adopt a rule that could lead to the liability of countless parties whose role in the infringement is nothing more than setting up and operating a system that is necessary for the functioning of the Internet'. However, to what extent it

---

77. For a more detailed discussion of the position of network operators in relation to copyright infringement issues, see Christopher Millard and Robert Carolina, 'Commercial Transactions on The Global Information Infrastructure: A European Perspective', *John Marshall Journal of Computer and Information Law*, vol. 14, No. 2, Winter 1996.

may have been significant that there were other defendants to the action who were clearly liable for direct infringement under the US Copyright Act is not clear.

A key question is whether jurisdiction should be determined by reference to where material originated, where it went along the way or where it ended up being displayed, stored or printed out. It may, of course, be correct to say that an infringement has taken place in more than one jurisdiction and under more than one law. Possibilities for 'forum shopping' will undoubtedly flow from this.

6.5 SCOPE OF PROTECTION FOR COMPUTER PROGRAMS AND DATA

6.5.1 Idea and expression, symbolism and functionality

In the United Kingdom there is no statutory rule that bars ideas from copyright protection.[78] However, the Software Directive[79] provides in art. 1.2 that 'Ideas and principles which underlie any element of a computer program, including those which underlie its interfaces, are not protected by copyright under this Directive'. The Copyright (Computer Programs) Regulations 1992 are silent on this point. However, a number of English, and other Commonwealth, precedents appear to exclude ideas *per se* from copyright protection.[80] The apparent logic behind the rule was illustrated by the Supreme Court of Canada in *Cuisenaire* v *South West Imports Ltd* [1969] SCR 208 with the observation that 'were the law otherwise, ... everybody who made a rabbit pie in accordance with the recipe of Mrs Beeton's cookery book would infringe the literary copyright in that book'.[81]

The claimed distinction then is between an idea that cannot be protected by copyright, such as the procedure for making a rabbit pie, and an expression of that idea, such as a written recipe describing the rabbit pie making process, which can be protected by copyright. In the case of a computer program, however, such a tidy analysis is not possible. Indeed, it may be that the statement that ideas can never be protected by copyright is a misleading over-simplification.[82] Take, for example, ideas such as the algorithms on which a program is based, or perhaps the methods or processes that the program implements. Because of the nature of the interaction between software and hardware, a program, unlike a page from a recipe book, can simultaneously be *symbolic* (i.e., a representation of instructions to be

---

78. Compare, for example, the position in the United States, where s. 102(b) of Title 17 USC provides 'in no case does copyright protection ... extend to any idea, procedure, process, system, method of operation, concept, principle, or discovery, regardless of the form in which it is described, explained, illustrated, or embodied in such work'.
79. Directive 91/250/EEC.
80. For example, in *Donoghue* v *Allied Newspapers Ltd* [1938] Ch 106, Farwell J stated unequivocally that 'there is no copyright in an idea, or in ideas'.
81. *Cuisenaire* v *South West Imports Ltd* [1969] SCR 208 at p. 212, citing Pape J in *Cuisenaire* v *Reed* [1963] VR 719.
82. This theme is developed in more detail in 6.5.6.

given to the computer) and *functional* (i.e., the means by which the computer is actually instructed to carry out operations). Lines of code that describe an operation or procedure can also be used to implement it. It is as though by putting the relevant pages from Mrs Beeton's cookery book into an oven one could produce a rabbit pie. This special characteristic of computer programs has a number of significant consequences in copyright law. One is that use of a program is almost impossible without copying and/or adaptation occurring (see 6.5.2). Another is that there may be no way to achieve functional compatibility between two or more items of hardware or software without reproducing a substantial amount of code to effect the desired interface or communication (see 6.5.3).

6.5.2   Infringement of program copyright by use of a program

In relation to conventional works, the 'use' of a legitimate copy of a work is not generally restricted by copyright. For example, the simple act of reading a book is not controlled by copyright. It is only on the occurrence of one of the specifically restricted acts, for example, the copying or adaptation of a substantial part of the book, that a question of infringement can arise. However, because computer programs in machine-code form are both symbolic and functional, normal use may necessitate such copying or adaptation. Loading or running a computer program typically entails the copying of part or all of the program from a disk (or other permanent storage medium) to the computer's random access memory (RAM) and central processing unit (CPU). Section 17(6) of the Copyright, Designs and Patents Act 1988 makes it clear that such copying of a work, even though it may be 'transient' or 'incidental to some other use of the work', is nevertheless an infringement of copyright if done without authorisation. Even screen displays generated during the running of a program may constitute infringing copies of copyright material. Because the restriction on copying applies even to simple use of a program, legitimate use can normally only take place pursuant to a licence or permission of some kind. Such a licence may be express or implied. Typically, a software house will seek to attach various conditions to a licence to use. A special provision in the 1988 Act dealing with transfers of second-hand copies of programs is dealt with in 6.5.9.

Hence, UK copyright law appears to give indirect protection to the ideas underlying a program by making the literal copying inherent in simple use of the program an infringing act. Thus, unlike the ideas and procedures described in a cookery recipe which can be used without infringing copyright in the recipe book, the ideas and procedures embodied in a computer program are regulated by copyright along with the code which implements them whenever the program is used. It is interesting to note, by way of comparison, that under United States copyright law the owner of a copy of a program does not need a licence to make or authorise the making of another copy or adaptation if doing so is 'an essential step in the utilisation of the computer program in conjunction with a machine'.[83]

---

83. Title 17 USC, s. 117. This derogation from the copyright owner's normal rights to prevent the making of copies and adaptations does not seem to apply where title to the physical copy does not pass to the software user.

A similar approach was adopted in the EU Software Directive,[84] though the deemed right to make copies or adaptations necessary for use seems to be subject to agreement to the contrary. Article 5.1 provides that 'In the absence of specific contractual provisions', copying and adaptation 'shall not require authorisation by the rightholder where they are necessary for the use of the computer program by the lawful acquirer in accordance with its intended purpose, including for error correction'. The words 'in the absence of specific contractual provisions' seem to make it clear that it remains open to a copyright owner to restrict by contract these acts of copying and adaptation necessary for use.[85] This is the interpretation adopted by the UK government in the implementing regulations. Whether copyright can also be used to prevent non-literal copying, for example, where a person analyses or reverse engineers a program and writes new but functionally equivalent code, is a rather more complex issue.

6.5.3 Copying, compatibility and reverse engineering

There may be a limited number of ways, in extreme cases possibly only one, of achieving a particular functional result using a specific configuration of hardware and/or software. Sometimes a single manufacturer can establish an almost universal standard or set of standards for carrying out particular operations, perhaps by being there first, by skilful marketing, by dominance in the industry, or sometimes by being truly innovative. Where, for whatever reason, a *de facto* industry standard has emerged, such as the BIOS ('basic input-output system') for IBM-compatible personal computers, the possibility of copyright being used to monopolise the specification of interfaces between hardware and hardware, hardware and software, software and software, and humans and software, has enormous policy implications. Much of the rapid growth and diversity that has characterised the computer industry in the last two decades has resulted from the widespread development of hardware and software products that are 'compatible' with those most popular in the market. Such compatible products frequently improve substantially on the products offered by the company that initiated the standard both in terms of price and performance, and often also in terms of innovation. A user who has invested in a particular 'environment' in terms of hardware, software, or training, will often wish to build on that investment without being tied into a particular supplier or suppliers for all future development purposes.

The development of compatible products can, of course, be effected in a number of ways with varying consequences in copyright terms. At one end of the spectrum, a clone may consist of or contain crude copies of key parts, or indeed the whole, of an established product. The maker of such a clone will

---

84. Directive 91/250/EEC.
85. Confusingly, the relevant recital is inconsistent with art. 5 and provides that 'the acts of loading and running necessary for the use of a copy of a program that has been lawfully acquired, and the act of correction of its errors, may not be prohibited by contract'. Presumably, art. 5 will prevail.

be vulnerable to be sued for infringement of copyright and a number of other intellectual property rights. Certainly, the literal copying of the whole or a substantial part of an existing program will almost invariably infringe copyright. At the other end of the spectrum, a developer of a compatible product may invest substantial resources in achieving functional compatibility by independent development without making a verbatim or literal copy of any part of the product that is being emulated. To ensure that it can be proved that the competing product is the result of such original labour and skill, a manufacturer may resort to a rigorous and exhaustively documented 'clean-room' procedure. Such a procedure would normally necessitate independent work being undertaken by two discrete groups of software engineers, the first analysing the product to be emulated and producing a functional specification, the second writing code to implement that specification.[86] In between these extremes of crude copying and sophisticated reverse engineering, there are various ways in which software may be developed using particular ideas or functions derived from pre-existing software products without any substantial literal copying taking place.

Various tests have been suggested for determining whether products developed using either of the latter two approaches will infringe copyright and a certain amount of judicial consideration has been given to these issues in the UK. However, most reported cases and current litigation in the area are concentrated in the United States. Much of the argument there has concerned the extent to which copyright law can provide protection against copying of either the 'structure, sequence and organisation' of a program, or of its 'look and feel'. The former concerns the internal structure and workings of a program, the latter its external appearance and user interfaces. Underlying both issues is the fundamental dichotomy in United States law between ideas, which cannot be protected by copyright, and expressions of those ideas, which can. Before looking briefly at some of the American cases, one other general issue should be noted.

6.5.4 Difficulties of proving non-literal infringement

A further consequence of the simultaneously symbolic and functional nature of software is that the traditional tests for establishing that copying of a work has occurred may be wholly inappropriate. It is by no means always the case that functional similarity between two programs is indicative of similarity in the underlying symbolic codes. To extend the rabbit pie analogy one final stage further, just because a rabbit pie looks, smells and tastes very similar to one made by Mrs Beaton is not in itself proof that both have been made from the same recipe. As Megarry V-C put it in *Thrustcode Ltd v WW Computing Ltd* [1983] FSR 502 at p. 505:

> ... where, as here, the claim is to copyright in the program itself, the results produced by operating the program must not be confused with the

---

86. For an interesting discussion of the issues, inherent in duplication of the functionality of the IBM BIOS see G. Gervaise Davis III, 'IBM PC Software and Hardware Compatibility' [1984] *EIPR* 273.

program in which copyright is claimed. If I may take an absurdly simple example, 2 and 2 make 4. But so does 2 times 2, or 6 minus 2, or 2 percent of 200, or 6 squared divided by 9, or many other things. Many different processes may produce the same answer and yet remain different processes that have not been copied one from another.

On the facts before it, the court was at a loss to see 'any real evidence of copying' (at p. 507) and accordingly dismissed the claimant's case. In *LB (Plastics) Ltd v Swish Products Ltd* [1979] FSR 145 at p. 149, Lord Wilberforce observed:

> The protection given by the law of copyright is against copying, the basis of protection being that one man must not be permitted to appropriate the result of another's labour. That copying has taken place, is for the plaintiff [claimant] to establish and prove as a matter of fact. The beginning of the necessary proof normally lies in the establishment of similarity combined with proof of access to the plaintiff's [claimant's] productions.

In *Cantor Fitzgerald International v Tradition (UK) Ltd* [1999] Masons CLR 157 Pumfrey J held, in finding that copyright infringement had occurred where 3,000 out of 77,000 lines of the claimant's code were copied by the defendant, that it is the function of copyright to protect the relevant skill and labour expended by the author of the work and that it follows that a copyist infringes if he appropriates a part of the work upon which a substantial part of the author's skill and labour was expended. It is not determined by whether the system would work without the copied code or the amount of use the system makes of the code.

This issue is of fundamental importance in the context of software copyright infringement. It is not enough for a claimant to allege that program code has been copied merely on the basis that a later program is similar to an earlier one in terms of its functionality or its appearance to a user. Actual copying of a substantial part is the key to copyright infringement under UK law.[87] In this case, Pumfrey J accepted that the general architecture of a computer program was capable of protection provided a substantial part of the programmer's skill and labour was used. Therefore, it was possible for specific software modules to be infringed, even though only a small proportion of the code had been copied.[88]

6.5.5 Infringement by non-literal copying under United States law

A full discussion of the many reported and pending American cases in the field of software copyright is quite beyond the scope of this chapter. However, a brief consideration of some of the issues that have been raised in the United

---

87. See *Catnic Components v Hill & Smith* [1982] RPC 182 at 223; followed *Ibcos Computers Ltd v Barclays Mercantile Highland Finance Ltd* [1994] FSR 275; *Cantor Fitzgerald International v Tradition (UK) Ltd and Others* [1999] Masons CLR 157.
88. See the comments of Colin Tapper at [1999] Masons CLR 265–266.

States may assist, sometimes by analogy, sometimes by way of contrast, in evaluating the position under UK copyright law.

In its landmark ruling in *Apple Computer Inc.* v *Franklin Computer Corporation* (1983) 714 F 2d 1240, the United States Court of Appeals for the Third Circuit confirmed unequivocally that computer programs in both source and object code are capable of protection as 'literary works' and that such protection extends to programs in machine code embedded in integrated circuit chips. The court then considered whether program copyright extended to operating systems, and in particular whether a merger of idea and expression would prevent Apple from claiming protection for various operating programs supplied with the Apple II microcomputer. The court ruled that 'If other programs can be written or created which perform the same function as an Apple's operating system program, then that program is an expression of the idea and hence copyrightable'.[89] In response to claims by the defendants that there was only a limited number of ways of writing a compatible operating system:[90]

> Franklin may wish to achieve total compatibility with independently developed application programs written for Apple II, but that is a commercial and competitive objective which does not enter into the somewhat metaphysical issue of whether particular ideas and expressions have merged.

The court concluded that operating system programs are not *per se* excluded from copyright protection.

Three years later, a different panel of judges in the same Third Circuit Court of Appeals addressed in rather more detail the application to computer programs of the idea–expression dichotomy. In *Whelan Associates Inc.* v *Jaslow Dental Laboratory Inc.* [1987] FSR 1 the claimants alleged that a program developed by the defendant in the PC language BASIC infringed their copyright in a similar program written in the minicomputer language EDL. It was accepted that no literal copying had occurred yet the Third Circuit ruled that substantial similarities between the BASIC and EDL programs in terms of their 'structure, sequence and organisation' provided sufficient grounds for a finding of infringement. As regards drawing a line between idea and expression, the court ruled that 'the line between idea and expression may be drawn by reference to the end sought to be achieved by the work in question'.[91] Where the desired purpose can be achieved in more than one way, then any particular means of achieving it will be expression, not idea. On the facts before it, the Third Circuit found that 'the idea of the Dentalab program was the efficient management of a dental laboratory... . Because that idea could be accomplished in a number of different ways with a number of different structures, the structure of the Dentalab program is part of the program's expression, not its idea.'

---

89. 714 F 2d 1240 at p. 1253.
90. Ibid., loc. cit.
91. [1987] FSR 1 at p 19.

The Third Circuit's analysis in *Whelan Associates Inc.* v *Jaslow Dental Laboratory Inc.* has been widely criticised by academic writers.[92] A particular concern has been that the court's 'sweeping rule and broad language extend copyright protection too far' by moving towards a degree of monopoly protection previously only given to patent holders.[93] An indication of how widely the *Whelan* ruling could be applied came in *Broderbund Software Inc.* v *Unison World Inc.* (1986) 648 F Supp 1127, where it was cited as 'stand[ing] for the proposition that copyright protection is not limited to the literal aspects of a computer program, but rather that it extends to the overall structure of a program, including its audiovisual displays'.[94] The last part of this statement is rather surprising, given that the *Whelan* case was about infringement of a copyright in program code (i.e., a literary work), not infringement of copyright in screen displays (i.e., audiovisual works). Moreover, in place of the structural analysis conducted by the *Whelan* court, the *Broderbund* court was more concerned with whether 'the infringing work captures the "total concept and feel" of the protected work'. Noting 'the eerie resemblance between the screens of the two programs', the court found that infringement had indeed occurred.[95]

An illustration of the flexibility of the 'total concept and feel' or 'look and feel' approach can be seen in the analysis of an Ohio District Court in *Worlds of Wonder Inc.* v *Vector Intercontinental Inc.* (1986) unreported. The case concerned allegations of infringement of copyright in a talking animated toy bear known as Teddy Ruxpin. The bear was designed to be used with cassette tapes containing a soundtrack together with software to control the bear's movements. The defendants, in competition with the claimant, produced various tapes containing stories and software for Teddy Ruxpin. The court found infringement of copyright in the bear as an audiovisual work on the ground that:[96]

> the general feel and concept of Teddy Ruxpin when telling a fairy tale is the same regardless of whether a WOW or Vector tape is used; the visual effects are identical, and the voices are similar, and the difference in stories does not alter the aesthetic appeal.... At least, the work created by the Vector tapes is a derivative work, if not an exact copy.

These and other look-and-feel cases set the scene for an action brought by Lotus against alleged infringers of copyright in the look and feel of the user interfaces of its enormously successful '1-2-3' spreadsheet product.

Before identifying the principal issues at stake in the Lotus case, however, consideration should be given to a move by a District Court in California to

92. For example, D. Nimmer, R. L. Bernacchi and G. N. Frischling, 'A Structured Approach to Analysing the Substantial Similarity of Computer Software in Copyright Infringement Cases' (1988) 20 *Ariz St LJ* 625.
93. Ibid at p. 630. See also, Ganz, '*Whelan* and "work made for hire" threaten job mobility' (1988) 4 *Computer Law Strategist* 1.
94. 648 F Supp 1127 at p. 1133.
95. Ibid., at p. 1137.
96. Transcript at p. 9.

limit the breadth of the monopoly given to software copyright owners. In
NEC Corporation v *Intel Corporation* (1989) 1 CCH Computer Cases 46,020,
the court confirmed that microcodes embodied in various Intel chips were
protected by copyright as computer programs, yet ruled that the reverse
engineering of those programs by NEC did not infringe the relevant copyrights.[97] The court found that 'overall, and particularly with respect to the
microroutines, NEC's microcode is not substantially similar to Intel's; but
some of the shorter, simpler microroutines resemble Intel's. None, however,
are identical'. To resolve the issue of whether those of the shorter microroutines which were similar infringed Intel's copyrights, the court placed great
emphasis on the possibility of a merger of idea and expression, not as a basis
for denying copyrightability but as a justification for the production of
substantially similar code:[98]

> In determining an idea's range of expression, constraints are relevant factors
> to consider.... . In this case, the expression of NEC's microcode was
> constrained by the use of the macroinstruction set and hardware of the
> 8086/88.... Accordingly, it is the conclusion of this court that the expression
> of the ideas underlying the shorter, simpler microroutines (including those
> identified earlier as substantially similar) may be protected only against
> virtually identical copying, and that NEC properly used the underlying ideas,
> without virtually identically copying their limited expression.

In *Lotus Development Corporation* v *Paperback Software International* (1990)
2 CCH Computer Cases 46,310, the District Court for the District of
Massachusetts was called upon to decide whether the defendant's software
package 'VP-Planner' infringed the copyright in Lotus's '1-2-3' package.
Both products are electronic spreadsheets intended to facilitate accounting
and other processes that involve the manipulation and display of numerical
data. District Judge Keeton identified three elements that appeared to him to
be 'the principal factors relevant to a decision of copyrightability of a
computer program such as Lotus 1-2-3'.[99] These were, first 'some conception
or definition of the "idea" — for the purpose of distinguishing between the
idea and its expression'. Secondly, the court must determine 'whether an
alleged expression of the idea is limited to elements essential to expression of
that idea (or is one of only a few ways of expressing the idea) or instead
includes identifiable elements of expression not essential to every expression
of that idea'. Finally, 'having identified elements of expression not essential
to every expression of the idea, the decision-maker must focus on whether
those elements are a substantial part of the allegedly copyrightable
"work"'.[100]

97. In addition, the court ruled that Intel's failure to ensure that chips containing its microcode
    were properly marked with appropriate copyright notices had resulted in a forfeiture of its
    copyrights (1 CCH Computer Cases at 60,845).
98. 1 CCH Computer Cases 60,853.
99. 2 CCH Computer Cases 46,310 at 62,264.
100. Ibid., loc. cit.

Interestingly, the District Court judge was fairly dismissive of the 'look and feel' concept. He did not find the concept 'significantly helpful' because it was a 'conclusion' rather than a means of reaching a conclusion. Instead, in applying his three-limb test, Judge Keeton looked at the 'user interface' of the two programs. He seemed to accept as a basis for analysis the claimant's description of the user interface as including such elements 'as the menus (and their structure and organisation), the long prompts, the screens on which they appear, the function key assignments [and] the macro commands language'.[101] Applying his three-stage test to these elements of the user interface, Judge Keeton found that neither the idea of developing an electronic spreadsheet nor the idea of a two-line moving cursor menu were copyrightable. Both elements thus failed to get beyond the first stage. The basic screen display of a 'rotated L' layout used in most spreadsheet packages to set out columns and rows failed to pass the second stage as 'there is a rather low limit, as a factual matter, on the number of ways of making a computer screen resemble a spreadsheet'. Similarly the use of a particular key to invoke the menu command system was found to be 'Another expressive element that merges with the idea of an electronic spreadsheet'.[102]

One element of the 1-2-3 package did, however, satisfy all three elements of the copyrightability test. The menu command system itself was capable of many types of expression and its precise 'structure, sequence and organisation' was 'distinctive'. Reaching the third element of his test, Judge Keeton found it to be 'incontrovertible' that the menu command system was a substantial part of the alleged copyrighted work:[103]

The user interface of 1-2-3 is its most unique element, and is the aspect that has made 1-2-3 so popular. That defendants went to such trouble to copy that element is a testament to its substantiality. Accordingly, evaluation of the third element of the legal test weighs heavily in favour of Lotus.

The court's conclusion was that it was 'indisputable that defendants have copied substantial copyrightable elements of plaintiff's [claimant's] copyrighted work ... therefore ... liability has been established'.[104]

However, subsequently, in *Brown Bag Software* v *Symantec Corp.* (1992) 960 F 2d 1465 the Ninth Circuit rejected the claimant's argument that the *Lotus* approach should be applied in deciding whether the graphical user interface of the defendant's outlining program infringed the claimant's copyright. Instead, the court held that it should engage in 'analytical dissection not for the purposes of comparing similarities and identifying infringement, but for the purposes of defining the scope of plaintiff's [claimant's] copyright'.[105] Thus, the court should first determine which elements are uncopyrightable, applying the idea–expression dichotomy and the merger

101. Ibid., at 62,266.
102. Ibid., at 62,268.
103. Ibid., at 62,269.
104. Ibid., at 62,271.
105. 1960 F 2d at 1475–6.

doctrine to each element. Only then should it compare the protectable elements of expression to determine whether infringement may have occurred.

Many district and circuit judges have been critical of the Third Circuit's approach in *Whelan Associates Inc.* v *Jaslow Dental Laboratory Inc.* to the separation of ideas, which may not be protected, from expressions which may be.[106] In *Plains Cotton Cooperative Association of Lubbock Texas* v *Goodpasture Computer Services Inc.* (1987) 807 F 2d 1256 the Court of Appeals for the Fifth Circuit 'declined to embrace' *Whelan*. Subsequently the Second Circuit, in *Computer Associates* v *Altai* (1992) 3 CCH Computer Cases 46,505, has commented that the *Whelan* approach to separating idea and expression 'relies too heavily on metaphysical distinctions'. Instead, the *Altai* court suggested that district courts would be 'well advised' to adopt a three-step procedure for determining substantial similarity of non-literal elements of computer programs. First, the court should break down the allegedly infringed program into its constituent structural parts. Secondly, the court should examine each of these parts for such things as incorporated ideas, expression that is necessarily incidental to those ideas, and elements that are taken from the public domain, thus sifting out all non-protectable material. Thirdly, 'left with a kernel, or possibly kernels, of creative expression after following this process of elimination, the court's last step would be to compare this material with the structure of an allegedly infringing program'.[107] This has become known as the 'abstraction-filtration-comparison' analysis.

The court concluded that 'we seek to ensure two things: (1) that programmers may receive appropriate copyright protection for innovative utilitarian works containing expression; and (2) that non-protectable technical expression remains in the public domain for others to use freely as building blocks in their own work'.[108] It is interesting to note that the court relied heavily on the Supreme Court's decision in *Feist Publications Inc.* v *Rural Telephone Service Co. Inc.* (1990) 113 L Ed 2d 358, noting that '*Feist* teaches that substantial effort alone cannot confer copyright status on an otherwise uncopyrightable work' and that 'despite the fact that significant labour and expense often goes into computer program flow-charting and debugging, that process does not always result in inherently protectable expression'.[109]

In recent cases it appears that the trend is shifting away from the 'look and feel' approach towards *Altai's* analytical three-step test. In *Gates Rubber Co.* v *Bando Chemical Industries Ltd* (1993) 4 CCH Computer Cases 46,971, the Court of Appeals for the Tenth Circuit formulated a refined version of the *Altai* test. The court suggested that before beginning the abstraction-filtration-comparison process it would normally be helpful for the court to compare the programs as a whole, as 'an initial holistic comparison may reveal a pattern of copying that is not obvious when only certain components

---

106. See, for example, *Comprehensive Technologies Int'l* v *Software Artisans Inc.* Civil No 90-1143-A (E.D. Va. 2 June 1992).
107. *Computer Associates* v *Altai*, transcript (22 June 1992) at 28.
108. Ibid., at 58.
109. Ibid., at 41.

are examined'.[110] The abstraction-filtration-comparison test itself remained comparable to the *Altai* version:[111]

First, in order to provide a framework for analysis, we conclude that a court should dissect the program according to its varying levels of generality as provided in the abstraction test. Second, poised with this framework, the court should examine each level of abstraction in order to filter out those elements of the program that are unprotectable. Filtration should eliminate from comparison the unprotectable elements of ideas, processes, facts, public domain information, merger material, *scénes à faire* material, and other unprotectable elements suggested by the particular facts of the program under examination. Third, the court should then compare the remaining protectable elements with the allegedly infringing program to determine whether the defendants have misappropriated substantial elements of the plaintiff's [claimant's] program.

Applying this test the court found that certain mathematical constants in a computer program were not protectable because they represented scientific observations of relationships that existed and were not invented or created by the claimant.

In the case of *Kepner-Trego* v *Leadership Software Inc.* (1994) 4 CCH Computer Cases 47,019, concerning management training software, the Court of Appeals, Fifth Circuit, held that non-literal aspects of copyrighted works may be protected. This decision was applied in *Engineering Dynamics Inc.* v *Structural Software Inc.* (1994) 4 CCH Computer Cases, 47,095 to apply to non-literal aspects of a computer program, reversing a district court's decision that input and output formats were uncopyrightable. The district court, in coming to its conclusion, had thought *Lotus* was 'persuasive' but had declined to follow the decision. The Court of Appeals for the Fifth Circuit stated that the district court had 'erred' and that the abstraction-filtration-comparison of *Gates Rubber* and *Altai* was appropriate on the facts albeit that:[112]

Describing this approach as abstraction-filtration-comparison should not convey a deceptive air of certitude about the outcome of any particular computer copyright case. Protectable originality can manifest itself in many ways, so the analytic approach may need to be varied to accommodate each case's facts.

Since *Engineering Dynamics*, *Altai's* abstraction-filtration-comparison analysis has tended to be applied more or less as a matter of course to determine the scope of copyright protection in cases involving non-literal copying.[113]

---

110. 4 CCH Computer Cases at 65,812.
111. Ibid., at 65,806.
112. 4 CCH Computer Cases at 66,555.
113. See, for example, *Cognotec Services Ltd* v *Morgan Guarantee Trust Company of New York* 862 F Supp 45, 49–51 (SDNY 1994) 5 CCH Computer Cases 47,143; *Mitek Holdings Inc.* v *ARCE Engineering Co. Inc.* 864 F Supp 1568, 1577–78 (SD Fla 1994) 5 CCH Computer Cases 47,203; *Bateman* v *Mnemonics Inc.* 79 F 3d 1532 (11th Cir 1996) 6 CCH Computer Cases 47,356; and *Country Kids'n Slicks Inc.* v *Sheen* 77 F 3d 1280, 1288–89 (10th Cir 1996).

6.5.6   Infringement by non-literal copying under UK law

As already noted, the extent to which ideas are excluded from protection under UK copyright law has perhaps tended to be exaggerated. Some commentators have suggested that there is, on the contrary, considerable scope for protection of ideas provided merely that they have been reduced to writing or some other material form. Laddie, Prescott and Vitoria, for example, identify the 'pithy catch-phrase' that 'there is no copyright in ideas or information but only in the form in which they are expressed' and comment:[114]

> A moment's thought will reveal that the maxim is obscure, or in its broadest sense suspect. For example, in the case of a book the ideas it contains are necessarily expressed in words. Hence, if it were really true that the copyright is confined to the form of expression, one would expect to find that anyone was at liberty to borrow the contents of the book provided he took care not to employ the same or similar language. This is not so, of course. Thus, it is an infringement of the copyright to make a version of a novel in which the story or action is conveyed wholly by means of pictures; or to turn it into a play, although not a line of dialogue is similar to any sentence in the book. Again, a translation of a work into another language can be an infringement; yet, since the form of expression is necessarily different — indeed, if it is turned into a language such as Chinese the translation will consist of ideograms — the only connecting factor must be the detailed ideas and information.

Laddie, Prescott and Vitoria also note that most of the cases commonly cited in support of the exclusion of ideas from protection were decided prior to the 1956 Act, many indeed prior to the 1911 Act, and would probably be decided differently today.[115] Similar scepticism about the blanket exclusion of ideas from copyright has been expressed in judicial circles. In *LB (Plastics) Ltd v Swish Products Ltd* [1979] FSR 145 Lord Hailsham of St Marylebone LC observed:

> ... it is trite law that there is no copyright in ideas. ... But, of course, as the late Professor Joad used to observe, it all depends on what you mean by 'ideas'. What the respondents in fact copied from the appellants was no mere general idea.

More recently, in *Plix Products Ltd v Frank M Winstone (Merchants)* [1986] FSR 63, a case concerning infringement of artistic copyright, Pritchard J of the High Court of New Zealand has suggested that the so-called 'idea–expression dichotomy' can perhaps best be understood by distinguishing two different kinds, or levels, of 'ideas'. The first type of idea, 'the general idea or basic concept of the work', cannot be protected by copyright.

---

114. Hugh Laddie, Peter Prescott and Mary Vitoria, *The Modern Law of Copyright and Designs*, 2nd edn, London: Butterworths, 1998 paras 2.73 and 2.75, footnotes omitted.
115. Ibid., paras 2.50–2.54.

Copyright can, however, subsist in the second type, namely 'the ideas which are applied in the exercise of giving expression to basic concepts'. As Pritchard J then observed (at pp 93–4):

The difficulty, of course, is to determine just where the general concept ends and the exercise of expressing the concept begins. . . . The basic idea (or concept) is not necessarily simple — it may be complex. It may be something innovative; or it may be commonplace, utilitarian or banal. The way the author treats the subject, the forms he uses to express the basic concept, may range from the crude and simplistic to the ornate, complicated — and involving the collation and application of a great number of constructive ideas. It is in this area that the author expends the skill and industry which (even though they may be slight) give the work its originality and entitle him to copyright. Anyone is free to use the basic idea — unless, of course, it is a novel invention that is protected by the grant of a patent. But no one can appropriate the forms or shapes evolved by the author in the process of giving expression to the basic idea. So he who seeks to make a product of the same description as that in which another owns copyright must tread with care.

This analysis has interesting implications for the debates relating to the development of compatible software by means of reverse engineering, and the emulation of the look and feel of the user interfaces of popular software packages. The UK courts may tend, like the High Court of New Zealand, to be concerned more with whether a significant amount of an author's labour and skill has been misappropriated, than with whether what has been taken is 'merely' an idea, though there is as yet insufficient case law in the UK to be sure. To date, there have been only three reported software copyright infringement cases under the 1988 Act and a number of reported interlocutory (pre-trial) rulings relating to alleged infringements.[116]

John Richardson Computers Ltd v *Flanders* [1993] FSR 497 was the first full English trial for alleged infringement of software copyright. The case concerned allegations of literal and semi-literal copying of the claimant's program as evidenced at the user interface level. The defendant had worked for the claimant when the claimant was developing his program and had later developed his own. The programs were for use by pharmacists and had a number of idiosyncratic user features and routines in common. Ferris J referred to US case law and commented:

at the stage at which the substantiality of any copying falls to be assessed in an English case the question which has to be answered, in relation to the

---

116. The interlocutory judgments are *Gates* v *Swift* [1981] FSR 57; *Sega Enterprises Ltd* v *Richards* [1983] FSR 73; *Systematica Ltd* v *London Computer Centre Ltd* [1983] FSR 313; *Thrustcode Ltd* v *WW Computing Ltd* [1983] FSR 502; *MS Associates Ltd* v *Power* [1988] FSR 242; *Leisure Data* v *Bell* [1988] FSR 367; *Total Information Processing Systems Ltd* v *Daman Ltd* [1992] FSR 171; *Shetland Times Ltd* v *Jonathan Wills and Another* [1997] SLT 669; and *Microsoft Corp.* v *Electro-Wide Ltd* [1997] FSR 580.

originality of the plaintiff's [claimant's] program and the separation of an idea from its expression, is essentially the same question as the United States court was addressing in *Computer Associates* v *Altai*. In my judgment it would be right to adopt a similar approach in England.

In deciding the case he drew on the filtration and comparison parts of *Computer Associates* v *Altai* (1992) 3 CCH Computer Cases 46,505, but rejected the abstraction test as inappropriate in the circumstances. The reliance he placed on United States law, which is, after all, based on a statutory bar on the grant of copyright protection for ideas, was somewhat surprising. Such an approach might result in computer programs being treated differently from other kinds of work. This would be an undesirable outcome both in terms of the functioning of copyright law and for the computer industry in its production of multimedia products. Moreover, the *Richardson* case was evidentially somewhat unclear. Ferris J did not attempt to compare the codes of the two programs, relying entirely on visual evidence at the user interface level. Although understandable given the complexities of the case and the genuine difficulty of comparing code, this tended to obscure what the work in issue really was.

The following year in *Ibcos Computers Ltd* v *Barclays Mercantile Highland Finance Ltd* [1994] FSR 275, Jacob J took a markedly different approach. He rejected the idea that United States precedents should be applied by the English courts, instead favouring a more traditional copyright analysis based on English legal principles. The facts were somewhat simpler than in *Richardson*, involving the literal or semi-literal copying of source code in an agricultural dealer system. Jacob J discussed at length not only the *Richardson* case, but also one of the interlocutory judgments, *Total Information Processing Systems Ltd* v *Daman Ltd* [1992] FSR 171. In that case Paul Baker QC, sitting as a deputy High Court judge, had not been prepared to find *prima facie* evidence of infringement notwithstanding admitted copying. He gave a preliminary ruling that there was no arguable case that the claimant had infringed copyright by copying various field and record specifications in the defendant's costing program. The defendant claimed, first, that the three-program package was a compilation, copyright in which was infringed when the claimant substituted its payroll program for the defendant's. Secondly, the defendant claimed that the copying of the specification of the files and records from the costing program infringed copyright in that program. The judge rejected the argument that the compilation was protected, partly because:[117]

> to accord it copyright protection would lead to great inconvenience. It would mean that the copyright owners of one of the components could not interface with another similar program to that of the other components without the licence of the compiler.

Regarding the specification that had been copied, he ruled that:[118]

---

117. [1992] FSR 171 at p. 179.
118. [1992] FSR 171 at pp. 180–1.

The part copied can be likened to a table of contents. It would be very unusual that that part of a book could be described as a substantial part of it. The specification in high-level language of fields and records in the data division tells one little or nothing about the costing program and so, in my judgment, cannot be regarded as a substantial part of it.

Both of these conclusions are curious. Regarding the first, it has never been a criterion for copyright protection that the partial monopoly afforded by a copyright must not lead to 'great inconvenience'. In *Ibcos Computers Ltd* v *Barclays Mercantile Highland Finance Ltd* [1994] FSR 275, Jacob J commented (at p. 290):

I cannot agree. Of course the owner of the copyright in an individual program could interface his program with that of another. What he could not do is to put his program into an *original* compilation of another without that other's licence. The same is true of any other copyright works, be they poems, songs or whatever.

Regarding the second of Mr Baker's conclusions, it seems quite likely that a detailed table of contents for a book could constitute not only a substantial part of a work but might even be a work in its own right. Similarly, a program specification could qualify as either a substantial part of a work or as a discrete work. Jacob J commented:[119]

Very often the working out of a reasonably detailed arrangement of topics, sub-topics and sub-sub-topics is the key to a successful work of non-fiction. I see no reason why the taking of that could not amount to an infringement. Likewise, there may be a considerable degree of skill involved in setting up the data division of a program. In practice, this is done with the operating division in mind and its construction may well involve enough skill, labour and, I add, judgment, for it to be considered a substantial part of the program as a whole.

Paul Baker QC further stated that there could be no copyright in the expression of an idea if the expression has a function and there is only one or a limited number of ways of achieving it. Jacob J took the view that, unlike United States law, English law does protect certain types of ideas. Rather:[120]

The true position is that where an 'idea' is sufficiently general, then even if an original work embodies it, the mere taking of that idea will not infringe. But if the 'idea' is detailed, then there may be infringement. It is a question of degree. The same applies whether the work is fictional or not, and whether visual or literary.

Paul Baker QC also suggested that copyright could not subsist in source code because the industry makes copious efforts to protect itself via confidentiality. Jacob J disagreed, saying:[121]

---

119. [1994] FSR 275 at p. 303.
120. Ibid., at p. 291.
121. Ibid., at p. 296.

I do not understand this observation. . . . Because people keep confidential material which would be of considerable use to pirates is no reason for saying that copyright does not protect it. . . . I unhesitatingly say that source code can be the subject of copyright.

Moving on to discuss *Richardson*, Jacob J noted that Ferris J had supported the United States approach of looking for the core of protectable expression and separating it from the unprotectable idea, leaving only 'expression' to be taken into account in determining substantiality. Jacob J found this method unhelpful. Instead, he returned to a more traditional English legal analysis, whereby ideas are not precluded from protection and the test is a question of degree, a 'good guide' being:

> the notion of overborrowing of the skill, labour and judgment which went into the copyright work. Going via the complication of the concept of a 'core of protectable expression' merely complicates the matter so far as our law is concerned. It is likely to lead to an overcitation of United States authority based on a statute different from ours.[122]

Jacob J's straightforward approach towards finding substantiality and his rejection of some of Paul Baker's views in *Total Information Processing Systems Ltd* v *Daman Ltd* were well received in the industry.

There are currently three trends that might result, generally, in a weakening of copyright protection for software. One trend which, if developed, would significantly weaken the scope of copyright protection for software is reliance on the principle of non-derogation from grant as a basis for permitting what would otherwise be infringing acts. The limited 'repair right' recognised by the House of Lords in *British Leyland Motor Corporation Ltd* v *Armstrong Patents Co. Ltd* [1986] AC 577 has been applied by the Official Referee's Court in *Saphena Computing Ltd* v *Allied Collection Agencies Ltd* [1995] FSR 616 to permit acts necessary for software maintenance which would normally infringe copyright.[123] However, Jacob J considered a similar issue in the *Ibcos* case and held that the right to repair held to exist in *British Leyland* could not be relied upon by analogy to establish a right to copy file transfer utilities.[124]

A second basis for a weakening of the monopoly given by copyright would rest on a development of competition law principles. How would a UK court respond if asked to decide on the scope of copyright protection in circum-

---

122. Ibid., at p. 302.
123. *British Leyland Motor Corporation Ltd* v *Armstrong Patents Co. Ltd* concerned the protection of the designs of functional objects, spare parts for cars, through artistic copyright in the underlying design drawings. This basis of claim has been severely restricted by the 1988 Act. On appeal in *Saphena Computing Ltd* v *Allied Collection Agencies Ltd* [1995] FSR 616, the Court of Appeal did not comment on the official referee's finding. See also *Canon Kabushiki Kaisha* v *Green Cartridge Company (Hong Kong) Ltd*, PLC, 1997, VIII(5), 78.
124. See also *Mars UK Ltd* v *Teknowledge Ltd (No. 2)*, *The Times*, 23 June, 1999 where it was held that British Leyland had been decided under the Copyright Act 1956 and there was no longer room for such a common law exception because there was now a complete statutory code to cover any exceptions.

stances where, for example, a single set of machine instructions was the only way to achieve a particular functional result, such as interfacing with a particular item of hardware or software? In such a case, it might be possible for the court to conclude that the subject matter in question is not protected by copyright due to lack of originality. However, a particular interface specification or procedure may be highly original and the result of considerable labour and skill. As has already been established, UK courts cannot invoke a 'merger doctrine' as a justification for excluding material from copyright on the ground that idea and expression have merged. In practice, however, a person who sought to use copyright as a basis for monopolising a *de facto* industry standard might be vulnerable to challenge under UK or EU competition law (see chapter 14).

A third, and related, consideration is the Software Directive.[125] Article 1(2) of the Software Directive requires all EU Member States to protect programs as literary works but to exclude from protection 'Ideas and principles which underlie any element of a computer program, including those which underlie its interfaces'. The Copyright (Computer Programs) Regulations 1992 contain no reference to the exclusion of ideas from copyright protection. This is presumably because the UK government believed that ideas were already excluded from protection as a result of judicial pronouncements to that effect. However, even if English law is already consistent with art. 1(2), there will remain considerable scope for dispute about what constitutes an 'idea' for the 'decompilation' right is so hedged about by restrictions as to give developers of compatible products limited comfort regarding risks that their reverse engineering activities may infringe copyright.

6.5.7 Decompilation of computer programs

During the Software Directive's turbulent passage through the EU legislative process, by far the most contentious issue concerned the new right to be given to users permitting them to decompile a program where necessary to achieve the interoperability of that program with another program. The complex compromise agreed by the principal protagonists, after many months of heated debate and lobbying, is now enshrined in art. 6 of the Directive. The wording of the Directive is altered somewhat in the Copyright (Computer Programs) Regulations 1992 but in effect, the provisions of art. 6(1) and (2) are implemented in full. The Regulations state that it is not an infringement of copyright for a 'lawful user' of a copy of a computer program which is 'expressed in a low level language' to convert it into a higher level language, so copying it, provided two conditions are met. These are that such decompilation is necessary 'to obtain the information necessary to create an independent program which can be operated with the program decompiled or with another program', which is defined as the 'permitted objective', and that 'the information so obtained is not used for any purpose other than the permitted objective'.

---

125. Directive 91/250/EEC.

Exercise of the decompilation right is hedged about by four further restrictions. The Regulations state that the two conditions described above are not met if the lawful user has the information necessary to achieve the permitted objective readily available to him; does not confine decompilation to acts necessary to achieve the permitted objective; supplies information obtained by decompiling to a third party to whom it is not necessary to supply it to achieve the permitted objective; or uses the information to create a program which is substantially similar in its expression to the decompiled program or to do any act restricted by copyright.[126]

Consistent with art 9(1) of the Directive, the Regulations render void any provisions which purport to prohibit or restrict the decompilation right.

6.5.8 Back-up copies of computer programs

Article 5(2) of the Software Directive provides that 'The making of a back-up copy by a person having a right to use the computer program may not be prevented by contract insofar as it is necessary for that use'. The Copyright (Computer Programs) Regulations 1992 have implemented art. 5(2). Section 50A of the Copyright, Designs and Patents Act 1988 permits the making of an additional copy of a program by a lawful user 'which it is necessary for him to have for the purposes of his lawful use'. In practice, most PC software must be loaded on to the hard disk of a PC before it can be run. The loading process often entails the 'explosion' of compressed files and the installation of the package for a particular configuration of hardware and software. The making of a back-up copy, in the sense of a verbatim copy of the original disks, may be unnecessary, as the original CD or disks will be available for back-up purposes. Thus, the back-up exemption may be of limited application.

6.5.9 Second-hand copies of works in electronic form

Section 56 of the Copyright, Designs and Patents Act 1988 contains a complex and somewhat convoluted statement of the rights to be enjoyed by a person taking a transfer from the original purchaser of a copy of a program or other work in electronic form. The provision is applicable where a copy of such a work 'has been purchased on terms which, expressly or impliedly or by virtue of any rule of law, allow the purchaser to copy the work, or to adapt it or make copies of an adaptation, in connection with his use of it'. Subject to any express terms to the contrary, where the copy is transferred to a third party, that person is entitled to do anything with the copy which the original purchaser was permitted to do. From the moment of transfer, however, any copy or adaptation retained by the original purchaser will be treated as an infringing copy. The same rules apply to any subsequent transfers made by the new owner and that person's successors in title.

---

126. Copyright, Designs and Patents Act 1988, s. 50B(3) inserted by the Copyright (Computer Programs) Regulations 1992, reg. 8.

Section 56 is not a model of clarity. Taking its application to computer programs, packaged software is typically distributed with a licence 'agreement' in which the software producer purports to retain title to part or all of the product. Where title to the physical copy of the program does not pass, it will make no sense to speak of the 'purchaser' of the copy. Moreover, the scope for inferring licences in this area is quite uncertain and thus the reference to terms which the purchaser has the benefit of 'impliedly or by virtue of any rule of law' is not particularly illuminating. In practice, quite apart from the theoretical question of whether or not there is a 'purchaser', it is likely to continue to be the norm for computer programs, and many other works published in electronic form, to be distributed with an express prohibition, or at least restriction, on transfers to third parties. In all such cases, the operation of s. 56 will be completely pre-empted.

6.6 MORAL RIGHTS

6.6.1 The nature of moral rights

The Berne Union, of which the UK is a member, provides for its members to give authors various 'moral rights'. Such rights are to be personal to the author or creator of a work and are to be capable of exercise independently of the economic exploitation rights in the work. For the first time in the UK, the Copyright, Designs and Patents Act 1988 gave the author of a work or director of a film the right, in certain circumstances, to be identified as such (s. 77). Relevant circumstances include commercial publication of the work or any adaptation of it. This right is otherwise known as the right of 'paternity'. Authors and directors also have the right to object to 'derogatory treatment' of their works (s. 80(1)), which right is otherwise known as the right of 'integrity'. Treatment of a work will be deemed derogatory 'if it amounts to distortion or mutilation of the work or is otherwise prejudicial to the honour or reputation of the author or director' (s. 80(2)). Two other moral rights give protection against false attribution of a work,[127] and the right to privacy of certain photographs and films (s. 85). With the exception of the false attribution right, which expires 20 years after a person's death, all of the moral rights continue to subsist for as long as copyright subsists in the work in question (s. 86). The rest of the discussion here will be focused on the rights of paternity and integrity as they apply to literary, dramatic, musical and artistic works.

6.6.2 Restrictions on scope

The right of paternity must be asserted in writing and will in most cases only bind third parties who have notice of it (1988 Act, s. 78). In the case of works created in the course of employment, the right does not apply to anything done by, or with the authority of, the employer or any subsequent owner of

---

127. I.e., the right not to have a work wrongly attributed to one (s. 84).

copyright in the work (s. 79(3)). The right of integrity is also severely cut back in relation to works created by employees, copyright in which originally vested in their employers (s. 82(1)).[128] Neither right applies, in any event, in relation to computer programs and computer-generated works (ss. 79(2) and 81(2)).

These exclusions appear, at first sight, to abrogate moral rights as they apply to works produced by the computer industry. Moral rights will, nevertheless, have significant implications for the computer and related industries and those who work in them. As already noted in this chapter, software packages, for example, are much more than computer programs for copyright purposes. While moral rights will not be available in respect of any programs and computer-generated works incorporated in a package nor any work owned automatically by an employer, moral rights will be available in respect of many other works produced on a commissioning basis. For example, a freelance technical author would be able to assert the right of paternity and object to unjust modification of published manuals or other documentation, and a freelance artist may make such claims with regard to published artwork. Moreover, moral rights will be applicable to many works that are included in databases and in that context it is difficult to see how the right of paternity could be exercised without becoming unduly cumbersome. Protection against false attribution applies to all categories of works but is less likely to cause problems in practice.

6.6.3 Consents and waivers

Although moral rights are 'inalienable' and thus cannot be assigned like the economic rights in a work,[129] a person entitled to moral rights can forgo the right to exercise the rights in part or completely. In general, it is not an infringement of moral rights to do anything to which the rightholder has consented. Moreover, any of the moral rights 'may be waived by instrument in writing signed by the person giving up the right'. Such waivers may relate to specific works or to works generally, may be conditional or unconditional, and may be made subject to revocation (1988 Act, s. 87). Given the potential difficulties that were identified in 6.6.2., it is probable that many organisations will include express consents or waivers of moral rights in their standard terms of business for commissioned works.

6.6.4 Remedies

Infringements of moral rights are actionable as breaches of statutory duty owed to the person entitled to the right (1988 Act, s. 103(1)). In relation to infringement of the right to object to derogatory treatment of a work, a court may grant an injunction requiring a disclaimer to be given, for example, on

---

128. The right will only apply if the author '(a) is identified at the time of the relevant act, or (b) has previously been identified in or on published copies of the work'. (s. 82(2)).
129. Although they do form part of an author's estate on death and consequently can pass to third parties under a will or on intestacy (s. 95).

publication, dissociating the author from the treatment of the work (s. 103(2)). In relation to the right of paternity, a court must, in considering what remedy should be given for an infringement, take into account any delay in asserting the right (s. 78(5)). Both of these qualifications on remedies have the effect of further limiting the potential commercial leverage which moral rights may confer on an author. Where, for example, a publisher has incurred considerable expense over a period of time in preparing a work for publication, instead of stopping publication because of derogatory treatment a court may merely order that a disclaimer be printed. Likewise, the author's right of paternity may effectively be undermined as a result of any delay in asserting the right.

6.7 CIVIL REMEDIES, CRIMINAL SANCTIONS AND PROCEDURAL MATTERS

6.7.1 Civil remedies

Copyright is a property right, and where infringement has been proved, the copyright owner can, subject to certain special rules, benefit from 'all such relief ... as is available in respect of the infringement of any other property right' (Copyright, Designs and Patents Act 1988, s. 96). In practice, the principal remedies are injunctions to prevent further breaches of copyright, damages for breach of copyright and orders for delivery up of infringing copies. Other remedies include accounts of profits (used relatively rarely because of the difficulty of proving the precise profits made) and orders for disposal of infringing copies which have been seized or delivered up to a claimant (see generally ss. 96–106 and 113–115).

Various court orders can be obtained at the pre-trial stage, in some circumstances without the alleged infringer being given any warning or opportunity to make representations to the court. One such order that has been used with particular success against audio, video and software pirates is the 'search order'.[130] Such an order can authorise a claimant to enter a defendant's premises, without prior warning, to seize evidentiary material which might otherwise be tampered with or disappear before trial. This is obviously a powerful remedy capable of abuse in the hands of overenthusiastic claimants and the courts now supervise its use quite strictly.[131]

Whilst a final injunction may be granted at trial, it is quite common in cases of alleged software copyright infringement for an 'interim' injunction to be

---

130. Formerly called an '*Anton Piller* order' after the case in which it was first obtained, *Anton Piller KG* v *Manufacturing Processes Ltd* [1976] Ch 55. For example of the grant of such an order in a case of alleged software piracy, see *Gates* v *Swift* [1981] FSR 57.

131. In another software copyright case, *Systematica Ltd* v *London Computer Centre Ltd* [1983] FSR 313 at p. 316, Whitford J observed that 'A situation is developing where I think rather too free a use is being made by plaintiffs [claimants] of the *Anton Piller* provision'. Subsequently, in *Columbia Picture Industries* v *Robinson* [1986] FSR 367 at p. 439, Scott J commented 'that the practice of the court has allowed the balance to swing too far in favour of the plaintiffs [claimants] and that *Anton Piller* orders have been too readily granted and with insufficient safeguards for respondents'. The court laid down a number of procedural safeguards which should be complied with to ensure minimum protection for defendants.

granted in pre-trial proceedings. An injunction may be prohibitory, for example, enjoining a defendant from copying or in any way dealing with the material that is the subject of the dispute.[132] Alternatively, or in addition, an injunction may be mandatory, for example, requiring delivery up of source code pending trial.[133]

As a general rule, damages for copyright infringement are intended to compensate a claimant for actual loss incurred as a result of the infringement. This might typically be calculated on the basis of royalties which would have been payable to the claimant had the defendant, instead of infringing copyright, obtained a licence for the acts in question.[134] The 1988 Act specifies one set of circumstances in which damages must not be awarded, and one in which they may be increased beyond the compensatory level. The former arises where it is shown that the defendant did not know and had no reason to believe that copyright subsisted in the work in question at the time of infringement. In such circumstances, 'the plaintiff [claimant] is not entitled to damages against him, without prejudice to any other remedy' (s. 97(1)). In other cases, however, the court may award 'such additional damages as the justice of the case may require' in all the circumstances, with particular reference to '(a) the flagrancy of the infringement, and (b) any benefit accruing to the defendant by reason of the infringement' (s. 97(2)).

6.7.2 Criminal sanctions

The 1988 Act sets out a number of categories of criminal copyright infringement which, in general, are intended to penalise those who deliberately infringe copyright with a view to commercial gain. Specifically, it is an offence, if done without a licence, to manufacture for sale or hire, import into the UK other than for private and domestic use, distribute in the course of business or otherwise 'to such an extent as to affect prejudicially' the rights of the copyright owner, an article which the offender knows to be, or has reason to believe to be, an infringing copy of a work (1988 Act, s. 107(1)(a), (b), (d)(iv) and (e)). On summary conviction the penalties for such an offence are imprisonment for up to six months and a fine not exceeding the statutory maximum, or both (s. 197(4)(a)).[135] On conviction on indictment the maximum penalties are imprisonment for up to two years or a fine.[136]

It is an offence, if done without a licence, to possess in the course of a business with a view to committing an infringing act, or in the course of business to sell or let for hire, to offer or expose for sale or hire, or exhibit in public, an article which the offender knows to be, or has reason to believe to

---

132. For example, *Raindrop Data Systems Ltd* v *Systematics Ltd* [1988] FSR 354; *Leisure Data* v *Bell* [1988] FSR 367.
133. For example, *Redwood Music Ltd* v *Chappell & Co. Ltd* [1982] RPC 109.
134. At the time of writing, the statutory maximum was £5,000.
135. At the time of writing, the statutory maximum was £5,000.
136. Section 107(4)(b). There is no statutory limit on the fine which may be imposed on conviction for one of these offences on indictment. In practice, however, the amount will be governed by the general principle that a fine should be within an offender's capacity to pay (*R* v *Churchill (No. 2)* [1967] 1 QB 190).

be, an infringing copy of a work (s. 107(1)(c), (d)(i), (ii) and (iii)). It is also an offence to make or possess 'an article specifically designed or adapted for making infringing copies of a particular copyright work' if the offender knows or has reason to believe that the article will be used to make infringing copies for sale or hire or use in the course of a business (s. 107(2)).[137] These latter categories of offences are only triable summarily and the maximum penalties are imprisonment for up to six months or a fine not exceeding level 5 on the standard scale, or both (s. 107(5)).[138]

Where a person is charged with any of the criminal offences under the 1988 Act, the court before which proceedings are brought may order delivery up of any infringing copy or article for making infringing copies (s. 108). The 1988 Act also provides for a magistrate, if satisfied that one of the offences which are triable either way has been or is about to be committed and that relevant evidence is in specified premises, to 'issue a warrant authorising a constable to enter and search the premises, using such reasonable force as is necessary' (s. 109). Moreover, where any of the offences is committed by a company 'with the consent or connivance of a director, manager, secretary or other similar officer ... or a person purporting to act in any such capacity' that person is also guilty of the offence, and liable to be prosecuted and punished accordingly (s. 110).

Taken as a whole, these criminal offences set high stakes for commercial copyright infringement and are intended to provide an effective deterrent against commercial infringement of copyright in software and other works. Moreover, a software pirate who fraudulently uses a trade mark may be convicted of a counterfeiting offence, the maximum penalty for which is 10 years' imprisonment.[139]

6.7.3 Presumptions

A prerequisite to a successful action for copyright infringement, whether in civil or criminal proceedings, is proof of authorship and ownership of the relevant copyright(s). For practical and procedural reasons, proof of such facts can sometimes constitute a substantial hurdle to a claimant or prosecutor, as the case may be. The 1988 Act provides that various presumptions will apply in proceedings relating to various types of copyright work. These include a presumption that where a name purporting to be that of the author of a literary, dramatic, musical or artistic work appears on published copies of the work, the named person shall, until the contrary is proved, be deemed to be the author. It is, moreover, presumed that the special rules as to first ownership of works created during the course of employment, etc. were not applicable and thus that the named person was the first owner (s. 104).

A special rule applies to copyright notices appearing on copies of computer programs. In litigation relating to program copyright, 'where copies of the

---

137. Interpretation of the equivalent civil infringement is discussed in 6.4.2.
138. At the time of writing, level 5 on the standard scale was £5,000.
139. Section 300 of the 1988 Act. An offender convicted on indictment may also be liable to pay an unlimited fine. The penalty limits for summary conviction are six months' imprisonment and a fine not exceeding the statutory maximum.

program are issued to the public in electronic form bearing a statement — (a) that a named person was the owner of copyright in the program at the date of issue of the copies, or (b) that the program was first published in a specified country or that copies of it were first issued to the public in electronic form in a specified year, the statement shall be admissible as evidence of the facts stated and shall be presumed to be correct until the contrary is proved' (s. 105(3)). This special presumption is likely, on occasions at least, to be of major assistance to claimant in civil cases and the prosecution in criminal proceedings. As a result, program copyright owners should ensure that they affix appropriate copyright notices to all copies of a program they publish and that any licensees are obliged to do likewise.

CHAPTER SEVEN

Property in Databases

Simon Chalton

7.1 THE CASE FOR LEGAL PROTECTION OF DATABASES

Databases are useful collections of materials which consequently have value independently of their several items of content. They are often creative, and are usually costly to compile, present and maintain. In the Information Society, they are of increasing economic importance.

Those who create databases, and those who invest in their development and maintenance, may reasonably expect to enjoy a return on their investments, but once a database has been made publicly available securing a financial return from it is likely to be difficult, if not impracticable, unless some form of property right is recognised in the database as such.

Traditionally, UK law has recognised copyright as protecting tables and compilations as literary works. More recently, the EU Directive on the legal protection of databases[1] has required the Member States of the European Union, and so the countries of the European Economic Area, to harmonise this form of copyright protection. The Directive also introduced a new form of *sui generis* right (so-called, because it is a right of its own special kind) to protect databases. The new right is complementary to copyright but can exist independently of it, and is known in the United Kingdom as 'database right'. This chapter gives a high level view of the UK law of copyright in relation to databases and other tables and compilations, of the development and provisions of the Directive and of the current UK law on the new *sui generis* database right.

---

1. Directive 96/9 of 11 March 1996.

7.2 DATABASE PROTECTION UNDER PRE-1998 UK LAW

The Copyright, Designs and Patents Act 1988 ('CDPA'), as at 31 December 1997, provided as follows:

Section 1(1)(a):	Copyright is a property right which subsists in ... original literary ... works.
Section 3(1):	... 'literary work' means any work, other than a dramatic or musical work, which is written, spoken or sung, and accordingly includes ... a table or compilation.
Section 9(1) and (3):	... 'author' in relation to a work means the person who creates it. In the case of a literary ... work which is computer-generated, the author shall be taken to be the person by whom the arrangements necessary for the creation of the work are undertaken.
Section 178:	'Computer-generated', in relation to a work, means that the work is generated by computer in circumstances such that there is no human author of the work.

Under the pre-1998 UK law, collections of materials in the form of tables or compilations were capable of protection by copyright as literary works. This principle still applies today and protects anthologies, dictionaries and other collections. These collections may be of works created by different authors, or of non-copyright materials derived from different sources. What is protected is the selection and/or arrangement of the collection. Copyright in the collection as such is distinct from copyright, if any, in the several items of content within the collection. As with all works, the collection as such must achieve the criterion of originality before it can qualify for protection by copyright. In the UK, this criterion requires that there shall have been sufficient skill, industry or experience applied in the production of the collection, which must not have been copied from another work. Mere random collections of information will not be protected nor will 'a selection or arrangement of scraps of information' not involving any real exercise of labour, judgment or skill.[2] However, a football pool betting coupon has been held to be protected,[3] as have railway timetables,[4] professional directories[5] and electrical circuit diagrams.[6]

In the United States, the Supreme Court has held that a listing of subscribers' names, addresses and telephone numbers in the white pages of

---

2. *G A Cramp and Sons Ltd v Frank Smythson Ltd* [1944] AC 329. And see JA Sterling and MCL Carpenter, *Copyright Law in the United Kingdom*, Sydney: Legal Books, 1986, at para. 210.
3. *Ladbroke (Football) Ltd v William Hill (Football) Ltd* [1964] 1 WLR 273.
4. *Leslie v Young and Sons* [1917] 2 KB 469.
5. *Waterlow Directories Ltd v Reed Information Services Ltd* [1984] FSR 64.
6. *Anacon Corporation Ltd v Environmental Research Technology Ltd* [1994] FSR 659.

a telephone directory does not contain any modicum of creativity, and so is not protected by copyright under the US Federal Copyright Act.[7] This is to be contrasted with the selection or arrangement of Yellow Pages classified directories, which have been held to be protected in the United States.[8]

The position under UK law down to 31 December 1997 may thus be broadly stated as:

(a) The selection and/or arrangement of a collection of materials may be protected by copyright as a literary work, whether or not the individual items of content in the collection are so protected.

(b) Where a collection is computer-generated, the person deemed to be the author of the collection, as a work, is the person who made the arrangements necessary for its creation.

(c) In any case, sufficient skill, industry or experience must have been applied by the author to production of the work as a collection if the work is to qualify for copyright protection (the so-called criterion of originality).

7.3 DEVELOPMENT OF THE DATABASE DIRECTIVE

The European Commission's 1988 Green Paper on Copyright and the Challenge of Technology[9] concluded that there was a need for Europe to give copyright protection to collections or compilations as such. The Green Paper also stated that the Commission was considering whether there was an additional need to protect collections or compilations which were not capable of qualifying for copyright protection.

The central difficulty found by the Commission in formulating a directive to harmonise the laws of the Member States on the legal protection of such collections was in reconciling the different approaches of, respectively, the copyright and authors' right systems of law on these issues. Civil law systems see authors' rights as recognitions of the author's creative intellectual activity: without such creativity, the application of time, trouble and expense are generally considered in civil law countries to be insufficient to justify protection. Furthermore, the absence of a human author precludes any possibility of human creativity, and so of protection. The same strict view is not taken in common law jurisdictions, but even in common law countries there is a growing tendency to emphasise the requirement of skill or creativity at the expense of the requirement of labour: in *Feist Publications Inc. v Rural Telephone Co. Inc.* (1991) 111 S Ct 1282 the US Supreme Court held that the application of 'sweat of the brow' was insufficient, in the absence of a modicum of creativity.

In May 1992 a first proposal for a directive[10] was issued by the Commission. It included provision for a new *sui generis* form of protection for

---

7. *Feist Publications Inc. v Rural Telephone Co. Inc.* (1991) 111 S Ct 1282.
8. *BellSouth Advertising & Publishing Corp. v Donnelly Information Publishing Inc.* (1991) US Ct of Appeals 11th Circuit No 89-5131, 933 F 2d 952.
9. COM (88) 172 final, 7 June 1988, at para. 215.
10. COM (92) 24 final — SYN 383, 13 May 1992.

compilations, but withheld the new protection from compilations of materials which were themselves protected by copyright. The new *sui generis* right was to protect against 'unfair' extraction, a concept which was re-expressed as 'unauthorised' extraction in an amended proposal issued in October 1993.[11]

After October 1993 major changes to the form of the proposed directive were made and a Common Position was reached in July 1995. On 11 March 1996 Directive 96/9 on the legal protection of databases[12] (the 'Database Directive') was adopted substantially in the terms of the Common Position and was required to be transposed into the laws of each of the Member States by 1 January 1998.

In August 1997 the Copyright Directorate at the Patent Office published draft implementing regulations under the European Communities Act, with a consultative paper. Following this consultation an amended draft was laid before Parliament. The amended draft was adopted as the Copyright and Rights in Databases Regulations 1997, SI 1977/3032 (the 'Database Regulations') which came into force on 1 January 1998.

The changes from the Commission's 1993 proposal, which were incorporated into the Database Directive and reflected in the Database Regulations, have simplified its provisions and have continued the concept of creating a new *sui generis* right, called in the Database Regulations 'database right'. This new right is to apply to all databases as defined by the Database Directive, including those which are accessible by other than electronic means and including databases of materials which are themselves protected by copyright. The new *sui generis* database right protects against unauthorised extraction or re-utilisation of the whole or a substantial part, evaluated qualitatively and/or quantitatively, of the contents of any such database.[13] In contrast with copyright in databases, the new *sui generis* database right requires substantial investment in a protected database but does not require intellectual creativity.

The simplifications achieved by the Commission in the adopted form of the Database Directive were welcomed, though there are parts of the Directive which are so broadly stated as to be potentially uncertain in their effect.[14] Since the *sui generis* right is new, elaboration by the Member States is needed beyond the provisions of the Directive. The process of elaboration has produced results which differ from Member State to Member State, so creating inconsistencies between the new laws adopted by different Member States. Optional provisions in the Directive have also resulted in disharmony.

7.4 THE SCOPE OF THE DATABASE DIRECTIVE

A major point of change from the form of the Commission's earlier proposals is extension of the Database Directive to all databases in any form, including those capable of being accessed by other than electronic means.

---

11. COM (93) 464 final — SYN 393, 4 October 1993.
12. OJ L77/20, 27 March 1996.
13. Database Directive art. 7.
14. For example, the meaning of the term 'lawful user of a database': see arts 8 and 9.

'Other means' includes the human eye, so extending the scope of the Database Directive to include collections of materials held, for example, in filing cabinets, provided that such collections fit within the remaining provisions of the Directive's definition of a database in art. 1(2):

'Database' shall mean a collection of independent works, data or other materials arranged in a systematic or methodical way and capable of being individually accessed by electronic or other means.

The inclusion of non-electronic databases avoids the difficulties which might otherwise have arisen from conflicts between legal provisions applying only to electronically accessible databases, as being within the scope of the Database Directive, and other provisions applying to similar or identical collections of materials but in non-electronic form, which would have been outside the Directive's scope. However, conflicts may still arise between legal provisions applying only to databases as defined by the Directive and those applying to collections which do not fall within that definition.

Although the CDPA protects tables and compilations as literary works, prior to the Database Regulations' coming into force it made no reference to databases as such. The Database Directive's definition of 'database' is narrower than the concept of a table or compilation. The Database Regulations have amended the CDPA so as to leave tables and compilations as a subclassification of literary works, and to add databases, as defined by the Database Directive, as a new and additional subclassification. This could have significant consequences. The form of protection available to a given collection may depend on the application of relatively complex classification criteria, for example whether or not the contents of the collection are 'independent' of one another. The resulting classification, either as a non-database table or compilation or as a database, will affect, amongst other things, the identity of the rightsholder, the term of protection, the applicable restricted acts and whether or not the collection is eligible for protection under the *sui generis* database right: see 7.5 below.

From the standpoint of UK database rightholders, generous transitional provisions included in the Database Directive and the Database Regulations allow those databases within the Directive's definition which, at 31 December 1996, qualified for UK copyright protection and which were in existence on 27 March 1998, the date of the Directive's publication, to continue to enjoy copyright protection under the pre-1998 UK law for the full copyright term of life of the author plus 70 years. This permitted continuing protection is notwithstanding that such databases may lack the necessary element of author's creativity required to meet the Directive's criterion for copyright protection,[15] and may be important for rightholders of computer-generated databases which lack a human creative author.

The copyright 70 year term is to be contrasted with the *sui generis* database right's 15 year term. Successive *sui generis* right terms of 15 years each,

---

15. Article 14(2).

available when a database is updated so as to create a substantial change to its contents,[16] may prove capable of producing indefinitely extendable protection outlasting the 70 year term allowed for copyright. This will be of particular value to databases such as telephone directories, statistical tables and factual compilations which may not attract copyright protection as lacking author's creativity but which need regular and costly updating. It may not help static databases, e.g., those in fixed electronic form such as databases marketed on CD-ROM, which are not capable of being updated or re-presented.

7.5   THE MEANING OF 'DATABASE'

The term 'database' is defined in art. 1(2) of the Database Directive as:

A collection of independent works, data or other materials arranged in a systematic or methodical way and capable of being individually accessed by electronic or other means.

A similar definition is contained in the Database Regulations. The significant elements in this definition are the references to 'independent works, data or other materials', to arrangement in a 'systematic or methodical' way, and to individual access 'by electronic or other means'.

'Independent works, data or other materials' is apparently intended to exclude from the definition works such as films, musical compositions and books which comprise distinct but related elements or materials (e.g., frames, movements or chapters) and which, though separately accessible, are interrelated within the collection. It may also exclude many tables or compilations already protected by copyright as literary works under UK law. 'Independent' is not defined, either in the Database Directive or in the Database Regulations. It is suggested that independence in relation to items of content in a collection should be judged from the standpoint of those items as they appear in the compiled collection: it is not sufficient for an item to be capable of being read or used by itself if reading or use of other items in the collection, or the collection as a whole, is dependent on reading or use of that item.

Arrangement in a 'systematic or methodical way' is an essential part of the definition, and may lead to difficulty. Some electronic databases are created in free form, leaving access dependent on a computer's searching capability to find relevant items. If there is no arrangement of material in a systematic or methodical way, a collection of materials may fail to qualify as a database: alternatively, it may be said that electronic arrangement of the database may be sufficient.

As mentioned at 7.4 above, access 'by electronic or other means' includes access by the human eye. Since the scope of the Database Directive extends to databases in any form,[17] collections of individual materials arranged in a

---

16. Article 10(3).
17. Article 1(1).

systematic or methodical way which are held in filing cabinets and capable of individual access by means of the human eye will apparently be included. By contrast, if the materials in a collection are not independent of each other or are not individually accessible that collection will apparently be excluded, though it may continue to be protected by copyright under UK law as a compilation.

The Database Directive expressly excludes from its protection computer programs used in the manufacture or operation of databases which can be accessed by electronic means.[18]

7.6 COPYRIGHT IN DATABASES

Article 3 of the Database Directive states that databases which, by reason of the selection or arrangement of their contents, constitute the author's own intellectual creation shall be protected as such by copyright, and that no other criteria shall be applied to determine their eligibility for that protection.[19]

The Database Directive refers to 'the expression of the database which is protectable by copyright', but does not define clearly what elements amount to protectable expression: presumably, the phrase is intended to include the expressed selection or arrangement, but not the ideas or concepts behind them.

To qualify for protection by copyright under the Directive, and to be subject to the Directive's requirement of human creativity, a collection of materials must first come within the definition of 'database' set out in art. 1(2).[20] In consequence, a collection of non-independent materials, not being a database within the meaning of the Directive, may be both outside the scope of the Directive and capable of attracting protection as a copyright compilation under the CDPA, provided that the collection conforms to the criterion of originality and other requirements of UK law.

The criterion of intellectual creativity for copyright protection of a database[21] under the Database Directive reflects a similar provision in the Software Directive,[22] namely that a computer program is only to be protected by copyright if it is original in the sense that it is the author's own intellectual creation, and that no other criteria are to be applied to determine its eligibility for that protection. Both provisions are in apparent conflict with s. 9(3) of the CDPA which provides that, in the case of a literary, dramatic, musical or artistic work which is computer-generated, the author shall be taken to be the person by whom the arrangements necessary for the creation of the work were undertaken. Section 178 of the CDPA defines 'computer-generated', in relation to a work, as meaning that the work is generated by computer in

---

18. Article 1(3).
19. Article 3(1).
20. Article 1(2) reads: 'a collection of works, data or other independent materials arranged in a systematic or methodical way and capable of being individually accessed by electronic or other means'.
21. Article 3(1).
22. Directive 91/250 on the legal protection of computer programs.

circumstances such that there is no human author of the work. The implication of these provisions in combination is that a computer-generated work, as
so defined, can attract copyright protection in the United Kingdom for the
benefit of the deemed author by whom the arrangements necessary for the
creation of the work were undertaken.

An exclusive criterion of originality for copyright, that a work shall be the
author's own intellectual creation, now applies to databases both under the
Database Directive and under the Database Regulations. No such express
provision was included in the Regulations implementing the Software Directive.[23]

Subject to generous transitional provisions in the Database Directive (see
7.8 below as to term of protection) a computer-generated collection conforming to the Directive's definition of a database may in future not qualify for
copyright protection either in the United Kingdom or in any other Member
State. Such a database will then be protectable only by the new *sui generis*
database right, and even that protection will be available only if the database's
maker can demonstrate substantial investment in the obtaining, verification
or presentation of its contents and is a national of a Member State or has
habitual residence in the territory of the Community.[24]

For those databases which qualify for copyright protection under the
Database Directive the copyright restricted acts provided for by that Directive[25] are familiar and comprise, in summary:

(a) Temporary or permanent reproduction by any means and in any form,
in whole or in part.

(b) Any form of distribution to the public, but subject to exhaustion of
the right to control resale of any copy of a database after that copy's first sale
within the Community by the rightholder or with his consent.

(c) Any communication, display or performance to the public.

(d) Translation, adaptation, arrangement and any other alteration.

(e) Reproduction, distribution, communication, display or performance
to the public of the results of any translation, adaptation, arrangement or
other alteration.

These restricted acts broadly control use of any electronic database where use
necessarily requires temporary reproduction in machine memory or on screen
of any part of the database. For non-electronic databases control may not be so
strong, but the risks to the rightholder of economic loss may not be so great.

Moral rights are outside the scope of the Database Directive.[26] Under UK
law, moral rights are capable of applying to databases as to other literary
works but do not apply to computer programs or to computer-generated
works.[27] The United Kingdom is to be free to continue these provisions, and

---

23. The Copyright (Computer Programs) Regulations 1992, SI 1992/3233.
24. Article 11.
25. Article 5.
26. Recital 28.
27. Copyright, Designs and Patents Act 1988, ss. 79(2) and 81(2).

other Member States are to be equally free to set their own laws for the application of moral rights to databases.

7.7 THE NEW *SUI GENERIS* DATABASE RIGHT

Whereas copyright protects the creativity of authors in the selection and arrangement of the contents of databases, the new *sui generis* 'database right' is designed to protect investment in databases by their makers. Recital 40 of the Database Directive states that the required investment 'may consist of the deployment of financial resources and/or the expending of time, effort and energy'. The Database Regulations define 'investment' as including any investment, whether of financial, human or technical resources'.[28] The investment made may be in the obtaining, verification or presentation of the contents of a database: these terms appear to be capable of including and extending beyond the selection or arrangement of database contents. The investment made must have been substantial, but substantiality may be measured either qualitatively or quantitatively, or both.[29]

The maker of a database in which there has been the necessary investment may also be an author of the same database, or may be a different natural or legal person. A database which is protected by copyright may also be protected by the new *sui generis* database right, but is not necessarily so protected if there has been no substantial investment in the obtaining, verification or presentation of the database's contents. Conversely, a database which is protected by the *sui generis* database right may also be protected by copyright, but is not necessarily so if the database lacks human creativity in the selection or arrangement of its contents. The *sui generis* database right cannot protect a collection which does not conform to the Database Directive's definition of a 'database', even though that collection may be protected by copyright under national law.

Both copyright and the *sui generis* database right can thus subsist in the same database but:

(a)   Each form of protection requires different criteria.
(b)   Each provides different forms and terms of protection.
(c)   Each may be vested in different rightholders.
(d)   Each affects the use of the contents of the database, but is expressly made independent of any copyright in such contents.[30]

Presumably, if part of the contents of a database comprises a subcollection of materials which itself qualifies for the *sui generis* database right, the protection by database right of that subcollection is independent of the protection of the parent compiled collection, whether by copyright or by the *sui generis* database right.

The *sui generis* database right protects against acts of extraction and/or re-utilisation of the whole, or of a substantial part of, the contents of the

---

28. Regulation 12(1).
29. Article 7 and reg. 13(2).
30. Article 3(2) (copyright) and art. 7(4) (*sui generis* right).

protected database.[31] 'Substantial' in this context is to be evaluated qualitatively and/or quantitatively.[32] 'Extraction' means the permanent or temporary transfer of all, or a substantial part of, the contents of a database to another medium by any means or in any form,[33] and 're-utilisation' means any form of making available to the public [of] all, or a substantial part of, the contents of a database by the distribution of copies, by renting, by on-line or other forms of transmission.[34] The definitions of 'extraction' and 're-utilisation' are exhaustive.

'Extraction' appears to include a permanent or temporary transfer of a substantial part of the contents of a database to machine memory for the purpose of processing as a necessary preliminary to searching or to screen display.[35] If these steps involve the temporary transfer of a substantial part of the database into machine memory in order to find and display a single item, control of extraction may have broadly the same effect on electronic use of a database as the copyright restricted act of temporary or permanent reproduction in whole or in part by any means and in any form.[36] Each of these rights may prove therefore to be sufficient to prevent electronic access to, or other electronic processing of, a protected database. The *sui generis* database right is however weaker than copyright in that it restricts only extraction of substantial parts, whereas copyright is expressed to restrict any reproduction in whole or in part, thus presumably also restricting reproduction of insubstantial parts.[37]

Both copyright and the *sui generis* database right appear to prevent searching of an electronic database to establish that a particular item of information is not represented in it (so-called meta information). This may prove to be a valuable control.

7.7.1 Limitations to the *sui generis* database right

The definition of 're-utilisation' distinguishes between on-line databases and databases which are made available to the public by the distribution of copies, including rental.[38] Such copies may be either electronic or printed, and their distribution may be by any means and is not restricted to sale or rental. However, the first sale of a copy of a database within the Community by the rightholder or with his consent exhausts the right to control resale within the Community of that copy.[39]

Taken literally, the first sale exhaustion provision does not appear to apply if property in a database copy is retained by the rightholder and that copy is provided on free loan to a user. Making available to the public a substantial

---

31. Article 7(1).
32. Article 7(1).
33. Article 7(2)(a).
34. Article 7(2)(b).
35. Recital 44.
36. Article 5(a). For copyright see chapter 6.4.2.1.
37. Article 5(a). But see *Cantor Fitzgerald International* v *Tradition (UK) Ltd* [2000] RPC 94 as to copyright and copying of a substantial part of a protected work under UK copyright law.
38. Article 7(2)(b).
39. Article 7(2)(b) and reg. 12(5).

part of the contents of a database is a restricted act only to the extent that availability is either 'by the distribution of copies, by renting, by on-line or [by] other forms of transmission'.[40] Public lending is expressly excluded from the meaning of either extraction or re-utilisation,[41] but making a copy of a database available for use for direct or indirect economic or commercial advantage, on terms that it will or may be returned, is not excluded.[42]

Once a database has been made available to the public, which availability may be by public lending, the maker of the database may not prevent a lawful user from extracting and/or re-utilising insubstantial parts of the database's contents for any purpose whatsoever.[43] This is subject to the qualification that, when a lawful user is authorised to extract and/or re-utilise only part of a database, this provision shall apply only to that part.[44]

This lawful user right is subject to further qualifications:

(a) The lawful user may not perform acts which conflict with normal exploitation of the database or unreasonably prejudice the legitimate interests of its maker.[45]

(b) The lawful user may not cause prejudice to the holder of a copyright or related right in respect of the works or services contained in the database.[46]

These qualifications are in broad terms and are not further defined or elaborated: they reflect the so-called three step test under art. 9(2) of the Berne Convention.

The concepts of a lawful acquirer of a computer program and of a person having a right to use a computer program were introduced by the Software Directive.[47] The United Kingdom's implementation of this latter Directive amended the CDPA[48] to provide that a person is a lawful user of a computer program if (whether under a licence to do any acts restricted by copyright in the program or otherwise) he has a right to use the program. The same principle is adopted by the Database Regulations, so that a lawful user is a person having a licence or other right to extract and/or re-utilise the whole or substantial parts of a database.[49] Where the database is in electronic form and a copy of it has been purchased, the provisions of the CDPA relating to transfers of copies of works in electronic form may apply,[50] but this section relates only to copyright; both the Database Directive and the Database Regulations prohibit contractual restraints on lawful user rights.[51]

---

40. Article 7(2)(b).
41. Article 7(2).
42. Regulation 12(2).
43. Article 8(1).
44. Ibid.
45. Article 8(2).
46. Article 8(3).
47. Directive 91/250 on the Legal Protection of Computer Programs, art. 5.
48. Section 50A(2).
49. Regulation 12(1).
50. Copyright, Designs and Patents Act 1988, s. 56.
51. Database Directive, art. 15 and Database Regulations, regs 10 (copyright) and 19 (database right).

The net result of these complex provisions appears to be:

(a) *sui generis* right enables the rightholder to prevent extraction and/or re-utilisation of substantial parts of a database otherwise than by public lending; but

(b) once that database has been made available to the public, the combined effects of the exhaustion of rights by sale of a copy of the database and the lawful user provisions will prevent the rightholder from using either the *sui generis* database right or a contract term to stop a subsequent lawful acquirer of a sold copy of the database from extracting or re-utilising insubstantial parts of the database for any purpose whatsoever.

This freedom for a lawful user to use insubstantial parts of such a database for any purpose whatsoever is subject to the two qualifications noted above and set out in arts 8(2) and 8(3) (conflict with normal exploitation and prejudice to rightholder).

These provisions may prejudice those who make databases available to the public by sale of distributed copies, for example electronic copies on CD-ROM or printed copies, and may favour those who license the use of their databases through on-line access agreements which impose confidence and contractual terms and which limit access to parts of a database. In preparing or renewing any licence or use agreement, regard should be had to art. 15 which makes null and void any contractual provision contrary to arts 6(1) and 8 (lawful user rights). This provision is reflected in the Database Regulations and their amendments to the CDPA.[52]

7.7.2 Exceptions to the *sui generis* database right

While much of the Database Directive is prescriptive and sets out provisions which Member States are required to adopt, certain exceptions to the *sui generis* right are permissive, and so optional.

These provisions allow Member States to create additional rights for lawful users of a database made available to the public to extract or re-utilise substantial parts of the contents of the database:

(a) for private purposes, where the extraction is of contents of a non-electronic database;

(b) for teaching or scientific research purposes, provided the source of the extraction is indicated and the extraction is only to the extent justified by the non-commercial purpose to be attained; and/or

(c) for purposes of public security or for the proper performance of an administrative or judicial procedure.[53]

These provisions apply only to the *sui generis* right,[54] and would not appear to permit, for example, the extraction of articles from a printed journal for

---

52. Regulations 15 and 19: Copyright, Designs and Patents Act 1988, ss. 50D and 296B.
53. Article 9.
54. Broadly similar optional exceptions to the copyright restricted acts are contained in art. 6.

private purposes if the extraction involves copying, and so copyright infringement, of the article itself. The copyright provisions of the Database Directive do not affect copyright in the contents of a database. Such copying may thus be fair dealing in the contents but, if done for a commercial purpose, may not be fair dealing in the database.[55] The Database Regulations set out exceptions to database right for public administration, which include use of databases for parliamentary and judicial proceedings, Royal Commissions and statutory enquiries, material open to public inspection on an official register, material communicated to the Crown in the course of public business, public records and acts done under statutory authority.[56]

The Database Regulations also include a special provision declaring that the doing of anything in relation to a database for the purposes of research for a commercial purpose is not fair dealing with the database.[57]

7.8 TERMS OF PROTECTION

The term of protection by copyright of databases under the Database Directive is as for other literary works, namely the author's life plus 70 years. This is not expressly stated in the Database Directive or the Database Regulations, but is a necessary consequence of recognising copyright for databases as literary works.

The term of protection under the *sui generis* right is 15 years from the 1 January of the year following the year in which the database was completed. If the database is made available to the public in any manner whatever during that period, the term of protection is extended so as to expire 15 years from the 1 January following the date on which the database was first made available to the public.[58]

It follows that, if a database was completed on 2 January 1999 and is first made available to the public on 31 December 2014, the initial term of protection will not expire until 1 January 2030.

If the making of a database was completed on or after 1 January 1983, and that database qualified for database right on 1 January 1998, its term of protection is 15 years from 1 January 1998.[59]

If at any time, either during the term of protection or after its expiry, any substantial change is made to the contents of a database which would result in the changed database being considered to be a substantial new investment then that database may qualify for its own 15 year term of *sui generis* protection.[60]

For these purposes:

(a) 'Substantial change' is to be evaluated either qualitatively or quantitatively.

---

55. Copyright, Designs and Patents Act 1988, s. 29, and Database Regulations, reg. 8 amending s. 29.
56. Database Regulations, sch. 2.
57. Ibid.
58. Articles 10(1), (2) and reg. 17(2).
59. Regulation 30.
60. Article 10(3) and reg. 17(3).

(b) 'Substantial change' includes any substantial change resulting from the accumulation of successive additions, deletions or alterations.

Databases, like telephone directories, which may lack the necessary quality of human creativity to achieve the criterion of originality for copyright protection under the Database Directive, may nevertheless achieve *sui generis* protection by virtue of substantial investment made in obtaining, verifying or presenting the contents of such databases.[61] Similar substantial investments made on updating of the database may qualify each updated version of the database for its own 15 year term.

The consequence may be that successive issues of an annually updated directory based around a common format or core of information may attract successive 15 year terms, to give in effect potentially perpetual *sui generis* database right protection, whether or not copyright protection is available. Such a directory could acquire a monopoly position, making it difficult commercially for a competing new directory to break into the market. This may have competition law consequences.[62]

The Database Directive does not attempt to deal with competition issues, and does not repeat the compulsory licensing provisions which were contained in earlier proposals in relation to the *sui generis* right. These provisions applied to databases which had been made publicly available either by a public body or by an entity enjoying a monopoly status derived from an exclusive concession granted by a public body. Instead, the Directive leaves these issues to be dealt with under Community competition law,[63] and is content to rely on the rights referred to at 7.7 above for lawful users of databases which have been made available to the public.[64]

7.9 TRANSITIONAL PROVISIONS

Databases created before 1 January 1998, the date on which the Database Regulations come into force, are protected by copyright under the Database Directive and the Database Regulations if they fulfil the requirements laid down by the Database Directive and the Database Regulations for copyright protection. This does not extend to UK databases in existence at 31 December 1997 which lack any element of author's creativity in their selection or arrangement. Such databases do not fulfil the Directive's requirements for copyright protection and, but for savings in the Directive and the Regulations, would have ceased to enjoy copyright protection under the Directive on 1 January 1998. The same principle applies to pre-1998 computer-generated UK databases, which would appear to have fallen out of copyright protection on 1 January 1998 and to have been left with only *sui generis* right.

---

61. Recital 40 and art. 7.
62. See art. 82 (formerly art. 86) of the European Treaty on abuse of a dominant position; *RTE & ITP* v *EC Commission* [1995] 4 CMLR 718 (the *Magill* case).
63. Recital 47.
64. Article 8.

To cushion this effect, the Database Directive provides[65] that where a pre-1998 database had been created and was protected by a copyright system in a Member State on or before the date of publication of the Directive (27 March 1996) but that database does not fulfil the Directive's eligibility requirement for copyright protection,[66] for example because the selection or arrangement of its contents does not constitute the author's own intellectual creation, the Directive shall not result in any curtailing in that Member State of the remaining term of protection afforded under that Member State's copyright system. This saving is reflected in the Database Regulations.[67]

This generous provision will allow UK computer-generated databases which qualified for UK copyright protection at 27 March 1996 to continue to do so for the full term of copyright remaining applicable to them. Such databases created after 27 March 1996 appear to be excluded from protection by copyright as from 1 January 1998.

For databases made after 1 January 1983 (i.e., during the 15 years prior to 1 January 1998), whether or not protected by copyright, the *sui generis* database right is to be available[68] provided that such databases meet the requirements for *sui generis* right, namely that they show a sufficiently substantial investment in obtaining, verification or presentation of their contents. Since *sui generis* right can apply to a database in addition to the protection of that database by copyright, UK computer-generated databases created on or after 1 January 1983 and in existence on 27 March 1996 can be protected both by copyright and by the *sui generis* right.[69] Computer-generated databases made after 27 March 1996, although apparently excluded from copyright protection as from 1 January 1998, will be capable of protection under the *sui generis* right.

For *sui generis* right, the term of protection will be 15 years from 1 January 1998.[70] Databases qualifying for *sui generis* right protection will have the possibility of creating successive new 15 year *sui generis* right terms by regular updating of their contents.

For databases in existence at 1 January 1998, the terms of protection provided both for copyright and for *sui generis* right are to be without prejudice to acts accomplished and rights acquired prior to 1 January 1998.[71]

7.10. RECIPROCITY AND THE *SUI GENERIS* RIGHT

The principle of national treatment will apply to copyright protection for databases which meet the originality and other requirements for protection by copyright under the Database Directive. This means that rightholders of copyright protected databases, whether nationals of Member States or

---

65. Article 14(2).
66. As set out in art. 3(1).
67. Regulation 29.
68. Database Directive art. 14(3) and Database Regulations reg. 30.
69. Combined effects of arts 14(1), 14(2) and 14(3).
70. Article 14(5).
71. Article 14(4).

nationals of other States which are members of the Berne Convention, will be entitled within Europe as elsewhere to copyright protection for their databases in accordance with the law of the Berne Union State in which an alleged act of infringement occurs. The same principle will apply to databases which meet the Berne Convention's requirement of first publication in a State which is a member of Berne.

Since the sui generis right is a creation of the European Union, this new right is to be available, broadly, only within that Union and only to nationals of Member States of that Union. This principle is elaborated by the Database Directive into a series of complex subrules.[72]

(a)   The right is to apply to databases whose makers or successors in title are nationals of a Member State who have their habitual residence in the territory of the Community.[73]

(b)   The right is also to apply to companies and firms formed in accordance with the law of a Member State and having either their registered office, central administration or principal place of business within the Community. Where only the registered office of the company or firm is within the Community, the company or firm's operations must have an effective and continuing link with the economy of one of the Member States.[74]

The Commission may put a proposal to the Council for extending *sui generis* right to third countries, and the Council may enter into negotiations with such countries providing that the term of protection so agreed does not exceed that available under art. 10 of the Database Directive (broadly, 15 years).[75]

7.11   CONCLUSIONS

Concerns have been expressed in the United Kingdom about the loss of the UK's copyright originality criterion of skill and labour, and the substitution of the higher standard of author's intellectual creation, thus potentially excluding computer-generated works of all kinds from copyright protection. This battle remains to be fought in relation to other forms of copyright protected works, but appears to have been lost in relation to computer programs and in relation to databases within the Database Directive's definition of a database. The skill and labour criterion will, however, continue to apply for the time being to other literary works, including tables and compilations not falling within the Directive's definition of a database.

The Database Directive's transitional provisions for copyright and *sui generis* right in databases have sweetened the pill:

(a)   Databases which were in existence on 27 March 1996 can continue to be protected in the United Kingdom under UK copyright law during the residue of their respective terms, namely the author's life plus 70 years.

---

72. Article 11.
73. Article 11(1).
74. Article 11(2).
75. Article 11(3).

(b) If a post-1 January 1993 database fails to qualify for copyright protection for lack of human creativity it can still qualify for *sui generis* database right protection if there has been sufficient investment by its maker in its obtaining, verification or presentation. The right of extraction under the *sui generis* database right is broad, and in some circumstances can amount to a right to control electronic searching of a database in much the same way as copyright controls transient copying, but subject to far-reaching lawful user rights which are likely to be widely available.

(c) The ability to obtain successive 15 year terms of protection under the *sui generis* database right makes the disparity between the author's life plus 70 years term allowed for copyright and the 15 years term allowed for the *sui generis* database right less significant, leaving exposed only collections of static, non-copyright protected collections of materials which are incapable of being updated or re-presented.

(d) The definitions of extraction and re-utilisation for *sui generis* right, combined with the traditional restricted acts for copyright, appear to give effective, though differently expressed, protection under each right against taking, adaptation, re-formatting and other forms of re-use of databases by digital manipulation. This protection would seem to be available both for databases created by human authors and for databases which are computer-generated. These, in practice, may turn out to be the most important provisions of all.

However, there remain latent uncertainties in relation to competition between authors and makers having different rights in the same database. Who will take priority? Can each block the other's right to use or to license the database to third parties? What will be the effect on commissioned databases?

The Commission sees the Directive on the Legal Protection of Databases as a major plank in its platform of harmonised intellectual property rights for the Information Society in Europe. As digitisation, the Internet, future information superhighways and the ability to store, forward, process and adapt large volumes of data emerge as commonplace realities, information is becoming a truly international commodity. Neither copyright nor *sui generis* right is intended to protect ideas or information as such, but control over processing of databases may provide a valuable form of secondary protection having that effect.

A remaining concern is uncertainty about the future of the *sui generis* right internationally. Should the European Commission have opted for national treatment? Will reciprocity in practice be negotiable with non-Union countries? Would it have been better for Europe to have been generous, and to have made the *sui generis* right applicable to all databases within the European Union, whether or not the rightholder is a Community national? The world seems to favour national treatment: a more generous approach by the European Union might have encouraged the development and use of non-European databases in the Union, to the general advantage of database rightholders, the public and the Union itself.

CHAPTER EIGHT

Protecting Confidential Information

Allison Coleman

One of the main features of computers is their ability to store, manipulate and transmit data in ways that could not be achieved with manual records and storage systems. A result of this is to focus attention on data and on the information it contains and to follow this with questions about its position within the protective regime of the law. For example, to what extent is information treated as a commodity in its own right? How can or does the law control its use or abuse? The questions are legion and the answers varied.

In this chapter we shall narrow the discussion and look at the extent to which the law protects one special category of information which might be stored on a computer, namely confidential information. This category is traditionally given special treatment in law, but the advent of computing has aggravated the risks of its unauthorised use, disclosure or manipulation. The computer hacker is potentially a more intrusive animal than the burglar or more traditional spy.

Information processed by computers can be of many types; for example it can be personal, business or governmental information, or perhaps a mixture of these. Similarly, information learned by computer operators and programmers can fall into any of these groups. Once information in any of those groupings is classified as confidential, certain general legal principles govern its use or disclosure by a confidant. In this chapter we shall look at these general principles, but within the general framework that there are sometimes special rules which apply to different types of confidential information. Where the rules diverge we shall look at the law relating to trade secrets rather than the rules which apply to the other categories of secrets, for this chapter is aimed primarily at managers and computer scientists working in industry and their advisers, rather than at civil servants and governmental agencies, and the confines of space make complete coverage impossible.

In the world of high technology it is unduly insular to consider only English law, for computers and modern telecommunications links allow information to be moved around the world and across jurisdictional boundaries in but the blink of an eye. Lawyers and information managers therefore need to be familiar with themes and developments in other countries. While the basis of this chapter will be the law of England and Wales we shall also make reference to the laws of other countries, notably the United States and Canada, and also to proposals for law reform, for the law is never static and new concepts introduced into other legal systems often have an impact on our own.

It would also be remiss to look only at the civil action for breach of confidence. When a valuable asset such as commercial information is misappropriated, e.g., by industrial espionage, the question arises as to whether a crime has been committed. We shall therefore look at the criminal laws and shall see that often, and rather surprisingly, the criminal law intervenes very little if purely information is 'stolen' or interfered with, as opposed to the tangible asset on which it is stored. This is an area which is ripe for reform, and in this context we shall look at the proposals of the Law Commission for England and Wales to create a new offence of unauthorised use or disclosure of a trade secret.

In other chapters it has sometimes been much easier to describe the law in its direct application to computers. For example, it is possible to analyse statutes and cases on copyright in computer programs. In the field of confidential information the law is generally old and computers are new, and there are not all that many English cases dealing specifically with computers and even fewer statutes. Thus it is necessary to describe the law of confidence in other contexts and to apply it to computers by way of analogy. However there has been a steady trickle of cases in the United States in the last few years. Many of these apply comparable principles to those of English law and they also provide useful factual examples. They will therefore be cited at appropriate points.

8.1 THE CIVIL ACTION FOR BREACH OF CONFIDENCE

In English law three conditions must be satisfied before a civil action for breach of confidence can succeed:[1]

(a) The information must be confidential.
(b) The information must have been disclosed in circumstances which give rise to an obligation of confidence.
(c) There must be an actual or anticipated unauthorised use or disclosure of the information.

A fourth factor is sometimes added, namely that the claimant must suffer detriment. However it is uncertain whether this is an element of the action or

---

1. *Coco v A.N. Clark (Engineers) Ltd* [1969] RPC 41 per Megarry J.

whether it is something which the court takes into account when deciding the appropriate remedy. In any event its significance was reduced by Lord Keith in *Attorney-General* v *Guardian Newspapers Ltd (No. 2)* [1990] 1 AC 109, who said:

> I would think it a sufficient detriment to the confider that the information given in confidence is to be disclosed to persons whom he would prefer not to know it, even though the disclosure would not be harmful to him in any positive way.[2]

Each of the three main elements of the action for breach of confidence will now be considered in turn.

8.1.1   What is confidential information?

Lord Greene MR in *Saltman Engineering* v *Campbell* (1948) 65 RPC 203 described confidential information as something which is not public property and public knowledge. This means that there is no need for absolute secrecy before information can qualify as confidential. Relative secrecy may suffice. Thus information may be confidential if it is inaccessible or if it is not readily available to the public. For example, programs developed to drive robots on a production line and known only to the employees of a particular firm may be confidential, as may be novel software methodologies[3] or even information which a journalist has gleaned by searching through old newspapers and publicly available documents such as birth certificates and wills. In the last example there is a new compilation of information or even a rediscovery of information which has ceased to be generally known. Either way, the law will protect the fruits of the journalist's labours until he chooses to put them into the public domain or until someone else does the same work and then puts the results of his own research into public circulation.

The extent of disclosure which will be needed before information comes into the public domain is a matter for determination by the court in the light of the facts of the case. However, once information is in the public domain it cannot be protected under confidentiality laws, as was decided in the UK *Spycatcher* case[4] and in the US case of *Public Systems Inc.* v *Towry and Adams* (1991) WL 184452 where the Alabama Supreme Court ruled that a commercially available spreadsheet program using public data could not be protected under Alabama trade secrecy laws.

The fact that relative secrecy is all that is needed before information can qualify as confidential contrasts with the requirement of absolute novelty in patent law where any prior publication, no matter how obscure, will destroy novelty and deny patentability.

The test of relative secrecy would seem to be an objective one, the matter being looked at by the court in the light of all the relevant circumstances. A

2. [1990] 1 AC 109 at 256.
3. *Healthcare Affiliated Services Inc.* v *Lippany* (1988) 701 F Supp 1142.
4. See *Attorney-General* v *Guardian Newspapers Ltd (No. 2)* [1990] 1 AC 109, but cf *Schering Chemicals* v *Falkman* [1982] QB 1.

different and more subjective test of confidentiality was suggested in *Thomas Marshall* v *Guinle* [1979] Ch 227 by Sir Robert Megarry V-C, a judge whose decisions will feature prominently in this chapter. He said that there were four elements which might be of assistance in identifying confidential information in a trade or industrial setting:

(a)   The information must be information the release of which the owner believes would be injurious to him or of advantage to his rivals or others.

(b)   The owner must believe the information is confidential or secret, i.e., not already in the public domain.

(c)   The owner's belief under the previous two heads must be reasonable.

(d)   The information must be judged in the light of the usage and practices of the particular industry concerned.

This test concentrates very heavily on the views of the 'owner' of the information. However, these views are objectively assessed under the third requirement that they must be reasonable, thus preventing overzealous protection of information which by objective standards is not the true subject matter of an action for breach of confidence.

8.1.2   Categories of confidential information

Any sort of information may be classified as confidential, but in practice confidential information tends to fall into three categories — personal information, governmental secrets and trade secrets. Whilst it is public policy to protect confidential information generally, each of these categories of information is also protected for special reasons which may not apply equally to the other classes. For example, the protection of personal information is closely tied up with the maintenance of privacy. Thus in *Argyll* v *Argyll* [1967] Ch 302, the Duke of Argyll was not able to publish in a newspaper the secrets of his marriage to the Duchess of Argyll. But English law, unlike for example the laws of North America, is remarkably reluctant to develop a full-blown action for the protection of privacy[5] and the extent to which the action for breach of confidence can fulfil this role is very limited.

The protection of governmental secrets gives rise to yet other public policy issues such as preservation of national security, international diplomacy, politics and the reputations of governments and of public figures; plus questions of the freedom of the press to publish information in their own commercial interests and/or in the interest of free and informed debate. One issue which has been highlighted is the attitudes of different governments to freedom of information and the preservation of secrecy. This is appositely illustrated by the pursuit of Mr Peter Wright through the courts of the world by the representatives of the Thatcher government in an attempt to prevent the publication of his book, *Spycatcher*.[6] This should be contrasted with the

---

5. See e.g., *Kaye* v *Robertson* [1991] FSR 62. However, data protection law offers an increasing
    level of privacy protection — see chapter 13.

6. See note 4, above.

abandonment of a case by the Wilson government after they lost at first instance in an action for breach of confidence against Richard Crossman for publishing Cabinet secrets.[7]

Trade secrets are valuable commercial assets and to a large extent they are protected for the same reasons as other intangible commercial assets such as patents and copyrights. These include rewarding innovation and effort, allowing recoupment of expenditure on research and development and curtailing unfair competition by limiting the opportunities for piracy. In the context of computing, trade secrets may include software or hardware specifications as well as more standard business information such as pricing policies, lists of customers and suppliers, the company's payroll, quotations and investments, any or all of which may be kept on an in-house computer or may be held on behalf of a client on the computer of a specialist bureau.

Because the protection of trade secrets will feature quite prominently in this chapter a definition should be attempted. It has proved notoriously difficult to define a trade secret, but one attempt at a non-exhaustive definition comes from the Report of the Alberta Institute of Law Research and Reform and a Federal Provincial Working Party, as amended in a draft statute adopted by the Canadian Uniform Law Conference in 1988.[8] This definition has the advantage of reflecting case law in England and Wales and in the United States of America, and thus can serve as an indicator of elements in all three jurisdictions. The draft statute states that:

(1) ... trade secret, means information that
   (i)   is, or may be, used in a trade or business,
   (ii) is not generally known in that trade or business,
   (iii) has economic value from not being generally known, and
   (iv) is the subject of efforts that are reasonable under the circumstances to prevent it from becoming generally known.
(2) For the purposes of the definition, trade secret 'information' includes information set out, contained or embodied in, but not limited to, a formula, pattern, plan, compilation, computer program, method, technique, process, product, device or mechanism.

The English Law Commission in their recent Consultation Paper on Misuse of Trade Secrets,[9] which considers whether there should an offence of misuse of a trade secret,[10] have suggested a somewhat looser definition of a trade secret. They think that the term should apply to information:

(a) which is not generally known;

---

7. *Attorney-General* v *Jonathan Cape* [1976] QB 752.
8. Report No. 46, *Trade Secrets*, 1986. That was, however, amended at a Uniform Law Conference in 1988. References in this chapter will be to the amended version. For the full text see A. Coleman, *The Legal Protection of Trade Secrets*, ESC/Sweet & Maxwell, 1992, Appendix 2(a).
9. Law Commission Consultation Paper No. 150, Legislating the Criminal Code, Misuse of Trade Secrets (25 November 1997).
10. See further section 8.4.3 below.

(b)   which derives its value from that fact; and
(c)   as to which its 'owner' has indicated (expressly or impliedly) his or her wish to preserve its quality of secrecy.[11]

The Law Commission then sought views on:

(a)   whether there should be an additional requirement that the information be used in a trade or business; and if so,
(b)   the extent to which the definition should exclude professional secrets, and
(c)   the extent to which the definition should extend to pure research.

The view of the present author is that the definition should include the trade or business element of (a) above, that it should not necessarily exclude professional secrets; and that pure research should be protected, provided that it has actual or potential economic value.

8.1.3   When will an obligation of confidence be imposed?

Generally, an obligation of confidence will be imposed whenever confidential information is disclosed for a limited purpose. The recipient of the information will then be under a duty to use the information for the limited purpose only, and if he discloses or uses the information for any other purpose he will be in breach of his obligation and is liable to be restrained by injunction or subject to other appropriate remedies. For example, in *Saltman Engineering* v *Campbell* (1948) 65 RPC 203, the claimants gave to the defendants confidential designs for tools which the defendants were to manufacture solely for the claimants. When the defendants manufactured the tools on their own account they were held to be in breach of an obligation of confidence. The court held that the designs had been handed over for a limited purpose only and the defendants were not entitled to use them or the information contained in them for any other purpose.

The same principles were applied in *Fraser* v *Thames Television* [1984] QB 44, where the claimants had disclosed in confidence to a television company an idea for their own show. When the defendants tried to use the idea for a series featuring other actresses without first obtaining the claimants' consent, they were held to be in breach of their obligation of confidence. A good example of the imposition of an obligation of confidence in the field of computers might be where a consultant programmer is brought in to develop programs which will be integrated with other programs devised in-house. Details of these programs will have to be disclosed to the consultant, but this disclosure is clearly for the sole purpose of work for that organisation and he or she will not be free to use the information in work for other clients.

Problems can sometimes arise in determining the issue of to whom a duty of confidentiality is owed. In *Fraser* v *Evans* [1969] 1 QB 349, the claimant,

---

11. Law Commission, op. cit., note 9, para. 1.29.

Fraser, wrote a report for the Greek government. His contract stated that he was to keep confidential any information that he acquired while compiling the report, but the Greek government did not enter into a reciprocal obligation to keep confidential information supplied by Fraser to them. After its delivery to the Greek government Fraser's report was leaked by an unknown source to a newspaper, which proposed to publish an article about it. Fraser thought that the article might damage his reputation and he sought to restrain its publication on the ground of breach of confidence. The court held that, on the facts, no one owed a duty of confidentiality to Fraser despite his own categorisation of the information as being sensitive. Similarly, in the US case of *Bush* v *Goldman Sachs* (1989) 544 So 2d 873, Bush had developed a computer model to restructure government bond debt through refunding. Bush was hired by one company to become part of its team tendering for the contract to reconstruct the bond debt of the city of Birmingham, Alabama. Bush's computer model was submitted to the city authorities as part of the tendering process. However, the contract was given to another company, Goldman Sachs. Goldman Sachs subsequently made use of Bush's model without his consent. However, an action for breach of confidence failed, first because Bush had failed to take positive steps to protect the confidentiality of the model, e.g., by express notice of confidentiality in the tendering documentation; and secondly the court held that the city authorities, which had undoubtedly passed on the information to Goldman Sachs, owed no duty of confidentiality to Bush. Because they owed no duty to Bush they did not act in breach of duty in passing on the information to Goldman Sachs, which likewise could also not be held liable.

Precedent has not limited the range of circumstances in which an obligation of confidence can arise; it is a question of fact to be decided in each case but there are guidelines. For example, in the commercial context a useful statement was made by Megarry J (as he then was) in *Coco* v *A.N. Clark (Engineers) Ltd* [1969] RPC 41. He said that where information of commercial or industrial value is given on a business-like basis or with a common object in mind such as a joint venture or the manufacture of articles by one party for another, the recipient is under a heavy burden if he seeks to refute the contention that he is bound by an obligation of confidence. Where confidential information falling into the other categories is disclosed this dictum is obviously not directly applicable, but use of the limited purpose test described above should overcome any difficulties.

In *Coco* v *A.N. Clark (Engineers) Ltd*, Megarry J gave another test for the circumstances giving rise to an obligation of confidence. He said that an obligation would lie when a reasonable man standing in the shoes of the recipient of the information would realise on reasonable grounds that the information was being given to him in confidence. It will be remembered that in *Thomas Marshall* v *Guinle* [1979] Ch 227, Megarry V-C (as he later became) had defined information which could be classified as confidential. There he viewed the situation from the standpoint of the 'owner' of the information, but now when faced with the other side of the coin he said that the circumstances which give rise to an obligation were to be viewed from the position of the reasonable recipient. This shift in emphasis from the 'owner' to the recipient reflects the bilateral nature of the obligation of confidence and the mixed elements of subjectivity and objectivity in the various tests. These take into account not only the views of the parties to the action but also the public interest in the maintenance of confidentiality. In certain circumstances even if information has been classified as confidential an obligation of confidence will not arise if, for example, it would be against the public interest to keep the information confidential or if such a restriction would prevent an ex-employee using the general knowledge and skill acquired in his former employment. The special position of employees will be considered in 8.2.3.1, but we shall now look in greater detail at the public interest which permits disclosure even of information which is otherwise classified as being confidential.

8.1.4   The public interest in disclosure

The cases show that there is a clear public policy in favour of protecting confidential information. However, in certain circumstances that policy is overturned by one which holds that it is in the public interest that even confidential information should be disclosed, either to the public as a whole, e.g., through the media, or to the appropriate authorities such as the police. For example, suppose a scientist has discovered a cure for AIDS or for cancer. Should he be allowed to lock it in his safe or store it on his computer with the intention of keeping it a secret for the rest of his life? If one of his employees proposes disclosing the secret in a medical journal, to a national newspaper or at a scientific conference, should the discoverer be able to restrain him from so doing by an action for breach of confidence? We shall look first at the factors which the court will take into account when assessing whether the disclosure is justified in the public interest, then consider the position of 'whistleblowing' employees and the protection given to them under the Public Interest Disclosure Act 1998 against victimisation by their employers following a public interest disclosure.

The test for determining the public interest in disclosure has varied over the years. An early and much-quoted dictum comes from the case of *Gartside* v *Outram* (1857) 26 LJ Ch 113, where Wood V-C said 'there is no confidence as to the disclosure of an iniquity'. From this there arose what became known as the 'iniquity rule', which basically meant that a confidant was justified in breaching confidentiality and disclosing information in the public interest if it was related to some misconduct, and the closer this misconduct came to criminal or unlawful activity the better. But this is a rather narrow basis on which to permit disclosure and it may not, for example, permit the disclosure of the cure for cancer referred to in the previous example, for there the discoverer who wishes to keep the information out of the public domain is guilty of no criminal or unlawful conduct even though most would probably castigate his intentions as immoral.

Lord Denning led a movement away from the iniquity rule in *Initial Services* v *Putterill* [1968] 1 QB 396, *Fraser* v *Evans* [1969] 1 QB 349 and *Schering*

Chemicals v *Falkman* [1982] QB 1, but there remained uncertainty as to the status of the old rule or the extent of any new rule until *Lion Laboratories* v *Evans* [1985] QB 526, where the Court of Appeal held that confidential information may be disclosed in circumstances where there was 'just cause or excuse', which is obviously a much broader notion than that of an iniquity.[12]

In *Lion Laboratories* v *Evans*, the claimant company manufactured computerised electronic equipment known as the Lion Intoximeter which was used by the police to measure the level of alcohol in the breath of people suspected of drunk driving. Readings from the machine were used as a basis for prosecution. Confidential internal memoranda produced by the company indicated that readings from the machines were often inaccurate. Two of the claimants' employees gave copies of the memoranda to a national newspaper, the Daily Express, which at that time was conducting a campaign against the use of the Intoximeter by the police. The claimants sought an injunction to restrain publication of the information by the newspaper on the grounds of breach of confidence and breach of copyright. The actions failed as the Court of Appeal held that there was a public interest in the disclosure of the information, as it might lead to the reappraisal of a device which had the potential for causing wrongful conviction for a serious offence. They said that the defence of public interest was not limited to cases involving disclosure of an iniquity, iniquity being just one example of the public interest exemption and not therefore an essential ingredient. The court based the defence on the wider ground of 'just cause or excuse' for disclosure, with the caution given by Lord Griffiths that the decision should not be treated as a 'mole's charter'. The court also made it clear that there was a difference between matters which, on the one hand, it was in the commercial interest of newspapers to publish and which might merely be of public interest to read and, on the other hand, matters which it was in the public interest to disclose. Only in the latter cases would the public interest permit disclosure of confidential information. Furthermore, the press might not always be the appropriate medium for a disclosure. In other cases it might be more appropriate to disclose the information to the police or other authorities. That was not, however, the case here where disclosure through the press would be allowed.

We do not know what happened to the employees in *Lion Laboratories*, but Yvonne Cripps in her book, *The Legal Implications of Disclosure in the Public Interest*,[13] chronicles a number of cases where the employees have lost their jobs as a result of the disclosure and effectively have been prevented from working for anyone else ever again. While equity may refuse an injunction to prevent the disclosure of information in the public interest, the common law has generally taken the approach that disclosure of confidential information is a breach of the implied duty of fidelity in the contract of employment, which may justify dismissal or other disciplinary action. The position of the

---

12. See also *W* v *Egdell* [1990] 1 All ER 835; and *Attorney-General* v *Guardian Newspapers Ltd (No. 2)* [1988] 3 All ER 545 at 659 per Lord Goff.

13. Yvonne Cripps: *The Legal Implications of Disclosure in the Public Interest: An Analysis of Prohibitions and Protections with Particular Reference to Employers and Employees*, 2nd edn, London: Sweet & Maxwell, 1994, ch. 1.

employee has however recently been improved by the Public Interest Disclosure Act 1998.[14]

The Public Interest Disclosure Act 1998 amends the Employment Rights Act 1996. The 1998 Act protects a 'worker' from being victimised by the employer when the worker makes what the Act calls a 'protected disclosure'. A 'worker' is an individual who works under a contract of employment, or who contracts 'to perform personally services for another party to the contract whose status is not by virtue of the contract that of a client or customer of any business undertaking carried on by the individual.'[15] Self-employed computing consultants are therefore not covered by the Act, but they have no need of its protection, as they cannot of course be dismissed or otherwise victimised by an 'employer'. Programmers seconded from other firms are however covered, for the PIDA[16] extends protection to, *inter alia*, agency and seconded employees; and also to many homeworkers and teleworkers, provided they do not ordinarily work outside Great Britain.[17]

A worker will be protected against victimisation for disclosure if the worker makes (a) a qualifying disclosure, (b) in certain prescribed circumstances. A 'qualifying disclosure' means any disclosure of information which, in the reasonable belief of the worker making the disclosure tends to show one or more of the following, which has occurred in the past, is occurring in the present, or is likely to occur in the future: a criminal offence; failure to comply with a legal obligation; a miscarriage of justice; danger to health and safety; environmental damage; or information showing concealment of any of these.[18] This is narrower than the 'just cause or excuse' test for public interest disclosure set out in *Lion Laboratories* (above) and reflects to a much greater extent the old and discredited 'iniquity' test. It is interesting that the legislature went for certainty of definition, rather than width of protection.

A qualifying disclosure made in appropriate circumstances to an appropriate person becomes a protected disclosure, entitling the worker to protection against victimisation. The PIDA lists six cases where a disclosure by a worker is a protected disclosure. Basically, the Act encourages private or semi-private disclosures, either to the employer, or to the person committing the wrongful act, and many employers have produced Codes of Practice on Public Interest Disclosure which also specify other persons to whom disclosures may be made and the way the matter is to be handled. Only if it is of a more serious nature, or if the private or semi-private route has failed, may the employee be justified in disclosing to a wider audience, such as the press, but in this case close attention needs to be paid to the minutiae of the Act, for there are many pitfalls for the public spirited, but poorly advised employee. Dismissal of an unprotected employee may not be unfair; and disciplinary action may not be in breach of contract. The 1988 Act therefore remedies many of the abuses

---

14. Hereafter, 'the PIDA' or the '1998 Act'.
15. Employment Rights Act 1996, s. 230.
16. Public Interest Disclosure Act 1998, s. 1, inserting a new s. 43K into the Employment Rights Act 1996.
17. Employment Rights Act 1996, s. 196(2), (3).
18. Public Interest disclosure Act s. 1; Employment Rights Act 1996, s. 43B.

highlighted by Cripps[19] and furthers the policy of permitting, and even encouraging, disclosure of otherwise confidential information in the public interest; but it is a cautious piece of legislation and it is to be hoped that the judiciary will not further restrict its ambit, for although they have defined public interest widely in the past, they have not also championed the rights of the victimised employee.

8.2 JURISDICTION

There has been much debate as to the jurisdictional foundation of the action for breach of confidence, but quite remarkably the courts seem free to draw on most of the available jurisdictional bases — contract, equity, property and tort. In many instances the facts will lead quite naturally to the application of one of these bases, in others there may be several possibilities. We shall now look at various jurisdictional bases and indicate the areas where they are most frequently employed in practice.

8.2.1 Express contractual obligations of confidence

Parties who are aware that information is confidential and that its unauthorised use or disclosure would be disadvantageous to them would be well advised to enter into express contracts of confidentiality with their confidants before making a disclosure. As well as setting out the terms on which the information is disclosed, the contract will also serve as a warning of both confidentiality and the serious intent of the discloser.

An express contract may be oral or in writing, although writing is clearly advantageous for evidential reasons. No particular form is necessary so long as the intent is clear, and it is common for the obligation of confidence to be set out in a letter or deed which, in practice, follows a fairly standard pattern. In return for the release of the information the confidant agrees to treat it as confidential and to use it only for the limited purpose intended. However, it is normal to qualify the agreement by providing that in three cases the obligation shall cease:

(a) If the information subsequently comes into the public domain other than by breach of confidence on the part of the confidant.

(b) If it was lawfully in the confidant's possession before the agreement.

(c) It was acquired by him after the agreement from a third party who was not also bound by an obligation of confidence to the present discloser.

Confidentiality clauses are also commonly found in contracts dealing with an array of other matters such as contracts for the supply or maintenance of hardware or software, consultancy contracts, and agreements for the provision of data services.

It is not necessary to define in the contract all of the information which is to be regarded as being confidential, and indeed this will rarely be possible

---

19. Note 13, above.

in practice. But if an injunction is sought to restrain breach of an obligation of confidence, it is important then to define carefully for the purpose of the proceedings information which is believed to be confidential and which it is alleged is, or is thought likely to be, improperly used or disclosed. For example, in *Amway Corporation Ltd* v *Eurway International Ltd* [1974] RPC 82,[20] the claimants alleged that all of the material in all of their sales promotion literature was confidential. The claim failed. The court held that the claimants had not disclosed the information to the defendants under an obligation of confidence, but even if they had, an injunction could not be granted to restrain use of such a generalised body of information or what the judge referred to as 'mere know-how'. The distinction between protectable confidential information and 'mere know-how' which cannot be protected is an important one, and is relied on heavily in employment cases as will be shown in a later part of this chapter.

Another useful device for protecting confidential information is what can be described as a 'black box' contract. In *Paul (Printing Machinery) Ltd* v *Southern Instruments (Communications) Ltd* [1964] RPC 118, the claimants supplied a telephone answering machine to one of the defendants under a contract for hire, which specified that the defendant was not to remove the machine from the address and position at which it was installed nor interfere in any way with the machine or with any of its electrical connections. In breach of this agreement one of the defendants allowed another defendant to remove it, take it apart and examine it. Damages would obviously not have been an appropriate remedy as the claimant clearly wanted to preserve the 'secrets in the box'. As a result the court granted an interlocutory injunction restraining the defendants from using or disclosing confidential information gleaned from the unlawful inspection.

This type of contract is obviously useful in the supply of computers or other technologically advanced equipment where the secret parts can be shielded from view. In the absence of such agreement the law of confidence will not prevent the purchaser of equipment from reverse engineering a machine or disassembling a program.[21] Even copyright laws do not prevent a competitor from taking the ideas behind, e.g., a computer program, copyright being aimed a protection of the form in which material is laid out rather than the ideas on which it is based.[22]

8.2.2 Implied contractual obligations

An obligation of confidence may also be implied into a contract. An implied term can provide the entire obligation of confidence or it may supplement an express term. An example of its supplementary role is *Thomas Marshall* v *Guinle* [1979] Ch 227 where an employee was subject to an express clause prohibiting the disclosure of confidential information

---

20. See also *FSS Travel and Leisure Systems Ltd* v *Johnson* [1999] FSR 505.
21. See, e.g., *Acuson Corp.* v *Aloka Co. Ltd*, 257 Cal Rptr 368, 209 Cal App 3d 1098, 209 Cal App 3d 425, 1989 Cal App Lexis 317, 1989, *The Software Law Bulletin*, vol. 2, p. 146.
22. See further chapter 6.

belonging to his employers. However, on the facts of the case the employee had been *using* the information for his own purposes and not *disclosing* it to others. The court held that the express term against disclosing confidential information could be supplemented by an implied term prohibiting its use.

Another case on the implied obligation of confidence, and one to which we shall return later, is *Schering Chemicals Ltd* v *Falkman* [1982] QB 1. The facts were that the claimant was a drug company which manufactured a drug called Primodos. It had been suggested that the drug could have harmful effects on unborn children, and as a result the claimant suffered bad publicity. It engaged the first defendant to train its executives in television techniques and to put across effectively the claimant's point of view. The first defendant engaged the second defendant to help with the training courses. The claimants supplied a large amount of information on the drug to the first defendant and that in turn was passed on to the second defendant. It was acknowledged that the first defendant had received the information in confidence, but it was never established whether the second defendant gave an express undertaking of confidentiality.

Shortly after the training course, the second defendant proposed making a television programme about the drug for Thames Television. Much of the information which was to be included in the film had been supplied by the claimant for the training course but, importantly, most of it was already available from public sources. The claimant sought an injunction to restrain use of the information, arguing that it had been obtained in circumstances imposing an obligation of confidence and to use it in the film would amount to breach of confidence.

Lord Denning MR, who dissented, refused to imply an obligation of confidence on the ground that the information was publicly available. Shaw and Templeman LJJ disagreed. Shaw LJ said that the second defendant owed a fiduciary duty to the claimant and described his conduct as a 'flagrant breach of an elementary duty to honour confidences'. He said that the law did not grant 'a licence for the mercenary betrayal of business confidences'. As for the argument that the information was in the public domain and thus not confidential, he said this was 'at best cynical; some may regard it as specious'.

Templeman LJ also held that the second defendant was under a duty of confidence, but instead of describing it as a fiduciary duty, he said, most importantly in the present context, that it was based on an implied promise. He said that the information had been given for one purpose only, and when the second defendant had agreed for reward to take part in the training course and had received the information from the claimant he came under a duty not to use that information, and in particular he impliedly promised not use it for the very purpose which the claimant sought to avoid, namely bad publicity or publicity which it reasonably regarded as bad. Rather unusually, although the information was already in the public domain it remained confidential as between the parties to the action, and as the second defendant could not republish or recycle it without causing further harm, he would be in breach of his obligation of confidence if he used the information for another purpose. Furthermore, as Thames Television had acted with full knowledge of the facts, they could be in no better position than the second defendant, and they too would be restrained from using or disclosing the information.

8.2.3 The different obligations of confidence owed by employees and consultants

8.2.3.1 Employees Employees both generate and acquire confidential information in the course of a contract of employment. The general principle is that the employee holds the confidential information for the benefit of the employer.

Employment contracts do, however, present special problems, as here the contractual obligation of confidence is subject to the qualification that an employee is, after the termination of the contract of employment, free to use general knowledge and skill either for the employee's own benefit or for the benefit of others. As a result, the confidential character of information is probably more closely scrutinised in these cases than in almost any others. One of the most difficult questions in this area of the law is to determine the dividing line between confidential information and general knowledge and skill. For example, is the knowledge acquired by a computer systems expert in the course of employment the employee's own to use as the employee pleases or is it an asset belonging to the employer? What is the position of firms of head-hunters who seek to persuade highly skilled personnel to leave their present employment and to use their expertise for the benefit of others in return for greater reward? In today's competitive environment expertise is a valuable commodity, but to what extent is it really readily saleable?

An employee's obligation of confidence may be found in the express or in the implied terms of the contract of employment. This was illustrated earlier by the case of *Thomas Marshall* v *Guinle* [1979] Ch 227, where it will be remembered that an express term prohibiting the disclosure of confidential information was supplemented by an implied term preventing the employee using that information. In employment cases the implied obligation of confidence is part of the more general implied obligation of good faith and fidelity which every employee owes to the employer. This obligation exists during the term of the contract, but very importantly, it also continues after employment ceases. It is at its clearest and strongest during the subsistence of the contract, for here as Gurry argues[23] the employee's interest in enhancing his or her knowledge and skill 'interlocks' with the duty to develop and improve the employer's business. At this stage Gurry shows that the obligation of fidelity owed by an employee to an employer can be expressed in three propositions:

(a) An employee is bound not to disclose or use confidential information received in the course of employment for purposes which are against the interests of the employer.

---

23. Francis Gurry, *Breach of Confidence*, Oxford: Oxford University Press, 1984, p. 179.

(b)   An employee must not compete with the employer or work for any of the employer's rivals.

(c)   The employee is bound to disclose to the employer any valuable information which the employee receives in his capacity as an employee and which is unknown to his employer, and this will include any confidential information which would further the employer's trade.

The first two propositions are illustrated by *Hivac v Park Royal Scientific Instruments Ltd* [1946] Ch 169, where five people who were employed by the claimants were working in their spare time for the claimants' rivals, the defendants. If this had continued they were almost certain to have disclosed to the defendants confidential information belonging to the claimants. As a result, the claimants succeeded in their action to restrain the defendants from continuing to employ the claimants' employees. Moonlighting is therefore discouraged.

After the contract of employment has been terminated the employee's implied duty of good faith and fidelity continues and he will still be required to keep confidential those secrets which he learnt during the former employment. However, at this stage the interest of the employee in using and developing general knowledge and skill usually diverges from the former employer's interest in the employer's own business. To return to the previous example, the computer systems expert whose skills have been head-hunted by a rival concern or who wishes to set up in business on his own account may not be prepared to make less than full use of all of the knowledge that he possesses, including knowledge of information classified by his former employer as being confidential, or indeed his new employment may be conditional on the full use of such knowledge. Here a number of policies conflict, namely the public policy in the maintenance of confidences as against policies favouring mobility of labour, the free flow of information and free competition. As a compromise, the first policy holds sway to the extent that a former employee is under a continuing obligation not to use or disclose confidential information belonging to the former employer, but the other policies ensure that he is free to use his general knowledge and skill.

There are a number of tests for determining the dividing line between confidential information and general knowledge and skill. In *Printers and Finishers v Holloway* [1964] 1 WLR 1, Cross J said the question was whether the information could 'fairly be regarded as a separate part of the employee's stock of knowledge which a man of ordinary honesty and intelligence would recognise to be the property of his old employer, and not as his own to do as he likes with'. More recently the Court of Appeal laid down guidelines in *Faccenda Chicken Ltd v Fowler* [1987] Ch 117. Neil LJ, giving the judgment of the court, said that in order to determine whether information could be classified as so confidential that an employee should not be allowed to use or disclose it for the benefit of a subsequent employer it was necessary to consider all the circumstances of the particular case, but the following were among those to which attention must be paid:

(a)   *The nature of the employment:* employment in a capacity where confidential information is habitually handled may impose a high obligation of confidentiality because the employee could be expected to realise its sensitive nature to a greater extent than if he were employed in a capacity where such material reached him only occasionally.

(b)   *The nature of the information itself:* in order to be protected the information must be of a highly confidential nature; no other information could be protected even by a covenant in restraint of trade. The court said it would clearly be impossible to provide a list of matters which would be protectable as trade secrets. Secret processes of manufacture were obvious examples, but innumerable other pieces of information were capable of being trade secrets even though the secrecy of some information may only be short-lived. In addition, the fact that the circulation of certain information was restricted to a limited number of individuals may throw a light on the status of the information and its degree of confidentiality.

(c)   *Whether the employer impressed upon the employee the confidentiality of the information.*

(d)   *Whether the relevant information can be easily isolated from other information which the employee is free to use or disclose:* this factor should not be regarded as conclusive, as might have been suggested in earlier cases, but like the other matters listed above it was one of the factors which the court should take into account.

The result of this is that if information is not categorised as confidential under these criteria then it forms part of the employee's general knowledge and skill, and it may be easier to apply the factors listed in *Faccenda Chicken Ltd v Fowler* to employees in high technology industries than it is to apply more general statements such as that in *Printers and Finishers v Holloway*. However, there are still many difficulties and each case must inevitably turn on its facts.

Neil LJ also made it clear that he was stating principles which would apply only when the ex-employee wanted to earn his living from use of the information in question. He left open the question of whether additional protection should be afforded if an ex-employee proposed not to use it in order to earn his living but merely to sell it to a third party. Such a distinction, if drawn, would be new to English law. It would also necessitate the development of a new set of principles of a complexity hitherto unforeseen. For example, what would be the position of a person who sold information in return for a consultancy for one day a week, or for one day a month, or for one day a year, or for just one day?

An alternative approach to reliance solely on an implied obligation to respect confidentiality, and hence a way around some of the difficulties described above, might be to use a contractual term to restrain the employee from working for competitors after he leaves his employment. However, the courts view such restrictions unfavourably and they will only be enforced if they are no wider than is reasonably necessary to protect the employer's interests in terms of the activities covered, the geographical area to which the restriction extends and the length of time it lasts.[24] For example, a hardware manufacturer whose business consisted solely of producing Automated Teller Machines for use in the banking industry in the UK would be unable to restrict one of its programmers from working for any other hardware manufacturer in the world for 10 years after leaving. It is important to note that if the restriction is too wide it is likely to be totally ineffective, thus allowing the employee to work for a direct competitor[25] and directing reliance back on the uncertain obligation of confidence. A better restriction would be against working on the production of Automated Teller Machines and connected hardware for any business marketing its equipment in the UK. The length of time of the restriction should not last beyond the date when the employer's secret technology is likely to become obsolete.

The principles for interpretation of restrictive covenants were recently restated by the Court of Appeal in *FSS Travel and Leisure Systems Ltd* v *Johnson* [1999] FSR 505. Here, the defendant employee was a computer programmer who had worked on the claimant employer's computerised booking system, a system which had been devised especially for the travel industry. The system comprised 2,852 separate programs which interacted with each other and were updated daily. The defendant had worked on 395 of them. It was a term of the defendant's contract of employment that for a period of one year after the termination of the contract, he would not work for any of the claimant's competitors. Mummery LJ, delivering the judgment of the Court of Appeal, said that the principles to be applied to cases such as the present were to be found in three cases: *Littlewoods Organisation* v *Harris* [1977] 1 WLR 1472; *Office Angels Ltd* v *Rainer-Thomas* [1991] IRLR 214; and *Lansing Linde Ltd* v *Kerr* [1991] IRLR 80. They were as follows. The court will never uphold a covenant taken by an employer merely to protect himself from competition by a former employee. Instead there must be some subject matter which an employer could legitimately protect by a restrictive covenant. However, protection could be claimed for identifiable objective knowledge constituting trade secrets belonging to the employer, but which the employee has learned (or even created) during the course of employment. By way of contrast, and as described above in the context of the implied obligation of confidence, protection could not be legitimately be claimed by way of a restrictive covenant for skill, experience, know-how and general knowledge acquired by an employee whilst working for the employer, even though that would better equip him to work for others in competition with the former employer. Once again, therefore, the critical question was whether the information the employer sought to protect came under the heading of trade secrets, or whether it was part of the employee's general knowledge and skill. Mummery LJ explained that in order to classify the information in question it was necessary to examine all of the evidence relating to the nature of the employment, the character of the information, the restrictions imposed on its dissemination, the extent to which it was in the public domain; the

---

24. *Nordenfeldt* v *Maxim Nordenfeldt Gun Co.* [1894] AC 535.
25. *Mason* v *Provident Clothing & Supply Co. Ltd* [1913] AC 724.

damage likely to be caused by its use and disclosure to a competitor; and the extent to which the information in question is readily separable from the employee's general knowledge and skill. But crucially, it was also necessary to be very precise in pleadings and to provide solid evidence in proof of trade secrets, and this the claimant in this case had failed to do. It was notable that witnesses had described the skills the defendant possessed and emphasised what he could do, rather than what he knew; and from this the court concluded that FSS Travel and Leisure Systems were claiming to be entitled to control the exercise, after the termination of the contract of employment, of the skill, experience, know-how and general knowledge of their former employee. This, the court would not allow them to do, and the covenant was held to be invalid. Witnesses for the employer should therefore be schooled not to use the modern skills based language, but to concentrate instead on hard fact.

Other ways in which an employee's competitive potential can be reduced and his ability to misappropriate trade secrets restricted is either to require a long period of notice to be given prior to termination of the contract, or to put the employee on 'garden leave'. 'Garden leave' entitles the employee to full pay and perks for a defined period (e.g., 12 months) so long as he does not work for anyone else. The employee may effectively be given a holiday. The enforceability of a garden leave clause and its ability to protect confidential information was first tested in *Provident Financial Group plc* v *Hayward* [1989] 3 All ER 298. At one time it was suggested that these clauses might be construed more flexibly than conventional restrictive covenants,[26] but more recently, in *William Hill* v *Tucker* [1999] ICR 291, Morritt LJ, giving the judgment of the Court of Appeal, said that they will be subject to similar controls to covenants in restraint of trade, for their effect is equally to keep an employee out of the labour market.

8.2.3.2 Consultants An increasing number of people are now working in the computing industry as consultants, i.e., as independent contractors rather than as employees. It is therefore necessary also to consider their position in relation to confidential information generated and acquired in the course of their work.

A well drafted contract for services to be provided by a consultant should always deal with the ownership of intellectual property rights generated in the course of the work and with the question of confidentiality. This is in the interests of both the consultant and the firm for which the work is to be done.

In the absence of express agreement it is necessary to fall back on ordinary principles of law. So far as confidential information is concerned this will be governed by implied contractual terms, as in the case of a contract of employment. A consultant should hold for the benefit of the firm for which he works all trade secrets generated or acquired in the course of the work and he should not use or disclose these trade secrets for any unauthorised purpose. Counterbalancing this is, however, the principle that a consultant,

---

26. *Credit Suisse Asset Management Ltd* v *Armstrong* [1996] ICR 882, CA, per Neill LJ.

like an employee, is entitled to use for his own benefit and for the benefit of others his general knowledge and skill. Thus again we meet the thorny issue of what is a trade secret and what is general knowledge and skill. Where does the dividing line lie?

In the case of an employee, *Faccenda Chicken* v *Fowler* [1987] Ch 117, laid down guidelines as to which information could be used for the benefit of the employee and others after termination of a contract of employment and which should be kept secret. However, there is nothing in *Faccenda Chicken* to indicate that those guidelines would apply equally to a consultant. If they do not apply, consultants are therefore in a different position to employees. Cases such as *Schering Chemicals* v *Falkman* [1982] QB 1, discussed above, *Deta Nominees* v *Viscount Plastic Products* [1979] VR 167, and *Surveys and Mining Ltd* v *Morrison* [1969] QdR 470, have taken a rather hard line with consultants who have acquired confidential information whilst working for one client and then subsequently used that information for their own benefit or for the benefit of others. In each of these case the courts have held that the consultant has acted in breach of an obligation of confidence.

If employees and consultants are treated differently several propositions follow. For example, while both consultants and employees can use their general knowledge and skill for the benefit of others, more information is likely to be held to be confidential and protectable in the case of consultants than in the case of employees. Viewing this from the point of view of a firm deciding to take on additional labour, it might be desirable therefore to take on independent contractors or consultants rather than to engage employees under short-term contracts.

8.2.4 The equitable obligation of confidence

There are many circumstances in which confidential information is disclosed and yet there cannot be said to be any contract between the discloser and confidant. This will normally be the case when personal confidences are exchanged between friends, and it will often be so when an inventor discusses an invention with potential financiers and business partners. In these circumstances any obligation of confidence will almost always be equitable. For example in *Coco* v *A N Clark (Engineers) Ltd* [1969] RPC 41, the claimant who had designed the 'Coco Moped' sought cooperation from the defendants in its development. The parties quarrelled before any agreement was reached, but features of the Coco Moped were later found in the defendants' mopeds. The court found that the information which the claimant gave to the defendants was not confidential but, had it been, Megarry J said that an equitable obligation would have been imposed if, applying the test which we met earlier, the circumstances were such that a reasonable man standing in the shoes of the recipient of the information would have realised on reasonable grounds that the information was being given to him in confidence.

Another example is *Seager* v *Copydex* [1967] RPC 349, where the claimant, in the course of negotiations for marketing one type of carpet grip which he had invented, disclosed his design for a second grip and suggested the name

'Invisigrip'. This disclosure would seem to have been unsolicited. Negotiations foundered and the defendants decided to develop and market a carpet grip of their own. This they also called 'Invisgrip' and its design closely resembled the second grip described to them by the claimant. The claimant succeeded in an action for unauthorised use of confidential information. The court said that even if the plagiarism by the defendants was unconscious there were too many coincidences and too many similarities for the court to conclude that there had been anything other than a misuse of information given to the defendants by the claimant. Equitable principles were also applied recently by the Irish courts in *House of Spring Gardens* v *Point Blank Ltd* [1985] FSR 327, where, because there were no Irish cases in point, the courts applied the doctrines of English law.[27]

8.2.4.1 Unsolicited disclosures Cases on the equitable obligation of confidence highlight the problems which can arise from unsolicited disclosures. Some firms regularly receive ideas from outsiders about new products or improvements to their existing ranges, and while it is not proper that they should make free use of all confidences that come their way their subsequent activities should not, at the other extreme, always be inhibited by a prior unsolicited disclosure. Strong representations were made to the Law Commission on this point.[28] Evidence to the Commission showed that many firms adopted elaborate procedures in order to avoid an obligation of confidence. Some firms required the person submitting the information to sign a form recognising that no obligation of confidence existed in relation to the information, the person submitting the information being limited to such rights (if any) which he may have to patent, copyright or design rights. Other firms were content to ensure that the person submitting unsolicited information appreciated that the recipient would remain free to exploit ideas involved if they had already been, or were in the future, independently discovered by the recipients or if they were in the public domain. In other words those firms who understood their legal position modified their relationship with the discloser of confidential information by express contract, whereas those who did not know the law often found themselves bound to respect confidentiality. To ameliorate the position of persons in the latter category the Law Commission recommended[29] that the law be changed, and that an obligation of confidence should come into existence only when the recipient of the information had given an express undertaking of confidence or where an undertaking could be inferred from the relationship between the parties or from the conduct of the recipient. However, this is arguably going too far and represents an unnecessary change. It is better to prefer confidentiality and to refute the obligation if necessary than to place barriers in the way of it arising in the first place.

---

27. See further A. Coleman, '*House of Spring Gardens* v *Point Blank: 'A Maze of Deception'"* [1988] *EIPR* 218.
28. Law Commission, *Breach of Confidence* (Law Com. No. 110, Cmnd 8388), London: HMSO, 1981, para. 5.3.
29. Ibid., para. 6.14.

8.2.5 Tortious obligations of confidence

So far tort has not featured very prominently in the cases on breach of confidence, but it assumes an important role in proposals for reform in three common law jurisdictions, England and Wales, Canada and the United States.[30] In each of these jurisdictions it has been suggested that henceforth, at least in certain areas, the action for breach of confidence should be based on tortious liability. In 1981 the English Law Commission recommended[31] that the present action for breach of confidence should be abolished and that it should be replaced by one new statutory tort of breach of confidence covering the unauthorised use or disclosure of confidential information. In contrast to the reforms in the United States and Canada, the English Law Commission recommended that the new action should apply to all categories of confidential information. In the United States and Canada the various categories of information are now often treated separately. There, for example, the law of privacy has burgeoned in recent years, affecting the protection of personal confidences, and reform bodies now suggest that trade secrets should also be treated separately, recognising the different interests involved and their greater affinity with the policies of intellectual property and unfair competition law than with the issues underlying, e.g., privacy and governmental information. In this section we shall be looking at the reforms of trade secrets law, following once again the theme of trade where the law diverges as between the different categories of confidential information.

In the United States and Canada the problem is that confidentiality is a matter for state or provincial law, unlike patents and copyrights which are regulated federally. As a result, although there is a common core of principles underlying the action for breach of confidence laws do diverge across the country. There have been two main sets of proposals for uniform laws for the United States. The first came in the *Restatement of the Law of Torts* published in 1939. Like the later English Law Commission Report this recommended that it should be a tort for a person to use or disclose a trade secret without privilege to do so. However, when the 1939 Restatement was updated the legal protection of trade secrets was omitted. The American Law Institute, which produces the Restatements, said that trade secrets had become a subject of such importance in its own right that it no longer belonged in that volume of the Restatement and that it should receive independent treatment in a separate Trade Practices Restatement, but regrettably this was never produced.

In a separate development in 1979 the US National Conference of Commissioners on Uniform State Laws recommended the adoption of another set of uniform laws on trade secrets set out in a Uniform Trade Secrets Act, which could be enacted by individual state legislatures. This has now been adopted (sometimes with amendments) in at least thirty five states.

The latest set of proposals for reform come from Canada in the joint Report of the Alberta Institute of Law Research and Reform and a Federal

---

30. See further Coleman, op. cit., note 8 above, ch. 2.
31. Law Commission Report No. 110 (see note 28), para. 6.2.

Provincial Working Party (see 8.1.2 above). The reforms suggested there reflect to a far greater extent the recent changes in US law than those recommended by the English Law Commission. This reflects a desire on the part of the Canadians to harmonise laws in North America, but it also means a break from Commonwealth jurisprudence which has traditionally been reflected in Canadian laws. At the date of writing no province of Canada has enacted the reform proposals, but the matter is by no means dead and changes are likely.

For present purposes one of the main differences between the various sets of proposals for law reform lies in the number of torts which each recommends. Both the Restatement and the English law Commission recommend one; the Alberta Institute and the US Commissioners recommend two. Common to all was the suggestion of a tort of unauthorised use or disclosure of a trade secret; but additionally the US Commissioners and the Alberta Institute recommend a second tort of improper acquisition of a trade secret. This latter tort is very important as it characterises as a separate tort the act of industrial espionage. Under the Restatement and the Law Commission proposals, improper acquisition *per se* is not a separate tort. No liability attaches until information improperly acquired is used or disclosed, although an injunction can of course be obtained to restrain anticipated use or disclosure. However, the improper acquisition of trade secrets is such an important issue that it is considered in much greater detail below where we shall look at both the civil and the criminal aspects of the subject. For the purposes of this section, however, it can be concluded that although tort is not an important jurisdictional base for the action for breach of confidence at the moment it is likely to become so in the future, and in some instances it may even supersede the contractual and/or equitable obligations of the current law.

8.2.6   Confidential information as property

A fourth jurisdictional base for the action for breach of confidence is in property. So far this has not featured prominently in English civil cases, although it has been used quite often in US cases. However, there have been many attempts to classify confidential information as property for the purposes of the criminal law in order to found charges of theft and other property-based offences. These will be considered at 8.4 below in the section on the criminal law. In the view of the present author, property in its traditional sense is not an ideal jurisdiction for the action for breach of confidence. Contract, tort and equity are more appropriate in that they focus on entitlement rather than ownership and this more accurately reflects rights over information than does property.

8.3   THE SPECIAL PROBLEM OF CONFIDENTIAL INFORMATION ACQUIRED BY IMPROPER MEANS

Before discussing the criminal law we shall consider first one rather surprising gap in the protection of confidential information by the civil law. This occurs where confidential information is acquired by improper means by a person such as a spy or computer hacker who is under no pre-existing obligation of confidence. As we have seen, the emphasis of the English action is on breach of an obligation of confidence. In cases where there is an obligation to respect confidentiality there are few problems in founding liability providing all the other elements of the action are present. To use the familiar example, an employee or ex-employee who misappropriates his employer's confidential information, e.g., in order to use it himself or to disclose to a trade rival, will be acting in breach of confidence and can be restrained by injunction or be subject to the other remedies of damages, an account etc.; and any third party who acquires information from the employee knowing that it has been disclosed in breach of an obligation will be similarly liable. Thus, the employee who gleans secrets from unauthorised use of a sector of his employer's computerised database can be made liable.

By way of contrast, where there is no obligation of confidence there can be no breach and no action. This causes problems, for example, where a spy gleans a secret from reading a confidential document, tapping a telephone or gaining unauthorised access to a computer network. The spy or hacker cannot, without a high degree of artificiality, be said to have voluntarily undertaken an obligation to respect the confidentiality of the information he has improperly acquired. Any obligation must be imposed involuntarily by the law, but here the law seems remarkably reluctant to intervene. A similar problem arises in the law of trusts. A trustee who misappropriates trust property acts in breach of a fiduciary obligation owed to a beneficiary under the trust. Breach of fiduciary duty allows the beneficiary to trace the property through other forms and into other hands. But if a thief who is not a trustee or other fiduciary misappropriates trust property, he breaks no fiduciary obligation and there is no right to trace in equity.

It is surprising that there have been few civil cases on the improper acquisition, use or disclosure of confidential information by persons who have no pre-existing obligation of confidence. After all, espionage is not particu-larly rare. For the lawyer looking for a precedent there are few guiding principles, only some broad ranging statements, but these are not necessarily helpful even though they are often cited in this context. For example, in *Millar v Taylor* (1769) 4 Burr 2303 it was said that an injunction would be granted to prevent:

> Surreptitious or treacherous publishing of what the owner never made public at all, nor consented to the publication of.... Ideas are free. But while the author confines them to his study, they are like birds in a cage which none but he have a right to let fly.

Millar v Taylor was, however, a case on the common law right of property in the copyright in an unpublished work and although sometimes cited in the context of breach of confidence and information law it cannot be relied on as authority in this particular field. Another broad statement is to be found in *Ashburton v Pape* [1913] 2 Ch 469, where Swinfen Eady LJ said:

The principle on which the Court of Chancery has acted for many years has been to restrain the publication of confidential information improperly or surreptitiously obtained or of information imparted in confidence which ought not to be divulged.

Also, in *ITC Film Distributors* v *Video Exchange Ltd* [1982] Ch 431, Walton J referred to a general rule that where A has improperly obtained possession of a document belonging to B the court will, at the suit of B, order A to return the document to B and deliver up any copies of it that A has made, and will restrain A from making use of such copies or the information contained in them. But again, although the dicta seems to be relevant both *Ashburton* v *Pape* and *ITC Film Distributors* v *Video Exchange Ltd* involved obtaining documents by a trick in order to use them in legal proceedings and arguably they are not directly applicable to the action for breach of confidence.

More recent cases have not clarified the position. In *Malone* v *Commissioner of Police of the Metropolis (No. 2)* [1979] Ch 344, the claimant's telephone was tapped by the Post Office at the request of the police. The claimant sought a declaration that he had a right of confidentiality in the information conveyed in the course of his telephone conversations and that recordings thereof were made in breach of confidence.

Sir Robert Megarry V-C, delivering the judgment of the court, drew a distinction between misuse of information (a) by a person to whom the information was intended to be communicated (where presumably the obligation of confidence would be governed by contract or by the normal equitable principles described above), and (b) by someone to whom the claimant had no intention of communicating anything. It is of course into this latter category that the spy and the telephone tapper fall. However, Megarry V-C did not distinguish those who deliberately set out to acquire information and those who come across it accidentally, which is arguably very important in deciding whether to attach liability, and in the course of his judgment many of the examples given were of those who accidentally overhear and maybe these examples even unfairly trivialise the problem.

He said that a person who utters confidential information must accept the risk of any unknown hearing that is inherent in the circumstances of communication. Those who exchange confidences on a bus or a train run the risk of a nearby passenger with acute hearing or a more distant passenger who is adept at lip reading; those who speak over the garden wall run the risk of the unseen neighbour in a tool shed nearby; office cleaners who discuss secrets in the office when they think everyone else has gone home run the risk of speaking within earshot of an unseen member of staff who is working late; those who give confidential information over an office intercommunication system run the risk of some third party being connected to the conversation.

His lordship then went on to say that he did not see why someone who has overheard some secret in such a way should be exposed to legal proceedings if he uses or divulges what he has heard. Furthermore, he said that no doubt an honourable man would give some warning when he realised that what he heard was not intended for his ears, but the court had to concern itself with the law and not with moral standards. Here he said he was dealing with only a moral precept and not with one that was legally enforceable.

Applying those general principles to telephone conversations, Megarry V-C argued that a speaker takes such risks of being overheard as are inherent in the system. By way of illustration he said that users of the telephone system knew that they might be overheard when using extension lines, private switchboards or as a result of 'crossed lines'. More modern examples not given by Megarry V-C would of course be misrouted electronic mail or hacking. His lordship said that in recent years so much publicity had been given to the deliberate tapping of telephone lines 'that it is difficult to envisage telephone users who are genuinely unaware of this possibility'. As a result he concluded that he did not see how it could be said that an obligation of confidence could be imposed on those who overhear a conversation 'whether by means of tapping or otherwise'. How, one might ask, would his lordship have viewed a case of computer hacking?

So far as tapping telephones was concerned, Megarry V-C expressly stated that he was only dealing with a case of authorised tapping by the police in connection with the detection of crime and his dicta on tapping must be limited accordingly,[32] but the judgment does remain disturbingly general on other methods of improper acquisition of confidential information and on the failure of the law to impose an obligation of confidence even where the improper acquisition is deliberate and for monetary gain.

In 1972, the Younger Committee (Cmnd 5012) concluded on the basis of the earlier cases that in English law it is highly uncertain whether a person who uses or discloses confidential information which he knows to have been improperly obtained can be made liable in an action for breach of confidence. They recommended that the law should be clarified and that an obligation of confidence should be imposed if the user or discloser of confidential information knew or ought to have known that it was obtained by illegal means. This was also the recommendation of the Law Commission in its preliminary Working Paper,[33] although there they referred to acquisition by unlawful means which they envisaged covering information obtained by means prohibited by the criminal law; taking without authority any object from which the information was obtained; and possibly also information obtained by means of a trespass to land. The Law Commission changed their minds on this after consultation, and in their Final Report[34] they said that improper acquisition should be only one of those circumstances which gave rise to an obligation of confidence and that obligation would be broken only by unauthorised use or disclosure. They also defined improper means much more narrowly than before. It is important to note in the present context that neither the Younger Committee nor the Law Commission in their Final Report suggested that the improper acquisition of confidential information in itself should be a tort, as is provided by the US Uniform Trade Secrets Act, recommended in Canada and discussed in 8.2.5. It is recognised that in most

---

32. Cf. *Francome v Mirror Group Newspapers* [1984] 1 WLR 892.
33. Working Paper No. 58.
34. Law Commission Report No. 110 (see note 28), para. 6.4 and Appendix A cl. 5.

circumstances it is the use or disclosure of the information which causes the greatest harm, and this may be the rationale of the conclusions of the Law Commission. However, in the view of the present author the earlier in the chain of activity the liability attaches the better. The Law Commission proposals have, of course, never been enacted and hence the problem in English law of trying to control the improper acquisition, use or disclosure of confidential information obtained in circumstances where there is no obligation of confidence remains.

One decision which could solve the dilemma, if it were followed here, is the Australian case of *Franklin* v *Giddins* [1978] QdR 72. The facts were that the defendant stole budwood cuttings from the claimant's genetically unique nectarine trees. An action was brought for the improper acquisition by the defendant of the confidential information embodied in the genetic coding in the wood. Dunn J in the Supreme Court of Queensland accepted that:

[t]he parent tree may be likened to a safe within which there are locked up a number of copies of a formula for making a nectarine tree with special characteristics ... when a twig of budwood is taken from the tree it is as though a copy of the formula is taken out of the safe.

Having thus classified it as a misappropriation of confidential information he went on to hold that the defendant had breached an obligation of confidence owed to the owner of the tree. He said, 'I find myself quite unable to accept that a thief who steals a trade secret, with the intention of using it in commercial competition with its owner, to the detriment of the latter, and so uses it, is less conscionable than a traitorous servant'.

Thus unconscionability was brought into play to found an action, but this is no less vague a term than many others which have been used as bases of the action for breach of confidence in equity in other circumstances. As Professor Gareth Jones has argued,[35] equity should not be past the age of child-bearing, and the action for breach of confidence should be capable of extension to protect confidential information obtained by improper means regardless of whether there is a pre-existing relationship of confidence.[36] This is particularly important now that information is assuming a greater role in technologically advanced communities. The defects of the present civil law leave a huge gap in the protection of confidential information in English law. This problem does not arise in the United States and would not arise in Canada if the reform proposals were enacted. In the next section we shall see that English criminal law also fails to punish the misappropriation of confidential information. There is an obvious need for reform.

---

35. (1970) 86 *Law Quarterly Review* 463, at pp. 482–3.
36. A similar view was expressed, *obiter*, by Lord Goff (a coauthor with Professor Jones of Goff and Jones, *The Law of Restitution*, 5th edn, London: Sweet & Maxwell, 1998, in *Attorney-General* v *Guardian Newspapers Ltd (No. 2)* [1988] 3 All ER 545 at 658–659; and see also Hull, *Commercial Secrecy: Law and Practice*, London: Sweet & Maxwell, 1998, pp. 139–148.

8.4   THE CRIMINAL LAW

The analysis in this part of the chapter inevitably cuts across the divisions drawn in preceding sections, for information can be misappropriated not only by persons who have never been bound by an obligation of secrecy, such as by strangers engaged in industrial espionage, but also by those already under an obligation of confidence such as employees who disclose the trade secrets of their employers to trade rivals. In the latter example, the prospect of making employees and ex-employees liable for misappropriating trade secrets shows perhaps even more poignantly than ever the need to distinguish carefully between an employee's general knowledge and skill, which he is of course entitled to use for the benefit of himself and others, and his employer's trade secrets which he cannot use or disclose, for in some legal systems the distinction could represent the line between criminal and legitimate activity.

Once again this account will concentrate mainly on the misappropriation of trade secrets. There are very different policy issues underlying the question of criminalising the acquisition of other categories of confidential information, and for reasons of space as well as emphasis no mention is made of the Official Secrets Act and the problems that it brings in its wake.

8.4.1   English law

In English law, if there is intentional interference with a tangible object, such as damage to or permanent deprivation of a computer disc or a piece of paper, or unauthorised entry onto land with intent to do specified acts in relation to tangibles or people, then various criminal offences may be committed. But if only information is 'taken' or interfered with by reading, memorising or photographing the tangible object on which the confidential information is stored, then no crime may be committed, unless it is a case of computer hacking, which is regulated by the Computer Misuse Act 1990.[37] As Sir Edward Boyle once remarked, 'It is not too much to say that we live in a country where . . . the theft of the board room table is punished far more severely than the theft of the board room secrets'.[38]

In English law, 'theft' of a trade secret is not a criminal offence. The main case is *Oxford v Moss* (1978) 68 Cr App R 183, where an undergraduate improperly obtained the proof of an examination paper before the examination was held. He read the paper and then returned it, retaining the information for his own use. He was charged with theft but was acquitted. Two reasons were given: first, for the purposes of the Theft Act 1968 information is not property, and only property can be stolen; and secondly, the university had not been permanently deprived of the tangible asset which had been taken, namely the piece of paper, and borrowing does not amount to theft. *Oxford v Moss* was followed in *R v Absolom* (1983) *The Times*, 14 September 1983, where a geologist was acquitted of a charge of theft after he

---

37. See further, chapter 9.
38. The Rt Hon Sir Edward Boyle MP (later Lord Boyle) cited in the Law Commission Consultation Paper No. 150, Legislating the Criminal Code: Misuse of Trade Secrets.

had obtained and tried to sell to a rival company details of Esso Petroleum's oil exploration off the Irish coast, information which was valued in evidence as worth between £50,000 and £100,000.

The emphasis in English law is clearly on the interference with a tangible asset, and because in neither *Oxford* v *Moss* nor *R* v *Absolom* was the owner of the information permanently deprived of such an asset there could be no successful prosecution for theft. However, even if a tangible asset such as a piece of paper or a computer disc is taken, the value of the tangible asset may in no way reflect the value of the information either in terms of damage to a business, if the secret is a trade secret, or of unwanted publicity if the information is of a personal nature; and if we look at the attitude of society towards crime, a charge of theft of a piece of paper worth pence is regarded as of far less importance than a charge of theft of information worth maybe thousands of pounds. Furthermore, when confidential information is misappropriated its owner loses the advantage of the exclusive right to control its use, yet this is not an asset protected by the English law of theft. All this is very strange.

Other criminal charges may of course be relevant. For example, where confidential information is obtained by hacking this will amount to a criminal offence under s. 1 of the Computer Misuse Act 1990. However, s. 1 does not apply when data storage media other than computers are accessed without authorisation such as filing cabinets, nor does it apply to access to programs or data which are, e.g., on disks lying on a shelf in an office. The wrong to which s. 1 is directed is a wrong against a particular computer, rather than being a wrong directed specifically and exclusively towards information as a commodity in its own right.

8.4.2 Scottish law

A similar approach has been taken in Scotland. In *Grant* v *Procurator Fiscal* [1988] RPC 41 the High Court of Justiciary said that there was no crime in Scots law of dishonest exploitation of the confidential information of another. Also, the court refused to exercise the inherent powers of the Scottish courts to create a new crime. In that case the defendant had made copies of computer print outs belonging to his employer and then offered to sell them to a rival concern. The print outs contained confidential information about the employer's customers. In the course of his judgment the Lord Justice Clerk said that while the defendant may have breached an express or implied obligation of confidence owed to his employer under the civil law it would be quite another thing to categorise such behaviour as criminal. If it was to be criminalised it was a matter for Parliament and not for the courts.

8.4.3 Reforms

Until recently, there were few calls for the reform of English law. In 1972, the Younger Committee[39] specifically rejected the suggestion that there

---

39. Cmnd 5012 at p. 149.

should be a new offence of theft of information, and when the Law Commission[40] were first asked to consider the law relating to breach of confidence their terms of reference limited them to the civil law alone. They made no recommendations for reform of the criminal law. By way of contrast the New Zealand Committee for Torts and General Law Reform said that the chief weakness of the New Zealand law relating to trade secrets was the lack of specialised criminal provisions. In the United States, many states have criminal statutes expressly protecting trade secrets;[41] and the Economic Espionage Act 1996 creates two federal offences of stealing trade secrets — one relating to the theft of trade secrets in general and the second aimed at economic espionage for the benefit of foreign governments. In Europe there are criminal offences in a number of Codes. For example art. 17(1) of the German Act Against Unfair Competition (UWG) of 1909[42] states that an employee who wrongfully communicates an industrial or commercial secret is liable to be imprisoned for up to three years and to pay a fine. Similar provisions are to be found in art. 418 of the French Penal Code and art. 162 of the Swiss Penal Code. In each of these Codes, communication of the secret to a foreigner increases the penalty. Interestingly, the civil laws of Japan dealing with the misappropriation of trade secrets have recently been re-formed but there have been no changes to the criminal laws. Prosecutions have however been obtained under general criminal laws such as larceny and embezzlement.

The English Law Commission have recently studied the problem anew and in 1997 they produced a Consultation Paper on the Misuse of Trade Secrets, as part of their on-going review of English criminal law.[43] They provisionally concluded that trade secrets were valuable commercial assets which were inadequately protected by the civil law and that there was no distinction in principle between the harm caused by the misuse of a trade secret and the harm caused by theft. They proposed a new offence which would be committed by a person who used or disclosed a trade secret belonging to another without that other's consent, providing that the defendant knew that the information in question was a trade secret belonging to another, and was aware that the other did not consent to the use or disclosure in question. Importantly, in view of the difficult distinctions which have to be drawn, they proposed that the new offence should not extend to the use or disclosure of information which, under the law of confidence, constitutes an enhancement of an employee's (or independent contractor's) personal knowledge, skill or experience. This qualification is very welcome. Also, the new offence should not cover the use or disclosure of information acquired by independent development or solely by reverse engineering. Furthermore, innocent third

---

40. Law Commission Report No. 110 (see note 28), para. 4.10.
41. E.g., California, Colorado, Massachusetts, Minnesota, New York, Texas, Ohio and Pennsylvania. See Law Commission Consultation Paper (note 9 above), Appendix B, for an account of the criminal laws of France, Germany, Italy, Switzerland, Bulgaria, Poland, Romania, Scotland, Australia, Canada, USA and Korea.
42. See Coleman, op. cit., note 8, ch. 7.
43. See note 9 above.

parties should not be liable, and no offence should be committed where the disclosure was in the public interest, this term being widely drawn. The new offence proposed by the Law Commission concerns the use or disclosure of a trade secret. However, they invited views on whether the criminal law should also be extended to cover the acquisition of a trade secret and if so, how this should be done. The Law Commission's provisional recommendations are to be welcomed as reform is urgently needed. However, given the low take-up rate of Law Commission proposals and only limited political interest in this area, the law is unlikely to change in the foreseeable future.

8.4.4   Canadian cases

Proposals to reform Canadian laws have similarly been slow to develop. There have been some interesting cases, but the proposals of the law reform bodies for legislative change have sat on the shelf for some considerable time. This is surprising given the changes to US federal laws in the form of the Economic Espionage Act 1996. In the Canadian case of *R v Offley* (1986) 28 CCC (3d) 1, the Alberta Court of Appeal followed the English decision of *Oxford v Moss* and held that confidential information could not be stolen. Here, the defendant had been asked by the representative of a union to obtain the details of the employees of an hotel. This information was contained in the employees' personal files and computer records held by the hotel company. They were regarded as being strictly confidential and were protected by the hotel's security arrangements. The defendant had contacted an employee of the hotel and asked him to copy the confidential information without removing or affecting the records themselves. The defendant was charged with three offences, namely counselling an employee of the hotel to commit fraud, theft and mischief to the private property of the hotel. The accused was acquitted on all three counts and the Crown appealed against the acquittals on the charges of counselling theft and counselling fraud. By a majority of two to one the Ontario Court of Appeal allowed the appeal and a conviction was entered for counselling theft.

Interestingly, the Ontario Court of Appeal in *R v Stewart* (1983) 42 OR (2d) 225, in contrast to the Alberta Court of Appeal in *Offley*, held that confidential information was property for the purposes of the offences of theft and fraud in Canadian criminal law. For example, Houlden JA said that while clearly not all information was property he could see no reason why confidential information that had been gathered through the expenditure of time, effort and money by a commercial enterprise for the purposes of its business should not be regarded as property and hence entitled to the protection of the criminal law. In *Offley* and *Stewart* we therefore have two contrasting decisions of two Courts of Appeal of Canadian provinces, the outstanding question being whether confidential information is property for the purposes of the criminal laws of Canada with its obvious implications also for the jurisdictional foundation of the civil obligation to respect confidentiality. The decision of the Supreme Court of Canada in *R v Stewart* (1988) 50 DLR (4th) 1, was therefore anxiously awaited.

On appeal, the Supreme Court of Canada rejected the notion that confidential information could be property. First, the Court said that although 'anything' (using that term in its technical sense in the Canadian Criminal Code) whether tangible or intangible could be the subject matter of a charge of theft, it must be of such a nature that it can be the subject of a proprietary right; and secondly, the property must be capable of being taken or converted in a manner that results in deprivation of the victim. Taking each of these elements in turn Lamer J, giving the judgment of the court, said that it had not been settled that property was the basis of the civil action for breach of confidence, but even if it had been it would not automatically follow that it would be so classified for the purposes of the criminal law. If it was property under the criminal law a large number of provisions of the Criminal Code would potentially apply to acts in relation to confidential information and a whole host of practical problems would ensue. He recognised that information of commercial value was in need of some protection under the criminal law, but this was a matter for Parliament and not for the courts. For policy reasons the court held that confidential information was not property for the purposes of the Canadian Criminal Code.

Secondly, the Supreme Court held that an intangible could not be 'taken' as such; nor could it be converted, as conversion required deprivation of its use and possession and if merely information was misappropriated (as opposed to the tangible on which the information was stored) then the alleged owner was not deprived of the information: henceforth, the information was merely shared. The only 'thing' that the victim would be deprived of was the confidentiality of the information and in the view of the court confidentiality could not be the subject of theft because it did not fall within the meaning of 'anything' as previously defined. Confidentiality could not be property, as it could not be owned only enjoyed. Furthermore, the court rejected the argument of Cory JA in the Ontario Court of Appeal that there was a right of property in confidential information which was the subject of copyright, as were the employer's confidential lists in this case. Lamer J explained that copying a list constitutes an infringement of copyright under the Copyright Act, but the rights provided in that Act could never be taken or converted as required by the theft provisions as their owner would never suffer deprivation. Once again, there would only be sharing and this was not enough.

The result of the Canadian Supreme Court decision in *Stewart* is that the question of criminalising the misappropriation of confidential information was referred back to the Canadian legislature. Those countries which do not already criminalise this type of conduct will inevitably have to consider doing so sooner or later, for with the growth in the use of computers and the development of information as a commodity in its own right the pressures will grow to afford information the same degree of protection as other valuable assets. In Canada there is already a set of proposals for legislative reform of this area of confidentiality. In 1986 the Alberta Institute of Law Research and Reform and the Federal Provincial Working Party recommended not only changes to the civil law but also the creation of new criminal offences relating to the misappropriation of trade secrets. These new offences have the advantage of being custom-built and hence avoid the difficulty of fitting intangible assets into an inappropriate conceptual framework which was developed to accommodate tangibles. Thus, the Report rejects the approach of the Ontario Court of Appeal in *Stewart* and argues that property should not form the basis for liability. We shall look at these proposals, as it is possible that they will be enacted in Canada in the next few years, albeit with amendments, and they also form a good starting point for reform in other common law jurisdictions.

8.4.5 Proposals for the reform of Canadian criminal law

First, it was decided that in order to achieve uniformity the same information should be protected under both the civil and the criminal law. Thus, the definition of a trade secret is set out in the earlier section of this chapter describing various categories of confidential information. Secondly, it is recommended that the new criminal offences should proscribe the non-consensual acquisition, use or disclosure of a trade secret, that term being used in the sense both of what might otherwise be called 'theft' of a secret and also of acts where the consent was fraudulently obtained, e.g., where the victim was duped. Therefore, there are two offences in the draft Bill covering the two aspects of non-consensual conduct, firstly a new s. 301.3(1) of the Criminal Code would provide that:

> Everyone who fraudulently and without colour of right acquires, discloses or uses the trade secret of another person, without the consent of that other person, with intent to deprive that other person (a) of control of the trade secret or (b) of an economic advantage associated with the trade secret is guilty of an indictable offence and is liable to imprisonment for ten years, or of an offence punishable on summary conviction.

Secondly a new draft s. 338.1(1) would provide that:

> Everyone who, by deceit, falsehood or other fraudulent means, whether or not it is a false pretence within the meaning of this Act, induces any person to disclose, or to permit another person to disclose or use, a trade secret, is guilt of an indictable offence and is liable to imprisonment for ten years, or of an offence punishable on summary conviction.

It was hoped by clearly defining the mental element which the accused must be shown to have that only the most reprehensible of conduct would be caught by the new provisions. As an additional safeguard, it is provided that no one commits an offence under s. 301.3 in respect of an acquisition, disclosure or use of a trade secret if:

> (a) the trade secret was acquired by independent development or by reason only of reverse engineering; or

(b)   the information was acquired in the course of that person's work, and the information is of such a nature that the acquisition amounts to no more than an enhancement of that person's personal knowledge, skill or expertise.

The proposed amendments to the Criminal Code contain two further offences aimed at, for example, the industrial spy who goes on what may be described as a 'shopping expedition' in order to acquire information, the precise character of which he does not know but which he thinks he may be able to sell or otherwise use. Subsequent reports suggest that these offences are not popular among those responsible for legislation and may be dropped from any draft Bills which come forward.

The Canadian proposals and the provisional conclusion of the Law Commission illustrate the moves in many countries to criminalise the misappropriation of trade secrets. Inevitably pressures from industry will mount to reform the law in this area, and the idea of adopting custom-built offences rather than extending existing property-based offences in order to found liability is a sound one. But there are strong reasons favouring the free flow of information and requiring the disclosure even of confidential information, and any shift in the balance needs to be carefully considered. Not least among the concerns are those affecting employees and the need to draw a very clear distinction between, on the one hand, the employer's trade secrets and, on the other hand, the employee's general knowledge and skill. Mobility of labour could be seriously damaged by overzealous prosecution of employees. This is particularly the case in high technology areas such as computing, where skills and knowledge so frequently merge.

CHAPTER NINE

Computer Crime

Ian Walden

9.1 INTRODUCTION

The proliferation and integration of computers into every aspect of society has inevitably led to computer-related criminal activities. The computer may constitute the instrument of the crime, such as in murder and fraud; the object of the crime, such as the theft of processor chips; or the subject of the crime, such as hacking and distributing viruses. This chapter is concerned with how criminal law has adapted and been amended to address some of the issues raised by the involvement of computers in criminal activities.

The first part of the chapter considers the offences under English law which are relevant to crimes involving the use of computers. Such offences are broadly divided into two categories. The first are traditional types of criminal offence which may be committed using computers, such as fraud. The second category are new offences which have been established specifically to address activities unique to a computer environment, such as distributing computer viruses.

The second half of the chapter will examine issues relating to the successful prosecution of perpetrators of computer crime. To date, relatively few cases have been brought before the courts. Such paucity is generally regarded as being due to a range of factors. First, there is a lack of reporting by victims, as commercial organisations avoid adverse publicity.[1] Secondly, a lack of

---

1. See the United States survey by CSI/FBI, which reported that only 32 percent of respondents who had suffered an intrusion had reported it to law enforcement agencies: quoted in National Criminal Intelligence Service, 'Project Trawler: Crime on the Information Highways', 1999, at para. 10.

adequate training within prosecuting authorities. Thirdly, the transnational nature of computer crime and the associated jurisdictional problems contribute to the complexity of investigating and prosecuting offenders. Finally, computers, particularly when networked, create significant forensic challenges to law enforcement agencies when obtaining evidence and subsequently presenting it before the courts.

9.2 TRADITIONAL CRIMINAL OFFENCES

It is obvious that computers may play a part in the commission of nearly every form of criminal activity, from fraud to murder. Therefore, this section will not review the broad range of English criminal law, but will focus on those areas of existing law which have given rise to particular problems where computers are involved, either because the legislation was drafted in an era before such technology was envisaged, or because statutory drafting has failed to be robust enough to appropriately address computer technology.

9.2.1 Fraud

Fraudulent activity is not substantially altered by the use of data communications; although a person's ability to cover his tracks may be enhanced. Computers may be involved in any aspect of the fraudulent process; e.g., alteration of the input of certain information, alteration of the operation of the computer through manipulation of certain programs, or, the output could be varied by computer. The computer is simply a modern tool by which the defendant's actions have been carried out.

In the majority of cases involving computer-related fraud, existing legislation has been an adequate instrument under which to prosecute. However, as with other areas of legislation, traditional statutory terminology can give rise to problems of definition not anticipated before computers appeared. In certain national jurisdictions, for example, for a fraud to be deemed to have occurred it is a necessary requirement to prove that a 'person has been deceived.[2]

Under English law, s. 15 of the Theft Act 1968 states:

(1) A person who by any deception dishonestly obtains property belonging to another, with the intention of permanently depriving the other of it, . . .

(4) For purposes of this section 'deception' means any deception (whether deliberate or reckless) by words or conduct as to fact or as to law, including a deception as to the present intentions of the person using the deception or any other person.

Case law has further defined 'deception' to mean 'to induce a man to believe a thing which is false, and which the person practising the deceit knows or believes to be false'.[3] Where innocent persons have been involved

---

2. E.g., German Penal Code, s. 263.
3. In the words of Buckley J in *Re London and Globe Finance Corp. Ltd* [1903] 1 Ch 728 at 732.

at some moment in the fraud, such as the processing of computer output, there does not appear to be any problem with prosecuting under s. 15 (e.g., *R v Thompson* [1984] 3 All ER 565). However, where the process is completely automated, the courts have indicated that no offence can be deemed to have taken place.[4] Where the machine has been deceived to obtain property, then the offence of theft is generally applicable. However, where a service is obtained from a machine, the absence of 'deception' is fatal to the founding of a criminal prosecution.[5] This problem has arisen in the Internet, where people have given false credit card details during an on-line registration process for accessing services such as CompuServe.[6] The Law Commission has recently examined this lacuna in English criminal law and has recommended that, rather than extending the concept of 'deception' to include machines,[7] a new offence related to theft should be established.[8]

The need to obtain property 'belonging to another' in the commission of a fraud also gave rise to a lacuna in English law in the House of Lords decision in *R v Preddy* [1996] 3 All ER 481. The court acquitted the defendants of mortgage fraud on the basis that the process of altering the accounting data recorded in the accounts of the lending institution and the mortgagor, by the amount representing the loan, did not constitute the obtaining of property 'belonging to another'. Instead, the court characterised the process as one where property, as a chose in action, is extinguished in one place and a different chose in action is created in another place. This decision required the government to push through emergency legislation creating a new offence of 'obtaining a money transfer by deception' to cover such activities.[9] However, *Preddy* illustrates the types of problem raised when trying to apply traditional criminal concepts to acts involving intangible information.

The principle that information *per se* is not 'property' was decisively upheld in *Oxford v Moss* (1978) 68 Cr App R 183.[10] In that case, a student had taken a copy of a forthcoming examination paper from a lecturer's desk, photocopied it, and returned the original. The second component of this decision was that the offence of theft had not been committed as the victim had not been permanently deprived of the asset, a copy had simply been taken.

---

4. See *Clayman*, Times Law Reports, 1 July 1972. See also *R v Moritz*, unreported 17–19 June 1981, Acton Crown Court; quoted in M. Wasik, *Crime and the Computer*, Oxford: Clarendon Press, 1991.
5. See the Theft Act 1978, s. 1.
6. Where the service is provided by a licensed telecommunication operator, an offence of fraudulent use of a telecommunication system would be applicable under the Telecommunications Act 1984, s. 42. see *Morgans v DPP* [2000] 2 WLR 386, HL.
7. Which is the approach adopted in the Value Added Tax Act 1994, s. 72(6): 'making use of a document which is false in a material particular, with intent to deceive, includes a reference to furnishing, sending or otherwise making use of such a document, with intent to secure that a machine will respond to the document as if it were a true document'.
8. See Law Commission Consultation Paper No. 155, *Legislating the Criminal Code: Fraud and Deception*, London: HMSO, 1999, paras 8.36–8.58.
9. Theft (Amendment) Act 1996. See also Law Commission Report, No. 243, *Offences of Dishonesty: Money Transfers*, London: HMSO 1996.
10. See further A. Coleman, chapter 8, 'Protecting confidential information'.

9.2.2 Criminal damage

The offence of criminal damage may obviously be relevant in many situations of computer misuse. The value of a computer system normally resides in the information it contains, both software and data, rather than the physical hardware.[11] An issue raised under the Criminal Damage Act 1971 was whether unauthorised deletion or modification of such information constituted 'damage' to property.[12] The question was examined in *Cox* v *Riley* (1986) 83 Cr App R 54, where an employee deleted computer programs from a plastic circuit card that were required to operate a computerised saw. The court stated that the property (i.e., the plastic circuit card) had been damaged by the erasure of the programs to the extent that the action impaired 'the value or usefulness' of the card and necessitated 'time and labour and money to be expended' to make the card operable.

This interpretation was upheld in *R* v *Whiteley* (1991) 93 Cr App R 25, where the defendant was convicted of causing damage through gaining unauthorised access into the Joint Academic Network system, used by UK universities, and deleting and amending substantial numbers of files. It was argued, on his behalf, that the defendant's activities only affected the information contained on a computer disk, not the disk itself. However, the court stated (at p. 28):

What the Act [Criminal Damage Act 1971] requires to be proved is that tangible property has been damaged, not necessarily that the damage itself should be tangible.

The alteration of the magnetic particles contained on a disk, whilst imperceptible, did impair the value and usefulness of the disk and therefore constituted damage. However, if the disk had been blank, any alteration would not necessarily be 'damage'.

Despite these successful prosecutions, the Law Commission considered that uncertainty continued to exist when prosecuting computer misuse under the Criminal Damage Act and, therefore, proposed the creation of a new offence under the Computer Misuse Act 1990.[13] One concern was the possibility of situations where it would be difficult to identify the tangible 'property' that had been damaged when altering data, e.g., deleting information being sent across the public telephone network. A second major concern was that police and prosecuting authorities were experiencing practical difficulties 'explaining to judges, magistrates and juries how the facts fit in with the present law of criminal damage'.[14]

---

11. Although the theft of computers for their processor chips has been significant during periods where market demand has exceeded supply.
12. Criminal Damage Act 1971, s. 1(1). Under s. 10(1), '"Property" means property of a tangible nature, whether real or personal...'.
13. See 9.3.4 below.
14. Law Commission, Report No. 186, Cmnd 819, London: HMSO, 1988, at para. 2.31.

9.2.3 Obscenity

Computer-based pornography is one of the most significant forms of computer crime. The obscenity laws have already been amended to take account of activities unique to a computer environment, such as the creation of 'pseudo-photographs'.[15] In addition to the obscenity laws, the act of sending such material across the public telephone network may constitute an offence (Telecommunications Act 1984, s. 43). In *R* v *Fellows; Arnold* [1997] 2 All ER 548, a court was required to consider whether the legislation pre-amendment would enable computer data to be considered a 'copy of an indecent photograph' and whether making images available for downloading from a web site constituted material being 'distributed or shown'. The court held that the statutory wording was drafted in sufficiently wide terms to encompass the use of computer technology.

9.2.4 Forgery

Under the Forgery and Counterfeiting Act 1981, s. 1 states:

A person is guilty of forgery if he makes a false instrument with the intention that he or another shall use it to induce somebody to accept it as genuine ...[16]

The leading English case involving computers was *R* v *Gold* [1987] 3 WLR 803. In this case, the defendants gained unauthorised access to BT's Prestel service and then discovered the password codes of various private mailboxes. The defendants were prosecuted under the Forgery Act, for creating a 'false instrument' by entering the customer's authorisation code to enter the system. However, the Court of Appeal decided that the electronic signals, that composed the identification code, could not be considered 'tangible' in the sense that a disk or tape was; and that they were held in the system for such a fleeting moment, that they could not be considered to have been 'recorded or stored'.

It is also interesting to note that the the Court of Appeal was critical of the application of the Act to such a set of circumstances:

The ... attempt to force these facts into the language of an Act not designed to fit them produced difficulties ... which we would not wish to see repeated.[17]

Such explicit recognition by the court system of the need to draft new legislation, as opposed to trying to bend traditional interpretations to fit

---

15. The Protection of Children Act 1978 and the Criminal Justice Act 1988 were amended by the Criminal Justice and Public Order Act 1994, s. 84. See also the recommendations made in House of Commons, Home Affairs Committee, *Computer Pornography*, 1st Report, Session 1993–1994 HC No. 126, London: HMSO, February 1994.
16. Under s. 8(d), an 'instrument' is defined as 'any disc, tape, sound-track or other device on or in which information is recorded or stored by mechanical, electronic or other means'.
17. [1988] AC 1063, at p. 1069.

computer technology, lent significant pressure to the calls for reform of the criminal law.

9.3 COMPUTER MISUSE ACT 1990

The Computer Misuse Act 1990 became law on 29 August 1990. The direct origins of the Act are found in the Law Commission report on 'Computer Misuse,[18] published in October 1989; additionally, the Scottish and English Law Commission's had published previous reports and working papers,[19] and a Private Member's Bill on the topic had been introduced during the previous parliamentary session. In December 1989, Michael Colvin MP introduced a Private Member's Bill with the tacit support of the government, closely following the Law Commission's recommendations.

The primary motivation for government support was probably a belief that if the United Kingdom did not follow the example of many of its European partners then the UK's position in the European information market could suffer. This is similar to the reason given by the government when it introduced the first Data Protection Act (DPA) into Parliament in 1983, when the Under-Secretary of State at the Home Office stated that the DPA will 'enable our own data processing industry to participate freely in the European market'.[20] The fear is that if the United Kingdom does not have adequate legal protection for both systems and data, this will restrict the growth of the domestic information technology industry.

The 1990 Act introduced three new categories of offence: unauthorised access to computer material; unauthorised access with intent to commit a further offence and unauthorised modification.

9.3.1 Unauthorised access

The s. 1 offence under the Computer Misuse Act 1990 of unauthorised access is the basic 'hacking' or 'cracking' offence. Commission of the offence requires the *actus reus* of causing 'a computer to perform any function'. Some form of interaction with the computer is required, but actual access does not need to be achieved. This broad formulation means that simply turning on a computer could constitute the necessary act.[21] The Act also does not define a 'computer', therefore potentially extending its scope to everyday domestic appliances and cars that incorporate computer technology. The Law Commission found general support for the view that to attempt such a definition would be 'so complex, in an endeavour to be all-embracing, that they are likely to produce extensive argument'.[22] This position is also adopted in other jurisdictions, such as France and Germany. One major exception to this

---

18. Report No. 186, Cmnd 819, London: HMSO, 1989.
19. Scottish Law Commission, '*Report on Computer Crime*', Cmnd 174, Edinburgh: HMSO, 1987 and Law Commission, Working Paper No. 110, *Computer Misuse* and Report No. 186, Cmnd 819, London: HMSO, 1988.
20. Statement of Lord Eton: 443 Parl. Deb., HL (5th ser.) 509 (1983).
21. Section 17(1) broadly defines 'function' to include alterations or erasure, copying or moving data, using it or producing output from the computer.
22. Law Commission, Report No. 186, Cmnd 819, London: HMSO, 1988, at para. 3.39.

approach is in the United States, where the Computer Fraud and Abuse Act contains the following definition:

> an electronic, magnetic, optical, electrochemical, or other high speed data processing device performing logical, arithmetic, or storage functions, and includes any data storage facility or communications facility directly related to or operating in conjunction with such device.[23]

The *mens rea* of the s. 1 offence comprises two elements. First, there must be 'intent to secure access to any program or data held in any computer'. Secondly, the person must know at the time that he commits the *actus reus* that the access he intends to secure is unauthorised. The intent does not have to be directed at any particular program, data or computer (s. 1(2)).

The first prosecution under the new Act addressed the nature of the *actus reus* under s. 1. In *R v Sean Cropp* (Snaresbrook Crown Court, 4 July 1991), the defendant returned to the premises of his former employer to purchase certain equipment. At some point when the sales assistant was not looking, the defendant was alleged to have keyed in certain commands to the computerised till granting himself a substantial discount. During the trial, the judge accepted the arguments of the defence counsel and held that s. 1(1)(a) required 'that a second computer must be involved'. He believed that if Parliament had intended the offence to extend to situations where unauthorised access took place on a single machine, then s. 1(1)(a) would have been drafted as 'causing a computer to perform any function with intent to secure access to any program or data held in *that or any other computer*'.

Such an interpretation would have seriously limited the scope of the Act, especially since the majority of instances of hacking are those carried out within organisations.[24] The critical nature of this distinction led the Attorney-General to take the rarely invoked procedure of referring the decision to the Court of Appeal. The Court of Appeal subsequently rejected the lower court's interpretation, stating that the 'plain and natural meaning is clear' (*Attorney-General's Reference (No. 1 of 1991)* [1992] 3 WLR 432, at 437F).

The s. 1 offence is punishable on summary conviction by a fine of up to £2,000 or six months in jail (s. 1(3)).[25] In addition, under s. 12, a person can be found guilty of the basic s. 1 offence where a jury could not find him guilty of an indictment under s. 2 or s. 3.

---

23. See 18 USC, s. 1030(e)(1) as amended in 1996. See also Singapore's Computer Misuse Act 1998, s. 2(1).
24. See Audit Commission Report, 'Ghost in the Machine: An Analysis of Fraud and Abuse', (1998); which found that nearly 25 percent of frauds were committed by staff in managerial positions. See http://www.audit-commission.gov.uk.
25. Under the Magistrates' Courts Act 1980, s. 44, a person who 'aids, abets, counsels or procures the commission by another person of a summary offence shall be guilty of the like offence', e.g., disclosure of passwords via a bulletin board. A prosecution under s. 1 is subject to certain time limits (s. 11(2) and (3)), which were not complied with in *Morgans v DPP* [1999] 1 WLR 968, DC.

9.3.2   Intent to commit a further offence

The s. 2 offence under the Computer Misuse Act 1990 involves the commission of a s. 1 offence together with the intent to commit, or facilitate the commission, of a further offence. A relevant further offence is one for which the sentence is fixed by law, e.g., life imprisonment for murder, or where imprisonment may be for a term of five years or more, e.g., a computer fraud.[26] The access and the further offence do not have to be intended to be carried out at the same time (s. 2(3)), and it also does not matter if the further offence was in fact impossible (s. 2(4)). Upon conviction, a person could be sentenced to imprisonment for up to a five year term (s. 2(5)). In Singapore similar legislation also grants a court the power to make an order against a person convicted of an offence to pay compensation to any party that has suffered damage from the offending activity,[27] which may provide an incentive to organisations to report such attacks.

The following cases illustrate the range of situations that may arise under the s. 2 offence:

(a)   In *R* v *Pearlstone*, Bow Street Magistrates' Court, April 1991, an ex employee used his former company's telephone account and another subscriber's account to defraud the computer-administered telephone system and place calls to the United States.[28]

(b)   In *R* v *Borg*, unreported March 1993, an investment company analyst was accused of setting up dummy accounts within a 'live' fund management system.[29] The alleged 'further offence' was expected to be fraudulent transfers into the dummy accounts. The defendant pleaded guilty.

(c)   In *R* v *Farquharson*, Croydon Magistrates' Court, 9 December 1993, the defendant was prosecuted for obtaining mobile telephone numbers and codes necessary to produce cloned telephones.[30] The computer system containing this information was actually accessed by his co-defendant Ms Pearce, an employee of the mobile telephone company, who was charged with a s. 1 offence. Farquharson was found to have committed an 'unauthorised access' even though he never touched the computer himself, but had simply asked Pearce to access the information.

9.3.3   Intent and authorisation

In May 1993, in the cases of *R* v *Strickland* and *R* v *Woods*, Southwark Crown Court, March 1993, the first classic 'hackers' were given six-month jail sentences for conspiracy to commit offences under s. 1 and s. 3 of the Computer Misuse Act 1990. The defendants activities were said to have

---

26. I.e., for a first offender at 21 or over.
27. Computer Misuse Act 1993 (amended in 1996 and 1998), s. 13.
28. Described in R. Battcock, 'Prosecutions under the Computer Misuse Act 1990', *Computers and Law*, no. 6, February/March 1996, p. 22.
29. See Battcock, ibid.
30. See Battcock, ibid.

caused damage, valued at £123,000, to computer systems ranging from the Polytechnic of Central London to NASA. In passing sentence the judge said:

> There may be people out there who consider hacking to be harmless, but hacking is not harmless. Computers now form a central role in our lives, containing personal details. . . . It is essential that the integrity of those systems should be protected and hacking puts that integrity in jeopardy.

Such judicial sentiment is critical if the Act is to have a significant deterrent effect.

However, one of the co-defendants in the same case, *Bedworth*, was acquitted by the jury because defence counsel successfully argued that the necessary *mens rea* for a charge of conspiracy was absent because the defendant was an 'obsessive' hacker. This case was widely publicised and was seen by many as a potential 'hacker's charter'.[31] However, the decision seems to have arisen from a mistaken choice by the prosecuting authorities to pursue an action for conspiracy, rather than a charge under the Computer Misuse Act.

In addition to the *Bedworth* case, the issue of prosecution for the inchoate offences of incitement or conspiracy with others to commit an offence (Criminal Law Act 1977, s. 1) arose in respect of the publication of the 'Hackers Handbook', a popular guide to current developments in this area. Following the 1990 Act coming into force, the publishers apparently decided to withdraw the book from circulation to avoid potential legal action.[32]

During passage of the Computer Misuse Bill, an attempt was made to add a provision whereby hackers would be able to offer a defence if computer users had not implemented security measures.[33] Whilst the amendment was rejected, the issue of the existence of security measures does arise in the context of establishing whether access was 'unauthorised'. Under the Act, an accused's access is considered to be unauthorised access if:

(a) he is not himself entitled to control access of the kind in question to the program or data; and

(b) he does not have consent to access by him of the kind in question to the program or data from any person who is so entitled. (Section 17(5))

Where the accused is external to the victim's organisation, showing knowledge of an absence of entitlement or consent is not generally an issue.

31. See for example 'Bedworth case puts law on trial', *Computing*, 25 March 1993, p. 7.
32. See E. Dumbill, 'Computer Misuse Act 1990 — recent developments', *Computer Law and Practice*, vol. 8, no. 4, 1992, p. 107.
33. See Standing Committee C, 14 March 1990. The following amendment was proposed by Harry Cohen MP: 'For the purposes of this section, it shall be a defence to prove that such care as in all the circumstances, was reasonably required to prevent the access or intended access in question was not taken'. In other jurisdictions, the presence of security measures is a necessary element of the offence: e.g., Norwegian Penal Code, s. 145, refers to persons 'breaking security measures to gain access to data/programs'.

However, where the accused is an employee of the organisation, the burden is upon the prosecution to show that the accused knew that 'access of the kind in question' was unauthorised, rather than a misuse of express or implied rights of access, e.g., an accounts clerk entering false expenses claims. As noted by the Law Commission:

> An employee should only be guilty of an offence if his employer has clearly defined the limits of the employee's authority to access a program or data. (Report No. 186, para. 3.37)

The interpretation of s. 17(5) was first considered in detail in *DPP* v *Bignell* [1998] 1 Cr App R. The case concerned two serving police officers who had accessed the Police National Computer (PNC), via an operator, for personal purposes. They were charged with offences under s. 1 of the Computer Misuse Act and convicted in the Magistrates' Court. They successfully appealed to the Crown Court against their conviction and this decision was the subject of a further appeal before the Divisional Court, which was dismissed.

The central issue addressed to the court was whether a person authorised to access a computer system for a particular purpose (e.g., policing) can commit a s. 1 offence by using such authorised access for unauthorised purposes (e.g., personal). The Crown Court asserted that the Computer Misuse Act was primarily concerned 'to protect the integrity of computer systems rather than the integrity of the information stored on the computers', therefore such unauthorised usage was not caught by the Act. The Divisional Court upheld this view. First, Astill, J stated that the phrase in s. 17(5)(a): 'access of the kind in question', was referring to the types of access detailed in s. 17(2): alteration, erasure, copying, moving, using and obtaining output. Secondly, the phrase 'control access' was referring to the authority granted to the police officers to access the PNC. He concluded that this interpretation did not create a lacuna in the law as the Data Protection Act 1984 contained appropriate offences in relation to the use of personal data for unauthorised purposes.[34]

This decision has attracted significant criticism and, as with *R* v *Sean Cropp*, was seen as significantly limiting the scope of the Act.[35] Aspects of the decision were re-examined by the House of Lords in *R* v *Bow Street Magistrate and Allison (AP), ex parte US Government* [1999] 3 WLR 620. The case concerned an extradition request by the US Government of an individual accused in a fraud involving an employee of American Express who was able to use her access to the computer system to obtain personal identification numbers to encode forged credit cards. As in *Bignell*, defence counsel argued that a s. 1 offence had not been committed since the employee was authorised to access the relevant computer system. The House of Lords, whilst agreeing

---

34. Data Protection Act 1984, s. 5(6). See generally chapter 13, on 'Data protection'.
35. E.g., D. Bainbridge, 'Cannot employees also be hackers?', *Computer Law and Security Report*, vol. 13, no. 5, 1997 pp. 352–354; and P. Spink, 'Misuse of Police Computers', *Juridical Review*, 1997, pp. 219–231.

with the decision in *Bignell*, rejected the subsequent interpretation of s. 17(5) made by Astill J.[36]

On the first issue, 'access of the kind in question', Lord Hobhouse stated that this phrase simply meant that the authority granted under s. 17(5) may be limited to certain types of programs or data, and did not refer to the kinds of access detailed in s. 17(2). Evidence showed that the employee at American Express accessed data in accounts for which she was not authorised, therefore the access she obtained was 'unauthorised access'. Secondly, 'control access' did not refer to the individual authorised to access the system, but the organisational authority granting authority to the individual. In the *Bignell* case, it was the Police Commissioner who exercised such control and, through internal manuals, specified that access was for police purposes only.

Whilst the decision in *Allison* clarifies the interpretation of 'control' under s. 17(5), the court's acceptance of *Bignell* would seem to perpetuate the uncertain jurisprudence under the 1990 Act. First, Lord Hobhouse stresses the point that in *Bignell* 'the computer operator did not exceed his authority' and therefore did not commit an offence (at 627G). This would seen irrelevant to the question of whether the Bignells were committing a s. 1 offence, since the operator is simply an innocent agent.[37] Secondly, Lord Hobhouse recognises that the concept of authorisation needs to be refined, as 'authority to secure access of the kind in question', and the example given is where access 'to view data may not extend to authority to copy or alter that data' (at 626F–G). On this reasoning, it seems incongruous that the court should hold, by implication, that authority to view the data may not also be limited to particular circumstances. The Bignells knew that they were only authorised to access the PNC for policing purposes and knowingly misrepresented the purpose for their request.

9.3.4 Unauthorised modification

The third substantive offence under the Computer Misuse Act 1990 is that of unauthorised modification of computer material (s. 3):

(1) A person is guilty of an offence if—
(a) he does any act which causes an unauthorised modification of the contents of the computer; and
(b) at the time when he does the act he has the requisite intent and the requisite knowledge.

Conviction could result in imprisonment for up to a five year term (s. 3(7)). The offence was principally promoted by the spate of publicity and fear surrounding the use of computer viruses.

The concept of damage in the Criminal Damage Act 1971 is amended by s. 3 to the extent that 'a modification of the contents of the computer' shall

---

36. This interpretation had been followed by the divisional court from which the appeal had been made: see *R* v *Bow Street Magistrates' Court, ex parte Allison* [1999] QB 847.
37. E.g., *R* v *Manley* (1844) 1 Cox 104.

not be regarded as damage, and therefore an offence under the 1971 Act, if it does not impair the 'physical condition' of the computer (s. 3(6)). In the case of removable data media, such as a computer disk or CD-ROM, deletion of data would only be an offence under s. 3 if the storage medium were in the computer (s. 17(6)). Once removed, any damage would be subject to the terms of the 1971 Act.

The 'unauthorised modification' offence creates a substantial discrepancy with the situation prior to the 1990 Act, since conviction under the Criminal Damage Act 1971 could be punishable by imprisonment for up to ten years (s. 4). In addition, liability for criminal damage could arise through the defendant 'being reckless as to whether any such property would be destroyed' (s. 1(1)), without the requirement for the prosecution to show intent. Such reckless damage is often a feature of 'hacking' cases, where a hacker inadvertently deletes or alters files and data during the course of his activities, causing the victim substantial loss. The restricted scope of the s. 3 offence significantly limits the penalties that such consequences can attract.

As with the s. 1 offence, the offence of unauthorised modification comprises three elements: 'unauthorised modification' of contents, 'requisite intent' and 'requisite knowledge'.

The first element can obviously be further broken down into 'unauthorised' and 'modification'. Whether an act is unauthorised or not is clearly a potentially difficult issue where the person carrying out the act is part of the organisation against whom the offence is being committed and has certain 'authorisation' to use the computer system in question.[38] The 'requisite knowledge' element, defined in s. 3(4) as knowledge that any modification he intends to cause is unauthorised, also relates to the question of authorisation. The interpretation provisions in the Act, at s. 17, provide guidance as to the nature of authorisation required under s. 3:

(8)   Such a modification is unauthorised if—
(a)   the person whose act causes it is not himself entitled to determine whether the modification should be made; and
(b)   he does not have consent to the modification from any person who is so entitled.

The nature of any 'modification' may be permanent or temporary (s. 3(5)) and is further elaborated at s. 17(7):

(7)   A modification of the contents of any computer takes place if, by the operation of any function of the computer concerned or any other computer—
(a)   any program or data held in the computer concerned is altered or erased; or
(b)   any program or data is added to its contents;
any act which contributes towards causing such a modification shall be regarded as causing it.

---

38. See the discussion of 'authorisation' at 9.3.3 above.

Subsection (2) elaborates the meaning of 'requisite intent':

(2) For the purposes of subsection (1)(b) above the requisite intent is an intent to cause a modification of the contents of any computer and by so doing—

(a) to impair the operation of any computer;

(b) to prevent or hinder access to any program or data held in any computer; or

(c) to impair the operation of any such program or the reliability of any such data.

As with the s. 1 offence, the intent need not be directed at any particular program, data or computer (s. 3(3)).

The issue of 'intent to impair' arose in the *Sean Cropp* case. In the Crown Court, the judge had agreed with the defence counsel's argument that the defendant's actions more appropriately fell under the unauthorised modification offence rather than that of unauthorised access. However, in the Court of Appeal, Lord Taylor put forward the opinion that the only form of modification that could be applicable to the defendant's actions was with respect to the impairment of the reliability of the data, and went on to note:

That would involve giving the word 'reliability' the meaning of achieving the result in the printout which was intended by the owner of the computer. It may not necessarily impair the reliability of data in a computer that you feed in something which will produce a result more favourable to a customer than the store holder intended.[39]

His sentiment seems clearly in favour of the more literal interpretation; and, as such, a conviction under s. 3 would have failed. This supports the Law Commission's opinion that 'the offence should not punish unauthorised modifications which improve, or are neutral in their effect'.[40]

The first major prosecution brought under s. 3 was *R v Goulden, The Times*, 10 June 1992. In this case, Goulden installed a security package on an Apple workstation for a printing company, Ampersand. The package included a facility to prevent access without the use of a password. Goulden made use of this facility as part of his claim for fees totalling £2,275. Due to the computerised nature of their printing operations, Ampersand were unable to function for a period of a few days. They claimed £36,000 lost business as a result of Goulden's actions, including £1,000 for a specialist to override the access protection. The court imposed a two-year conditional discharge on Goulden and a £1650 fine. The judge also commented that Goulden's actions were 'at the lowest end of seriousness'!

In *R v Whitaker*, Scunthorpe Magistrates Court, 1993,[41] the courts were required to consider the extent to which the unauthorised modification

---

39. *Attorney-General's Reference (No. 1 of 1991)* [1992] 3 WLR 432, at 438A.
40. Report No. 186, op. cit., note 22, at para. 3.72.
41. See Battcock, op. cit., note 28.

offence could be applied against an owner of intellectual property. The case concerned a software developer and his client and arose when the developer initiated a logic bomb designed to prevent use of the software following a dispute over payment. The defendant programmer argued that since under the contract he had retained all intellectual property rights in the software (title transferred upon payment), he had the requisite right to modify the software. The court held that, despite the existence of copyright in the software, the nature of the development contract constituted a limitation on the exercise of the developer's rights. The court did recognise, however, that such an action would have been permitted if it had been explicitly provided for in the contract, i.e., the licensee was made aware of the consequences of a failure to pay. He was therefore found guilty of an offence under s. 3. This was an important decision as the software industry is increasingly resorting to such techniques as a means of ensuring payment for their services.

The first prosecution of a virus writer, one of the original targets of s. 3, was of *Christopher Pile*, aka the 'Black Baron', in 1995 (unreported, Plymouth Crown Court, 1995).[42] One interesting feature of the case was that Pile was guilty of the offence even though he had no knowledge of which computers were affected by his virus (e.g. 'Pathogen') and had not targeted any specific computer.

In the comparatively short time since coming into force, the Computer Misuse Act 1990 has been successfully applied against the range of offences for which it was envisaged. However, uncertainties continue to exist over the attitude of the judicial authorities to convicting for such offences. In terms of increasing the effectiveness of the Act, further successful prosecutions will give organisations the confidence to make use of the Act to pursue offenders.

9.4 INTERNATIONAL HARMONISATION

Computer crime has an obvious international dimension. It has been seen as necessary, therefore, to ensure that legal protection is harmonised internationally. Over recent years, attempts have been made through international organisations to achieve a harmonised approach to legislating against computer crime and thereby try to prevent the appearance of 'computer crime havens'.

From 1983 to 1985, an *ad hoc* committee of the OECD discussed the need for international harmonisation of criminal laws with respect to computer-related economic crime. After further joint work with the Working Party on Information, Computers and Communications Policy (ICCP), a final report was published in 1986.[43] The Report lists five categories of offences which it believes should constitute a common approach to computer crime.

The Council of Europe has also considered this field. A select committee of experts, the European Committee on Crime Problems, was established in

---

42. See Battcock, op. cit., note 28.
43. 'Computer-Related Criminality: Analysis of Legal Policy in the OECD Area', Report DSTI-ICCP 84.22 of 18 April 1986.

December 1985 to consider the legal issues raised by computer crime. The final report was published in September 1989.[44] As part of the Committee's work, it produced guidelines for national legislatures on a 'Minimum List of Offences Necessary for a Uniform Criminal Policy'.[45] These eight offences were seen by all Member States to be the critical areas of computer misuse that required provisions in criminal law. In addition, the Report put forward an 'optional list' of four offences that failed to achieve consensus among Members, but were thought to be worthy of consideration.[46] The Report was published with a Council of Ministers Recommendation urging governments to take account of the Report when reviewing and initiating legislation in this field.[47]

Over recent years, the Council of Europe has shifted its attention to the issue of prosecution of computer crime and the particular problems faced by law enforcement agencies. In 1995, it adopted a Recommendation addressing issues of search and seizure, the admissibility of evidence and international mutual assistance.[48] The Council of Europe is currently developing a Convention on 'Cyber Crime' which will also address issues of mutual assistance, extradition and, potentially, the interception and decryption of internet-based communications.[49]

Issues of criminal law have historically been outside the competence of the European Union.[50] However, under Title VI of the Treaty on European Union issues of 'police and judicial cooperation in criminal matters' have now been brought within the EU's sphere of activities. At a special meeting of the European Council in October 1999 'on the creation of an area of freedom, security and justice in the European Union', Member State governments agreed that efforts should be made to reach common positions with respect to definitions of criminal offences and appropriate sanctions for particular areas of crime, including computer crime.[51] In the area of enforcement, a draft Convention on Mutual Legal Assistance is currently being prepared.[52]

---

44. 'Computer-related crime', Report by the European Committee on Crime Problems, Strasbourg, 1990.
45. The list of offences: computer fraud; computer forgery; damage to computer data or computer programmes; computer sabotage; unauthorised access; unauthorised interception; unauthorised reproduction of a computer programme; and unauthorised reproduction of a topography.
46. I.e., alteration of computer data or computer programmes; computer espionage; unauthorised use of a computer; and unauthorised use of a protected computer programme.
47. Recommendation No. R(89)9, 13 September 1989.
48. Recommendation No. R(95)13, 'concerning problems of procedural law connected with information technology'.
49. See Draft Convention on Cyber-crime (Draft No. 19), released for public discussion 27 April 2000: http://www.coe.fr.
50. However, see the Commission-funded study COMCRIME: 'Legal aspects of Computer-related Crime in the Information Society', January 1998: http://www2.echo.lu/legal/en/crime/crime.html.
51. Press Release C/99/0002, Presidency conclusions, Tampere European Council, 15–16 October 1999.
52. See Home Office Consultation Paper, 'Interception of Communications in the United Kingdom', Cmnd 4368, HMSO, London: June 1999, at para. 6.2.

9.5 JURISDICTIONAL ISSUES

Inevitably, computer crime will often have an extraterritorial aspect to it, i.e., it involves persons and acts in different countries. This can give rise to difficult jurisdictional issues. Addressing these difficulties has required legislators to provide explicitly for extraterritorial jurisdiction in certain situations. In the Computer Misuse Act 1990 extraterritorial jurisdiction is provided for through the concept of a 'significant link' existing with the domestic jurisdiction. An offence will have been committed if either the accused, the accessed computer or the unauthorised modification is in the domestic jurisdiction.[53]

The Citibank fraud is illustrative of some of the issues which can arise when prosecuting transnational criminal activities. In 1994 Citibank suffered a significant breach of security in its cash management system,[54] resulting in funds being transferred from customer accounts into the accounts of the perpetrator and his accomplices. The eventual sum involved was $12 million, although the vast majority, $11.6 million, was transferred subsequent to the discovery of the breach as part of the efforts to locate the perpetrators. After significant international cooperation between law enforcement agencies and other organisations, including the local St. Petersburg telephone company, an individual was identified. Vladimer Levin was arrested in the United Kingdom and, after appeals, was subsequently extradited to the United States (*R v Governor of Brixton Prison and another, ex parte Levin* [1996] 4 All ER 350, HL).

In an action for extradition the applicant is required to show that the actions of the accused constitute a criminal offence exceeding a minimum level of seriousness in both jurisdictions, the country from which the accused is to be extradited and the country to which the extradition will be made.[55] In the Citibank case, Levin was accused of committing wire and bank fraud in the United States. No direct equivalent exists in English law, and therefore Levin was charged with 66 related offences, including unauthorised access and unauthorised modification under the Computer Misuse Act 1990. However, even where similar offences exist, a particular computer-related activity may not be deemed to fall within the terminology of existing criminal law.[56] Levin's counsel argued, for example, that one of the offences cited by

---

53. Sections 4 and 5. Sections 6 and 7 addresses the territorial scope for the inchoate offences, i.e., conspiracy, attempt or incitement. See also the Criminal Justice Act 1993, Part I, which provides for jurisdiction for certain offences, such as fraud, on the basis of a 'relevant event' occurring in England and Wales (Part I came into force on 1 June 1999 only).

54. The system, called the 'Financial Institutions Citibank Cash Manager' (FICCM), provided large institutional customers with dial-in access from any geographic location to the on-line service, based on a system in Parsipenny, New Jersey. Once accessed, customers could carry out a range of financial transactions, including the execution of credit transfers between accounts.

55. The offence must be punishable by a minimum 12-months imprisonment in both States (sometimes referred to as the 'double criminality' principle): Extradition Act 1989, s. 2. See also Computer Misuse Act 1990, s. 8(1). Also *R v Bow Street Magistrates' Court, ex parte Allison* [1998] 3 WLR 1156, where the court held that ss. 2 and 3 of the Computer Misuse Act 1990 were extradition crimes (confirmed by the House of Lords, at 625G).

56. See 9.2.4 above.

the extradition applicant, under the Forgery and Counterfeiting Act 1981, had not been committed based on an earlier decision by the English courts in *R* v *Gold* [1987] 3 WLR 803.[57]

A second jurisdictional issue revolved around the question of *where* the offences were held to have taken place. Defendant's counsel claimed that the criminal act occurred in St. Petersburg at the moment when Levin pressed particular keys on the keyboard instigating fraudulent Citibank transfers, therefore Russian law applied. Counsel for the extradition applicant claimed that the place where the changes to the data occurred, the Citibank computer in Parsipenny (United States), constituted the place where the offence took place. The judge decided in favour of the applicant on the basis that the real-time nature of the communication link between Levin and the Citibank computer meant that Levin's keystrokes were actually occurring on the Citibank computer.[58] A message-based system of communication, such as email, might have produced a different result. In *Governor of Pentonville Prison, ex parte Osman* [1989] 3 All ER 701, the court held that the sending of a telex constituted the act of appropriation and, therefore, the place from where the telex was sent was where the offence was committed (at case report, lines 295e–f).

9.6 FORENSIC ISSUES

The investigation of computer crimes and the gathering of appropriate evidence for a criminal prosecution can be an extremely difficult and complex issue, due primarily to the intangible and often transient nature of the data, especially in networked environments. The technology renders the process of investigation and recording of evidence extremely vulnerable to defence claims of errors, technical malfunction, prejudicial interference or fabrication. Such claims may lead to a ruling from the court against the admissibility of such evidence.[59] A lack of adequate training of law enforcement officers may exasperate these difficulties.

The execution of search warrants, under s. 14 of the Computer Misuse Act 1990 or s. 8 of the Police and Criminal Evidence Act 1984, and the seizure of material can give rise to problems where the relevant material is held on a computer system being used at the time of the search, since any attempt to seize the material for further examination may result in either the loss or alteration of the evidence.[60] In addition, the volume of material potentially contained on the hard disk of a computer may raise issues as to the scope of the warrant, particularly in respect of legally privileged items.[61]

Investigation and obtaining evidence in cross-border computer crimes usually requires mutual assistance between national law enforcement

---

57. See also the *Levin* case at 360e–361e.
58. Ibid., at 363a.
59. Police and Criminal Evidence Act 1984, s. 78.
60. See generally the 'Good Practice Guide for Computer Based Evidence; published by the Association of Chief Police Officers, March 1998.
61. See *R* v *Chesterfield Justices and others, ex parte Bramley*, Times Law Reports, 10 November 1999, [2000] 2 WLR 409, DC.

agencies. Such mutual assistance is currently governed by the Criminal Justice (International Co-operation) Act 1990, which provides for the provision of evidence and extends the powers of search and seizure to materials relevant to an overseas investigation or proceedings.[62]

Under the Police and Criminal Evidence Act 1984, a constable may require 'any information which is contained in a computer and is accessible from the premises to be produced in a form in which it can be taken away...'.[63] This provision would seem to enable law enforcement officers to obtain information held on remote systems, since the reference to 'a computer' would seem to extend to a remote computer which can be accessed via another computer on the premises. However, where the remote computer is based in another jurisdiction, important issues of sovereignty and territoriality can arise.[64]

In the early 1990s, certain electronic bulletin boards, containing potentially illegal material such as virus code, began placing messages at the point of access to the site stating that 'law enforcement officials are not permitted to enter the system'. Such a warning has been considered to be an effective technique in restricting the police from monitoring the use made of such bulletin boards.[65] In 1994, the Computer Misuse Act 1990 was amended to enable law enforcement agencies to log onto electronic bulletin boards without themselves committing a s. 1 offence of unauthorised access.[66]

The interception of data during transmission across a communications network is subject to the regime established under the Interception of Communications Act 1985, which makes it an offence to intercept a communication being carried by means of a public telecommunications system without a warrant issued by the Secretary of State (s. 2). The regime is not primarily designed to tackle the activities of those intercepting communications in the furtherance of their criminal activities;[67] rather its purpose is to control the interception practices of law enforcement agents and the use of intercepted material as evidence.[68] The Government has recently published a bill reforming the interception regime, including provisions requiring 'com-

62. E.g., to obtain evidence from overseas for use in the United Kingdom, it is usually necessary to obtain a 'letter of request' (also referred to as a 'commission rogatoire') from a court: Criminal Justice (International Co-operation) Act 1990, s. 3.
63. Section 19(4). See also s. 20, which extends this provision to powers of seizure conferred under other enactments.
64. See United Nations 'Manual on the prevention and control of computer-related crime', paras 261–267, published in the *International Review of Criminal Policy*, Nos. 43 and 44, 1996: http://www.ifs.univie.ac.at/~pr2gq1/rev4344.html.
65. See Home Affairs Committee Report No. 126, *Computer Pornography*, op. cit., note 15, p. xii, paras 31–32.
66. The Criminal Justice and Public Order Act 1994, s. 162 'Access to computer material by constables and other law enforcement officers', amending s. 10 of the Computer Misuse Act 1990.
67. The Act would not cover 'electronic eavesdropping', where emissions from computer VDU screens are surreptitiously received and reconstituted for viewing on external equipment. See generally, O. Lewis, 'Information Security & Electronic Eavesdropping — a perspective', *Computer Law and Security Report*, vol. 7, no. 4, 1991, pp. 165–168.
68. The Act was designed to bring English law into line with the European Convention on Human Rights following the decision in *Malone* v *United Kingdom* [1984] 7 EHRR 14.

munication service providers' to ensure their systems have on-going intercept capability, as well as obligations to provide relevant communications data in the course of a lawful investigation.[69]

Prosecutors will often be challenged to prove the reliability of the computer-derived evidence presented. Auditable procedures may need to be adhered to, often supported by independent expert witnesses, to show that the computer systems generating any evidence, either under the direct control of the investigators (e.g., a seized hard disk) or remotely accessed (e.g., a website), were operating properly; that a link can be made between the evidence and the accused;[70] and how the evidence was collected and maintained by the investigators until trial.[71]

9.7 CRIMINAL EVIDENCE

It is beyond the scope of this chapter to discuss the rules relating to the admissibility of real and hearsay evidence into court.[72] However, until recently, English law had special rules governing the admissibility of computer records in criminal proceedings. These rules presented a potential obstacle in the prosecution of computer-related crime and continue to be relevant in respect of issues concerning the probative value of computer-derived evidence.

Under the Police and Criminal Evidence Act 1984, all computer evidence had to comply with s. 69:

(1)   In any proceedings, a statement in a document produced by a computer shall not be admissible as evidence of any fact stated therein unless it is shown—

(a)   that there are no reasonable grounds for believing that the statement is inaccurate because of improper use of the computer;

(b)   that at all material times the computer was operating properly, or if not, that any respect in which it was not operating properly or was out of operation was not such as to affect the production of the document or the accuracy of its contents; ...

To satisfy a court that the s. 69(1) conditions had been met, it was necessary to obtain either a signed statement or oral testimony from a person who occupies 'a responsible position' in relation to the operation of the computer system.[73]

---

69. See Regulation of Investigatory Powers Bill 2000.
70. *R* v *Woollhead*, The Herald, 9 March 1995 (quoted in Spink, op.cit., note 35).
71. See P. Sommer, 'Evidence from Cyberspace: Downloads, Logs and Captures', *Journal of Financial Crime*, 5(2), 1997, pp. 138–152; and 'Digital Footprints: Assessing Computer Evidence', *Criminal Law Review*, special edition, December 1998, pp. 61–78.
72. See *R* v *Wood* (1983) 76 Cr App R 23, which held that when computers are operating in a mechanistic way, as automatic recording systems or simply as calculating tools, the evidence is real, not hearsay. See also *R* v *Governor of Brixton Prison and another, ex parte Levin* [1997] 3 WLR 117, HL, at 121D. See generally, Cross and Tapper on Evidence, 9th edn, London: Butterworths, 1999.
73. Police and Criminal Evidence Act 1984, sch. 3, pt. II, paras 8 and 9.

The broad nature of the language used in s. 69(1) presented obvious opportunities for a party to challenge computer-derived evidence. The conditions were therefore the subject of significant consideration by the courts. The House of Lords considered the scope of s. 69 in *R v Shephard* [1993] 1 All ER 225. The case concerned the theft of goods from a store and the defence was that the goods had been paid for. The central item of evidence tendered by the prosecution was the till rolls produced for the relevant day, which showed that the particular combination of items which the defendant was alleged to have stolen had not been purchased from the store on that day. As the tills were essentially computers, the evidence produced from them had to meet the s. 69 requirements.[74] The House of Lords held that the courts would not in any circumstances presume that the s. 69 conditions were met, but there was an 'affirmative duty' on the party tendering the evidence to show that the conditions were complied with.[75]

In a networked environment, one issue that arises is the extent to which s. 69(1) had to be complied with in respect of each and every machine involved in the processing of the evidential information. Even identifying the relevant computers would be problematic in an open environment such as the Internet. In *R v Cochrane* [1993] Crim LR 48, the court upheld an appeal against a prosecution for theft of monies from a building society's cash machines because the Crown were unable to adduce evidence about the operation of the company's mainframe computer as well as the cash machine itself. However, in *R v Waddon* (Southwark Crown Court, 30 June 1999), the court held that the computers involved in the transmission of an image across the Internet were 'mere post boxes', therefore the only s. 69 certificate that the prosecution needed to provide was from the computer from which the image had been obtained.

In the *Levin* case, defence counsel challenged certain evidence presented by Citibank on the grounds that since the accused had improperly used the computer, the requirements of s. 69(1)(a) could not be satisfied. The court rejected this argument stating that 'unauthorised use of the computer is not of itself a ground for believing that the statements recorded by it were inaccurate'.[76]

Section 69(1)(b) states that the computer must have been 'operating properly' at the 'material time'. Evidence showing compliance with the conditions must therefore relate to the relevant time. In *Connolly v Lancashire County Council* (1994) RTR 79, audit records were submitted with respect to the correct operation of a computerised weighing bridge. However, the records related to an examination of the weighbridge system carried out

---

74. One issue addressed by the House of Lords was whether the s. 69 conditions applied to all computer records or only hearsay computer evidence. The court held that the requirement extended to all forms of computer evidence: see *R v Shephard* [1993] 1 All ER 225 at 228j–230d.

75. Ibid., at 228h. See also *R v Aylesbury Crown Court ex parte Lait* [1998] Masons CLR 264, where the prosecution failed to ask the relevant witness whether the computer, an Intoximeter, was 'operating properly', and therefore failed to discharge the 'affirmative duty'.

76. *Levin* case, op. cit., note 72, at 359c. It is interesting to note that the judge refers to the recording of statements, whereas s. 69(1) is only concerned with the production of statements.

nearly three months prior to the date of the alleged offence. The records were not therefore accepted by the courts as evidence that the system was operating properly at the 'material time'.

Another issued addressed in *Shephard* was what sort of person should be able to certify or provide oral testimony that the system was 'operating properly'. Computers are highly complex machines which could potentially require expert evidence from a number of different people, particularly in a networked environment. However, the House of Lords stated that it was sufficient that the 'responsible person' was 'familiar with the operation of the computer'. In *Shephard*, this meant the store detective, since she was able to state that to her knowledge the system had not suffered any problems on the relevant day.[77]

A final aspect that has been addressed by the courts is the admissibility of computer evidence where a part of the computer is found to be malfunctioning. In *DPP* v *McKeown and Jones* [1997] 1 WLR 295, an Intoximeter used to analyse the amount of alcohol in a person's breath was found to have an inaccurate clock. In the Divisional Court, the defendants successfully argued that the clock's inaccuracy rendered the statement detailing the level of alcohol present inadmissible on the grounds that s. 69(1)(b) could not be complied with. However, this was overturned by the House of Lords, with Lord Hoffmann stating (at 302G):

A malfunction is relevant if it affects the way in which the computer processes, stores or retrieves the information used to generate the statement tendered in evidence. Other malfunctions do not matter.

Despite the generally favourable attitude of the courts to the admission of computer-derived evidence, considerable disquiet had been voiced against the s. 69 conditions. In response, the Law Commission recently proposed reform of the rules to re-introduce the pre-1984 maxim *omnia praesumuntur rite esse acta*, a common law presumption that things have been done properly.[78] The presumption would effectively shift the burden of proof with respect to the reliability of computer evidence from the party submitting the evidence to the party against whom the evidence is being adduced. A similar reform was adopted with respect to the admissibility of computer evidence in civil proceedings by the Civil Evidence Act 1995, repealing the special provisions for computer evidence under s. 5 of the Civil Evidence Act 1968. The reform of s. 69 was enacted under the Youth Justice and Criminal Evidence Act 1999.[79]

---

77. See also *T* v *Ipswich Youth Court* (1998) LawTel, 22 October 1998, where an IT security manager was accepted as being sufficiently familiar with the computer system; also in *R* v *Ana Marcolino* (1999) LawTel, 28 April 1999, a risk supervisor met the test.
78. See Law Commission consultation paper No. 138, *Evidence in Criminal Proceedings: Hearsay and Related Topics*, London: HMSO, 1995 and Law Com No. 245, London: HMSO, 1997, part XIII and recommendation 50.
79. Section 60, which provides 'Section 69 of the Police and Criminal Evidence Act 1984 . . . shall cease to have effect'. The provision came into force on 14 April 2000: The Youth Justice and Criminal Evidence Act 1999 (Commencement No. 2) Order, SI 1034/2000, para. 2(a).

9.8 CONCLUDING REMARKS

Public perception of computer crime contrasts sharply with reality. The news and entertainment media have promoted the image of the 'hacker' as an almost 'Robin Hood'-like figure attacking the computers of big brother organisations. The reality of computer crime is that such activities encompass a broad range of perpetrators: the traditional criminal fraternity, exploiting the power of a new tool; disgruntled employees utilising their inside knowledge; the curious and thrill-seekers treating the medium as a challenge; and those engaged in industrial espionage and information warfare.

Nation States have generally needed to react to the phenomena of computer crime by updating their criminal law, whether through amendments to existing statutes or the adoption of *sui generis* offences. However, prosecutors, the judiciary and juries continue to struggle to comprehend the nature of computer-related crime and computer-derived evidence. Over recent years, policy makers have shifted their focus from the need for appropriate offences to the needs of law enforcement agencies in a networked environment.

From a commercial perspective, computer misuse legislation is a final resort to which companies are generally reluctant to turn. The impact that such a prosecution may have on a company can be substantial, often affecting the systems upon which the company is reliant, consuming considerable management time and effort, and generating adverse publicity.

Perpetrators of computer crime usually exploit weaknesses in the systems either being used or attacked. Inadequate security procedures — physical, organisational and logical — continue to be a central feature in the vast majority of examples of computer crime. The growth of the Internet, with the prospect of 'always-on' connectivity for large segments of population, presents very significant new and enhanced security threats to individuals and society as a whole, as well as challenges to law enforcement agencies.

CHAPTER TEN

Electronic Commerce

Chris Reed and Lars Davies

10.1 WHAT IS ELECTRONIC COMMERCE?

The advent and subsequent growth of the Internet has made electronic commerce a very fashionable topic, both in terms of business-to-consumer sales and, increasingly, business-to-business electronic commerce. Yet it would be a mistake to assume that electronic commerce is a new phenomenon. Prior to the development and widespread commercial use of the Internet, other technologies based on private or closed electronic networks were already in use to provide electronic communications between commercial entities which in turn were used to enter into binding agreements or contracts.

Electronic Data Interchange (EDI), a system of electronic communications between commercial parties where the communications take place over a closed system and are governed by a set of previously agreed contracts, was perhaps the most commonly used technology. Other communications systems existed and continue to exist within certain defined industries, and these too constitute a form of electronic commerce. Quite aside from these closed networks, new techniques and protocols are being developed that allow users to create virtual private networks or VPNs across the Internet; these too can and almost certainly will be used in a manner similar to those of closed networks.

The Internet, by contrast, is an open network which permits communication between parties without the need for both to subscribe to the same closed network. Due to its widespread use and purportedly well educated and affluent user group, it is an attractive medium for both business-to-business and business-to-consumer commerce. Quite aside from the possibility of using it to make contracts, the wide reach of the Internet presents an attractive medium through which commercial entities can advertise and market their wares.

Given the increasing use of electronic networks by commercial entities, all of which have differing aims and uses, what aspects of this use amount to electronic commerce? What does the term mean?

Though the question is easy to ask it is very hard to answer, or at least to answer in a definite manner. This is not due to any difficulty in understanding what is meant by the question. Rather it is due to the difficulty of categorising the subject matter into discrete topic areas.

Electronic network activity is very simple to define in a generic sense. It can be summarised as activities carried out across some form of electronic network, such as the Internet or the closed networks used for EDI, whatever those activities may be. Electronic commerce presents much more of a problem[1] as its definition depends on the differing views taken as to what is and what is not commerce or commercial activity. Taken at its most generic sense electronic commerce could be said to comprise commercial transactions, whether between private individuals or commercial entities, which take place in or over electronic networks. The matters dealt with in the transactions could be intangibles, such as data or information products,[2] or tangible goods such as books and T-shirts. The only important factor is that some or all of the various communications which make up these transactions take place over an electronic medium. The communications could involve any part of the commercial process, from the initial marketing to the placing of orders and even through to the background transaction processing.[3] Whether these communications take place via EDI, or across other forms of electronic network such as the Internet or indeed a combination of these systems, is irrelevant. All that matters is that the commercial transactions utilise some form of electronic communication.

10.2   GENERAL ISSUES

10.2.1   Contract formation

The question of contract formation across electronic networks is problematic to say the least. This is due not only to the interjurisdictional issues that arise

---

1. See the discussion in *Defying Definition*, US Department of Commerce.
2. Data products are often combinations of both the tangible and the intangible, for instance a CD-ROM which contains a database.
3. The *Sacher Report*, OECD 1997, p. 20 gives a generic yet comprehensive definition which forms a good starting point from which to proceed:

    Definitions of electronic commerce vary considerably, but generally, electronic commerce refers to all forms of commercial transactions involving organizations and individuals that are based upon the processing and transmission of digitized data, including text, sound, and visual images. It also refers to the effects that the electronic exchange of commercial information may have on the institutions and processes that support and govern commercial activities. These include organizational management, commercial negotiations and contracts, legal and regulatory frameworks, financial settlement arrangements, and taxation among many others.

as a natural result of the borderless nature of the networks, but also to the issues that arise when considering the terms of any contract that might be formed. Such issues arise because of the need to consider any overriding legislation which may affect the freedom to contract in the jurisdiction in which the contract was formed or under the law chosen in the contract.

The ease and flexibility of communicating across electronic networks allows users to enter into agreements with each other with little if any difficulty. The issue is therefore not whether the users can enter into agreements. The issue that must be addressed is whether these agreements can constitute contracts.[4] Though it is valid to ask what *law* applies to contracts formed across electronic networks, which courts have *jurisdiction* and what *terms* apply, these are not the most important issues. The fundamental question, and one which is rarely asked, is *whether or not* a contract was actually formed. This naturally leads to the questions of *where* that contract was formed and *when*.[5] Until these questions are answered it makes no sense to even attempt to ask what laws or jurisdictions apply. If contracts were not formed then any discussion on which laws apply is completely irrelevant. This is an obvious point, perhaps, but one which is often missed.

The basic principles of contract law are very well understood and can be applied readily to most traditional contracting scenarios to give answers to these questions. Unfortunately, applying these principles to electronic commerce across electronic networks often poses more questions than answers. This occurs as a result of the fact that applying standard contractual principles to electronic transactions can either provide unwelcome results, or in the worst case a series of mutually contradictory results.

One of the main requirements of contract law, at least from a commercial point of view, is that it should provide for some degree of certainty as to the relationship and obligations that lie between the contracting parties. The degree of certainty may not, and indeed need not, be absolute. What is required is sufficient certainty so that the risks and obligations are ascertainable and thus the parties can engage in a risk/benefit analysis and decide whether or not to proceed with their agreements.

In any contract the parties need to be able to determine several factors, whether these are implicit or explicit. These are rules of contract formation, choice of law, choice of jurisdiction, terms and conditions, enforceability of the agreement, the identities of the contracting parties, whether the contract can bind third parties, and, perhaps most important of all, whether or not a contract has actually been formed.

Not all electronic transactions or communications result in the formation of a contract. Although a number of attempts have been made to classify

---

4. Agreements that are legally enforceable in a Court of Law as opposed to simply having moral force.

5. It is of no use whatsoever to suggest that somewhere in the soup of electronic communications that make up a series of messages a contract was formed but it is not known exactly where or when; just that a contract was somehow formed. In order for a contract to exist the exact instant when it came into existence must be identifiable, and not merely be a vague and nebulous occurrence. It must be a definite and identifiable event.

electronic messages according to the different legal problems raised,[6] for our purposes it is sufficient to note three broad categories, set out below.

10.2.1.1 The transmission of mere information Generally, the sender does not intend a message of this type to have legal consequences. Examples might range from the trivial:

'Our Chairman will arrive on the 15.20 flight'

to the vital:

'Maximum safe operating pressure = 130 p.s.i.'

The only legal problem arising from this type of message is the potential liability where the sender owes a duty to the recipient to take care to ensure that the information is correct, and as a result of his carelessness the recipient suffers loss.[7]

10.2.1.2 The transmission of unilateral notices This type of communication will be intended to have a legal effect and will in most cases be made in performing an existing contract. Typical examples of this category might be invoices, which are often a prerequisite for payment, or a notice under a charterparty that a ship is ready to load, thus fixing the laytime and demurrage periods.

The sort of legal questions that this type of communication will raise are threefold:

(a)   Is it effective as a notice? This will often depend on whether the notice is required to be in writing, or if a signature is required.

(b)   When (and possibly where) does it take effect, i.e., is the sending or receipt the legally significant point?

(c)   If its sending or contents are disputed, can these facts be proved?

One important unilateral notice is the Customs declaration. The penalties for false or non-declaration are severe, so the legal effect of such a notice is easily apparent. The required form and contents of Customs declarations are set out in national legislation, which will thus answer the question of whether it is possible to replace the paper documents with an electronic transmission.

---

6. For example, Goode and Bergsten identify five types of communication:
   (a)   Communications having no legal significance.
   (b)   Communications having legal significance.
   (c)   Communications operative to transfer ownership, control or contract rights.
   (d)   Communications required by law.
   (e)   Communications requiring legal authority or licence.

   'Legal questions and problems to be overcome', in Thomsen & Wheble, *Trading with EDI: the Legal Issues*, London: IBC, 1989, pp. 131–133.
7. *Hedley Byrne v Heller & Partners* [1963] 2 All ER 575.

Over recent years many jurisdictions have introduced systems for electronic customs declarations which are designed to produce the necessary evidence and authentication for these documents.[8]

10.2.1.3 Contract formation messages[9]   Where, for example, goods are ordered using an electronic message, the intended result will be the formation of a contract. In most cases such messages are part of a series including negotiation, ordering and acceptance. This type of communication raises the largest number of legal questions, in particular:

(a)   Can this particular type of contract be formed using electronic messages? There may be requirements such as writing or signature, depending on the national legislation. For example, in the United Kingdom a contract of marine insurance must be embodied in a marine insurance policy signed by the insurer,[10] and in the United States a contract for the sale of goods for a price of $500 or more must be evidenced in writing and signed by the party against whom it is to be enforced.[11]

(b)   When, and more important where, was the agreement made? This may decide which national law is to apply to the contract or which court has jurisdiction, if there is no effective choice of law or forum clause.

(c)   If the terms of the contract are later disputed, will it be possible to prove what was agreed?

Unless particular formalities such as writing are specifically required (see 10.2.3.1 below), the general rule of English law and of most other jurisdictions is that a contract is formed when the parties reach an agreement on its terms — this can be done orally, as our everyday experience in shops demonstrates. There is thus no theoretical objection to using electronic messages for this purpose. In English law, the process of formation is analysed into two stages: the offer, when one party sets out the terms on which he is prepared to contract, either in one document or by express or implied reference to a preceding course of negotiations; and the acceptance, when the other party agrees to these terms without attempting to amend them in any way. If both parties satisfactorily perform their side of the bargain there is no need to involve the law. However, there are three types of dispute which might arise, and which can be resolved by examining the formation process:

(a)   One party believes a contract to have been concluded, but the other disputes it.

(b)   Both agree that a contract has been formed, but disagree as to its terms.

(c)   The parties disagree as to when and where the contract was formed.

---

8. E.g., the UK HM Customs & Excise CHIEF system — www.hmce.gov.uk/bus/customs/chief.htm.
9. See also L.J. Davies, *Contract Formation on the Internet: shattering a few myths*, ch. 6, in Lilian Edwards & Charlotte Waelde, *Law & the Internet: regulating cyberspace* Oxford: Hart Publishing, 1997.
10. Marine Insurance Act 1906, ss. 22–24.
11. Uniform Commercial Code, s. 201(1).

In order to understand how English law will deal with these disputes, a number of basic principles of contract law must be borne in mind:

(a)   Unless otherwise stated, an offer remains open for a reasonable time or until it is accepted or rejected by the other party.

(b)   An offer may be withdrawn (unless there has been some payment to keep it open, i.e., an option) at any time before it is accepted, but this withdrawal is only effective when it reaches the other party.[12]

(c)   A counter offer, i.e., the suggestion of different terms, brings the original offer to an end, and no contract is formed until the new offer is accepted.[13] If the parties engage in a so-called 'battle of the forms' where each purports to contract on its own terms, the set of terms that applies will be those contained in the last offer made before acceptance.[14]

(d)   The contract is formed when, and where, acceptance takes place.

In applying these principles to electronic communications, it must also be noted that whilst offers and withdrawals of offers must actually be communicated to the other party[15] the rules governing acceptances are quite different. Where acceptance is made by some instantaneous means such as face to face communication or telephone, it too must actually reach the offeror. It has been held that telex communications are instantaneous, and thus contracts made by telex are made where the telex is received.[16] This rule is certain to apply to electronic communications where there is a direct link between the parties. The contract formation law of other jurisdictions will differ in detail. All these issues are normally addressed in national laws, and most jurisdictions adopt roughly similar principles.

The position may, however, be different if the network across which the transmission is made stores the acceptance message for an appreciable period before it is delivered to the offeror. As common law lawyers learn at an early stage, if an acceptance is made in written form the 'postal rule' applies. This provides that the acceptance takes place *when the letter is posted*, whether or not it ever arrives.[17] Might the postal rule apply to such an electronic message of acceptance?

There are two justifications suggested for the postal rule. The first is that it is an *ad hoc* method for solving what is inevitably a difficult question (if the rule were that the letter had to be received, would it be relevant that it arrived but was never read, or not read before withdrawal of the offer?). Even if this justification is the correct one, the dictum of Lord Brandon in *Brinkibon Ltd v Stahag Stahl und Stahlwarenhandelgesellschaft mbH* [1982] 1 All ER 293 suggests that the postal rule might apply to electronic acceptances:

---

12. *Byrne* v *Van Tienhoven* (1880) 5 CPD 344.
13. *Hyde* v *Wrench* (1840) 3 Beav 334.
14. *Butler Machine Tool Co.* v *Ex-Cell-O Corporation* [1979] 1 WLR 401.
15. *Byrne* v *Van Tienhoven* (1880) 5 CPD 344.
16. *Entores Ltd* v *Miles Far East Corporation* [1955] 2 QB 327.
17. *Adams* v *Lindsell* (1818) 1 B & Ald 681; *Household Fire Insurance* v *Grant* (1879) 4 Ex D 216.

The cases on acceptance by letter and telegram constitute an exception to the general principle of the law of contract [on grounds of expediency]. . . . That reason of commercial expediency applies to cases where there is bound to be a substantial interval between the time when the acceptance is sent and the time when it is received. In such cases the exception to the general rule is more convenient, and makes on the whole for greater fairness, than the rule itself would do.[18]

The second justification is that the offeror has impliedly agreed that the accepting party may entrust the transmission of his acceptance to an independent third party, the postal authorities, and that therefore the offeree has done all that the offeror requires for acceptance when he posts his letter. This too would suggest that acceptance takes place when the message is received by the system provider's computer. The clearest analogy to using a store and forward messaging system is with acceptance by telegram; it is necessary for the message actually to be communicated to the telegram service, normally by telephone (an instantaneous method of communication), but once it has been received by the service acceptance is complete.[19]

The postal rule is not unique to Anglo-American law; for example, in Spain the postal rule applies to acceptances in commercial transactions,[20] though in non-commercial transactions an acceptance is not effective until it is received.[21] Other jurisdictions apply the requirement of receipt to all types of contract.[22]

Where the postal rule applies, the authors' opinion is that the time of acceptance is the time the electronic message was received by the network, and the place of acceptance will therefore be that node of the network which received the message. In most cases this is likely to be in the same jurisdiction as the acceptor, but not inevitably — it is easy to conceive a Scottish company accepting an offer from a US company using a closed electronic messaging system such as an EDI system, or indeed a private network based on an open electronic network such as the Internet,[23] where the message of acceptance is sent to a computer in England. The contract would be formed in England, and subject to agreement to the contrary might therefore be subject to English law, at least in respect of its formation. Fortunately, the English courts have accepted that it is permissible for the parties to stipulate what acts will constitute acceptance,[24] which suggests that it would be beneficial for electronic commerce contracts to provide exactly when a message will be taken to have effect and which law is to govern the performance of the contract. Where the electronic transaction is subject to a different law, it will

---

18. At p. 300.
19. *Re London & Northern Bank* [1900] 1 Ch 200.
20. Spanish Commercial Code, art. 54.
21. Spanish Civil Code, art. 1262(2).
22. See, e.g., Swiss Code of Obligations, art. 35; Italian Civil Code, art 1335. The Italian Code adopts a further refinement, that it is sufficient for the acceptance to reach the offeror's premises provided he is then likely to receive it.
23. For example virtual private networks or VPNs that operate across the Internet.
24. *Holwell Securities Ltd v Hughes* [1974] 1 WLR 155.

be necessary to assess whether, under that law, it is possible for the parties to agree what steps will lead to the formation of a valid contract and include an appropriate term to that effect in their contract. With regard to the EDI community there appears to be general agreement that an EDI message should not have operative effect until it is received.[25]

Within Europe, many of these uncertainties should be reduced when Directive 2000/31/EC on electronic commerce is implemented in national law. Article 9(1) provides:

> Member States shall ensure that their legal system allows contracts to be concluded by electronic means. Member States shall in particular ensure that the legal requirements applicable to the contractual process neither create obstacles for the use of electronic contracts nor result in such contracts being deprived of legal effectiveness and validity on account of their having been made by electronic means.

The directive does not attempt to define the formation process, but art. 10(1) requires the supplier to explain to the customer the steps which will give rise to a contract and make its terms available, while art. 11(1) requires orders to be acknowledged and provides that both these communications are only effective when received.

10.2.2 Evidential problems

10.2.2.1 Admissibility There are three reasons why a record produced by a computer might be inadmissible as evidence:

(a)   because it is not an original;
(b)   because it is hearsay; or
(c)   because some rule of law prevents the evidence from being adduced.

The Civil Evidence Act 1995 removed all of these potential problems, so far as English law is concerned. Section 1 of the Act simply abolishes the hearsay rule, and s. 8 provides that where a statement in a document is admissible, it may be proved by producing a copy of the document (even if the original is still in existence) and that the number of removes between a copy and the original is irrelevant (i.e., it may be an nth generation copy). Furthermore, under s. 9, documents which form part of the records[26] of a

---

25. UNCID Rules, art. 7(a).
26. Note that not all business documents are 'records'. *H* v *Schering Chemicals* [1983] 1 All ER 849, the leading case on the meaning of 'record', indicates that a document, irrespective of its form, will only be a record if:

  (a)   it effects a transaction or is a contemporaneous compilation of information derived from primary sources which is intended to serve as a record of events; and
  (b)   it is a comprehensive compilation, rather than a selection of source information.

  If a document is not a comprehensive record of what has occurred, or, even if comprehensive, was not intended to serve as a primary source of information on that matter, it will not be a record. Thus the majority of computer records will fall under s. 8 rather than the more favourable provisions of s. 9.

business (defined very widely) are automatically admissible[27] and the absence of an entry in those records can be proved by an appropriately signed certificate.[28] The admissibility problems for computer records will thus disappear, for new litigation at least, and the focus of litigation will now be on what should be the real question, the authentication of the relevant records.

Other jurisdictions treat the question of admissibility differently, although it is now rare for a court to refuse to admit a computer record as evidence. Many common law jurisdictions have specific rules, either statutory or derived from case law, which permit the admission of computer records as exceptions to the hearsay rule. Thus US law has a business records exception to its hearsay rule, which allows the computer evidence to be admitted if:

(a) The computer equipment used was standard equipment, or if modified, was reliable.

(b) The data were entered in the regular course of business at or near the time of the events recorded by persons having personal knowledge of the events recorded.

(c) Adequate measures were taken to insure the accuracy of the data during entry, storage and processing.

(d) The printouts were prepared in such a manner as to ensure their accuracy.[29]

The Australian courts have taken a robust approach, holding that 'Courts should ... be prepared to facilitate proof of business transactions generated by computers',[30] and South Africa has passed the Computer Evidence Act 1983 which allows the admission of computer records as evidence without imposing any special technical conditions, the court deciding what weight is appropriate to be given to the evidence.

In Civil law jurisdictions the general rule is one of freedom of proof, so that electronic records are admissible in most legal proceedings. However, in some cases national record keeping laws make detailed provisions as to the form and content of documents, and occasionally that country's law of evidence may also give those documents a particular evidential status. Loss of this status can be a disincentive to using methods of electronic messaging, whether EDI or some other system. For example, the laws of both France and Belgium provide that if accounts comply with the constraints imposed by law, their contents are presumed to be accurate unless the contrary is proved. Article 213 of the Austrian Commercial Code provides for a presumption that accounts which comply with the legal constraints are *prima facie* accurate, and it is necessary for evidence to the contrary to be adduced if the accuracy of the accounts is to be put in question. Austrian law also contains a general presumption that, as against the signatory, signed documents are accurate

27. A certificate signed by an officer of the business is required under s. 9(2) so as to demonstrate that the document forms part of its records.
28. Section 9(3).
29. Scott, *Computer Law*, New York: Wiley, 1984, §10.20.
30. *ANZ Banking Group* v *Griffiths* (1990) 53 SASR 256.

unless the signatory produces evidence to counter this presumption. Such a signature must be by hand or, in exceptional cases, via a stamp on a hard copy document. This presumption cannot, therefore, apply to electronic messages.

Some laws also give special evidential status to hard copy documents. This is the case in Italy, where for some transactions a 'document' needs to be produced to assert or enforce rights and the law makes it clear that the only valid form a 'document' can take is hard copy. The same is true for Greece.

In no country is it compulsory to produce proof in the form of these particular documents, but there is a clear benefit in using them if possible as the burden of disproof is placed on the other party.

Even where electronic records can amount to 'documents', they may receive a lower evidential status than a signed hard copy document. This is the case in Germany, and in Portugal signed documents are presumed against the signatory to be accurate until the contrary is proved. A further problem is where the law requires that originals of documents are produced, as in Spain's Civil Procedure Act. This has not yet been tested in the courts — indeed, in all the Civil law States there is a general, though reducing, uncertainty about the evidential efficacy of electronic records.

10.2.2.2   Authentication

Basic principles   Authentication means satisfying the court:

(a)   That the contents of the record have remained unchanged.

(b)   That the information in the record does in fact originate from its purported source, whether human or machine.

(c)   That extraneous information such as the apparent date of the record is accurate.

As with paper records, the necessary degree of authentication may be proved through oral and circumstantial evidence, if available, or via technological features of the system or the record. Non-technical evidence will include a wide variety of matters:

> In an ideal world, the attorney would recommend that the client obtain and record countless bits of evidence for each message so that it could later be authenticated in court — autographs, fingerprints, photographic identification cards, attestations from witnesses, acknowledgements before notaries, letters of introduction, signature guarantees from banks, postmarks on envelopes, records of the return of acknowledgements and so forth.... . [These] observations on conventional messages should apply equally to electronic messages.[31]

Technical evidence might come from system logs, particularly if they are specifically designed with this end in mind, or through embedded features of the record itself such as digital signatures.[32] For some years now the US

---

31. B. Wright, '*Authenticating EDI: the location of a trusted recordkeeper*' (1990) 6 *CL&P* 80.
32. Reed, '*Authenticating Electronic Mail Messages — some evidential problems*' [1989] *MLR* 649.

courts have taken a relaxed approach to the authentication of computer records, refusing to exclude computer-related evidence merely because corruption or alteration is theoretically undetectable.[33]

Where records are kept in physical form, i.e., on paper, there is normally little difficulty in convincing the court that the document produced as evidence is the same document as was originally stored. If the document is signed, it can be produced to prove the fact of sending and the contents of the message. The sender's physical signature will prove that he is responsible for it, and any alteration to its contents should be apparent on its face. The problem with electronically stored messages, however, is that alteration is simple and leaves no traces. Unless these messages can be as well-authenticated as physically signed documents, their value as evidence of the communication is somewhat problematical.

This is because electronic records consist of a stream of numbers (normally in ASCII or some proprietary code[34]) representing the letters of the message (plus, possibly, control characters that define format, emphasis, etc.). When a record is edited, the new version is saved to disk and replaces the old version. The change in the stream of numbers cannot normally be discovered by examining the record itself.

The problems occur when the apparent sender of the message denies that he was responsible for it or where he alleges that his own record of the message differs from the recipient's record. There is nothing in the record itself that authenticates it, and so the court will be forced to assess its authenticity solely by reference to any oral and circumstantial evidence that may be available. It must also be remembered that most of the records will be copies, and there is thus a need to prove that each is an *authentic* copy of the message. The obvious way of so doing is to give oral evidence to that effect, and it is clear that failure to do so will render the copy inadmissible.[35]

Authentication provisions in contracts between the parties   Practising lawyers seem generally to agree that it is worth including a provision in all electronic commerce agreements (e.g., in the Interchange Agreement for EDI transactions) which states that messages which comply with the archiving and authentication procedures of the agreement (and where appropriate, of any specified network provider's User Handbook) are deemed to be admissible and *prima facie* accurate.[36] The efficacy of the provision as to authentication is inevitably uncertain, but although the courts may be unwilling to allow the parties to devise their own law of evidence in a contract, a provision of this

---

33. *US* v *Vela* 673 F 2d 86 (1982), *US* v *Sanders* 749 F 2d 195 (1984).
34. The American Standard Code for Information Interchange is used for most microcomputer communication. Each 8-bit binary word represents a letter of the alphabet or some control or graphics character. For example, in ASCII code A = decimal 65, a = decimal 97, carriage return = decimal 13 etc. EBCDIC (Extended Binary Coded Decimal Interchange Code) is the proprietary format used in IBM mainframes and minicomputers. See H. Cornwall, *Hacker's Handbook III*, London: Century, 1988, pp. 10–14 and Appendix IV.
35. *R* v *Collins* (1960) 44 Cr App Rep 170.
36. See Rowbotham, 'EDI: the practitioner's view', *International Financial Law Review*, August 1988, p. 32.

type might be effective to raise an estoppel preventing the parties from disputing admissibility and accuracy (see 10.2.3.1 below).

Authentication through third party records   If communications are monitored by the network operator, as might occur for EDI transactions, the log of this monitoring could provide a useful level of authentication. The monitoring system should record (a) the identity of sender and recipient of the message, and (b) the message contents. So far as (b) is concerned, it should not be necessary to record the entire text of the message, so long as sufficient information is retained so that any alterations can be detected. The strongest authentication evidence would come from such monitoring by an independent third party.

A good example of such a system was the SEADOCS project developed at Chase Manhattan Bank,[37] abandoned some years ago. This system was intended to overcome the problem of the multiple sale of cargoes at sea, when the shipping documents often fail to reach the ultimate purchaser until some time after the goods themselves. The written documents were deposited with the SEADOCS Registry and all subsequent transfers made electronically. These transfers were authenticated by three tests:

(a)   Each party's message must be confirmed by at least one or more other messages.

(b)   Messages are re-filed to the presumed sender and must be re-acknowledged.

(c)   Each message has a header code which is unique to sender and message as it must contain an element from the prior sender and from the computer acknowledgement message ...[38]

If there was any dispute as to whether a message was sent or as to its contents, the SEADOCS Registry records would be available as evidence of what actually occurred.[39] The Bolero system[40] is a more recent and sophisticated example of a system which provides authentication via an intermediary's records, which also operates in the international trade arena.

It is quite feasible to set up such a system on a less specialised intermediary system, or to use any features of the system which have evidential value, even if they were not designed with authentication in mind.[41] However, a log

37. See A. Urbach, 'The Electronic Presentation and Transfer of Shipping Documents' in R. Goode (ed), *Electronic Banking — the Legal Implications*, London: Institute of Bankers & Centre for Commercial Law Studies, 1985, p. 111.
38. Ibid., p. 121.
39. Other systems fulfilling the same function are found in the field of electronic banking — see A. Arora, *Electronic Banking and the Law*, London: IBC, 1988, ch. 7; Reed, *Electronic Finance Law*, Cambridge: Woodhead Faulkner, 1991.
40. See www.boleroltd.com.
41. It is possible to compel the production of information in the hands of a third party by serving a *subpoena duces tecum*, but this can only be done on notice and the court has jurisdiction to refuse the order if it would be unreasonable, oppressive or otherwise not proper. In any event it will ensure that the third party is properly reimbursed by the parties for his expenses, which in such a case would be substantial — see *Senior v Holdsworth, ex parte ITN* [1976] QB 23.

would only be useful as evidence if it contained some record of the message's contents; otherwise it could only prove that *some* message was sent by one party and received by the other, and where there has been a series of messages it will not be much help in proving that the one in question was sent and received. The technology which would enable providers of communications networks to retain this information already exists, and the facility will no doubt be introduced wherever there is sufficient demand to make it economically viable.

Where the network operator is unable to provide authentication evidence, for example in Internet communications, the necessary authentication evidence should be found in the document itself. This already happens to some extent with telex and fax communications, as in each case the transmitting and receiving machines send messages identifying themselves. It could be argued that, so far as the transmitting machine is concerned, these messages amount to a signature. In *Clipper Maritime Ltd v Shirlstar Container Transport Ltd (the 'Anemone')* [1987] 1 Lloyd's Rep 546 Staughton J, considering whether a telex might constitute a guarantee in writing and signed for the purpose of the Statute of Frauds, said obiter:

> I reached a provisional conclusion in the course of the argument that the answerback of the sender of a telex would constitute a signature, whilst that of the receiver would not since it only authenticates the document and does not convey approval of the contents.[42]

However, the point was in the end not relevant and he did not pursue the matter further. If he had, three points should have been recognised:

(a)   The identification messages of telex and fax machines only identify the *machine*, not the sender.
(b)   It is quite possible to program a telex or fax device to send a false identification message.
(c)   If the message is stored on disk it is possible to edit the contents and amend the identification message to take account of the alteration.

In the case in question there was no dispute that the telex had been sent nor as to its contents, so only the first point would be relevant to the question of signature. If in another case there were to be such a dispute, all three points would weigh strongly against any suggestion that the telex could be treated as signed.[43]

What is really required, therefore, is some method of authenticating the message while permitting the sender and recipient to store it on their own computers. This might be achieved through cryptographic techniques.

---

42. At p. 554.
43. On this point in relation to email see B. Amory and Y. Poullet, '*Computers in the law of evidence — a comparative approach in civil and common law systems*', (1987) 3 *Computer Law and Practice* 114, p. 118.

Cryptography for authentication The fact that electronic messages are transmitted as a stream of digital information makes it possible to use cryptographic techniques to authenticate a message. This is achieved by performing a mathematical function on the message content, or part of it, which could only have been effected by the sender. To be effective, the encrypted version must be producible by the sender alone, and any attempt to change the content of the message and re-encrypt it must in practical terms be impossible. Encryption techniques are a fundamental part of the technology of digital signatures (see 10.2.3.1 below).

The two main cryptographic candidates for this purpose are the Data Encryption Standard (DES)[44] and the RSA[45] cipher. DES is normally effected in hardware, and requires a 64-bit key which is common to sender and recipient and kept secret from all others, which is used to scramble the message to such a degree that it is computationally infeasible[46] to unscramble it without knowing the key. The fact that a message is DES encrypted is therefore extremely strong evidence that it could have emanated only from one or other of the key holders. This, however, does not authenticate it fully as both parties have the key. Either could alter the contents of the message and then re-encrypt it. The alteration would be undetectable, and the court would still be left with two messages, each claimed to be authentic.

In order for encryption to be effective for authentication purposes it must be a 'one-way function', i.e., for a message from A to B, A must be able to encrypt and B to decrypt, but B must be unable to re-encrypt the message. This is possible within DES using complicated techniques such as the Lamport-Diffie signature[47] or the Rabin signature.[48] All these techniques suffer from two drawbacks; (a) they are difficult to implement and require complicated validation procedures, and more importantly (b) each message requires a unique key to effect the signature. Although they are theoretically capable of producing an acceptable signature which authenticates the document, the practical difficulties of administration and of devising and recording a number of unique keys every time a signature is required make DES inappropriate for regular use.

Probably the best candidates for digital signatures are 'public key' cryptosystems such as RSA. These cryptosystems were devised so as to enable secret communications without the two parties having to agree on an encryption method and exchange keys. This cypher requires three numbers: N, K_p (the

---

44. National Bureau of Standards FIPS Publication 64 (1977), ANSI X3.92-1981.
45. Named after its inventors — see R.L. Rivest, A. Shamir and L. Adleman, '*A method of obtaining digital signatures and public key cryptosystems*', (1978) 21 *Communications of the ACM* 120.
46. Computational infeasibility means that although the message can in theory be decoded, the amount of time this would take is so large that for practical purposes the encryption can be regarded as secure. For DES the time required to break the code using a computer that checks one potential key per microsecond, operating 24 hours a day, is on average over 1,000 years — see B. Beckett, *Introduction to Cryptology*, Oxford: Blackwell, 1988, p. 277.
47. D. Longley and M. Shain, *Data and Computer Security — dictionary of standard concepts and terms*, New York: Macmillan, 1987, p. 193.
48. Ibid., p. 281.

public key, used for encryption) and K_s (the secret key, used for decryption). The numbers N and K_p are published to form the recipient's public key, but K_s is kept secret. The sender of a message encrypts it by raising the digital form of the message to the power K_p and then calculating the result modulus N (i.e., the remainder when (message) raised to the power of K_p is successively divided by N until it will no longer divide). The recipient decrypts the message using the formula (encrypted message) to the power K_s modulus N. Because of the way K_p, K_s and N are derived it is computationally infeasible to calculate K_s knowing only K_p and N.

Because the encryption formula is symmetrical it is possible to encrypt a message using the sender's private key K_s and decrypt it with K_p, and thus effect a digital signature. The sender encrypts his message using K_s. When it is received, the recipient decrypts the message using the sender's public key, K_p and N. As only the sender could have encrypted the message, if both encrypted and plaintext versions are produced in court the judge can check the identity of the sender by decrypting the message and checking it against the plaintext version. This also authenticates the contents of the message, as if the recipient alters the contents he will not be able to re-encrypt the message so that it decrypts with K_p and N. In the present state of cryptological knowledge, provided N is sufficiently large it is harder to forge an RSA digital signature than a written one. In civil cases the burden of proof is merely the balance of probabilities, and the mathematical basis of the RSA cipher is clearly strong enough to discharge that burden.[49]

Authentication in practice   Authentication in practice may be easier than this discussion suggests. English criminal law imposes a high standard of proof[50] and yet in *R v Spiby* (1990) 91 Cr App R 186, the English Court of Appeal was prepared to presume that a computer was recording evidence accurately when its operator (a hotel manager) testified that he was unaware of any problems in operation, and in the absence of any evidence by the defendant that there was any question of malfunction. This approach was approved by the House of Lords in *R v Shephard* [1993] AC 380. It is likely, therefore, that authenticity will be presumed if:

(a)   the user can produce a human witness to testify that the system was operating properly at the relevant time; and

(b)   the other party to the litigation is unable to adduce evidence to counter this presumption.

---

49. If N has more than 200 digits it is calculated that, using a computer which eliminated one potential factor of N every microsecond, the task would on average take longer than the expected lifetime of the universe — see B. Beckett, *Introduction to Cryptology*, Oxford: Blackwell, 1988, ch. 9. Note, though, that it is possible to check keys at a much faster rate than this, but that increases in computing power can be countered by increasing the key length. An increase of one bit in key length doubles the effective time required to break the encryption of that message.

50. I.e., proof beyond a reasonable doubt, as opposed to proof on the balance of probabilities as required in civil cases.

In order to ensure that an appropriate audit trail exists, and to produce evidence which will tend to authenticate records of electronic messages, it is common to provide in Interchange Agreements what records the parties will keep, and whether particular categories of message are to be acknowledged by the receiving party (including provisions on what that acknowledgement should consist of). These records will assist in resolving disputes over the existence or content of electronic messages.

10.2.3 Formalities in the underlying transaction

It has already been pointed out (see 10.2.1.3 above) that certain types of contract require particular formalities to be observed if they are to be enforceable. The most common of these are that the contract must be made or evidenced in writing or in a document, and that it must be signed.

10.2.3.1 *Writing, documents and signatures*

General problems Unless there is legislation which specifically provides to the contrary,[51] 'writing' under English law requires the communication to be in some visible form.[52] However, if all that is required is a 'document'[53] then, unless this is also defined in the legislation or case law governing the transaction to require visible form, there seems no reason why it might not be produced electronically.[54] Most other countries' laws also require certain types of transaction to be made in writing and signed. This is often limited to sales of real property, but in Greece a wider range of commercial transactions require written and signed documents. France has a particular problem in that transactions carried out by persons other than *traders* need written proof if their value exceeds 5,000 francs.[55] This presents a problem for the retail use of electronic messaging, but can also affect commercial use because professionals such as architects are not classified as traders.

In an attempt to deal with problems of formalities, it is worth including a provision in the electronic commerce contract which provides:

(a) That all communications between the parties are deemed to be in writing.

(b) That use of the prescribed authentication procedures is deemed to be the signature of the appropriate party.

Whether the first provision is legally effective must be open to doubt — as most national laws are adamant that 'writing' demands visible marks on a

---

51. E.g., art. 1(4)(b) of the Unidroit Convention on International Factoring 1988 defines notice in writing to include 'any other telecommunication capable of being reproduced in tangible form'.
52. Interpretation Act 1978, sch. 1.
53. In civil proceedings this is defined as 'anything in which information of any description is recorded': Civil Evidence Act 1995, s. 13.
54. See Bergsten and Goode, 'Legal questions and problems to be overcome', in Thomsen & Wheble, *Trading with EDI: the Legal Issues*, London: IBC, 1989, pp. 136–138.
55. French Civil Code, art. 1341.

physical carrier it might seem to be equivalent to providing that 'for the purposes of this contract, night shall be deemed to be day'. However, in the common law jurisdictions at least, a provision of this type may raise an estoppel between the parties to the Interchange Agreement, and thus prevent either of them from denying the validity of an electronic transaction on the ground that the law requires the transaction to have been made in writing. This would be the case even though both parties know that under their law the electronic messages do *not* amount to writing.[56] It should be noted, though, that:

(a)   The estoppel will not bind a third party, who will be able to plead the lack of writing as a defence and, as a corollary, will not be able to found his own action on the estoppel.
(b)   The estoppel will not be effective if the result would be to declare valid a transaction which is in fact *void* according to the law for lack of formalities.[57] This will not be so, however, if the requirement for writing is imposed by the law solely to protect the parties to the transaction, as opposed to the public interest.[58]

By contrast, the second provision stands a good chance of being effective if national law does not specifically demand that signatures be in manuscript form. For example, because English law permits signatures to be typewritten or made via a stamp,[59] there seems no reason to insist on a handwritten signature. Attention should instead be focussed on the purpose of the signature; to authenticate the message as originating from the purported sender. If this is a correct statement of the function of a signature under English law[60] cryptography (see 10.2.2.2 above) offers the possibility of producing digital signatures that are more difficult to forge than hand-writing.[61]

56. 'The full facts may be known to both parties; but if, even knowing those facts to the full, they are clearly enough shown to have assumed a different state of facts *as between themselves* for the purposes of a particular transaction, then their assumption will be treated, as between them, as true, in proceedings arising out of the transaction. The claim of the party raising the estoppel is, not that he believed the assumed version of the facts was true, but that he believed (and agreed) that it should be *treated as true*'. Spencer Bower & Turner, *The Law Relating to Estoppel by Representation* 3rd edn, London: Butterworths, 1977, p. 160, citing *Newis* v *General Accident Fire & Life Assurance Corporation* (1910) 11 CLR 620 at p. 636 per Isaacs J (High Court of Australia).
57. See, e.g., *Swallow & Pearson* v *Middlesex County Council* [1953] 1 All ER 580.
58. Spencer Bower & Turner, *The Law Relating to Estoppel by Representation*, 3rd edn, London: Butterworths, 1977, pp. 142–144.
59. See, e.g., *Chapman* v *Smethurst* [1909] 1 KB 927.
60. See *Goodman* v *J. Eban Ltd* [1954] 1 QB 550, [1954] 1 All ER 763; *London County Council* v *Vitamins, Ltd*; *London County Council* v *Agricultural Food Products Ltd* [1955] 2 QB 218, [1955] 2 All ER 229; *Ringham* v *Hackett and Walmsley* (1980)10 Legal Decisions Affecting Bankers 206; *Bartletts de Reya (A Firm)* v *Byrne*, The Times, 14 January 1983, 127 SJ 69.
61. Digital signatures are mathematical functions of the digital form of a message. In order to act effectively as a signature they must be producible only by the sender. In theory, all digital signatures are capable of forgery — what gives them their effectiveness is that it is *computationally infeasible* to do so.

Digital signatures   The issue of authentication, and consequently the use of digital signatures, is vital for two reasons. Parties who wish to engage in electronic commerce and enter into an electronic contract will not usually have any means of verifying the other's identity. Quite aside from the issue of establishing the validity of each other's purported identity to their mutual satisfaction the parties must have some way of authenticating or signing contracts in an electronic form as evidence of intent if nothing else. These two requirements are separate and need to be treated as such.

Parties can agree between themselves whether or not they will accept a data string[62] as evidence of intent. In effect they can themselves agree on the validity of an electronic signature between themselves. However their agreement will not bind a third party unless that third party agrees to be so bound.

Though the parties might agree between themselves to accept a digital signature, the signature itself may not necessarily prove to be acceptable before a court. The uncertainty on this point has so far proved to be a major stumbling block to the widespread use of digital signatures. In order to be effective parties must be able to sign documents electronically or digitally and to enforce these signatures before a court of law. The digital or electronic signatures must be as acceptable as hard copy signatures and accorded the same rights before a court of law.

In order to determine whether digital signatures may be used the situation regarding hard copy signatures must be examined to determine whether it is possible to use digital versions. Unfortunately the situation regarding hard copy signatures is not particularly clear. Though it is possible to define what a signature is in civil jurisdictions, common law jurisdictions cannot do so. Instead they look more to the function of the signature for a particular class of document.[63]

Specifically the signatures must have validity before a court of law. As with ensuring the sufficiency of electronic data or electronic messages for contract formation, this is an area which the parties cannot deal with between themselves. Regulatory intervention is the most effective way of ensuring that the electronic form of a signature is held to be legally valid and so treated as a hard copy equivalent.

The starting point for most electronic signature laws is art. 7(1) of the UNCITRAL Model Law on Electronic Commerce 1996, which provides:

Where the law requires a signature of a person, that requirement is met in relation to a data message if:

   (a)   a method is used to identify that person and to indicate that person's approval of the information contained in the data message; and

   (b)   that method is as reliable as was appropriate for the purpose for which the data message was generated or communicated, in the light of all the circumstances, including any relevant agreement.

---

62. In other words a digital or electronic signature.
63. A signature is only recognised as such if it fulfils the functions of a signature that are required by that document.

This text does not mandate any particular technological signature method. However, the current trend in laws and legislative proposals is to link the question of signature validity with certification of identity, and to introduce licensing schemes for Certification Authorities. This enables national law to recognise as valid ID certificates issued by a foreign Certification Authority by approving the relevant licensing scheme.

Over the next few years a global system of digital signature law will largely have been put in place. Already there is legislation in Germany,[64] Singapore[65] and numerous US states,[66] to name but a few of the jurisdictions which have introduced legislation. The general shape of the global digital signature regime is already becoming clear:

(a) An important element is the establishment of a digital signature infrastructure, in which bodies known as Certification Authorities take evidence of a person's identity (e.g., by requiring production of a passport or identity card), and then issue an electronic ID certificate which links that person to his digital signature key. In many instances voluntary licensing schemes are introduced, and a digital signature which refers to an ID certificate issued by a licensed Certification Authority may be given greater legal weight.[67]

(c) The second part of the regime is the introduction of laws which define as valid[68] any digital signature which is supported by an ID certificate issued by a qualifying Certification Authority. These laws may be technology-neutral, in the sense that they do not prescribe a particular technical standard which must be adopted but merely describe the requirements which a certificate and its issuing Certification Authority must meet. Some laws, however, mandate the use of particular technical standards.[69]

---

64. Digital Signature Act (Signaturgesetz) and Ordinance (Signaturverordnung) 1997.
65. Electronic Transactions Act 1998.
66. A useful introduction to the US approaches is set out in the American Bar Association Digital Signature Guidelines, Chicago: ABA, 1996.
67. See arts 2 and 5 of EU Directive 1999/93/EC on a Community framework for electronic signatures, OJ L13 p. 12, 19 January 2000.
68. Note that the UK's Electronic Communications Act 2000 does not follow this trend. Although it is likely to result in a voluntary licensing scheme for Certification Authorities (see www.fei.org.uk/fei/news/newintro.htm for details of the scheme project), it does not specifically validate resulting digital signatures. Instead, clause 7(1) provides only that such a signature shall be 'be admissible in evidence in relation to any question as to the authenticity of the communication or data or as to the integrity of the communication or data'. This approach in practice produces the result that an electronic signature is legally equivalent to a handwritten signature because under English law a handwritten signature is merely an evidential method of authenticating a document — see Reed, *Digital Information Law: electronic documents and requirements of form*, London: CCLS, 1996, ch. 5. However, the UK solution will be less satisfactory to digital signature users than that adopted in art. 5(1) of Directive 1999/93/EC on a Community framework for electronic signatures, OJ L13 p. 12, 19 January 2000, which in addition to making them admissible as evidence provides that certain types of certified signature shall 'satisfy the legal requirements of a signature in relation to data in electronic form in the same manner as a handwritten signature satisfies those requirements in relation to paper-based data'.
69. E.g., Utah Digital Signature Rules (r. 154–10 of the Utah Commerce, Corporations and Commercial Code) r. 301(4)(a); German Digital Signature Act (Signaturgesetz) § 14(4),

10.2.3.2   Record keeping requirements   A user is likely to see little benefit from adopting electronic commerce if the record keeping requirements of its national law or the law of its trading partner force him to use paper documents in order to comply with the law. As a general rule, record keeping laws are mandatory, and if they prohibit electronic record keeping there is little that can be done. However, if electronic commerce is possible under a country's record keeping laws, then in respect of EDI the Interchange Agreement should set out what records each party is to keep, and the information that each is to supply to the other, so as to enable both parties to keep their records in accordance with the law.

The accounting laws of Europe fall broadly into two types: those which permit, or at least do not prohibit, the keeping of accounts in electronic form; and those which require accounts to be maintained on paper. This split is, interestingly, largely geographical. The northern States tend to fall into the first category, while the southern States (with the exception of Spain) fall into the second.

Thus Denmark has accounting laws which specifically facilitate computerised record keeping, requiring only that the annual accounts should be in hard copy form,[70] and Ireland[71] and the UK[72] specifically permit computerised accounting. Belgium still retains some hard copy requirements, but the trend is clearly towards permitting the use of electronic documents. This is not universal in the Northern European countries, however, as in some cases there is still a legacy of accounting or tax laws which require the production or receipt of paper (see below).

In the southern States, accounting laws generally require the books of account to be maintained on paper. France, stretching from the North Sea to the Mediterranean, is a hybrid case. Electronic accounts have been permitted since 1983,[73] but in the end need to be printed out to comply with the law. In Italy accounting records can probably be kept electronically, though this is an interpretation of the law which has not been tested in the courts, but it is clear that the information in those records will still need to be printed out in order to produce the compulsory hard copy books.[74]

Greece is the most extreme case, with very complicated and formal accounting requirements. In order to ensure these are complied with when accounts are computerised, accounting software is subject to stringent regulation and software suppliers can be fined if they fail to comply with the law.[75] Computerisation of accounting in Greece is unusual in that it is merely an automated method of producing the compulsory hard copy books.

Most of the countries which permit accounts to be kept electronically do so without restriction, other than that the accounts must satisfy the com-

---

continued
    German Digital Signature Ordinance (Signaturverordnung, made under § 19 Digital Signature Act 1997, in force 1 November 1997) § 16(6).
70. Danish Book-Keeping Act 1986 and Instruction No. 598 of 1990.
71. Irish companies (Amendment) Act 1977, s. 4.
72. UK Companies Act 1985, s. 723(1).
73. French Decree of 29 November 1983, art 2(2).
74. Italian Civil Code arts 2214 *et seq.*
75. Greek Code of Fiscal Elements, arts 22–25.

pany's auditors. However, German law contains stringent requirements to ensure that the accounting software prevents subsequent alteration, and in Belgium formal accounts must be kept in hard copy form, though working accounts can be electronic.[76] Belgian law therefore contains special provisions which allow credit institutions to keep bank account records, records of insurance policies etc. in electronic form and prove them by producing copies.

The laws of some European States, however, have not been amended to permit modern forms of book keeping. The need to maintain printed books of account was restated recently in Italy in a Supreme Court decision,[77] and in Portugal a number of categories of obligatory accounts must be kept on paper.[78] Some categories of books must be sealed and authenticated by a government official before they can be used in the courts or government offices so as to comply with the Portuguese Stamp Tax Act.[79] However, the Portuguese Government appears to be attempting to interpret existing laws to permit electronic record keeping, although the compulsory categories of paper records still remain on the statute book. Articles 10 and 11 of the Norwegian VAT Act require sales documents to be issued in writing and in duplicate. As no input VAT can be deducted in the absence of such a document[80] this provision is a formidable barrier to the adoption of electronic commerce within this jurisdiction. In addition, Norwegian law requires annual accounts to be presented on paper with sequentially numbered pages,[81] and in Sweden a choice must be made between maintaining vouchers (such as invoices) or accounting records in electronic form.[82] Even in Austria, which does not formally require accounting records to be kept in any particular form, the tax authorities can require printouts at any time and the annual accounts must be signed,[83] which implies a manuscript signature on paper and therefore hard copy accounts. Article 11 of the Austrian VAT Act also requires invoices to be 'documents', which demands that they be in hard copy format. However, the Ministry of Finance has ameliorated the harshness of this rule by permitting regular EDI users to produce summary invoices as hard copy for VAT purposes. The same will probably hold true for electronic commerce providers in general.

UK legislation contains extensive requirements for writing and signatures,[84] though in general these apply to communications with governmental and

76. Belgian Act of 17 July 1975.
77. Cass. 16 November 1991 (Italy).
78. Portuguese Commercial Law Act 1988, art. 25.
79. Portuguese Stamp Tax Act, arts 130, 195 and 196.
80. Norwegian VAT Act, art. 25.
81. Norwegian Accountancy Act, art. 6.
82. Recommendation U 89:2 Bokföringsnämnden, the Swedish official commission of accountancy, whose recommendations have legal force. If the choice to keep accounting records in electronic form is made, they must be stored in such a way that a printout can be produced at any time.
83. Austrian Commercial Code, art. 194.
84. See generally Reed, *Digital Information Law: electronic documents and requirements of form*, London: CCLS, 1996.

administrative bodies rather than commercial communications. The Electronic Communications Act 2000, section 8 will confer on ministers the power to repeal many of these provisions, although as yet no proposals for what should be repealed have been produced.

10.2.4 Compliance with national laws

In theory there is no limit on the circumstances in which jurisdiction might claim to apply its laws to the electronic commerce activities of a supplier from a different jurisdiction, although practical enforcement of those laws against a foreign enterprise may be difficulty or impossible. However, governments usually attempt to limit the extraterritorial effect of their laws through the principle of comity, which requires that a state should not claim to apply its legislation to persons within another state unless it is reasonable to do so. The standard approach to maintaining comity is to apply a state's laws only to *activities* undertaken within the state, but determining the location where electronic commerce activities take place is extremely difficult. Traditional tests for localisation of commercial activities look for particular trigger events, the most common of which include:

(a)   the place of delivery of products sold;
(b)   the place where services were performed;
(c)   the place where a purchaser took steps towards concluding a contract; and
(d)   whether the supplier 'targeted' the jurisdiction in question.

All of these are largely metaphysical concepts where products and services are supplied on-line, or where products are advertised and contracts concluded via a website.

Increasingly, there is a recognition that attempts to localise electronic commerce activities are inappropriate, and that some alternative basis for maintaining comity must be found. The most promising alternative seems to be that of accepting 'country of origin' regulation, coupled with an appropriate degree of harmonisation or convergence of national laws.

The most striking example of country of origin regulation is found in arts 3 and 4 of Directive 2000/31/EC on electronic commerce, which provide:

Article 3
1.   Each Member State shall ensure that the Information Society services provided by a service provider established on its territory comply with the national provisions applicable in the Member State in question which fall within the coordinated field.
2.   Member States may not, for reasons falling within the coordinated field, restrict the freedom to provide Information Society services from another Member State.
    . . .

Article 4
1. Member States shall ensure that the taking up and pursuit of the activity of an Information Society service provider may not be made subject to prior authorisation or any other requirement having equivalent effect.
. . .

A number of exceptions to this principle are set out in the Annex to the Directive, but its general effect can be expressed quite simply. An electronic commerce business in one Member State is free to do business with residents of every other Member State provided that it complies with its own national laws, even if its activities would contravene the laws of the purchaser's Member State. Thus, for example, a UK electronic commerce business cannot be subject to action for breach of Germany's Act Against Unfair Competition simply on the ground that its website is visible to German customers and it does business with German consumers.

This adoption of the country of origin principle is only possible because of the large degree of harmonisation which has already taken place in fields such as consumer protection, and because the Directive's other provisions on commercial communications (arts 6 and 7) and the provision of information about the business (art. 5) introduce common controls on the potentially controversial aspects of these activities. How far the principle will be adopted on a global scale depends very much on the degree to which the economic pressures exerted by electronic commerce result in convergence of these aspects of other jurisdictions' laws.

10.3 BUSINESS-TO-BUSINESS ELECTRONIC COMMERCE

Business-to-business electronic commerce has, until recently, been undertaken solely via proprietary networks, and is usually referred to as Electronic Data Interchange (EDI). Open networks, and in particular the Internet, are increasingly becoming the communications medium of choice for business, and the term EDI is likely to fall gradually into disuse. This has not yet occurred, however, and so in this section the term EDI is used for convenience of expression.[85]

EDI is, at the simplest level, nothing more than a technology for exchanging information. One computer is linked to another and a stream of data is sent across the link. At this level, the only distinction from, say, a fax message is that the recipient can easily edit his copy.

Where EDI becomes interesting, both commercially and legally, is if the messages are structured in such a way that they can be processed automatically.[86] The most common use of such messages is to carry out trade,

---

85. The replacement term has not yet been settled upon, although 'B2B electronic commerce' (business-to-business) appears to be growing in use. Its equivalent for consumer transactions is 'B2C'.
86. This is somewhat different to networking methods, such as the Internet where a large proportion of messages are meant to be processed by the human mind. However, the technologies exist that can easily be put into use to allow messages to be structured in such

particularly international trade, and it is in this sense that the term EDI is most commonly used. This also gives rise to the alternative term 'paperless trading', which is particularly common in the United States.[87]

Structured EDI messages offer their users two potential benefits, benefits which can be of immense commercial value:

(a)   The abolition (or near abolition) of the physical, paper documents which previously effected the transaction. Estimates of the costs involved in producing and processing this paper range as high as 10 percent of the value of the goods.

(b)   The complete automation of the ordering/delivery/payment cycle.

10.3.1   Replacing paper

To take an example, suppose a motor manufacturer has a need to purchase parts from a supplier. In a paper-based system a human being examines the stock inventory, decides which parts are needed, and informs the purchasing department. The purchasing department issues an order to the supplier. Payment may need to be effected through a documentary credit, necessitating further communications between the manufacturer, one or more banks, and the supplier. Once the supplier has the parts ready to ship he must engage a carrier, thus generating further documentation which must be processed by all the parties involved in the transaction.

The EDI ideal is quite different. Here the manufacturer's stock control system automatically generates the order when stocks of any part are low. The order is sent without any human intervention to the supplier's computer, which accepts the order and commences manufacture. The payment mechanism is set up in a similar way, again with little or no human intervention, as is the contract of carriage. To perform the contract the only physical movement is that of the goods from the supplier's premises to those of the manufacturer. All the messages which would have been placed on paper and circulated along the chain of banks to the manufacturer are replaced by structured EDI messages which are processed automatically, the relevant portions being copied to accounting and other computer systems.

This technology exists and is in use, though not in quite such a perfect form as the example above. The benefits it brings are increasing the pressure for its adoption, as large customers force their suppliers to adopt EDI. The time saved in the ordering process makes 'Just in Time' ordering possible, cutting stocks held to the bare minimum. It also offers the flexibility of production seen in the Japanese motor industry where a production line can be switched from one model to another in a very short space of time. The manpower savings are also potentially large, as EDI prevents the redundant manual processing of information in stock control, purchasing and accounts departments.

---

continued
        a way that they too can be processed automatically. Not only is this increasingly being used
        by interactive sites on the Internet but it is possible to create a virtual private network across
        the Internet that behaves in a manner similar to EDI.
87.   See, e.g., Wright, *The Law of Electronic Commerce*, Boston: Little, Brown & Co., 1991.

To achieve this aim, the legal relationships set up by lawyers must make it possible to carry out the transaction without needing to generate any paper. Whether this is possible or not will depend very much on the legal barriers which are posed by the national laws involved, and whether those barriers can be surmounted by provisions in the Interchange Agreement (see 10.3.4 below). If the provisions of national laws make it necessary to document discrete parts of the transaction on paper or, worst of all, require duplication of, e.g., invoices by generating them as both EDI messages and hard copy, the client will need to be advised so that he can decide whether the use of EDI for that transaction is appropriate.

10.3.2   EDI and networks

Whilst it is possible to set up dedicated EDI links with each of one's trading partners, this rarely makes sense in practice. The volume of communications is likely to be too small to be economical. For this reason most EDI users communicate via a Value Added Network Service (VAN), although as mentioned above the Internet is increasingly favoured as a communications technology. Most of the issues discussed in this section do not apply to Internet communications because there is no identifiable network provider who can be made responsible for elements of the communications process.

In the VAN model the user's computer system generates the messages to the network, rather than directly to the intended recipient. The network's computer systems ensure, using the address information which is part of the message structure,[88] that the message is delivered to the addressee's computer. The delivery may be near-instantaneous or may take several hours, depending on the number of time zones which separate the parties and the level of service contracted for. In most cases there will be an element of 'store and forward' which, as we have seen, raises potential problems when forming contracts using EDI.

Additionally, the VAN may not be the only network involved, as the technology exists for a sender using one VAN to communicate with an addressee using another via a 'gateway' between the two VANs. The address segment of the message contains the information required to route the message to the gateway, and thence to the addressee across his own VAN. Linking VANs in this way raises interesting liability questions, as the nature of the legal relationship between the sender and the addressee's VAN is unclear.

10.3.3   Network agreements

The legal issues raised by EDI[89] fall into two basic categories; those that arise between the user and the network provider(s) and those that arise between

---

88. See Walden (ed), *EDI and the Law*, London: Blenheim OnLine, 1989, Appendix E for examples of message structures.
89. These problems have been examined on an international scale in TEDIS, *The Legal Position of the Member States with respect to Electronic Data Interchange*, Brussels: EC Commission 1991, and subsequent publications under the project.

users themselves. The relationship between a user and the VAN to which he connects is primarily contractual. Sa'id Mosteshar identifies four main responsibilities of the network provider:

(a) Conveyance of the message in the correct format and protocol.
(b) Safeguarding against corruption of the message.
(c) Securing that the message is conveyed to the recipient.
(d) Preserving the confidentiality and security of the message.[90]

The method by which these responsibilities are to be carried out will largely be covered by the User Handbook, the technical manual for connecting to the VAN. It is most likely that the contract between user and network provider will contain an obligation that the user's communications with other users of the network should comply with the technical and operational requirements of the User Handbook, but even if this is not expressly stated it is likely that the users will be contractually bound to each other under the principle in *Clarke* v *Dunraven* [1897] AC 59. The effect of the agreement will be to create a contract between each user and all the other users, either because entering into the agreement amounts to a standing offer to future users to be bound which is accepted by joining the system, or perhaps more logically, by impliedly giving the system provider authority to contract as agent on behalf of the user.

The contract may also make express provision for the level and quality of service to be provided, though in most cases VAN operators will seek to exclude much, if not all, of their liability for breach of these obligations.[91] These exclusions will be subject to the Unfair Contract Terms Act 1977, and may also be limited in scope by the terms of the network operator's telecommunications licence.

The VAN operator's contractual liability to the user will primarily be based on the Supply of Goods and Services Act 1982, s. 13 which will imply into the contract an obligation to take reasonable care in supplying the service contracted for. This obligation may be breached in a number of ways:

(a) if the system goes down;
(b) if a message is not transmitted;
(c) if it is sent to the wrong person;
(d) if it is intercepted or copied by an unauthorised person; or
(e) if it is garbled in transmission.

---

90. Mosteshar, '*Liability issues of EDI*', in Walden (ed), *EDI and the Law*, London: Blenheim OnLine 1989, p. 50.
91. One of the few exceptions to this practice is Swift, the Society for Worldwide Interbank Financial Telecommunications. Swift is a closed network for electronic funds transfer, used only by the banks which own it or organisations sponsored by a member. Swift limits its liability to 3,000 million Belgian francs per loss or series of losses caused by Swift's negligence, error or omission — see Petre, '*Network Providers*' (1990) 7 *Computer Law & Practice*, p. 8, note 18.

In each case, however, the system provider will only be liable for breach of the implied term if the problem was caused by a lack of care. Such negligence might take one of two forms; a failure to be sufficiently careful in selecting the hardware and software which comprises the system, or a failure to take sufficient care in operating the system. Provided the hardware and software are from reputable sources, then unless the system provider is also the designer of the hardware or software a defect in either will not normally render him in breach.

Although there is no doubt that this term will be implied into the contract between the system provider and each user, it is less clear that the users are providing services to each other. It is probable that their contractual liability to other users, in the absence of a formal interchange agreement, is limited to observing the terms of their agreement with the VAN operator.

10.3.4 Interchange agreements

The purpose of an interchange agreement is to set out the terms on which the communicating parties agree to undertake EDI.[92] It is important to make a distinction between the interchange agreement, which deals only with the details of the communication process, and the underlying commercial trans-action such as a sale of goods, which is entered into and performed using that communication process. Although in the United States it is not uncommon for both to be dealt with in the same agreement, this practice arose from the way EDI has developed there, through large customers forcing their suppliers to trade with them via EDI. In Europe the practice has been rather different. Industry groupings such as ODETTE[93] or CEFIC[94] have developed proto-cols for EDI, and this has focussed attention on the communications aspect of EDI rather than the underlying transaction. This separation makes theoretical and practical sense, as EDI can be used for many different types of underlying transactions without changing the agreement on interchange.

As the purpose of the interchange agreement is to bind the parties to a particular, structured form of communication, there are a number of issues which it must address. Because different industry sectors will inevitably have different specific requirements, no universal standard is achievable. However, a number of organisations have produced model interchange agreements which provide a useful starting point for negotiations, and on an international level the International Chamber of Commerce has produced the *Uniform Rules of Conduct for Interchange of Trade Data by Teletransmission* (the UNCID Rules). Within the EC, DG XIII initiated the TEDIS[95] project which examined the technical and legal issues involved in EDI. As part of its work,

---

92. The Interchange and User agreements inherent in EDI set this system apart from the general use of the Internet where agreements to cover the use and provision of networking services cover only the access from the user to the provider's network and usually warrant nothing further. With EDI the provider can guarantee a level of service and messaging reliability. Without the use of VPN technologies Internet Service Providers can only warrant the performance of their own systems and not those of other ISPs.
93. The motor industry.
94. The chemicals industry.
95. *Trade Electronic Data Interchange Systems*, OJ L 285, 8 October 1987.

TEDIS produced a model interchange agreement whose suggested provisions reflect best practice among the EDI community.[96]

Although there is insufficient space in this chapter for a detailed examination of interchange agreements[97] it is useful to set out the main areas which such an agreement should cover:

(a)   A requirement to adhere to the technical procedures of the chosen communication link. This is normally done by reference to the VAN User Handbook. Where the Internet is used, these matters will need to be dealt with in detail in the Interchange Agreement rather than being left to a third party document.

(b)   Agreement on a particular protocol for the message format, e.g., an EDIFACT message.

(c)   Agreement on acknowledgements of messages and any confirmations of their content that are required.

(d)   Agreement on which of the parties takes responsibility for the completeness and accuracy of the communication. As we have already seen, it is likely that the parties will wish the received version of a message to be operative, rather than that transmitted. For this reason it will be important that the technical safeguards listed in (a) to (c) above are incorporated to ensure that transmission takes place and that errors are immediately detected. Whilst message corruption is almost certain not to produce an apparently sensible message with an entirely different meaning, it is quite conceivable that a £ symbol could be replaced by a $ symbol, or that an entire block could be lost. As, in general, it is the received version which is operative, the onus to ensure correct transmission must be on the sender.

(e)   Agreement on security and confidentiality.

(f)   Agreement on data logs and the storage of messages.

(g)   Agreement on which country's law is to apply to the communications process.

10.4   BUSINESS-TO-CONSUMER ELECTRONIC COMMERCE

Commercial electronic commerce, where both parties to any contract are businesses, is the easiest situation to deal with as the parties can in general agree to what they wish with few constraints. In general where two or more commercial entities enter into agreements at arms' length then they can usually agree to whatever terms they so wish. The position can differ considerably with other types of contract, notably where one of the parties acts as a consumer.

Consumer protection legislation, such as that commonly found within EU Member States,[98] often imposes limits on the terms and conditions that may be excluded or varied and these cannot be overridden by agreement. Any

---

96. European Commission Recommendation of 19 October 1994 relating to the legal aspects of electronic data interchange (94/820/EC), OJ L338, 1994.

97. For more detail see Walden (ed), *EDI and the Law*, London: Blenheim OnLine, 1989, chs 5, 6.

98. See the Council Directive 93/13/EEC of 5 April 1993 on unfair terms in consumer contracts. This is implemented within the United Kingdom by the Unfair Terms in Consumer Contracts Regulations 1994, SI 1994/3159.

terms which attempt to avoid the legislative provisions are automatically void. The position is somewhat different within the United States where it is possible, in some circumstances, to contract out of the provisions provided certain formalities are met.

In its early versions the Distance Selling Directive[99] presented several problems for businesses that wished to sell goods or supply services to consumers, the problems principally being in the requirement to provide prior information about the contract to the consumer in written form. This would automatically negate some of the benefits of contracting over the Internet, namely the elimination or reduction of large amounts of paperwork. This has now changed to a requirement to provide the required information in any way appropriate to the means of communication,[100] a vast improvement on the previous versions. The Directive also gives consumers the right, in certain circumstances, to withdraw from the contract within seven days from the date of performance of the contract[101] and requires that consumers receive written confirmation[102] of the information previously supplied prior to the contract[103] itself.

In order to determine whether or not overriding terms and conditions apply the law and jurisdiction of the contract must be determined, as the rules of that jurisdiction will determine the question. This holds even if the parties have attempted to predetermine the jurisdiction and governing law. Such an agreement can only be valid if the choice is not void within the applicable law of the contract itself.[104] In reality, however this will rarely pose a problem as

---

99. Directive 97/7/EC of the European Parliament and of the Council of 20 May 1997 on the protection of consumers in respect of distance contracts.
100. Article 4(2).
101. Article 6(1). The date from which the seven day period runs depends on whether the contract is for the sale of goods or the supply of services.
102. Article 5(1).
103. Articles 5 and 6 still pose problems for some Internet contracts. Where the contract is clearly for the sale of goods then no real issues arise as the information required by art. 5 can be supplied on delivery of the goods themselves under art. 6(1). Where the contract is clearly for the supply of services then again no issues arise. Indeed art. 5(2) removes the requirement for written confirmation where the 'service is to be performed through the use of a means of distant communication'. However, the situation is not so clear cut when it comes to supplying information, computer code or software over the Internet. The Directive does not explicitly define these as either services or goods, though it does make mention of what could be regarded as shrink-wrapped software, that is software packages bought off the shelf or by mail order or whatever, in art. 6(3). The issue here is that there is some confusion as to the status of computer code or software. Software or computer code which is stored and supplied on a physical medium such as a tape or disk would most probably be treated as a good, in the same way as a music tape, record or CD is treated as a good. The value is in the intangible information contained in the medium and not the medium itself. However, the confusion arises when looking at information, computer code or software that is supplied electronically over the Internet as a stream of bits. If this is held as a good, then art. 5(1) might present a problem, as the benefits sought by transacting over the Internet, of paperless transactions, is reduced. If this is held as a service then art. 5(1) may not apply through art. 5(2). Some EC competition law cases seem to point to the electronic supply of computer code or software as being a supply of a service, as does EU VAT law, but the courts have yet to decide the matter.
104. As an example in the United Kingdom see the Unfair Contract Terms Act 1977, s. 27(2).

in general the law of a contract for a consumer transaction will be held to be that of the consumer.[105]

Consumer regulation is an all pervasive topic which has several aims. Contrary to many views, commercial concerns often welcome some degree of consumer protection. Not only does it give consumers the confidence to interact and enter into commercial transactions with the commercial entities, but it also informs the commercial entities of what they can do and how they can act.

One view of the regulatory framework for consumer protection is that its purpose is to provide some redress in the balance of bargaining power between the consumer and a commercial entity. The idea is simply that the consumer should not be overreached by the commercial entity[106] and to this end commercial entities are often prevented from excluding certain rights and warranties that are granted to the consumer. Another object is to provide a competitive regulatory framework within which the consumers and commercial entities are free to interact as they wish. So long as neither breaches the framework, the parties will have freedom to operate within that framework to contract for that which each party wants.

The framework can also be viewed as a form of protection for commercial entities. By operating within the consumer protection framework, the liabilities of the commercial entities for faults or flaws in their services or goods may be capped or controlled.

The general perception of electronic commerce among consumers is that it poses a greater degree of risk than other more standard forms of commerce. Consumer protection measures could help to allay these fears and encourage

---

105. For instance see the suggested amendments to the Convention of 27 September 1968 on Jurisdiction and the Enforcement of Judgments in Civil and Commercial Matters concerning the question of jurisdiction for electronic consumer contracts OJ L 299, 31 December 1972, p. 32.

106. The Unfair Terms in Consumer Contracts Regulations 1994, SI 1994/3159 go further than the Unfair Contract Terms Act 1977 in that it applies to any contractual term in a consumer contract rather than simply to exclusion clauses. Regulation 3 makes this quite clear:

Terms to which these Regulations apply:
(1) Subject to the provisions of Schedule 1, these Regulations apply to any term in a contract concluded between a seller or supplier and a consumer where the said term has not been individually negotiated.
(2) In so far as it is in plain, intelligible language, no assessment shall be made of the fairness of any term which—
(a) defines the main subject matter of the contract, or
(b) concerns the adequacy of the price or remuneration, as against the goods or services sold or supplied.
(3) For the purposes of these Regulations, a term shall always be regarded as not having been individually negotiated where it has been drafted in advance and the consumer has not been able to influence the substance of the term.
(4) Notwithstanding that a specific term or certain aspects of it in a contract has been individually negotiated, these Regulations shall apply to the rest of a contract if an overall assessment of the contract indicates that it is a pre-formulated standard contract.

It shall be for any seller or supplier who claims that a term was individually negotiated to show that it was.

the take up of electronic commerce. This would bring benefits to all actors in the activity, to the economic development of the jurisdiction, to the economic activity of the commercial entities, and to a greater degree of freedom of choice for the consumer.

Consumer protection need not be seen as a burden. Indeed in some jurisdictions where consumer protection is quite weak commercial entities have taken it upon themselves to offer consumers extra rights or warranties over those of competitors. The effect has been to establish a quality or superior feel to the product or service. The service becomes regarded as superior and so attracts more customers. A similar result could easily occur in electronic commerce.[107]

Paradoxically, electronic commerce will most likely be an area where under-regulation could have as detrimental an effect as over-regulation for a jurisdiction. If a jurisdiction were to provide no consumer protection, or a degree of consumer protection which was perceived as being inadequate, then consumers and users might not wish to enter into transactions with commercial entities situated in that jurisdiction. Commercial entities would then be faced with three possibilities. They could remain in the jurisdiction and lobby for greater consumer protection; they could themselves offer a degree of consumer protection as a selling point to attract consumers; or they could move to a jurisdiction which offered a greater degree of consumer protection. Due to the current perception of consumers that electronic commerce bears a greater degree of risk than other forms of commerce, commercial entities would most probably move to a jurisdiction with stronger consumer protection simply in order to allay those fears. The option of simply offering a degree of protection would not be realistically available, as this would only be enforceable by contract if at all.

Similar issues would face commercial entities which faced overbearing consumer protection regulations. Should the regulations prove to be too burdensome the commercial entity can easily move to another jurisdiction to conduct trade.

10.5 REGULATORY ISSUES

10.5.1 Payment[108]

All the major banks now offer electronic banking products to their corporate customers, which allow accounts to be manipulated from a PC at the customer's premises. These permit payments to be made through:

---

107. This might occur through self-regulatory schemes which audit the electronic commerce website and operations for consumer protection compliance. For an early example of such a certification scheme see the UK *Which?* Webtrader certification scheme, at http://www.which.net/webtrader/index.html.

108. This section concentrates on the UK position only. Recommendations for legislation at an international level can be found in the UNCITRAL Legal Guide to Electronic Funds Transfers (New York: 1987) and the UNCITRAL Model Law on International Credit Transfers 1992.

(a) BACS, which operates a three day clearing cycle;
(b) CHAPS, for same day inter-UK payment; and
(c) SWIFT for same-day (or near same-day, depending on time differences) payment internationally.

These products can be used for making payments arising out of electronic transactions, but a number of points need to be noted:

(a) It is likely to be difficult, perhaps impossible, to link an electronic networking system, such as EDI or an Internet-based system with the electronic banking product, as the banks generally insist in their terms and conditions that the electronic banking service can only be accessed using the software provided by the bank. The reasons for this are:
    (i) to preserve the integrity of the banks' own systems, using the inbuilt security features of the software; and
    (ii) to ensure that the bank does not make payments following unauthorised instructions apparently emanating from a customer for which it would be liable to the customer — again, this is linked to the security and authentication features of the software.
Payments made in this way will therefore require some manual input, though the software in question may allow the payment data to be prepared on disk and uploaded for manual authorisation. This may not be too great a disadvantage, as the security risks of completely unsupervised payment are obvious.

(b) Electronic payments are normally irrevocable. So far as traditional payment methods such as cheques are concerned, it is clear that the bank makes payment as its customer's agent, and therefore its authority as agent to pay can be withdrawn at any time until the payment is made.[109] However, certain types of paper payment, in particular the use of cheques with a cheque card, are not capable of countermand by the customer. The reason for this is the agreement by the customer, as part of the terms and conditions for the issue of the card, that he will not countermand cheques which are guaranteed with that card. There is some doubt whether this stipulation does in fact prevent countermand of the cheque, but whether it does or not the effect so far as the customer is concerned is the same.[110] It is therefore clear that if the bank includes in its contract with the customer an obligation not to countermand electronic payments, that obligation will be in practice effective to prevent the customer stopping payment. Such an obligation is likely to be found in the terms and conditions of all electronic banking products.

---

109. Bills of Exchange Act 1882, s. 75, codifying the pre-existing common law — see e.g., *Williams* v *Everett* (1811) 14 East 582; *Warlow* v *Harrison* (1859) 1 E&E 309.
110. If the customer is not able to countermand the cheque, the cheque will be paid and the bank will be entitled to debit his account. If he is entitled to countermand the cheque, he will be in breach of his contract with the bank and thus liable to pay damages. As the bank, by issuing the card to the customer, makes a unilateral contract with payees who accept the cheque card as guarantee (*Carlill* v *Carbolic Smoke Ball Co.* [1893] 1 QB 256), it will be contractually obliged to pay those people. The loss it suffers by reason of the customer's breach of the obligation not to countermand is therefore the amount it is forced to pay out, i.e., the value of the cheque.

Even if there is no express agreement that the payment may not be countermanded, the customer would have to give actual notice to the bank that it is to stop payment,[111] before the payment is made and almost certainly at a reasonable time before payment so as to give the bank the opportunity to process the countermand.[112] It seems clear from the leading cases on revocation of payments[113] that payment cannot be countermanded once the banks become irrevocably committed to each other to process the transfer through the clearing system. The time at which this occurs will depend very much on the payment method selected by the customer. As a general rule, both CHAPS and SWIFT messages are irrevocable once confirmed by the recipient, but BACS messages may be revoked until part way through the second day of the clearing cycle.

(c)   The effect of an electronic payment in discharging the underlying debt may be rather different from its paper analogy. For example, although the receipt of a cheque by the creditor is a conditional discharge of the debt, the mere issue of a payment instruction by the payer does not as a general rule discharge the obligation. The essence of payment is that the funds should be available to the recipient for his unfettered use. If for some reason of national law or banking practice the money is not available to the creditor,[114] the fact that it has been transferred to his bank will not amount to payment, and thus not discharge the debt.[115]

Whether any particular form of payment is conditional or unconditional depends on the terms of the contract under which payment is due, and in general will need to be inferred from the surrounding circumstances. In *Re Charge Card Services Ltd* [1986] 3 All ER 289. Charge Card Services operated a credit card scheme, 'Fuel Card', for the purchase of petrol and other motor supplies from garages. On the company's liquidation the question arose as to whether the use of the card discharged the user's liability to pay the garage, so that the garages were left to prove in the liquidation, or whether it was conditional payment so that on the liquidation of the company the condition was not fulfilled and the garages' rights to payment from the users revived. The court held that because the card was generally used to pay for small purchases where the supplier and customer were not known to each other, and there was no obligation on the customer to supply his address, the intention of the contract between garage and card user was that use of the card would amount to complete payment:

[T]he supplier and customer have for their mutual convenience each previously arranged to open an account with the same company, and agree

---

111. *Curtice v London City and Midland Bank Ltd* [1908] 1 KB 293.
112. Penn, Shea and Arora, *Banking Law Vol. I*, London: Sweet & Maxwell, 1987, para. 6.26.
113. See *Momm v Barclays' Bank International Ltd* [1976] 3 All ER 588; *Delbrueck and Co. v Manufacturers Hanover Trust Co.* (1979) 609 F 2d 1047.
114. See, e.g., *The Chikuma* [1981] 1 All ER 652. In this case, through the peculiar provisions of Italian law, the money transferred to the recipient's account was only available to him in the first instance on payment of interest to the bank. The court held that this did not amount to payment of the obligation.
115. See Goode, *Payment Obligations in Commercial and Financial Transactions*, London: Sweet & Maxwell and Centre for Commercial Law Studies, 1983, pp. 11–19.

that any account between themselves may, if the customer wishes, be settled by crediting the supplier's and debiting the customer's account with that company ... [T]he customer must be discharged, at the latest, when the supplier's account with the company is credited, not when the supplier is paid.[116]

The question which therefore needs to be answered, which can only be done by interpretation of the agreement between creditor and debtor for electronic payment, is whether the creditor has agreed to accept some third party's contractual obligation as satisfaction of the debt, or whether the agreement requires the funds actually to become available to the creditor. This point can be important because the effect of an electronic payment message sent from one bank to another is that:

(i)   the message does not normally transfer any funds as between the banks *per se*;

(ii)   instead, the message gives rise to a contractual obligation on the sending bank to clear that payment through the central bank (e.g., the Bank of England) at some later time (the close of business for CHAPS transfer, the close of the clearing cycle for BACS transfers).

If the proper interpretation of the agreement between creditor and debtor is that creditor has agreed that receipt of a payment message by his bank amounts to payment, he has effectively agreed to the substitution of the sending bank's obligation for that of the debtor, so that the debt is discharged.

This can be important in a transaction where late payment gives rise to legal rights, such as the right to bring a charterparty to an end, as payment would have been made perhaps some days before the funds actually became available to the creditor. This occurred in *Mardorf Peach & Co. Ltd* v *Attica Sea Carriers Corporation of Liberia* [1976] 2 All ER 249, 255, where the Court of Appeal held that payment was complete when the debtor's bank's payment order (which the arbitrator found to be equivalent to payment in cash) was received by the creditor's bank. Here, the obligation to pay was expressed to be by payment into the payee's account. The case illustrates that the agreement between debtor and creditor as to the mode of payment is definitive; if the payee agrees that payment to his agent (i.e., his bank) will suffice, payment will be complete when the agent receives the funds.

(d)   Current electronic funds transfer systems have no method of ensuring that payment is made only against the security of documents of title. Electronic payments are simply internal accounting exercises on the computers involved, and until dematerialised bills of lading and other documents of title are devised, no electronic equivalent of the letter of credit is possible.[117]

Business customers will be able to use the electronic banking products discussed above to make payment for electronic transactions, but it is still not

116. [1986] 3 All ER 289, 304 per Millett J.
117. See Reed, *Electronic Finance Law*, Cambridge: Woodhead Faulkner, 1991, ch. 8.

common for consumer customers to manage their bank accounts in this way. An electronic commerce supplier which wishes to receive electronic payment from its consumer customers will therefore need to use some third party service, such as a credit card provider. It is clearly possible to accept credit card payments using any electronic networking service, or even using the Internet, as all that is required is for the purchaser to transmit his card number and expiry date. This is already common practice when purchasing by telephone. However, because electronic messages are transmitted by copying them to all the computers in the chain of transmission, electronic credit card payments present major security risks to the card holder. Visa and Mastercard have for some time been working on systems which are intended to reduce these risks. As an alternative, payment in digital cash[118] should also become an effective way of receiving payment from consumers.

10.5.2 Advertising and promotion

Advertising regulations present a great problem to entities involved in offering commercial services across the Internet or some other public electronic network. The issue does not really occur with EDI as the purpose of EDI is to transport and process electronic messages according to a predetermined agreement and for a predetermined process. By contrast, the Internet is simply a vast communications medium that is available to the public. EDI tends to be private to a small and defined user group and EDI messages are not made available to the public.

Almost every jurisdiction has advertising regulations of some form which aim to control not only the content of the material that is published in the form of an advertisement, but also the subject matter that may be advertised. These controls can vary, from requiring the material to be presented in the national language through to requiring certain information to be presented in a certain form. The penalty for breaching the controls can vary from a civil offence to a serious criminal offence. Except where these controls originate from an international forum, they invariably apply only to the relevant jurisdiction.

By placing a web page containing an advertisement on the Internet a commercial entity is effectively advertising across the globe. As such it will almost certainly be in breach of an advertising regulation in a jurisdiction somewhere on the planet irrespective of whether or not it complies with the regulations of the jurisdiction within which the advertisement was placed on the Internet. As a consequence it may well be held to be in breach of various advertising regulations in differing jurisdictions simply because users in that jurisdiction may access the page. Two particular areas of advertising will cause regulators a great deal of concern.

---

118. See Reed & Davies, *Digital Cash — the legal implications*, London: Centre for Commercial Law Studies, 1995, published under the Information Technology Law Unit's *Internet Law Research Project*; Laura Edgar, 'Electronic Payment Systems', ECLIP Research Paper (1999), http://www.jura.uni-muenster.de/eclip/.

10.5.2.1 Financial advertising Regulations which purport to control financial advertising can be very stringent,[119] and incorrect information published in an advertisement will result in a breach of the regulations. One of the major attractions of the Internet is the ease with which users can offer financial services to other users no matter their actual geographic location. Most users can pay for these services by using credit cards, bank transfers and the like, without having any real regard to their actual physical location.[120] Though this availability is obviously a great leap in competition within the markets for financial services, financial service regulators may have great cause for concern. Financial advertising regulations are not designed to keep the advertising of such services to a minimum so much as to protect investors from fraud and malpractice and to prevent them from being mislead or exposed to undue risk without their knowledge.

Some investors are highly informed about financial markets and are quite able to make decisions for themselves regarding the risks and pitfalls of investment opportunities, and consequently need little regulatory protection. Most investors, however, are not that sophisticated. One of the problems of financial advertising on the Internet is that in general it does not target specific investors but rather is open to all who access it. It targets all potential investors. Regulators will thus have a wholly valid interest in attempting to regulate financial advertising to ensure that the unsophisticated investor is protected or at least warned of the dangers inherent in unknown or poorly understood financial products and services.

Within the United Kingdom the Financial Services Authority takes the pragmatic and realistic view that the Internet is simply a means of communication. Consequently this has the immediate effect of bringing within its remit any activity controlled by the Financial Services and Markets Act 2000 which is carried out over the Internet. Indeed the Authority holds that the provisions of the Act apply equally to the Internet as they do to other forms of communication.[121] In the main this causes few problems and could be seen as an enlightened position although it partly comes about by accident due to the wide drafting adopted within certain definitions of the Act itself. The result is that the financial regulations, and in particular the securities laws and regulations, automatically apply to the Internet.

Were this to be the only issue arising from the view expressed by the Financial Services Authority then this would be all that there is to analysing the regime within the United Kingdom aside from a description of that regime itself. Fortunately, or unfortunately as the case may be, the use of the Internet in the area of financial services, and securities in

---

119. See the Financial Services and Markets Act 2000, ss. 19 and 21.
120. The limitations are not so much to do with the physical location of the users as to do with the ease with which the users can pay for the services. Providing that they can make payment in the required form or currency, users may effectively purchase products from wherever they choose. Whether or not they will incur tax or other liabilities is besides the point.
121. See 'Carrying on investment business over the Internet' and 'Treatment of material on overseas Internet World Wide Web sites accessible in the UK but not intended for investors in the UK', Guidance 2/98, both available from www.fsa.gov.uk.

particular, raises issues which pose difficult problems for the Financial Services Authority.

The Financial Services and Markets Act which replaces the Financial Services Act 1986, has been drafted partly with the Internet in mind. However, though this is the stated case the Internet itself is not specifically regulated within the new Act. Instead the aim has been to draft the Act in such a manner that its provisions remain as far as possible technologically neutral in order to future proof these provisions against future technical developments, both in terms of services and the underlying technologies irrespective of how these services are offered. It is in providing for this flexibility that the specific nature of the Internet was taken into account when the Act was drafted.

The Act itself aims to build upon and extend the regime that currently exists under the Financial Services Act 1986. This regime covers most, if not all of the activities concerning securities over the Internet through the accident of wide drafting rather than by design. One consequence of this is the wide jurisdiction which exists under the present regime and which proves somewhat problematical.

10.5.2.2 Medical advertising As with other forms of commercial activity so too for pharmaceutical and biotechnology companies the Internet presents an attractive medium to attempt to circumvent the standard restrictions that currently exist within different jurisdictions and advertise directly to the consumer.[122] The rules differ quite widely between jurisdictions as different regulators take differing views on what should and should not be allowed. Some regulators simply monitor and police the statements and claims made concerning authorised medical products and treatments, whilst others strictly prevent any publication or dissemination of information to consumers about such products in all but the most limited cases.

Within the United Kingdom the restrictions and controls on advertising[123] medicines are particularly stringent. Quite aside from the general controls placed on advertising medicines[124] to the medical profession, the specific

---

122. A recent attempt was made by a Canadian biotechnology company to use the services of a United States Agency to spam (send unsolicited commercial electronic mail or unsolicited news data) to thousands of users on the Internet using user lists obtained from Internet Service Providers. They attempted to do this using a mail server in the United Kingdom. The posting of the messages within the United Kingdom fell foul of the Medicines Act 1968.

123. Section 92 of the Medicines Act 1968:

   (1) Subject to the following provisions of this section, in this Part of this Act 'advertisement' includes every form of advertising, whether in a publication, or by the display of any notice, or by means of any catalogue, price list, letter (whether circular or addressed to a particular person) or other document, or by words inscribed on any article, or by means of a photograph, film, sound recording, broadcast or cable programme, or in any other way, and any reference to the issue of an advertisement shall be construed accordingly.

124. The Medicines Act 1968, s. 95 grants Ministers the appropriate powers to introduce regulations to prohibit the advertising of medicines. It is a criminal offence to breach the regulations promulgated under this section.

advertising to the general public is strictly controlled or, more usually, absolutely prohibited.[125] The regulations are designed to prevent consumers from coming in to contact with information about which they would not be able or have the knowledge to make an informed judgment. Medical professionals, on the other hand, are specifically trained and have the requisite knowledge to be able to make informed opinions about medical products and treatments. Thus the regulations are designed to restrict most of the advertising to the professional journals that are aimed at these professionals as they are best placed to make the required decisions on the merits of the products or services.

Where direct advertising to consumers is allowed, the regulations control the type of information that is allowed and the way in which the information itself may be displayed. By setting out these stringent requirements consumers are protected from being unduly swayed towards or against a medical treatment or product without seeking medical advice, an action which could have a serious and detrimental effect on their health and well being.

Quite aside from controlling the type of information which is published to consumers, the regulators also have the valid wish to limit access to medical treatments and products in their jurisdictions to those which have been tested and approved by them. In some circumstances this may be to control the costs to a public health scheme of providing those treatments. In the majority of cases, however, any restriction has to do with valid concerns over the suitability and safety of the treatment in question. Making information about medical treatments available across the Internet, and in some cases making the treatments themselves available, would circumvent these controls which are put in place for the reasons of public safety.

10.5.3 Jurisdiction

A general rule of contract formation is that parties are free to contract as they wish, including the freedom to agree the laws and the jurisdiction[126] which they wish to govern the contract. They do this not only to ensure that they will know the laws which govern the contract but also that they know the rules and procedure of the courts which may have to determine any dispute that arises as a consequence of the contract. However, the fact that the parties can choose the law or jurisdiction does not necessarily mean that the choice

---

125. See the Medicines (Advertising of Medicinal Products) Regulations 1975, SI 1975/298; the Medicines (Advertising of Medicinal Products) (No. 2) Regulations 1975, SI 1975/1326, as amended by the Medicines (Contact Lens Fluids and Other Substances) (Advertising and Miscellaneous Amendments) Regulations 1979, SI 1979/1760; and the Medicines (Labelling and Advertising to the Public) Regulations 1978, SI 1978/41, as amended by the Medicines (Advertising) Regulations 1994, SI 1994/1932, as amended by the Medicines for Human Use (Marketing Authorisations Etc.) Regulations 1994, SI 1994/3144. Aside from controlling the wording and descriptions which can be applied to various medicines the regulations also strictly prohibit certain medicines from being marketed or advertised to the general public.

126. These are two separate issues. Parties can choose a jurisdiction without choosing a law or choose a law without choosing a jurisdiction, but this is rare and can be dangerous.

is valid or enforceable[127] and this is why the actual location of the contract formation has such an important bearing on this matter. The contractual terms which purport to define the law and jurisdiction must be valid and the question of validity is determined by the laws of the jurisdiction in which the contract is formed regardless of any term within the contract itself. This point is often forgotten but it is vital. Every jurisdiction has rules which govern the freedom of parties to choose the law or jurisdiction[128] of a contract and it is these rules which will determine whether or not the terms or choices themselves are valid.[129]

The borderless nature of the Internet gives rise to legal issues for commercial transactions which occur over, or in some way involve use of the Internet. If a transaction takes place between computers or parties in different jurisdictions then the question arises as to which laws govern the transaction? This is compounded by the problem that the involvement of different jurisdictions is not immediately apparent. Another question which must be asked is where was the contract formed, or even was a contract formed at all? The question which must always be asked is does the jurisdiction in which any agreement was entered into recognise that agreement as a legally valid contract?

Attempts have been made to deal with the question of choice of law and jurisdiction in electronic contracts. Some of the more interesting are the attempts made in the draft revision of the Uniform Commercial Code. Articles 2, 2A and 2B contain several interesting elements. Most particularly

---

127. The Unfair Terms in Consumer Contracts Regulations 1994, SI 1994/3159, reg. 3(7) states that:

> These Regulations shall apply notwithstanding any contract term which applies or purports to apply the law of a non member State, if the contract has a close connection with the territory of the member States.

128. The Brussels Convention is one such example. This applies to Member States of the European Union and governs the choice of jurisdiction for civil and commercial matters within the European Union. Put very simply the Convention operates in one of three ways. The basic rule, in sch. 1 of the Convention, is that the defendant must be sued in his local court, with the meaning of the word 'local' dependent on whether the defendant is an individual or a company. For a few matters, the Convention stipulates an exclusive jurisdiction which cannot be altered by contract. For many other matters the Convention implies a choice of jurisdiction where no explicit choice to the contrary exists, and this means that for that class of contract the parties can agree to contract out of the Convention; that is they can override the Convention but must do so explicitly. An example is the rules governing contracts. Here the general rule is that the relevant jurisdiction is that in which the contract is to be performed. If there are many jurisdictions where the contract is performed, then the relevant jurisdiction is that in which the dispute arises. If, however, the contract could be performed in several different jurisdictions as opposed to being required to be performed in those jurisdictions then the situation is confusing. The way in which the Convention is interpreted differs in different jurisdictions within the European Union. The English courts hold that there is a choice of jurisdictions, namely those where the contract could be performed, and it is for those jurisdictions to seize jurisdiction. The Scottish courts hold that the relevant jurisdictions are those in which the contract was performed. A subtle difference, perhaps, but an important one nevertheless.

129. The choice may be valid but the term in which that choice is made may itself be invalid. In this case the whole term falls apart and the choice disappears into the great courtroom in the sky. Equally the term may be valid but the choice of law invalid. The term survives but is completely ineffective.

perhaps are the inclusions of provisions to deal with the default choice of law and jurisdiction[130] of any contracts entered into which come under the code. Though the provisions are interesting they would appear to be unworkable in most jurisdictions outside of the United States and its commonwealth and in any case the draft revision will only bind States and territories that enact the provisions. The call by the United States for the international adoption of the UNCITRAL Model Law would help in enabling the common provisions to be satisfied and so be applicable in many more jurisdictions. The Model Law, however, does not go so far as to attempt to solve the jurisdictional questions. Indeed the Model Law would be an incorrect forum to do so as it is simply concerned with the mechanisms of contract formation. It should not deal with jurisdictional issues in a prescriptive manner as these are issues which are within the sole competence of individual States to adjudicate according to their own rules on the conflicts of laws.

10.6 CONCLUSIONS

The law governing electronic commerce in all of its flavours is very much in its infancy, as is clearly demonstrated by the lack of case law on the subject. By the time of the next edition of this book, however, it is likely that there will be a large volume of legislation which deals specifically with electronic commerce issues. In the interim many of the potential problems, once they are properly identified, can be overcome quite simply through the mechanism of properly drafted contracts. This is a task for which the commercial lawyer is ideally suited, and lawyers will play a crucial role in facilitating the inevitable spread of electronic commerce amongst the trading community.

---

130. Section 2B–108:

    (a) A choice-of-law term in an agreement is enforceable.

    (b) If an agreement does not have a choice-of-law term, the following rules apply:

        (1) In an access contract or a contract providing for delivery of a copy by electronic communication, the contract is governed by the law of the jurisdiction in which the licensor is located when the contract becomes enforceable between the parties.

        (2) A consumer contract not governed by subsection (b)(1) which requires delivery of a copy on a physical medium to the consumer is governed as to the contractual rights and obligations of the parties by the law of the jurisdiction in which the copy is located when the licensee receives possession of the copy or, in the event of nondelivery, the jurisdiction in which the receipt was to have occurred.

        (3) In all other cases, the contract is governed by the law of the State with the most significant relationship to the contract.

    (c) If the jurisdiction whose law applies as determined under subsection (b) is outside the United States, subsection (b) applies only if the laws of that jurisdiction provide substantially similar protections and rights to the party not located in that jurisdiction as are provided under this article. Otherwise, the rights and duties of the parties are governed by the law of the jurisdiction in the United States which has the most significant relationship to the transaction.

    (d) A party is located at its place of business if it has one place of business, at its chief executive office if it has more than one place of business, or at its place of incorporation or primary registration if it does not have a physical place of business. Otherwise, a party is located at its primary residence.

CHAPTER ELEVEN

The Liability of Internet Service Providers and Internet Intermediaries

Andrew Charlesworth and Chris Reed

11.1 INTRODUCTION

This chapter will consider the issue of the liability of Internet Service Providers (ISPs). Commercial ISPs[1] are without doubt the highest profile grouping of what are termed Internet Intermediaries that is, those organisations that provide access to, and services on, the Internet. This is undoubtedly due, in large part, to the fact that the public is being constantly bombarded with publicity (and CD-ROMs) by some of the larger players in the commercial ISP market. However, other types of intermediaries such as index portals, auction web sites and online shopping malls are all now increasingly vying for our attention. Whilst this chapter will concentrate on commercial ISPs, it will also consider in passing some of the legal issues arising from the increasing convergence between commercial ISPs and these other types of Internet Intermediary. It will examine the circumstances in which an ISP might face legal liability for either its provision of Internet services, or for its provision of certain types of information content. In the latter case the developing consensus on the limitations that can or should be placed on liability for information content will be considered.

---

1. That is, ISPs that provide Internet access for a fee, as opposed to businesses that provide their employees, or universities that provide staff and students, with Internet access as part of their employment or course of study.

11.2   WHAT IS AN INTERNET SERVICE PROVIDER?

When one examines the issue of the legal liabilities of ISPs, one has first to determine what is currently understood by the term 'ISP'. Initially, the answer to this question would seem quite straightforward, but if one engages in just a little research, almost immediately any answer begins to take on more complex dimensions. For example, the Webopedia[2] provides the following definition of an ISP:

> ... a company that provides access to the Internet. For a monthly fee, the service provider gives you a software package, username, password and access phone number. Equipped with a modem, you can then log on to the Internet and browse the World Wide Web and USENET, and send and receive e-mail.
>
> In addition to serving individuals, ISPs also serve large companies, providing a direct connection from the company's networks to the Internet. ISPs themselves are connected to one another through Network Access Points (NAPs).[3]

On its face this would seem like a reasonably adequate definition of an ISP, one that many Internet users might once have recognised as fitting perfectly the company that provided them with access to the Internet. However, beyond the 'provides access to the Internet' of the opening sentence, today this definition appears both simplistic and inaccurate, for as the Internet hardware and software technologies have developed and become more sophisticated, so too have the standard business models of the companies that provide access to it. Now, therefore, the answer to the ISP question posed above has become a much more complex one than that which might have been given five years ago.

Contemporary ISPs may supply solely Internet access,[4] such companies being referred to as access-only ISPs, interactive computer service providers (ICSPs),[5] or enhanced service providers (ESPs).[6] However, increasingly they may provide a bundle of communications services including telecommunications[7] and television.[8] They may provide access via traditional telecommunications systems requiring an analog dial-up modem,[9] via traditional telecommunications systems using ADSL[10] Modems or ISDN Terminal

---

2. Online dictionary and search engine at http://www.pcwebopedia.com/.
3. See http://www.pcwebopedia.com/TERM/I/ISP.html.
4. E.g., Freeserve (http://www.freeserve.net/) and AOL (http://www.aol.com).
5. US Telecommunications Act 1996, 47 USC § 223(e)(6).
6. Werbach, 'Digital Tornado: The Internet and Telecommunications Policy', March 1997, *FCC OPP Working Paper No. 29*, at pp. 32–33.
7. E.g., British Telecom (http://www.bt net/ and AT&T http://www.att.net).
8. E.g., COGECO (http://www.cgocable.net) and Cox Communications (http://www.cox.com).
9. See notes 4 and 7, above.
10. Asymmetric Digital Subscriber Line. 'Asymmetric Digital Subscriber Lines (ADSL) are used to deliver high-rate digital data over existing ordinary phone-lines. A new modulation technology called Discrete Multitone (DMT) allows the transmission of high speed data. ADSL facilitates the simultaneous use of normal telephone services, ISDN, and high speed data transmission, e.g., video': Kimmo K. Saarela, *ADSL*, http://www.cs.tut.fi/tlt/stuff/adsl1/pt_adsl.html at http://www.cs.tut.fi/tlt/stuff/adsl/node5.html.

Adapters[11] to provide high speed service,[12] through a broadband cable network requiring a cable modem,[13] or through a combination of dial-up and satellite service.[14] They may provide just a connection to the Internet,[15] or they may provide other services through 'portal sites' via the worldwide web (WWW),[16] where the actual services are usually supplied by third parties.[17] Technical innovations are appearing apace, and developments such as Hotline[18] mean that even the 'standard' software set ups provided by ISPs, usually based around a WWW browser, may be far from a permanent fixture.

To take two examples:

(a) *America Online, Inc.*: America Online, Inc. operates two worldwide Internet services, America Online, with more than 19 million members, and CompuServe, with more than 2.2 million members. It owns several leading Internet brands including ICQ, AOL Instant Messenger and Digital City, Inc.; the Netscape Netcenter and AOL.COM portals; the Netscape Navigator and Communicator browsers; AOL MovieFone, a movie listing guide and ticketing service; Spinner Networks and NullSoft, Inc., leaders in Internet music; and Digital Marketing Services (DMS), the leader in online incentive marketing programs and online custom market research. In conjunction with Sun Microsystems, the Company produces end-to-end e-commerce and enterprise solutions for Internet companies.[19]

(b) *Cogeco Cable, Inc.*: Cogeco Cable, Inc., Canada's fourth largest cable operator, and @Home Network[20] provide high-speed Internet services in key

---

11. Integrated Services Digital Network. 'ISDN allows multiple digital channels to be operated simultaneously through the same regular phone wiring used for analog lines. The change comes about when the telephone company's switches can support digital connections. Therefore, the same physical wiring can be used, but a digital signal, instead of an analog signal, is transmitted across the line. This scheme permits a much higher data transfer rate than analog lines: Ralph Becker, *ISDN Tutorial*, http://www.ralphb.net/ISDN/index.html at http://www.ralphb.net/ISDN/advs.html.

12. E.g., Bell Sympatico High Speed Edition (http://hse.sympatico.ca/en/fs_main.htm), British Telecom Home Highway (http://www.homehighway.bt.com/).

13. E.g., The @Home network and its franchises (http://www.home.com/), Cable London (http://www.cablelondon.co.uk/residential/internet/index.html), and Cable Internet (http://www.cableinet.net/).

14. E.g., DirecPC (http://www.direcpc.com).

15. E.g., West Dorset Internet (http://www.wdi.co.uk/), CIX Ltd (http://www1.cix.co.uk/).

16. Portal sites offer preselected, ready-made links throughout the Internet, essentially making the information source transparent to the user. Such portals are content aggregators. They add value to that content by organizing it within a unified framework.

17. E.g., AOL's Compuserve (http://www.compuserve.com/gateway/default.asp), Demon Internet Ltd (http://www.demon.net/).

18. See Hotline Communications Ltd (http://www.BigRedH.com/index2.html).

19. See AOL's corporate website at http://corp.aol.com and its SEC 10K filing for 1999 at http://www.sec.gov/Archives/edgar/data/883780/0000883780-99-000063.txt.

20. @Home Network distributes high-speed interactive services to residences and businesses using its own network architecture and a variety of transport options including the cable industry's hybrid-fibre coaxial infrastructure. The cable connection provides users with significant increases in speed over conventional Internet services. Since its founding in 1995, @Home Network has reached affiliate agreements with 14 leading cable companies in North America.

markets in Canada called Cogeco@Home. Cogeco Cable Inc. rebuilt its cable television systems with a hybrid-fibre coaxial architecture to support @Home Network's proprietary national broadband infrastructure. The majority of the Cogeco@Home subscribers are already subscribers to Cogeco's cable TV programming. The service does not use a phone line, but transmits data over existing television cable wiring using a cable modem.[21] The cable Internet service does not require a manual log in and operates on a 24/7 basis for a fixed fee. The service currently comes with a proprietary WWW based front end, which Cogeco@Home uses to provide additional content and services, although this can be ignored in favour of the standard suite of Internet-related software (or perhaps Hotline).[22]

So it appears from even a brief examination of the ISP industry that the commercial operations that form its constituents exhibit diverse characteristics in both their business models and the technology used. In addition, industry players often come from a range of existing commercial and regulatory backgrounds. This has led to differing expectations, both in terms of the degree to which ISPs can and should be regulated, and also with regard to the extent to which they can be held liable for the activities of their users. In order to understand the background to this diversity, it is useful to first consider the regulatory market frameworks within which ISPs have developed.

11.3   AN ISP'S REGULATORY LIABILITY

It is important at this point to distinguish between the liability for failing to comply with the sectoral regulatory requirements, considered in this section, and the liability for activities carried out when operating within the bounds of those requirements, considered below. The former, unlike the latter, clearly does not affect all ISPs equally, but has played, and continues to play, a large part in shaping the nature of the market for ISP services, primarily through the promotion of competition. The transformation of the Internet in the United States and the United Kingdom, the two countries considered here, has seen it move from an essentially government-funded and publicly-owned institution to an institution that is largely privately-owned and corporately-dominated. The process by which this has occurred has been heavily influenced by the activity or inactivity of national regulatory bodies, usually in the telecommunications sector, in placing limitations on some key players while encouraging the rapid expansion of others.

11.3.1   Regulatory models — the United States

The potential for regulatory divergence between groups of ISPs is particularly clear in the United States. Here, differential treatment of the telecommuni-

---

21. The term 'Cable Modem' is somewhat misleading, as the device works more like a Local Area Network (LAN) interface than a modem. For further details, see Rolf V. Østergaard, *Cable Modem Tutorial* (http://www.cable-modems.org/tutorial/).
22. See COGECO's corporate website at http://www.cgocable.net/index.html.

cations, cable and data services sectors, by the federal government, has resulted in an effective three-way split in the regulation of ISP services in the United States. This split has its roots in the Federal Communications Commission's longstanding perception that, unlike the situation in the market for basic telecommunications services, where there has been extensive regulation, the growth of both cable and computer-based data services in the United States would be best facilitated by not extending 'common carrier' status to them, and by keeping federal regulation of such services to a minimum.[23]

11.3.1.1 Telecommunications company ISPs Telecommunications companies are treated as 'common carriers' under Title II of the Communications Act 1934, with its attendant liabilities, and are heavily federally regulated.[24] As a 'common carrier' a telecommunications company is obliged to sell other companies, such as access-only ISPs which will be competing with the ISP services of the telecommunications company, the rights to use their network facilities.[25] On the positive side, while common carriers are obliged to carry any message and are not permitted to discriminate against either the content of a message or against the person sending it, because they act simply as a conduit for transporting information from one location to another, they have largely been freed of liability for the content provided by their users and subscribers.[26]

11.3.1.2 Cable company ISPs Cable service providers are not treated as 'common carriers', in part because cable systems were originally built and operated to meet the demands of consumers for video and other programming. This meant that the cable companies were exercising editorial discretion concerning the content, information, programming and services that they offered. They are regulated,[27] although the majority of that regulation still takes place at the municipal rather than federal level, with cities operating as franchisers.[28] The lack of 'common carrier' status means that they are not generally obliged to open their networks to potential ISP competitors. However, as the technological convergence between their services and those of the telecommunications companies increases, to the point where both groups may be able to offer basic telecommunications, Internet connectivity

23. For an excellent short overview of the history of FCC non-intervention in this area, see J. Oxman, 'The FCC and the Unregulation of the Internet', July 1999, *FCC OPP Working Paper No. 31.*
24. See The Common Carrier Bureau, part of the Federal Communications Commission, at http://www.fcc.gov/ccb.
25. Title II of the US Communications Act 1934 requires common carriers to offer service under tariff to all who request it on rates, terms and conditions that are just, reasonable, and nondiscriminatory. 47 USC §§ 201–205.
26. For a brief overview of the purpose of common carrier status, see E.M. Noam, 'Beyond Liberalization II: The Impending Doom of Common Carriage', at http://www.vii.org/papers/citinoa5.htm.
27. See 47 USC §§ 521–561.
28. See, for example, the situation in *AT&T, TCI, et. al. v City of Portland* cited at note 30, below.

and TV/video, there is increasing pressure on them, in particular from the access-only ISPs, to accept some form of 'common carrier' status by offering third party access to local cable television lines for Internet use.[29] Not unnaturally, given the recent massive investment in infrastructure made by the cable companies, they are less than enthusiastic about the possibility of having to open up their networks to what they perceive as freeloading competitors.[30] The access-only ISPs argue that their pursuit of open access to, or 'unbundling' of, the cable companies networks is simply in line with the deregulatory aims of the omnibus US Telecommunications Act of 1996. This interpretation, however, flies in the face of both the majority of commentators' opinion[31] and the wording of the Communications Act of 1934, as amended by the 1996 Act.[32]

11.3.1.3 Access only ISPs Access only ISPs, like AOL, are considered to provide an 'information service' or 'enhanced services' as opposed to the basic telephony service, and as such have been left largely unregulated, although they are not necessarily immune from new legal measures. They are not currently considered to be 'common carriers' either by the legislature,[33] the Federal Communications Commission (FCC) or the US courts.[34] They

---

29. See further, arguing against open access, D.B. Kopel, 'Access to the Internet: Regulation or Markets?', *Heartland Policy Study No. 92*, at http://www.heartland.org/studies/kopel-ps.pdf; M.C. Hochman, 'Beware What You Ask For', *American Lawyer Media, Inc. Intellectual Property Magazine* at http://www.proskauer.com/pubs/articles/isp_regulation.html; contrast F. Bar, *et al.* 'Defending the Internet Revolution in the Broadband Era: When Doing Nothing is Doing Harm', *E-conomy Project Working Paper 12*, at http://e-conomy.berkeley.edu/pubs/wp/ewp12.pdf.
30. See *AT&T, TCI, et. al* v *City of Portland and Multnomah County*, (D Ore 3 June 1999) Case No. CV 99-65-PA; *AT&T, et. al.* v *City of Portland*, US Court of Appeals, 9th Circuit, Appeal No. 99-35609. The case stems from AT&T's acquisition of TCI and its network of high-speed, broadband cables. The City of Portland imposed an 'open access' requirement as a condition to the transfer of TCI's local cable lines. AT&T sued claiming the city did not have the jurisdiction to require the company to open its cable lines. In June 1999, AT&T lost the case, but at the time of writing is appealing the decision to the Court of Appeals for the 9th Circuit. The FCC has filed an *amicus curiae* brief essentially supporting AT&T's position. See http://www.techlawjournal.com/courts/portland/19990816fcc.htm.
31. Op. cit., note 29, above.
32. Section 621(c) expressly prohibits the imposition of 'common carrier or utility' regulation on a cable system by reason of its provision of cable services. See M.C. Hochman, 'Beware What You Ask For', op. cit., note 29, above.
33. For example, the Telecommunications Act of 1996 specifically provides that '[n]othing in this section shall be construed to treat interactive computer services as common carriers or telecommunications carriers'. 47 USC § 223(e)(6).
34. See *Alan M Howard, et. al.* v *America Online, Inc., et. al.*, CV 97-1642-AAH, 14 May 1998 also at http://legal.web.aol.com/decisions/dlpriv/howard.html; *Religious Technology Center* v *Netcom On-Line Communication Services, Inc.*, 907 F Supp 1361 (ND Cal 1995), (the defendant, an Internet access provider, Netcom, did not fit within the definition of 'common carriers' under the Copyright Act, which was analogous to the Communications Act definition); *CompuServe, Inc.* v *Cyber Promotions, Inc.*, 962 F Supp 1015 (SD Ohio 1997) (CompuServe could not be viewed as a public utility, to which the public would have a right to reasonable access, because CompuServe did not provide an 'essential good or service to the general public' and did not occupy a 'monopolistic or oligopolistic position in the relevant marketplace').

have, however, received significant attention from the FCC, which in 1971 decided that computers providing data processing services over the telephone network would not be regulated under the 'common carrier' regulations; that the FCC only had limited jurisdiction over such services under Title I of the Communications Act 1934; and then only where they were transmitted over the telephone networks.[35] This was followed in 1980 by further FCC intervention in the form of 'structural safeguards' which maintained the policy that large telephone companies could only provide enhanced services through separate subsidiaries; and the introduction of the concepts of 'basic' and 'enhanced' service.[36] Basic service, regulated under the 'common carrier' regulations, is the offering of 'a pure transmission capability over a communications path that is virtually transparent in terms of its interaction with customer supplied information'. Enhanced services include data processing services and hybrid forms of communications. In 1983, the FCC decided that enhanced service providers would be exempt from the access charge requirements of long distance carriers even where they used a local telephone service to originate and terminate interstate communications,[37] a decision extended in 1996.[38]

11.3.2   FCC policy

To summarise the above, non-telecommunications company ESPs/ISPs are not currently telecommunication common carriers and are thus not regulated under Title II of the Communications Act 1934. Where ESP/ISPs transmit their service over a telephone network they are subject to limited FCC jurisdiction under Title I, but are not where other methods of transmission are used. ESP/ISPs are 'end users' of the telephone network and do not pay the access charges of long distance carriers. As will be discussed later in this chapter, while both the cable companies and the access-only ISPs have been unenthusiastic about accepting any form of common carrier status, this could have potentially left them open to much wider content liability than that imposed on the telecommunication companies. The telecommunications ISPs are, unsurprisingly, unhappy about their position with regard to the cable and access only ISPs. However, the rise in competition from those sectors has arguably expedited the roll out of broadband services, such as ISDN and ASDL, by the telecommunications companies as they seek to counter the developing threat to their markets.

With regard to the future, the FCC appears unlikely to drop its policy of benign non-regulation of both the cable ISP and access-only ISP sectors, as it regards the exponential growth of the Internet in the last decade as having

---

35. *First Computer Inquiry*, Final Decision, 28 FCC 2d 267 (1971).
36. *Second Computer Inquiry*, Final Decision, 77 FCC 2d 384 (1980).
37. MTS and WATS Market Structure, Memorandum Opinion and Order 97 FCC 2d 682 (1983).
38. See Access Charge Reform, Notice of Proposed Rule Making, Third Report and Order, and Notice of Inquiry, CC Docket 96-262 (24 December 1996), http://www.fcc.gov/Bureaus/Common_Carrier/Notices/1996/fcc96488.txt, at para. 282.

been significantly spurred by the overall lack of federal regulation. Its main concerns appear to be to prevent the development of anticompetitive behaviour, to ensure that such regulation as is implemented is not disproportionate to the problems it aims to solve, and over time to reduce the regulation of the telecommunications sector in line with the development of unregulated new technologies.[39]

11.3.3   Regulatory models — the UK

In the UK, the regulatory position is somewhat different, and the type of differentiation between the three categories of ISPs found in the US is less obvious, although there are parallels. This is due in part to the following factors:

(a)   The general UK telecommunications regulatory and policy framework has been allowed to have a larger impact on policy relating to the provision of cable and Internet services, and the active encouragement of regulatory divergence between telecommunications company ISPs, cable company ISPs, and access-only ISPs, on the grounds of stimulating competition, has been less noticeable.[40]

(b)   Despite early deregulation in 1984, and the government drive to encourage competition in the telecommunications sector, the UK provision of network services has been, and remains, dominated by one player, BT.[41] Thus, much of the regulatory effort by OFTEL[42] has been focused on preventing anti-competitive behaviour on the part of BT, by regulating pricing and forcing BT to allow its competitors, in both the basic and enhanced services sectors, access to its network.

(c)   The UK government has acknowledged the process of convergence between the telecommunications, broadcasting and information industries and intends to further narrow the differences between broadcasting and telecommunications regulatory approaches.[43]

In short, the historical development of the UK telecommunications sector has differed significantly from that of the US. The inevitable overlap between the activities of the telecommunications companies and cable companies was acknowledged at an early stage. Indeed, when telecommunications were deregulated in 1984 BT was permitted to invest in cable and it had the largest interests in cable of any UK company by 1989. However, it took a strategic

---

39. J. Oxman, 'The FCC and the Unregulation of the Internet', *op. cit.*, note 23, above at pp. 25–26.
40. See A. Graham, 'Public Policy and the Information Superhighway: The Case of the UK', paper prepared for the Harvard/GIIC Symposium on 'National Initiatives for Information Infrastructure', 25–27 January 1996 at http://ksgwww.harvard.edu/iip/GIIconf/graham.html.
41. See OFTEL Consultative Document 'Provision of Services over Telecommunications Networks', OFTEL, 1996 at http://www.oftel.gov.uk/competition/promote/contents.html.
42. The regulator for the UK telecommunications industry (http://www.oftel.gov.uk/).
43. See DTI: 'Broadband Britain: A Fresh Look at the Broadcast Entertainment Restrictions', London, DTI & DCMS, April 1998 at para. 14.

decision to leave the cable market, and by the summer of 1999 had sold all its cable interests. Perhaps guided by the perception that, despite surface dissimilarities, the core functions of cable and telecommunications companies as network operators, as well as basic and enhanced service providers, were essentially the same, the UK government never permitted the same degree of regulatory divergence to appear between telecommunications ISPs and cable company ISPs, and in as much as there are any differences, these are already in the process of being removed.

Some other significant differences between the US and UK situations also exist. Access-only ISPs in the UK do not receive the favourable treatment meted out to their US counterparts, with the high cost of telecommunications to the ISPs, and the measured usage charges levied on end users, serving to depress somewhat the demand for Internet services.[44] Also, despite explosive growth in the mid to late 1990s, cable network companies still have a comparatively limited penetration into the UK consumer markets for tele-communications and Internet service, with most of the development still taking place in the larger urban areas.[45]

11.3.4 UK policy

The direction the UK will take with regard to the regulation of what is increasingly coalescing into an 'information industry', where companies, whether telecoms, cable or access-only ISP, may provide one, some, or all of the processes of network service, basic services, and enhanced data services, has already been spelt out. Government policy will be based on the principle of 'co-regulation' where government will define the public policy objectives and the industry will deliver solutions through self-regulatory processes, formal regulation will only be used where co-regulation is ineffective.[46] The overall aims of the UK regulators, if not the methods of achieving those aims, are thus much the same as those of their US counterparts; the encouragement of competition, limited new regulation, and a move towards a cohesive information industry policy.

11.4   OTHER ASPECTS OF ISP LIABILITY

In their most basic form, ISPs are the 'glue' that binds the Internet together, via their supply of TCP/IP packet switching services, which allow third parties to communicate data packets across the 'network of networks'. To facilitate

---

44. J. Oxman, 'The FCC and the Unregulation of the Internet', *op. cit.*, note 23 at pp. 17–18.
45. Although the five main UK cable providers, Atlantic Telecom, Cable & Wireless, NTL, Eurobell and Telewest Communications, claim via their industry website that 'Over 12 million homes in Britain are already passed by cable networks, and over 4.5 million customers are already subscribing to one or more of the services offered by Cable companies', http://www.cable.co.uk/.
46. Patricia Hewitt MP, Address to the *Scrambling for Safety 3.5* Conference, 23 September 1999, at http://www.dti.gov.uk/cii/elec/speech.html.

such information transactions, ISPs will provide services to one or more of the parties, including fundamental communications services such as access and information storage. ISPs, and indeed other Internet Intermediaries, may also provide additional services to facilitate transactions between end users, such as the provision of search facilities and indexes. Where these basic or additional services are found to be defective, liability will normally be based on the established legal principles of contract and tort, although it may not be immediately apparent how best to apply existing principles to forms of service previously unconsidered by legislators and the courts. Indeed, in the case of certain types of enhanced service, such as those involving provision of software, the courts may struggle to determine whether the service provided is in fact legally to be considered a 'service'.[47]

A more problematic issue is raised by the role of ISPs and other intermediaries in relaying information through their systems. Determining their liability for loss of the information stored in relayed packets is one matter, determining liability for the nature of the information content of those packets, where that content has been determined by a third party, is quite another. ISPs and other intermediaries usually operate using software which processes information automatically. As such, they are usually transferring the information without obtaining, or seeking to obtain, knowledge of either its content, or the nature of the transaction of which it is a part. This lack of knowledge, however, does not necessarily render them immune to legal action where the third party information content infringes another third party's rights, for there are often good reasons for aggrieved claimants to pursue the intermediary rather than the other third party:

(a)   Information intermediaries are often seen as potentially more lucrative targets for litigation than the originators of the offending information content. This perception may be based on the unofficial first rule of litigation 'Never sue poor people' or, in the case of large intermediaries, because the claimants suspect that it will be cheaper for the intermediary to pay them to drop the case than to fight it.

(b)   The question of jurisdiction may play a role, for example if the originator of the offending information is in a foreign jurisdiction while the intermediary is in the claimant's home jurisdiction, or if the intermediary is in a jurisdiction that has a reputation for favourable outcomes in cases similar to that brought by the claimant.[48]

(c)   The outcome the claimant desires may be more effectively obtained by action against the intermediary. For example, where the desired outcome is the prevention of further access to the offending information, taking action against one originator may have minimal effect, whereas action against the intermediary may result in complete or partial blocking of all potential

---

47. Consider the difficulties faced by the court in *St. Albans City and District Council* v *International Computers Ltd* [1996] 4 All ER 481. See further chapter 1, section 1.2.1.14.

48. Consider, for example, the well-publicised possibility of jurisdiction or forum shopping in libel cases. See F. Auburn, 'Usenet News And The Law' [1995] 1 *Web JCLI* at http://webjcli.ncl.ac.uk/articles1/auburn1.html.

originators.[49] Action against an intermediary may also be part of a wider strategy by a claimant to 'chill' the willingness of other intermediaries to carry the same information.[50]

11.5 AN ISP'S LIABILITY TO ITS CLIENTS

Any intermediary who provides Internet transaction services is faced with the risk that his actions or inaction may result in the failure of the transaction. In such circumstances, it may be that he will be forced to compensate one or other of the parties to that transaction for any resulting losses. For ISPs that risk is two-fold: first, there may simply be a communications failure which prevents the transaction from ever taking place, this may be considered a failure of 'basic service provision'; secondly, there may be a failure of some additional service, for example, a loss of stored data such as a website, this may be considered as a failure of an 'enhanced service provision'. This service may be offered to the parties by the ISP, or by a third party Internet Intermediary through the ISP. In addition to provision of service liability, an ISP may owe other legal obligations to a party availing itself of its services, not least in the area of consumer protection. Another obligation that has received much media and industry attention in recent years, not least because of its importance to the development of e-commerce, is that of informational privacy. This may be granted by law, as in the case of the EU Data Protection Directive and attendant national legislation,[51] or may be incorporated or implied into the contract between ISP and user.[52]

11.5.1 Basic service provision

Any claim that an intermediary should compensate communicating parties for a transmission failure must identify a duty on the part of the intermediary to ensure that such failures would not occur. Unless there is specific legislative provision for imposing liability on Internet Intermediaries, this

---

49. This was the aim of the Bavarian Länder government when it took action against CompuServe officials in 1995 attempting to stop CompuServe providing access from within Germany to neo-Nazi newsgroups (mainly in the United States). This achieved some limited measure of success, as CompuServe was initially forced to suspend worldwide access to those newsgroups. See U. Sieber, 'Criminal Liability for the Transfer of Data in International Networks — New Challenges for the Internet (part I)' (1997) 13 *Computer Law and Security Report*, p. 151. However, given the distributed nature of the Internet, the wide array of intermediary options for accessing information on it, and the perception of many governments that allowing such cases to be brought might damage Internet growth, such apparent victories are all too likely to be transitory, as indeed was the victory here. CompuServe Ex-Official's Porn-Case Conviction Reversed, Associated Press, 17 November 1999.
50. See *Religious Technology Center v Netcom* (1995) 33 IPR 132.
51. European Union Council Directive 95/46/EC on the Protection of Individuals with regard to the Processing of Personal Data and on the Free Movement of Such Data, OJ 1995 L281/31 (http://www2.echo.lu/legal/en/dataprot/directiv/directiv.html). See chapter 13.
52. See, for example, Sprint Canada's terms and conditions at http://www.sprint.ca/general/terms.php3 and http://www.sprint.ca/general/privacy.php3.

duty could only come about via contract or the law of tort. For many types of intermediary, there will be no contractual relationship between them and communicating parties. In the case of commercial ISPs, the relationship between each communicating party and its ISP is highly likely to be governed by express contracts whose terms will define the ISP's liability for communications failures. However, this may not always be the case; for example, if company X provides its employees with Internet access through a commercial ISP, communications made in furtherance of X's business which were lost would normally be covered by the terms of the contract between the X and the commercial ISP. Private communications made by X's employees would likely fall outside that contractual relationship, and thus any remedy for loss of their communications would likely lie in tort.[53] Equally in universities, which often act as ISPs for their staff and students, there is unlikely to be a contract for service between the university and its users.[54] Where there is an express contract between a communicating party and its ISP, the terms of that contract are likely to attempt to limit the extent of the ISPs liability to the bare minimum that the ISP's lawyers think will pass muster in the courts.[55] For example:

Kingston Internet Ltd's Terms and Conditions
for the Provision of Karoo Dial service
(http://www.kingston-internet.net/karooterms.html)

[. . .]

9.1   We warrant that We will use all reasonable care and skill in carrying out Our obligations under this Agreement. All other conditions, warranties and obligations implied by statute, common law or otherwise and any liabilities arising therefrom are excluded to the extent permissible by law.

9.2   You acknowledge that We do not exercise control over or monitor in any way the content of any information, data or software which is stored or transmitted via the Service or which You send or receive. We exclude all liability for the accuracy or inaccuracy of any information or data stored or transmitted through the Service, or the sending or receipt or failure to send or receive any information, data or software.

9.3   We will not limit Our liability to You for death or personal injury caused by any of Our acts or omissions, or those of Our employees or agents acting in the course of their employment.

---

53. Employers appear increasingly loathe to permit employees to use company Internet access for personal business, whether this is because of liability issues or simply to stop employees wasting time web surfing and e-mailing their friends is not clear.

54. It is noticeable that many university regulations and guidelines now contain statements such as 'Whilst every reasonable endeavour is made to ensure that the computing systems are available as scheduled and function correctly, no liability whatsoever can be accepted by Academic Services Computing for any loss or delay as a result of any system malfunction, howsoever caused'.

55. See further in the context of Y2K liability, E. Macdonald, 'Y2K and Contractual Exemption Clauses', 1999, (2) *The Journal of Information, Law and Technology* (JILT), http://www.law.warwick.ac.uk/jilt/99-2/macdonald.html.

9.4   Our liability to You for damage to Your tangible property caused by the negligence of Us, Our employees or agents, acting in the course of their duty shall be limited to £1 million in respect of any one event or series of connected events.

9.5   In any event apart from Clause 9.3, We will not be liable to You in contract, tort, negligence or otherwise for any loss of business, contracts, profits, or anticipated savings or for any other special, indirect or consequential loss whatsoever, even if such loss was reasonably foreseeable, or We have been advised of the possibility of Your incurring the same.

9.6   Apart from Clauses 9.3 and 9.4, Our maximum aggregate liability in contract, tort, negligence or otherwise arising out of, or in connection with, this Agreement shall be limited in respect of any one event or series of two or more connected events to an amount equal to £50,000 and to an amount equal to £100,000 in respect of all claims under this Agreement.

In the unlikely event that the ISP's contract contains no express terms as to liability, or if the express terms are voided as exclusion clauses, most jurisdictions' laws of contract will imply a term that the ISP must take reasonable care in the provision of services to its user.[56] That is, an ISP can be liable for a basic service failure, such as failing to process a communication, but only if a competent ISP could reasonably have been expected not to have failed. The mere fact that a failure has occurred would not by itself be enough to ground a successful action, as in normal operations computing technology can fail at times, sometimes catastrophically, and often for no apparent reason.[57] Thus in the majority of circumstances, an ISP would only be liable to its clients if the failed transmission resulted from a failure on the part of the ISP to take sufficient care in selecting the hardware and software which comprises its system, or to take sufficient care in operating the system. In a situation where the hardware and software used by the ISP have been sourced from reliable suppliers, and have been operated within appropriate bounds by suitably qualified staff, then unless the ISP has played a part in designing that hardware or software, defects in either, no matter how serious, will not normally result in a judicial finding of breach.[58]

11.5.2   Enhanced service provision

Increasingly, ISPs have begun to offer services that go well beyond the simple carriage of information packets, and in doing so have begun blurring the line

---

56. E.g., UK Supply of Goods and Services Act 1982, s. 13. Some ISPs explicitly spell this out. For example, BT Internet Terms and Conditions (http://guest.btinternet.com/html/termsconditions.html):

> 11.3 In performing any obligation under this Contract, our duty is only to exercise the reasonable care and skill of a competent Internet service provider.

57. See I. Peterson, *Fatal Defect: Chasing Killer Computer Bugs*, New York: Time Books, 1995. Mission critical software or services may however be held to a higher standard by the courts. See also G. Hughes, 'Reasonable Design', 1999, (2) *The Journal of Information, Law and Technology* (JILT), http://www.law.warwick.ac.uk/jilt/99-2/hughes.html.

58. See further generally, chapter 5 of I. Lloyd, and M. Simpson, *Law on The Electronic Frontier* Hume Papers on Public Policy: vol. 2, no. 4. Also at http://www.strath.ac.uk/Departments/Law/dept/diglib/book/.

between themselves and information content providers. A key reason for this evolution is that as the competition between ISPs has increased, consumers of ISP services have become more sophisticated and cognizant of the fact that many ISPs in effect provide an identical service.[59] There has thus been an accelerating trend amongst ISPs towards the provision of 'enhanced services' that they hope will sufficiently differentiate them from their competitors in the eyes of potential clients. Such enhanced services are sometimes available to all comers via the WWW, but can be restricted to the ISPs clients.[60] They may include the provision of:

(a)   Customised software for accessing Internet services, including parental controls, dedicated chat rooms, roaming capabilities, and instant messaging.
(b)   Space on the ISP's servers for client web pages, and data storage.
(c)   Information services such as news, weather, and financial data.

The development by ISPs of such increasingly complex business models has obvious implications for increasing their potential legal liabilities. To take, as an example, the situation of America Online, Inc. Their relationship with an end user might involve:

(a)   *Subscription to one of their two Internet services* — e.g., AOL or CompuServe — either with or without AOL supplied Internet access. This relationship would be governed by the service contract that the end user agreed with America Online, Inc.[61]
(b)   *Use of their software* — e.g., the WWW browser, Netscape Navigator; or their messaging system, AOL Instant Messenger. This might be governed by the service contract, if the end user is an America Online, Inc. Internet service client, or by the software's click through license agreement, displayed prior to installation of the software.[62]
(c)   *Access to their web portals* — e.g., the Netscape Netcenter and AOL.com portals. This may be governed by the portal website's terms of

---

59. Indeed, the ISP market has increasingly come to resemble the US telecommunications market in that a wide range of suppliers offering virtually identical services are pursuing a finite set of consumers. In that market, the advertising for services has become so complex that the average consumer will often struggle to determine which service in fact offers the 'best value'. Some people might suggest that this consumer confusion is exactly what most of the companies want, as a clear comparison between their services would reveal how little they differ in scope and price.

60. AOL, for example, offers a range of pricing packages for its services. A client can purchase:
    (a)   Four pricing variants on basic access to AOL's services, plus Internet access.
    (b)   Additional premium services, on top of one of the four basic variants.
    (c)   Access to AOL's services and premium services, via another ISP.

    A range of informational services are also available for free from AOL's webpage, to anyone with Internet access.

61. See AOL Terms of Service, Spring 1998 at http://www.cc.gatech.edu/classes/ cs8113e_99_winter/aol-tos.html. For current documentation from America Online, connect to AOL and enter the keyword: TOS.

62. See, e.g., Netscape Client Software End User License Agreement at http://www.netscape. com/download/client.html.

use,[63] although it might be argued that the client was given insufficient notice of the terms and conditions of use to be bound by them.[64]

(d) *Access to their Internet movie listing guide and ticketing service* — AOL MovieFone. This, at present, does not appear to be governed by any specific agreement between the user and AOL, although provision of inaccurate information or invalid tickets might have tortious implications in the former case, and would certainly have contractual implications in the latter.

In the case of services provided by an ISP for which there are no express contract provisions, or where the services are in fact provided by a third party intermediary, the avenue for potential legal redress is less certain. Where the ISP is providing a non-contractual service, or the service is being delivered by other Internet Intermediaries who have no express contract with a end user, there are only limited circumstances in which a contractual duty might be owed. In some cases the courts may be prepared to imply a contract between the intermediary and the end user. This is rare, but not unknown, at least in the common law jurisdictions, even where the parties have had no previous dealings.[65] Much would turn on the closeness of the relationship between the intermediary and end user.

For example, where the intermediary was an Internet host supplying the ISP with transmission facilities, and his sole connection with an end user of the ISP was the reception of information packets for onward transmission, it seems unlikely that a court would be prepared to imply a contract between him and that end user in the event of a loss of information. That would involve the implication of contracts between every Internet host and all users whose packets arrive at their servers. Taken to its logical conclusion, this would potentially produce millions of individual contracts, none of whose terms could easily be identified as they would all need to be implied by the courts.

Additionally, in jurisdictions where the applicable law recognises the concept of enforceable contractual obligations for the benefit of a third party, this might create a contractual duty owed by a host to the customers of those ISPs with which it has an express interconnection agreement (e.g., if it provides the ISP with a connection to the Internet on a chargeable basis).[66] However, even if such a contractual duty were found to exist, again it would be at most a duty to take reasonable care in the forwarding of packets. Proof of breach would always be extremely difficult.

If bringing a successful case against our Internet host intermediary would be difficult in contract, it would be even less likely in tort, due to the extreme

---

63. See, e.g., Netscape Communications Corporation Legal Information at http://www. netcenter.com/legal_notices/index.html.

64. *Thornton* v *Shoe Lane Parking* [1971] 2 QB 163.

65. In the United Kingdom see *Clarke* v *Dunraven* [1897] AC 59 (a yacht owner's act of entering for a sailing race created an implied contract between himself and all the other entrants in which they agreed to abide by the rules of the race).

66. For the UK, see now the Contracts (Rights of Third Parties) Act 1999, discussed in chapter 3, section 3.3.

difficulty of demonstrating that the intermediary owed the user a tortious duty of care. This is because losses resulting from an information transaction are highly likely to be pure financial losses, and many jurisdictions will not impose a duty of care to avoid pure financial losses unless there is some clear pre-existing non-contractual relationship between the parties. The fact that the Internet operates using a packet-switching protocol (TCP/IP) allowing individual information packets from the same communications to be routed via a multiplicity of different routes and hosts to ensure the best chance of delivery means that a user cannot predict with any certainty which intermediaries will be involved in the transaction, other than his ISP and that of the party with whom he is communicating, as such there can be no duty of care to him on the part of the other hosts involved. Even if the failure or malfunction of Internet communication at issue were to have the capacity to cause physical injury or property damage, it would not be foreseeable that a failure on their part might cause such loss. This is because the intermediaries involved in transporting the communication would have no knowledge of the nature of the transaction, as it would appear as just a set of not necessarily related packets to them. Foreseeability of this kind is normally a prerequisite for a duty to arise. Even if, by some means it could be proven that a particular intermediary did owe a duty to one or other of the communicating parties, the fault-tolerant nature of the Internet would tend to militate against any breach of that duty causing loss. In the common law jurisdictions at least, this will mean that there is insufficient causal link between the breach and the loss, which will be unrecoverable as being too remote.

11.5.3   General consumer protection

Some of the marketing and sales activities of ISPs may also draw the attention of national consumer protection and trade bodies. For example, many of the larger ISPs such as America Online, Inc., and Prodigy attempt to attract new clients by the use of 'free trial' offers. These often promise users hundreds of free hours of Internet access and the use of enhanced membership-only services.[67] However, the nature of the terms and conditions attached to these 'free trials', the advertising copy used to promote an ISP's services, or the actual business practices of the ISP may on occasion breach consumer protection laws. An example of this could be seen when, in May 1997, America Online. Inc. (AOL), CompuServe, Inc., and Prodigy Services Corporation reached a consent agreement[68] with the Federal Trade Commission (FTC) in the United States, over a list of allegations including:

---

67. A recent (January 2000) Canadian AOL promotion promised 540 free hours, although the small print pointed out that the free time had to be used within one month of joining, and the 'free time' had thus been calculated on a usage rate of 18 hours a day, 7 days a week!

68. 'A consent agreement is for settlement purposes only and does not constitute an admission of a law violation. When the Commission issues a consent order on a final basis, it carries the force of law with respect to future actions. Each violation of such an order may result in a civil penalty of $11,000.' See http://www.ftc.gov/opa/1997/9705/online.htm.

(a)   That all three firms' 'free trial' offers could result in charges which they had not adequately notified their clients about in violation of the Federal Trade Commission Act (FTCA).[69]

(b)   That AOL failed to inform consumers that 15 seconds of connect time was added to each online session, resulting in additional undisclosed charges. This was exacerbated by AOL's practice of rounding up online sessions to the next full minute, meaning many consumers unknowingly ran up extra charges for online time.[70]

(c)   That AOL informed consumers who chose automatic debiting that their bank accounts would not be debited without their authorisation, but in fact accounts were debited without authorisation, thereby violating both the FTCA and the Electronic Funds Transfer Act 1978 (EFTA).

(d)   That all three firms failed to obtain appropriate consumer authorisation before making electronic withdrawals from the accounts of consumers, and failed to give consumers advance notice of monthly amounts to be electronically withdrawn from their accounts, in violation of the EFTA.[71]

The terms of the FTC's consent agreement in those cases mean that US ISPs:

(a)   Must not misrepresent the terms or conditions of any online service trial offer.

(b)   Must not represent that an online service is free unless they disclose clearly and prominently in their instructional materials any obligation to take action to avoid charges, and in all advertisements inform consumers where that disclosure is available.

(c)   Must disclose clearly and prominently during the final registration process and prior to consumers incurring any financial obligation, the terms of all mandatory charges that consumers will incur as a result of using the online services.

(d)   When they use an automatic membership enrollment or renewal plan, must disclose clearly and prominently any obligation of consumers to cancel to avoid charges and to provide consumers with at least one reasonable means of cancelling their memberships.

(e)   Must obtain consumers' written authorisation before initiating any electronic fund transfer and notify consumers in advance about electronic fund transfers varying in amount from previous transfers.

The interest shown by the FTC in this area is unlikely to decrease, for as the provision of Internet services becomes an increasingly mainstream

---

69. Clients were not told that they had to affirmatively cancel their membership during the trial period — when they failed to cancel they were automatically enrolled as members, and charged monthly membership fees.

70. For example, an online session of 2 minutes and 46 seconds, with the 15-second supplement, would make 3 minutes and 1 second, which would then would be billed by AOL as a 4 minute session.

71. See File Nos. AOL–952 3331 (http://www.ftc.gov/os/1997/9705/ameronli.htm); Compu-Serve–962 3096 (http://www. ftc.gov/os/1997/9705/compuser.htm); Prodigy–952 3332 (http://www.ftc.gov/os/1997/9705/prodigy.htm).

business sector, ISPs, like businesses in any other high profile, high penetration consumer sector, can expect increasing scrutiny of their actions by consumer protection authorities, and other consumer watchdogs.

11.5.4 Privacy

Information privacy has become a high profile issue on the Internet, not least because many users are concerned about the secondary purposes to which data collected about them via ISPs and other Internet Intermediaries might be put. In the European Union (EU), the Data Protection Directive[72] has required Member States to put in place strict rules on how, why, and when personal data may be collected, and the uses to which it may be put.[73] The following aspects of the Directive are of particular relevance to ISPs with operations in the EU. It applies to most situations where data are processed wholly or partly by automatic means. The only major exception to this rule is data processed by natural persons in the course of private and personal activity.[74] The term 'processing' is defined widely, effectively covering every aspect of personal data use from collection to destruction.[75] Processing of data is legitimate only in certain specified situations, and must comply with data protection principles contained in the Directive. Certain data such as indications as to 'racial or ethnic origin, political opinions, religious or philosophical beliefs, trade union membership and health or sex life' are regarded as particularly sensitive, and may only be processed with the explicit consent of the data subject.[76] The Directive requires that individuals whose data are processed must be provided with certain information, for example, about the purpose of processing; and that they should have the right of access to their personal data, and the right to have inaccurate data amended, erased or destroyed.[77] Individuals are also provided with rights to object to lawful processing of their data and to their data being used for direct marketing purposes.[78] With regard to transfers of data outside the EU and EEA, the Directive sets detailed conditions for transfer of personal data to third party countries, forbidding transfers where, subject to limited exceptions, non-Member States fail to ensure an 'adequate level of protection'. The key exception is when the transfer of data is 'necessary for the performance of a contract between the data subject and the controller' and the data subject has

---

72. Council Directive 95/46/EC on the Protection of Individuals with Regard to the Processing of Personal Data and on the Free Movement of Such Data, OJ 1995 L 281/31, p. 31 (http://www2.echo.lu/legal/en/dataprot/directiv/directiv.html).
73. See D. Bainbridge, *EC Data Protection Directive*, London: Butterworths, 1996; F.H. Cate, *Privacy in the Information Age*, Washington D.C.: Brookings Institution Press, 1997; and A. Charlesworth, 'Implementing the European Data Protection Directive 1995 in UK Law: The Data Protection Act 1998', (1999), 16(3) *Government Information Quarterly* 203 at pp. 230–231.
74. Article 3(1)–(2), in note 72, above.
75. Article 2(b), note 72, above.
76. Article 8, note 72, above.
77. Articles 10–12, note 72, above.
78. Article 14, note 72, above.

been informed of both this and the fact that the country receiving the export does not provide 'an adequate level of protection'.[79]

This latter requirement has been the subject of considerable disagreement between the United States and the EU,[80] for while the United States has a number of privacy-related laws, and the concept of privacy in the sense of 'the right to be let alone'[81] has long been accepted in principle by the US legal system as a constitutional right, it has rarely received much support in regard to informational privacy.[82] The US approach to informational privacy on the Internet has instead focused upon promoting self-regulatory mechanisms, as exemplified by the growth of new on-line industry self-regulatory bodies such as TRUSTe,[83] the Online Privacy Alliance[84] and BBBonline.[85] Both the US and EU approaches to informational privacy stem from a common belief based on a set of fair information practices that can be traced back at least to the OECD's *Guidelines on the Protection of Privacy and Transborder Data Flows of Personal Data*.[86] However, the key difference between them is that the European approach offers credible oversight and enforcement mechanisms, and legal redress for the individual, while the US self-regulatory approach thus far does not.

A European ISP is obliged to ensure that the data it collects about its clients is: processed fairly and lawfully; obtained and processed only for specified and lawful purposes; adequate, relevant, and not excessive; accurate and up-to-date; kept only while it is required; processed in accordance with the rights of data subjects; protected against unauthorised or unlawful processing and against accidental loss, destruction, or damage; and not transferred to a country or territory without an equal level of protection for personal data. If it breaches those rules, it may be subject to legal action brought by those affected by the breach, or by a national data privacy authority. A US ISP or Internet Intermediary, in contrast, is only obliged by law to provide specific data privacy protection to children.[87] However, as the

---

79. Articles 25 and 26, note 72, above.
80. See A. Charlesworth 'Data Privacy in Cyberspace: Not National vs International but Commercial vs Individual', in *Issues in Internet Law*, Edwards & Waelde (eds), Oxford: Hart Publishing, 2000.
81. The phrase drawn from the seminal article by S.D. Warren, & L.D. Brandeis, 'The Right to Privacy: the Implicit made Explicit', (1890) 4 *Harvard Law Review*, p. 193.
82. For an excellent discussion of the historical and philosophical development of privacy theory in US law, see further S. Scoglio, *Transforming Privacy: A Transpersonal Philosophy of Rights*, New York: Praeger 1998. Also P.M. Schwartz, and J.R. Reidenberg, *Data Privacy Law*, Charlottesville: Michie, 1996.
83. See http://www.Truste.org/.
84. See http://www.privacyalliance.org.
85. See http://www.BBBonline.org/.
86. OECD's *Guidelines on the Protection of Privacy and Transborder Data Flows of Personal Data*, Paris: Organization for Economic Co-operation and Development, 1980.
87. Under the Children's Online Privacy Protection Act 1998, which comes into force in April 2000. This Act deals with commercial web sites or on-line services aimed at children under 13 that collect personal information from children, and general audience web sites aware that they are collecting personal information from children. The rules apply to individually identifiable information about a child that is collected on-line, such as full name, home address, e-mail address, telephone number or any other information that would allow someone to identify or contact the child, and other types of information — for example,

US public has grown increasingly concerned about privacy issues,[88] US ISPs and other intermediaries have tended to publish 'privacy policies' and 'privacy statements' that are submitted for approval to one or more of the industry self-regulatory bodies. The problem from the US public's point of view is that when breaches of those 'privacy policies' and 'privacy statements' have occurred, both the policies and the activities of the industry self-regulatory bodies have been repeatedly demonstrated to be meaningless.[89] This is not to say that ISPs and Internet Intermediaries can breach individuals' informational privacy at will, for if they make untrue claims about their privacy policies, they may still be subject to action by the FTC for misleading business practices.[90]

The impact that breach of an ISPs privacy policy may have, and the lack of protection afforded US citizens for such breaches, was graphically demonstrated in the 1998 case of *McVeigh* v *Cohen* 983 F Supp 215 (DDC 1998).[91] Here, a sailor in the US Navy challenged his discharge by the Chief of Naval Personnel, on the ground that he was a homosexual. Discharge proceedings against McVeigh had begun after a Navy investigation resulting from the discovery that he was using a 'screen name' of 'boysrch' to access AOL's services, and to send e-mail. In his AOL 'profile'[92] McVeigh had listed his name as 'Tim' and his marital status as 'gay.' A Navy officer, having received this information from a third party, ordered a Navy paralegal to telephone AOL and obtain the profile owner's name. When the paralegal called AOL's customer service, he represented himself as a friend of the sailor, and did not reveal his Navy affiliation. The customer service representative then provided the sailor's full name to the Navy paralegal. This was clearly in breach of AOL's policy regarding its members' privacy, but the issue of AOL's legal liability, if any, for the disclosure is less clear cut.

The Electronic Communications Privacy Act of 1986 ('ECPA')[93] provides some degree of privacy protection to the extent that it bars certain unwanted

---

continued

   hobbies, interests and information collected through cookies or other types of tracking mechanisms when they are tied to individually identifiable information.

88. See L. Gurak, *Persuasion and Privacy in Cyberspace: The Online Protests over Lotus Marketplace and the Clipper Chip*, Yale University Press, 1999, at pp. 19–31. See also M.J. Culnan, 'Self-Regulation on the Electronic Frontier: Implications for Public Policy', in *Privacy and Self-Regulation in the Information Age*, 1997, http://www.ntia.doc.gov/reports/privacy/Selfreg1.htm.

89. See A. Charlesworth, 'Data Privacy in Cyberspace: Not National vs International but Commercial vs Individual', op. cit., note 80, above.

90. 13 August 1998, the Federal Trade Commission (FTC) announced that it and GeoCities, a provider of free home pages on the Internet with over two million members and a TRUSTe member, had agreed on a consent order to settle the first FTC case of privacy violation. See *In re GeoCities*, 63 Fed Reg 44,624 (FTC, 1998) or http://www.ftc.gov/opa/1998/9808/geocitie.htm for details of the consent order.

91. Also http://www.loundy.com/CASES/McVeigh_v_Cohen.html. See further C.T. Karafm, '"Don't Ask, Don't Tell"; A Discussion of Employee Privacy in Cyberspace in Light of *McVeigh* v *Cohen, et al*', 3 Va JL & Tech 7 (Fall, 1998), http://vjolt.student.virginia.edu at http://scs.student.virginia.edu/~vjolt/graphics/vol3/vol3_art7.html.

92. An AOL listing associated with an individual screen name and available to all AOL members.

93. Electronic Communications Privacy Act of 1986, Pub L No. 99–508, 100 Stat 1848.

intrusions into an individual's use of electronic communications media. Title II of the Act specifically deals with the unauthorised access and disclosure of stored wire or electronic communications.[94] However, the ECPA only deals with governmental intrusions, it does not apply to unauthorised non-governmental third party inquiries into information in the possession of an ISP.

The potential liability of an ISP for an unauthorised disclosure under the ECPA revolves around a three-stage test:

(a) Whether the information disclosed is the 'contents' of a communication in storage with or carried or maintained on the service;[95] or if it is simply 'a record or other information pertaining to a subscriber to or customer of such service'.[96]

If it is 'contents' of a communication in storage with or carried or maintained on the service, the information cannot be released to government entities without suitable authorisation, or to non-governmental entities not otherwise exempted from the provisions of the Act. If it is a record or other information pertaining to a subscriber to or customer of such service, the information cannot be released to government entities without suitable authorisation, but may be released to non-governmental entities.[97]

(b) If the information is the 'contents' of a communication in storage or carried or maintained on the service, whether it could still be legitimately disclosed to the person or entity requesting the disclosure.

A government entity can force disclosure of the 'contents' of a communication in storage with or carried or maintained on an ISP's service by obtaining a warrant,[98] court order,[99] or administrative subpoena.[100] In addition, again after obtaining proper authorisation, a government entity can also force disclosure of the 'name, address, . . . telephone number . . . and the type of services the subscriber or customer utilized'.[101]

ISPs are also protected from liability under the Act where they disclose the contents of a communication in storage with or carried or maintained on their service to an addressee, an intended recipient or an agent of the addressee or recipient;[102] or the disclosure is made with the lawful consent of the originator, addressee, intended recipient or the ISP subscriber.[103]

(c) Whether the person or entity making the disclosure believed that the party requesting the disclosure was in fact a person or entity to which it could be legitimately disclosed.

---

94. 18 USC §§ 2701–2710.
95. 'Contents' are defined as including 'any information concerning the substance, purport, or meaning' of any wire, oral, or electronic communication. 18 USC § 2510(8).
96. 18 USC § 2703(c)(1)(A).
97. An ISP 'may disclose a record or other information pertaining to a subscriber to or customer of such service (not including the contents of communications. . .) to any person other than a governmental entity'. 18 USC § 2703(c)(1)(A).
98. 18 USC § 2703(a) & § 2703(b)(2)(A).
99. 18 USC § 2703(b)(2)(B)(i).
100. 18 USC § 2703(b)(2)(B)(ii).
101. 18 USC § 2703(c)(1)(B), (C).
102. 18 USC § 2702(b)(1).
103. 18 USC § 2702(b)(3).

The major hurdle for an individual seeking to hold an ISP liable for unlawful disclosure of the 'contents' of a communication in storage with or carried or maintained on the ISP's service is that the unlawful 'conduct ... is engaged in with a knowing or intentional state of mind'.[104] In other words, if the ISP states that it or its representatives believed that the disclosure was lawful, in the absence of compelling evidence to the contrary, that will be a defence, as negligent disclosure does not appear to be a offence under the Act.

In the *McVeigh* case, it would seem clear that a government entity was involved, and that the proper authorisation for the disclosure of either the 'contents' of a communication in storage with, or carried or maintained by AOL, or the 'name, address, ... telephone number... and the type of services the subscriber or customer utilized' was not present. However, if the information that their customer service representative disclosed was the 'contents' of a communication, AOL might argue that they honestly believed that the Navy paralegal was in fact an intended recipient of a communication from McVeigh, the Act not setting any reasonableness standard for such an alleged belief. If the information was simply 'a record or other information pertaining to a subscriber to or customer of such service', the failure of the Navy paralegal to identify his government entity status would again appear to allow AOL to argue that their representative had simply assumed he was a non-governmental third party. The fact that such an assumption was wrong would not be enough to meet the requirement that the unlawful disclosure was 'engaged in with a knowing or intentional state of mind'.

It has been argued that making changes to the current regime, such as changing the ECPA standard of liability for unauthorised disclosures of content and non-content information to a 'negligence' standard;[105] clarifying the liability of government entities who solicit information from ISPs without properly identifying themselves;[106] and providing an ECPA companion statute outlawing unauthorised non-governmental third party access to an individual's communications and personal information held by ISPs;[107] would provide a suitable method of determining ISP liability and protecting individual privacy. While this approach would be perfectly in line with the piecemeal US approach to privacy legislation, it is arguable that a rather more elegant, and comprehensive, solution for the protection of personal privacy on the Internet, including personal data held by ISPs and other Internet Intermediaries, would be the adoption of omnibus data privacy legislation similar to that of the EU. This would, at a stroke, remove the artificial divide between 'contents of a communication' and 'a record or other information', and clarify the position of government and non-government entities. Certainly, if a

---

104. 18 USC § 2707(a).
105. C.T. Karafin, ' "Don't Ask, Don't Tell"; A Discussion of Employee Privacy in Cyberspace in Light of *McVeigh* v *Cohen, et al*', op. cit., note 91, above.
106. Ibid., at para. 45.
107. Ibid., at para. 46.

European ISP was placed in a similar position to that of AOL and it had disclosed McVeigh's personal details, it would be liable for a breach of his privacy, and for such damages as the claimant suffered as a result of that breach.[108]

11.6 INFORMATION CONTENT — CIVIL LIABILITY

The range of laws that impose civil, or in some cases criminal, liability in respect of information content is extremely wide. However, in most jurisdictions, a common feature of such laws is that mere intermediaries will not be held liable for their contravention in the same way as an individual who originates the information, or who instigates its transmission or copying. In many circumstances, as with the concept of 'common carrier' status commonly applied to telecommunications companies in the United States, if the intermediary simply provides a regular service for information transport, without discriminating as between types of users, or exercising any control over the information content, he is likely to be granted a degree of immunity from information content laws. In contrast, newspaper publishers who exercise editorial functions, in deciding both who and what will and will not be published, expose themselves to the full gamut of information content legislation: from the obvious aspects such as copyright, obscenity and indecency, and defamation through to the intricacies of advertising and securities laws, and obscurities such as the law relating to blasphemy.

The difficulty with Internet Intermediaries and ISPs is that the nature of the forms of communication that they provide often go well beyond the simple carriage of information commonly found with basic telecommunication services, without necessarily remotely approaching the degree of carrier involvement to be found in the communications process in the print and broadcast media. In the basic telecommunications model, information, for instance in the form of words spoken into a telephone mouthpiece, is digitised at point A and transferred by the telecommunications company to point B, where it is converted back to sound at a telephone earpiece. Information about that transmission, such as the locations from which it was made and at which it was received, and its duration, is stored by the telephone company, but only for billing purposes. Unless the call is the subject of a wiretap, the telephone company will not store the actual transmission, copy the transmission, or make it available to others.[109] Most ISPs, on the other hand, provide facilities for the storage, copying and retransmitting of information, and many also exercise significant controls over the nature of the information transmitted via various of their functions, barring on their own initiative

---

108. See for example s. 13 of the UK Data Protection Act 1998, which provides that data subjects have the right to claim compensation for damage caused by any breach of the Act and also for distress where this is inflicted by virtue of damage caused by any breach of the Act.

109. Of course with enhanced telephone services, such as voice mail, this distinction may be less clear.

certain types of topics and information,[110] and at times, certain words.[111]

This has led to a certain degree of international judicial and legislative uncertainty as to the precise standard to which ISPs and other Internet Intermediaries (IIs) should be held with regard to responsibility for the content of their services. Although, as will be seen, this uncertainty initially led to cases where ISPs were effectively held to broadcast and print media standards of liability for content, the international trend is moving towards a much more limited standard, one which is, in some instances, not dissimilar to the 'common carrier' standard alluded to above. The main reason for this shift in attitude has been increasing legislative action relating to the Internet on the part of many national governments, which have been concerned to ensure that the application of existing national laws to Internet Intermediaries will not unnecessarily impede the growth of electronic commerce.

In general terms, an intermediary's liability for the information content of communications or resources which have originated from a third party will be derived from one or more of three types of activity, copying, possession or transmission. In the case of copyright infringement, carrying out any of the three actions without the permission of the copyright owner will potentially be an infringing act. In the case of obscenity or indecency laws the act of copying may not give rise to liability, but possession and transmission may. In terms of defamation law, making copies of or possessing potentially defamatory content is unlikely to raise liability issues, but the act of transmission probably will.

11.6.1 Intellectual property: copyright

Of all the areas of law associated with the Internet, copyright law is probably the most widely discussed, the most widely breached, and the least fully understood by anybody but intellectual property lawyers. A very basic formulation of the way that most nations' copyright laws relate to electronic communications is that 'there will be a copyright infringement when an individual copies a work held in electronic format without the authority of the copyright holder'.[112]

---

110. See J. Kornblum, 'AOL fixes serial killer site' CNET News.com, 12 September 1997 (US website on serial killers removed by ISP) http://news.cnet.com/news/0-1005-200-322092.html; J. Kornblum, 'ISP censorship seen as trend' 18 September 1997, (a UK website containing Euskal Herria Journal, a Basque-separatist publication removed by ISP) http://news.cnet.com/news/0-1005-200-322275.html.

111. 'America Online, in an attempt to crack down on vulgar on-line language, filtered for the word "breast" and deleted files containing it. A breast cancer patient in Vermont with an AOL account found that her files had been deleted, and when she attempted to create a new file, AOL "flashed her a message that she could not use vulgar words"'. 'Names & Faces', *Washington Post*, 2 December 1995, at C3 (' "Breast" Reconstruction'). Cited in R. Cannon, 'The Legislative History of Senator Exon's Communications Decency Act: Regulating Barbarians on the Information Superhighway', (1996) 49 *Federal Communications Law Journal* 51, http://www.law.indiana.edu/fclj/pubs/v49/no1/cannon.html.

112. Berne Convention art. 9(1):

Authors of literary and artistic works ... shall have the exclusive right of authorising reproduction of these works, in any manner or form.

UK Copyright, Designs and Patents Act 1988, s. 16(1):

The key problem with this formulation, as far as ISPs and IIs are concerned, is that both the TCP/IP protocol underlying the Internet, and the technologies which overlay it rely extensively, if not entirely, on the ability to make copies of information. Thus ISPs and IIs can only operate by copying information. If the II is merely part of the communications chain, it copies received packets into memory (and probably onto disk) and then sends fresh copies to the next host in the chain. If it is hosting a resource, it initially makes a copy of that resource onto its disks, and then makes further copies when the resource is requested by a user. If those copies are of a work protected by copyright, the intermediary, by making copies not specifically authorised by the rightsholder, is technically infringing that copyright.

It was argued that such transient, or evanescent copies, in RAM, because of their lack of permanence, could not be said to breach copyright.[113] In fact, many copyright laws can be, and have been, interpreted such that even supposedly evanescent copies in computer memory can be deemed to be sufficient copying for a finding of infringement.[114] Of course, in the course of their daily operations, many ISPs and IIs will make not just evanescent copies in RAM, but will make further copies on a range of storage media, for example, hard discs when caching a resource, or DAT tapes when making backup copies of a resource. The first US court to consider the matter, in *Playboy Enterprises* v *Frena*, 839 F Supp 1552 (MD Fla, 1993)[115] held that a bulletin board operator who encouraged users to use the board to upload and download images in which Playboy owned copyright, had infringed Playboy's copyright by the direct copying the system undertook when storing and transmitting images. The problem with this particular interpretation of what precisely is taking place when information is being uploaded or downloaded from Internet hosts is that although, as a matter of technical fact, the host is

---

continued

The owner of the copyright in a work has ... the exclusive right ... (a) to copy the work   ...

17 USC § 106:

... the owner of copyright under this title has the exclusive rights ... (1) to reproduce the copyrighted work....

113. Especially important under US law, where 17 USC s. 101 states ' "Copies" are material objects, ... in which a work is fixed by any method ... and from which the work can be perceived, reproduced, or otherwise communicated, either directly or with the aid of a machine or device' and 'A work is "fixed" in a tangible medium of expression when its embodiment ... is sufficiently permanent or stable to permit it to be perceived, reproduced, or otherwise communicated for a period of more than transitory duration'.

114. *MAI Systems Corp.* v *Peak Computer Inc.* 991 F 2d 511 (9th Cir, 1993) cert. *dismissed*, 114 S Ct 671 (1994). (copyrighted software program at issue was 'fixed' in RAM because the computer user was able to view a representation of the program's information, including the system error log, after loading the program into the computer's RAM); *Triad Systems Corp.* v *Southeastern Express Co.*, 31 USPQ 2d 1239 (NDC, 1994); *Advanced Systems of Michigan Inc.* v *MAI Systems Corporation* 845 F Supp 356, 363 (ED Va, 1994). See A. Morrison, 'Hijack on the road to Xanadu: The Infringement of Copyright in HTML Documents via Networked Computers and the Legitimacy of Browsing Hypermedia Documents', 1999, (1) *The Journal of Information, Law and Technology* (JILT), http://www.law.warwick.ac.uk/jilt/99-1/morrison.html.

115. Also http://www.Loundy.com/CASES/Playboy_v_Frena.html.

copying or reproducing the work, via its software, the commands that are being sent to that software instructing it to make the copies are in fact given by a third party. In other words, a third party is operating the host's computer system remotely. Thus, when instructions to make an infringing copy of information are sent to an Internet host by a third party, the owner of the host will very likely have neither knowledge of the infringement relating to that information, nor any intent to infringe that information.[116]

This lack of knowledge, or lack of intent, was often emphasised by the ISPs in the early case law. However, they were soon to discover that it did not necessarily mean that they would escape liability for the infringement. The judiciaries in the United Kingdom and the United States, for example, have long tended towards a position that lack of intention to infringe is not a defence in copyright actions. In some of the ISP cases, it appears that that rigid position may have shifted slightly, with the courts recognising that there might be a minimal mental element in copyright infringement — the intention to make a copy. This position was exemplified by the case of *Religious Technology Centre* v *Netcom On-Line Communications Services Inc.*, 907 F Supp 1361 (ND Cal, 1995).[117] Here, an infringement action was brought by representatives of the Church of Scientology (CoS) against Netcom, an ISP, which hosted a newsgroup, *alt.religion.scientology*, to which a customer had posted verbatim extracts of material in which the CoS claimed copyright. The judge expressly rejected the allegation that the ISP had infringed directly and refused to follow *Playboy Enterprises* v *Frena*, on the ground that Netcom could only be guilty of direct infringement if it had caused the infringing copies to be made:

> the mere fact that Netcom's system incidentally makes temporary copies of plaintiffs [claimants] works does not mean Netcom has caused the copying.[118]

In *Playboy Enterprises, Inc.* v *Webbworld* 968 F Supp 1171 (ND Tex, 1997),[119] however, the judge noted the principle raised in the *Netcom* case that an ISP or II might not have any control over the information to which it gave access, but concluded that:

> Even the absence of the ability to exercise such control, however, is no defense to liability. If a business cannot be operated within the bounds of

---

116. See *Marobie-FL Inc. d/b/a Galactic Software* v *National Association of Fire Equipment Distributors and Northwest Nexus Inc.* 983 F Supp 1167 (ND Ill., 13 November 1997) (defendant not guilty of direct infringement because it did not initiate the copying of claimants work, its systems were merely used to create a copy by a third party). Also http://www.Loundy.com/CASES/Marobie_v_NAFED.html.

117. Also http://www.Loundy.com/CASES/RTC_v_Netcom.html.

118. *Religious Technology Centre* v *Netcom On-Line Communications Services Inc.*, 907 F Supp 1361 (ND Cal, 1995), at 1368. See further on contributory infringement, E.A. Burcher and A.M. Hughes, Casenote, 'Religious Tech. Ctr. v Netcom On-Line Communications, Inc.: Internet Service Providers: The Knowledge Standard for Contributory Copyright Infringement and The Fair Use Defense, (1997) 3 *Rich. J.L. Tech.* 5, http://www.richmond.edu/~jolt/v3il/burhugh.html.

119. Also http://www.loundy.com/CASES/PEL_v_Webbworld.html.

the Copyright Act, then perhaps the question of its legitimate existence needs to be addressed.

Whilst this might perhaps be true of the website that the defendants in *Webbworld* ran, as it provided subscription access to images obtained from adult newsgroups, which are notorious for egregious copyright infringements,[120] it was a harsh approach to the copyright liability position of the average ISP. However, even if the trend in US cases[121] tended to suggest that ISPs, and other IIs, such as BBS operators, should escape direct liability, it was clear that they might still be held to be contributory or vicarious infringers where they are vicariously liable for the users' acts or have authorised or contributed to the copying.[122]

Vicarious liability is predicated upon a pre-existing relationship between the defendant and the direct infringer, and not on the defendant's involvement in the infringing activity — the link essentially being that the defendant potentially benefits from the infringer's activities.[123]

If someone has the 'right and ability' to supervise the infringing action of another, and that right and ability 'coalesce with an obvious and direct

---

120. See also *Playboy Enterprises, Inc. v Russ Hardenburgh, et al.*, 982 F Supp 503 (N.D. Ohio, 25 November 1997) (a bulletin board service operator was held liable for infringement of the copyright in Playboy's images, on the basis of his executive position, and his authority to control the BBSs content — there was no evidence that he personally approved the uploading of the images. He was also liable for contributory infringement as he had at least constructive knowledge that infringing activity was likely to be occurring on the BBS).

121. The trend in other jurisdictions is more difficult to ascertain, either because there have been no cases decided, or because the cases that have been decided carry uncertain precedental value. See H. Paynter, and R. Foreman, 'Liability of Internet Service Providers for Copyright Infringement', (1998) 21(2) *University of NSW Law Journal* at http://www. austlii.edu.au/au/other/unswlj/thematic/1998/vol21no2/paynter.html.

122. See *Sega Enterprises Ltd v Sabella*, 1996 WL 780560 (ND Cal 1996); *Sega Enterprises Ltd v MAPHIA*, 948 F Supp 923 (ND Cal 1996) (BBS operators knew their boards were being used to copy Sega's games and actively participated in that use by soliciting users to upload games and selling copiers to assist in the making of copies). Also *Marobie-FL Inc.* op. cit., note 117 (defendant not vicariously liable for copyright infringement unless it has the right and ability to supervise the infringing activity and also has a direct financial interest in such activities). See further K. Tickle, 'The Vicarious Liability of Electronic Bulletin Board Operators for the Copyright Infringement Occurring on Their Bulletin Boards', (1995) 80 *Iowa Law Review* 391.

123. The most common example would be that of employer and employee, but any relationship in which the defendant expects to benefit from the infringer's acts might give rise to vicarious liability, thus, for example, vicarious liability could arise from an independent contract or via a licence, e.g., *PRS v Bradford Corporation* [1917–1923] Mac CC 309; *Australasian PRA v Miles* [1962] NSWR 405 (liability of an organiser of an entertainment for infringement of performance rights by musicians); *Shapiro, Bernstein & Co. v H.L. Green Co.*, 316 F 2d 304, 307 (2d Cir, 1963) (a company leasing floor space to a record department was liable for the record department's sales of 'bootleg' records despite absence of actual knowledge of infringement, because of company's beneficial relationship to the sales). See also the 'dance hall cases', *Dreamland Ball Room, Inc. v Shapiro, Bernstein & Co.*, 36 F 2d 354 (7th Cir, 1929); *Famous Music Corp. v Bay State Harness Horse Racing & Breeding Ass'n, Inc.*, 554 F 2d 1213 (1st Cir, 1977); *KECA Music, Inc. v Dingus McGee's Co.*, 432 F Supp 72 (WD Mo, 1977).

financial interest in the exploitation of copyrighted materials — even in the absence of actual knowledge' that the infringement is taking place — the 'supervisor' may be held vicariously liable for the infringement. Vicarious liability is based on a connection to the direct infringer (not necessarily to the infringing activity).[124]

Yet in the case of ISPs, it is unlikely that a court will find sufficient relationship between a user and a transmission host to ground such liability.[125] Equally, even though a defendant may appear to authorise infringement by providing the necessary facilities for copying knowing that some users of that service will use it to make infringing copies,[126] this will probably not be sufficient to persuade a court that authorisation is intended, in circumstances where the equipment might also be used for non-infringing purposes and where the provider cannot control the use made by the copier.[127] The US doctrine of contributory infringement is based on 'the basic common law doctrine that one who knowingly participates or furthers a tortious act is jointly and severally liable with the prime tortfeasor ...'[128] and thus the defendant must (a) have knowledge of the infringement, and (b) have induced, caused or materially contributed to the third party's infringing conduct.[129] This was a key point raised by the court in the *Netcom* case. Here it was held that if Netcom had knowledge that infringing material was passing through its servers and failed to take action to prevent the dissemination of that material, it might be liable as a contributory infringer. The deciding factor would be the host's actual knowledge of the infringement:

[If the host] cannot reasonably verify a claim of infringement, either because of a possible fair use defense, the lack of copyright notices on the copies, or the copyright holder's failure to provide the necessary documentation to show that there is a likely infringement, the operator's lack of knowledge will be found reasonable and there will be no liability for contributory infringement for allowing the continued distribution of the works on its system.[130]

---

124. Information Infrastructure Task Force. Working Group on Intellectual Property Rights. Intellectual Property and the National Information Infrastructure: The Report of the Working Group on Intellectual Property Rights, Bruce A. Lehman, Chair. ISBN 0-9648716-0-1.
125. *Cubby Inc.* v *CompuServe Inc.* 776 F Supp 135 (SDNY, 1991).
126. *Moorhouse* v *University of NSW* [1976] RPC 157.
127. *CBS Songs UK Ltd* v *Amstrad* [1988] RPC 567; *Sony Corp. of America* v *Universal Studios, Inc.* 464 US 417 (1984). See, however, the contrary argument voiced in F. Macmillan *et al.*, 'Copyright Liability of Communications Carriers', 1997, (3) *The Journal of Information, Law and Technology* (JILT), http://elj.warwick.ac.uk/jilt/commsreg/97_3macm/.
128. *Screen Gems-Columbia Music, Inc.* v *Mark Pi Records Inc.* 256 F Supp 399 (SDNY, 1966), cited in K.A. Walton, 'Is a Website like a Flea Market Stall? How *Fonovisa* v *Cherry Auction* Increases the Risk of Third-Party Copyright Infringement liability for Online Service Providers', (1997) 19 *Hastings Comm. Ent. L.J.*, 921 at p. 926.
129. *Gershwin Publishing Corp.* v *Columbia Artists Management, Inc.* 443 F 2d 1159, 1162 (2d Cir, 1971); *Sega Enterprises Inc.* v *MAPHIA* 857 F Supp 679 (ND Cal, 1994).
130. *Religious Technology Centre* v *Netcom On-Line Communications Services Inc.* 907 F Supp 1361,

The uncertain state of affairs that was developing out of the case law in the United States led ISPs to hope that the Working Group on Intellectual Property Rights, set up in 1994 as part of the Department Of Commerce's Information Infrastructure Task Force, would support their assertion that on-line service providers should not be held liable for copyright infringement, since they had no way of policing what was transmitted on their networks. The ISPs argued that:

(a)   The volume of material on any ISP's system was too great to monitor or screen.

(b)   Even if an ISP was willing and able to monitor the material on its system, it would not be able to reliably identify infringing material.

(c)   Failure to shield ISPs would impair communication and availability of information.

(d)   Exposure to liability for infringement would drive ISPs out of business, causing the Net to fail.

(e)   The law should impose liability only on those ISPs who assumed responsibility for the online activities of their subscribers.

However, when that Working Group reported in 1995,[131] the ISPs were dismayed to discover that the concerns of a more powerful lobby group, that of the copyright owners, had won the day. The Working Group decided that it would be undesirable to reduce the copyright liability of ISPs as this might prematurely halt the development of marketplace tools that could be used to lessen their risk of liability and the risk to copyright owners, although they suggested that circumstances under which service providers should have reduced liability might be identified in the future.

The Working Group noted that:

(a)   Millions of files travel through a network in a given day, but believed that other industries were faced with similar situations and coped without reduced liability.[132]

(b)   On-line service providers could take appropriate action when notified of the existence of infringing material on their systems and therefore limit their liability for damages to those for innocent infringement.

(c)   On-line service providers were in the best position to know the identity and activities of their subscribers and to stop unlawful activities.

---

continued
  1374 (ND Cal, 1995). For a detailed analysis of the potential liability of intermediaries as contributory infringers see E.A. Burcher & A.M. Hughes, Casenote, '*Religious Tech. Ctr.* v *Netcom On-Line Communications, Inc.*: Internet Service Providers: The Knowledge Standard for Contributory Copyright Infringement and The Fair Use Defense', op. cit., note 118, above.
131. Information Infrastructure Task Force. Working Group on Intellectual Property Rights. Intellectual Property and the National Information Infrastructure: The Report of the Working Group on Intellectual Property Rights, op. cit., at note 124, above.
132. The position of photo processing laboratories, for example.

(d)   Other businesses with similar risk factors had been able to take appropriate precautions to minimise their risk of liability through indemnification agreements and insurance.

In the event, the legislative response to the recommendations of the Working Group on Intellectual Property Rights, and their proposed amendments to the Copyright Act was muted,[133] not least because of the protests that some of the other proposed measures provoked.[134] It was not until the passage of the Digital Millennium Copyright Act of 1998 (see below), that the issue of ISP liability for copying was addressed by the US legislature to the satisfaction of US ISPs.

Under UK law, the fact that an ISP is in possession of infringing copies made by a third party may, in some circumstances, lead to liability for infringement of the copyright owner's rights. This liability is known as secondary infringement, and stems from s. 23 of the Copyright, Designs and Patents Act (CDPA) 1988. This states that there will be an infringement where the possession is in the course of a business; and the defendant knows or has reason to believe that the material held is an infringing copy. Most ISPs clearly operate on a commercial basis, and will thus fall within the definition of a business under the first leg of the test.[135] However, the question of possession remains uncertain. If an ISP is merely routing information packets constituting infringing material, it is unclear whether the transient possession will suffice for s. 23 liability, or whether more long-term possession is necessary. Certainly, even if possession could be proven, it would be extremely difficult for the rightsholder to prove that an ISP had specific knowledge about the copyright status of individual packets. An ISP's liability arising from possession is therefore likely to be limited by practical constraints to circumstances where it hosts resources, such as webpages and Usenet postings, or where it provides caching services.

The question of knowledge is less certain. Copyright infringement has long been endemic on the Internet,[136] either because users are unaware of the restrictions imposed by copyright, or because they are aware of the limited likelihood of their being held to account for infringement. As a result, almost every ISP, and especially those which host third party websites, carry Usenet newsgroups, and cache resources will inevitably have a certain number of infringing copies on its servers. Yet the fact that there is a high likelihood of infringing copies, does not mean that an ISP can be automatically held to have sufficient knowledge of any particular infringement to give rise to

---

133. Although the NII Copyright Protection Act of 1995 was considered by the both the Senate and House of Representatives in the 104th Congress, it was not passed by either house and was not reintroduced in the 105th Congress. See for criticism of the Act, W.M. Melone, 'Contributory Liability for Access Providers: Solving the Conundrum Digitalization Has Placed on Copyright Laws', (1997) 49 (2) *Federal Communications Law Journal* at http://www.law. indiana.edu/fclj/pubs/v49/no2/melone.html.

134. For a brief overview of other criticisms, see P. Samuelson, *The Copyright Grab*, Wired 4.01, January 1996.

135. Copyright, Designs and Patents Act 1988, s. 178.

136. Indeed, on the more exotic Usenet hierarchies, such as alt.binaries.pictures.erotica.* and alt.binaries.warez.* the scale of infringement is such that over 90 per cent of postings are likely to involve infringing material.

liability under s. 23. The cases under the legislation prior to the CDPA 1988[137] give strong support to the theory that actual knowledge of the infringement in question is required,[138] and that a general constructive knowledge that some copies may be infringing will not be sufficient.[139]

This can make determining the liability of an ISP, in circumstances where the rightsholder claims that the ISP was given notice of infringing material, difficult to determine. If the notice identifies specific infringing material, such as a .jpg or .gif picture file on a webpage, or a computer program on a 'warez' FTP site, the matter is easy to resolve, as the ISP can either delete or block access to the resource, reducing the likelihood of the rightsholder bringing legal action. If the ISP were to refuse to delete or block access to the resource the rightsholder would have no difficulty proving continued possession with actual knowledge. However, this circumstance is probably the exception rather than the rule, as with many infringements the rightsholder may only be able to determine that the infringing material is being distributed via a particular newsgroup or third party website, and its notice can only indicate that if an ISP carries that newsgroup or caches resources requested from the website, it will come into possession of infringing copies.[140] In those circumstances, it would seem that the UK courts would be unwilling to accept that a notice couched in such general terms would be sufficient to fix a person with knowledge such that any infringing copies which appeared on their systems would be capable of leading to liability.[141]

The issue of liability for further transmission of infringing materials is equally fraught. An ISP may undertake two forms of transmission which have copyright implications. These are forwarding packets received from another host; and transmitting a copy of a resource hosted by the intermediary, following a user request. This transmission involves copying of the material, and thus can be considered as a potential infringement. However, the copies made are evanescent, with the ISP's copy normally being deleted once the material has been sent and while such copying can result in an infringement under the laws of some jurisdictions,[142] this is by no means a universally accepted rule,[143] and some jurisdictions have explicitly stated that it does not infringe.[144]

---

137. Copyright Act 1956, s. 5 — infringement by importation, sale etc. of copies known to be infringing.
138. *Hoover plc* v *George Hulme Ltd* [1982] FSR 565.
139. *Columbia Picture Industries* v *Robinson* [1987] Ch 38.
140. For an example of an even vaguer notice, consider the form letter sent by Lucasfilm to hundreds of ISPs regarding infringing materials from the film *Star Wars: Episode I — The Phantom Menace*, discussed in D. Goodin, 'Star Wars rekindles Net debate', *CNET-News.com*, 2 May 2 1999, http://news.cnet.com/news/0-1005-200-341957.html.
141. *Hoover plc* v *George Hulme Ltd* [1982] FSR 565 (under the Copyright Act 1956).
142. See, e.g., UK Copyright, Designs and Patents Act 1988, s. 17(6).
143. '[T]he treatment of temporary acts of reproduction is generally still not addressed, with the result of significant legal uncertainty with respect to the exploitation of protected subject matter in the electronic environment'. *Proposal for a European Parliament and Council Directive on the harmonization of certain aspects of copyright and related rights in the Information Society*, COM (97) 628 final, 10 December 1997, p. 15.
144. *Religious Technology Centre* v *Netcom On-Line Communications Services Inc.* 907 F Supp 1361, 1368 (ND Cal, 1995).

A further potential complication can be found in the fact that rightsholders are often granted, as part of their jurisdiction's copyright 'bundle of rights', an exclusive right of distribution. It is arguable therefore that the transmission of infringing packets of information might breach this exclusive right. In practice, however, it would appear that the protection afforded under this right would not, in most cases, stretch to cover digital transmissions. This is primarily because most statutory formulations of that right are not couched in suitable terminology:

> In legal terms, it is generally accepted that the distribution right, which only applies to the distribution of physical copies does not cover the act of transmission. Also the reproduction right does not cover the act of transmission as such, but only the reproductions which take place in this context.[145]

Thus, the exclusive right might be limited to the distribution of physical copies of a work, ruling out distribution of intangible digital copies, or mean that the nature of digital transmission may not meet the requirement for 'distribution to the public'. To further complicate matters, each jurisdiction's law will include exceptions to the right whose applicability in a digital environment is uncertain.[146]

In short, in the absence of specific new legislation the courts, both in the United States and elsewhere,[147] appear to be moving towards the position that Internet Intermediaries should not be strictly liable for the copies they make of information held on, or passing through, their servers. As a result,

---

145. *Proposal for a European Parliament and Council Directive on the harmonization of certain aspects of copyright and related rights in the Information Society*, op. cit., note 143, above, at p. 20.

146. See further, Explanatory Memorandum to the *Proposal for a European Parliament and Council Directive on the harmonization of certain aspects of copyright and related rights in the Information Society*, op. cit., note 143, above, at p. 21.

147. In the Netherlands in 1996, a copyright infringement case brought by the Church of Scientology against an ISP was dismissed on the ground that ISPs 'do no more than give the opportunity of communication to the public, and that, in principle, they can exert no influence over, nor even have knowledge of, what those having access to the Internet through them, will supply' — *Decision N 96/160*, 12 March 1996. However, a more recent court decision suggests that the Dutch courts may be moving towards an approach similar to that of the United States. In *Religious Technology Center v Dataweb B.V.*, No. 96/1048 (Dist Ct of the Hague, Civil Law Sector, 9 June 1999) it was held that, while ISPs are not publishers of the infringing work by virtue of providing the technological means to enable publication by others, if they are notified of infringing material and then either fail to remove it or fail to deny access to the infringer they will be liable for copyright infringement. Perhaps more worryingly for ISPs, the court also held that there is copyright infringement when an ISP has a link on its computer system, which leads to the reproduction of the material, and is aware of the infringing material.

On 1 March 1999, a Belgian service provider was convicted of copyright violation in the Hasselt Criminal Court and ordered to pay 500,000 BF in damages after subscribers used the service to upload illicit copies of Novell software. The service provider argued that he could not be held responsible for files uploaded to his system by other users and that the volume of software uploaded meant that controls could not be implemented. The court ruled that the time required to perform these checks did not detract from the provider's legal responsibility.

circumstances where liability for carrying infringing copies where a user carried out the original infringement will be limited to those where the ISP or II has actively encouraged its users to transport infringing material via its facilities,[148] or where the ISP or II has actual knowledge of the infringement and has failed to take reasonable steps to try and prevent it.[149] Yet it remains entirely possible that not all courts in all jurisdictions will be inclined to reach this essentially pragmatic position, and for this reason recent national and international proposals for granting intermediaries statutory immunity (see below) are likely to be the most effective way to clarify the position of ISPs.

11.6.2 Defamation

The primary difficulty with establishing an ISP's liability for defamation is that national defamation laws differ so widely. It is possible to state with some certainty that in most, if not all, jurisdictions, the fundamental basis of defamation liability is the publication of untrue information, that liability will be based on the extent of the damage to the reputation of the person referred to in that information, and that a person's reputation cannot be damaged unless the information is disseminated to people other than the author. Once one ventures beyond these basic principles, national defamation laws rapidly diverge. English law[150] imposes liability regardless of whether the publisher of a statement knew or ought to have known it was defamatory[151] whereas under Finnish law a distinction is made between intentional and negligent defamation.[152] Unlike English law, Scots law[153] provides that the defamatory statement need only be communicated to the pursuer for an action to lie and justify an award of at least nominal damages.[154] Under US law a statement referring to a public figure will only be defamatory if malice can be proved on the part of the maker of the statement.[155] These national differences make it difficult for an Internet publisher to assess in advance whether material is likely to give rise to liability.

Because of these disparate divergences, the differing provisions of national law will not be considered in detail here, and the discussion below will start from the assumption that an ISP has transmitted a defamatory statement, either from a website which it hosts or caches, or as one of the hosts in the transmission chain from the offending website. The potential risk to ISPs of transmitting defamatory information is high, because of the way in which the Internet works and, more importantly, because of the ways in which users

---

148. *Sega Enterprises Inc.* v. *MAPHIA* 857 F Supp 679 (ND Cal, 1994).
149. *Religious Technology Centre* v *Netcom On-Line Communications Services Inc.* 907 F Supp 1361 (ND Cal, 1995).
150. See further D. Price, *Defamation: Law, Procedure and Practice*, London: Sweet & Maxwell, 1997.
151. *Hulton & Co.* v *Jones* [1910] AC 20.
152. Finnish Penal Code.
153. See further K. Norrie, *Defamation and Related Actions in Scots Law*, London: Butterworths 1995.
154. *Mackay* v *McCankie* (1883) 10 R 537.
155. *New York Times Co.* v *Sullivan* 376 US 254 (1964).

communicate using the Internet technologies.[156] The important question is whether that risk of (usually inadvertent) transmission translates into liability on the part of the ISP in addition to the original author of the statement.

In the traditional media, publishing is seen as requiring positive input on the part of the publisher (such as arranging for the printing of a work, sending out copies, selling copies, etc.). This positive input approach meshes with the approach of those legal authorities that define publication as the communication of the statement to at least one person other than the claimant.[157] However, in the consideration of copyright in 11.6.1 above, it was noted that many Internet-based transactions are neither initiated nor controlled by the ISP, as the commands that are being sent to the ISP's hardware and software instructing it to make the copies are in fact given by a third party. The process can be described thus:

(a)   the user (or the user's software) issues a request to the intermediary's computer system;
(b)   software has been set up by the intermediary which automatically responds to such a request with no human intervention;
(c)   that software transmits the information requested from the intermediary's system to the user.

This has provided the courts with two potential perspectives as to the process that is occurring, either:

(a)   the user is controlling the software running on the ISP's system, and is thus responsible for the transmission; or
(b)   the transmission is undertaken by software which is in the possession of and under the overall control of the ISP, making it responsible for the transmission.

The latter perspective was recently adopted by the UK courts in *Godfrey* v *Demon Internet Ltd, The Times*, 20 April 1999. Here the defendant ISP was sued for a defamatory statement carried in a newsgroup hosted on its server. Demon argued that it was not a publisher, as it merely provided the infrastructure necessary for the newsgroup posters to exchange views. The court, in rejecting this line of defence, held that because Demon had chosen to receive and store the newsgroup, and had the power to delete messages from it, it was at common law a publisher, subject to any specific defences under the Defamation Act 1996 (see below).

While Demon's defence with regard to newsgroups failed, where ISPs do not store defamatory material in readily ascertainable forms like newsgroups or webpages, or simply transmit the material, it is not really accurate to say that they 'publish' it in the sense that we would understand it in the physical world. The term 'publication' in national libel laws, however, sometimes is

---

156. See L. Edwards, 'Defamation and the Internet' in Edwards and Waelde (eds), *Law and the Internet: regulating cyberspace*, Oxford: Hart Publishing, 1997, pp. 184–188.
157. *Halsbury's Laws of England*, 4th edn, London: Butterworths, vol. 28, 'Libel and Slander' para. 60.

used in a more technical legal sense to include the role of those persons who play an important role in the dissemination of the statement In general, this broader interpretation means that, in addition to the author of the statement, publishers and editors are nearly always liable, and in some jurisdictions some degree of liability may also be imposed on distributors, such as printers, booksellers, and libraries and newsagents.[158]

Assessing the liability of ISPs with regard to the transmission of defamatory material thus involves an examination of the functions, or business practices, that the ISPs themselves have adopted, as this will often influence the application of the law by the courts. There are essentially three levels of activity that can be separated out:[159]

(1)   *The ISP as 'information carrier'.*   Here the ISP merely moves information from one place to another, without examining its contents. Most jurisdictions recognise that certain types of organisation have such a limited role in the dissemination of statements that they should be granted immunity from defamation claims. Classic examples of such organisations are postal services and telecommunications organisations (see the discussion of 'common carrier' status above). A number of US cases have held that where an ISP acts as an information carrier, taking no steps to monitor or control the content of the information it conveys to users, it will not be liable for third party defamatory statements.[160]

(2)   *The ISP as 'information distributor'.*   Here the ISP's main function is the transportation of information, but the law presumes the ISP to have had the opportunity of examining the content of that information. The actual operational difference between an 'information distributor' ISP and an 'information carrier' ISP may be negligible. Thus the difference in their liability is based entirely on a legal presumption. Where a jurisdiction adopts an 'information distributor' model of defamation liability, the ISP will usually

---

158. E.g., *Goldsmith* v *Sperrings Ltd* [1977] 1 WLR 478, CA (newsagent). 'The defence of innocent dissemination was the UK common law's response to the occasional injustice strict application of this rule produced. This defence relieved distributors (but, perversely, not printers) of liability, if they had no control over the content of the offending publication and neither knew nor should have known that an item they distributed contained or was likely to contain defamatory statements.' D. Vick, and L. Macpherson, 'An Opportunity Lost: The United Kingdom's Failed Reform of Defamation Law', (1997) 49 *Federal Communications Law Journal* at http://www.law.indiana.edu/fclj/pubs/v49/n03/vick.html.

159. See also L. Edwards, 'Defamation and the Internet', in Edwards and Waelde (eds), *Law and the Internet: regulating cyberspace*, Oxford: Hart Publishing, 1997, p. 192 and C. Waelde, L. Edwards, 'Defamation and the Internet: A Case Study of Anomalies and Difficulties in the Information Age', (1996) 10 (2) *International Review of Law Computers and Technology* 263.

160. *Cubby Inc.* v *CompuServe Inc.* 776 F Supp 135 (SDNY, 1991) (ISP's chosen mode of activity in passing on information from third parties unmodified and unexamined rendered it more like a distributor than a publisher, and thus not liable for allegedly defamatory statements made by a subscriber in posting to newsgroup); *Lunney* v *Prodigy Services Co.* 683 NYS 2d 557 (ISP could not be held liable for defamation and intentional infliction of emotional distress arising out of a third party's offensive e-mail to a Boy Scout leader that appeared to originate with the claimant. The court applied as precedent, a New York State court libel decision dealing with telephone and telegraph companies, *Anderson* v *New York Telephone Co.* 35 NY 2d 746).

have a legal obligation to meet certain additional conditions in order to avoid liability. Simply taking no steps to monitor or control the content of the information it conveys to users will leave it exposed to liability. Following the passage of the Defamation Act 1996, UK defamation law is a clear example of the information distributor model. Here ISPs will generally not be considered to be publishers,[161] but will not escape liability unless they are able to demonstrate that they did not know and had no reason to believe the statement was defamatory,[162] and that they took 'reasonable care in relation to its publication'.[163]

(3) *The ISP as 'information controller'.* Where an ISP makes a concerted effort to examine the information content it transmits, and to take action to prevent transmission if the content is unlawful, it will be liable if that 'editorial' function fails to stop the transmission of a defamatory statement.[164] This would certainly be the position under UK law,[165] and most likely under many other countries' laws.

The liability of ISPs in the first and third categories is fairly clear. However, difficulties can arise when a jurisdiction's laws blur the line between the second and third categories. The UK Defamation Act 1996 provides a salutary example of this. ISPs are obliged to take some minimum steps to monitor information content to obtain liability protection under s. 1(1), and once they are apprised of defamatory content on their servers they must take all reasonable steps to remove or deny access to it.[166] Yet, if UK ISPs begin monitoring in any depth, they open themselves to the contrary risk that they fall outside s. 1(3), and will thus treated as publishers.[167]

In some circumstances ISPs may in the course of their activities either directly or inadvertently open themselves to the risk of defamation for which they are responsible as a publisher. The direct risk comes where the ISP provides the type of sophisticated information services and resources such as those found in the popular portal services, including news and sports reports. If the ISP produces its own material or, as is more common, buys it in from another content provider,[168] inasmuch as it makes a decision what news to publish from those sources, it operates as a regular publisher.

---

161. Defamation Act 1996, s. 1(3).
162. Defamation Act 1996, s. 1(1)(b).
163. Defamation Act 1996, s. 1(1)(c).
164. *Stratton Oakmont, Inc. v Prodigy Services Co.* 23 Media Law Rep (BNA) 1794, 5 CCH Computer Cases ¶47,291 (NY Sup Ct, 1995) (defendant bulletin board claimed in its advertising that it offered a family service, and that all its discussion groups were moderated. When the moderation process had failed, because Prodigy held itself out as exercising editorial control, the court held that it was liable for a statement defaming the claimant). D. P. Miranda, 'Defamation in Cyberspace: Stratton Oakmont, Inc. v Prodigy Services Co.', (1996) 5 *Alb LJ Sci & Tech* 229.
165. UK Defamation Act 1996, s. 1(2): ' "editor" means a person having editorial or equivalent responsibility for the content of the statement or the decision to publish it'.
166. *Godfrey v Demon Internet Ltd*, The Times, 20 April 1999.
167. See further L. Edwards, 'Defamation and the Internet', in Edwards and Waelde (eds), *Law and the Internet: regulating cyberspace* op. cit., note 159, above, at p. 194.
168. AOL, for example, appears to obtain the news content for its portal site primarily from Reuters and The Associated Press. See http://www.aol.com.

A less obvious risk arises where the ISP provides more basic information resources, such as collections of links, as might be compiled through automated Web searches. Here there is some potential for ISPs to fall foul of a lesser-known type of defamation, that of 'legal innuendo'. This describes a situation where words or pictures, which by themselves lack defamatory meaning, may be perceived as defamatory by readers or viewers who draw inferences by combining that information with other information already known to them.[169] In some circumstances an innuendo will clearly be intentional,[170] in others the innuendo may arise by happenstance.[171] From the point of view of ISPs, it is important that an innuendo may arise not just from one piece of information, but the combination of two or more.[172] One way in which this might happen on the Internet would be a link from a website relating to some criminal activity, to another site relating to a person who had been suspected, but never convicted, of that criminal activity.[173] Equally, the inclusion of a particular link or links in a topic-specific webpage might give rise to an unintended innuendo by suggesting to a person browsing the webpage that some of those linked to shared the opinions of the others. Such a page could be created by using software agents, such as 'web spiders' or 'robots' to comb the Internet to obtain the URLs of webpages containing particular combinations of words. Thus, for example, a webpage put together based on the topic of euthanasia, might have links to sites maintained by doctors specialising in care for the elderly or incurably ill, and to sites advocating the legalisation

---

169. *Tolley v Fry* [1931] AC 333 (the claimant, an amateur golfer was caricatured in an advertisement with the advertiser's chocolate bar displayed prominently in his pocket, the court held that a viewer of the advertisement who understood the rules relating to amateur golf would draw the inference that the claimant had endorsed the product, thus forfeiting his amateur status, and was therefore playing in amateur tournaments under false pretences).

170. In 1986 Lord Gowrie sued *The Star* over the following comment on his departure from the Cabinet:

> There has been much excited chatter as to why dashing poetry scribbling minister, Lord Gowrie, left the cabinet so suddenly. What expensive habit can he not support on a salary of £33,000? I am sure Lord Gowrie himself would snort at the suggestion that he was born with a silver spoon round his neck.

Lord Gowrie claimed that the quote implied that he had taken drugs. The court agreed. Case cited in Scott-Bayfield, J, *Defamation: Law and Practice*, London: FT Law & Tax, 1996.

171. An innocent intention or knowledge will be no defence to a person who makes a statement which has a defamatory meaning for those to whom he makes it: *Hulton Co. Ltd v Jones* [1910] AC 20.

172. *Monson v Tussauds Ltd* [1894] 1 QB 671 (the court held that a waxwork statue of the claimant holding a gun, when placed just outside the Chamber of Horrors at Madame Tussauds, and combined with the information that the man was charged with murder before a Scottish court but the case was found not proven, was defamatory).

173. For example, a website on the racketeering activities of the Mafia and its associates, which had a link to a site relating to Frank Sinatra (who cannot now be libelled under UK libel law, as the law does not apply to the deceased) would potentially have been defamatory under UK law. Under US law, following the 'public figure' test in *New York Times Co. v Sullivan* 376 US 254 (1964), such a case would be harder to make out.

of euthanasia and its practice even before legalisation. Should the webpage by its context and content suggest to visitors that the doctors in question were in favour of, or engaged in, euthanasia for elderly or incurable patients, that could give rise to a defamatory innuendo. Under English law, at least, unintended innuendoes may also arise in other ways.[174] Whilst the case law in this area is limited, and no Internet-related cases arguing innuendo, intentional or otherwise, yet appear to have surfaced, it is arguable that the very nature of the Internet and WWW significantly increases the future risk of accidental defamations.

It will be clear from the foregoing that the question of where publication takes place is vital to determining the jurisprudence under which the intermediary will or will not liable be for the defamation. Because there is such wide divergence between different national laws, the potential ability of a claimant to choose between jurisdictions (jurisdiction hopping or shopping) takes on increased importance. With regard to Internet publication, there are essentially two possibilities as to where publication takes place, either the place where the message was transmitted, or where it was received. Given that the justification for libel laws is to ensure redress for acts of communication which cause an individual to be shamed, ridiculed, held in contempt, lowered in the estimation of the community, to lose employment status or earnings, or otherwise suffer a damaged reputation, it would seem logical to assume that this 'damage' takes place at the point where it is viewed by the user, and that the reader's jurisdiction is thus the one in which publication occurs. However, as we have already seen, the courts may not subscribe to the view of an Internet communication being sent to the viewer, preferring instead to view the transaction as one where the viewer's software collects the statement from the machine on which it has been stored. In the former case, publication would take place in the user's jurisdiction, in the latter case in the publisher's.

As regards libel actions in the traditional print media, the UK courts appear to take the line that publication will be deemed to have occurred in every jurisdiction in which the publisher ought to have foreseen it would be made available. This excludes copies brought privately into jurisdictions where it was not otherwise foreseeable that the publication would be made available.[175] This makes sense from both a practical point of view, in that a print media publisher will be aware of both the distribution chain for his product, and the number of physical copies made, and from a pragmatic legal point of view, in that the potential damage done to an individual's reputation by the

---

174. *Hulton & Co.* v *Jones* [1910] AC 20 (defendant claimed that the libel complained of had been written as a piece of fiction, and that he had named one character 'Artemus Jones' in utter ignorance of the existence of the claimant, a barrister who shared that name, the court found him liable — incidentally it has since been suggested that 'the writer of the article knew Jones and disliked him' — P. Mitchell, 'Artemus Jones and the Press Club', (1999) 20 The Journal of Legal History) *Cassidy* v *Daily Mirror Newspapers Ltd* [1929] 2 KB 331 (where a reference to a lady's husband in the company of another lady 'whose engagement has been announced' was held to defame the wife).

175. *Shevill and others* v *Presse-Alliance SA* [1992] 1 All ER 409 (CA), [1995] All ER (EC) 289, [1995] 2 WLR 499 (ECJ).

odd personal copy that is transported into jurisdictions not served by the publisher, will necessarily be limited.

Of course this analysis does not transfer well to modes of electronic distribution, such as websites, Usenet newsgroups, and e-mail list/expanders/ exploders. A website allows individuals accessing it to make multiple copies, and transport those copies back to their own jurisdiction. Usenet newsgroups propagate messages from newserver to newserver across the world. E-mail list/expander/exploder software allows an individual to send a single e-mail message to a server, and have the software make copies and distribute them to multiple recipients.

As regards a website there appear to be two options available to deal with the issue of which jurisdiction governs for the purposes of deterring defamation liability, namely to assume that either:

(a)   Publication is made in all jurisdictions where it is foreseeable that the information may be transported by a user, and where it actually is transported. As regards the WWW, this will effectively mean every jurisdiction in the world.

(b)   Publication is made in the location where the information is stored and from which it is received. Thus, a website in the US would publish only in the US, and be subject only to the appropriate US state defamation laws.

However, the first option seems unsatisfactory, as it potentially opens the publisher to liability to a claimant in an unlimited number of jurisdictions. The second option appears more workable, but fails to deal adequately with a situation where, for example, a US-based website actively markets its services to other countries by providing a local access node or regional webpages. In any event, the two options do not provide a suitable model for dealing with either e-mail lists or Usenet news groups.

It is possible that these perceived difficulties will not prove as intransigent as they appear, as some current developments suggest that the issue of where publication takes place may become of decreasing importance. In *Shevill and others* v *Presse-Alliance SA* [1995] 2 WLR 499, the European Court of Justice held that where the Brussels Convention 1988 applies,[176] a defamation action may be brought both where the publication occurred and where the claimant suffered damage to his reputation. The latter place is most likely to be interpreted as where the defamatory statement was read, i.e., the location of the viewer. On that basis, ISPs (and authors) will inevitably be exposed to liability in every country of the world, although *Shevill* suggests that a court may only award compensation for the damage to the claimants reputation in its jurisdiction, and not damages for all losses worldwide. In the case of Internet defamation, that will probably be sufficient to make it worthwhile for intermediaries to be sued in a 'claimant-friendly' jurisdiction. Indeed, in

---

176. Where the Brussels Convention does not apply, the English courts have the power to stay proceedings on the ground that there is insufficient connection with the jurisdiction, e.g., if the publication in England is small in comparison to worldwide publication: *Berezovsky* v *Forbes Inc.*, *The Times*, 19 January 1998.

Shevill the Advocate-General of the European Court of Justice expressed exactly this point, saying:

... the English courts could even find themselves in danger, by reason of their 'generosity' towards victims of defamation, of becoming the natural choice of forum in such matters.[177]

The difficulties that ISPs currently face with regard to defamation are increasingly being ameliorated by the development of national and international rules exempting them from liability. Whilst, as in the case of the UK Defamation Act 1996, the rules are not always as helpful as might be expected, the general trend is towards affording ISPs the same type of protection as is afforded telecommunications companies and postal services (see below).

11.7 INFORMATION CONTENT — CRIMINAL LIABILITY

11.7.1 Obscenity/indecency

If one were to take media reports about Internet information content at face value, one might be justified in believing that the primary activity on the Internet is the provision, distribution, and downloading, of obscene and indecent materials, notably pictorial pornography.[178] Whilst it is certainly possible to locate such material with relative ease,[179] media statements as to its prevalence usually considerably overstate its role and status on the Internet. Despite this, the result of the extensive coverage that the topic has received has placed the question of ISP liability for its possession and transmission firmly on the political agenda. There are, however, a number of difficult issues to address when considering the issue of liability. To begin with, there is no international understanding or definition of the type of material that would be considered 'obscene', 'indecent', or even 'pornographic'.

In the US, 'obscenity' is limited to sexual material, and requires the material to appeal to the prurient interest, as defined by reference to the standards of the local community, and to depict sexual conduct defined by the applicable state law. The three-part test set out by the Supreme Court in *Miller* v *California* 413 US 15 (1973) is:

(a) whether the average person, applying contemporary community standards, would find that the work, taken as a whole, appeals to the prurient interest,

---

177. Opinion of Advocate General Leger, para. 56.
178. And not just the media, see M. Rimm, 'Marketing Pornography on the Information Superhighway', 83 *Georgetown Law Journal*, June 1995, pp. 1849–1934 (archived on the WWW at http://TRFN.pgh.pa.us/guest/mrstudy.html). This study caused immense controversy when first published, making the cover of TIME magazine and being widely quoted in during the passage of the ill-fated US Communications Decency Act. However, it was rapidly exposed as, at best, methodologically flawed. See http://www2000.ogsm.vanderbilt.edu/cyberporn.debate.html for more details.
179. Yahoo, the popular US webindexing site, contains a number of index pages to such material. See for example http://www.yahoo.com/Business_and_Economy/Companies/Sex/Directories/.

(b)   whether the work depicts or describes, in a patently offensive way, sexual conduct specifically defined by the applicable state law, and

(c)   whether the work, taken as a whole, lacks serious literary, artistic, political, or scientific value.

This test is not based on the potential effects of the material, but on whether it contravenes locally determined standards of acceptable sexual depiction. This leads to the somewhat unfortunate result that material which is unobjectionable in one US state may be viewed as obscene in another, with potentially deleterious effects for the publishers. In the traditional media, publishers can largely avoid falling foul of locally determined standards, by adjusting their distribution networks accordingly. For an ISP or other II, this distribution control approach may simply be untenable, as those using or accessing a potentially objectionable Internet service might be based any-where in the US.[180]

In the UK, by contrast, the term is not limited to sexual material, but applies to any material whose:

effect ... is, if taken as a whole, such as to tend to deprave and corrupt persons who are likely ... to read, see or hear the matter contained or embodied in it.[181]

Thus, while the depiction of sexual acts in pictorial or textual form is the most obvious form of potentially obscene material, UK case law demonstrates that action can also be taken against pamphlets and books about the use of drugs,[182] and material showing scenes of violence.[183]

Equally, the question of the standard that one might use to establish whether material is, or is not, 'pornography' is a highly contentious one and one that over the years has created some unusual alliances.[184] An example of

---

180. This problem is clearly demonstrated by the case of *United States* v *Thomas* 74 F 3d 701 (6th Cir), cert. denied, 117 S Ct 74 (1996), where a bulletin board operator was extradited from California to Tennessee to face criminal charges. It was stated in argument that the material, which was stored on a computer in California, was not obscene by Californian community standards, but the court determined that the appropriate standards by which to test for obscenity were the standards of Tennessee, the place in which the material was received and viewed.

181. The Obscene Publications Act 1959, s. 1(1).

182. *John Calder (Publications) Ltd* v *Powell* [1965] 1 All ER 159 (book concerning the life of a junkie in New York held to be obscene); *R* v *Skirving and another* [1985] 2 All ER 705 (book concerned with the use and abuse of the drug cocaine and contained detailed explanations, instructions and recipes for obtaining the maximum effect from ingesting cocaine held to be obscene).

183. *DPP* v *A. & B.C. Chewing Gum Ltd* [1967] 2 All ER 504 (depiction of violent activity on chewing gum cards held liable to tend to deprave or corrupt children, and thus to be obscene).

184. For example, on this issue, but one would suspect few others, US feminist writers Catherine McKinnon (author of *Only Words*, Cambridge, Mass: Harvard UP 1994), and Andrea Dworkin (author of *Pornography: Men Possessing Women*, London: The Women's Press 1981), agree with US Christian fundamentalist groups that certain materials are pornographic, though for very different reasons.

the type of definition that may be used is 'offensive, degrading, and threatening material of an explicitly sexual or violent nature'. However, it is clear from the debates and the case law over the years that one person's 'offensive, degrading, and threatening material' may well be another's great work of literature,[185] great work of art,[186] protected social, political, or sexual statement, or holiday snaps.[187]

Where child pornography is concerned, while most jurisdictions are united in their prohibition of it, their national standards tend to be equally divergent. The rationales often provided for prohibiting such pornography include that children may be harmed in the making of the materials; that the materials may be used to persuade children that sexual activity with adults is acceptable; and that the material may encourage paedophiles to act out their fantasies. Thus, while broadly speaking, depictions of minors engaged in sexual conduct will usually be held to be unlawful *per se*, regardless of local community standards, or the likelihood that the depictions might deprave and corrupt there are significant differences between national rules.[188] Hence, depictions of adults who appear to be minors, and computer manipulated depictions based on non-obscene images of minors and adults may be prohibited in some jurisdictions,[189] in others the actual participation of a minor may be required.[190] Equally, in some jurisdictions,[191] only pictorial

---

185. For example Lady Chatterley's Lover: *R* v *Penguin Books* [1961] Crim LR 176; Last Exit to Brooklyn: *R* v *Calder & Boyars Ltd* [1969] 1 QB 151.
186. In June 1998, British police seized a book, *Mapplethorpe*, from the library at the University of Central England. It contained photographs of homosexual activity and bondage scenes taken by the internationally renowned photographer and artist Robert Mapplethorpe. Despite the fact that the book was widely acknowledged as serious artistic work, the police told the University that its contents might contravene the Obscene Publications Act 1959. In the event, no charges were brought.
187. There have been a number of reports of film processors reporting to the police pictures of nude children taken by family members on holiday. These reports are however difficult to substantiate.
188. In Canada, the situation has been complicated by the case of *R* v *Sharpe*, where the British Columbia Court of Appeals upheld a lower court ruling that the Canadian federal child pornography law, as currently drafted, breaches constitutional rights that guarantee freedom of expression and the protection of privacy, It said the law is also flawed because it has the potential to penalise people for possessing and creating material that may merely be the products of the imagination and not intended for distribution. The court stated that 'Making it an offence to possess expressive material, when that material may have been created without abusing children and may never be published, distributed or sold, constitutes an extreme invasion of the values of liberty, autonomy and privacy protected by the rights and freedoms enshrined in the Charter', Court of Appeal for British Columbia in *R* v *Sharpe* (BCCA 1999 416), judgment of 30 June 1999, para. 171. See further, Anon, 'Kiddie-porn law headed to top court: B.C. appeal judges decide 2-1 in favour of man found with child pornography', *The Globe and Mail*, 1 July 1999, and http://www.courts. gov.bc.ca/jdb-txt/ca/99/04/c99-0416.html.
189. Adults depicted as minors, (US) 18 USC § 2256(B); computer manipulated depictions, (UK) Protection of Children Act 1978, and s. 160 of the Criminal Justice Act 1988, both as amended by ss. 84 and 86 of the Criminal Justice and Public Order Act 1994; (US) 18 USC § 2256(C). The constitutionality of the Child Pornography Protection Act 1996's prohibition on possession of child pornography was recently upheld by the United States First Circuit Court of Appeals in *US* v *Hilton*, 167 F 3d 61.
190. See *R* v *Sharpe*, op. cit., note 188, above.
191. E.g., the United Kingdom legislation.

child pornography is covered, whilst in others written child pornography is also illegal.[192] There is also no international agreement on the age of sexual consent. In the UK a minor for these purposes is a person under 16 years of age, but in Tennessee[193] and Canada,[194] the relevant age is set at 18 years.

This plethora of laws and approaches to obscene and indecent material can place ISPs and IIs in a difficult position with regard to its possession and transmission, particularly where those ISPs have an international presence, such as AOL and CompuServe. They may find themselves being held liable in one jurisdiction in which they operate, for activities that are perfectly legal in their other jurisdictions of operation. As former CompuServe Germany general manager, Felix Somm, discovered to his cost, such situations might have costly consequences. Somm resigned from CompuServe Germany in June 1997 after being indicted on 13 counts of distributing on-line pornography and other illegal material by a Bavarian court.[195] He was charged even though he had no direct role in disseminating the material on the Internet. The charges followed an investigation in 1995, when prosecutors forced CompuServe to shut down access to more than 200 Internet newsgroups, some of which were suspected of displaying child pornography. In February 1998 he was given a two-year suspended sentence by the Munich district court. The court's decision came despite the fact that Germany had passed a law since his indictment providing a degree of protection for ISPs from criminal liability for carrying illegal material on their services.[196] The key issue for ISPs to elicit, therefore, is their liability for the possession and transmission of obscene and indecent materials in their sphere of operations.

11.7.1.1 Possession by an ISP In principle, in most jurisdictions, mere possession of an obscene article will not constitute an offence. That having been said, some jurisdictions, such as the United Kingdom, do make a distinction between child pornography and other obscene or indecent material, with the possession of the child pornography constituting an offence in and of itself.[197] Where mere possession is not criminalised, prosecutors must usually show that some further element of intent is involved, this usually

---

192. E.g., New Zealand where child pornography is addressed in the Films, Videos and Publications Classification Act 1993, No. 94 — SNZ 1993. Publication is defined in this respect to include written materials.
193. Tennessee Code § 39-17-901(8).
194. Section 163.1(1)(a) of the Canadian Criminal Code, RSC 1985, c. C-46.
195. Criminal case of Felix Bruno Somm, File No: 8340 Ds 465 JS 173158/95, Local Court (Amtsgericht) Munich. The conviction was reversed on appeal in 1999.
196. The German Information and Communication Services Act 1997 (otherwise known as the German Multimedia Law), *Gesetz zur Regelung der Rahmenbedingungen für Informations- und Kommunikationsdienste (Informations- und Kommunikationsdienste-Gesetz IuKDG): Bundestagsdrucksache 13/7934 vom 11.06.1997*; approved by Bundestag (13 June 1997) and Bundesrat (4 July 1997); valid from 1 August 1997, onwards. See http://www.iid.de/rahmen/iukdgbt.html (German) and http://www.kuner.com/data/reg/multimd3.htm (English translation).
197. See the UK Criminal Justice Act 1988, s. 160 as amended by Criminal Justice and Public Order Act 1994, s. 84(4) to cover 'pseudo photographs', California Penal Code § 311.11(a).

being an intent to distribute or exhibit the article. Sometimes that intent alone is sufficient to ground a criminal action,[198] whereas in some jurisdictions a more specific intent, that of distribution for gain must be proven.[199] Where child pornography is at issue, possession with intent to distribute is normally regarded as a more serious offence than mere possession.[200]

In circumstances where the basis of liability is possession, ISPs will only run the risk of liability for third party content if they host or cache the offending material on their servers. In this situation, the act of possession will be committed in the jurisdiction where the server is physically located. It is possible that there may be a further risk involved where the ISP controls a server from a different jurisdiction, if the determination as to the jurisdiction in which the material is held is made by reference to the place of control, rather than the physical location of the data. As yet, however this type of issue does not appear to have arisen in any legal proceedings.

If an ISP is found to be in possession of obscene or indecent material, a prosecutor may also then have to additionally prove that the ISP knew that the file held on its server was unlawful.[201] Proving this with regard to an ISP's hosted and cached resources might very well prove difficult as it would, in most circumstances, almost certainly be uneconomic for an ISP to check all its files for obscene content. Under the UK Obscene Publications Act 1964 it is a defence for the accused to show that he has not examined the article and thus has no reasonable grounds for suspicion that his possession of it amounted to an offence. Whether this suggests that UK ISPs should simply abdicate any responsibility for checking of content is a moot point, for a criminal court might take the view that a deliberate policy of not undertaking any scrutiny of content negated the defence of lack of reasonable grounds for suspicion. It could be argued that, as an ISP will, at the very least, have electronic records of the titles of files it is hosting, and the domain names of sites from which information is cached, it should be capable of identifying at least some suspicious file and domain names. An alternative approach, and one seemingly favoured by UK ISPs has been a combination of hotlines for individuals to report illegal materials, and other self-regulatory mechanisms such as Codes of Conduct for their clients, with coordination through a UK self-regulatory body for ISPs, the Internet Watch Foundation.[202] Whilst this approach almost certainly cannot totally prevent the storage and transmission of illegal material via an ISP's servers, it would appear to have reduced the amount of such material on UK ISPs to a level with which the authorities and law enforcement agencies are willing to live, whilst not imposing too rigorous an economic burden on the ISPs themselves.

Where intent to distribute is required for liability, the issue of whether an ISP, whose primary role is the transmission of data packets, has the requisite

---

198. See, e.g., California Penal Code § 311.2(a); under § 311.2(b) possession with intent to distribute for gain, where the subject is a minor, is a more serious offence.
199. See, e.g., the UK Obscene Publications Act 1964, s. 1(2).
200. See the California Penal Code § 311.1(a) (possession with intent to distribute), § 311.2(b) (intent to distribute for commercial consideration).
201. See, e.g., the California Penal Code § 311.11(a).
202. See http://www.iwf.org.uk/, especially http://www.iwf.org.uk/stats/stats.html.

intention by virtue of possessing a copy of the file arises. This issue was handled in UK law by amendments to the Obscene Publications Act 1964 s. 1(2).[203] However, because the s. 1(2) offence is only committed if the intention is to distribute for gain, a website host will only be criminally liable under this section if it has paid subscribers, and possibly only if access to the offending website requires a separate subscription.

11.7.1.2 Transmission by an ISP It is clear that the primary purpose of most obscenity laws is to prevent the distribution of pornographic material, presumably on the ground that if individuals are prevented from distributing it, at least some of the motivation for producing it in the first place will be lost. As such the laws clearly target distributors over possessors. This is where the aims of the legislators and courts clash most obviously with the role of ISPs, as the primary purpose of ISPs is the paid transmission of information. From the ISPs' point of view, and depending upon their particular business model, the more people sending and receiving information, or the more information that is sent, the better, regardless of the content of that information. Legal measures that slow the flow of information, dissuade people from using the medium, or impose higher costs on the service are all undesirable. From the lawmakers' point of view, for national content laws to have any meaning, they must be applied to all media, or the distributors of undesirable content will simply shift their focus to the weakly-regulated medium. The difficulty lies in determining what constitutes reasonable regulation within a new medium, and in ensuring that the financial burden of any regulation does not destroy the growth of that medium.[204]

Three different approaches to that dilemma can be ascertained from existing laws. The first approach criminalises the knowing distribution of obscene material.[205] This approach allows ISPs to plead ignorance of the content of the material that they host or re-transmit, providing that they do not monitor the contents of their servers. Problems may arise, however, if the relevant law defines knowledge to include constructive knowledge.[206] Hosting Usenet newsgroups such as those in the alt.binaries.pictures.erotica.* hierarchy, or alt.sex.bestiality, or webpages with names such as *.supersex.com/cumming.html and *.gang-bang.com/hardcoreXXX/Ebony would suggest, fairly strongly, constructive knowledge. The second approach criminalises

---

203. See s. 168 and sch. 9, para. 3, Criminal Justice and Public Order Act 1994.

204. For an interesting, if unconventional, assessment of this balance see Johnson, 'Pornography Drives Technology: Why Not to Censor the Internet', *Federal Communications Law Journal*, vol. 49, no. 1, November 1996, http://www.law.indiana.edu./fclji/pubs/v49/no1/johnson.html.

205. See, e.g., the Tennessee Code, § 39-17-902(a) of which provides:

It is unlawful to knowingly ... prepare for distribution, publish, print, exhibit, distribute, or offer to distribute, or to possess with intent to distribute or to exhibit or offer to distribute any obscene matter. ...

206. See the Tennessee Code § 39-17-901(1):

'Actual or constructive knowledge': a person is deemed to have constructive knowledge of the contents of material who has knowledge of facts which would put a reasonable and prudent person on notice as to the suspect nature of the material.

distribution of obscene material for gain, subject to a defence of lack of knowledge or reasonable suspicion of contents.[207] This would potentially catch ISPs who carried the Usenet newsgroups and websites listed above, but would seem to permit ISPs not to have to filter all the files, on and transmissions to and from, their systems. The third approach criminalises knowing distribution of obscene material, but provides a specific exemption from liability for intermediaries who merely provide access to other servers without participating actively in the production or distribution of the material.[208]

This model is gradually becoming more prevalent, a recent example being the German Federal Law to Regulate the Conditions for Information and Communications Services 1997 ('the Multimedia Law'). Under art. 5(3) of the Multimedia Law, ISPs are provided with a blanket immunity from liability except insofar as they are aware that certain material is unlawful and fail to comply with a legal duty to block access to it.[209] Intermediaries who host material, however, are liable under art. 5(2) for unlawful content if (a) they know that the content is unlawful, and (b) it is technically possible for the intermediary to block access and it is reasonable to expect such blocking to be effected.[210] Liability for material distributed from the intermediary's own servers, e.g., from a hosted website, remains based on knowledge of the intermediary. The effect of this approach is to provide criminal sanctions against an intermediary who knowingly hosts or caches obscene material, but removes the danger of liability from those intermediaries who merely act as transmitters of third party originated packets, whatever the intermediary's state of knowledge. This degree of immunity, however, may be predicated on a fairly simple ISP business model, where the ISP simply provides Internet access. Providing more sophisticated services may still leave an ISP or II open to more stringent rules.[211]

---

207. See, e.g., the UK Obscene Publications Act 1959 s. 2(1).
208. See, e.g., the California Penal Code § 312.6(a):

> It does not constitute a violation of this chapter for a person or entity solely to provide access or connection to or from a facility, system, or network over which that person or entity has no control, including related capabilities that are incidental to providing access or connection. This subdivision does not apply to an individual or entity that is owned or controlled by, or a conspirator with, an entity actively involved in the creation, editing, or knowing distribution of communications that violate this chapter.

209. German Multimedia Law 1997, art. 5(4):

> any duties to block the use of illegal content according to the general laws remain unaffected, insofar as the service provider gains knowledge of such content . . . .

210. See F.W. Bulst, 'Hear No Evil, See No Evil, Answer for No Evil: Internet Service Providers and Intellectual Property — The New German Teleservices Act', [1997] *European Intellectual Property Law Review* 32.
211. This appears to be the situation in France, where the French Telecommunications Law of July 1996 provides those supplying basic ISP services with a limited immunity for content liability. In the situation where an intermediary hosts webpages for third parties, an increasingly common option for ISPs, a recent court ruling has held that in providing file storage and transfer facilities at the disposal of the public the intermediary is no longer a mere access provider, and becomes responsible for the content of its site even in the absence of knowledge: Tribunal de grande instance de Paris, référé, 9 juin 1998 et Cour d'appel de Paris, 14ème Chambre, section A, 10 février 1999, *Affaire Estelle Hallyday c. Altern* (France) (http://www.legalis.net/legalnet/judiciaire/decisions/ca_100299.htm).

Some jurisdictions impose criminal liability for the transmission of obscene, indecent or other unlawful material through their national telecommunications laws. Since Internet communications are often carried across telecommunications networks, these laws will also potentially be applicable. Examples of such laws are 18 USC § 1465[212] and the UK Telecommunications Act 1994, s. 43.[213] Such offences are usually only committed by the sender of the material, which suggests that an ISP, which merely transmits packets originating outside its systems, cannot be liable. Matters become less certain when the ISP hosts a website — it may be perceived that the ISP does send the material, in that its software responds to requests for the obscene resource by transmitting it to the requesting user,[214] although it would seem more logical to decide that the true sender is in fact the controller of the resource.

In general, it would seem that many ISPs are unenthusiastic about the storage and transmission of hard- or soft-core pornography regardless of their legal position. In countries like the United Kingdom, this may be partially over concerns about their liability, but may also be because ISPs wish to avoid the service disruption that law enforcement visits tend to cause, feel that association with pornographic material would be damaging to their potential client market, or simply find that the high rate of accesses to hosts that contain pornography tends to be disruptive to the operation of the computer on which the material is stored.

With regard to the way in which future ISP content regulation will develop, the EU provides an interesting example. This lack of consensus between the EU Member States with regard to what constitutes obscene and indecent material, combined with the difficulties of imposing national rules on an international and thus a jurisdictional medium suggests that, in conformity with the doctrine of subsidiarity, legislative action would be best taken at European Union level. However, when in 1996, the Commission initiated debate on the issue,[215] it soon became apparent that the EU would struggle to provide a workable legislative response to all aspects of the regulation of Internet content. That debate did, however, identify several key issues:

---

212. Offence of using a means of interstate commerce for the purpose of transporting obscene material.
213. Offence of using a public telecommunications system to send grossly offensive, threatening or obscene material. See T. Gibbons, 'Computer Generated Pornography', [1995] 9 *International Yearbook of Law Computers and Technology* 83.
214. This may be the correct interpretation of the UK Indecent Displays (Control) Act 1981, s. 1(1), which creates an offence of publicly displaying indecent matter in public or in a manner which permits it to be visible from any public place (s. 1(2)). Although s. 1(3) exempts places which exclude those under 18 and make a charge for admission, this does not apply to the s. 1(1) offence. It has been suggested that this might impose liability for websites, on the grounds that they can be accessed from terminals in public places: see G. Smith (ed.), *Internet Law and Regulation*, 2nd edn, London: FT Law & Tax, 1997, p. 260.
215. See European Commission, *Communication to the European Parliament, The Council, The Economic and Social Committee and the Committee of the Regions: illegal and Harmful Content on the Internet*, COM (96) 487. Brussels, 16 October 1996, http://www2.echo.lu/legal/en/internet/content/content.html; and, European Commission, *Green Paper on the Protection of Minors and Human Dignity in Audiovisual and Information Services*, Brussels, 16 October 1996, http://www2.echo.lu/legal/en/internet/content/content.html.

(a)   That self-regulation would play a essential role in content control.[216]
(b)   That 'illegal content' was going to be easier to categorise for legislative purposes than 'harmful content'.[217]
(c)   That to be truly effective, any system of Internet content regulation would have to be global.[218]
(d)   That responsibility for content should rest with producers and distributors, and not with intermediaries such as ISPs.[219]

Legislative initiatives, of the type seen in the United States,[220] to regulate Internet content do not appear to have been seriously considered, the consensus being that a multi-level approach to content regulation would be a more effective way forward. This was reflected in the Union's decision not to take the legislative approach via a regulation or directive, but rather to adopt, by Council Decision, an Action Plan to promote the safer use of the Internet.[221] The Action aims to:

(a)   Encourage both industry and users to develop and implement adequate systems of self-regulation by building on existing hot-line initiatives, improving liaison with law enforcement agencies, encouraging further initiatives on self-regulation including the implementation of Codes of Conduct,[222] and the promotion of a system of visible quality labels.

(b)   Strengthen developments by supporting various means of filtering and rating to provide users with a range of tools to protect themselves and their families against undesirable material. This will include the validation of rating systems for European content providers, the integration of rating into the content creation process, assessing the benefits of these technical solutions and the provision of third party rating systems.

(c)   Prepare the ground for awareness actions to be carried out by the Member States, including alerting and informing parents and teachers, through their relevant associations.

(d)   Evaluate the impact of Community measures, to asses legal implications and coordinate with similar international initiatives, and to foster cooperation, exchange of experiences and best practices.

(e)   Promote coordination across Europe and between actors concerned.

(f)   Ensure compatibility between the approach taken in Europe and elsewhere.

---

216. See European Commission Working Party Report (1996), 'Illegal and Harmful Content on the Internet', http://www2.echo.lu/legal/en/internet/content/wopen.html.
217. See The European Parliament, *Resolution on the Commission communication on illegal and harmful content on the Internet* (COM (96) 0487 — C4-0592/96).
218. Ibid.
219. See Ministerial Declaration, Global Information Networks, Ministerial Conference, Bonn, 6–8 July 1997 at paras. 41–43, http://www2.echo.lu/bonn/final.html.
220. European Commission Working Party Report, op. cit. footnote 216 above, at notes 11 and 12.
221. Decision No. 276/1999/EC of the European Parliament and of the Council of 25 January 1999 adopting a multiannual Community action plan on promoting safer use of the Internet by combating illegal and harmful content on global networks, OJ 1999 L33/1, http://www.ispo.cec.be/ecommerce/oj/1999/1999L33/276_1999CE_es.pdf.
222. As suggested in Recommendation 98/560/EC on the protection of minors and human dignity, 24 September 1998, OJ 1998 L270/1.

Thus far, within the EU Member States themselves, there appears to have been a disinclination to engage in any wide-ranging legislative changes with regard to Internet content regulation, and to rely on industry self-regulation. Where there has been legislative activity, it has more often had the aim of limiting the liability, if any, of ISPs, than of penalising IIs and end users. This is not to say that those providing or obtaining material considered illegal or harmful, via the Internet, may do so with impunity. As the recent case of *R v Waddon* (1999) in the United Kingdom demonstrated, national courts are perfectly capable of using existing laws to cover Internet activities, even if some of the law has to be fairly liberally interpreted in the process.[223]

11.7.2   Publication restrictions

Another information content area where the potential criminal liability of ISPs remains uncertain, due largely to a lack of decided case law, is that of criminal contempt of court.[224] Criminal contempts essentially fall into five categories:

(a)   The publication of materials prejudicial to a fair criminal trial.
(b)   The publication of materials prejudicial to fair civil proceedings.
(c)   The publication of materials interfering with the course of justice as a continuing process.
(d)   Contempt in the face of the court.
(e)   Acts which interfere with the course of justice.

Whilst the law of contempt of court has been largely developed by the judiciary through the common law, it has been modified to some extent by the Contempt of Court Act 1981.[225] This makes it an offence of strict liability to publish a publication which:

includes any speech, writing, broadcast, cable programme or other communication in whatever form, which is addressed to the public at large, or any section of the public[226]

where such a publication:

---

223. See http://news2.thls.bbc.co.uk/hi/english/sci/tech/newsid%5F382000/382152.stm. See also *R v Fellows*; *R v Arnold* [1997] 2 All ER 548, CA.
224. In England and Wales, a distinction is drawn between 'civil' and 'criminal' contempts. In broad terms, civil contempt relates to circumstances where parties breach an order of court made in civil proceedings, for example injunctions or undertakings, and as such are not relevant here. Criminal contempt, in contrast, is aimed at various types of conduct that might interfere with the administration of justice, and is designed to have both a punitive and deterrent effect. See G. Smith, (ed) *Internet Law and Regulation*, London: FT Law & Tax, 1996; and A. Charlesworth, 'Criminal Liability' in C. Armstrong (ed), *Electronic Law and the Information Society*, London: Library Association, 1999, pp. 120–149.
225. However the Contempt of Court Act 1981 does not codify or replace entirely the common law. It does, however, apply to Scotland (s. 15).
226. Contempt of Court Act 1981, s. 2(1).

creates a substantial risk that the course of justice in the proceedings in question will be seriously impeded or prejudiced.[227]

The fact that it is a 'strict liability' offence means that an offence occurs even where the person making the publication did not intend to interfere with the course of justice. The broad definition of 'publication' would cover USENET messages, e-mail messages sent to mailing lists and WWW pages. The publication of material relating to a case will only be an offence where it occurs when the case is still *sub judice*. The statutory 'strict liability' rule is only applied during the period that the case is 'active' and the definition of 'active' is laid down in the Act. However, in circumstances where an individual knows, or has good reason to believe, that proceedings are imminent, and publishes material which is likely or calculated to impede or prejudice the course of justice before the point laid down in the Act as the time when the case is 'active', may still constitute a common law contempt.

Actions which would commonly draw charges of contempt include:

(a) Publication of material that prejudges the case, especially where it makes the express or tacit assumption that the accused in a criminal trial is guilty.[228]

(b) Publication of material which is emotive or disparaging, especially where there is an insinuation of complicity or guilt by association.

(c) Publication of material which is likely to be inadmissible at trial, such as previous convictions, or mention of evidence likely to be excluded as having been improperly obtained.[229]

(d) Publication of material such as a photograph of the defendant, where the issue of identification forms part of the trial proceedings.

(e) Publication of material hostile or abusive towards potential witnesses with the intention of coercing them into not testifying, or disclosure of witnesses' names following a court order that their names should not be disclosed if there was a danger that lack of anonymity would prevent them from coming forward.[230]

(f) Publication of jury deliberations.

(g) Publication of material breaching reporting restrictions in cases such where in open court there is identification of children involved in the proceedings, or identification of rape victims.[231]

(h) Publications of material relating to court proceedings closed to the public, including where there is an issue of national security.

Defences to the 'strict liability' offence are:

(a) A person will not be guilty of contempt of court under the strict liability rule as the publisher of any matter to which that rule applies if at the

---

227. Contempt of Court Act 1981, s. 2(2).
228. See *A-G* v *TVS Television, The Times*, 7 July 1989, DC.
229. See *S-G* v *Henry* (1990] COD 307.
230. See *R* v *Socialist Worker Printers and Publishers Ltd, ex parte A-G* [1975] QB 637, DC.
231. See *Pickering* v *Liverpool Daily Post and Echo Newspapers plc* [1991] 1 All ER 622, HL.

time of publication (having taken all reasonable care) he does not know and has no reason to suspect that the relevant proceedings are active.[232]

(b) A person will not be guilty of contempt of court under the strict liability rule as the distributor of a publication containing any such matter if at the time of publication (having taken all reasonable care) he does not know that it contains such matter and has no reason to suspect that it is likely to do so.[233]

(c) A person is not guilty of contempt of court under the strict liability rule in respect of a fair and accurate report of legal proceedings held in public, published contemporaneously and in good faith.[234]

The enforcement of the law of contempt has been rendered more difficult in modern times, by the ability of individuals to publish material, in both traditional[235] and digital media, in countries outside the court's jurisdiction. The Internet has in many ways exacerbated this situation. A prime example of this concerns the 1993 murder trials in Ontario, Canada, of Karla Homolka and Paul Bernado. During the trial of Karla Homolka for the murders of two teenaged girls, Kristen French and Leslie Muhaffy, the court ordered a publication ban on reports of the trial in Ontario, in order to ensure a fair trial for Homolka's husband Paul Bernado (a.k.a. Paul Teale), also charged with the murders.[236] Despite the ban, however, information was widely available due to coverage by US newspapers, cable and TV stations, and at least one website based at a US university.[237] A Usenet newsgroup set up to disseminate and discuss information about the trial, alt.fan.karla-homolka, was censored by many Canadian universities, which were concerned about their liability to contempt proceedings.[238]

Whilst denying access to webpages is more difficult than cutting off newsgroups, it has been suggested with regard to the Internet, that where the court cannot bring contempt proceedings against the original publisher, it may seek to do so against the ISP that distributed the material within the court's jurisdiction. If this approach were to be adopted, it would potentially create similar problems to those found in libel cases, where ISPs have argued that the sheer volume of e-mail traffic, or the vast number of WWW pages on

---

232. Contempt of Court Act 1981, s. 3(1).
233. Ibid., s. 3(2).
234. Ibid., s. 4(1).
235. Consider, for instance, the *Spycatcher* saga, where the book in question was freely available outside the UK, but could not be published or excerpted in the UK. The judicial ban was imposed by preliminary injunction to ensure that the main trial, where the UK government sought to prevent publication of the allegations made in the book, was not rendered meaningless by prior publication in the UK. It is likely that a similar UK publication ban today would be rendered ineffective by web publication within hours. See, for example, the events surrounding the case *Nottinghamshire County Council v Gwatkin*, (High Court of Justice, Chancery Division, 3 June 1997), and *Cyber-Rights & Cyber-Liberties (UK) Newsletter* Issue Number 2, June 1997 at http://www.leeds.ac.uk/law/pgs/yaman/newslet2.htm.
236. See Action No. 125/93, *R v Bernardo* [1993] OJ No. 2047 at http://www2.magmacom.com/~djakob/censor/mediaban.txt. Also C. Walker, 'Cybercontempt: Fair Trials and the Internet', (1997–8) 3 *Oxford Yearbook of Media and Entertainment Law* 1.
237. Information from http://www.cs.indiana.edu/canada/karla.html.
238. Information from http://www.cs.indiana.edu/canada/BannedInCanada.txt.

their systems make it impossible to check them all for possible libelous statements. It would seem likely however that, as with libel, the courts are likely to look favourably (with regard to punitive sanctions) on those ISPs and other IIs who, once notified that material likely to constitute the basis for a contempt offence is held on their systems, do everything in their power to remove it as rapidly as possible. It has been further suggested that the s. 1 defence available in defamation actions under the Defamation Act 1986 should be available by analogy in contempt proceedings. That would, in theory, exempt from liability those who merely operate the machinery by which electronic publications are distributed. However, this thesis is naturally cast into grave doubt by the decision in *Godfrey* v *Demon Internet Ltd*, *The Times*, 20 April 1999.[239]

11.8 CONCLUSIONS

The discussion throughout this chapter provides some indication that despite the often quite sharp differences between national laws relating to ISP liability, there remain some common trends. In most jurisdictions, in situations where ISPs are transmitting information to and from third parties and are hosting information for that particular purpose, there appears to be a growing consensus amongst legislators and judges that they should not be held absolutely liable for breaches of the law committed by their users.

Liability is tending to be imposed in circumstances where:

(a)   The ISP knows, or has reason to believe, that the information content it is transmitting is unlawful.

(b)   Regardless of the ISP's knowledge, it benefits directly from the transmission.[240]

A third, and, it appears, increasingly unpopular reason for imposing liability is where:

(c)   The ISP fails to take reasonable steps to determine if the information content it transmits is unlawful.

However, it is arguable that, even in the three circumstances outlined, the imposition of liability is inappropriate for Internet transactions. All were developed out of the rules applying to physical world transactions where an intermediary will necessarily have closer connections with the parties engaging in a particular transaction, and will usually have the time to ascertain the necessary information concerning the status of the parties and the legality of the transaction. ISPs, on the other hand, have neither the time during the processing of an individual transaction, nor the ability to subject the volume of transactions to scrutiny, that would make such liability viable. An ISP may be able to identify the source of an individual transmission and the nature of

---

239. See section 11.6.2.
240. That is, it receives benefits beyond the indirect benefit that it receives from Internet access fees.

the information transmitted, but to be able to do this for any meaningful numbers of transactions is beyond the scope of current technology. In short, the Internet's infrastructure and technical protocols were simply not designed to facilitate the type of intermediary practices that physical world legal liability requires. As national governments have come to understand that insisting on imposing such liability might significantly restrict the growth of desirable on-line developments such as e-commerce, there has been an increasing trend towards granting Internet intermediaries and ISPs much greater immunities and limitations on their liability for third party content. There are thus some key conclusions that can be drawn from the developments thus far.

11.8.1 The sectoral regulatory burdens on ISPs will continue to decline for basic services

The clear lesson from the regulatory models extant in the US and UK is that neither national governments nor their regulatory agencies are inclined, in the absence of anticompetitive behaviour, to impose any further regulatory burdens on ISPs, at present, whether they are telecoms ISPs, cable ISPs, or access only ISPs. Indeed, existing regulatory frameworks appear to be being either relaxed or actively dismantled as the convergence between the various strands of the 'information industry' continues. In part, this is due to a general shift in government ethos, with its emphasis on competition and self-regulation, and the move away from centrally planned industrial development, but it also owes something to the internationalisation (or globalisation) of the information industry, and to the belief that, thus far, benign non-regulation has played a significant part in the rapid commercial development of the Internet. As such, it seems likely that the sectoral regulatory burdens of ISPs of any stripe will continue to decrease for the foreseeable future.

11.8.2 The legal liability of ISPs will continue to decline for their basic services

As with the question of sectoral regulation, the issue of ISPs' legal liability for content has not escaped the notice of legislators and regulators. The media is full of sound bites from politicians, industrialists and pundits, all emphasising the crucial economic importance of the development of Information Superhighway services and e-commerce activities. It has become almost an article of faith now that retaining differing liability models across national boundaries will create substantial uncertainty for ISPs as to the scope and extent of their potential liabilities, and that this will act as a major disincentive to market entry or the provision of new services, if not rapidly addressed.[241]

---

241. 'The development of electronic commerce could potentially be impeded by illegal and harmful content issues where users fear unwanted content, and where network service providers fear the liability they will take on if they are expected to be responsible for the content that flows across systems.' OECD Policy Brief, 'Electronic Commerce', No. 1-1997, November 1997.

The obvious way to solve this problem is to grant ISPs and other intermediaries some degree of immunity from liability. The difficulty with this approach is in coordinating the various national efforts, given that there is often disagreement about the circumstances in which such immunities should arise and their limitations. Governments have thus far managed to determine some broad international principles for action, but implementing those principles in a coherent fashion across differing jurisdictions will inevitably prove more difficult:

Declaration of the Bonn Ministerial Conference on
Global Information Networks, 6-8 July 1997[242]

[. . .]
41.   Ministers underline the importance of clearly defining the relevant legal rules on responsibility for content of the various actors in the chain between creation and use. They recognise the need to make a clear distinction between the responsibility of those who produce and place content in circulation and that of intermediaries.

42.   Ministers stress that the rules on responsibility for content should be based on a set of common principles so as to ensure a level playing field. Therefore, intermediaries like network operators and access providers should, in general, not be responsible for content. This principle should be applied in such a way that intermediaries like network operators and access providers are not subject to unreasonable, disproportionate or discriminatory rules. In any case, third-party content hosting services should not be expected to exercise prior control on content which they have no reason to believe is illegal. Due account should be taken of whether such intermediaries had reasonable grounds to know and reasonable possibility to control content.

43.   Ministers consider that rules on responsibility should give effect to the principle of freedom of speech, respect public and private interests and not impose disproportionate burdens on actors.

Beyond such sweeping statements of principle, the international political process has been slow to reach practical agreements, this has meant delays in implementing national and international rules that define and limit the responsibility of ISPs and Internet Intermediaries. ISPs and Internet Intermediaries have thus tended to opt for some degree of self-help in this matter, primarily by the use of contract law to attempt to limit the extent of their liability. However, while this approach may have some utility within the ISP's own national jurisdiction, the use of contracts to control liability in multiple jurisdictions, with varying contract laws, leaves the ISP little better off in terms of certainty about the extent to which it is capable of controlling its liability, while posing the risk of providing an illusory sense of security. In particular, there are problems with:

(a)   Forming the contract between an ISP and a user. It is not practicable for an ISP to engage in a drawn out contractual negotiation with its users,

---

242. See http://www.echo.lu/bonn/final.html.

nor is it desirable for an ISP to have a signed paper contract for its dealings with each user. The most efficient and cost effective method of forming contracts with its users governing their dealings with each other will be electronically. However, just as liability laws have not yet caught up with the realities of electronic intermediaries, so contract law lags behind the need for contract formation technology. Some jurisdictions will simply not recognise the legality of electronically concluded contracts, and even where such contracts are feasible, the precise effects of contract formation technologies such as 'click through' contracts on webpages are difficult to gauge State to State.[243]

(b)   Determining what can actually be excluded under contract law. Even where an ISP has concluded a contract successfully with an end user, its attempts to limit its own liability may be frustrated by judicial oversight of 'unfair' or 'unacceptable' contract terms.[244] The differences in national approaches to this issue makes drafting a universally applicable limitation of liability almost impossible.

(c)   The restrictions imposed on liability exclusion by consumer protection laws. In many jurisdictions, consumer protection laws exist which will render void contractual terms that purport to exclude liability if the user is a consumer.[245]

If the ISP is in a position to conclude an effective contract with the user, it will likely only be effective to exclude or limit the intermediary's liability to that user. Whilst indemnity clauses are increasingly popular in ISP contracts, for example:

Kingston Internet Ltd's Terms and Conditions for the
Provision of Karoo Dial service
(http://www.kingston-internet.net/karooterms.html)

6.2   You must not use or allow the Service or your web space to be used for storing, sending or receiving any material which is obscene, menacing, threatening, offensive, abusive, indecent, defamatory, fraudulent, criminal or which infringes the rights of any other party including any intellectual property rights.
[...]

---

243. *Commission proposal for a European Parliament and Council directive on certain legal aspects of electronic commerce in the internal market*, COM (1998) 586 final, 98/0325 (COD), 18 November 1998, Explanatory Memorandum, pp. 11–12.

244. E.g., the UK Unfair Contract Terms Act 1977 gives UK courts the power to declare many types of exclusion or limitation terms to be unenforceable, particularly terms that attempt to exclude contractual or tortious obligations of care (s. 2(2)) and terms that are contained in written standard form contracts (s. 3), where the court considers these to be unreasonable (s. 11). See also The Unfair Terms in Consumer Contracts Regulations 1999 (SI 1999/2083) which came into force on 1 October 1999 to ensure UK law conforms with Directive 93/13/EEC on Unfair Terms in Consumer Contracts, OJ L 95, 21 April 1993.

245. E.g., the Directive 93/13/EEC on Unfair Terms in Consumer Contracts, OJ L 95 21 April 1993 provides that a term is unfair if (a) it has not been individually negotiated and (b) contrary to the requirement of good faith, it causes a significant imbalance in the parties rights and obligations arising under the contract, to the detriment of the consumer (arts. 6 and 7).

394 The Liability of Internet Service Providers and Internet Intermediaries

6.5   You will indemnify Us and hold Us harmless against any claim brought by a third party arising out of the breach by You of clauses 2.2, 6.1 and 6.2 or in any way connected with Your use of the Service or Your web space.

The actual utility of these clauses is probably limited, as:

(a)   They too will be subject to mandatory consumer protection rules such as the UK Unfair Contract Terms Act 1977 and the EC Directive on Unfair Terms in Consumer Contracts.
(b)   Even if valid, the ability of the ISP defending a content liability action to obtain adequate financial recompense from the offending end user is likely to be limited.

Most importantly they will have no effect on any criminal liability of the ISP for transmitting third party content. Many of the claims against an ISP will be made by persons with whom the ISP has no opportunity of forming a contract, and thus contractual approaches to liability control will clearly fail to provide ISPs with the degree of immunity which it is generally accepted that they require.

Some governments have been quick to recognise that substantial law reform will be required to satisfactorily resolve the liability of ISPs and other Internet intermediaries. The United States, in particular, has been quick to act to introduce particular immunity relating to copyright, as have some other jurisdictions, although the US legislation thus far provided falls some way short of a comprehensive and coherent statement of ISP liability. The EU has engaged in a more considered examination of the legal differences between European national laws with regard to e-commerce, and while its progress towards actual legislation has thus been delayed, the result of that examination are several draft and enacted Directives relating to electronic commerce.[246] The draft directive on copyright in the Information Society provides a specific exemption for certain types of copyright infringement, and the Directive on certain legal aspects of electronic commerce in the Internal Market contains a comprehensive proposal for an EU-wide framework for determining intermediary immunities.

11.8.2.1   Copyright liability immunity   Liability for copyright infringement has been specifically addressed by a number of jurisdictions, not just because of the difficulties that it poses for Internet Intermediaries, but also because of sustained pressure from major rightsholders concerned to ensure that their interests are not undermined by digital copying. Much of that legislation reflects the tensions between those two groupings, who while not exactly opposed to each other's point of view, have each been wary to ensure that any concession made to the other does not potentially damage their own interests. The resulting legislation thus tends to display two main threads:

---

246. See further http://www.ispo.cec.be/Ecommerce/Welcome.html.

(a)   That ISPs will be granted a carefully crafted limited immunity from liability for copyright infringement.

(b)   That rightsholders will be granted greater powers over digital copying of their works than has been granted to any previous type of work.

A particularly good example of this approach can be seen in the Online Copyright Infringement Liability Limitation Act 1998, part of the Digital Millennium Copyright Act 1998[247] which was designed to ratify the WIPO Copyright Treaty of 1996. It inserts a new § 512 into the US Copyright Act, Title 17 USC, which briefly put, provides immunity to ISPs and Internet intermediaries who transmit infringing material if their role is only to:

(a)   transmit the infringing packets;
(b)   automatically cache information requested by third parties;
(c)   host third party resources; or
(d)   provide search and location tools for resources located elsewhere.

Thus, an ISP is simply not liable for the transmission of infringing data through its servers as long as the servers transmit the information automatically and the contents are not altered by the ISP. The immunities granted are however hedged around with detailed conditions, primarily that the ISP:

(a)   does not actually know, nor should be expected to know, that the material on its server, is infringing;
(b)   does not receive a direct financial benefit from the posting of the infringing material; and
(c)   responds expeditiously to remove or disable access to the infringing material when made aware of its presence.

In order for an ISP to limit its liability under the Act, it must designate an agent for notification of claimed infringements by providing contact information to the Copyright Office and also by making that information available to users online.

The EU initially took a rather simpler approach to this problem in its draft directive on copyright in the Information Society:

Proposal for a European Parliament and Council Directive
on the harmonization of certain aspects of copyright and related rights
in the Information Society, COM (97) 628 final, 10 December 1997[248]

Commentary to Article 5, p. 36
3.   Article 5(1) introduces an obligatory exception to the right of reproduction for certain technical acts of reproductions that are integral to a technological process and made for the sole purpose of executing another

---

247. See The Digital Millennium Copyright Act of 1998: US Copyright Office Summary at p. 9 (December 1998), available at http://lcweb.loc.gov/copyright/legislation/dmca.pdf.
248. See http://www.europa.eu.int/comm/dg15/en/intprop/intprop/copyen.pdf.

act of exploitation of a work. When applying this exception, or any other exception listed in this Article, the 'three step test', as set out in paragraph 4 of this Article, has, of course, also to be met. The purpose of Article 5(1) is to exclude from the scope of the reproduction right certain acts of reproduction which are dictated by technology, but which have no separate economic significance of their own. It applies notably to the on-line environment, but also to acts of reproduction taking place in the context of the use of a protected subject matter in off-line formats. In such cases, it is appropriate to limit the scope of the reproduction right and only protect those acts of reproduction which are of a separate economic relevance. Such an obligatory exception at Community level is vital as such short lived reproductions ancillary to the final use of a work will take place in most acts of exploitation of protected subject matter, which will often be of a transnational nature. For instance, when transmitting a video on-demand from a database in Germany to a home computer in Portugal, this retrieval will imply a copy of the video, first of all, at the place of the database and afterwards, in average, up to at least a hundred often ephemeral   acts of storage along the transmission to Portugal. A divergent situation in Member States with some requiring authorization of such ancillary acts of storage would significantly risk impeding the free movement of works and services, and notably on-line services containing protected subject matter.

Article 5 — Exceptions to the restricted acts set out in Articles 2 and 3
    1.   Temporary acts of reproduction referred to in Article 2 which are an integral part of a technological process for the sole purpose of enabling use to be made of a work or other subject matter, and having no independent economic significance, shall be exempted from the right set out in Article 2 [Reproduction Right].
    . . .
    4.   The exceptions and limitations provided for in paragraphs 1, 2 and 3 shall only be applied to certain specific cases and shall not be interpreted in such a way as to allow their application to be used in a manner which unreasonably prejudices the rightholders' legitimate interests or conflicts with the normal exploitation of their works or other subject matter.

However, the initial version of the draft Directive met with considerable resistance both in the European Parliament and amongst the Member States. There was considerable disagreement amongst national governments about the scope of some of the directive's proposals, notably the exemptions in art. 5. The United Kingdom, for example, asked for a substantial re-discussion of all exemptions and proposed to delete the draft exemptions in arts 5.1–5.3. Failure of the Member States to agree on the whole issue of the exemptions has meant that a Common position, which was expected in June 1999, was considerably delayed. As matters currently stand under the amended proposal:

Amended proposal for a European Parliament and Council Directive on the harmonization of certain aspects of copyright and related rights in the Information Society, Commission of the European Communities, Brussels, 21.05.1999. COM (1999) 250 final, 97/0359/COD[249]

Article 5 — Exceptions to the restricted acts set out in Articles 2, 3 & 4
1. Temporary acts of reproduction referred to in Article 2, such as transient and incidental acts of reproduction which are an integral and essential part of a technological process, including those which facilitate effective functioning of transmission systems, whose sole purpose is to enable use to be made of a work or other subject matter, and which have no independent economic significance, shall be exempted from the right set out in Article 2 [Reproduction Right].

The current additions to art. 5(1) do not appear to unduly change its meaning, with the effect being that temporary copying by intermediaries, such as packet transmission and caching, will not amount to infringement in the Member States. An additional restriction on these immunities in both the United States and the EU is that an ISP must ensure, when it provides access to Internet resources, that it preserves all technical rights management information attached to those resources, i.e., information used to prove the copyright ownership of the work or to track licensed users.[250]

11.8.2.2 General immunity The first general immunity provisions for ISPs were introduced by the United States, via the Communications Decency Act (CDA) of 1996. The provisions, which provide that immunity, were not in fact supposed to be the main thrust of the Act. It drafters intended the CDA to introduce new criminal offences of knowingly creating, sending, transmitting or displaying obscene or indecent materials to minors, or knowingly permitting the use of one's telecommunications systems for these purposes. The ISP immunity provisions in § 230 were added to overrule the decision in *Stratton Oakmont, Inc.* v *Prodigy Services Co.* 23 Media Law Rep (BNA) 1794, (NY Sup Ct, 1995)[251] which had made it risky for an ISP to exercise any monitoring of the content it carried, such as introducing blocking or filtering technology, without rendering itself potentially liable as an editor or publisher, and thus becoming responsible for any third party content that it carried. The drafters intended ISPs who acted as 'Good Samaritans' by 'protecting' their users from obscene or indecent materials using such technologies, to escape any resulting liability.[252]

---

249. See http://www.europa.eu.int/comm/dg15/en/intprop/intprop/copy2.htm.
250. Article 7, draft directive; 17 USC § 512(i).
251. See section 11.6.2 and note 164, above.
252. The Senate conference report on § 230 states:

> This section provides 'Good Samaritan' protections from civil liability for providers or users of an interactive computer service for actions to restrict or to enable restriction of access to objectionable online material. One of the specific purposes of this section is to overrule *Stratton Oakmont* v *Prodigy* and any other similar decisions which have treated such providers and users as publishers or speakers of content that is not their own

Regrettably for the CDA's drafters (but in a ruling greeted with applause worldwide), the new criminal offences were struck down in *A.C.L.U.* v *Reno* 929 F Supp 824, 830–838 (ED Pa, 1996)[253] as the court felt its 'indecent transmission' and 'patently offensive display' provisions abridged 'the freedom of speech' protected by the First Amendment as it lacked the precision that the First Amendment requires when a statute regulates the content of speech. However, the striking down of the criminal provisions left the immunity provisions untouched:

US Communications Decency Act 1996, 47 USC § 230

SEC. 230. *Protection for Private Blocking and Screening of Offensive Material.*[254]

(a)   *Findings*: The Congress finds the following:

(1)   The rapidly developing array of Internet and other interactive computer services available to individual Americans represent an extraordinary advance in the availability of educational and informational resources to our citizens.

(2)   These services offer users a great degree of control over the information that they receive, as well as the potential for even greater control in the future as technology develops.

(3)   The Internet and other interactive computer services offer a forum for a true diversity of political discourse, unique opportunities for cultural development, and myriad avenues for intellectual activity.

---

continued

because they have restricted access to objectionable material. The conferees believe that such decisions create serious obstacles to the important federal policy of empowering parents to determine the content of communications their children receive through interactive computer services. S Conf Rep No. 104–230, at p. 435 (1996).

253. Affirmed 117 S Ct 2329 (1997).
254. The definitions used in this section are:

(1)   *Internet:* The term Internet means the international computer network of both Federal and non-Federal interoperable packet switched data networks.

(2)   *Interactive computer service:* The term interactive computer service means any information service, system, or access software provider that provides or enables computer access by multiple users to a computer server, including specifically a service or system that provides access to the Internet and such systems operated or services offered by libraries or educational institutions.

(3)   *Information content provider:* The term information content provider means any person or entity that is responsible, in whole or in part, for the creation or development of information provided through the Internet or any other interactive computer service.

(4)   *Access software provider:* The term access software provider means a provider of software (including client or server software), or enabling tools that do any one or more of the following:
(A)   filter, screen, allow, or disallow content;
(B)   pick, choose, analyze, or digest content; or
(C)   transmit, receive, display, forward, cache, search, subset, organize, reorganize, or translate content.

(4)   The Internet and other interactive computer services have flourished, to the benefit of all Americans, with a minimum of government regulation.

(5)   Increasingly Americans are relying on interactive media for a variety of political, educational, cultural, and entertainment services.

(b)   *Policy*: It is the policy of the United States—

(1)   to promote the continued development of the Internet and other interactive computer services and other interactive media;

(2)   to preserve the vibrant and competitive free market that presently exists for the Internet and other interactive computer services, unfettered by Federal or State regulation;

(3)   to encourage the development of technologies which maximize user control over what information is received by individuals, families, and schools who use the Internet and other interactive computer services;

(4)   to remove disincentives for the development and utilization of blocking and filtering technologies that empower parents to restrict their children's access to objectionable or inappropriate online material; and

(5)   to ensure vigorous enforcement of Federal criminal laws to deter and punish trafficking in obscenity, stalking, and harassment by means of computer.

(c)   *Protection for Good Samaritan Blocking and Screening of Offensive Material*:

(1)   Treatment of publisher or speaker: No provider or user of an interactive computer service shall be treated as the publisher or speaker of any information provided by another information content provider.

(2)   Civil liability: No provider or user of an interactive computer service shall be held liable on account of—

(A)   any action voluntarily taken in good faith to restrict access to or availability of material that the provider or user considers to be obscene, lewd, lascivious, filthy, excessively violent, harassing, or otherwise objectionable, whether or not such material is constitutionally protected; or

(B)   any action taken to enable or make available to information content providers or others the technical means to restrict access to material described in paragraph (1).

(d)   *Effect on Other Laws*:

(1)   No effect on criminal law: Nothing in this section shall be construed to impair the enforcement of section 223 of this Act, chapter 71 (relating to obscenity) or 110 (relating to sexual exploitation of children) of title 18, United States Code, or any other Federal criminal statute.

(2)   No effect on intellectual property law: Nothing in this section shall be construed to limit or expand any law pertaining to intellectual property.

(3)   State law: Nothing in this section shall be construed to prevent any State from enforcing any State law that is consistent with this section. No cause of action may be brought and no liability may be imposed under any State or local law that is inconsistent with this section.

(4)   No effect on communications privacy law: Nothing in this section shall be construed to limit the application of the Electronic Communications Privacy Act of 1986 or any of the amendments made by such Act, or any similar State law.

§ 230 has been tested a number of times in subsequent litigation, but at present the US courts appear to consider that it provides complete immunity from civil actions for defamation,[255] even where the ISP pays the author for the right to provide access to the defamatory material,[256] and it has also been successfully used as a defence in a civil action alleging negligence in failing to prevent continued solicitations to purchase child pornography made via an ISP's system:[257]

Zeran v America Online Inc.
129 F 3d 327 (4th Cir, 1979) pp. 330–31

By its plain language, sec. 230 creates a federal immunity to any cause of action that would make service providers liable for information originating with a third-party user of the service. Specifically, sec. 230 precludes courts

---

255. *Zeran v America Online Inc.*, 129 F 3d 327 (4th Cir, 12 December 1979), affirming 958 F Supp 1124 (ED Va, 21 March 1997), cert. denied (ISP not liable for allegedly defamatory postings by one of its subscribers. The claimant maintained that ISP was negligent in permitting anonymous postings by a subscriber accusing claimant of publishing materials 'glorifying' the Oklahoma City bombing. The superior court affirmed that the claim was preempted by s. 230(c)(1) Communications Decency Act 1996 (CDA), immunising Internet Service Providers from 'distributor liability'. Imposing liability would create a disincentive for providers to review content for potentially objectionable material, and would thus frustrate one of the CDA's chief aims. Also if liability were incurred merely upon an ISP being notified of allegedly improper material, it would place a burden of investigation and judgment far greater than that on traditional print publishers — an impossible burden in the Internet context, and a clear invitation to third parties to foment lawsuits and leverage settlements by merely sending notice and demanding action.); *Aquino v ElectriCiti* 26 Media L Rep 1032 (San Francisco Supr Ct, 1997) (claimant sued claiming an ISP had failed to take action against a subscriber who sent messages to a Usenet group allegedly defaming claimants by associating them with a previous child abuse investigation. The court dismissed the action under the Communications Decency Act's 'safe harbour' provisions for Internet Service Providers, citing the rule in *Zeran v America Online Inc.*; *Kempf v Time, Inc.*, No. BC 184799 (LA Supr Ct, 11 June 1998) (claimants admission that defendant ISP played no role in creating or developing allegedly libellous material, meant action against the ISP dismissed under the 'safe harbor' provisions of the CDA); *Ben Ezra, Weinstein & Co. v America Online Inc.*, No. CIV 97-485 (DN Mex 1 March 1999) (BW&C sued for defamation, alleging that AOL published incorrect and defamatory information on the Internet concerning BW&C's publicly traded stock. The court held that AOL 'clearly qualifies' for Internet service provider immunity under § 230 of the CDA).
256. *Blumenthal v Drudge*, 992 F Supp 44 (DDC, 1998) (ISP shielded from liability as a content provider for allegedly defamatory statements about the claimant written by columnist under contract to ISP and published on ISP's service. Court held following *Zeran v America Online* that the safe harbor provisions of the CDA absolutely precluded state common law defamation actions against Internet service providers).
257. *Doe v America Online Inc.*, No. 25 Media L Rep 2112 (Fl Cir Ct, 1997) (ISP liability shield provision of CDA protected ISP from liability for subscriber's use of chat room to advertise pornographic images of 11-year-old boy).

from entertaining claims that would place a computer service provider in a publisher's role. Thus, lawsuits seeking to hold a service provider liable for its exercise of a publisher's traditional editorial functions — such as deciding whether to publish, withdraw, postpone or alter content — are barred.

The purpose of this statutory immunity is not difficult to discern. Congress recognized the threat that tort-based lawsuits pose to freedom of speech in the new and burgeoning Internet medium. The imposition of tort liability on service providers for the communications of others represented, for Congress, simply another form of intrusive government regulation of speech. Section 230 was enacted, in part, to maintain the robust nature of Internet communication and, accordingly, to keep government interference in the medium to a minimum . . . .

None of this means, of course, that the original culpable party who posts defamatory messages would escape accountability. . . . Congress made a policy choice, however, not to deter harmful online speech through the separate route of imposing tort liability on companies that serve as intermediaries for other parties' potentially injurious messages.

Blumenthal v *Drudge and America Online Inc.*
992 F Supp 44 (DDC 1998)

If it were writing on a clean slate, this Court would agree with plaintiffs [claimants]. AOL has certain editorial rights with respect to the content provided by Drudge and disseminated by AOL, including the right to require changes in content and to remove it; and it has affirmatively promoted Drudge as a new source of unverified instant gossip on AOL. Yet it takes no responsibility for any damage he may cause. AOL is not a passive conduit like the telephone company, a common carrier with no control and therefore no responsibility for what is said over the telephone wires.[258] Because it has the right to exercise editorial control over those with whom it contracts and whose words it disseminates, it would seem only fair to hold AOL to the liability standards applied to a publisher or, at least, like a book store owner or library, to the liability standards applied to a distributor.[259] But Congress has made a different policy choice by providing immunity even where the interactive service provider has an active, even aggressive role in making available content prepared by others. In some sort of tacit quid pro quo arrangement with the service provider community, Congress has conferred immunity from tort liability as an incentive to Internet service providers to self-police the Internet for obscenity and other offensive material, even where the self-policing is unsuccessful or not even attempted.

---

258. See David J. Goldstone, 'A Funny Thing Happened On The Way To the Cyber Forum: Public vs. Private in Cyberspace Speech', (1998) 69 *U. Colo. L. Rev.* 1, 40–48.
259. See Douglas B. Lufflnan, 'Defamation Liability For On-Line Services: The Sky Is Not Falling', (1997) 65 *Geo. Wash. L. Rev.* 1071, at pp. 1083–35; David R. Sheridan, '*Zeran* v *AOL* And The Effect Of Section 230 Of The Communications Decency Act Upon Liability for Defamation On The Internet', (1997) 61 *Alb. L. Rev.* 147, at pp. 167–77.

... While it appears to this Court that AOL in this case has taken advantage of all the benefits conferred by Congress in the Communications Decency Act, and then some, without accepting any of the burdens that Congress intended, the statutory language is clear: AOL is immune from suit, and the Court therefore must grant its motion for summary judgment.

It seems clear that § 230 has taken on a life of its own, considerably beyond that which its legislative drafters intended, but despite some disquiet on the part of the courts and others,[260] about the extremely broad immunity that it appears to provide, in none of the judgments thus far has there been a suggestion that that immunity will be overturned or eroded by the judiciary. Indeed in *Lunney* v *Prodigy Services Co.* 683 NYS 2d 557 a New York court decided it did not even need to consider § 230 in deciding the outcome of an on-line libel case, deciding it instead on the basis of a prior New York state court libel decision dealing with telephone and telegraph companies, *Anderson* v *New York Telephone Co.* 35 NY 2d 746 and treating the ISP concerned essentially as a common carrier. Thus, it would seem that if the United States wishes to reduce the level of immunity currently granted to ISPs, fresh legislation would be required.

Such legislation may not be forthcoming, as in the interim other jurisdictions have introduced, or proposed, extensive immunities for ISPs and other Internet intermediaries. These immunities extend both to copyright infringement and criminal law, as well as to civil actions for torts such as defamation:

Singapore Electronic Transactions Act 1998

10. Liability of network service providers

(1) A network service provider shall not be subject to any civil or criminal liability under any rule of law in respect of third-party material in the form of electronic records to which he merely provides access if such liability is founded on—

a. the making, publication, dissemination or distribution of such materials or any statement made in such material; or

b. the infringement of any rights subsisting in or in relation to such material.

(2) Nothing in this section shall affect—

a. any obligation founded on contract;

b. the obligation of a network service provider as such under a licensing or other regulatory regime established under any written law; or

c. any obligation imposed under any written law or by a court to remove, block or deny access to any material.

(3) For the purposes of this section—

'provides access', in relation to third-party material, means the provision of the necessary technical means by which third-party material may be accessed and includes the automatic and temporary storage of the third-party material for the purpose of providing access;

---

260. See I.C. Ballon, '*Zeran* v *AOL*: Why the Fourth Circuit is Wrong', *Journal of Internet Law*, March 1998 at http://www.finnegan.com/pubs/internet/zeranvaol.htm.

'third-party', in relation to a network service provider, means a person over whom the provider has no effective control.

The scope of this immunity, while remarkable by Singaporean standards of media control,[261] only extends to packet transmission and caching. It is clear from the definition of 'provides access' in s. 10(3) that the Act will not grant immunity for hosting third party resources, because such hosting would not be 'automatic and temporary storage' of those resources. It does, however, reflect a growing recognition, even in relatively autocratic nations, that ISPs have to be granted some form of immunity from liability for the content they carry, if national ambitions for e-commerce are to be achieved.[262] Both the German Multimedia Law and the draft EU directive on electronic commerce go rather further in granting immunity to both transmission and resource hosts as well as to packet transmitters and cache operators:

German Multimedia Law 1998 art. 5
(trans. Christopher Kuner, www.kuner.com)

Responsibility
(1) Service providers are responsible under the general laws for their own content which they make available for use.
(2) Service providers are only responsible for third-party content which they make available for use if they have knowledge of such content and blocking its use is both technically possible and can be reasonably expected.
(3) Service providers are not responsible for third-party content to which they merely provide access for use. The automatic and temporary storage of third-party content because of a user access constitutes the provision of access.
(4) Any duties to block the use of illegal content according to the general laws remains unaffected, insofar as the service provider gains knowledge of such content while complying with the obligation of telecommunications secrecy under Art. 85 of the Telecommunications Law, and blocking is both technically possible and can be reasonably expected.

This law makes a clear distinction between hosting resources, in which case immunity under art. 5(2) will be lost where the intermediary knows the nature of the information content and fails to take reasonable steps to block access, and transmission and caching, where according to art. 5(3) knowledge appears to be irrelevant.

---

261. Consider Endeshaw, 'Singapore gets to grips with the Internet', (1996) 7 *Journal of Law and Information Science* 208; the Singapore Broadcasting Authority (Class Licence) Notification 1996, http://www.sba.gov.sg/work/sba/internet.nsf, and the Singapore Broadcasting Authority Internet Code of Practice (November 1997), http://www.sba.gov.sg/work/sba/internet.nsf/pages/code.
262. See S.B. Hogan, 'To Net or Not to Net: Singapore's Regulation of the Internet', (1999) 51 *Federal Communications Law Journal* 430, http://www.law.indiana.edu/fclj/pubs/v51/no2/hoganmac.PDF.

Commission Proposal for a European Parliament and Council Directive on Certain Legal Aspects of Electronic Commerce in the Internal Market, Com (1998) 586 final, 98/0325 (COD), 18 November 1998

Section 4 — Liability[263] *of intermediary service providers*

Article 12 — Mere conduit

1. Where an Information Society service is provided that consists of the transmission in a communication network of information provided by a recipient of the service, or the provision of access to a communication network, Member States shall ensure that the service provider is not liable for the information transmitted, on condition that the provider:

    (a)   does not initiate the transmission;

    (b)   does not select the receiver of the transmission; and

    (c)   does not select or modify the information contained in the transmission.

2. The acts of transmission and of provision of access referred to in paragraph 1 include the automatic, intermediate and transient storage of the information transmitted insofar as this takes place for the sole purpose of carrying out the transmission in the communication network, and provided that the information is not stored for any period longer than is reasonably necessary for the transmission.

3. This Article shall not affect the possibility for a court or administrative authority, in accordance with Member States' legal systems, to require the service provider to terminate or prevent an infringement.

Article 13 — Caching

1. Where an Information Society service is provided that consists of the transmission in a communication network of information provided by a recipient of the service, Member States shall ensure that the service provider is not liable for the automatic, intermediate and temporary storage of that information, performed for the sole purpose of making more efficient the information's onward transmission to other recipients of the service upon their request, on condition that:

    (a)   the provider does not modify the information;

---

263. Page 28 of the Explanatory Memorandum for the original proposal (COM (1999) 427 final) stated that the immunities in arts. 12 and 14 extended to criminal liability, and the subsequent version of the text (COM (1999) 427 final) clarified that this covered art. 13 as well. However, the enacted text does not mention criminal liability in respect of these immunities, and recital 26 states:

> Member States, in conformity with conditions established in this Directive, may apply their national rules on criminal law and criminal proceedings with a view to taking all investigative and other measures necessary for the detection and prosecution of criminal offences, without there being a need to notify such measures to the Commission.

The question whether intermediaries will be granted immunity for criminal prosecutions as well as for civil actions is therefore left to the Member States when implementing the Directive, although the global trend suggests that they will face pressure to cover criminal as well as civil liabilities.

(b)   the provider complies with conditions on access to the information;
(c)   the provider complies with rules regarding the updating of the information, specified in a manner widely recognised and used by industry;
(d)   the provider does not interfere with the lawful use of technology, widely recognised and used by industry, to obtain data on the use of the information; and
(e)   the provider acts expeditiously to remove or to disable access to the information it has stored upon obtaining actual knowledge of the fact that the information at the initial source of the transmission has been removed from the network, or access to it has been disabled, or that a court or an administrative authority has ordered such removal or disablement.
2.   This Article shall not affect the possibility for a court or administrative authority, in accordance with Member States' legal systems, to require the service provider to terminate or prevent an infringement.

Article 14 — Hosting

1.   Where an Information Society service is provided that consists of the storage of information provided by a recipient of the service, Member States shall ensure that the service provider is not liable for the information stored at the request of a recipient of the service, on condition that:
(a)   the provider does not have actual knowledge of illegal activity or information and, as regards claims for damages, is not aware of facts or circumstances from which the illegal activity or information is apparent; or
(b)   the provider, upon obtaining such knowledge or awareness, acts expeditiously to remove or to disable access to the information.
2.   Paragraph 1 shall not apply when the recipient of the service is acting under the authority or the control of the provider.
3.   This Article shall not affect the possibility for a court or administrative authority, in accordance with Member States' legal systems, to require the service provider to terminate or prevent an infringement, nor does it affect the possibility for Member States to establish procedures governing the removal or disabling of access to information.

Article 15 — No general obligation to monitor

1.   Member States shall not impose a general obligation on providers, when providing the services covered by Articles 12, 13 and 14, to monitor the information which they transmit or store, nor a general obligation actively to seek facts or circumstances indicating illegal activity.
2.   Member States may establish obligations for Information Society service providers promptly to inform the competent public authorities of alleged illegal activities undertaken or information provided by recipients of their service or obligations to communicate to the competent authorities, at their request, information enabling the identification of recipients of their service with whom they have storage agreements.

From the above examples, it is possible to extract four types of ISP activity for which one or more jurisdiction now considers immunity to be necessary:

(a)   The transmission of resources from a third party server to a user (regardless of whether or not they are a customer of the ISP).

(b)   The automatic storage of copies of user-requested resources, so that future requests for the same resource can be provided from a local cache rather than from a more distant server.

(c)   The hosting of resources, control over which is exercised by a third party, normally a customer, rather than by the ISP itself.

(d)   The provision of search and directory facilities which enable users to locate and access third party resources.

It is obvious that in most cases there will be limits to this immunity from liability, and again, clear patterns are being to emerge as to situations where immunity will be lost:

(a)   If the ISP fails to comply with a court order, such as an injunction to block access to, or requiring the removal of, unlawful material.

(b)   If the ISP exercises positive control over the information content, for example by editing it.

(c)   Non-editorial modifications will also prevent the immunity arising, for example, the removal of copyright management information.

(d)   If the ISP hosts a resource, where the unlawful nature of the resource becomes known to the intermediary and it fails to take reasonable steps to remove access to that resource.

At present the US stands alone in granting absolute immunity from civil liability under the Communications Decency Act 1996. As already noted, it might be considered that altering that immunity would be a retrograde step — certainly the ISPs would view it as such. However, as both the court in *Blumenthal*,[264] and several commentators have noted,[265] § 230, as it currently stands, does not in fact perform the function that Congress intended it to, by encouraging ISPs to exercise more editorial control over the content they make accessible to their subscribers. Rather the provision of absolute immunity, whether an ISP attempts to edit content or not, removes a significant motivation to exercise editorial control — the threat of legal consequences:

Congress has conferred immunity from tort liability as an incentive to Internet service providers to self-police the Internet for obscenity and other offensive material, even where the self-policing is unsuccessful or not even attempted.[266]

In any event, on a general basis, worldwide, the likelihood of ISPs being held liable for the content of material that they have simply stored and/or transmitted appears to be decreasing. This is not just because of the

---

264. *Blumenthal* v *Drudge*, op. cit., note 256, above.
265. See I.C. Ballon, '*Zeran* v *AOL*: Why the Fourth Circuit is Wrong', op. cit., at note 260, above, and Anon, 'The Implications of the Good Samaritan Provision on Defamation Law', at http://www.law.yale.edu/infosociety/papers/defamation.html.
266. *Blumenthal* v *Drudge*, op. cit., note 256, above.

realisation on the part of legislatures that overenthusiastic regulation will retard the development of desirable aspects of Internet use such as e-commerce, but because ISPs are becoming more active in influencing the legislative and legal processes to protect their interests. ISP representative groups such as the Commercial Internet eXchange (CIX) and the Internet Watch Foundation (IWF) have engaged in highly successful lobbying to ensure that legislators acknowledge their members' interests. Examples of the influence wielded can be seen in the funding by CIX of the ACLU's successful challenge to the Communications Decency Act 1996, and the role played by CIX in the passage of a version of the Digital Millennium Copyright Act that reduced its regulation of ISPs and other website providers to just about the minimum acceptable to copyright holders. For the moment, however ISP's remain wary about the possible imposition of further liability for their services, and keen to ensure that future regulation is both limited and lighthanded.

11.8.3 The standard business model for ISPs will continue to add more enhanced services and new areas of sectoral regulation and legal liability will arise out of the convergence between ISPs and other industry sectors

Even as ISPs have begun to obtain legislative immunity for their basic service provision, they have, as is amply exemplified by the proposed AOL/Time Warner/EMI merger, already begun to diversify into a wide range of business activities, many of which will incur additional potential liabilities. When one examines a company such as AOL, it may become increasingly difficult to separate its provision of 'basic services' from the range of additional or 'premium' services which it supplies. AOL's users may use a fraction of its services, or all of them — Internet connection, software, information services, website etc. — and thus the impact of § 230 in the United States may not be insignificant in this regard.

However, in general, the liability of intermediaries for the information content and services they supply to users on their own account is a matter which can in most instances be left to existing laws to determine. These intermediaries are usually in a direct relationship with the information source, and can decide whether to provide the information or services as a matter of commercial judgment. Liability questions will play some part in making that judgment, but are not so fundamental as to require international action immediately.

Some other issues of potential ISP liability do perhaps merit some further thought, for instance, the liability of ISPs for facilitating the growth of unsolicited commercial e-mail (UCE or spam). This has certainly been aided by both the aggressive marketing techniques of some ISPs, who offer free trials of their software and access, whilst exercising minimal control over what is done with that access.[267] As 'spammers' have become more sophisticated

---

267. The author receives on average about 50 UCE a month, many sent from major ISPs such as Prodigy and AOL, most from temporary accounts.

in their approaches, they may use a temporary account with one ISP with e-mail addresses faked to appear as if they came from another ISP. The problems that this can cause for the ISP whose address is faked, range from having to deal with irate users from around the world complaining about junk mail, to the possibility that their own users will lose functionality due to blacklisting by other ISPs.[268] How this may be dealt with if ISPs refuse to adopt more effective practices to stem such abuse remains to be seen.

---

268. Global Online, a Japanese ISP, alleged that they had such difficulties with this particular problem from people using AOL accounts that, in January 2000, they were forced to temporarily block all e-mail from AOL to their users. Additionally they found that e-mail from their users was blocked from other ISPs' systems, because those ISPs were erroneously under the impression that the UCE was, in fact, emanating from Global Online's users. See http://home.gol.com/index_e.html.

CHAPTER TWELVE

Employment Rights in an Information Society

John Angel and David Engel

12.1 INTRODUCTION

Employment lawyers are used to considering employment rights largely in the context of unfair dismissal, redundancy, discrimination and trade union laws. In this chapter it is argued that the new Information Society demands an extension of the fields of law traditionally viewed as employment law in the light of radical technological developments in our society.

What do we mean by an Information Society? First, it is one where an increasing proportion of society's wealth is made up of 'information' rather than tangible goods. Secondly, it is one which enables much of traditional work, commerce and leisure to be undertaken anywhere and at any time at a person's choice. This is being achieved largely through digital technology which converts information, including sound, images, (even smells) as well as text, into similar formats for transporting anywhere at incredible speeds through broadband telecommunications systems. It is no less than an 'information revolution', on a par, in the writers' view, with the industrial revolution of the last century. Already today, a person can take his multimedia computer and mobile phone to most places in the world and communicate by voice or visually, without the need to plug into anything. The person could be in an open field in the country, or on a desert island, and for all intents and purposes be able to operate as if in an office or a shopping centre. This is sometimes known as the virtual office or virtual shopping.

Returning to some form of reality, although this may be virtual reality, this chapter examines how laws relating to the new Information Society impinge on employment rights. The analysis will be divided into two parts. First, the statutory protection of intellectual property (IP) rights, which should be familiar ground, although not regularly examined, by employment lawyers. Secondly, management of the employment relationship requires an understanding of new fields of law which are becoming important because of the need to deal with new problems arising from the radical changes described above.

12.2   CONTRACT OF EMPLOYMENT

Before considering the two part analysis, there needs to be a brief review of the basis of any employment relationship, namely the contract of employment. Such contracts comprise both express and implied terms. When it comes to an information age the only constant is continuing change brought about by new technology and the need to be flexible to stay competitive. Most employment contracts today have express flexibility and mobility clauses to facilitate this constant need for change. Even where they are absent, the courts are predisposed towards flexibility where the purpose is the efficient running of the enterprise.

In *Cresswell* v *Board of Inland Revenue* [1984] IRLR 190 a group of tax officers brought an action against the Inland Revenue for refusing to pay them unless they worked a new computerised system for administering the new PAYE (pay as you earn) system. The court found that the employer had not broken the contract since there was an implied contractual duty on the employees' part 'to adapt themselves to new methods and techniques' of working. The employer had in turn an obligation to train the employee, if the change required it.

The *Cresswell* case related to doing the same job but using a computer. Where the job definition is required to change substantially, then unless there is an express flexibility clause covering the change, employers cannot insist on a unilateral variation of the contract. However, the dismissal of an employee who refuses to accept such a change would not necessarily be unfair. Where the old job, in effect, disappears because the requirement to do the job has ceased or diminished, this may be a redundancy situation, and provided the dismissal is carried out in a way which is procedurally fair, then an employer can dismiss without breaching the law.[1] Even if there is not a redundancy situation, insisting on changes to the job might still be fair where there is a business need for reorganisation.[2]

Increasingly in this information age, workers are not employees, but independent contractors. In order to maintain flexibility and keep costs down, many enterprises use contractors for specialist requirements as and when needed, and only retain a 'core' workforce. How is the status of a worker determined? Historically, the test to determine whether a contact was one of employment or for services was whether or not the employer controlled or

---

1. Employment Rights Act 1996, s. 98(1), (3), and see *Polkey* v *A E Dayton Services Ltd* [1987] IRLR 503, HL.
2. Employment Rights Act 1996, s. 98(4).

had the right to control the job that the employee did and the way it was done. The 'control' test became outdated with a more skilled workforce and the concept of empowerment, and the courts then considered the extent to which workers were an 'integral part of the business' as opposed to being merely an accessory to it. More recently, the courts have moved to a multiple factor test, one which retains the test of control, but combines it with a test of mutual obligation. So, factors like whether or not there is an entrepreneurial element in the relationship,[3] the degree of control, the risk of loss and chance of profit, the provision of equipment, methods of tax and national insurance payment, and the parties intentions,[4] are matters which will be taken into account.

The implementation of the European Working Time Directive[5] by the Working Time Regulations 1998,[6] which gives entitlements to 'workers', together with DTI guidelines,[7] helps further define who are the genuinely self employed. Someone who is pursuing a business activity on his or her own account is such a person and factors to be taken into account to determine this include:

(a)   Whether they are paid on the basis of an invoice or similar demand for payment rather than receiving wages.
(b)   How they are taxed.
(c)   Whether they can decide not to accept work.
(d)   Whether they are free to do the same type of work for more than one employer.
(e)   Whether they provide their own tools and equipment.
(f)   Whether they have their own helpers.
(g)   What degree of financial risk they take.
(h)   What degree of responsibility for investment and management they have.
(i)   Whether and how far they have an opportunity of profiting from sound management in the performance of their task.

As will be appreciated from the following discussion, employment status is a key factor in an Information Society.

12.3   INTELLECTUAL PROPERTY RIGHTS AND EMPLOYEES

12.3.1   Copyright

The fundamental property laws of an Information Society are those which relate to intellectual property, and the most important IP right is 'copyright'.

---

3. *Market Investigations Ltd v Minister of Social Security* [1968] 3 All ER 732; *Nethermere (St Neots) Ltd v Taverna and Gardiner* [1984] IRLR 240, CA.
4. *O'Kelly v Trusthouse Forte plc* [1983] IRLR 369, CA.
5. EC 93/1040.
6. SI 1988/1833.
7. Guide to the Working Time Regulations, September 1998, URN 98/894.

One of the big issues with all proprietary rights relates to their ownership. The general rule under the Copyright, Designs and Patents Act 1988 (CDPA)[8] is that information (which may be literary, dramatic, musical or artistic) which amounts to an original work, such as a book, marketing brochure, CD or a legal opinion, will first be owned by the person who creates it. The legal standard in the United Kingdom for establishing 'copyright' is low and does not involve any element of creativity, only that the work has not been copied. All such works are made by people, except computer-generated works. Where these people are employees who make the works during the course of their employment, the employer is the owner of copyright in the work.[9]

Two issues arise here. Firstly, with the increasing use of contractors, who owns the copyright? This is particularly relevant where a work is created by a number of people, some of whom are employees and some contractors. For example, in *John Richardson Computers Ltd* v *Flanders* [1993] FSR 497 there was a dispute over the copying of a computer program and the claimant first had to establish that he owned the copyright in the program. This was quite difficult because the program was developed over a period of time by different people, some employees, some contractors (of whom some were ex-employees), and generally the software company had not entered into express assignments of intellectual property rights. The court found that the claimant had an equitable interest in nearly all parts of the program not developed by employees, and that the contractors held their rights in trust for the company. However, there is no guarantee of such a finding which depends on the facts of each case. The increasing use of contractors in all parts of business makes it much more difficult to protect company property, and could give rights to some workers which previously were taken for granted as being 'owned by the employer'.

If the employer wishes, he may allow the employee to be the first owner of the copyright under the CDPA.[10] In these times of scarce expert hi-tech resources, some employees will be in strong negotiating positions and may insist on owning their own works.

The second issue relates to whether or not the work is undertaken 'in the course of employment'. In these days of home working, possibly using one's own computer, it will not be so obvious whether the work has been undertaken by an employee in the course of employment. The position may be apparent from the job description. However, the trend towards more general descriptions with increased flexibility and mobility, could make this more uncertain. A basic test is whether the skill, effort and judgment expended by the employee in creating the work are part of the employee's normal duties (express or implied) or within any special duties assigned to him by the employer. If the answer is 'no', then the employee will be the first owner of the work, even if he has used his employer's equipment or received help from the employer. In *Stephenson Jordan & Harrison Ltd* v *MacDonald* [1952] RPC 10 an employed accountant gave some lectures which he later

---

8. Copyright, Designs and Patents Act 1988, ss. 9, 11(1).
9. Ibid., s. 11(2).
10. Ibid., s. 11(2).

incorporated into a book. It was held that, even though his employer had provided secretarial help, the copyright in the lectures belonged to the accountant because he was employed as an accountant to advise clients and not to deliver public lectures. However, part of the book was based on a report that the accountant had written for a client of his employer, and it was held that the copyright in this part belonged to the employer. So employers need to draft job descriptions carefully and keep them up to date. Also, where there is any doubt as to first ownership, agreement should be reached before the employee starts the work.

Today many works are created by computers. Where the computer assists a person in making the work, the rules on ownership are the same as for any other work. Where the computer generates the work without human intervention, the author is 'the person by whom the arrangements necessary for the creation of the work are undertaken'.[11] If such an author is an employee, then the employer ownership rule applies.

In an Information Society much of our knowledge and information is obtained from published databases such as law reports and journals. The articles or cases in such databases are usually owned by their authors, where copyright also usually resides, unless they are employees. However, the compilation (arrangement and selection) of such material may also give rise to copyright.[12] In some EU countries, the intellectual effort involved in compiling a database is regarded as too low for the work to attract copyright. As a result of the inconsistent approach in Member States and the recognition of the need to protect the investment of makers of databases, which can so easily be copied in this technological age and which are regarded as economically and socially beneficial to the EU, a Directive to protect makers has been adopted.[13] Under art. 3(4), a database created by employees in the execution of their duties following instructions given by employers will entitle the employer to exercise all economic rights in the database, unless otherwise provided by contract. The Directive has now been implemented in England by the Copyright (Rights in Databases) Regulations 1997.[14] Databases that do not qualify for copyright might qualify for the new *sui generis* or database right under these Regulations. Again there is the usual provision that a database made by an employee in the course of his employment will (in the absence of any agreement to the contrary) automatically be the property of the employer.

One final and rather different point on copyright relates to the use of works rather than their creation. Under the CDPA, organisations which in the course of business possess copyright materials without a licence may be guilty of a criminal offence.[15] This is a considerable problem with computer software, which can so easily be copied if not properly controlled. Most organisations go in fear of committing such an offence, particularly as employees often install software on their workstations and it is common

---

11. Ibid., s. 9(3).
12. Ibid., s. 3(1)(a).
13. Directive on the legal protection of databases (93/C 308/01). See chapter 7.
14. SI 1997/3032.
15. Copyright, Designs and Patents Act 1988, s. 107(1).

practice to copy software from someone else's PC. Where an employer knows such activity is going on and copyright is being infringed, then not only the company but also the directors and officers of the company will be committing an offence. Today, software audits are a regular feature of asset management systems designed to reduce this risk.

12.3.2 Moral rights

The Berne Convention incorporated a new set of IP rights based on continental systems known as 'moral rights',[16] and these were introduced into English law by the CDPA. They provide authors with two rights: to be identified as the author of a copyright work (right of paternity),[17] and to object to any derogatory treatment of the work (right of integrity).[18] However, there are a number of exceptions which include employees who produce works in the course of their employment. Employees have no right of paternity nor of integrity in relation to such works unless the author/employee had at some time been identified with the works; and even here the extent of the right is simply to insist that there is a clear and reasonably prominent indication that the work has been subjected to treatment to which the author has not consented.[19] Other exceptions relate even to contractors, like reporting current events,[20] publications in newspapers, magazines or similar periodicals[21] and computer programs, including computer-generated works.[22]

Moral rights generally operate to allow a person to be identified with his own work or to object to interference with the work. There is also a right against false attribution which involves the converse situation.[23] This right is not affected by employment status, although it is unlikely to apply to employees if their names are not associated with copyright works in the first place, because they have no moral rights.

It is questionable whether a signatory to the Convention can exclude moral rights for employees, as there is no such right under art. 6 *bis*, and it would be interesting to see the result of a challenge before the European Court of Human Rights (or soon in the UK courts, as per the Human Rights Act 1998). Some EU countries do not exclude moral rights for employees, so those employers with European workforces may find that different rules apply.

12.3.3 Patents

Copyright is not the only IP right subject to 'the employer ownership' rule. Employees' inventions will belong to their employers, even where they are

---

16. Article 6 *bis* of the Paris text of the Berne Convention for the Protection of Literary and Artistic Works, 24 July 1971.
17. Copyright, Designs and Patents Act 1988, s. 77.
18. Ibid., s. 80.
19. Ibid., ss. 79(3), 82.
20. Ibid., ss. 79(5), 81(3).
21. Ibid., ss. 79(6), 81(4).
22. Ibid., ss. 79(2), 81(2).
23. Ibid., s. 84.

made outside normal duties, where the task is specifically assigned to the employee and an invention might reasonably be expected to result from carrying out those duties.[24] Also, an invention made in the course of the employee's duties which, at the time of making the invention, was such that the employee had a special obligation to further the interests of the employer's undertaking, will belong to the employer.[25] The rule will not apply where the invention is made outside the employee's normal duties and where he has not been assigned any relevant specific duties; for example, a salesperson inventing a new product.[26]

What is less well known is that an employee who has made an invention can claim compensation from the owning employer where a patent has been granted in certain circumstances. These are where the patent is of 'outstanding benefit' to the employer, having regard, *inter alia*, to the size and nature of the employer's undertaking, and if it would be just for the employee to be awarded compensation of an amount representing a 'fair share' of the benefit derived or expected to be derived by the employer from exploiting the patent itself or by assigning it.[27] A claim for compensation can be made under the Patent Rules.[28] Cases normally go before the Comptroller of Patents who determines the amount of compensation according to the provisions set out in the Patents Act.[29] These provisions also apply where the invention initially belonged to the employee and he has subsequently assigned it to the employer or granted an exclusive license to him.

Employees rarely seem to use this right. This is surprising considering the number of registered patents and applications for patents made each year, and the fact that some patents can make enormous sums for their owners, for example in the pharmaceutical industry. No doubt, one of the difficulties is that inventions are not made single-handedly, and there may be problems deciding who should receive compensation and how it should be shared between employees in, say, a research and development team. Also, it is difficult for employees to determine whether the patent is of outstanding value as all the evidence tends to be held by the employer. Patent attorneys or agents are careful to find out whether employees could have a claim at the time of preparing the application and will try to ensure employees are 'compensated' at this stage before any outstanding value can be established. Any payments made would be taken into account by the Comptroller, and morally and ethically employees tend to consider they have received recompense and do not take matters further. Not surprisingly, there have been few cases and of the reported decisions not a single employee has succeeded.[30]

---

24. Patents Act 1977, s. 39(1)(a).
25. Ibid., s. 39(1)(b).
26. E.g., *Harris' Patent* [1985] RPC 19, *Reiss Engineering Co. Ltd v Harris* [1985] IRLR 232 where the inventor of a valve made while he was working out his redundancy notice was the manager of the valve department.
27. Patents Act 1977, ss. 40, 41.
28. SI 1990/2384, rule 59 using Patents Form 2/77.
29. Patents Act 1977, s. 41(4).
30. Examples include *Memco-Med Ltd's Patent* [1992] RPC 403, *GEC Avionics Ltd's Patent* [1992] RPC 107 and *British Steel Plc's Patent* [1992] RPC 117.

Common reasons given for failure include the fact that, where an employer is very large, it is difficult to show outstanding benefit, as even relatively large revenues attributed to the patent will still be very small compared to annual turnover.

One way of avoiding the compensation provisions is for the employer not to apply for a patent and to rely on the law of confidence. Furthermore, a contracting-out clause in relation to inventions owned by the employee or the compensation provisions, will be unenforceable against an employee,[31] unless a trade union, of which the employee is a member, negotiates a payment for compensation for inventions in a collective agreement.[32]

12.3.4 Design rights[33]

Both registered (aesthetic appeal) and unregistered design (utilitarian, including semi-conductor chips) rights are subject to the employer ownership rule.[34] This goes even further with unregistered designs where the commissioner is the first owner.[35]

12.3.5 Confidential information

So far we have examined the old rules, which employment lawyers will be familiar with even if they are not referred to regularly. They will become increasingly important as information plays a more important role in wealth creation. However, there is a newer analysis being prompted by the advent of the Information Society.

The starting point is in the law of confidence. This subject has already been covered in chapter 8 but will be further analysed and extended here in a way which is particularly relevant to the subject of this chapter.

Employees both generate and acquire confidential information in the course of employment. The concern here is with confidential information associated with industrial and commercial activity, often known as 'trade secrets'. The general principle is that the employee holds the confidential information for the benefit of his employer. However, relying on this principle in employment relationships presents special problems as the contractual obligation of confidence (whether express or implied under the duty of good faith) is subject to the qualification that an employee is, after the termination of his employment, free to use his 'knowledge and skill' either for his own benefit or for the benefit of others. This remains true even though during his employment such information which is learned must be treated as confiden-

---

31. Patents Act 1977, s. 42.
32. Ibid., s. 40(3).
33. Under the proposed Council directive on the legal protection of designs C142/7 14 May 1996 computer programs were excluded from protection. This directive was adopted on 13 October 1998. OJ L289, pp. 28–35.
34. Registered Designs Act 1949, s. 2(1B) as amended by the Copyright, Designs and Patents Act 1988; and ibid., s. 215(3) as amended by the Design Right (Semiconductor Topographies) Regulations SI 1989/1100.
35. Copyright, Designs and Patents Act 1988, s. 215(2).

tial. Some trade secrets, however, are so confidential or can be described as so entitled to protection that a continuing duty of confidence applies even beyond the termination of employment. This classification was considered by the court in *Faccenda Chicken Ltd v Fowler* [1985] 1 All ER 724.

The problem is distinguishing between trade secrets and knowledge and skills employees can take with them. In *Fowler* the Court of Appeal laid down guidelines as to how to determine whether information could be classified as confidential. The court said attention should be paid to:

(a)   The nature of the information itself, e.g., a secret process or confidential customer list.

(b)   The nature of the employment, e.g., higher obligation on a more senior employee or one who habitually handles sensitive data.

(c)   Whether the employer made it known to the employee that the information was of a confidential nature, e.g., by marking it confidential.

(d)   Whether the information can be easily isolated from other information the employee is free to use.

The problem with this approach to classification is that it provides little guidance as to what precisely distinguishes a trade secret from information in the second category (skill and competence), although it does show that such information will be given less protection. In *Lansing Linde Ltd v Kerr* [1991] 1 All ER 418 the court spoke in terms of information that would be liable to cause real harm if it was disclosed to a competitor, provided it was used in a trade or business and the owner had either limited the dissemination of the information or at least not encouraged or permitted widespread publication. The court stressed the need to take account of the changing nature of the business and the need to take account of 'the wider context of highly confidential information of a non-technical or non scientific nature'.

The computer industry has provided some examples of cases which can help us understand this difficult issue. In the South African case *Northern Office Microcomputers v Rosenstein* [1982] FSR 129/4 the Supreme Court recognised the difficulty in deciding where to draw the dividing line. The court considered that computer programs, which were not commonplace, should be eligible for protection as trade secrets. However, the protection given by the law of trade secrets in the context of ex-employees should be of a limited nature only, and that all that should be protected was the employer's 'lead-time', the time to develop the program. In other words, the advantage the employer has in getting his product to market first should be protected and nothing more. The court went on to find that, in many cases, the employer's trade secrets were no more than the result of the application by an employee of his own skill and judgment, but if the employee was engaged specifically to produce that information then it could still amount to a trade secret. But, if the material was commonplace, there would be nothing to stop the ex-employee deriving the same or similar material again as long as he did not simply copy his employer's material. The employee would not have to 'wipe the slate of his mind clean' on the termination of his employment.

In *Ibcos Computers* v *Poole* [1994] FSR 275 the court observed that source code of a computer program is normally kept confidential by software houses and that customers do not themselves usually get such code — itself being held to be confidential by the court.

These cases also involved questions of copyright infringement and substantial copying of computer programs which were worked on by an ex-employer. In the *John Richardson Computers Ltd* v *Flanders* case [1993] FSR 497 it was accepted that the employee/programmer had a deep knowledge of the claimant's program, and that while he could not carry in his memory substantial parts of the source code, he would have remembered all the main routines. Despite this finding it was held there was no substantial copying. Breach of confidence was not pleaded. If it had been, the claimant might have succeeded in confidence where he did not in copyright law.

More recently in *FSS Travel & Leisure Systems Ltd* v *Johnson* [1998] IRLR 382 an employer in the business of designing and marketing software for the travel industry attempted to constrain a computer programmer from joining a competitor. The Court of Appeal dealt with the question of whether an employer has trade secrets which are legitimately protectable by the imposition of a restrictive covenant against an employee. The court had to decide whether there are trade secrets which can fairly be regarded as the employer's property, as distinct from the skill, experience, know-how and general knowledge which can fairly be regarded as the property of the employee to use without restraint for his own benefit or in the service of a competitor. The court found that the distinction necessitates examination of all the evidence relating to the nature of the employment, the character of the information, the restrictions imposed on its dissemination, the extent of use and disclosure in competition to the employer. In each case it is a question of examining closely the detailed evidence relating to the employer's claim for secrecy and deciding, as a matter of fact, on which side of the boundary line it falls. It is not sufficient for the employer to assert a claim that it is entitled to an accumulated mass of knowledge which in the relevant business, the use and dissemination of which is likely to harm the employer.

In *PMS International plc & McKenhnie plc* v *Whitehouse & Willenhall Automation Ltd* [1992] FSR 489 drawings, quotations, price costings and business strategies were considered to rank as trade secrets. In *Faccenda Chicken* v *Fowler* [1985] 1 All ER 724, more mundane information such as sales information, convenient routes to customers, and customer orders was found not to be of a confidential nature, relying on the implied duty of fidelity.

However, there must be a fine line between such information and trade secrets. An express provision in a contract of employment, or a clear indication that the employer regards such information as confidential, may tip the balance and provide an additional cause of action in computer program copying cases, which often involve ex-employees.

Another weakness of confidentiality is its difficulty in enforcement, whether or not there is an express provision in the contract, particularly in post termination situations. As a result there is an increasing trend towards introducing non-competition or restraint of trade clauses in contracts of employment for employees at all levels, which can be easier to enforce provided they are reasonable.[36]

The new employer can also be liable for the ex-employee's misuse of confidential information. This was the position in *Ibcos Computers v Poole* [1994] FSR 275, where Barclays Mercantile Highland Finance were aware that Mr Poole had taken the source code. Where such a breach is discovered, the new employer would be advised to disregard the code developed in breach. It may require re-engineering the program through a clean room approach as was done by the employer in the US case *Computer Associates v Altai* 23 USPQ 2nd 1241 (2nd Cir, 1992). This only left the copyright claim which is much more difficult to prove, particularly for non-literal copying.

What is the position of consultants? A well-drafted contract for services should always deal with ownership of intellectual property rights generated in the course of the consultant's work, as will be appreciated from the discussion so far. Also, it should deal with the question of confidentiality. In the absence of express agreement it is necessary to fall back on ordinary principles of law. So far as confidential information is concerned this will be governed by implied contractual terms, as in the case of a contract of employment. A consultant should hold for the benefit of the company for which he works, all trade secrets generated or acquired in the course of the work, and he should not use or disclose these trade secrets for any unauthorised purpose. Counter-balancing this is the principle that a consultant, like an employee, is entitled to use for his own benefit and for the benefit of others his general knowledge and skill. So again there is the thorny issue of what is a trade secret and what is general knowledge and skill. Where does the dividing line lie? Cases like *Schering Chemicals Ltd v Falkman Ltd* [1982] QB 1 would suggest that a rather harder line is taken by courts with consultants who have acquired confidential information in the course of work undertaken for others. In *Schering Chemicals* consultants were used to undertake damage limitation sales training for the defendant in relation to a drug which had been withdrawn from the market. Their contract included a confidentiality clause. They in turn contracted out some of the training to the defendant, who also accepted the information was confidential. The defendant used the confidential information to make a film for TV. The defendant was held to be in breach of an obligation of confidence to the claimant with whom he had no direct contract, even though the disclosures in the film were found to be in the public interest, but only where the information was not from public sources. Could this make it even more attractive for firms to use contractors?

The point should be made that the obligation of confidence arising from a contract of employment is not all one way. In many cases, the employer will owe a duty of confidence to his employee. An employer will hold information concerning an employee such as performance rating, salary and career details. This information should not be divulged to others without the employee's

---

36. Except in the circumstances found in *Rock Refrigeration Ltd v Jones, The Times*, 17 October 1996.

permission, except where disclosure is permitted by express provision (e.g., attachment of earnings), or implied (e.g., salaries paid by a bureau). The protection given by data protection laws will be discussed later in the chapter.

The obligation of confidence here could be considered as an extension of the duty of mutual respect and trust between employees and employers. There are few cases on this aspect of the employer's duty. In *Dalgleish v Lothian and Borders Police Board* [1991] IRLR 422, CS, a local authority sought information on the names and addresses of persons employed by another public sector body, for the purposes of ensuring payment of taxes. A Scottish court granted an interdict (injunction) restraining the disclosure of the information on two alternative grounds. First, that the contract of employment did not authorise such disclosures and secondly, under the general principles of confidentiality irrespective of contract.

Another illustration could be where employers operate suggestion schemes. An employee could be said to have waived his rights, if any, in the information he has disclosed under such a scheme if his employer uses the information. However, if the employer does not use the information it seems that a duty of confidence could arise. In *Prout v British Gas plc* [1992] FSR 478 an employee submitted an idea for a new design of a bracket for warning lamps placed around excavations. The bracket was supposed to be vandal-proof. Mr Prout was given an award by British Gas under a suggestion scheme, but later the company said it had no interest and agreed to allow Mr Prout to apply for a patent on his own behalf. In spite of this, British Gas later decided to use the suggestion. On the issue of confidence it was held that there was a contractual or equitable duty of confidence imposed on the employer. Although this duty would normally end once the idea was used in public for the first time without objection from the employee, a fresh duty could arise if the employee gave notice to apply for a patent and would continue until the filing date of the application. In this particular case it was held that the employer was in breach of confidence by making use of the invention.

This case has interesting implications for employers who do not use 'ideas' coming from their employees. There is no copyright protection in ideas, only in original works. So the rule that the employer owns IP rights does not apply. If we assume employees are under a duty of good faith to disclose ideas which could be beneficial to the employer's business, then where the employer does not use or rejects the idea, is the employee free to use or exploit it? In an information age this is a serious issue. The answer may depend on whether the idea itself is confidential information, which is the only IP right (other than perhaps patents) which can protect, in effect, ideas.

The duty of confidence has already proved to be an important right in the Information Society. Like other common law rights it has demonstrated adaptability in the face of new technology. However, it is not reliable enough as once confidential information is in the public domain, the protection is lost. This can easily happen in these days of the Internet.

12.4 MANAGING THE EMPLOYMENT RELATIONSHIP

The nineteenth century concept of master and servant, in which the employer issued instructions which had to be obeyed by the employee, and in which the employer was only liable for the employee's actions when carrying out those instructions, is very far from the current legal situation. There are important new constraints on the employer's freedom to organise the way in which employees work with information technology, and by providing them with that technology the employer is subject to new liability risks.

12.4.1 Data protection

The converse of the duty of confidence, discussed at 12.3.5 above, is the employer's obligations in respect of employee information. This is a question of data protection and privacy. Many employers today hold personal data of their employees and contractors on computer. What is less well considered is that video surveillance combined with swipe cards, active badges and satellite monitoring of the location of mobile phones or other uses of the latest technology to monitor the behaviour, location and activities of employees, may also involve the processing and collection of personal data. These new technologies allow for the creation of increasing and more sophisticated information sources on workers including continuous monitoring and surveillance at the workplace.

In order to collect and process such data employers as data controllers are required to notify the Data Protection Commissioner. Employers are required to comply with the provisions of the Data Protection Act 1998,[37] which from an employment rights point of view means, *inter alia*:

(a)   Collecting and processing personal data fairly and lawfully by obtaining consent from employees in, say, the contract of employment or recruitment application form.[38]

(b)   Only using the data for personnel administration and not for a non-obvious purpose[39] without specific consent.

(c)   Not disclosing the information in a way which is incompatible with the purpose (confidentiality considerations are additional to this obligation).[40]

(d)   Ensuring the personal data are accurate and kept up-to-date.[41]

---

37. There were transitional provisions which meant that for some systems there was only a need to comply with the Data Protection Act 1984 for a period before the 1998 Act became applicable. The 1998 Act implements Directive 95/46/EC on the protection of individuals with regard to the processing of personal data and on the free movement of such data and became law in the United Kingdom on 1 March 2000.

38. First Data Protection Principle, sch. 1, Data Protection Act 1998. See also *CCN Systems Ltd v DPR* delivered in February 1991 (NLJ 1991, 141 (6499), 497–98).

39. Although the data could be used for other registered purposes the Data Protection Tribunal has found this cannot be for a non-obvious purpose unless the employee is aware of this at the time the data are collected: *Innovations (Mail Order) Ltd v DPR* delivered on 29 September 1993, [1994] 10 CLSR, 260. Second Data Protection Principle.

40. Second Data Protection Principle.

41. Fourth Data Protection Principle.

(e)   Not holding the data for longer than is necessary for employment administration — this calls into question how long the records of ex-employees can be held on computer after employment terminates.[42]

(f)   Providing employees with a right of access to their personal data at reasonable intervals and without undue delay or expense.[43]

(g)   Allowing employees to have their data rectified, erased or blocked if inaccurate or not complying with the above principles.[44]

(h)   Taking security measures to guard against unauthorised access, alteration disclosure or destruction of personal data and against accidental loss or destruction of such data.[45]

(i)   Transferring personnel records across national boundaries by multinational enterprises outside the European Economic Area is prohibited unless subject to a derogation.[46]

(j)   Sensitive data are prohibited from being revealed, which includes personal data relating to racial or ethnic origin, political opinions, religious and philosophical beliefs, trade union membership, health and sex life and criminal convictions, although subject to exceptions[47] including where this is required under employment laws for example the Fair Employment laws in Northern Ireland.

(k)   Employees will have the right not to be subject to decisions which significantly affect them which are based on automatic processing of data intended to evaluate such matters as performance at work, reliability, conduct etc.[48] and also have the right to be informed of the logic behind the automatic processing of such decisions, where the automatic processing constitutes the sole basis for any decision which significantly affects the employee.[49]

Employees have a right of access to their personal data,[50] so it makes sense to have a data access procedure in, say, the staff handbook. Employers can charge a small fee per request.[51] Most employers today have the ability to provide employees with a print out of the personal data held. All computer-held data has to be disclosed unless it is exempted.[52]

In addition to computer records most manual personnel records will also be covered by the Data Protection Act 1998, although there are lengthy transitional provisions.[53]

---

42. Fifth Data Protection Principle. It can be argued at least for six years as the limitation period for contractual claims.
43. Sixth Data Protection Principle and Data Protection Act 1998, s. 7.
44. Sixth Data Protection Principle and Data Protection Act 1998, s. 14.
45. Seventh Data Protection Principle.
46. Eighth Data Protection Principle and the Data Protection Act 1998, sch. 4.
47. Ibid., sch. 3.
48. Ibid., s. 12.
49. Ibid., s. 7(d).
50. Ibid., s. 7.
51. The Data Protection (Subject Access) (Fees and Miscellaneous Provisions) Regulations 1999 (SI 2000/191).
52. Data Protection Act 1998, sch. 7.
53. See definition of 'relevant filing system' in s. 1 of the Data Protection Act 1998 and ibid., sch. 8 for transitional provisions.

Data Protection Registrar v *PLP Motors Ltd*[54] illustrates the overlap between data protection and confidentiality. The defendant recruited an employee from one of his competitors. Shortly after joining the company, the employee passed on names and addresses of his former employer's customers to the defendant's marketing department. This information was used in a direct marketing campaign, and the Data Protection Registrar received a complaint from a recipient of the mailshot. The Registrar brought proceedings against the defendant under the Data Protection Act 1984 for obtaining the information unlawfully. The company was found to have misused the data and was fined £2,500 plus £200 costs. Usually claims that ex-employees have taken customer information have been based on the misuse of trade secrets. However, such claims are difficult to prove and are potentially expensive. A criminal prosecution under the Data Protection Act will be at someone else's expense and may be quicker.

There is also a Directive on data protection specifically aimed at telecommunications,[55] which could limit the ways employers monitor employees calls where it affects the privacy of calling parties.

Much of this new 'privacy' legislation is designed to protect individuals against the greater possibilities of abuse in an Information Society.[56]

12.4.2 Teleworking

As considered earlier in this chapter, the Information Society facilitates very different ways of working, and many of the issues of teleworking have been widely discussed. In addition to covering employment status and associated rights, this topic also covers health and safety issues which are not restricted to the normal place of work, taxation, insurance, planning law and telecommunications, as well as intellectual property and data protection matters already discussed in this chapter. Most of these matters are discussed in detail in a number of articles and publications[57] and the authors do not wish to repeat the issues here.

However, there are a number of matters which should be mentioned here, as raising important practical issues which the employer who adopts teleworking will need to address:

(a) The physical distance between the employer and the workers, as well as between the workers themselves, will be a catalyst for the implementation

---

54. Decision given on 24 April 1995 (Data Protection Registrar's Annual Report, p. 48).
55. Directive concerning the processing of personal data and the protection of privacy in the telecommunications sector, in particular the integrated services digital network (ISDN) and in the public digital mobile networks (OJ C 315/30, 24 October 1996) which has been implemented in England by the Telecommunications (Data Protection and Privacy) Regulations 1999 (SI 1999/2093).
56. See the Bangermann Report on 'Europe and the global information society' which can be found at www.ispo.cec.be/infosoc/backg/bangermann.html.
57. See Dr Ian Walden, 'The legal implication of teleworking in the United Kingdom', Centre for Commercial Law Studies, QMW University of London; and 'The Teleworking Handbook — New Ways of Working in the Information Society', sponsored by the EC and others.

of data recording devices, thereby allowing for remote control by the employer. This in itself poses a risk to privacy, some of the issues of which are discussed in section 12.4.5.12 below.

(b)   Employers as licensees of intellectual property rights, will usually have the right to allow employees to use, for example, software as part of a site or other licence on or off the employer's premises and on an employee's own computer. Company confidential information will also be held on such equipment by employees. The termination of the employment relationship will give rise to a number of issues, from protecting the company's property to ensuring there are no breaches of licence agreements. These issues will usually be covered by the contract of employment and personnel procedures on termination, including getting undertakings from employees to the effect that there are no breaches. Software and digital information are always difficult to check, particularly as even deleted files can be recovered. However, it is important to be able to demonstrate that action has been taken so that licenses are not breached, and such assurances are often obtained in termination agreements which may also include the right to enter the employee's premises to make any appropriate seizures.

(c)   Health and safety legislation relates to places of work under the employer's control.[58] Although teleworking centres may be covered, the employee's home is another matter. However, two regulations which have arisen from the EC Framework Directive for the 'introduction of measures to encourage improvements in the health and safety of workers at the workplace' are relevant to teleworking. They are the Workplace (Health, Safety and Welfare) Regulations 1992 and the Health and Safety (Display Screen Equipment) Regulations 1992.[59] In particular, the latter seems to relate to employees using workstations, regardless of to whom they belong and wherever used. It may be good practice for safety officers to make periodic inspections of teleworking environments to check compliance with standards and to reserve a right to do so in the contract of employment.

(d)   Finally, the Working Time Regulations[60] will have some impact on the flexibility of teleworking, although they do not seem to apply to the self employed and many other categories of workers. If opt-out agreements are used they will only be effective if up-to-date records are maintained, which will increase the need to computerise record keeping, particularly for those who work remotely.

12.4.3   Computer misuse

Most computer crimes are committed by employees. Under the Computer Misuse Act 1990, discussed more fully in chapter 9, unauthorised access to computer material is an offence.[61] This is commonly known as 'hacking'. In some organisations, employees play around with their computers and find it fun to break someone's password. Many confidential matters are discovered

---

58. Health and Safety at Work Act 1974, s. 2(1), (2).
59. SI 1992/2792.
60. SI 1998/1833.
61. Computer Misuse Act 1990, s. 1.

by employees hacking into parts of the business system to which they are not entitled. These are likely to be offences provided for under a company's disciplinary procedure. They can also be reported to the police as possible computer crimes. However, the difficulty lies in knowing what has been authorised. Where the contract of employment is not clear on the position, it may prove difficult to bring a prosecution. This may be a particular problem where authorised employees write down their passwords in an accessible place, or even disclose them to other employees, as in such a situation the offending employee will have received no warning from the system that his or her access is unauthorised.

Before 1990 only a civil action could be taken. For example in *Denco Ltd v Joinson* [1991] IRLR 63, EAT, an employee who had limited access to the firm's computer found out the password of another employee which gave greater access. Late one night, while legitimately using the computer for his own work, he used the password and tried (unsuccessfully) to gain access to certain financially important information. He had worked for the company for 21 years and was dismissed for gross misconduct. The EAT found that

in the modern industrial world if an employee deliberately used an authorised password in order to enter or attempt to enter a computer known to contain information to which he is not entitled, then that of itself is gross misconduct which *prima facie* will attract summary dismissal, although there may be some exceptional circumstances in which such a response might be held unreasonable. Basically this is a question of 'absolutes' and can be compared with dishonesty. However, because of the importance of preserving integrity of the computer with its information it is important that management should make it abundantly clear to its workforce that interfering with it will carry severe penalties.

Unauthorised modification of computer material, is also a criminal offence.[62] Such action can cause severe damage to a business. It is not unknown for aggrieved employees to damage company property physically, but the damage is usually minor. Such an employee could cause much greater harm through a computer by, for example, introducing a virus.

The business risks involved in this computer age are potentially great and a good employer will bring them to an employee's attention, say in a staff handbook, to the effect that not only could offending actions be subject to disciplinary action, but that they could also be criminal offences. In addition, a good employer will insert banner warnings on screen, for example:

'The programs and data held on this screen are the property of . . . and are lawfully available to authorised users for authorised company purposes only. Access to any data or program must be authorised by the company.'

'It is a criminal offence as well as an act of gross misconduct to secure unauthorised access to any program or data in, or make any unauthorised

---

62. Ibid., s. 3.

modification to the contents of, this computer system. Offenders are liable to be summarily dismissed and subject to criminal prosecution.'

'If you are not an authorised user disconnect immediately.'

12.4.4 Interception of communications

In many organisations it is normal practice to read incoming and outgoing mail. In some organisations telephone calls are recorded or e-mails checked, usually to verify instructions given over the phone or as part of a training programme. As any such communication is generally seen as part of the employer's business activity and there are no general rights to privacy within employment in the UK, except in relation to the processing of personal data, it has been seen as a limited employment issue. However, in *Halford v United Kingdom* [1997] IRLR 471 the European Court of Human Rights found that the interception by an employer of an employee's office telephone calls was a violation of art. 8 of the European Convention on Human Rights which provides that 'everyone has the right to respect for his private and family life, his home and his correspondence'. The court went on to find that telephone calls made from business premises may be covered by notions of 'private life' and 'correspondence' within the meaning of art. 8. As no warning had been given to the employee that calls made on the telephone in her office used for private calls would be liable to interception, the employee would have had a reasonable expectation of privacy for such calls and therefore art. 8 was applicable. The Convention's provision is now in the process of being implemented directly into English law by the Human Rights Act 1998, which means it will be able to be enforced directly by English courts. However, the Act only affects public authorities and not every employer.

Outside employment,[63] monitoring of communications is illegal unless subject to a police warrant under the Interception of Communications Act 1985.[64] An employer engaged in running a public telecommunications system, like BT, who otherwise than in the course of its duties intentionally intercepts, discloses[65] or modifies or interferes with the content of a message sent by the system,[66] whether voice or data, will be guilty of a criminal offence. Also it is an offence to receive a wireless communication without a license.[67] As this is what happens with most mobile telephones, many employees would appear to be committing an offence. Fortunately, the DTI has issued class licenses under the Telecommunications Act 1984 which

---

63. Telephone conversations made from home were found by the court in *Halford v United Kingdom* [1997] IRLR 471 to be covered by the notions of 'private life' and 'correspondence' within the meaning of art. 8 of the Convention.
64. The 1985 Act is currently being considered for reform and a consultation process has taken place. A Regulation of Investigatory Powers Bill has been published by going through the Parliamentary process.
65. Telecommunications Act 1984, s. 45.
66. Ibid., s. 44.
67. Wireless Telegraphy Act 1949, s. 5.

legally permit employees or anyone else to use mobile phones.[68] These class licences impose confidentiality conditions on employers which have resulted in Oftel issuing guidance in relation to the monitoring of employee phone calls.[69]

12.4.5 E-mail and the Internet

Increasingly organisations of all sizes are giving their employees access to e-mail and the Internet.

E-mail is a cheap and effective means of communication internally and also with customers, suppliers and business partners. Access to the Internet enables employees to carry out research on a wide variety of topics and, increasingly, to participate in business-to-business e-commerce. Recent estimates suggest that in the UK at least 3.3 million employees have access to the Internet at work.

However, the provision of such access can expose organisations to legal liability in a number of ways.

12.4.5.1 Defamation The law of defamation applies to electronic communication, on the whole, in just the same way as it does to other forms of communication. There is very little legally different about 'cyberlibel'. However, the nature of e-mail and other Internet communication (e.g., newsgroups, bulletin boards and chat rooms) can create its own particular problems.

First, it is a potentially risky combination of the spontaneous and the permanent. On the one hand, most people appear to regard e-mails as more akin to the spoken than the written word. Typically their style is informal, their content unpredictable. Employees tend to give the content of an e-mail rather less thought than they would give to a formal typed office memorandum or a letter on company notepaper. On the other hand, there is a permanent record of such messages. Contrary to the impression of many users, hitting the 'send' or even the 'delete' button, does not mean that the message disappears into the ether. It is of course preserved on servers and on back-up tapes. In many organisations, back-up tapes can be held for as long as a year.

Secondly, the ease with which material can be forwarded and copied to any number of users on the Internet means that publication may be far wider than originally intended by the initial sender of the message. That problem increases exponentially when one considers newsgroups and websites which may be read by tens, or even hundreds, of thousands of users anywhere in the world.

Thirdly, the specialised nature of many bulletin boards and websites means that publication may well be targeted at precisely those individuals and organisations to whom its publication is most damaging for the victim. That will tend to increase the damages to which the victim is entitled.

---

68. The Self-Provision Licence (SPL) under the Telecommunications Act 1984, s. 7. Also see the Telecommunications (Fraud) Act 1997.
69. See Oftel press release ref 47/99 issued on 19 August 1999.

What is actionable?   Defamation is a strict liability tort; knowledge and intention are irrelevant. An untrue statement of fact which damages the reputation of a person, or company, will be actionable, provided that the victim of the libel is identifiable and it has been published to a third party (i.e., to a party other than the victim). For example, an e-mail from an employee to a supplier which is defamatory of the supplier would not be actionable at the suit of the supplier.

A statement need not be obviously insulting in order to amount to a libel. It could, for example, simply be a suggestion that a competitor is in financial difficulties[70] or is unprofessional in the conduct of its business.[71]

Defamation in permanent form is libel; defamation in transient form (e.g., spoken words) is slander. While the point has not yet been tested before the courts, defamation by e-mail and by publication on the Internet is most likely to be libel.

Publication   For the purposes of defamation law, 'publication' means the dissemination of a libel, whether such publication is innocent or not. It includes transmission by e-mail, inclusion on a website on the worldwide web or the posting of a message to a bulletin board or news group.

Accordingly an Internet Service Provider (ISP) which carries on its server a news group containing a defamatory posting from a third party is the publisher of that posting and is therefore *prima facie* liable 'even if the [ISP] was ignorant of the defamatory material'.[72]

Who is liable?   The author of the libellous message will be liable for the damage it causes to the reputation of the victim. In most cases, damage is presumed. Unlike most types of claim, there is no requirement for the victim to demonstrate financial loss.

However, the concept of 'publication' is important in defamation law, because not only the author but also the 'publisher' is directly liable. The author's employer may therefore also be liable. Indeed, the employer may be caught in something of a double bind.

On the one hand, the employer may be liable on the normal principles of vicarious liability for the actions of the employee as *author* if the employee was acting in the course of his employment. Even if an act is expressly prohibited, the employer may still be vicariously liable for it if it was within the scope of the employment or for the purposes of the employer's business. An employer may also be liable for the acts of non-employee contract workers. The employer will only be able to escape such liability if it can demonstrate that the employee was acting outside the scope of his employment in, for example, sending a defamatory e-mail.

But that does not necessarily get the employer off the hook under defamation law. The employer may also be directly liable as *publisher*. Whilst this point has not yet been tested before the courts, it would certainly be

70. *Borella* v *Penfolds Wines* (1992) 7 WAR 492; *Aspro Travel Ltd* v *Owners Abroad Group Plc* [1996] 1 WLR 132, CA.
71. *Drummond-Jackson* v *BMA* [1970] 1 WLR 688, CA.
72. *Godfrey* v *Demon Internet* [1999] IT&CLR 282.

argued by the claimant that the employer which owns the computer hardware and enters into the agreement with the ISP to provide access to the Internet was a 'publisher' and therefore directly liable.

In many cases the employer is more likely than the author to be in the firing line simply because it is perceived to have deeper pockets or because, given the nature of Internet communication, the author may be difficult to trace or if traceable may be resident outside the jurisdiction.

The new Internet defence   However, relief may be at hand for *organisations* which might otherwise find themselves liable as publisher. The Defamation Act 1996 s. 1 provides a new statutory defence of innocent dissemination. The defence is available provided that the defendant satisfies all the following criteria:[73]

(a)   it was not the author, editor or publisher of the statement complained of; *and*

(b)   it took reasonable care in relation to its publication; *and*

(c)   it did not know, and had no reason to believe, that what it did caused or contributed to the publication of a defamatory statement.

A defendant will not be considered an author, editor or publisher if it is only involved:

(a)   in operating or providing any equipment, system or service by means of which a statement is retrieved, copied, distributed or made available in electronic form;[74] or

(b)   as the operator of, or provider of access to, a communications systems by means of which a statement is transmitted, or made available, by a person over whom it has no effective control.[75]

Whether an employer had 'no effective control' over the author of the e-mail may be an important issue. This is a question of fact for the jury.[76] In deciding whether the defendant has satisfied the reasonable care and knowing contribution test, the court will consider:[77]

(a)   the extent of the defendant's responsibility for the content of the statement or the decision to publish it;

(b)   the nature or circumstances of the publication; and

(c)   the previous conduct or character of the author, editor or publisher.

Unlike the old common law defence of innocent dissemination, therefore, and by total contrast with the position in the United States, the onus is firmly

---

73. Defamation Act 1996, s. 1(1)(a)–(c).
74. Ibid., s. 1(3)(c).
75. Ibid., s. 1(3)(e).
76. *MORI* v *BBC & Anor*, 17 June 1999 (unreported).
77. Defamation Act 1996, s. 1(5)(a)–(c).

on the defendant to show that it satisfies those criteria. Any employer which does not have the necessary policies and procedures in place is unlikely to be successful in that regard. It will have to be shown that it had taken 'reasonable care' in relation to publication of the statement complained of and also that it had not knowingly contributed to the publication of a defamatory statement. That is likely to mean that the employer will have to take such steps as are reasonably practicable to ensure that employees do not disseminate defamatory material by e-mail or on the Internet, for example by implementing and — equally importantly — enforcing a watertight code of practice for computer usage. Further, the 'previous conduct or character' provision places an additional burden on the employer if a particular employee is known to be a maverick. In such circumstances, precautions would need to be more stringent, culminating perhaps in denial of access.

It is worth noting that in the UK the position of such electronic 'innocent disseminators', including ISPs, is wholly different from their position in the US, where there is case law and statute[78] which makes their position much stronger.

In addition to the new defence under the Defamation Act 1996, the usual defences to an action for defamation still apply, namely:

(a)   That the words complained of are in substance true.

(b)   That they are fair comment (i.e., an honest expression of opinion) on a matter of public interest based on facts which are true, such facts being known to the reader, and not motivated by malice.

(c)   Qualified or absolute privilege.

(d)   Consent to publication.

Truth is a complete defence to an action for defamation. However, the onus is on the defendant to prove that the statement was true, by way of evidence admissible in court. There is often a gap between truth and proof.

Fair comment is also a complete defence, but the requirement that it be comment on a matter of public interest means that it is unlikely to apply to industry gossip, let alone office tittle-tattle. This defence is in any event vitiated by evidence of malice on the part of the defendant. Malice may mean not just spite, but also any improper motive (e.g., to gain an unfair commercial advantage) or recklessness as to the truth or falsity of the statement.

Qualified privilege may arise, broadly speaking, where the author has a duty to communicate the statement and the recipient has a corresponding interest in receiving it, and again there is no evidence of malice. This defence may well apply to e-mail within an organisation concerning, for example, employment references or competitor activity.

12.4.5.2 Infringing copyright   The rules relating to copyright are discussed in detail in chapter 6.

---

78. See e.g., *Cubby Inc.* v *Compuserve Inc.* 776 F Supp 135 (SDNY, 1991), *Lunney* v *Prodigy Services* [1998] WL 999836 (NYAD 2 Dept) and s. 230 of the Communications Decency Act 1996 (incorporated in s. 509 of the Telecommunications Act 1996).

Most information and programmes which may be downloaded from the Internet will consist of a combination of various copyright works. For example, in the case of a computer game, there is likely to be copyright not only in the programme and the executable code, but also in the graphics, the sound effects and the music.

Primary infringement Primary infringement of copyright occurs when a person, without the permission of the copyright owner, does, or authorises another to do, any one of a number of acts prohibited under the Copyright, Designs and Patents Act 1988 (CDPA).[79] That most likely to be relevant to Internet users is to 'copy' the work. Copying includes 'storing the work in any medium by electronic means'.[80] It is also includes making transient copies, as will inevitably be the case in the operation of a computer system.

Although information on the Internet can freely be read, the owner of the copyright and material on a website may not have given permission for copies of the data to be made. Copyright in such information is likely to vest in its originator or in the website owner. Accordingly, the downloading and/or printing of any material from a website may constitute infringement of copyright.

The Internet, of course, operates on the basis of almost constant copying by one computer of material on another computer. Liability is therefore likely to turn not on whether copying took place, but on whether there was a licence for such copying, i.e., whether the person copying did so with the express or implied consent of the copyright owner.

Much information put onto the Internet is expressly allowed to be copied. Where such permission is granted, naturally no infringement of copyright will occur. However, where there is no express permission it may be difficult to argue that there is an implied licence. Users should look out for any signs of copyright reservation, such as the @ sign or the words 'Copyright reserved'.

Where an employee downloads an executable programme, such as a computer game, or a music track, which he would otherwise have to pay for, it is very unlikely that a licence to copy will be implied. In those circumstances, the employee would be liable for infringement of copyright and, unless it could show that the employee was not acting within the scope of his employment, the employer may also be liable on normal principles of vicarious liability (see under 12.4.5.1, 'Who is liable'?, above).

Similarly, if material downloaded from a website is incorporated into the employer's own corporate material and used for commercial purposes, the employer could be liable to pay damages to the copyright owner.

Copyright infringement can also occur where text is copied into or attached to an e-mail message.

Secondary infringement In addition to primary infringement, a person also infringes copyright in a work, if, in the course of business, he possesses an article which is an infringing copy,[81] provided he does so with a 'guilty mind'. This is known as secondary infringement.

---

79. Copyright, Designs and Patents Act 1988, s. 16.
80. Ibid., s. 17(2).
81. Ibid., s. 23.

The test for a guilty mind is whether on the facts known by the defendant any reasonable person would have known the material was an infringing copy. The onus would therefore be on the claimant to show that the employer knew, or had reason to believe, that it had on its system an infringing copy of a copyright work.

By contrast with the requirement under the Defamation Act 1996 for the defendant to show reasonable care, under the CDPA there is no minimum standard of care. In each case, the onus would be on the claimant to prove that the defendant knew that the infringing material was on its system and was being used in the course of business.

Secondary infringement can also take place by providing the means for a third party to make infringing copies. This might apply where, for example, an employee downloads a computer game and then transmits it over the Internet to a third party with a view to their making copies of it.

In certain circumstances, there may be criminal liability for infringement of copyright, though prosecutions tend to be directed at those seeking to trade in counterfeit goods.

12.4.5.3 Confidentiality The very speed and efficiency of electronic communication can make a breach of confidence all the more likely. Employee access to e-mail and the Internet can give rise to problems of confidentiality in two ways.

First, there is a risk that the employer's confidential information may lose the protection of confidentiality if it is inadvertently put into the public domain. Secondly, the employer may find itself liable to a third party for breach of confidence as a result of failing to keep confidential information which was provided to it by that third party in confidence.

Breach of confidence Rules relating to confidentiality are discussed in detail in chapter 8. In respect of protecting confidential information where company employees with access to the Internet also have access to confidential information, as will almost invariably be the case (see 12.3.5 above), the employer will wish to ensure that the practice and procedure applicable to the disclosure of such information outside the company applies to communication by e-mail and on the Internet in the same way it does to other forms of communication. One example of this is the confidentiality notice which is commonplace on faxes, but not yet very widely used on e-mails. The legal effect of such a notice is to make it easier for the sender to demonstrate that the person to whom the information was communicated (whether the addressee or an unintended recipient of the e-mail) owed it a duty of confidence, and will therefore strengthen the sender's position should it need to enforce that confidentiality.

An equally serious potential problem for many employers is that if information is imparted to an employee in circumstances where a duty of confidence arises (whether in contract or otherwise), and such information is then communicated by the employee to a third party who makes unauthorised use of it, an action may lie against the employer for breach of confidence at the suit of the confider.

The ease with which e-mails may be copied and forwarded can make this a particular problem. If, for example, a client or supplier sends an e-mail to an employee containing confidential information and the employee forwards that e-mail over the Internet to a third party, the client or supplier may have a cause of action for breach of confidence both against the employee in question and, subject to the principles of vicarious liability already discussed, against the employer.

The only effective defence to an action for breach of confidence is that there was a public interest in its disclosure. That test may well be difficult to satisfy in a commercial context. There is also a defence of disclosure of inequity, which has recently been widened to a defence of 'just cause or excuse', but neither is likely to be of assistance except in a genuine whistle blowing situation.

12.4.5.4 Sexual harassment Sexual harassment means unwanted conduct of a personal nature, or other conduct based on sex, affecting the dignity of men and women at work.[82] This can include unwelcome physical, verbal or non-verbal conduct. It is unwanted if such conduct is unacceptable, unreasonable and offensive to the recipient. Sexual attention becomes sexual harassment if it is persisted in once rejected by the recipient. However, a single act, if sufficiently serious, can also constitute harassment.[83]

Sexual harassment may be committed by way of a computer in two ways: directly, for example by use of e-mail to send harassing messages to the victim; and indirectly, by creating a hostile workplace from the victim's perspective. In other words, the distribution of sexually explicit material by computer may constitute sexual harassment in much the same way as placing pin-ups on a factory wall. If the display of such material, from the victim's perspective, causes offence, it will constitute harassment.

Employer's liability The employer is vicariously liable for the discriminatory acts of its employees done in the course of employment.[84] Where a situation is in the employer's control, the employer therefore has a duty to protect employees from acts of harassment and may be vicariously liable to employees for failure to do so. 'In the course of employment' has been given a wide meaning by the courts in sexual harassment cases.[85] It may therefore include the transmission of e-mail outside working hours.

An employer can also be liable for discriminatory acts done by third parties which affect its employees, where those third parties are sufficiently within the control of the employer.[86]

The employer will have a defence if it can show that it took such steps as were reasonably practicable to prevent the employee from doing the act in the course of his employment. The onus is on the employer to show that it

---

82. Council Recommendation No. 92/131/EEC and see *British Telecommunications plc* v *Williams* [1997] IRLR 668, EAT.
83. *Bracebridge Engineering Ltd* v *Darby* [1990] IRLR 3, EAT.
84. Sex Discrimination Act 1975, s. 41(1).
85. See *Chief Constable of Lincolnshire Police* v *Stubbs* [1999] IRLR 81, EAT.
86. See *Burton and Rhule* v *De Vere Hotels* [1996] IRLR 596, EAT (a case of racial harassment).

attempted to prevent either the particular act complained of or that kind of act in general.

In addition, the failure of an employer to react in a responsible fashion to a complaint of sexual harassment may amount to a breach of the implied term of mutual trust and confidence.[87]

The prudent employer will therefore have in place an e-mail policy prohibiting anything which could amount to sexual harassment, as well as providing warnings and education on sexual harassment generally. It may well also wish to make use of software which can, for example, exclude or restrict access to certain types of material available on the Internet.

Finally, it is worth noting that in recent cases the existence of e-mail records has made it easier for complainants to prove their claims for sexual harassment.

12.4.5.5 Racial harassment[88]   The Race Relations Act 1976[89] contains provisions in relation to racial harassment similar to those relating to sexual harassment outlined above. Again, harassment may be carried out by way of e-mail and the use of computers generally.

As with sexual harassment, the employer may be vicariously liable for racial harassment, even that perpetrated by third parties, where the situation in which the harassment occurs is sufficiently within the control of the employer.

Further, it is a criminal offence for a person to publish written material, which is likely to include e-mails that are threatening, abusive or insulting if he intends thereby to stir up racial hatred, or having regard to all the circumstances, racial hatred is likely to be stirred up thereby.[90]

12.4.5.6 Inadvertent contract formation   Where it appears to an outside party that an employee has authority to negotiate or enter into an agreement, then the employer will be bound by the employee's actions. The fact that the employee in question may not in fact have had such authority is immaterial, provided that the other contracting party acted reasonably in assuming that he did. This is the principle of 'ostensible authority'.

---

87. See *W A Goold (Pearmak Ltd) v McConnell* [1997] IRLR 516, EAT.
88. Also blasphemy is a criminal offence consisting in the publication of contemptuous, reviling, scurrilous or ludicrous matter relating to God, Jesus Christ, the Bible or the Church of England. There must be an intention on the part of the publisher to publish, but he need not intend that the words amount to blasphemy: *Whitehouse v Lemon* [1979] AC 617, 68 Cr App Rep 381, HL.

   However, it is not blasphemous to speak or publish opinions hostile to the Christian religion, or to deny the existence of God, if the publication is couched in decent and temperate language: *Whitehouse v Lemon* [1979] AC 617, 68 Cr App Rep 381, HL. In other words, criticism couched in reasonable language is allowed. Other religions, and arguably even Christian denominations other than the Church of England, are not protected by the law of blasphemy. To this extent the law of blasphemy is plainly outmoded and most employers will in any event wish to prohibit the downloading or circulation of material offensive to any religious beliefs. In any event, prosecutions for blasphemy are extremely rare.
89. Race Relations Act, s. 32.
90. Public Order Act 1986, s. 19.

This principle applies to communication by e-mail just as it does to any other form of communication. E-mails are generally identified as originating from a particular company. In the absence of any disclaimer on the e-mail, in most cases a third party would be acting reasonably if it assumed that the e-mail was sent with the authority of the employer. The employer would therefore be bound by any agreement entered into, or more likely perhaps varied, by e-mail.

12.4.5.7 Negligent misstatement The law imposes a duty of care on a person or organisation providing advice, where the recipient of such advice reasonably relies upon it.

Since an e-mail is likely to be identifiable as emanating from the employer, advice provided by an employee by e-mail will be of the same legal effect as that provided in a letter on company stationery. If the advice reasonably appears to the recipient to have come from the employer, the recipient will be entitled to rely upon it, even if the employee was not authorised (or specifically forbidden) to provide such advice.

In such circumstances, the employer may be liable under the principles of vicarious liability and/or agency.

In certain circumstances, a third party may also be entitled to rely on the advice, even if he is not the person to which the advice was directed, if it was reasonably foreseeable to the adviser that such a third party would rely on the advice. This might apply to an e-mail copied to a third party or a posting to a news group.

12.4.5.8 Negligent virus transmission While most companies are now fairly scrupulous about checking incoming e-mails and their attachments for viruses, the same care is not always taken in relation to outgoing material.

However, where a virus is accidentally transmitted to another organisation, for example in an e-mail attachment sent by an employee, the employer may well be liable to the third party for any damage caused as a result, if the employer had been negligent in allowing the virus to be transmitted. An intentional introduction of a virus would be a criminal offence — see further chapter 9.

12.4.5.9 Obscene material Publication of an obscene article is a criminal offence.[91] A person publishes an article who, *inter alia*, distributes, circulates, gives or lends it.[92] Further, the Obscene Publications Act 1959 was specifically amended in 1994[93] to make it clear that where the matter is data stored electronically, publication takes place where that data is transmitted.

Accordingly, where an employee downloads obscene material from the Internet and then circulates it to his colleagues, he commits a criminal offence. In addition, it is likely that where an obscene article is downloaded and subsequently distributed by email, that will constitute the offence of distribution.

---

91. Obscene Publications Act 1959, s. 2 (as amended).
92. Obscene Publications Act 1959, s. 1(3).
93. Criminal Justice and Public Order Act 1994, s. 168(1), sch. 9, para. 3.

A 1995 decision of the Court of Appeal in *R* v *Fellows* [1997] 2 All ER 548 suggests that the fact that obscene material is simply stored on a system may amount to 'passive' publication. On the face of it, therefore, the employer could be criminally liable for obscene material held on its computer system.

However, it should be borne in mind that obscene material is not the same as pornography, let alone the sort of 'adult' material available in top-shelf magazines. An article is deemed to be obscene only if its effect is such as to tend to deprave and corrupt persons who are likely, in all the circumstances, to read or see it.[94] Whether a particular article is obscene is a question of fact for the court in each particular case. The purpose or intention of the publisher is immaterial. These days, obscenity is likely to be fairly narrowly defined. It is, for example, a much narrower concept than sexual explicitness. The prosecution must also show that it tended to deprave and corrupt the target audience. That is unlikely to be the case where, for example, it simply repels and disgusts the audience.

It is a defence to show that the defendant:

(a)   had not examined the article; and
(b)   did not have reasonable cause to suspect that publication of it would make him or her liable to be convicted of an offence.[95]

It is not therefore sufficient for the employer simply to close its eyes to the material held on, or being transmitted via, its system. The employer is likely to be required to show that:

(a)   it did not know that the material was likely to be obscene; and
(b)   this absence of knowledge was not due to negligence.

12.4.5.10   Child pornography   Under the Protection of Children Act 1978 (as amended), it is a criminal offence for a person to distribute, show or have in his possession indecent photographs or 'pseudo-photographs' (i.e., computer-generated photographs) of children.[96] The viewing on a PC, downloading and transmission of child pornography will all constitute criminal offences.

The employer may be guilty where the offence occurred with the consent or connivance of, or — more importantly — was attributable to any neglect on the part of, any director, manager, company secretary or other officer of the company.[97] In such circumstances, the negligent director or manager may be prosecuted as well as the company itself.

A child means any person who appears in the photograph to have been under the age of 16. The Act does not define indecency, but it is thought that indecency is to be determined solely by considering the photograph, rather

---

94. Obscene Publications Act 1959, s. 1(1).
95. Ibid., s. 2(5).
96. Protection of Children Act 1978, s. 1(1) as amended by Criminal Justice and Public Order Act 1994, ss. 84(1), (2), 168(3), sch. 11.
97. Protection of Children Act 1978, s. 3(1).

than the surrounding circumstances.[98] Whether the material is indecent is a matter entirely for the court; it is exclusively within the province of the jury or, on summary trial, the magistrates to determine and safeguard current standards of propriety.[99]

12.4.5.11 Improper use of a public telecommunication system It is a criminal offence[100] to:

(a)   Send, by means of a public telecommunication system, a message or other matter that is grossly offensive or of an indecent, obscene or menacing character.
(b)   Send by those means, for the purpose of causing annoyance, inconvenience or needless anxiety to another, a message that the defendant knows to be false, or persistently makes use for that purpose of a public telecommunication system.

Section 43 was included in the Telecommunications Act 1984 primarily to deal with 'nuisance' telephone calls and other harassment by means of the telephone. At the time it was enacted, plainly Parliament could not have envisaged the widespread use today of email. However, e-mails sent via the Internet are certainly transmitted via a public telecommunications system and the courts have been willing to infer that Parliament intended pre-Internet statutes to catch equivalent activities which have only become technologically feasible subsequent to their enactment.[101] It is therefore likely that anyone who uses e-mail in a manner which is caught by either of the definitions above is committing a criminal offence.

12.4.5.12 Privacy There is in England and Wales no right to privacy. Quasi-privacy rights are to some extent conferred by the laws of confidence, trespass, harassment and data protection. There is also a right to privacy against the State, or organs of the State, under the European Convention for the Protection of Human Rights,[102] which will be incorporated into English law when the Human Rights Act 1998 comes into force.

Given that access to e-mail is provided to employees for the performance of their duties, e-mail is no more private than letters on company business sent out on company stationery.

The position may be slightly less straightforward where there is evidence of a contractual entitlement on the part of the employee to use e-mail for personal communications, or even where such use has simply been tolerated. However, even in those circumstances, the employee will not necessarily be

---

98. See *Kosmos Publications Ltd* v *DPP* [1975] Crim LR 345.
99. *R* v *Stamford* [1972] 2 All ER 427, CA.
100. Telecommunications Act 1984, s. 43.
101. See *Attorney General's Reference (No. 5 of 1980)* [1980] CLY 538 and *R* v *Fellows* [1997] 2 All ER 548.
102. European Convention for the Protection of Human Rights and Fundamental Freedoms, art VIII.

entitled to privacy in the content of his personal e-mails unless there had been express agreement to that effect. In order to avoid misunderstandings, as a matter of best practice it undoubtedly makes sense for the employer to remind employees that e-mail is not a private form of communication.

The only decided case in this area, *Halford* v *UK* (1997) 24 EHRR 253 takes matters no further. As discussed earlier in the chapter a complaint was brought in the European Court of Human Rights by a senior police officer for breach of art. 8 of the European Convention for the Protection of Human Rights, because certain of her telephone calls had been covertly recorded by her employer. However, it should be remembered that this case was decided on its own particular facts. First, the employer was an emanation of the State (or, in the language of the Human Rights Act 1998, a 'public authority') which gave Ms Halford a right of action which would not have been available to her had she worked for a private company. The same will apply when the Human Rights Act 1998 comes into force. Secondly, in the *Halford* case, the telephone which had been 'tapped' had been provided to her by her employer *specifically for her private use*. Plainly that would not apply to an e-mail system provided for work-related purposes.

It is possible that the legal landscape may gradually change once the Human Rights Act 1998 has come into force. The Act provides[103] that it is unlawful for a public authority to act in a way which is incompatible with a Convention right, which would include the right to privacy under art. 8 of the Convention. A public authority is defined[104] as 'any person certain of whose functions are functions of a public nature'. That is why it does not give any right of action against private sector employers. However, a public authority also includes any court.[105] It is possible that the creation of an obligation on the court not to act in a way incompatible with the right to privacy under the Convention will result in the gradual development in England and Wales of a law of privacy on a case by case basis. It will not, however, give potential claimants a new cause of action for infringement of privacy (except against the State and public authorities).

Private sector employers should not, therefore, be under the misapprehension that when the Human Rights Act 1998 comes into force in October 2000 it will create a new right of privacy for employees. Public authorities, by contrast, must have regard to the provisions of the Act.

12.4.5.13   Time wasting   A recent survey[106] of 191 of the largest international companies found that 84 percent of employees were given unlimited access to the Internet. On average such employees spent 30 minutes a day browsing the Internet for non-business purposes. Half of them accessed pornographic websites during working hours. The survey estimated that such time-wasting was costing each of those companies at least £2.5 million a year.

Plainly this has important implications for the management and profitability of companies. Such abuse of Internet access may also constitute grounds

---

103. Human Rights Act 1998, s. 6.
104. Human Rights Act 1998, s. 6(3).
105. Human Rights Act 1998, s. 6(3)(a).
106. Survey conducted by InfoSec reported in *The Daily Telegraph* on 10 April 1999.

for dismissal and has already been the subject of an Employment Tribunal decision; a number of other cases are pending.[107]

12.4.5.14 Spamming 'Spamming' is Internet jargon for the transmission of unsolicited e-mail. Spamming is not just a marketing tool; bulk spamming can be used as an aggressive weapon to disable a target's e-mail system by overwhelming it with e-mail and bulky attachments. Employees could put themselves or their employer at risk if they put the organisation on external mailing lists, except for approved business reasons.

12.4.5.15 Corporate culture Even where the downloading or circulation of material from the Internet does not give rise to direct liability, e.g., soft-core pornography which is not being used in a way which constitutes sexual harassment, the employer will often take the view that the circulation of such material does not accord with company culture and principles of best practice.

Such considerations are even more likely to be uppermost in the employer's mind if such material is transmitted outside the company, for example to a customer or supplier. This applies just as much to a non-commercial organisation, such as an academic institution, as to companies. Such conduct has already formed the basis for numerous dismissals of employees.

12.4.6 Disclosure of computer records in legal proceedings

12.4.6.1 The duty to disclose relevant documents Increasingly, e-mail records are being used to telling effect as evidence in legal proceedings. As soon as legal proceedings are commenced, or a party is placed on notice that legal proceedings against it are contemplated, it is under a duty to the court to preserve all documents relevant to the claim. In the course of proceedings, and in some cases before proceedings are commenced, it will be obliged to disclose such documents. That obligation covers:

(a) documents on which a party relies; and
(b) any documents which:
    (i)   adversely affect a party's own case;
    (ii) adversely affect another party's case; or
    (iii) support another party's case.[108]

Documents include electronic records, such as e-mails. All relevant e-mails, including in particular those unhelpful to the employer's case, would therefore have to be handed over to the other side.

Indeed the other party to proceedings might apply to the court for an order that electronic records, such as e-mail messages, which are likely to be deleted in the normal course of business be preserved and hard copies handed over

---

107. *Franchi* v *Focus Management Consultants Ltd*, Electronic Business Law 1999, vol. 1, no. 8, p. 13 (LTL 26 January 2000, unreported).
108. Civil Procedure Rules, Part 31.6.

to them. The High Court made just such an order in the United Kingdom's first major e-mail libel action, *Western Provident Association* v *Norwich Union*, 21 September 1995 (unreported).

For the avoidance of doubt, where there are no legal proceedings in contemplation, no blame can be attached to an employer for wiping the backup tapes at regular intervals. However, deliberate and knowing destruction of such records after proceedings have begun could amount to a contempt of court punishable by a fine and/or sequestration of the company's assets.

12.4.6.2 Legally privileged emails A document, including an e-mail, which is protected by legal privilege need not be disclosed in proceedings. Broadly speaking, a document will be protected by legal privilege if:

(a)   it is a confidential communication between a lawyer (including the employer's in-house lawyer) and his client which came into existence for the purpose of providing or receiving legal advice (whether or not litigation is pending or contemplated); or

(b)   it is a confidential communication between a lawyer and his client or a third party which came into existence for the sole or dominant purpose of advising in relation to contemplated or pending litigation.

It is said by some that the insecure nature of Internet communication means that communication by e-mail amounts to a waiver of privilege. However, privilege cannot be waived inadvertently. Unless it was reasonably anticipated that material transmitted by e-mail would be read by a third party, such communication should remain privileged.

However, care should be taken where the same message is communicated to a third party. For example, an e-mail which is privileged because it was addressed to a lawyer, would lose that privilege if a copy of it was sent to another recipient within or outside the organisation. Having regard to the copying and forwarding facilities on e-mail systems, caution should therefore be exercised.

12.4.7   Jurisdictional issues

The global nature of Internet communication creates a number of jurisdictional problems. In theory, it gives rise to liability in every jurisdiction from which the relevant material may be accessed. In practice, however, liability will be restricted to those jurisdictions in which the claimant has suffered damage and/or the defendant is established.

So far as defamation is concerned, it is likely that publication occurs on the user's PC on which the material is downloaded or the e-mail message read and on the printer on which any hard copy is made. The claimant would therefore have a cause of action only in the jurisdiction in which publication had taken place or in which the defendant was based.

Accordingly, if defamatory material is sent by e-mail from abroad to a computer user in England and Wales, or was posted to a news group or a website, and the claimant has a reputation in England and Wales, then the English court will probably have jurisdiction, even if the material originated outside the United Kingdom. However, if the claimant has no connection with England and Wales (e.g., a Turkish television star completely unknown in the United Kingdom) then our court is unlikely to accept jurisdiction.

In *Mecklermedia Corp.* v *DC Congress* [1998] 1 All ER 148 the English and US claimants brought proceedings for passing off in England in respect of the phrase 'Internet World', their rights in which they said was damaged by the defendant's website, which was operated from Germany with a URL incorporating the words 'Internet World'. The English court decided it had jurisdiction because the damage to the claimants' goodwill occurred in England, despite the fact that the website was on a server abroad.

Further, it is now well established[109] that where a libel is published in a number of EU Member States, the claimant may sue either in the State where the publisher is based and claim for damage suffered in all EU Member States, or in the courts of each Member State in which the libel was published, but only in respect of the harm caused in that Member State.

The net effect of such developments may well be that claimants will be tempted to 'forum shop'. This point needs to be borne in mind particularly by multinationals, which may be sued wherever they have a corporate presence. It may be open to the claimant, often a business rival, to bring proceedings in the country whose law is best suited to its case or whose courts are most likely to make a generous award of damages.

12.5 CONCLUSION

The new Information Society will bring with it the need to protect the changing nature of the wealth of organisations which will be increasingly information based. Changing ways of working and new technologies will question traditional ownership rules and facilitate easy abuse, making it more difficult to protect this wealth. Getting the basis of the employment relationship right, whether with employees or contractors, will be a key factor to ensuring that there is a smooth transition through the information revolution. Traditional ways of viewing employment rights will need to be reconsidered, and extended in the light of these changes.

---

109. *Shevill* v *Press-Alliance SA*, Case 68/93 [1995] ECR 415.

CHAPTER THIRTEEN

Data Protection

Ian Walden

Throughout this chapter the reader will be introduced to elements which go towards an understanding of data protection law. The first part will give consideration to the nature of the subject itself, primarily from a European perspective, as well as reviewing international instruments addressing data protection issues. The second part will focus on UK law, specifically the Data Protection Act 1998.

13.1 DEFINITIONS

Data protection law as a distinct legislative field is predominantly a European phenomenon. Currently such laws exist in some 25 European countries,[1] and of these, a number have already revised or amended their original legislation. Outside of Europe other industrialised nations have adopted data protection laws, such as Australia, Japan and Canada, however they are in the minority of trading nations and their laws tend to be less all-embracing than the European approach.

One of the most straightforward definitions of 'data protection' is given in the British government's explanatory report, appended to the draft of the Council of Europe Convention on Data Protection:

---

1. Austria, Belgium, Czech and Slovak Republics, Denmark, Finland, France, Germany, Greece, Guernsey, Hungary, Iceland, Ireland, Isle of Man, Italy, Jersey, Luxembourg, The Netherlands, Norway, Poland, Portugal, Spain, Sweden, Switzerland and the UK.

... the legal protection of individuals with regard to automatic processing of personal information relating to them.[2]

An alternative definition of data protection legislation has been proposed by the Office of the Data Protection Registrar. The Deputy Registrar has defined data protection as 'fairness legislation', not requiring a balance between data users and data subjects, but simply being fair to an individual.[3]

However, an expanded definition of data protection has been put forward by a number of 'third-world' countries. It has been suggested that data protection is a legal regime that should also be applied to information pertaining to States. Resolutions at Latin American and African conferences have proposed that 'information and knowledge affecting national sovereignty, security, economic well being and socio-cultural interests should be brought within the ambit of data protection'.[4]

Indeed, until the recent European Union (EU) Directive[5], the British government's definition would not have been sufficient to cover the variations of data protection legislation within Europe, or between industrialised nations. Some countries, such as Denmark, Austria and Italy extend the protection afforded under data protection laws to legal persons, such as companies and trade unions, as well as individuals. In other countries, including France and the Netherlands, data protection laws have always applied to manual records, as well as computer data. While in non-European countries, such as Australia and Japan, data protection laws are limited to public sector data processing activities, not the private sector.

It is also necessary to distinguish data protection from the related, but distinct, areas of privacy and data security. A simple distinction between data protection and privacy is made in the Lindop Report,[6] when it gives an example that the use of inaccurate or incomplete information when decision-making, although within the proper scope of data protection, is not necessarily a privacy issue. Whilst data security is part of the requirements of adequate data protection, it also covers issues of computer crime, as well as ensuring that computer systems are protected from physical disasters.

Within Europe, the 1981 Council of Europe Convention on Data Protection has been the foundation upon which national legislation and the 1995 EU Directive has been constructed. Two distinct motives underpin the 1981 Convention: the threat to individual privacy posed by computerisation; and the desire to maintain a free flow of information between trading nations. The Convention therefore attempts to reconcile art. 8 of the European Human Rights Convention, concerning an individual's right to privacy, with the

---

2. *Convention for the Protection of Individuals with regard to Automatic Processing of Personal Data*, Strasbourg, 28 January 1981 (Cmnd 8341), London: HMSO, 1981, Explanatory Report, p. 5.
3. CBI Conference, London, 4 March 1988.
4. Intergovernmental Bureau for Informatics, TDF 270, p. 55.
5. See footnote 31 below.
6. *Report of the Committee on Data Protection*, (Chairman: Sir Norman Lindop) (Cmnd 7341), London: HMSO, 1978, para. 2.03.

principle of free flow of information, enshrined in art. 10 of the Human Rights Convention protecting freedom of expression.

Indeed, in the course of the Parliamentary debates on the United Kingdom Data Protection Act 1984, the Under-Secretary of State at the Home Office clearly puts forward these two objectives:

> ... the Bill is drafted to fulfil two purposes. The first is to protect private individuals from the threat of the use of erroneous information about them — or indeed, the misuse of correct information about them — held on computers. The second is to provide that protection in a form that will enable us to satisfyrthe Council of Europe Convention on Data Processing so as to enable our own data processing industry to participate freely in the European market.[7]

13.2 DATA PROTECTION AND PRIVACY

Since the Warren and Brandeis formulation of privacy as the 'right to be let alone',[8] a great amount of effort has been devoted to establishing an exhaustive definition of the constituent components within the concept of 'privacy'. The United Nations Declaration of Human Rights at art. 12, for example, states that every individual has a right to privacy, yet fails to define the term. However, what does seem to be agreed upon is the extent to which the meaning of 'privacy' is dependent on a nation's culture.

The classic contrast to the British attitude to privacy is Sweden. On the one hand, Sweden has had 'freedom of information' legislation since 1776, but they also have a social system based on the existence of a mandatory, unique personal identifier for each citizen, something which would not be acceptable in this country at the present time.

However, what is the difference between the principles upon which data protection legislation is based and justified, and those that lie behind the 'right to privacy'? The 1978 Lindop Report on Data Protection acknowledged the following distinction:

> a data protection law should be different from that of a law on privacy: rather than establishing rights, it should provide a framework for finding a balance between the interests of the individual, the data user and the community at large.[9]

Such a balancing act can be easily recognised in the two motives behind the Council of Europe Convention.

Despite this difference between the concept of data protection and privacy, developing data protection case law can extend the scope of the legislation to wider questions regarding an individual's 'right to privacy'. In Germany, a Constitutional Court decision declared unconstitutional an act which had

---

7. Parliamentary Debates (Hansard), Lords, 5th ser., vol. 443, col. 509 (statement of Lord Eton).
8. See S.D. Warren, and L.D. Brandeis, 'The Right to Privacy', *Harvard Law Review*, pp. 193–220, vol. IV, no. 5, 1890.
9. Lindop Report (see note 6), at p. xix.

authorised the government to undertake a comprehensive population census. The court declared that each data subject has a right to 'determine in general the release and use of his or her personal data'; therefore establishing a constitutional right of individual 'informational self-determination.[10] The decision also led to a fundamental review of the German Data Protection Act. It has also been noted that some judicial opinion within the European Commission of Human Rights has begun to use the Council of Europe Convention on Data Protection to enliven and strengthen art. 8 of the Human Rights Charter.[11]

A related question concerns the nature and manner of the relationship between data protection legislation and freedom of information laws. For example, the exercise of a citizen's access rights to documents on the activities of a particular public official could lead to infringements of the individual's privacy. In recognition of such interaction, some countries have adopted a single statutory framework to address both issues, such as Canada.[12] In the UK, the Freedom of Information Bill 1999 will amend the Data Protection Act 1998 in a number of ways, including placing the regulatory enforcement powers with the Data Protection Registrar.

13.3 INTERNATIONAL ACTIVITY

The nature of the global economy inevitably means that large amounts of personal data cross national borders every day, either over communication networks, such as the Internet, or through the manual transfer of media, such as hard disks within notebook computers. Such transfers will predominantly occur in the absence of any form of control or supervision by any regulatory authority. However, such transfers could obviously pose a threat to individual privacy, since national data protection laws may be circumvented by transferring data to a so-called 'data haven', which lacks such legislation.

In order to prevent organisations from avoiding data protection controls, and therefore guaranteeing a free flow of information, international governmental organisations have become involved in attempting to obtain international harmonisation for data protection legislation; including the Council of Europe, the OECD, the United Nations and the European Union.

13.3.1 The Council of Europe

The Council of Europe has been the major international force in the field of data protection since the 1981 'Convention for the Protection of Individuals with regard to Automatic Processing of Personal Data' was agreed upon.[13]

---

10. Judgment of 15 December 1983, Bundesverfassungsgericht [BVerfG], 65 Entscheidungen des Bundesverfassungsgericht [BverfGE] 1, at p. 43.
11. P. Hustinx, 'The role of the Council of Europe', Privacy, Laws and Business Conference on Data Protection in Ireland, The Netherlands and Switzerland, 19 October 1988. See Application No. 9248/81.
12. E.g., in British Columbia, the Freedom of Information and Protection of Privacy Act 1992 (SBC 1992, ch. 61, amended by SBC 1993, ch. 46, 1993).
13. See note 2, above.

The majority of the 41 Council of Europe Members have signed the Convention, and have therefore accepted an obligation to incorporate certain data protection principles into national law. The Convention came into force on 1 October 1985 when five countries had ratified it: Sweden, Norway, France, Federal Republic of Germany and Spain.

The Council of Europe has been involved in this area since 1968, when the Parliamentary Assembly passed Recommendation 509 (68), asking the Council of Ministers to look at the Human Rights Convention to see if domestic laws gave adequate protection for personal privacy in the light of modern scientific and technical developments. The Council of Ministers asked the Committee of Experts on Human Rights to study the issue, and they reported that insufficient protection existed.

A specialist Committee of Experts on the Protection of Privacy was subsequently asked to draft appropriate resolutions for the Committee of Ministers to adopt. Resolution 22 (1973) covered the 'ground rules' for data protection in the private sector while Resolution 29 (1974) focused on the public sector.

In 1976, the Committee of Experts on Data Protection was established. Its primary task was to prepare a Convention on the protection of privacy in relation to data processing abroad and transfrontier data processing. The text of this Convention was finalised in April 1980, and opened for signature on 28 January 1981.

The Convention is based around a number of basic principles of data protection, upon which each country is expected to draft appropriate legislation. Such legislative provision will provide for a minimum degree of harmonisation between signatories, and should therefore prevent restrictions on transborder data flows for reasons of 'privacy' protection.

Since 1981, the Committee of Experts on Data Protection has been primarily involved in the drafting of sectoral rules on data protection. These form part of an ongoing series of recommendations issued by the Committee of Ministers designed to supplement the provisions of the Convention.[14]

The major weakness of the Convention is its lack of enforceability against countries that fail to uphold the basic principles. No enforcement machinery was created under the Convention, and therefore any disputes have to be resolved at the diplomatic level.

13.3.2 OECD

The Organisation for Economic Cooperation and Development was established in 1961, and currently comprises 29 of the leading industrial nations. The nature of the organisation has meant that interest in data protection has

---

14. Recommendations already published include the use of personal data in 'automated medical data banks' (R (81) 1); 'scientific research and statistics' (R (83) 10); 'direct marketing' (R (85) 20); 'social security records' (R (86) 1); 'the police sector' (R (87) 15); 'employment records' (R (89) 2) and 'payment' (R (90) 19); 'the communication to third parties of personal data held by public bodies' (R (91) 10); 'telecommunication services' (R (95) 4) and 'protection of privacy on the Internet' (R (99) 5).

centred primarily on the promotion of trade and economic advancement of Member States, rather than 'privacy' concerns.

In 1963, a Computer Utilisation Group was set up by the third Ministerial Meeting. Aspects of the Group's work concerned with privacy went to a subgroup, the Data Bank Panel. This body issued a set of principles in 1977. In the same year, the Working Party on Information Computers and Communications Policy (ICCP), was created out of the Computer Utilisation and Scientific and Technical policy groups. Within this body, the Data Bank Panel became the 'Group of Government Experts on Transborder Data Barriers and the Protection of Privacy'. Its remit was 'to develop guidelines on basic rules governing the transborder flow and the protection of personal data and privacy, in order to facilitate the harmonisation of national legislation'.

The OECD guidelines were drafted by 1979, adopted September 1980, and endorsed by the UK government in 1981.[15]

The guidelines are based, as with the Council of Europe Convention, upon eight, self-explanatory, principles of good data protection practice. The guidelines are simply a recommendation to countries to adopt good data protection practices in order to prevent unnecessary restrictions on transborder data flows and have no formal authority. However, some companies and trade associations, particularly in the United States and Canada, have formally supported the guidelines.

13.3.3 The United Nations

The United Nations has only focused on the human rights aspects of the use of computer technology comparatively recently. In 1989, the General Assembly adopted a set of draft 'guidelines for the regulation of computerized personal data files'.[16] These draft guidelines were subsequently referred to the Commission on Human Right's Special Rapporteur, Mr Louis Joinet, for redrafting based on the comments and suggestions received from member governments and other interested international organisations. A revised version of the guidelines were presented and adopted in 1990.[17]

The guidelines are divided into two sections. The first section covers 'Principles concerning the minimum guarantees that should be provided in national legislations'. These 'principles' echo those put forward by both the Council of Europe Convention and the OECD guidelines,[18] except for three additional terms:

(a)   'Principle of non-discrimination' — sensitive data, such as racial or ethnic origin, should not be compiled at all.

---

15. Organisation for Economic Cooperation and Development, *Guidelines on the Protection of Privacy and Transborder Flows of Personal Data*, Paris: OECD, 1980.
16. Resolution 44/132, on 15 December 1989.
17. Adopted by the Commission on Human Rights, Resolution 1990/42 (6 March 1990); subsequently by the UN Economic and Social Council, Resolution 1990/38, 14th Plenary Session (25 May 1990), and finally by the UN General Assembly, Resolution 45/95, 68th Plenary Session (14 December 1990).
18. See section 13.4.5 below.

(b) 'Power to make exceptions' — justified only for reasons of national security, public order, public health or morality.

(c) 'Supervision and sanctions' — the data protection authority 'shall offer guarantees of impartiality, independence *vis-à-vis* persons or agencies responsible for processing ... and technical competence'.

The second section considers the 'application of the guidelines to personal data files kept by governmental international organisations'. This requires that international organisations designate a particular supervisory authority to oversee their compliance. In addition, it includes a 'humanitarian clause', which states that:

> a derogation from these principles may be specifically provided for when the purpose of the file is the protection of human rights and fundamental freedoms of the individual concerned or humanitarian assistance.

Such a clause is intended to cover such organisations as Amnesty International, who hold large amounts of personal data, but would be wary of sending information out to a data subject on the basis of an access request made while the person was still imprisoned.

13.3.4 European Union

Despite interest and involvement in data protection and privacy issues for nearly two decades, from both the European Parliament and the Commission, the emergence of a Directive concerning this area only appeared in 1990.

The European Parliament's involvement in data protection issues has primarily been through its Legal Affairs Committee, though the issue has been subject to parliamentary questions and debates for the past 10 years. In 1976, the European Parliament adopted a resolution calling for a Directive to ensure that 'Community citizens enjoy maximum protection against abuses or failures of data processing' as well as 'to avoid the development of conflicting legislation'.[19]

In 1977 the Legal Affairs Committee established the Subcommittee on Data Processing and the Rights of the Individual. The Subcommittee, produced the 'Bayerl Report' in May 1979.[20] The resultant debate in the European Parliament led to recommendations being made to the Commission and the Council of Ministers concerning the principles that should form the basis of the Community's attitude to data protection.[21] These recommendations called on the European Commission to draft a Directive to

---

19. Resolution on the protection of the rights of individuals in connection with data processing; OJ C100, 3 May 1976, p. 27.
20. Named after the rapporteur. Report on the Protection of the Individual in the Face of the Technical Developments in Data Processing, 1979–1980 Eur.Parl.Doc. (No. 100) 13 (1979).
21. OJ C140, 5 June 1979, p. 34.

complement a common communications system, to harmonise the data protection laws and to secure the privacy of information on individuals in computer files.

In July 1981, the European Commission recommended that all Members sign the Council of Europe Convention and seek to ratify it by the end of 1982.[22]

A second parliamentary report, the 'Sieglerschidt' Report, was published in 1982.[23] The report noted 'that data transmission in general should be placed on a legal footing and not be determined merely by technical reasons'.[24] It recommended the establishment of a 'European Zone', of members in the EEC and Council of Europe, within which authorisation prior to the export of data would not be needed. It also indicated that initiatives, such as a Directive, were still necessary. Following the report, a resolution was adopted by the European Parliament, on 9 March 1982, calling for a Directive if the Convention proved inadequate.[25]

In July 1990, the European Commission finally published a proposed Directive on data protection.[26] It was published as part of a package of proposals, which included a recommendation that the European Community adheres to the Council of Europe Convention on data protection,[27] a declaration applying data protection principles to Community institutions,[28] a draft Directive addressing data protection issues in the telecommunications sector,[29] and a draft Council decision to adopt a two-year plan in the area of security for information systems.[30]

After considerable controversy and political debate at all stages of the legislative process, the general framework Directive on data protection was finally adopted by the European Parliament and Council on 24 October 1995[31]. Member States had to implement the Directive by 24 October 1998,

---

22. Commission Recommendation of 29 July 1981, relating to the Council of Europe Convention for the protection of individuals with regard to automatic processing of personal data, OJ L246/31, 29 August 1979, 81/679/EEC.
23. Second Report on the Protection of the Rights of the Individual in the Face of Technical Developments in Data Processing, E.P.Doc. 1-548/81, 12 October 1981.
24. Ibid., at p. 7.
25. OJ C87, 5 April 1982, p. 39.
26. OJ C277, 5 November 1990.
27. However, see the European Court of Justice Opinion No. 2/94 [1996] 2 CMLR 265 that the Community cannot adhere to the European Convention on Human Rights.
28. Commission Declaration on the application to the institutions and other bodies of the European Communities of the principles contained in the Council Directive concerning the protection of individuals in relation to the processing of personal data (COM (90) 314 final, OJ C277/74, 5 November 1990. This is now incorporated in the Treaty of Amsterdam, art. 286, and the Council has an obligation to establish an independent supervisory body for Community institutions.
29. Finally adopted in 1997: Directive 97/66/EC of the European Parliament and of the Council concerning the processing of personal data and the protection of privacy in the telecommunications sector, OJ L24, 30 January 1998, p. 1. Implemented in the United Kingdom by the Telecommunications (Data Protection and Privacy) Regulations 1999, SI 1999/2093.
30. Adopted as Council Decision 92/242/EEC of 31 March 1992, in the field of information security, OJ L123, 8 May 1992.
31. Directive 95/46/EC on the protection of individuals with regard to the processing of personal data and on the free movement of such data, OJ L281, 23 November 1995, p. 31.

although only five managed to adopt legislation by that date.[32] The provisions of the Directive shall be considered below in the context of the United Kingdom's implementing statute: the Data Protection Act 1998.

The primary justification for Commission action was as part of the Single Market programme, under art. 100a of the EU Treaty. In 1990, only eight of the (then) twelve Member States had passed data protection legislation. Even between these eight considerable divergence existed in terms of the scope of protection; the nature of the obligations imposed on data users and the restrictions on use and export of data. Such differences were seen as a potential obstacle to the development of an integrated European Information Market. The Commission also expressed its desire to protect the rights of individual data subjects, 'and in particular their right to privacy' (art. 1(1)). The Directive is therefore limited to the protection of natural persons, rather than legal persons.[33]

13.3.5   Transborder data flows

Despite the international initiatives outlined above, many important trading nations still lack comprehensive data protection laws, extending in particular to private sector use of personal data, such as the United States and Japan. Where countries do not have legislation, or indeed where the level of protection is of a different nature (e.g., extending only to public sector data), an issue arises as to whether transfers of personal data should be permitted to jurisdictions that do not have 'equivalent' or 'adequate' protection?

Where a recipient country does not have substantive data protection legislation, could an individual's rights be ensured through other means? Where a functional rather than strictly legal approach is adopted, a transfer could take place to countries without specific legislation where it can be shown that other forms of protection exist in the recipient country, such as constitutional or sectoral legal provisions and/or that the real risk to personal data is low, due to one or a combination of alternative forms of control, such as industry self-regulatory codes of practice, data security measures or contractual protection.

Over recent years. particular interest has been shown in the use of contractual terms between the sender and recipient of the personal data as a mechanism for achieving 'equivalent' protection. In 1992, the Council of Europe's Committee of Experts on Data Protection published a set of model contractual provisions which are designed to replicate, as far as possible, the principles of the Convention on Data Protection in a set of enforceable contractual provisions.[34] The clauses are primarily intended for situations where a 'Contracting Party' to the Council of Europe Convention receives a

---

32. I.e., Greece, Italy, Portugal, Sweden and the UK, although the UK had not implemented the legislation.

33. However, the telecommunications data protection directive (note 29, above) does confer certain rights upon 'subscribers', who may be natural or legal persons (art. 2(a)).

34. Council of Europe, 'Model Contract to ensure equivalent data protection in the context of transborder data flows', (T-PD (92) 7), October 1992.

request to export personal data to a State, which has not legislated for data protection. Subsequently, other organisations have issued such model terms, designed specifically to achieve 'adequate' protection as required under EU data protection legislation.[35]

The major question with contractual safeguards is whether such provisions can be sufficiently enforceable by, or on behalf of, the data subject whom they are intended to protect. The data user exporting the data is unlikely to suffer damage from any breach of such contractual terms, and therefore has little incentive to either police the agreement or sue for any breach. In addition, until recently, the primary obstacle under English law to a third party, such as a data subject, acting against the importing data user has been the 'privity of contract' rule, whereby only the parties to a contract can enforce its obligations.[36]

The use of contractual terms to achieve harmonised protection for personal data between jurisdictions is a solution being strongly promoted by industry. Companies perceive contractual terms as a practical means of providing for data protection in jurisdictions where the adoption of comprehensive data protection laws appears unlikely. The widespread adoption of such terms will, however, depend on the attitude of the appropriate national data protection authorities.[37]

13.4 THE UNITED KINGDOM DATA PROTECTION ACT 1998

13.4.1 A history of legislative activity

In 1961, Lord Mancroft introduced a 'Right of Privacy' Bill. This Bill can be seen to mark the beginning of a 23-year history which finally led to the successful passage of the Data Protection Act 1984. This first private member's Bill was followed by four others until the government finally decided to establish a formal committee of inquiry into this area.

In May 1970, a Committee on Privacy was appointed under the Chairmanship of Kenneth Younger (the Younger Report). The Committee's purview was limited to the private sector despite the Committee's request that it be reviewed. The final report was completed and presented to Parliament in July 1972.[38]

During its establishment, the Committee set up a special Working Party on Computers. The Working Party (at para. 580) concluded that:

> Put quite simply, the computer problem as it affects privacy in Great Britain is one of apprehensions and fears and not so far one of facts and figures.

---

35. E.g., International Chamber of Commerce, Model clauses for use in contracts involving transborder data flows (1999): www.icc.org.
36. The Contracts (Rights of Third Parties) Act 1999 has removed this obstacle.
37. See the following report adopted by the Working Party comprising the EU Member State data protection authorities, established under art. 29 of Directive 95/46/EC: 'Transfers of personal data to third countries: applying Articles 25 and 26 of the EU data protection directive' (24 July 1998). See generally: http://europa.eu.int/comm/dg15/en/media/dataprot/adopted.htm.
38. *Report of the Committee on Privacy* (Cmnd 5012), London: HMSO, 1972.

Indeed, their report went on to note that the most credible anxieties were those held about computers in the *public* sector, an area outside the Committee's scope. The Committee noted that the main areas of public concern were with universities, bank records and credit agencies. The Committee recommended that an independent body (standing commission) composed of computer experts and lay persons should be established to monitor growth in the processing of personal information by computer, as well as the use of new technologies and practices.

In response to the Younger Report, the government promised a White Paper. However, it was three years before the White Paper, *Computers and Privacy* (Cmnd 6353) was presented to Parliament in December 1975. In it, the government accepted the need for legislation to protect computer-based information. Despite the concerns expressed in the Younger Report with regard to manual records, the government felt that computers posed a special threat to individual privacy:

> 6.   The speed of computers, their capacity to store, combine, retrieve and transfer data, their flexibility, and the low unit cost of the work which they can do have the following practical implications for privacy:
> (1)   they facilitate the maintenance of extensive record systems and the retention of data on those systems;
> (2)   they can make data easily and quickly accessible from many distant points;
> (3)   they make it possible for data to be transferred quickly from one information system to another;
> (4)   they make it possible for data to be combined in ways which might not otherwise be practicable;
> (5)   because the data are stored, processed and often transmitted in a form which is not directly intelligible, few people may know what is in the records, or what is happening to them.

The government also issued a second White Paper, entitled *Computers: Safeguards for Privacy* (Cmnd 6354), which agreed with the comments made by the Younger Report with regard to the concerns generated by public sector information.

Rather than establish a standing commission to monitor the use of personal data, the White Paper proposed legislation to cover both public and private sector information systems. The creation of a Data Protection Authority was also proposed, to supervise the legislation and ensure that appropriate safeguards for individual privacy were implemented. In order to provide a detailed structure for the proposed data protection authority, the government established a Data Protection Committee, under the chairmanship of Sir Norman Lindop, which reported in 1978.[39]

The Lindop Report proposed that a number of data protection principles should form the core of the legislation, with the Data Protection Authority

---

39. See note 6, above.

being responsible for ensuring compliance with those principles. In particular, the Authority would be required to draft codes of practice for various sectors, based on consultations with interested parties and associations, which would then become law, as statutory instruments. Failure to comply with a code would lead to criminal sanctions. Overall, the Lindop Report was concerned to produce a flexible solution which would not act so as to hold back the growing use of computers within both the public and private sector.

After the fall of the government in 1979, legislation on data protection was further delayed. Finally, in 1982, the government issued the White Paper, *Data Protection: The Government's Proposals For Legislation* (Cmnd 8539). The approach put forward in the White Paper was much less thorough than that proposed in the Lindop Report. The idea of a Data Protection Authority was replaced by an individual Registrar of Data Protection. The White Paper also rejected the idea of statutory codes of practice. Although they saw the value of such codes, the government felt that the length of time necessary to create an adequate range of statutory codes of practice would be unacceptable.

The Data Protection Act of 1984 received the Royal Assent on 12 July 1984. The provisions of the Act were phased in over a three-year period, with the Act becoming fully operational on 11 November 1987.

The Data Protection Act 1998 received Royal Assent on 16 July 1998. The Act enables the government to comply with its obligation to implement EU Directive 95/46/EC. It repeals the 1984 Act, although transitional provisions in the 1998 Act effectively mean that processing carried out prior to 24 October 1998 will continue to be subject to the 1984 Act until October 2001. The 1998 Act did not enter into force until 1 March 2000, when the necessary ministerial orders under the Act had been drafted.[40]

The following sections primarily consider the provisions of the 1998 Act, although some of the detailed procedural aspects have yet to be finalised. However, reference will also be made to the 1984 Act, since much of the case law that has arisen under the Act will continue to be applicable when considering how such legislation impacts on the processing of personal data.

13.4.2 Terms

The Data Protection Act 1998 is concerned with personal data. 'Personal data' consists of data that relates to a 'living individual' who can be identified from that data, or from that and other data or information in the possession of the data user. 'Data' includes information processed by computers, 'relevant filing systems' and 'accessible records'.[41]

In contrast to the Data Protection Act 1984, the term 'relevant filing system' extends the scope of the legislation to manual records as well as computer records. To constitute a 'relevant filing system', the set of

---

40. For all the relevant primary and secondary legislation, see *Encyclopedia of Data Protection*, S. Chalton, S. Gaskill, H. Grant and I. Walden (eds), London: Sweet & Maxwell: looseleaf.
41. Under the government's proposed freedom of information bill (see section 13.2, above) the definition will be further extended to include information recorded by a public authority (clause 60).

information must be 'structured, either by reference to individuals or by reference to criteria relating to individuals, in such a way that specific information relating to a particular individual is readily available' (s. 1).

The term 'accessible records' has been incorporated in order that the UK government can comply with the European Court of Human Right's decision in *Gaskin* v *United Kingdom*, (1989) 12 EHRR 36. In this case, the court held that certain records relate to 'private and family life' in such a way that the issue of access falls within the ambit of art. 8 of the European Convention on Human Rights. The government has defined the types of records which it believes fall within the scope of the *Gaskin* decision, including health and educational records (s. 68 and sch. 12).

Under the 1984 Act, the processing of personal data is limited to processing 'by reference to the data subject'.[42] Such a limitation is not present in the 1998 Act's definition of processing which follows the all-encompassing definition in Directive 95/46/EC.

The 1998 Act is primarily concerned with three categories of persons:

(a) 'Data subjects': the individual which is the subject of the personal data.

(b) 'Data controllers': a person who, whether alone, jointly or in common with others, 'determines the purposes for which and the manner in which' the data are processed.[43]

(c) 'Data processor': a third party simply processes personal data on behalf of a data controller without controlling the contents or use of the data.

Under the regime established by the EU Directive 95/46/EC, a key concept is that of 'data subject's consent'. If the data controller obtains consent then he is able to process the personal data. The Directive defines 'data subject's consent' as being freely given, specific and informed. It supplements this in the substantive provisions when referring to consent as being 'unambiguously given'. Such terminology seems to provide little opportunity for a data controller to rely on the implied consent of the data subject. Significantly, however, the 1998 Act does not include any definition of 'consent'. In justification of this position, the Government has stated:

The Government are content for the issue of whether consent has been validly given to be determined by the courts in the normal way .... It is better for the courts to decide according to ordinary principles of law than for the Act to contain specific consent provisions.[44]

---

42. See *Equifax Europe Ltd* v *Data Protection Registrar* (1991) case DA/90 25/49/7, where the Data Protection Tribunal held that the phrase 'processing by reference to data subject' meant that 'the object of the exercise is to learn something about individuals'.
43. In *Data Protection Registrar* v *Francis Joseph Griffin* (QB, 22 February 1993), *The Times*, 5 March 1993, the court held that limitations imposed on an individual's use of personal data for his own purposes, either contractual or professional, does not necessarily prevent him from being a separate registerable 'data user' under the 1984 Act.
44. Comments made by Mr Hoon (Parliamentary Secretary, Lord Chancellor's Department), 12th sitting of Standing Committee D, 4 June 1998 (morning).

However, this absence may provide data controllers with greater flexibility with respect to claiming the consent of the data subject through implication, although the courts would have to consider the terminology used in the Directive when interpreting the application of the Act.

Provisions concerning so-called 'sensitive data' were contained in the 1984 Act, but were never brought into operation by the Secretary of State.[45] Under the new Act, s. 2 defines eight categories of 'sensitive personal data', including data concerning a person's racial or ethnic origin; their political and religious beliefs; trade union membership; physical and mental health and criminal convictions. The processing of sensitive data is subject to additional controls.[46]

13.4.3   Data protection principles

The Data Protection Act 1984 was built around certain data protection principles, and the EU Directive 95/46/EC and the Data Protection Act 1998 reiterate this approach. These principles are intended to be good practices that data controllers should comply with in order to protect the data they hold, in both their interests and those of their data subjects. These principles are fundamental to an understanding of the basis of data protection law in Europe. The 1998 Act contains a limited redraft and renumbering of the 1984 principles, and data controllers have a duty to comply with the principles, except where an exemption exists (s. 4(4)).

The first principle requires fair and lawful processing, with the additional requirement that one of the conditions in sch. 2 (and sch. 3 where sensitive data is processed) are present. These conditions primarily relate to the issue of lawful processing. Schedules 2 and 3 therefore substantially extend the concept of 'lawful' processing under the 1984 Act (see further section 13.4.8 below).

The basic position under schs 2 and 3 is that, except where the data controller has the consent of the data subject, the processing of personal data must be 'necessary' for the stated purposes, such as 'the performance of contract to which the data subject is a party'. The burden will be upon the data controller to show evidence of such necessity.

Under the EU Directive, a data controller is required to provide certain information to the data subject, either when the data are collected from the data subject (art. 10), or where the data were not obtained from the data subject (art. 11). These provisions have been incorporated into the Act within the concept of 'fair' processing, as part of the interpretation provisions. As with 'lawful' processing, this constitutes a significant extension to the interpretation of 'fairness' under the 1984 Act.

In *Innovation (Mail Order) Ltd* v *Data Protection Registrar* (29 September 1993; case DA/92 31/49/1) the Data Protection Tribunal stated that fair obtaining' means that at the time that information is collected, the data user needs to inform the data subject of certain matters that will enable the

---

45. Data Protection Act 1984, s. 2(3).
46. See the Data Protection Act 1998, sch. 3 and The Data Protection (Processing of Sensitive Personal Data) Order 1999 (SI 417/2000).

individual to decide whether to provide the information or not. In particular, this includes information about the intended uses for the data, unless such use could be considered obvious.

Whilst the Directive refers only to the data controller providing such information to the data subject, 'except where he already has it', the Act also enables the data controller to comply with the obligation by making the information 'readily available' to the data subject. The manner in which this phrase is interpreted may have important implications for a controller in terms of the procedural mechanisms it establishes, such as the use of Intranet-based techniques to disseminate information to employees.

Where the data controller has not obtained the data from the data subject themselves, the controller is exempt from the requirement to provide information where it would involve either 'disproportionate effort', or the recording or disclosure is required under a non-contractual legal obligation.[47]

Under the second principle, data controllers must obtain data only for specified and lawful purposes, and must not carry out any further processing which is incompatible with those purposes. For example, a contravention of this principle would be for an organisation to register the holding of personal data for purposes of personnel management, and use it additionally for marketing purposes.

The third principle requires a data controller to only hold personal data that is 'adequate, relevant and not excessive in relation to that purpose or those purposes'.

The fourth principle requires that all personal data 'shall be accurate and, where necessary, kept up to date'. If, for example, an organisation purports to keep a list of undischarged bankrupts, but makes no effort to seek information on persons discharging themselves from bankruptcy, it will be contravening this principle.

The fifth principle states that personal data 'shall not be kept for longer than is necessary for that purpose or those purposes'. This principle implies that data should be destroyed when the specified purpose(s) for which they were collected has been achieved.

The sixth principle requires processing to be carried out in accordance with the rights of data subjects under the Act (see section 13.4.6 below).

The seventh principle addresses issues of data security, requiring data controllers to take 'appropriate technical and organisational measures' against unauthorised or unlawful processing, and accidental loss, destruction or damage to the data. Regard must be had to the state of technological development and the cost of implementing such measures. Data controllers should also take measures to ensure that employees are reliable and, if using a data processor, contractual obligations must be provided for to ensure that the processor implements security measures.

The obligation upon data controllers not to transfer personal data to countries which do not have an 'adequate' level of protection, as required by

---

47. See The Data Protection (Conditions under Paragraph 3 of Part II of Schedule 1) Order 1999 (SI 185/2000).

the Directive's art. 25, is implemented in the Act through a new eighth principle:

> Personal data shall not be transferred to a country or territory outside the European Economic Area unless that country or territory ensures an adequate level of protection for the rights and freedoms of data subjects in relation to the processing of personal data.

The principle is accompanied by an interpretation section (sch. 1, pt. II) and by sch. 4, which details situations where the principle is not applicable.

Data controllers will also be required to notify the Commissioner of those countries outside the European Economic Area to which they transfer, or intend to transfer, personal data. This will enable her to take proactive steps against transfers to countries perceived as providing inadequate protection. The eighth principle will require an assessment of 'adequacy' on a country-by-country basis.

In procedural terms, where a data controller intends to transfer personal data, the first issue that will need to be addressed is whether the transfer falls within one of the criteria specified in sch. 4. If it does, then the eighth principle would not be applicable.

Schedule 4 substantially echoes the derogations provided for under art. 26(1) of the Directive. Article 26(2) provides an additional circumstance arising where a Member State, through the offices of the Data Protection Commissioner, authorises 'a transfer or a set of transfers of personal data to a third country which does not ensure an adequate level of protection'. Such authorisations will only arise where the data controller 'adduces adequate safeguards'. The initiative is clearly upon the individual data controller to seek such authorisation before making a transfer.

Under the Act, the Directive's art. 26(2) has been implemented through two distinct procedural situations:

(a)   the transfer 'is made on terms of a kind approved by the Commissioner'; or

(b)   the transfer 'has been authorised by the Commissioner'.

The former is addressed to the possibility that the Commissioner could approve the use of certain contractual terms, which would then be considered suitable to cover a 'set of transfers' carried out by the data controller over a period of time (see section 13.3.5 above). The latter procedure seems to presume some form of case-by-case prior authorisation process.

The Commissioner is required to notify the European Commission and the other Member States of all approvals and authorisations granted. Objections may be lodged against such decisions and the European Commission, through its Committee procedure under art. 31, may make a determination prohibiting such an authorisation. Therefore, any approval or authorisation a data controller obtains from the Commissioner must be viewed as qualified, subject to this consultation process.

Where a transfer *does* fall within the scope of the eight principle, then a data controller will need to assess whether the 'country or territory' to which the transfer is to be made ensures an adequate level of protection.[48] The interpretation provision, pt. II of sch. 1, provides a non-exclusive list of criteria relevant to the making of such an assessment, echoing the terminology of art. 25(2). Of particular interest is para. 13(g), which states:

> any relevant codes of conduct or other rules which are enforceable in that country or territory (whether generally or by arrangement in particular cases).

This is phrased in broad enough terms to include contractual mechanisms, as rules may be 'enforceable' through contractual agreement. Such an interpretation suggests that contractual mechanisms governing transborder data flows will be a factor both in cases where the eighth principle applies and where it does not. The advantage of the former approach is avoidance of the notification procedure.[49]

13.4.4   The Data Protection Commissioner

The Data Protection Act 1998 renames the existing supervisory authority: the Data Protection Registrar has become the Data Protection Commissioner.[50] The Commissioner has a number of duties and enforcement powers under the Act. The Registrar had a duty to promote observance of the data protection principles under the Data Protection Act 1984. This has been significantly broadened to a general duty to promote 'good practice':

> 'good practice' means such practice in the processing of personal data as appears to the Commissioner to be desirable having regard to the interests of data subjects and others, and includes (but is not limited to) compliance with the requirements of this Act (s. 51(9)).

One mechanism for such promotion will be the development of codes of practice. Under the 1998 Act, the Commissioner can draft such codes herself, rather than merely encourage trade associations to do so (s. 51(3)(b)). This is likely to be an important implementation tool for the Commissioner and will result in a proliferation in the number of codes.[51] Under the proposed orders, compliance with a code of practice is likely to confer a number of procedural benefits. The Commissioner has the power to carry out 'good practice'-based assessments, with the consent of the data controller (s. 51(7)).

---

48. Although the data controller will need to consider any 'Community finding' regarding adequacy (Data Protection Act 1998, sch. 1, pt. II, para. 15).
49. See generally, guidance note, 'The Eighth Data Protection Principle and Transborder Data Flows' (July 1999, Version 1).
50. The first Registrar was Eric Howe. He was replaced by Elizabeth France in August 1994.
51. There are currently some 30 codes of practice. See the *Encyclopedia of Data Protection*, note 40, above.

In terms of investigating compliance with the Act, the Commissioner can issue an 'information notice' against a data controller requiring the provision of specific information (s. 43). Where necessary, the Commissioner can apply to a court for a warrant to access, search and seize material held by an individual or organisation (sch. 9). The Commissioner can instigate a prosecution for an offence under the Act. However, the Commissioner cannot commence civil proceedings against a data controller where a data subject's statutory rights have been breached.

The Act also provides the Commissioner with the ability to serve an 'enforcement notice' against a data user that has failed to observe any of the data protection principles (s. 40). The notice specifies the nature of the breach that has occurred and outlines the measures that will need to be taken in order to correct the breach. If the data user fails to comply with the notice, then an offence is committed (s. 47).

Any person who is, or believes himself to be, directly affect by any processing of personal data may require the Commissioner to carry out an 'assessment' of whether the Act is being complied with (s. 42). If the Commissioner has been provided with sufficient information to identity the relevant processing, then she has a duty to make such an assessment,

Under the 1984 Act, a Data Protection Tribunal was established to hear appeals by data controllers against any notice issued against them by the Registrar. Data subjects had no such right of appeal. This position is maintained under the 1998 Act, although data subjects will now have the right to appeal to the Tribunal where they are 'directly affected' by the issuance of a certificate exempting data from the Act's provisions for reasons of national security (s. 28(4)–(5)).

13.4.5   Data controller notification

Under the Data Protection Act 1984, the Registrar was required to establish a public register of all data users and computer bureaux. The principal functions of the register were to identify systems and facilitate supervision and compliance with standards (as well as generating fee income!). The Office of the Data Protection Registrar initially estimated the number of registrations to be around 300,000; however, just over half that number were received.[52] Much criticism was levelled at the registration process from both data users and subjects.

Under the Data Protection Act 1998, data controllers will be required to continue to notify the Data Protection Commissioner in a similar fashion to the existing registration system, although, as stated by the Home Office, 'notification will be an element of the main regime rather than triggering application of that regime.[53] The Act prohibits processing without notification (s. 17), except:

---

52. The number of registered data users in July 1999 was 225,440: see Data Protection Registrar's Fifteenth Annual Report, p. 41 (1999).
53. See Home Office Consultation Paper on Notification Regulations, August 1998, at para. 8.

(a)   Manual data processed as part of a 'relevant filing system' or an 'accessible record'.

(b)   Where the Secretary of State has, in 'notification regulations', exempted categories of processing from the notification obligation as 'unlikely to prejudice' data subject rights and freedoms.[54]

(c)   Where the processing is for the *sole* purpose of maintaining a public register.

Such notification shall include 'the registrable particulars' (e.g., name, address and description of purposes for which the data are being processed: s. 16(1)) and 'a general description of measures to be taken for the purpose of complying with the seventh data protection principle'. Controllers also have a duty to notify the Commissioner of any changes relating to such matters. The Commissioner shall maintain a register of notifications which shall be made available to the public for inspection, although this will include only the 'registrable particulars', not the information relating to data security measures (s. 19(2)). Considerable controversy has surrounded the need to supply a description of security measures. Data controllers will obviously be concerned to limit the amount of information disclosed; whilst the Commissioner will want to obtain sufficient detail to make the process meaningful.

Where processing is considered 'assessable processing', under the terms of an order to be issued by the Secretary of State, such processing will be considered likely either to cause 'significant damage or distress to data subjects', or to 'prejudice the rights and freedoms of data subjects' (s. 22). The government has indicated that it is considering whether such controls may be necessary for processing involving data matching, genetic data and private investigation activities. Processing such data will require the data controller to notify the Commissioner, as with any other form of data, but then delay commencement for a period of 28 days, which can be extended for a further 14 days by the Commissioner. Whilst the Commissioner is unable to prohibit such processing, she will be able to issue an enforcement notice where the processing is considered to be non-compliant with the Act.

One innovation under the Directive, imported from German data protection law,[55] is the possibility that a controller may be exempted from the notification obligation through the appointment of a 'personal data protection official' to act as an internal supervisory authority. However, the government found little private sector enthusiasm for the idea and, therefore, the Act simply grants the Secretary of State the power to issue an order at some point in the future.[56]

In contrast to the 1984 Act, exemption from notification does not take the relevant processing outside of the terms of the Act, and data controllers will

---

54. See The Data Protection (Notification and Notification Fees) Regulations 1999 (SI 188/2000), reg. 3 and schedule.
55. Gesetz zur Fortentwicklung der Datenverarbeitung und des Datenschutzes (Bundesgesetzblatt 1990 I, p. 2954), at s. 28.
56. Government White Paper, *Data Protection: The Government's Proposals* (Cm 3725), London: HMSO, July 1997, at para. 5.11.

still be required to comply with the data protection principles. In addition, even where a data controller is exempt from notification, processing only manual data or under the 'notification regulations', the data controller may be required to provide details of its 'registrable particulars' to any person which submits a request in writing (s. 24(1)). Such information is to be provided free of charge, within 21 days. The potential burden involved in meeting this obligation may convince many data controllers to notify voluntarily their details to the Commissioner (s. 18).[57]

Three categories of offence arose under the 1984 Act with respect to the register of data users: non-registration,[58] defective registration information[59] and acting outside of a register entry. However, the 1998 Act only specifies offences for a failure to notify the Commissioner and a failure to give notification of any changes in the 'registrable particulars' (s. 21). No offence arises directly from acting outside the terms of the data controller's notification, although a provision may be placed in the 'notification regulations' and failure to comply may be an offence. Such processing may also breach the second data protection principle.

13.4.6 Data subjects' rights

The Data Protection Act 1998, extends and amends existing rights given to data subjects and provides data subjects with additional rights, in line with Directive 95/46/EC.

Under the Act, a data subject is entitled to be informed by any data controller whether processing of his personal data is being carried out and to be given copies, 'in an intelligible form', of any such data (s. 7). However, the requirement to provide information to the data subject is significantly enhanced over that required under the existing regime. Under the new Act, the following information must be supplied:

(a)   the personal data being processed;
(b)   the purpose(s) for which data are being processed;
(c)   the recipients or classes of recipients to whom data may be disclosed; and
(d)   where relevant, the logic involved in any automated decision taking.

In the event that the data subject then requests a copy of such information, the data controller must also provide the data subject with 'any information available to the data controller as to the source of those data'.

Under the Data Protection Act 1984, information relating to purpose, source and recipients is only indirectly and imperfectly made available to the data subject through the data user's registration entry. The Act's provisions, however, require the direct provision of specific information on a per request basis. This will require significant additional processing overhead for data controllers responding to subject access requests.

---

57. Ibid., at para. 5.10.
58. E.g., s. 5(1): holding personal data when not registered.
59. E.g., s. 6(6): furnishing false or misleading registration details.

The 1998 Act goes on to address the problem of the provision of information which includes personal data relating to another individual. Coverage of the issue is in considerably greater detail than the 1984 Act, possibly reflecting the problems experienced by data users in the past.

In determining whether 'information relating to another individual who can be identified from that information' will be disclosed through the subject access request, the data controller must take into account 'any other information which, in the reasonable belief of the data controller, is likely to be in, or come into, the possession of the data subject making the request' (s. 8(7)). This is likely to prove difficult for data controllers to apply and it may require them to demand further information from the data subject prior to responding to their access request. A data controller is obliged to provide such information to the data subject as he can without 'disclosing the identity of the individual concerned'.

The 1984 Act only permitted disclosure of third party identifying information where the data user was 'satisfied that the other individual has consented'. This is extended under the 1998 Act to include situations where 'it is reasonable in all the circumstances to comply with the request without the consent of the other individual'. The Act elaborates a non-exhaustive list of factors that may be relevant to such a determination, such as any duty of confidentiality owed to the other individual (s. 7(6)). A data controller will need to establish appropriate internal procedures to handle subject access requests for information which contain data on third parties, in order to evidence the appropriateness of any decision to disclose or withhold data.

The Act provides the Secretary of State with the ability to prescribe different levels of fees and periods for the supply of information to the data subject, including no fee. However, the current maximum fee of £10 per request remains the default position.[60]

The information supplied to a data subject under an access request shall be in 'permanent form', unless the data subject agrees otherwise or 'it is not possible or would involve *disproportionate effort*'. In the absence of guidance from the Commissioner, or any judicial interpretation, data controllers will have to decide how to implement this phrase.

Under the 1984 Act, organisations have received far fewer access requests than might have been expected. Public sector data users have generally had considerably more requests than the private sector.

Three distinct new rights are granted to data subjects by the 1998 Act. Under art. 14(a) of the Directive, a data subject has the right to object to the processing of his data 'on compelling legitimate grounds' and, if the complaint is 'justified', the data controller is obliged to stop such processing. The Act has specified the scope of such legitimate grounds as causing, or is likely to cause (a) 'substantial damage or substantial distress to him [the data subject] or to another', and (b) such damage is 'unwarranted' (s. 10(1)). Where such circumstances arise, the data subject may give notice to the data

---

60. See The Data Protection (Subject Access) (Fees and Miscellaneous Provisions) Regulations 1999 (SI 191/2000), para. 3.

controller in writing and, in the event of dispute, apply for a court order requiring the data controller to stop such processing.

Article 14(b) of the Directive grants data subjects a specific right to object to processing for the purpose of direct marketing, 'or to be informed before personal data are disclosed for the first time to third parties or used on their behalf for the purposes of direct marketing'. The Act clearly implements the first part of this provision, by granting the data subject a right to require the data controller to cease processing for the purposes of direct marketing (s. 11(1)). However, the further element (in quotations) is not present in the Act, which would appear to be a significant limitation of the rights being granted to the data subject.

Data subjects have a new right in respect of automated decision taking, such as credit reference scoring and the use of psychometric testing for screening applicants (s. 12). The Act gives data subjects an entitlement to notify a data controller not to take decisions which 'significantly affect' the data subject and are based 'solely' on automated processing. In the absence of notification, a data controller must proactively notify the individual, 'as soon as reasonably practicable', where such a decision *was* taken and give them the opportunity to require the data controller to 'reconsider the decision or to take a new decision otherwise than on that basis'. However, this right of notification does not apply where the Secretary of State has exempted particular circumstances, or the following conditions are met:

(a)   the decision is an aspect of entering into, or performing, a contract with the data subject (s. 12(6)(a)); or

(b)   the automated decision-making is required under an enactment (s. 12(6)(b));

and:

(c)   the decision grants the request of the data subject (s. 12(7)(a)); or

(d)   steps have been taken to protect the data subject's interests, e.g., there is a procedure for appeal (s. 12(7)(b)).

The operation of these provisions seem unnecessarily complex, which will create compliance uncertainties and procedural overheads for data controllers, whilst also offering minimal effective protection for data subjects.

The 1998 Act extends the grounds upon which a data subject may recover compensation. Under the 1984 Act, compensation may only be awarded by a court in situations of inaccuracy, loss, destruction or unauthorised disclosure or access.[61] The 1998 Act substantially broadens this right to '*any* contravention by a data controller of *any* of the requirements of this Act' (s. 13). As with the 1984 Act, compensation can extend to any 'distress' suffered by the individual, although only as a supplement to damage. Compensation may be for distress alone only where the contravention relates to processing for the 'special purposes' (see section 13.4.7 below). It has been suggested

---

61. Data Protection Act 1984, ss. 22–23. 'Unauthorised' relates to the data user's authorisation, not the data subject's.

that this provision may not comply with the Directive because the concept of 'damage', under art. 23(1), has been interpreted too narrowly. The European Commission's art. 29 Working Party on data protection has stated:

> It should be borne in mind that 'damage' in the sense of the data protection directive includes not only physical damage and financial loss, but also any psychological or moral harm caused (know as 'distress' under UK and US law).[62]

Whether the government's interpretation is non-compliant, or whether such issues of restitution are beyond the competence of EU law, may have to be resolved before the European Court of Justice.

It should also be noted that a data subject may have a right to take the government to court for a failure to protect an individual's rights under the Directive, and this could rise to a compensatory award.[63] Alternatively, where the data controller is a 'public authority', an action could be brought under the Human Rights Act 1998.[64]

The 1984 Act gave data subjects the right to apply to the courts for an order requiring a data controller to rectify or erase inaccurate data. The 1998 Act extends this to rectification, erasure, destruction and blocking of incomplete and inaccurate data (s. 14).

The Directive also requires that data subjects be given the right to 'obtain from' data controllers notification to third parties, to whom data have been disclosed, of any rectification erasure and blocking, unless this is impossible or involves a 'disproportionate effort' (art. 12(c)). However, the 1998 Act has qualified this provision. Imposition upon a data controller of an obligation to notify third parties lies within either the discretion of the court, or an enforcement notice issued by the Commissioner, but not with the data subject. This would seem to be potentially non-compliant with the Directive.

An important new right for data subjects, beyond the requirements of the Directive, is the issue of enforced subject access. This is the practice whereby potential employees ask individuals to supply them with a copy of their criminal record, obtained through the exercise of the individual's subject access right to the Police National Computer. The Registrar has indicated her disapproval of such practices, but was unable to prevent them under the 1984

---

62. Working Document, 'Judging industry self-regulation: When does it make a meaningful contribution to the level of data protection in a third country?', Adopted by the Working Party on 14 January 1998.

63. E.g., Case C-6, 9/90, *Francovich and Others* v *Italy* [1991] ECR 1-5357.

64. Human Rights Act 1998, s. 6(1): 'it is unlawful for a public authority to act in a way which is incompatible with a Convention right'. Section 8 states that a court may grant 'such relief or remedy, or make such order, within its powers as it considers just and appropriate', including an award of damages (subject to a general limitation that the principles applied by the European Court of Human Rights must be taken into account (s. 8(4)). In *Gaskin* v *United Kingdom*, 12 EHRR 36, the court awarded £5000 as compensation for non-pecuniary injury in respect of emotional distress and anxiety (paras 57–58), even though the claim for pecuniary damage was rejected.

Act.[65] The government's White Paper announced its intention to prohibit such practices and the 1998 Act creates an offence where the requirement relates to criminal records, prison records and DSS records (s. 56). Where 'health records' are concerned any contractual term requiring the provision of such information is rendered void (s. 57). The offence contains the following features:

(a)   The data subject has to have been required to provide the information, rather than such information being requested.

(b)   It applies in only certain types of situations: employment, placing of contracts and the provision of goods, facilities or services to the public.

(c)   Defences exist where the requirement was authorised by law, or was in the public interest.[66]

However, the offence will not be brought into operation until ss. 112, 113 and 115 of the Police Act 1997 have been brought into force. These provisions provide for the establishment of a criminal records agency to issue 'criminal record certificates'. These certificates will provide an alternative mechanism for the obtaining of criminal conviction data and, therefore, the practice of enforced subject access will be allowed to continue until the new system has been established.

13.4.7   Exemptions

Three broad categories of exemption are provided for in the Data Protection Act 1998:

(a)   General exemptions, e.g., processing of personal data for reasons of national security.

(b)   Exemptions from the 'subject information provisions', under s. 7 and the information obligations under the first data protection principle, e.g., crime and taxation.

(c)   Exemptions from the 'non-disclosure provisions', e.g., data made public under enactment (s. 34) or required by law or in connection with legal proceedings.

The latter two categories may obviously overlap.

One of the most significant new exemptions relates to personal data processed for the 'special purposes', defined under s. 3 of the Act as the purposes of journalism, artistic purposes and literary purposes. This exemption arises from art. 9 of Directive 95/46/EC, which stresses the need to

---

65. See Data Protection Registrar's Guidance Note 21, 'The use of the subject access provisions of the Data Protection Act to check the criminal records of applicants for jobs or licences', GN21-JB-3/89; see also The Tenth Report of the Data Protection Registrar (June 1994), Appendix 2.

66. The public interest defence does not include the prevention or detection of crime, due to the Police Act 1997 (Data Protection Act 1998, s. 56(4)).

balance the right of privacy against the need to protect freedom of express-ion.[67] However, it also reflects wider government policy, which places a high priority upon the protection of freedom of expression and a clear intention not to allow data protection laws to risk such freedom. This exemption is also be affected by the Human Rights Act 1998.

Data processed for a 'special purpose' will be exempt from compliance with certain of the Act's requirements, including the data protection principles, the subject access right, and the right of rectification, blocking, erasure and destruction. However, these exemptions will only operate where all of the following conditions apply:

(a)   The processing is *only* for one or more of the 'special purposes'.
(b)   The processing is 'with a view to publication'.
(c)   The data controller 'reasonably believes' that publication is in the public interest, 'having regard in particular to the special importance of freedom of expression'.[68]
(d)   The data controller 'reasonably believes' that compliance with the exempted provisions would be incompatible with the 'special purposes'.

The data controller will be concerned to ensure that it maintains appropri-ate records in the event that reliance on the exemption was challenged.

Where a data subject commences civil proceedings against a data control-ler, the controller can raise a defence based on this exemption. In such an event, the court would be obliged to stay the proceedings pending a determination by the Commissioner whether the processing is only for the special purposes or with a view to publication. The Data Protection Registrar has strongly criticised the complexity of the mechanism by which this exemption will operate, since it shifts the burden of proof between the various parties and could provide the data controller with a legitimate mechanism to delay proceedings for an unnecessary period of time.

Research data may be exempt from the subject access provisions. The research exemption includes data held for 'statistical and historical purposes'. As with the 'special purpose' exemption, certain conditions must exist:

(a)   the data are not to be processed 'to support measures or decisions with respect to particular individuals'; and
(b)   'substantial' damage or distress must not be, or be likely to be, caused (collectively referred to as the 'relevant conditions'); and
(c)   the research results 'are not made available in a form which identifies data subjects'.

---

67. See Recommendation 1/97, 'Data protection law and the media', of the art. 29 Working Party (note 37, above).
68. An assessment of whether such a belief was reasonable will take into account any relevant, or designated, code of practice (Data Protection Act 1998, s. 32(3)), e.g., Press Complaints Commission Code of Practice, see The Data Protection (Designated Codes of Practice) Order, SI 418/2000.

Under the Directive, the processing of data for purely domestic purposes is considered outside of the scope of its application. The Act provides that data controllers processing personal data 'only for the purposes of that individual's personal, family or household affairs (including recreational purposes)' are exempt from the data protection principles, the rights of data subjects (pt. II) or the notification obligations (pt. III). However, they may be subject to an 'information notice' or 'special information notice' issued by the Commissioner.

For private sector data controllers, the most important new exemptions concern:

(a) 'Confidential references' given or to be given for the purposes of either (a) the education, training or employment, or prospective education, training or employment of the data subject, (b) the appointment or prospective employment of the data subject to an office, or (c) the provision or prospective provision of a service by the data subject.[69]

(b) Processing for the 'purposes of management forecasting or management planning'.

(c) Processing relating to the provision of a 'corporate finance service'.

(d) Processing 'of records of the intentions of the data controller in relation to any negotiations with the data subject' (sch. 7).

Management forecasting and planning is not defined, which leaves data controllers with a potentially broad, although uncertain, scope to withhold information. However, under both the management and negotiation exemptions, the data controller will need to show that providing subject access 'would be likely to prejudice' the activities in question.

13.4.8 Enforcement

The Data Protection Act 1998 creates or gives rise to the possibility of criminal prosecution under five different categories of offence:

(a) Processing without notification.
(b) Notification information must be accurate.
(c) Failure to comply with a notice.
(d) Unlawful obtaining or procurement of data.
(e) Requiring the provision of certain records.

These offences can be further divided into offences of strict or absolute liability; and those which require the data user to have acted 'knowingly or recklessly.[70]

---

69. The recipient of the reference would be subject to the Data Protection Act 1998, s. 7(4), regarding 'information relating to another individual', e.g., references given in confidence could not be disclosed.

70. See *Data Protection Registrar* v *Amnesty International (British Section)*, *The Times*, 23 November 1994, for an interpretation of the concept of 'recklessness'. See also [1995] Crim LR 633.

In addition, under s. 61 of the Act, as well as the company being prosecuted for an offence, a 'director, manager, secretary or similar officer' can also be found personally liable, where the offence was committed with 'the consent or connivance of or to be attributable to any neglect on the part' of any such individual.

Under the Data Protection Act 1984, the vast majority of prosecutions were brought against data controllers who have failed to register or to renew their registration. In 1996, in *R v Brown* [1996] 1 All ER 545, the House of Lords gave an important judgment on the interpretation of the word 'use' in s. 5(2)(b) of the Act:

A person in respect of whom such an entry is contained in the register shall not ... (b) hold any such data, or use any such data held by him, for any purpose other than the purpose described in the entry ....

The case involved a police officer who was also associated with a debt collection agency. It was alleged that, on two occasions, he obtained information from the police national computer relating to the ownership of certain cars relating to two debtors being pursued by the agency. On the first occasion, the car was owned by a company, and therefore no personal data was retrieved. In the second, no evidence was shown that he had made subsequent use of the information retrieved. He was charged on two counts, one of improper use and attempted improper use in contravention of s. 5(2)(b) of the 1984 Act. At his first trial he was found guilty, and he appealed to the Court of Appeal. They upheld his appeal and the case then came before the House of Lords.

The central issue before the Lords was whether the retrieval of personal data onto a screen constituted 'use' under the Act. The Lords decided, by a three-to-two majority, that the natural and ordinary meaning of the word 'use' should be adopted. 'Use' was therefore seen to require some element of subsequent use, which could not be shown to have taken place in this case. Lord Griffiths, dissenting, argued that a broad construction should be taken otherwise the purpose of the Act would not be achieved: to protect an individual's right to privacy.[71] The decision was seen as a serious limitation in the protection afforded by the 1984 Act.

Under the 1984 Act, a number of appeals against 'enforcement notices' were made by data users to the Data Protection Tribunal. Of these cases, the most interesting concerned the credit reference industry and the utility industry.

The former Registrar was in a long-running dispute with the four United Kingdom credit reference agencies concerning the definition of what information it is 'fair' for the agencies to consider when assessing a persons eligibility for credit. In particular, the Registrar had been concerned over the use of information relating to past residents of a person's accommodation. In *CCN Systems Ltd v Data Protection Registrar* (25 February 1991) case DA/90

---

71. *R v Brown* [1996] 1 All ER 545, at p. 554, paras. g–j.

25/49/9 the Registrar had issued an enforcement notice to the appellants, requiring them to cease to provide information relating to applicants for credit that was based purely on their address. The practice of CCN and other credit reference agencies was to provide not only details of the applicant's credit record, but also details of others (whether they bear the same name or not) who formerly or subsequently resided at the applicant's current or previous address. CCN appealed against this notice on the ground that the processing they undertook was not unfair.

The case was concerned primarily with the issue of what is 'fair processing'. The question was whether the processing undertaken by the appellants extracted data which were *relevant* to the decision whether to grant credit. CCN argued that such data were relevant to the credit decision because, on the statistical evidence present, adverse information against third parties at the same address increased the likelihood *in the aggregate* that applicants in that category would default on the loan. On the other hand, the Registrar argued that the proper test was whether the information was relevant *to the particular applicant*, and it was clear that for any individual case such third party information did not generally increase the risk of default. In coming to its judgment on this point, the tribunal held:

> In our view, in deciding whether the processing ... is fair we must give first and paramount consideration to the interests of the applicant for credit — the 'data subject' in the Act's terms. We are not ignoring the consequences for the credit industry of a finding of unfairness, and we sympathise with their problems, but we believe that they will accept that they must carry on their activities in accordance with the principles laid down in the Act of Parliament.

The tribunal therefore held that CCN's processing was unfair in this respect, and disallowed the appeal on that point. It was particularly influenced by the fact that in some cases the inquirer never saw the raw data, and thus had no opportunity to make a separate assessment of their relevance, because CCN offered a number of credit scoring systems which gave the inquirer only a credit score, based in part on this third party information.

However, the Tribunal did hold that the enforcement notice had been too wide, as certain types of third party information would be relevant and thus fairly extracted if there was a clear connection with the applicant for credit. The enforcement notice was therefore amended so as to permit the extraction of certain types of third party information, such as individuals who have the same surname.

The most important principle to be extracted from this judgment is that 'fairness' must always be assessed in relation to the data subject. The mere fact that such processing is to the advantage of the data user is not a relevant consideration.[72]

---

72. See further Data Protection Registrar's Guidance Note 27, 'Views of the Data Protection Registrar concerning the revised enforcement notices issued against four credit reference agencies by the Data Protection Tribunal (February, 1993).

Enforcement notices have also been issued against companies in the gas and electricity industries. In *British Gas Trading Ltd* v *Data Protection Registrar* (24 March 1998),[73] the Registrar took action against the gas supplier over the use of its customer data for marketing purposes. The Data Protection Tribunal was required to consider whether such processing was both unlawful and unfair, in breach of the first principle.

On the issue of lawfulness, the Registrar has stated that processing requires that '. . . a data user must comply with all relevant rules of law, whether derived from statute or common law . . .'.[74] The Tribunal was therefore asked to consider whether such processing could be considered unlawful by virtue of either (a) a statutory limitation on use of the data rendering the processing *ultra vires*, (b) breach of an implied contractual provision, or (c) breach of an equitable obligation of confidence between British Gas and its customers. The Tribunal held that none of these obligations were present and, therefore, the processing was not unlawful.

On the issue of fair processing, two key issues arose. First, with respect to whether customers had been appropriately informed that their data would be used for marketing purposes, the Tribunal held that it was not unfair to process customer data for marketing gas and gas-related products, including electricity, since it may be considered 'reasonably obvious' to customers that their personal data may be used in that way. However, disclosure of such data to third parties for marketing purposes would not be fair. Second, British Gas provided customers with the opportunity to 'opt-out' of having their data used for marketing purposes, through the use of a separate form sent with customers bills. On this issue the Tribunal held that it would be unfair for British Gas to imply consent from a customers failure to return this opt-out form, since customers would have to positively send the form back to British Gas even though they may pay their bill through another mechanism (e.g., their bank) which does not require communication with British Gas. As subsequently stated by the Registrar:

> The fact that the data subject must 'signify' their agreement means that there must be some active communication between the parties. Data controllers cannot infer consent from non-response to a communication, for example from a customer's failure to return or respond to a leaflet.[75]

13.5 CONCLUSION

Data protection law became a high-profile political issue during the late 1970s and early 1980s, as European countries began to adopt legislation and companies voiced fears that the spread of such laws would act as an obstacle

---

73. See also *Midlands Electricity plc* v *Data Protection Registrar* (7 May 1999), http:// www.open.gov.uk/dpr/ or the *Encyclopedia of Data Protection*, note 40, above.
74. See Data Protection Registrar's Guideline 4, 'The Data Protection Principles' (Third Series, November 1994) at para. 1.18.
75. Data Protection Registrar, *An Introduction to the Data Protection Act 1998*, October 1998, at ch. 3, section 1.6.

to the international flow of data, even as a deterrent to the adoption of computer systems altogether. Reality, particularly in the age of the Internet, would suggest that such fears were unfounded. However, the adoption and implementation of the EU data protection Directive has given new life to the debate. Currently, a trade row is brewing between the EU and the United States over the extent to which US companies can avoid potential restrictions on international data flows by agreeing to abide by a set of self-regulatory principles.[76]

When the first national data protection law was passed in Sweden in 1973, the major privacy fears were generated through the use of large mainframe computers. Currently, it is developments such as the Internet, CCTV and the use of genetic data which are some of the major areas of concern. Such rapid technological change renders data protection law vulnerable to an accusation of obsolescence. However, the promotion of general principles of good information practice, together with an independent supervisory regime, should enable the law to maintain sufficient flexibility to achieve an appropriate balance between the need to protect the rights of individuals to control how data about them is used, and the needs of an increasingly networked economy.

---

76. See the 'Safe-harbor' initiative issued by the US Department of Commerce (November 1999): www.doc.gov. See also Opinion 7/99 (3 December 1999) of the art. 29 Working Party (note 37, above).

CHAPTER FOURTEEN

European Computer Law

Tim Cowen and Justine Campbell

14.1 INTRODUCTION AND KEY DEVELOPMENTS

14.1.1 The 1992 legislative program

A great deal has been written on the national aspects of computer law, but comparatively little is available on the European aspects of procuring, selling and distributing computers and computing equipment. Nonetheless, these aspects have become more and more important, particularly in the context of the 1992 program of European legislation aimed at completing the single market and the recently-announced program intended to enhance the Information Society. All of these legislative developments need to be seen in the context of the following underlying aims of the Treaty of Rome:

(a) To abolish the proliferation of differences between national computer laws and nationalistic purchasing practices, which act as disguised barriers to free trade (arts 28, 49–55 and 94).[1]

(b) Following the abolition of these barriers, to ensure free and open competition through the application of European Communittee (EC) competition law (arts 81–89).

(c) To support the development of a single internal market (art. 95).

(d) To promote a common commercial policy in the relations of the European Economic Communittee (EEC) to non-Member States (art. 133).

---

1. Unless otherwise described, all of the Treaty article numbers in this chapter reflect the amendments resulting from the entering into force of the Treaty of Amsterdam on 1 May 1999.

These objectives were to be realised step by step following the publication of the Commission's White Paper in 1985.[2] In that Paper, the Commission presented an extensive programme for the completion of the single internal market by 31 December 1992. The intention was that by that date, all restrictions on the free movement of goods, persons, services and capital within the European Community should be eliminated.[3]

This ambitious programme could only be realised with the aid of the Single European Act (SEA), which came into force on 1 July 1987.[4] The SEA amended the Treaty of Rome. One of the major changes was to clear the log-jam of legislation on which agreement had not been reached in the Council of Ministers. The SEA achieved this by changing the voting rules so that, under art. 100a (now 95) more legislation could be enacted by a qualified majority of Member States rather than by unanimity.[5] The Maastricht Treaty creating the European Union (EU) built on this process of gradual integration of the Member States, and the progress towards a single currency and common security, defence and foreign policy continues at the time of writing. The Treaty introduced a more complex co-decision procedure for harmonisation measures.

As part of its 1992 initiative the EC authorities took a number of initiatives to harmonise computer law within Europe. Amongst the most important were:

(a)   The Council Directive on the Approximation of the Laws, Regulations and Administrative Provisions of the Member States Concerning Liability for Defective Products as amended by Directive 1999/34/EC of the European Parliament and of the Council of 10 May 1999.[6]

(b)   The Council Directive on the Protection of Semiconductor Product Designs issued on 16 December 1986.[7]

(c)   The Council Directive on Approximation of Trade Mark Laws.[8]

(d)   The Council Directive on the Legal Protection of Computer Programs adopted by the Council of Ministers on 14 May 1991.[9]

(e)   The Council Directive Concerning the Protection of Individuals in Relation to the Processing of Personal Data adopted on 24 October 1995.[10]

---

2. For a more detailed discussion of this development see Corinna M. Wissels. 'European Community Law' in A.P. Meijboom and C. Prins (eds), *The Law of Information Technology in Europe*, Deventer: 1991, p. 3 *et seq.*

3. The majority of the measures proposed for completion of the Single Market have now been enacted, though additional measures appear from time to time as part of the process of fine tuning the market. Up-to-date information can be found on the European Commission's WWW server, http://europe.eu.int/.

4. Single European Act, OJ L169, 1987.

5. See P. Pescatore, 'Some Critical Remarks on the Single European Act' 24 *CML Rev* 19; J. Lodge, 'The Single European Act: towards a New Euro-dynamism' (1986) 24 *Journal of Common Market Studies* 203.

6. 85/374/EEC, OJ L210, 7 August, 1985, pp. 0029–0033.

7. 87/54/EEC, OJ L24, 27 January 1987, p. 36.

8. 89/104/EEC OJ L40, 11 February 1989, p. 1.

9. 91/250/EEC OJ L122, 17 May 1991, p. 42.

10. 95/46/EEC OJ L281, p. 31.

(f)   The Council Directive on the Legal Protection of Databases.[11]

The 1992 programme now affects both the EC and the European Free Trade Area (EFTA) Member States, since the creation of the European Economic Area (EEA) on 2 May 1992. EFTA States will now implement EC regulations into national law in the same way as EC Member States. Some of the former EFTA States have become full members of the EU.

Before the 1992 programme of legislation, Member States often did not comply with their fundamental Treaty obligations, and supplementary regulations were needed to supplement these obligations. The 1992 program of legislation was created to achieve this aim. The fundamental Treaty rules are addressed briefly below. Where relevant the specific regulations are referred to, and other chapters of this book provide greater detail on the specific regulations. This chapter is primarily concerned with the following areas:

(a)   The free trade provisions of the EC Treaty and the basic obligations on governments and government bodies to purchase from any EC supplier.

(b)   The competition rules which apply to ensure that barriers to free trade are not re-erected by agreements between businesses, and which impose obligations on all concerned in the sale and distribution of computer products throughout the Community.

14.1.2   The 1999 Communication on the single market

In November 1999, the Commission adopted a Communication setting out its strategy for the internal market over the next five years.[12] The Communication notes those single market objectives which have not been particularly successful to date, including:

(a)   Slow progress on a single market patent development.
(b)   Remaining barriers to free movement from lack of tax harmonisation.
(c)   State aid expenditure, which continues to distort the single market.

The main objectives of the new strategy include:

(a)   Enhancing the efficiency of the EU's product and capital markets: The Commission has specified a number of priority targets, including establishing a dialogue with industry and consumers to develop an integrated framework for electronic commerce (see below), developing proposals for a Community patent and for a directive on the patentability of software before June 2000; and developing proposals for legislation announced in the recent review of Telecommunications Legislation.

(b)   Improving the business environment: The Commission also aims to remove all remaining barriers to free trade and free movement of goods,

---

11. 96/9 EEC OJ L77, 27 March 1996, p. 20.
12. Communication from the Commission to the European Parliament and the Council, COM 1999 (464), Brussels, 5 October 1999.

services and persons by introducing measures to modernise excise duty and VAT legislation, and by pressing for effective implementation by all Member States of internal market directives.

The targets outlined by the Commission are intended to be updated annually.

14.1.3 Electronic commerce

Another essential priority recognised in the Commission's action plan is the need to adapt the single market framework to new challenges and opportunities such as electronic commerce (e-commerce). The Commission's intention is to propose legislative initiatives and non-legislative initiatives to meet these priorities.

It is predicted that the European on-line market is estimated to reach 45 billion Euros in revenue by 2002.[13] E-commerce in Europe in general faces certain difficulties not faced by the United States, particularly its lack of homogeneity, with vast differences in development stages between Member States which were early adopters of the internet boom (e.g., Scandinavian countries) and many smaller Member States with considerably further to go in ensuring mass internet access.

This diversity has limited the ability of local operators to expand beyond national borders and European on-line retailers have generally taken narrower focuses, generating the majority of their sales in their home markets. In addition, exports are very low. The EU is trying to encourage the development of e-commerce across Europe for all European citizens and to strengthen the competitive position of European e-business when compared to the United States.

The Commission has set itself a very ambitious agenda to aim to push through all the e-commerce legislation by the end of 2000 in order to help the EU to catch up with the United States on the Internet economy. The Commission has committed to implement directives on copyright, distance selling of financial services, electronic money, e-commerce, the Brussels and Rome Conventions that cover contractual law, and an on-line disputes settlement procedure for e-commerce. In addition, the EU hopes to set up a new 'dot' EU domain for Internet addresses.

14.2 THE FREEDOM TO TRADE THROUGHOUT THE EUROPEAN UNION

Perhaps the most important amendment to national laws governing the information technology industry, and which led to a degree of harmonisation of those laws, derives from the Treaty of Rome itself. Articles 30 (now 28) and 59 (now 49) to 66 (now 55) of the Treaty abolished disguised barriers to free trade within the European Community.

---

13. Boston Consulting Group, 'The race for on-line riches — e-retailing in Europe'.

The Treaty established a customs union in which duties were eliminated between Member States and a common customs tariff was adopted in trade relations with non-EEC Member States. As a customs union, the free-movement provisions concerning both goods and services apply not only to goods originating within the Community, but also to products which have entered the Community from non-member countries, once those products are in 'free circulation' within a single Member State. A substantial percentage of computer products or components are manufactured outside the Community. Once these products have lawfully[14] entered the Community, in their subsequent trade between Member States it is possible to rely on the free-movement provisions to the same extent as if those goods had originated within the Community.[15]

The origin of products may, however, be of significance if a Member State invokes art. 134, which may entitle it to prevent the free circulation of goods from another Member State. Substantial investment into the EC from Far Eastern companies occurred during the 1980s and early 1990s and some of the resulting products may be affected by these rules. The basic rule that defines the origin of goods was in Regulation 802/68, now repealed by Council Regulation 2913/92 of 12 October 1992 establishing the Community Customs Code. This provides that a product that is wholly obtained or produced in one country originates there. Goods produced in two or more countries are regarded as originating in the country where the last substantial process or operation that is economically justified was performed, having been carried out by an undertaking equipped for the purpose, and resulting in the manufacture of a new product or representing an important stage in manufacture.

In practice, a Community transit system has been introduced to facilitate internal Community transit and external Community transit (an exporter must make a 'T1' declaration for exports, whereas a 'T2' declaration is used for internal Community transit where the goods are in free circulation).

14.2.1 Measures which restrict the free movement of goods

Lifting the barriers to free trade may prompt a Member State to protect its national (domestic) industry. One mechanism for restricting the extent to which overseas competition may compete with domestic industry is to impose disguised restrictions on non-domestic goods. Such restrictions are abolished under art. 28 of the Treaty. Article 28 has been interpreted very widely and any measure which affects trade in goods between Members States may fall within its prohibition. Measures such as labelling or origin-marking, differing product standards, import licences or 'buy national campaigns' can fall within art. 28. Directive 70/50/EEC[16] provides guidance on those measures which

---

14. EEC Treaty, art. 24, which requires import formalities to have been complied with and customs duties or charges having equivalent effect to have been levied without reimbursement of such duties or charges.
15. Regulation 802/68, OJ English Sp. Ed. 1968 (I), p. 15.
16. OJ Sp. Ed. 1970 (I), p. 17 (technically only applies to measures in force at the end of the transitional period, which has now ended). Referred to by the European Court of Justice in *Torfaen Borough Council* v *B & Q plc* (case 145/88) [1990] 2 QB 19.

can be regarded as infringing art. 28. The European Court of Justice had widened the scope of art. 28 to encompass 'all trading rules enacted by member States which are capable of injuring directly or indirectly, actually or potentially, intra-Community trade'.[17] It is of no consequence that the trading rules in question are applicable to both imports and products which have been produced domestically if the *effect* is to discriminate against imports. Products which can be valued in money and which are capable of forming the subject of commercial transactions will be regarded as 'goods' under art. 28. This is a wide definition and may encompass products, which in other areas of law would be regarded as services.[18] It is likely, although undecided, that computer software would be regarded as 'goods' if transported around the Community on disk or some other form of hardware (including firm-ware). However, if the software is used for providing a service between Member States such as an e-mail service or a remote data-processing service, it may be more appropriate to seek to rely on the equivalent rules concerned with the freedom to provide services under arts 49 to 55 of the Treaty (see section 14.2.3 for further discussion).

14.2.2 Exceptions and limitations

Article 30 of the EC Treaty permits government or government authority to impose or maintain restrictions in breach of art. 28 on the grounds of:

(a) public morality;
(b) public policy or public security;
(c) protection of health and life of humans, animals or plants;
(d) protection of national treasures possessing artistic, historic or archae-ological value; or
(e) protection of industrial and commercial property.

In addition, there is an obligation imposed on the government bodies concerned that any exemptions to the principles of free movement should not constitute a means of arbitrary discrimination or a disguised restriction on trade. Exemptions to the free movement rules are to be restrictively interpreted and measures taken should not be disproportionate to their objective. Once the Community authorities have issued harmonising measures, it becomes impossible for a government body to rely on an equivalent national law to justify restrictive conduct. However, the European Court of Justice has recognised certain further grounds for excluding goods from particular territories. In particular, it has recognised the following as potential justifications for restrictions on the free movement of goods:

---

17. *Procureur du Roi* v *Dassonville* (case 8/74) [1974] ECR 837 at p. 852. In some recent cases the European Court of Justice appears to have qualified the broad interpretation of art. 28 given above. See *Keck* (cases C-267 and 268/91) [1995] 1 CMLR 101 and *Punto Cas* v *Sindaco* (cases C-69 and 258/93 [1994] 1 ECR 2355).
18. *Commission* v *Italy* (case 7/68) [1968] ECR 423.

(a)   fiscal supervision;
(b)   public health;
(c)   fairness of commercial transactions;
(d)   protection of the consumer;
(e)   environmental protection.[19]

14.2.3   Freedom to provide services: article 49

Article 49 of the Treaty guarantees, as a general rule, the freedom to provide crossborder services. In *Italy* v *Sacchi* (case 155/73) [1974] ECR 409 the European Court of Justice held that a television signal should be regarded as a provision of services. It is likely that transborder computer services or telecommunications services would be regarded as services falling within the definition of art. 50. Indeed this is the basis for the Commission's Directive (90/388/EEC) on telecommunication services liberalisation. Such services must be provided for remuneration and must not fall within the rules concerning the free movement of goods, capital or persons.

In order to rely on the free movement of services provisions contained in the Treaty a national must be 'established' in one of the EC Member States. This may normally be accomplished by setting up a company.

Article 49 is subject to limitations, which may be invoked by member States or government bodies on the grounds of:

(a)   activities concerned with the exercise of official authority (art. 44);
(b)   public policy, public security or public health (art. 46);
(c)   non-economic public interest exceptions, e.g., where copyright owners have 'performance' rights in the services concerned.

14.2.4   Public procurement

Public bodies are the biggest purchasers of information technology in most parts of Europe. The prohibitions contained in arts 28 and 49 of the EEC Treaty are the bases for the specific public procurement rules. In its 1985 White Paper, the Commission identified concerns about the purchasing practices of government bodies.[20] In summary, these concerns were:

(a)   The authorities concerned purchased on a national basis which led to the continued partitioning of national markets contrary to the single market objective.

---

19. The 'mandatory requirements' which may provide a basis for a Member State to justify a restriction on the freedom of movement of goods were originally identified in *Rewe-Zentral AG* v *Bundesmonopolverwaltung für Branntwein* (case 120/78) [1979] ECR 649. Environmental protection was recognised in *Commission* v *Denmark* (case 302/86) [1988] ECR 4607.
20. See International Institute for Legal and Administrative Technology, *Public Procurement*, Cologne: 1990, p. 14 *et seq.*; Brechon and Moulenes, *Les Marchés Publics Européens* (Droit Communautaire, droit comparé), Dossiers et documents de la Revue française de Droit administrative, Paris: 1989, pp. 37–69.

(b)   The EEC Treaty as a whole, and arts 28 and 49 in particular, lays down basic rules, which mean that discrimination by governments and government bodies in favour of national suppliers is illegal. However, these rules were ignored in practice.

A particular example of such discrimination occurred when the Dundalk Urban District Council required all tenders for the construction of a water main to comply with Irish standards. Only one company had obtained such approval and, perhaps unsurprisingly, that was an Irish company. A Spanish manufacturer tendering pipes which met an equivalent international standard, complained to the Commission, which took Ireland to the European Court of Justice, where Ireland was held to have breached art. 28.[21] This case demonstrates the application of the underlying Treaty rules. However, specific rules that supplement the Treaty have now been created so that the rules are more widely observed.[22] The following have now been adopted:

(a)   The Council Directive of 17 December 1969 on the Supply of Goods to the State and other Authorities.[23]
(b)   The Council Directive of 21 December 1976 on the Coordination of Procedures for the Award of Public Supply Contracts.[24]
(c)   The Council Directive of 22 March 1988 amending Directive 77/62/EEC relating to the Coordination of Procedures on the Award of Public Supply Contracts and repealing certain provisions of Directive 80/767/EEC.[25]
(d)   The Council Directive of 14 June 1993 Coordinating Procedures for the Award of Public Supply Contracts.[26]
(e)   The Council Directive of 21 December 1989 on the Coordination of the Laws, Regulations and Administrative Provisions Relating to the Application of Review Procedures to the Award of Public Supply and Public Works Contracts.[27]

14.2.4.1   Applicability of the Directives   The Public Supply Directives apply to all public supply contracts of a value of at least 200,000 Euros. The sectors of telecommunications, energy, transport and water were expressly excluded. A separate Directive (90/53/EEC) was issued to cover the sectors excluded from the previous regime and has become known as the 'excluded sectors Directive'. It is concerned with both supplies and works, and applies the EC procurement rules to the telecommunications, energy, transport and water sectors from 1 January 1993.

---

21. *Commission* v *Ireland* (case 45/87) [1988] ECR 4929.
22. See Elke Schmitz, *Das Recht der öffentlichen Aufträge im Gemeinsamen Markt*, Baden-Baden: 1972, p. 128 *et seq.*
23. Directive 70/32/EEC, OJ L13, 19 January 1970, p. 1.
24. Directive 77/62/EEC, OJ L13 of 15 January 1977, p. 1.
25. Directive 88/295/EEC, OJ L 127, 20 May 1988, p. 1.
26. Directive 93/36/EEC, OJ L 199, 9 August 1993, pp. 1–53.
27. Directive 89/665/EEC, OJ L395 of 30 December 1989, p. 33.

14.2.4.2 Main elements   The Directives state that public bodies have generally to award their supply contracts by open tendering, i.e., tendering which
is open to all interested suppliers. Selective tendering or negotiations with
chosen suppliers are only lawful in some special circumstances described in
the Directives; the use of these procedures must be justified by the public
body in a report. This choice of open tendering is contrary to previous
practice in the United Kingdom, which has been to award the bulk of
contracts by selective tendering.[28]
   The Directives additionally stress the importance of transparency. Public
bodies are required to publish announcements of an award in the Official
Journal of the EC. Furthermore, they have to announce their award decisions
and the total sum of expected purchases for the year.

14.2.4.3 Public telecommunications contracts   As mentioned above, the Directives on public supply contracts do not apply to telecommunications. This
exemption proved to be unsatisfactory so the EC authorities created a
separate Directive to deal with public telecommunications contracts.[29]
   This Directive applies to all public bodies' contracts for telecommunication
products (including software) and services; the relevant threshold is 600,000
Euros. Contracting entities have to define technical specifications by reference
to European standards; they are free to choose open, selective or negotiated
tendering procedures. In addition, they have to publish a list of their total
anticipated procurement during the next 12 months. The Directive allows the
bodies to which it applies, which are known as 'contracting entities', to
maintain approved lists of contractors competent to carry out particular work.
The contract has to be awarded to the tenderer who submitted the lowest
assessed tender, i.e., the tenderer whose tender offers the best overall value for
money. According to the Directive, the contracting entities may refuse to
award a tender on the grounds of non-EC origin under certain circumstances.

14.2.4.4 Council Decision 87/95/EEC   On 22 December 1986, the Council
announced its Decision on standardisation in the field of information technology and telecommunications.[30] This Decision calls for the mandatory use
of European and international standards by public sector authorities. Contracts for information systems of value above 100,000 Euros must refer to
these standards. This obligation is not binding upon orders concerning
'innovative' systems or if an adherence to the standards would lead to an
'uneconomic solution'.
   The Decision is binding upon the EC Member States, which have to
transform it into national law. In March 1988 a number of function standards

---

28. International Institute for Legal and Administrative Technology, *Public Procurement*,
    Cologne: 1990, p. 81 *et seq.*
29. Council Directive on Public Procurement in the Sectors of Water, Energy, Transport and
    Telecommunications, 90/351/EEC, OJ L297, 25 October 1990, p. 1. There is also a second
    Directive on coordination of public procurement regulations with regard to these four
    sectors: Council Directive 93/38/EEC OJ L199, 9 August 1993, p. 84.
30. Decision 87/95/EEC, OJ L36, 7 February 1987, p. 31.

were published by the UK Central Computer and Telecommunications Agency (CCTA) which are now used as mandatory standards under Decision 87/95/EEC.

14.2.5 EC law remedies

According to the Remedies Directive (89/665/EEC) of 21 December 1989, the Member States have to set up a judicial or administrative authority, which examines alleged infringements against the EC public procurement regulations. This authority must be able:

(a) to suspend the award procedure;
(b) to cancel unlawful decisions;
(c) to order the removal of discriminatory specifications; and
(d) to grant damages to injured parties.

In addition to the Remedies Directive (89/665/EEC), arts 28 and 49 of the Treaty may be relied upon in national courts and it is possible to complain to the European Commission to ensure that the national authority complies with the Member State's treaty obligations. This may provide an effective practical remedy where, for example, a supplier considers he has been discriminated against as a result of the nationalistic purchasing practices of the government authority or where a supplier suffers from some other form of discrimination by government authorities.

In *Francovich* v *Italy* (cases C-6 and 9/90) [1991] ECR I5357, the European Court of Justice held that directly effective provisions (such as arts 28 and 49) may be relied upon by individuals against the State. It also reviewed the issue of State liability and held that the principle of Member State liability for damage resulting from infringements of Community law was inherent in the EEC Treaty. Some uncertainty still remains over the full extent of a Member State's liability, but, following *Brasserie du Pêcheur SA* v *Germany* (cases C-46 and 48/93 [1996] QB 404 and *R* v *HM Treasury, ex parte British Telecommunications plc* (case C-392/93) [1996] 3 WLR 203, it is clear that it is possible to claim damages against a Member State for its failure to observe its Treaty obligations, including arts 28 and 49. This might be of considerable importance in the context of the public procurement regime as an additional weapon against a Member State body such as a local authority.

14.3 EC COMPETITION LAW

The objects of EC competition law can be regarded as twofold. Article 3 of the EC Treaty provides that:

> For the purposes set out in art. 2, the activities of the Community shall include, as provided in this Treaty and in accordance with the timetable set out therein:

(a)   the elimination, as between Member States, of customs duties and of quantitative restrictions on the import and export of goods, and of all other measures having equivalent effect; . . .
(b)   the institution of a system ensuring that competition in the common market is not distorted.

The European Court of Justice has held that the competition rules should be construed in the light of the aims and intentions expressed in these provisions. The first aim is to preserve and create unrestricted competition between businesses as a stimulant to economic activity. The Treaty recognises, and there is a presumption in favour of, a 'free market' economic policy.[31]

The second intention is that the economic benefits of the market should be available to all, and that the market should truly be regarded as a 'common' market, or to adopt more recent terminology, a 'single' market. The second intention is that competition policy should be used as a method of prohibiting agreements which create obstacles to trade between Member States. The aim of provisions such as arts. 28 and 49 of the EEC Treaty was to abolish government restrictions on the movement of goods and services across Member States' borders. The competition rules strike down agreements which attempt to divide markets or re-erect such barriers to trade.

14.3.1   EC Treaty competition rules

Articles 81 to 89 of the EEC Treaty are the principal Treaty provisions which contain the competition rules. The broad scheme of these provisions is as follows:

Article 81 prohibits all agreements and restrictive practices, decisions by associations of undertakings and concerted practices which may affect trade and which have as their object or effect the prevention, restriction or distortion of competition within the Community.

Article 82 prohibits all abuses of 'dominant' or 'monopoly' power in the Community.

Articles 83 and 85 provide the basis for the EC Council of Ministers, acting by qualified majority and after consulting the European Parliament, to adopt implementing Regulations and Directives. This machinery has been used to grant the Commission its powers of monitoring and enforcement.

Articles 87 to 89 provide the Commission with supervisory responsibilities and powers in relation to government grants and aids to industry throughout

---

31. As the Commission stated in its First Report on Competition Policy: 'An active competition policy pursued in accordance with the provisions of the Treaties establishing the Communities makes it easier for the supply and demand structure continuously to adjust to technological development. Through the interplay of decentralised decision-making machinery, competition enables enterprises continuously to improve their efficiency, which is the *sine qua non* for a steady improvement in living standards and employment prospects within the countries of the Community.'

the Community. These are the so-called 'State aid' rules. The Commission can only allow aids to be permitted where certain economic and social objectives are fulfilled. One intention is to prevent governments providing incentives to inefficient national champions or industries.

14.3.2 Article 81(1)

Article 81 deals with collusion or cooperative behaviour between independent businesses. The scheme of the article is to render unenforceable and to prohibit all such arrangements or practices and provide for an exemption for particular types of beneficial arrangements (art. 81(3)). In order to take advantage of the exemption, the economic benefits must outweigh the anticompetitive effects.

Infringement of art. 81(1) will arise where the following are fulfilled:

(a) some form of cooperation occurs between undertakings, being either an agreement, decision or concerted practice; and

(b) that cooperation has as its object or effect the restriction of competition within the Common Market; and

(c) that cooperation has some effect on trade between Member States; and

(d) that cooperation is not de minimis.

Infringement of art. 81 has the consequence that the restrictive provisions are void and the Commission is entitled to impose fines of up to 10 percent of the combined group worldwide turnovers of the undertakings concerned. Where an agreement is found to be unenforceable, it may also be the case that benefits (money, goods or services) conferred under a void clause or contract will be irrecoverable (see below).

However, as indicated above, exemptions are available from art. 81(1). These exemptions are only available on limited grounds and may be granted to an individual agreement following a notification or where the agreement corresponds to an exemption for a particular category of agreements (known as a 'block exemption') (see section 14.3.3 below).

14.3.2.1 Cooperation between undertakings 'Undertakings' means any entity, regardless of legal form, carrying on activities of an economic nature (whether or not profit-making).[32] 'Undertakings' have been taken to include individuals carrying on economic activities, partnerships, companies, sporting bodies and committees.[33] Whether or not companies in the same economic group are separate undertakings for the purposes of EC competition law will depend on whether the companies are economically independent. The factors to take into account will be the level of shareholding, and the extent to which the business plans and policies of the subsidiary are controlled by the parent and

---

32. *Höfner and Elser* v *Macrotron GmbH* (case C-41/90) [1991] ECR 1-1979.
33. *Distribution of Package Tours during the 1990 World Cup*, OJ 1992 L326/31 paras 43–58.

whether the subsidiary's decision-making responsibilities are truly independent.

This issue is critical in determining whether or not arrangements between them constitute an agreement between undertakings or merely an intra-group agreement. Where they are regarded as being within the same economic unit, e.g., parent and subsidiary or two companies having the same parent, they will not be regarded as infringing art. 81. Companies can be held responsible for the acts of their subsidiaries, an issue which can be of critical importance where the parent company is outside the jurisdiction. In calculating the level of fine, the question of what constitutes the 'undertaking' is critical. For example, if a 51 percent owned subsidiary follows the parent company's instructions and as a result infringed art. 81(1), both parent and subsidiary can be fined for the infringement and the fines could amount to 10 percent of the combined turnover of the parent and the subsidiary.

14.3.2.2 Agreement or concerted practice An 'agreement' will usually be easy to identify. It will include a contract or other form of written arrangement such as 'heads of agreement' or memoranda of understanding. There is no requirement that the agreement should be legally binding. Oral and written arrangements and gentlemen's agreements may amount to an agreement within the meaning of art. 81(1). Where an agreement has been ended but the parties to that agreement continue to abide by its terms, it can be viewed as a concerted practice. The distinction between an agreement and a concerted practice is often unclear and the essential common factor between the two is that they involve undertakings determining commercial policy not independently but taking into account the activities or intentions of competitors. 'The importance of the concept of a concerted practice does not thus resolve so much from the distinction between it and an agreement as from the distinction between forms of collusion falling under art. 81(1) and mere parallel behaviour with no element of consultation'.[34] The European Court of Justice has defined a concerted practice as:

> A form of coordination between undertakings which, without having reached the stage when an agreement properly so-called has been concluded, knowingly substitutes practical cooperation between them for the risks of competition.

Evidence of a concerted practice may be found by the Commission from a number of sources. Parallel behaviour may not, by itself, amount to a concerted practice, but where such parallel behaviour occurs in circumstances where the perpetrators meet together, follow each other's prices and there is limited circumstantial evidence of collusion, the Commission has found a concerted practice.[35] In addition, a regular participant in this type of meeting would have to provide corroborative evidence in order to convince the

---

34. *Polypropylene*, OJ L230 18 August 1986, para. 87.
35. *Imperial Chemical Industries Ltd v Commission* (case 48/69) [1972] ECR 619.

Commission that it had not subscribed to the anticompetitive initiatives agreed at the meeting. The fact that the undertaking had not put the initiative into effect would not be sufficient defence and it would have to be established that the undertaking did not have any anticompetitive intention when attending the meeting and that the other participants were aware of this.[36]

In practice, a company must be extremely careful to ensure that direct or indirect contact with competitors does not lead to any limitation of competition.

A decision of an association of undertakings would typically include trade association resolutions and recommendations. Such activities, if they fulfil the other criteria of art. 81(1), will be regarded either as an agreement (in consequence of the general internal regulations or constitution of the trade association) or as a concerted practice between the members of the association. The Commission, in an appropriate case, may find in addition to the members that the association itself has committed an infringement of the rules. As with agreements, there is no requirement that a decision should be legally binding.

What may appear to be unilateral conduct by one party can also be caught by art. 81(1). It would appear that at first sight that a non-dominant undertaking could act unilaterally without the risk of infringing the competition rules. However, in certain circumstances the Commission can characterise what might appear to be unilateral behaviour as in reality being behaviour which can be attributed to an underlying agreement or concerted practice.

14.3.2.3   Object or effect   Article 81(1) prohibits all agreements/concerted practices the object or the effect of which is to prevent, restrict or distort competition. These words are alternative and not cumulative requirements. The authorities would first look at the terms of an agreement to determine whether its object can be seen to be the restriction of competition. If an agreement has an anticompetitive object, it is not strictly necessary for it to have an anticompetitive effect. The rationale is that some agreements are so obviously anticompetitive in their object that the Commission should not be expected to waste resources determining whether or not they have an *anti*-competitive effect. There is therefore, strictly, no need for an agreement to have an anticompetitive effect to infringe art. 81(1), it need only have that 'object'.[37] To establish whether an agreement has an anticompetitive effect a market analysis is required, taking into account the nature and quality of the products covered by the agreement, the severity of the clauses intended to protect a supplier or distributor, the opportunities available for other commercial operators to supply the same products etc.

14.3.2.4   Effect on trade between Member States   Because the effect on trade test is merely a jurisdictional hurdle designed to ensure that agreements which interfere with the pattern of trade between Member States and thus,

---

36. *.Atochem* v *Commission* (case T-3/89) [1991] ECR 11/867
37. *Societé Technique Minière* v *Maschinenbau Ulm* (case 56/65) [1966] ECR 235. See also *Établissements Consten SA* v *Commission* (cases 56 and 58/64) [1966] ECR 299.

affect single market objectives, are caught by art. 81(1), the EC authorities have interpreted this concept widely and it is relatively easily satisfied. For example, agreements may be caught if it is reasonable to anticipate that they will affect the pattern of trade in the future even if they do not currently do so.[38]

14.3.2.5 De minimis The effect of an agreement on both inter-State trade and on competition within the Common Market must be appreciable. As has been described above, restrictions on competition must be judged in relation to be market in question, e.g., restrictive clauses in a software licence would need to be looked at in the context of the software market as a whole.[39] The Commission has clarified this issue by an advisory notice on agreements of minor importance.[40] The notice first published in 1986 was replaced by a new notice published on 9 December 1997.[41] The updated notice is intended to enhance legal certainty by clarifying the text and making it easier to apply.

Under the new notice, quantitative criteria and not turnover thresholds are applied to determine whether or not an agreement will have an appreciable effect. Horizontal agreements are outside the scope of art. 81(1) where the aggregate market share held by all participating undertaking does not exceed 5 percent. For vertical agreements, the aggregate market share must not exceed 10 percent. This of course requires an often complex exercise of defining the relevant market in order to assess market share. There is a discretion to claw back agreements if they involve price fixing, limiting production of sales or fixing resale prices. When the criteria set out in the notice are satisfied, there is no need to notify the agreement.

14.3.2.6 White Paper on the Modernisation of the EC Competition Rules The wide interpretation by the Commission of the jurisdictional criteria and the rapid accession of new Member States has led to an enormous workload for the Commission's Competition Directorate, resulting in a huge backlog of agreements notified for review. The Commission has adopted various techniques to try and reduce its workload, including issuing a number of 'block exemptions' to give a blanket clearance for certain types of agreements (see below).

In addition, it has recently launched its White Paper on *Modernisation of the Rules Implementing Article 81 and 82 of the EC Treaty*.[42] The White Paper addresses the need for fundamental reform of the current procedural framework, particularly in relation to the notification and exemption of agreements under art. 81(1) and 81(3).

The two guiding principles under which the Commission is seeking to reform the competition laws are:

---

38. *AEG v Commission* (Case 107/82) [1983] ECR 3151 at para. 60.
39. *Völk v Établissements Vervaecke Sprl* (case 5/69) [1969] ECR 295.
40. OJ C231, 1986, p. 2.
41. OJ 1997 C372/13.
42. OJ 1999 C132/1 [1999] 5 CMLR 208.

(a)   focusing the Commission's actions on the essentials; and
(b)   bringing the decision-making power closer to the European citizen in order to increase the acceptance of competition policy.

The Commission's proposals include:

(a)   that it should relinquish its monopoly over granting exemptions;
(b)   that art. 81(3) should be directly applicable before national courts and national competition authorities; and
(c)   that the current notification system be abolished.

These proposals are very radical and for companies and their advisers will involve considerable changes in their strategy and approach to the application of the competition rules. With abolition of the notification system it will not be possible to notify agreements at all and the safe haven which was offered by notification to the Commission and the reliance on immunity from fines will no longer be available. The Commission wants undertakings to make their own assessment of the compatibility of the restrictive practices with community law, in the light of the legislation in force and the case law. Companies will therefore have to be more self-reliant. It is likely that the proposals in the White Paper will not be put into effect even if they are finally agreed, until 2003.

14.3.2.7 Typical agreements caught by Article 81(1) Article 81(1) lists examples of types of agreement which it prohibits. These are agreements which:

(a)   'directly or indirectly fix purchase or selling prices or any other trading conditions'. This includes price-fixing agreements between competitors about the prices at which goods or services are to be supplied to customers. Direct influences on pricing policies are also prohibited. Information exchanges between competitors which disclose prices, discounts or other business secrets will be viewed as reducing the normal risks of competition and creating cooperation in practice.
(b)   'limit or control production, markets, technical development or investment', e.g., agreements between competitors about which of them is to supply particular customers or territories. Price-fixing agreements are often supported by quotas so that each party can maintain its share of demand. Such agreements are likely to be prohibited.
(c)   'share markets or sources of supply'. Market-sharing has been referred to above. Joint purchasing agreements by which competitors agreed to combine their buying power are, equally, prohibited. Collective aggregate discounts are also likely to be condemned.

Export bans, i.e., clauses in agreements that prevent parties from exporting goods from one Member State to another are also regarded as a serious violation of art. 81. Care should be taken in computer agreements that clauses intended to ensure compliance with national security law obligations, e.g., to prevent the sale of high-tech products to the former Eastern bloc countries, do not go further than is necessary, and restrict resale within the Community.

In addition, although the Commission does not necessarily object to all of them, agreements for the creation of joint ventures, long-term purchase, supply or distribution agreements, subcontracting agreements, agency agreements, industrial property licences and agreements for joint purchase and joint sale agreements may all infringe art. 81(1).

14.3.2.8 The treatment of horizontal and vertical agreements Horizontal agreements in which competitors agree or conspire to fix prices or share market or restrict production etc. will almost always have an anticompetitive object or effect. Any consideration of possible counter balancing beneficial effects of an agreement is undertaken under art. 81(3). Most agreements are not found as a whole to fall outside art. 81(1) but instead the Commission tends to find art. 81(1) to apply and to undertake a rigorous assessment under Article 81(3). This approach can have serious detrimental effects including lack of legal certainty because of the delays in reviewing many of these agreements. It has been urged that the Commission should undertake a more sophisticated analysis under art. 81(1). In the case of *European Night Services* v *Commission* (cases T-374, 375, 384 and 388/94), the Court of First Instance (FI) held that the Commission made an incorrect and inadequate assessment in its decision to exempt the agreement under art. 81(3) subject to conditions. The case involved agreements between four rail companies to provide overnight passenger rail services between the United Kingdom and through Continental Europe through the Channel Tunnel. The applicants appealed the decision of the Commission to the CFI, which emphasised that the conditions in which an agreement operated must be taken into account in assessing whether or not it breached art. 81(1) in the first place. The CFI annulled the Commission's decision, stating that the Commission had not demonstrated that the agreement restricted competition and that there was any need therefore for an exemption under art. 81(3).

Vertical agreements have been a controversial subject in recent years in EC competition law. Because they are not made between competitors, they are less obviously anticompetitive than horizontal agreements and, in particular, distribution arrangements are quite often procompetitive. Since the decision of the European Court of Justice in *Consten and Grundig* v *Commission* (cases 56 & 58/64) [1966] ECR 299; [1966] CMLR 418, it has been accepted that vertical agreements between independent undertakings are capable of falling within the scope of art. 81. There is some conflict between community goals in this area and while the Commission recognises that vertical agreements are often procompetitive, giving producers and distributors protection in launching new products and certainty needed for them to make investment etc., they also often involve territorial exclusivity for distributors. These territorial restrictions conflict with the Commission's aim of creating a single market.

The new Vertical Restraints Block Exemption is described further at section 14.3.3.1 below.

14.3.2.9   Common clauses   A number of clauses may be regarded as having the object or effect of restricting competition contrary to art. 81(1):

Exclusivity. An exclusivity obligation would usually restrict the seller or licensor from competing with the reseller or licensee. It may also restrict the seller or licensor from selling to firms other than the reseller or licensee, either within or outside a particular territory. A licensee or reseller may be restricted from competing with other licensees or resellers in other territories.

Exclusivity obligations in contracts for the resale or goods (as opposed to agreements which involve the licensing and sublicensing of intellectual property rights) may benefit from the exclusive distribution or exclusive purchasing block exemptions. Where the licensee of intellectual property rights is concerned, there used to be two block exemptions separately covering know-how and patents. There is now a combined block exemption covering technology, the Technology Transfer Regulation 240/96. This block exemption covers patent and know-how licensing and also any licensing of software, trade mark and other intellectual property rights which 'contributes to the achievement of the objects of the licensed technology'.

Non-compete. Non-compete provisions may well infringe art. 81(1). However, it may be economically efficient for a reseller to be forced to concentrate his sales on the goods in question. In consequence, non-compete provisions are exempted under the technology transfer and the new vertical restraints block exemptions.

No-challenge clauses. Clauses where the licensee is prohibited from challenging the validity of the licensed intellectual property right. These are always blacklisted by block exemptions.

Post-term use provisions. Provisions where the duration of the licensing agreement is automatically prolonged beyond the expiry of intellectual property rights existing at the time the agreement was entered into. These are also blacklisted.

Royalty calculation clauses. Agreements under which the licensee is charged royalties on products which are not entirely or partially produced by means of the intellectual-property-based process in question (specifically in relation to patents and know-how) or where the licensee is charged royalties on the use of know-how or confidential information which has entered into the public domain otherwise than by the fault of the licensee.

Quantity restrictions. Where the quantity of licensed products one party may manufacture or sell is restricted or where other quantitative restrictions on the exploitation of the intellectual property rights in question are imposed.

Price and discount restrictions.

Customer restrictions. Where one party is restricted as to the type or class of customer he may serve.

Grant-back arrangements. Where the licensee is obliged to assign or grant back all the improvements to intellectual property rights which are created independently from the licensed intellectual property rights and are not part of the licensed intellectual property rights. These may be permissible under block exemption if non-exclusive mutual grants of improvements occur.

Tying restrictions. Where the licensee is required to accept goods or services which he does not want as a condition of entering into an intellectual property right licence, e.g., a requirement to obtain maintenance or support for licensed software. However, such a restriction may be acceptable when it can be shown that it is necessary for the technically satisfactory exploitation of the product concerned.

Export restraints. Where one or other of the parties is required to refuse (without objective reason) to meet demand from users or resellers in other Member States of the Community.

14.3.2.10   Acceptable cooperation   The Commission issued in 1968 a 'notice on cooperation agreements' which sets out categories of agreement it considered did not fall within art. 81(1). This notice may provide useful guidance but its terms are narrowly construed by the Commission. The following are the categories of acceptable cooperative activity:

(a)   *Information exchanges,* e.g., exchanges of market research, comparative studies of enterprises or industries and the preparation of statistics and calculation models, provided that this information does not lead to coordination of market behaviour. The line may be difficult to draw and extreme caution should be exercised where an information exchange is proposed.

(b)   *Financial cooperation,* e.g., accountancy cooperation, the provision of credit guarantees, debt collection and consultancy facilities on business and tax matters.

(c)   *Sharing* of production, storage and transport facilities.

(d)   *Tendering* on cooperation in the execution of orders, where either the parties are not in competition with each other or, where they are competitors, they would not be able individually to execute a given order.

(e)   *Joint selling* or joint provision of after-sales services, but only where the partners are not actual or potential competitors.

(f)   *Joint advertising,* provided that there is no restriction on individual advertising.

(g)   *Common quality symbols or labels,* where the label is available to all competitors on the same conditions.

14.3.2.11   Agreements outside the scope of Article 81(1)   Apart from the Commission's notice on cooperation agreements, it has issued notices on agency[43] and subcontracting.[44] These are, in the same way as the notice on agreements of minor importance, helpful for the parties but are not binding on either the Commission or the European Court. In its agency notice the

---

43.   24 December 1962.
44.   OJ C1, 3 January 1979, p. 2.

Commission stated that agreements between principal and agent do not infringe art. 81(1). In several cases since, both the Commission and Court have made it clear that it is difficult to rely on this exception. In order to come within the exception the agent must take instructions in detail from the principal and not be a firm capable of acting in its own name and on its own behalf. The test is difficult to apply and will not apply to dealers which are independent firms. The agency notice has been under review by the Commission for some time. Subcontracting arrangements are those arrangements by which the contractor sets out in detail the products he wishes a subcontractor to manufacture. The subcontracting notice may be valuable in the context of software development agreements since it may entitle firms commissioning software to obtain exclusive rights over the software once it has been developed.

14.3.2.12 Selective distribution Selective distribution is widely used in the computer industry for the distribution of both hardware and software. A system of selective distribution, i.e., the appointment of distributors which are 'selected' on objective criteria relating to the quality of the distributor, will be compatible with art. 81(1) provided that:

(a) The products concerned are sophisticated, e.g., computer products which require a high level of expertise or back-up services.

(b) The qualitative criteria for the appointment of distributors relate to the technical capability to supply the goods or services in question and the suitability of their premises.

(c) The qualitative criteria must be applied in a non-discriminatory way — any qualified reseller who wishes to join the system must be admitted.[45]

(d) No 'quantitative' restrictions may be included, i.e., no restrictions may be included on the number of resellers admitted to the system and restrictions on the geographic location of dealers cannot be included. If such restrictions are included, the system may be suitable for individual exemption under art. 81(3) or the franchise block exemption should be considered.

Selective distribution systems are likely to create higher prices to the consumer and to restrict, to an extent, the outlets for a particular product. An obligation can be imposed on authorised resellers to sell only to other authorised resellers or end-users and the supplier may refuse to admit insufficiently-qualified dealers to the network.[46]

In the context of distribution of computers, the Commission accepted that no infringement of art. 81(1) occurred for IBM's selective distribution system for personal computers (PCs).[47] The following were important to the Commission's decision:

---

45. *AEG* v *Commission* (case 107/82) [1983] ECR 3151. A fine of 1 million ECUs was imposed where a qualified reseller was refused admission.
46. *Metro* v *Commission (No. 1)* [1970] ECR 1875.
47. OJ L118, 1984, p. 24.

(a)   IBM PCs were sophisticated products and customers were unsophisticated (although this may change over time).

(b)   The capabilities and price of the IBM PC meant that it was likely to be sold to business and professional users who required information on:

(i)   the type of services a computer may offer;

(ii)   how computers work and the capabilities of the software; and

(iii)   the costs, benefits, advantages and disadvantages of alternative systems.

The Commission accepted certain criteria for the appointment of dealers:

(a)   Dealers needed to have appropriate space for demonstration purposes and were required to keep at least one PC available for demonstration purposes.

(b)   Dealers were required to show ability to provide customers with technical support and training.

(c)   Dealers had to employ sales staff experienced in the use of PCs or willing to be trained (one week) in IBM's PCs.

(d)   Dealers were to provide service facilities and experienced staff trained in servicing IBM's PCs.

(e)   Dealers had to show an ability to run a PC-sales business.

14.3.2.13   Intellectual property   It is possible to argue that certain contractual restrictions, relating to the 'essential subject matter of intellectual property rights' do not restrict competition. This approach identifies the essence of an intellectual property right and then regards any clause which relates to that right as being outside the scope of art. 81(1). For example, copyright protection entitles the copyright owner to restrict the reproduction of the copyright work. An agreement between a supplier and a distributor which involves a copyright licence, such as a software licence, would usually restrict the distributor from copying, except for back-up purposes, and may also impose restrictions on end-users from making copies other than back-up copies. Since the copyright owner is legitimately entitled to impose such a requirement as it relates to copyright in the software being licensed, those 'restrictions' which relate to 'copying' cannot be regarded as infringements of art. 81(1). Obligations are often imposed in software licences preventing a licensee from modifying the software, reverse engineering the object code, or sublicensing or assigning without the permission of the licensor. Such obligations could in the past be regarded as not infringing art. 81(1) since they could be viewed as relating to the essential subject matter of the copyright which was being licensed.

Following the Commission's Directive (91/250/EEC) on the scope of copyright protection given to software, the 'essential subject matter' of the software has been defined. Restrictions on modification or reverse engineering which go beyond the Directive may now be regarded as restrictions of competition.

Any restrictions which relate to the exercise of the copyright which is being licensed may be struck down if they appreciably restrict competition and trade between member States and hence infringe art. 81(1).

14.3.2.14 Nungesser In a number of cases, the European Court of Justice has held that contractual provisions giving a degree of protection against competition do not fall within art. 81(1) if they are necessary to establish competition in the first place. This is a 'but for' test; but for a restrictive clause, no competition would exist since no agreement would be entered into.[48] In its judgment in *L.C. Nungesser KG v Commission* (case 258/78) [1982] ECR 2015, the European Court of Justice considered an exclusive licensing agreement which had appointed a licensor for a particular territory but prevented the licensor from competing with the licensee or granting further licences in the territory in question. The European Court of Justice held that no restriction within art. 81(1) arose and stated that its reasoning could apply to agreements involving intellectual property rights but only where the subject matter of the contract involved the introduction of something 'new' into the territory in which it was being marketed, and in the circumstances the products in question involved significant research and development. Without the restrictions the licensor would not have entered into the agreement — the restrictions were vital to secure the risk of launching the new product.

It is possible to develop this argument by analogy and regard source code to be similar, in economic terms, to the basic maize seed which was at issue in *Nungesser*, since they both involve considerable research and development. On this basis a licensor could restrict the reseller from sublicensing source code.[49]

14.3.2.15 Coditel In its judgments concerning *Coditel*,[50] the European Court of Justice considered that exclusivity and prohibition on resale outside an exclusive territory did not infringe art. 81(1). The particular characteristics of the market and the intellectual property right concerned were taken into account. It is possible to regard this case as one that was concerned with performance rights, which are subject to copyright protection in many Member States. Without relying on his performance right the licensor would be unable to predict actual or probable royalty levels for films, which have been licensed.

This characteristic of films, that they can be shown a number of different times to different sizes of audience, influenced the European Court of Justice to hold that in the circumstances:[51]

---

48. *Société Technique Minière v Maschinenbau Ulm* (case 56/65) [1966] ECR 235 (otherwise known as the indispensable inducement rationale).
49. See also *SPRL Louis Erauw-Jacquery v SC La Hesbignonne* (case 27/87) [1988] 4 CMLR 576.
50. *Coditel SA v Ciné Vog Films (No. 1)* (case 62/79) [1980] ECR 881; *Coditel SA v Ciné Vog Films (No. 2)* (case 262/81) [1982] ECR 3381.
51. See also cases concerning copyright protection such as *Basset v Sacem* (case 402/85) [1987] ECR 1747 and *Ministère Public v Tournier* (case 395/87) [1991] 4 CMLR 248.

The right of the copyright owner ... to require fees for any showing of a
film is part of the essential function of the copyright in this type of literary
or artistic work.

Many types of information technology products may benefit from this
approach. Protection may be available for different parts of a computer
system. A restriction may be imposed on the distribution of computer
software as part of the right to prevent copying. In addition, provided the
performance-right type of copyright protection is available (and this is usually
only the case where the work is shown or broadcast to the public), performance of that software may be regarded in a similar way to the performance of
a film. In such cases, restrictions on licensees which limit the place of
performance (site restrictions), the number of performances (e.g., limitation
on the use of software to a particular computer system) and the performance
of that software via remote terminals or via a number of remote terminals may
be regarded as falling outside art. 81(1).

The *Coditel* and *Nungesser* cases may be regarded as examples of a 'rule of
reason' approach which is being applied in the computer/communications
industry. In the United States, a 'rule of reason' is applied to contracts under
the Sherman Act 1980. Section 1 of the Act prohibits, as illegal, contracts
which are in restraint of trade or commerce and these are found to infringe
the section *per se*. Other agreements are examined under the rule of reason,
under which the pro and anticompetitive effects of the agreement are
balanced against each other. The Court of Justice has adopted this approach
in other industries in a number of cases. (As a recent example, see *Delimitis*
v *Henninger Bräu* (case C-234/89) [1991] ECR I-935.)

14.3.2.16 Mergers and joint ventures   In addition, there are a number of
Commission notices dealing with the application of competition law to joint
ventures, including one on the concept of 'full function' joint ventures under
the EC Merger Regulation.[52] This notice replaces the previous notice on the
distinction between concentrative and cooperative joint ventures and addresses what type of joint venture is covered by the EC Merger Regulation,
what may fall outside the scope of the Merger Regulation and what may fall
instead within the scope of arts 81(1) and (3).

14.3.3   Exemption: Article 81(3)

Article 81(3) provides for exemptions from art. 81(1). As mentioned above,
an exemption may be available for an individual agreement on notification or
for an agreement satisfying the terms of a block exemption Regulation. Article
81(3) provides that two positive and two negative conditions must be
satisfied. An exemption will be available if:

---

52. Commission Notice 98/C 66/01 on the concept of full-function joint ventures under Council
    Regulation (EEC) No. 4064/89 on the control of concentrations between undertakings.

(a)   the agreement contributes to improving the production or distribution of goods or to promoting technical or economic progress; and

(b)   consumers are allowed a fair share of the resulting benefit; and

(c)   only those restrictions in the agreement which are 'indispensable' to the attainment of the objectives of the agreement are imposed on the undertakings concerned; and

(d)   the undertakings concerned are not afforded the possibility of eliminating competition in respect of a substantial part of the products in question.

All four of these requirements must be satisfied if an agreement is to benefit from an exemption. Exemptions are available either on an individual basis or may be published in the form of Regulations by the Commission exempting categories of agreements which fall within the terms of the regulation. Such exemptions are known as 'block exemptions'. The following points should be noted about block exemptions:

(a)   Unless expressly permitted, any restriction contained in an agreement which falls outside the terms of the block exemptions may mean that the entire agreement falls outside the block exemption.

(b)   The Commission specifies permitted and non-permitted clauses — the block exemption may not be sufficiently flexible for many types of commercial agreements.

The most important block exemptions are briefly described below.

14.3.3.1   Vertical restraints block exemption   The new EC block exemption on vertical restraints[53] came into force on 1 January 2000, although most of the clauses do not take effect until 1 June 2000. The new block exemption will apply to vertical agreements for the sale of goods and services completed by undertakings with a market share of less than 30 percent. It replaces three previous block exemption regulations: those applicable to exclusive distribution, exclusive purchasing and franchising agreements, from 1 June 2000. These block exemptions expired on 31 December 1999 but in order to avert a legal vacuum the new regulation prolongs them until 1 June 2000.

Vertical agreements are defined as agreements or concerted practices entered into between two or more undertakings, each of which operates for the purposes of the agreement at a different level of the production level or supply chain, and relating to the conditions which the parties may purchase, sell or re-sell certain goods or services.

Agreements between competing undertakings will not benefit from the exemption. The new block exemption contains a 'black list' of restrictions, which if they exist will prevent the block exemption from applying to the whole of the agreement or practice. These include:

---

53. Commission Regulation No. 2790/1999 of 22 December 1999 on the application of Article 81(3) of the EC Treaty to categories of Vertical Agreements and Concerted Practices [1999] OJ L336/21.

(a) *Restrictions on resale prices* — where the buyer's ability to determine its sale price is restricted, this will prevent the block exemption from applying.

(b) *Non-compete obligations* — any non-compete obligations exceeding five years will not benefit from the exemption.

This is intended to balance the need for a more economic-based approach to vertical restraints against the Commission's competition policy and to ensure that business is offered legal certainty and acceptable enforcement costs.

Given the fact that it is notoriously difficult to define markets in the IT and communications industries, the application of the law is inevitably uncertain. For industry, while the intention behind the law is intended to relax the previous 'strait-jacket' of complex rules, one potential consequence is a lack of certainty over whether the law prohibits certain agreements or not. (See further below for discussion of market analysis).

14.3.3.2 Specialisation agreements[54] A block exemption is granted to agreements under which the parties accept 'reciprocal obligations':

(a) to specialise in the manufacture of one product and to leave to the other party the manufacture of another product; or

(b) to manufacture certain products or to have them manufactured jointly only.

A non-reciprocal obligation to cease productions is not within the Regulation. Care needs to be taken to decide whether an agreement is a specialisation agreement and not a market-sharing agreement. This block exemption is subject to a threshold — the undertaking concerned must not represent more than 20 percent of the market for such products in a substantial part of the Common Market. There is also a turnover threshold.

14.3.3.3 Research and development agreements[55] Three types of agreement may be exempted under the research and development (R&D) block exemption:

(a) Joint R&D products or processes and joint exploitation of the results.

(b) Joint exploitation of the results of R&D jointly carried out under a prior agreement or plan between the parties.

(c) Joint R&D without subsequent exploitation.

Exploitation includes manufacture, and licensing of intellectual property rights, but not distribution or selling.

14.3.3.4 Technology transfer[56] Exclusive and other patent and know-how licences are exempted under this block exemption. It also covers ancillary

---

54. Regulation 417/85, OJ L53, 1985, p. 1.
55. Regulation 418/85, OJ L53, 1985, p. 5.
56. Regulation 240/96 OJ L31, 1996, p. 2.

licences of trade marks, software and other intellectual property rights which contribute to the objects of the licensed technology. However, it does not cover pure software licences. This block exemption replaces the former know-how and patent licence block exemptions from 1 April 1996.

Patent licensors can provide exclusive licences and prevent licensees fulfilling unsolicited orders for up to five years (from the date the product first enters the market) in other licensed territories and from actively seeking orders in other licensed territories for the period of the patent. Know-how agreements can prevent competition with other licensees by restricting fulfilment of unsolicited orders for five years and from actively seeking orders for 10 years. Price restriction, restrictions on R&D, maximum sales restrictions, non-mutual exclusive licences of improvements and export bans are all blacklisted by the Regulation and will prevent an agreement obtaining the benefit of the block exemption.

14.3.3.5 Intellectual property licensing generally As indicated above, a number of common clauses in intellectual property licences are likely to infringe art. 81(1). These clauses do not benefit from exemptions in relation to technology licensing and they are likely to be prohibited in the context of copyright (software) and trade mark licensing. The existing block exemption regulations may, however, provide arguments for the individual exemption of information technology agreements containing software. Such arguments will only be appropriate when applying for individual exemption in the context of an agreement with similar economic benefits to a patent or a know-how licence.

14.3.4 Community and domestic competition law

Many of the Member States of the EC have formulated their own competition policy in recent years and have based their new competition legislation on EC rules. Where domestic competition law differs from EC law the general rule is that Community law takes precedence. Article 5 of the Treaty specifically imposes a duty on Member States to ensure the fulfilment of Treaty obligations, to facilitate the achievement of the Community's tasks and abstain from any measure which could jeopardise the attainment of the Treaty's objectives. The Commission's notice on cooperation addresses the need to avoid conflicts between national and community authorities. For example, where conduct is prohibited by art. 81(1) but is permitted by the domestic competition law, the community law will prevail and the conduct cannot be permitted by the national authorities.

14.3.5 Article 82

Article 82 of the EEC Treaty is concerned with unilateral activity by one party occupying a dominant position. It provides that:

> Any abuse by one or more undertakings of a dominant position within the Common Market or in a substantial part of it shall be prohibited as

incompatible with the Common Market insofar as it may affect trade between Member States.

A 'dominant position' is defined in qualitative terms:[57]

> A position of economic strength enjoyed by an undertaking which enables it to hinder the maintenance of effective competition in the relevant market by allowing it to behave to an appreciable extent independently of its competitors and customers and ultimately of consumers.

A number of factors are to be taken into account in order to establish whether a particular undertaking is in a dominant position:

(a)   the market share of the undertaking and of its competitors;
(b)   the undertaking's supply and/or purchasing power;
(c)   technical knowledge and expertise of the undertaking;
(d)   availability of raw materials and supplies;
(e)   the scale of the undertaking's activities — its capital and resources;
(f)   exclusionary effect of any sales or distribution networks;
(g)   intellectual property right protection;
(h)   customer dependence;
(i)   the exclusionary effect of government licences (such as telecommunications licences limiting the number of competitors in a particular market).

14.3.6   Market analysis in the technology sector

Often, particularly in fast moving communications and technological markets, it is extremely difficult to identify the relevant market, both to assess market shares to assess the applicability of block exemptions and to assess dominance. Complex economic analysis is often required. Dominance cannot exist in the abstract but always exists in relation to a relevant market and therefore is essential to identify the relevant product market, the geographical market and the temporal market.

Dominance is assessed in relation to a relevant market which comprises the products which may be regarded as substitutable by users (demand substitutability) and in relation to the ability of suppliers or manufacturers to switch from one product to another (supply substitutability). A product market can only exist in relation to a particular geographic area where the conditions for competition are sufficiently similar. The temporal element of market definition is of enormous significance for technology and communications markets since short term success may be short lived; in other words, short term dominance may be overtaken by new technological or market developments. As a practical guide, a dominant position is not normally found unless the market share of the business concerned is substantial, typically above 40 or 50 percent. The overriding criteria are the structure and state of the market in economic terms. Barriers to entry and supply-side

---

57. *Michelin* v *Commission* (case 322/81) [1983] ECR 3461.

substitutes are now recognised to be of greater significance than they formerly were. However, in relation to the computer industry, the relevant market may be narrowly defined, or even defined in terms of a single computer supplier's products, services or software. The more narrowly defined the market, the higher a particular supplier's market share. Also, a supplier may find itself dominant in the spare parts or maintenance services markets for its own products.

Finding dominance in the technology and communications sectors is particularly difficult due to the following economic factors:

(a)   Unlike traditional industries where economies of scale are such that a critical mass can be achieved, in many parts of the 'high-tech' sector economies of scale continue to increase with each unit of production. In other words the costs of producing an extra product are relatively small and, for example, the production of an extra piece of software is an insignificant incremental cost. As a consequence, there is no such thing as efficient scale, and if a company writes a successful piece of software it can easily 'dominate' the market.

(b)   Externalities can be high. For example, the benefit to all users of an e-mail system, or a telephony system, continues to increase with the number of members of the system. This has given rise to the concept of 'tipping' whereby once a firm achieves a particular size the entire market 'tips' into that firm's products as it becomes less valuable to remain on another system. This has a spiralling effect, as the 'dominant' product continues to increase in popularity and hence, maintains and strengthens its dominant position.

(c)   Technological discontinuity shifts can occur. For example, suppliers of records and record players would probably have been regarded by competition authorities as occupying the record and record player markets. Of course such an analysis may ignore substitutes that have different qualities and different prices but nevertheless meet the same demand, such as CD's and CD systems. The CD and CD system is a technological discontinuity that makes the analysis of dominance in the record market particularly difficult.

(d)   Speed of change: Since new products can reach the market quickly, they may become entrenched and speed of market change may make them difficult to dislodge. Conversely new products may overtake them and short term dominance may be short lived.

14.3.6.1   Types of abuse   A number of types of abusive conduct are listed in art. 82:

... directly or indirectly imposing unfair purchase or selling prices or other unfair trading conditions, limiting production, markets or technical development, discrimination by applying dissimilar conditions to equivalent transactions, or similar conditions to dissimilar transactions, tying practices by which unrelated products are only supplied together.

Practical examples of abuses in the computer industry would include:

(a) *Predatory pricing*, where a computer manufacturer lowers its price below its average variable cost of production, or sets its prices between average variable and average total cost, with an intent to eliminate a competitor. The test approved here is taken from *Re AKZO Chemie BV* [1986] 3 CMLR 273, which may be the appropriate test for companies manufacturing goods, but not for highly capital intensive information technology or telecommunications companies.

(b) *Monopoly pricing*, where a company prices its products with no relation to costs or the likely reaction of competitors and obtains 'excessive' profits.

(c) *Discriminatory prices*, charging different prices to different customers without any cost justification for the difference, e.g., a pricing structure under which ex-factory sale prices of products vary depending on the member State to which they are ultimately sold.

(d) *Unfair, anticompetitive or discriminatory terms or conditions*, such as arrangements whereby a purchaser of a product (hardware) is obliged to purchase from the dominant supplier unrelated products (other add-on hardware, or software, or maintenance services, or a complete range of other products).

(e) *Restrictions on resale.*

(f) *Refusal to deal*, e.g., refusal by a dominant supplier to continue to deal with a long-standing customer for no objective reason.

14.3.6.2 British Telecommunications   The European Court of Justice had occasion to consider the position of British Telecommunications (BT) at the time when it was a statutory corporation. A complaint was lodged with the European Commission by Telespeed,[58] which wished to take advantage of lower tariffs in the United Kingdom than existed in other parts of Europe. Before the formation of BT, the Post Office had incorporated in its standard terms of service certain restrictions on re-forwarding messages in this way. The Commission held that BT held a statutory monopoly at the time, and was therefore in a dominant position. In addition, the refusal to permit message re-forwarding services was considered to be an abuse.[59]

14.3.6.3 IBM   Although it has never been established, the Commission has alleged that IBM was in a dominant position under Article 86. The allegation related to the market for IBM's System/370 central processing units and operating system. The allegation was made that the dominant position in relation to those two products allowed IBM to control the market for the supply of compatible products. The allegations of abuse involved:

(a)   Failure to supply other manufacturers with interface information.

(b)   Not offering System/370 central processing units without a capacity of main memory included in the price (memory tying or memory bundling).

---

58. *Italy v Commission* (case 41/83) [1985] ECR 873.
59. OJ L360, 21 December 1982, p. 36.

(c)   Not offering System/370 central processing units without basic software included in the price (software tying or software bundling).

(d)   Discriminating between different users of IBM software, i.e., refusing to supply certain software installation services to users of non-IBM central processing units.

The Commission eventually accepted IBM's undertakings in relation to these issues, and in particular in relation to interface information and memory bundling.

The IBM proceedings[60] are an illustration of the Commission's general approach to defining markets in very narrow terms.[61] From this approach, it is possible that:

(a)   A relevant market may be very narrowly defined in terms of a manufacturer's own products.

(b)   A hardware manufacturer may find itself in a dominant position over the supply of interrelated software, e.g., interface information.

(c)   Operating system software may be the relevant market when examining the effect on the downstream applications programs.[62]

Particular care will need to be taken in marketing and pricing policies which might be regarded as abusive.[63]

14.3.6.4   Magill   The motive behind the particular method chosen to enforce intellectual property rights is important, as can be seen from the Commission's decision in *Magill TV Guide/ITP* OJ 1989 L78/43. Here the defendant television companies used copyright in their programme listings to prevent Magill from publishing a weekly programme guide for Ireland. Copyright in these listings had already been established, and the defendants were granted an injunction against Magill. The Commission also found a history of taking similar action against other intending publishers of weekly guides.

The Commission held that the companies were in a dominant position with regard to their programme listings (a very narrow market definition), and that by enforcing their copyright in this manner they were abusing that position. The defendants argued that their current policies of licensing only same-day publication was necessary to ensure that all their programmes were adequately listed, but the Commission rejected this submission, noting that the same effect could be produced by conditions in any licences to publish weekly

---

60. *International Business Machines Corporation* v *Commission* (case 60/81) [1981] 3 CMLR 635, [1984] 3 CMLR 147.
61. The Commission's reasoning in *Hilti AG* v *Commission* (case T-30/89) [1991] ECR II-1439 indicates that hardware components and spare parts may be in separate markets. See also *Digital/Krenzle* (case IV/M.057) (1992), which identified personal computers and workstations as separate markets.
62. See *IBM France/CGI* (case IV/M.336), the Commission's Microsoft settlement (Press Release IP 94/653) and *EDS/SD Scicon* (case IV/M.112) [1993] 4 CMLR M77.
63. A legitimate business objective such as the leveraging of software sales via a strong presence in hardware may amount to an abuse. Also, arbitrary refusals to license intellectual property rights may constitute an abuse (*Volvo AB* v *Erik Veng (UK) Ltd* [1989] 4 CMLR 122).

listings, and that in practice none of the defendants were willing to grant such licences:

> [The] Commission concludes that the current policies and practices of ITP, BBC and RTE in relation to their respective advance weekly listings are *intended* to protect and have the effect of protecting the position of their individual TV guides, which do not compete with one another or with any other guides .... By limiting the scope of their licensing policies so as to prevent the production and sale of comprehensive TV guides ... they restrict competition to the prejudice of consumers.

The case has been affirmed by the Court of First Instance of the EC on substantially the same grounds,[64] and that judgment has reiterated the principle that EC competition law prevails over the national rights to exploit intellectual property:[65]

> ... while it is plain that the exercise of the exclusive right to reproduce a protected work is not in itself an abuse, that does not apply when, in the light of the details of each individual case, it is apparent that such right is exercised in such ways and circumstances as in fact *to pursue an aim manifestly contrary to the objectives of article 86 (now Article 82)*. In that event the copyright is no longer exercised in a manner which corresponds to its essential function, within the meaning of article 30 of the Treaty, *which is to protect the moral rights in the work and ensure a reward for the creative effort*, while respecting the aims of, in particular, article 86 (now Article 82). In that case, the primacy of Community law, particularly as regards principles as fundamental as those of the free movement of goods and freedom of competition, prevails over any use of national intellectual property law in a manner contrary to those principles.

In the judgment of the European Court of Justice in the *Magill* case (6 April 1996), the court held that although the refusal to grant a licence does not, by itself, constitute an abuse, the exercise of the exclusive right may, in exceptional circumstances, be abusive. In the *Magill* case behaviour of the TV broadcasters consisted in relying on their copyright to prevent Magill or any other third party from publishing weekly information on their programmes. The European Court of Justice noted that the Court of First Instance has listed three categories of circumstances in support of the conclusion that the refusal to grant the licence was abusive:

(a) The refusal prevented the appearance on the market of a new product for which there was no adequate substitute, although there existed specific, constant and regular potential demand for that product on the part of consumers. This creates a state of dependence on the guides published by each of the three broadcasters.

(b) There was no justification for the refusal to licence, either by reference to the broadcasters' activities in TV broadcasting or in publishing.

---

64. *Independent Television Publications Ltd* v *Commission* (case T-76/89) [1991] 4 CMLR 745.
65. [1991] 4 CMLR 745, at pp. 767–8 (emphasis added).

(c)   The broadcasters 'reserve to themselves the secondary market of weekly television guides by excluding all competition on that market'. Indeed, they denied to third parties access to the 'basic information', which constituted the indispensable raw material for creating such a guide.

A number of information technology industry representatives have sought to confine the case to its facts. However, although the court says that it is only 'in exceptional circumstances' that the refusal to grant a licence can be considered an abuse, its judgment gives rise to the possible conclusion that none of the circumstances which it lists as 'exceptional' were truly exceptional. First, Magill's product was not particularly new or innovative (TV guides are widely published by the BBC and ITV and many other broadcasters). Secondly, the lack of justification centres on the essential subject matter of copyright. The justification was that it was the BBC and ITV's right to refuse to supply. It seems from the *Magill* case that an additional objective concerning the reservation of a secondary market to the broadcasters is questionable. The broadcasters did not exclude the development of the market, but limited its development by restricting information and the use which might be made of that information.

Although the software industry generally has sought to distinguish *Magill*, a cautious approach would indicate that it is highly relevant to the supply of information whether in digital or other form where such a supply restricts the development of a secondary market.

14.4   SANCTIONS AND REMEDIES

If an agreement infringes art. 81(1) or conduct is an abuse under art. 82, the agreement will be void and the Commission is entitled to impose fines of up to 10 percent of the combined group worldwide turnovers of the companies concerned.

Very significant fines have to date been levied by the Commission in cases taken under art. 82. For example, the members of the Trans-Atlantic Conference Agreement were fined Euro 273 million in 1999, having been found guilty of abuse of their joint dominant position.[66]

The scope of invalidity is a matter for national law. Under English law, the doctrine of severance would apply to cut out or 'blue-pencil' the restrictive provisions in the agreement. The court would then be required to decide whether the resulting agreement is one the parties should be held to perform or whether the restrictions are fundamental and strike the heart of the agreement. It is likely that clauses which are of considerable commercial importance, such as exclusivity, would, if found to infringe art. 81(1), be struck out and the resulting agreement may be rendered unenforceable. In a technology transfer, this risk of unenforceability is probably of more serious commercial concern than the risk of fines.[67]

It also appears likely now that benefits (money, goods or services) conferred under a void clause or contract may be irrecoverable. In *Gibbs Mew plc* v

---

66. *TACA* OJ L95/1, 1999, [1999] 4 CMLR 1415.
67. See also *Irish Aerospace (Belgium)* v *Euro Control* (10 June 1991, unreported).

Gemmel [1990] 01 EG 117 for example, the English Court of Appeal rejected a restitutionary claim for the recovery of sums paid by a publican-tenant under a beer supply agreement which the publican had alleged to be in breach of art. 81. The claim was rejected for various reasons including on the basis that it is contrary to public policy to assist a claimant in recovering benefits conferred under an illegal contract, including one which breaches art. 81. Consequently, any restitutionary claim will be barred by the illegality of the agreement. There is limited precedent[68] to support an action for damages for breach of EC law. A third party which has lost business as a consequence of a restrictive agreement might wish to take such action.

Recently, the Commission has encouraged individuals affected by anticompetitive practices or abuses of dominant positions to take actions in national courts. However, an effective and perhaps cheaper remedy is to lodge a complaint with the Commission where infringement of the rules is suspected. The Commission has very wide search and seizure powers which may be used to establish the truth of the complaint. This is a very real benefit where conduct complained of relates to activity in Continental Europe where the inability to obtain discovery of documents may severely constrain the ability of a claimant to bring a case in court.

Breaches of Member State obligations may entitle an individual to damages where that breach has resulted in loss. A Member State's failure to comply with art. 28 or art. 49 or even its failure properly to implement a Directive, may also form the basis for a damages action in a national court.[69]

---

68. *Garden Cottage Foods Ltd* v *Milk Marketing Board* [1984] AC 1390.
69. *Francovich* v *Italy* (cases C-6 and 9/90) [1991] ECR I-5357: *Brasserie du Pêcheur SA* v *Germany* (cases C-46 and 48/93) [1996] QB 404; *R* v *HM Treasury, ex parte British Telecommunications plc* (case C-392/93) [1996] 3 WLR 203.

Index